Early Modern Ireland

Early Modern Ireland: New Sources, Methods, and Perspectives offers fresh approaches and case studies that push the field of early modern Ireland, and of British and European history more generally, into unexplored directions.

The centuries between 1500 and 1700 were pivotal in Ireland's history, yet so much about this period has remained neglected until relatively recently, and a great deal has yet to be explored. Containing seventeen original and individually commissioned essays by an international and interdisciplinary group of leading and emerging scholars, this book covers a wide range of topics, including social, cultural, and political history as well as folklore, medicine, archaeology, and digital humanities, all of which are enhanced by a selection of maps, graphs, tables, and images.

Urging a reevaluation of the terms and assumptions which have been used to describe Ireland's past, and a consideration of the new directions in which the study of early modern Ireland could be taken, *Early Modern Ireland: New Sources, Methods, and Perspectives* is a groundbreaking collection for students and scholars studying early modern Irish history.

Sarah Covington is Professor of History at the Graduate Center and Queens College of the City University of New York, and director of the Irish Studies program at Queens College. In addition to two books and numerous articles on early modern England and Ireland, she is the author of a forthcoming book that will explore the political, folkloric, literary, and religious afterlives of Oliver Cromwell in Ireland over three centuries.

Vincent P. Carey teaches European history at the State University of New York at Plattsburgh in upstate New York. He has published extensively on sixteenth-century Ireland and is currently finishing a book tentatively titled *Murder on the Border of the Pale: A Sixteenth-Century Irish Micro-History.*

Valerie McGowan-Doyle is Professor of History at Lorain County Community College and Adjunct Associate Professor of History at Kent State University. She is the author of *The Book of Howth: Elizabethan Conquest and the Old English* (2011) and coeditor of *Elizabeth I and Ireland* (2014). Her current research examines violence against women in early modern Ireland.

Early Modern Ireland

New Sources, Methods, and Perspectives

**Edited by
Sarah Covington, Vincent P. Carey,
and Valerie McGowan-Doyle**

Routledge
Taylor & Francis Group

LONDON AND NEW YORK

First published 2019
by Routledge
2 Park Square, Milton Park, Abingdon, Oxon OX14 4RN

and by Routledge
52 Vanderbilt Avenue, New York, NY 10017

Routledge is an imprint of the Taylor & Francis Group, an informa business

British Library Cataloguing-in-Publication Data
A catalogue record for this book is available from the British Library

Library of Congress Cataloging-in-Publication Data
Names: Covington, Sarah, 1965– editor. | Carey, Vincent, editor. | McGowan-Doyle, Valerie, editor.
Title: Early modern Ireland: new sources, methods, and perspectives / edited by Sarah Covington, Vincent P. Carey and Valerie McGowan-Doyle.
Description: Abingdon, Oxon; New York, NY: Routledge, 2019.
Identifiers: LCCN 2018038793 |
Subjects: LCSH: Ireland—History—16th century. | Ireland—History—17th century. | Ireland—Historiography. | Ireland—History—Sources.
Classification: LCC DA935 .E27 2019 | DDC 941.505—dc23
LC record available at https://lccn.loc.gov/2018038793

ISBN: 978-0-8153-7393-3 (hbk)
ISBN: 978-0-8153-7394-0 (pbk)
ISBN: 978-1-351-24301-8 (ebk)

Typeset in Bembo
by codeMantra

MIX
Paper from
responsible sources
FSC
www.fsc.org   FSC® C013056

Printed and bound in Great Britain by
TJ International Ltd, Padstow, Cornwall

For Nicholas Canny

Contents

Figures

Foreword

New Directions for Early Modern Ireland

Nicholas Canny

One of my pleasant surprises of recent years was when some colleagues in the United States arranged to dedicate three sessions of the 2016 annual meeting of the Renaissance Society of America to discuss my published work and explain how it had influenced their own writing.[1] I naturally traveled to Boston for the occasion, and when the organizers of the sessions later decided to edit a volume on possible new directions for the study of early modern Ireland, I had no choice but to switch my customary role as historian to that of clairvoyant to imagine what new directions scholars of the future are likely to follow.

Once I engaged with the task, I found myself reflecting on what academic new directions I had discerned in the study of the history of Ireland in the sixteenth and seventeenth centuries (and of early modern history more generally) since 1970 and 1971, when my first research papers appeared in print.[2] As I did so, I came to recognize that I have lived through two careers and that it was only after I had embarked upon the second one that the traditional molds were really shattered. Any changes that occurred previous to then were in scale, as more scholars from more diverse training experiences took up the study of the subject, and in the increasing willingness of scholars from the various disciplines, especially in literature and history, to work with each other in cautious cooperation.

These subtle and incremental changes that proceeded apace over an extended interlude stood in sharp contrast to the new directions in the study of humanities disciplines that came into effect quite suddenly (or so it appeared to me) over the course of my second career. Most of these were the product of directives from the top, were frequently enabled by technology, and were backed by individuals and agencies determined to make them the recognized pathways for future study.

The start of my first career can be dated either from those publications of 1970 and 1971 or from my appointment in January 1972 to my first academic posting at University College, Galway (now National University Ireland, Galway [NUIG]). This appointment led to a fairly conventional, and some would say, successful, academic career, in which I dedicated myself to teaching and writing history, and to undertaking the administrative chores associated with furthering the study of history, both within my own institution and at national and international levels. Given the precarious state of the Irish economy in the 1970s, I considered myself lucky and privileged to have been appointed to a permanent post at a relatively young age, and even more so because I was elevated rapidly on the career ladder and was well rewarded by the standards of that time. Luck would have featured in any contemporary appraisal of my progression because 'merit' was only one factor that entered into the choice of people for almost all public appointments in the Ireland of those days, and academics, no less than judges, senior civil servants, and members of the medical profession, were expected to be upholders of the *status quo* in a society of limited opportunity. This recognition of academics as pillars of society meant that once people were appointed to permanent positions and steered clear of 'gross moral turpitude', they were not answerable to any external, or indeed internal, discipline or monitoring besides their own consciences. Many university teachers of the day equated this laxity with liberalism and considered proposals to introduce any inspection of teaching and research activity, or any salary differentials based on performance, to be threats to academic freedom.

Despite this permissive and incentive-free environment, I, like some others of my generation, strove to improve the Irish university system by providing better instruction to our students than we had received a generation earlier. For me, this resulted in a heavy teaching load, but I also sustained a steady research output, despite having to suffer in working conditions, most notably library holdings, that were inadequate by any standards. This proved possible because I devoted most of my vacation times to archival investigation and because I secured a sequence of research fellowships that enabled me to free myself from my academic responsibilities at critical junctures and spend time writing and keeping abreast with advances in my subject at some of the world's best research institutions. Then, as I became more senior and established internationally, I resolved to reduce my teaching and administrative responsibilities at age sixty and take more time off to engage in research and writing before I reached the mandatory retirement age of sixty-five. My purpose then was to complete a book that I am now unlikely ever to write, comparing English with French writing on the natural history of the West Indies during the sixteenth and seventeenth centuries.[3]

This plan was defeated by a sequence of factors, the first being that the Irish government of the time, prompted and supported by Chuck Feeney of Atlantic Philanthropies, decided, for the first time since Ireland had achieved partial independence in 1922, to make a substantial investment in building a research infrastructure and research programs in Irish universities on a competitive basis. As these plans unfolded, I was called upon by Galway's university president of the day to head up a proposal for research funding in the Humanities as part of an institutional bid for support. The proposal that I authored with assistance from colleagues was found convincing by the external adjudicators of the competition. This, for me, meant that instead of taking time off to complete the book I had in mind, I became saddled with the responsibility of encouraging and monitoring the work of fellow academics and research students in a brand new humanities research center.

This experience was, for me, novel and even stimulating, but what I could not have anticipated was that it exposed me to being conscripted in 2005 and, against my better judgment, to serving the university as Vice President for Research from then until 2008. Appointment to the vice presidency forced me to sever my connection with undergraduate teaching, which I had always enjoyed, because it would have been impossible for me to fulfill my responsibility to students once I found myself, by rotation, serving for a year as Chair of the Committee of the Vice Presidents for Research of Ireland's seven universities. The principal responsibility of this committee during that year was to coordinate the research bids of Ireland's universities when the government, again with financial support from Atlantic Philanthropies, made an even greater allocation of money available to support research in universities on a competitive basis, this time with the proviso that bids for funding should have a significant multi-institutional collaborative dimension.

It was only when the committee of Vice Presidents for Research undertook the coordination of these bids that I became aware of the extent to which colleagues in the various Science, Medicine, and Engineering disciplines of Ireland's universities had broken from the nonchalance of the past and considered themselves to be competitors for research funding, both internationally and nationally. Moreover, I found that to this end, those colleagues were willing to have their work measured by the H Index (a calculus of which I was previously unaware) and could, with unblushing certainty, proclaim the benefits to society of whatever research they had in hand and the social cataclysm that would ensue if their every demand was not met.

This exposure to the revolutionary change in outlook that had been adopted by large sectors of Ireland's academic community acted as shock therapy for me since my closest academic interactions, up to this point, had been with fellow humanists who, when they did engage with research, still cherished the notion of *ars gratia artis*. Moreover, the funding demands of humanities scholars did not usually extend beyond calls for greater library resources and for more time release from departmental duties so they could get on with personal research. I too was afflicted with these limited ambitions, which meant that, initially, I experienced difficulty in persuading my fellow Vice Presidents for Research, who were all scientists, engineers, and medical researchers, that some of the funding being released for competition by the government should be earmarked to support research activity and research infrastructure for the benefit of scholars in the arts, humanities, and social sciences. The most disheartening moment for me, when I did begin to make my case, was when one colleague, in an effort to be helpful as well as polite, blurted out that assigning some money for a competition to support research in economics would be worth considering.

In the event, and in response to the known research priorities of researchers in the arts and humanities in their own institutions, my opposite numbers from Trinity College Dublin, and Maynooth University supported the idea that a substantial tranche of the total spending should be assigned to a competition for research support in that area. This spurred interested humanities scholars in the universities to formulate research proposals, with the result that all but one of the seven universities benefited from the recurrent elements of this fund. More importantly, the enduring legacy for research in the arts and humanities from this round of funding was the construction of the Long Room Hub at Trinity College Dublin; The Moore Institute for Research in the Humanities and Social Studies at the National University Ireland, Galway; and the building for *An Foras Feasa* at Maynooth University. Further infrastructural as well as human support designed to benefit all arts and humanities institutions and repositories throughout Ireland came with the establishment at the Royal Irish Academy (RIA) of the Digital Humanities Observatory (DHO), which, since then, and with further funding from another round of research money, has morphed into the Digital Repository of Ireland (DRI).

This outcome satisfied me that there had been some positive outcome from the abandonment, or at least postponement, of my personal research because my interventions at the policy level had made it possible for humanities scholars in all of Ireland's universities to make a bid to improve their research funding and facilities. What I could not have anticipated was that once the appetites of these scholars for research money had been whetted, they were, in effect, following their colleagues in science, engineering, and medicine across the threshold into an academic world where their efforts thereafter, whether they involved teaching, research, or administration, would be quantified and monitored. The objectives of the functionaries appointed to undertake this metrification of effort were either to calculate the positive academic and social outcomes that had derived from public investment in research or to use the data they amassed to enhance the standing of each of Ireland's universities in international league tables of universities that ranked them according to agreed quantifiable criteria.

My familiarity with such procedures was honed during my stint, from 2005 to 2008, as Vice President for Research at NUIG, when, as already mentioned, I was responsible for formulating institutional research proposals; my knowledge was further enhanced when I served as president of the RIA from 2008 to 2011, and then, from 2011 to 2016, as one of a group of twenty-two researchers appointed by the European Commission to oversee the management of the European Research Council (ERC) as members of its Scientific Council. During these various service interludes, I became necessarily familiar with how procedures are agreed upon for appraising the quality of research bids and with the methods by which the relative merits of researchers are calculated based on their publication record. A critical appraisal of the methods being employed for such tabulations led logically to a study, first, of the means by which the integrity of research proposals and outcomes can be monitored, and then of the extent to which the public sharing of data necessarily forms part of the procedure by which assurances can be given of the integrity of the research that has been supported by the various funding agencies. The more I learned, the more I came to understand why the creators of research indices had set about establishing a rank order of journals and publishers because their performance indicators would be meaningless if there was no general acceptance of such a hierarchy. It was then also that I learned something of how the societal impact of research can be appraised and the means by which research findings can be communicated to the widest possible audience, ideally free of charge by open access. This, as I now appreciate (and I did serve for two years as Chair of the Open Access Committee of the ERC, and even published a paper on the subject),[4] is ideal because it is the investment being made by the tax-paying public in public universities and in research funding that is the principal enabler of almost all research conducted in Europe.

During my various periods of service, I frequently remonstrated about the inapplicability of some of these practices to research activity in the arts and humanities, and as I did so, I became acquainted with the rich philosophical literature on the subject. However, I quickly discovered that for almost every philosophical objective raised to measuring research activity in arts and humanities disciplines, there is an equally plausible counterargument and none more persuasive than that which holds that if researchers in the arts and humanities wish to avail themselves as equals for research funding that derives from the public purse, they must become reconciled to having the merit and integrity of their work scrutinized in the same way as the research conducted by colleagues in Science, Medicine, and Engineering. Moreover, there seems to be no escape from the logic that those whose tax contributions cover the salary costs of almost all academics in Europe, as well as the research funding that is distributed among them on a competitive basis, must be prepared to give that same public access free of charge to the research findings that result from this investment.

Scholars in North America, where much of the support provided to researchers in the arts and humanities comes from private sources, are frequently taken aback by the way in which research in Europe is becoming bureaucratized. However, if they look more closely into what is happening in their own institutions, they will come to appreciate that what is happening in Europe is also their future. Their colleagues in Science, Medicine, and Engineering, and their librarians, have been trendsetters in metrification, especially so since universities in North America were the first to become obsessed with ranking as a national, if not international, pursuit. And scholars in North America will see little that is novel about some of the new directions that I believe are already changing the way in which research in the humanities generally, and therefore also on early modern Ireland, is being approached.

The first major change in Ireland is that where, in the past, relatively few of those holding academic positions produced significant bodies of research, almost all now subscribe to the 'publish or perish' ethos that was previously mockingly associated with universities in North America. The immediate consequence of this is that the quantity of work being published, even on as narrowly defined an area as early modern Ireland, has increased dramatically, as has the number of publishers and journals where research outcomes can be read in print or online. The increase in the quantity of work being published has escalated further because of the number of early-stage researchers who are being appointed to multiyear postdoctoral positions, either in a stand-alone capacity or as members of research teams being led by holders of major grants, usually from the Irish Research Council (IRC) or from the ERC.

The other factor that has already transformed humanities research practice in Ireland, and therefore also on early modern Ireland, is that a considerable body of research material, to which access could previously be had only in major research libraries and archives, has now become available in digital form online, in professionally edited printed compilations, or both. This has been made possible because of the greater availability of research funding in Europe to create such compilations and because Irish universities are better able to subscribe to commercially sponsored repositories such as Early English Books Online (EEBO). Technological developments and know-how have also made it possible for researchers to extract from digitized sources knowledge that would not previously have been attainable. Such developments have further boosted research output and made it possible to address new research questions, relating, for example, to the prevalence of speech patterns or word occurrences in particular bodies of print or manuscripts to which answers might be found through the data mining of digitized texts.

Those researchers who succeed in winning large research grants, sometimes extending to millions of euros to be spent over five years, can be even more ambitious and employ, for example, aerial photography or even satellite imaging to gain a better understanding of questions relating to matters as various as the outcome of battles and sieges or ecological or climatic change as it impacted upon Ireland over the course of the 'little ice age'.[5] The availability of large research grants also enables greater cross-disciplinary investigations into previously unanswerable questions. Up to now, archaeology has been the discipline where practitioners were most confident in their ability to shed light on the lives of those who left no or few written records; but archaeologists of Ireland seem also to have recognized the possibilities that the study of the early modern centuries in Ireland hold for the investigation of issues of wider interest, notably cultural shifts and cultural encounters, which have made them willing in turn to work with historians on these subjects.[6] Historians of the future are also likely to take inspiration from the ability of archaeologists to think big and expansively, and to look beyond the humanities to make use of techniques developed by biologists, medical researchers, and scientists of marine and land environments when these make it possible to establish the age of buildings or objects; to track changes in land use over the medium and long terms; to identify the precise locations of manufacturing activity with their associated technologies; and to shed light on the lives of the poor and of women—what food they might have eaten or prepared, and what diseases afflicted them. And those humanist scholars who appreciate or have mastered these techniques are most likely to broaden our understanding of the past when they relate the information they can glean from the natural archive to what has survived in the written record, which, as has already been mentioned, is now more readily available in printed and well-indexed editions and in digitized form.

Some of the contributions in this collection, like a few of the chapters in the recently published second volume of the *Cambridge History of Ireland*, treating of the years 1550–1730,[7] exemplify the way in which our knowledge of what happened in early modern Ireland can be enriched through the adoption of these new approaches. And it is also clear that researchers associated with these new approaches enjoy many more opportunities than traditional scholars to engage with popular audiences because they work with physical objects from the past and with contemporary maps and images, and with charts, tables, and data sets compiled by themselves (or their research assistants) from an extensive range of sources. They are thus better equipped than traditional scholars to mount museum or traveling exhibitions; to supply visual material related to their research for television programs; or even to construct visitor centers, which are highly esteemed by the calculators of 'societal impact'.

It was during my five years' service with the ERC that I became fully informed on the endless range of technologies, including, for example, DNA sampling, the word mining of digitized texts, and the deployment of techniques used by dental pathologists to establish the diet of people long since dead—all of which are being used extensively by humanist scholars to shed light on social conditions in the past, and even to explain the course of past events. We have noted that some scholars who work on early modern Ireland are already using some of these techniques, and I predict that many of the breakthroughs in the years ahead will derive from the further deployment of such technologies. However, I have become aware from my time with the ERC, and from conversations with senior scholars from a range of disciplines, that there are also shortcomings associated with such approaches. One is that of cost, and historians frequently gasp at the amount of money expended by archaeologists in establishing concrete proof of some detail of which they were already aware from printed sources. Historians tend also to be suspicious of the readiness with which archaeologists presume that material proof of cultural exchanges between peoples is evidence that they were well disposed toward each other. Many historians are dubious as well about the willingness of archaeologists, and scholars associated with cultural studies, to put their expertise at the disposal of the tourist industry for the creation of visitor centers, which can provide no more than a snapshot of society at a particular moment in time, and which, in a sense, negates the work of historians who are concerned with explaining change over time. Another problem is that some scholars who seek to be 'cutting-edge researchers' become so fascinated with the technologies they employ that they become more concerned with displaying their capabilities than with providing answers to questions about the past. And another concern is that an increasing number of scholars consider the creation of data sets and online compilations to be ends in themselves rather than resources that may be used by them, or others, to address research questions.

While it is correct to celebrate the fact that some limited funding for research in humanities disciplines (including some very large grants) is being made available for competition by the European Union and by some national research councils, including the IRC, this has necessarily resulted in the scholarly work of individuals being monitored by the institutions in which they are employed as well as by the funding bodies that allocate grants to researchers on a competitive basis. One purpose behind institutional monitoring is to force more academic staff to become, and remain, 'research active', and, in sharp contrast with the past, most hiring and promotional decisions in Irish universities are now contingent on applicants' being able to demonstrate their ability to attract research money and/or to have scholarly work published by 'high impact' journals and publishing houses. All such monitoring proceeds from the premise that more means better and that the reputational hierarchy of publishing outlets is a reliable guide for decision-making.

One consequence of such pressures is that a great number of scholars in institutional employment, and particularly those early-stage researchers who survive financially by moving from one research grant to its successor, choose to undertake projects that are likely to yield quick results and early publications, and that draw upon resources that are readily to hand, ideally in well-indexed or digitized editions, and that lend themselves to sampling. Many scholars are also attracted to projects that will provide them with the opportunity to display their proficiency at using 'cutting edge' technologies, and this too is quite understandable since their technological proficiency may well secure them employment outside academia at a time when career positions in humanities disciplines are in steady decline. Such selectivity in the choice of research topics means that large-scale projects that require painstaking research in scattered archives and repositories that might take twenty or more years to complete are unsuitable for early-stage researchers seeking to advance, or launch, their careers. This has not, as yet, caused any major problem for the overall study of early modern Ireland because there are other scholars at hand who undertake these time-consuming projects, while they also take advantage of what has been achieved by those who have compiled user-friendly research resources or have added to the existing store of knowledge through the use of the new technologies.

Among those who show a willingness to persist with long-term projects are some senior scholars in Irish universities who refrain from involvement in team research and from the wearisome business of grant application but still possess the burning desire to solve research questions and contribute to new knowledge. Another group of scholars who, over the past decade, have been making a major contribution to our understanding of the total range of experiences of Irish people during the early modern centuries have been those based in continental universities, more frequently in Spain and France, who seem totally dedicated to searching in the archives to trace the careers of Irish men and women who lived out their lives in their host countries or in the empires that these host societies were in the process of creating overseas. To these might be added scholars from universities in North America, who, once they have met the criteria for promotion to a full professorship (usually two well-reviewed books), are at liberty to take on whatever research subject they may wish, regardless of scope and time. And yet another category includes those who, like myself, have entered upon a publishing career in retirement, where the only regulatory control rests with their own ability to remain alive in reasonable physical and mental health.

This brief conspectus of my own careers and of the changes that I consider to have impacted upon the study of early modern Ireland during the half century they span suggest that we are better placed than ever before to progress into a fresh and deeper understanding of developments in early modern Ireland. The advantages we enjoy over all previous generations are that we are more numerous than ever before, that we come from more varied backgrounds and experiences than our predecessors, that we have more scholars who are linguistically proficient than has been customary, and that we have altogether more scholars who are equipped to engage in cross-disciplinary investigation and use cross-domain technologies to extract new knowledge from unwieldy sources. Under these circumstances, it would be presumptuous of me to establish any research agenda other than to conclude, as I did for my contribution to the *Cambridge History of Ireland*, that 'the future lies with those practitioners who search ceaselessly after fresh knowledge, and employ sophisticated methods and new perspectives that will aid the understanding of how and why people acted as they did in that very turbulent age'.[8]

Notes

1 The Renaissance Society of America, *Annual Meeting Program*, Boston, 31 March–2 April 2016, pp. 243, 260, 278.
2 Nicholas Canny, 'Hugh O'Neill and the changing face of Gaelic Ulster', in *Studia Hibernica* 10 (1970), 7–35; Canny, 'The Flight of the earls, 1607', *Irish Historical Studies* 17 (1971), 380–399.
3 I have abandoned the subject because further work on it would require me to spend extensive time in foreign archives, which is not feasible in retirement. However, I did publish two papers from my preliminary research: Nicholas Canny, 'The Representation of Slaves and Slavery in the Writing on the West Indies during the Early Modern Centuries: French and English Contributions Compared', in Wim Klooster (ed.), *Migration, Trade, and Slavery in an Expanding World: Essays in Honor of Pieter Emmer* (Leiden: Brill, 2009), pp. 197–224, and

Canny, 'A Protestant or Catholic Atlantic World? Confessional Divisions and the Writing of Natural History', The Raleigh Lecture to the British Academy for 2017, *Proceedings of the British Academy* 181 (2012), 83–121.

4 Nicholas Canny, 'Opening Access to Archaeology', *Forum; Open Access und Open Data*, in *Archäologische Informationen* 38 (2015), 21–29.

5 The concept of the 'little ice age' is now well integrated into literature on the early modern world and is the key to appreciating Geoffrey Parker, *Global Crisis: War, Climate Change & Catastrophe in the Seventeenth Century* (New Haven: Yale University Press, 2013).

6 See, for example, Audrey Horning, *Ireland in the Virginian Sea: Colonialism in the British Atlantic* (Chapel Hill: University of North Carolina Press, 2013).

7 Jane Ohlmeyer (ed.), *The Cambridge History of Ireland*, II, *1550–1730* (Cambridge: Cambridge University Press, 2018), especially chapters by Clodagh Tait; Mary O'Dowd; Susan Flavin; Jane Fenlon; William O'Reilly; Annaleigh Margey; Mícheál Ó Siochrú, with David Brown; and Francis Ludlow, with Arlene Crampsie.

8 Ohlmeyer (ed.), *Cambridge History*, II, p. 663.

Acknowledgments

The coeditors wish to thank the Renaissance Society of America, which sponsored three panel sessions in honor of Nicholas Canny at its annual meeting in March 2016. The following essays were commissioned in the wake of those sessions and the ideas and discussions that emerged from them. We are grateful to David Armitage, Ralph Bauer, Martin Burke, Thomas Herron, and Maryclaire Moroney, who also participated in those panels. We also wish to express our gratitude to Laura Pilsworth and Morwenna Scott for supporting this volume and for their patience in helping it along.

Contributors

David Brown is a research fellow at Trinity College Dublin. He is the author of *Trade, Finance and Lobbying: The Adventurers for Irish Land, 1642–1660* (forthcoming) and coeditor, with Micheál Ó Siochrú, of *Books of Survey and Distribution* (forthcoming). He is currently researching digital tools for the automated transcription of handwritten texts.

Marc Caball is Associate Professor at University College Dublin School of History. Among his recent publications are *Kerry, 1600–1730: The Emergence of a British Atlantic County* (2017); 'Language, Print and Literature in Irish, 1550–1630' in Jane Ohlmeyer (ed.), *The Cambridge History of Ireland, volume II 1550–1730* (2018); and 'Creating an Irish Identity: Print, Culture, and the Irish Franciscans of Louvain' in Liam Chambers and Thomas O'Connor (eds.), *Forming Catholic Communities: Irish, Scots and English College Networks in Europe, 1568–1918* (2018).

Ruth A. Canning is Lecturer in History at Liverpool Hope University. She is the author of *The Old English in Early Modern Ireland: The Palesmen and the Nine Years' War, 1594–1603* (forthcoming) as well as essays on various aspects of Ireland and the Old English during the late Elizabethan period. Her current research examines the sociopolitical impact of war on identity formation amongst the Old English population.

Nicholas Canny held an Established Chair of History at the National University of Ireland, Galway, 1979–2009, where he was the founding director of the Moore Institute for Research in Humanities and Social Studies, a position he held from 2000 to 2011. He was elected President of the Royal Academy 2008–11 and was a member of the Scientific Council of the European Research Council from 2011 to 2016. His major book on Irish history is *Making Ireland British, 1580–1650* (2001), and he is currently completing *Imagining Ireland's Pasts: Early Modern Ireland through the Centuries* (forthcoming).

Vincent P. Carey teaches European history at the State University of New York at Plattsburgh in upstate New York. He has published extensively on sixteenth-century Ireland and is currently finishing a book tentatively titled *Murder on the Border of the Pale: A Sixteenth-Century Irish Micro-History*.

Marie-Louise Coolahan is Professor of English at the National University of Ireland, Galway. She is the author of *Women, Writing, and Language in Early Modern Ireland* (2010) as well as articles and essays about women's writing, early modern identity, and textual transmission. She is currently Principal Investigator of the ERC-funded project *RECIRC: The Reception and Circulation of Early Modern Women's Writing, 1550–1700* (www.recirc.nuigalway.ie).

Sarah Covington is Professor of History at the Graduate Center and Queens College of the City University of New York, and director of the Irish Studies program at Queens College. In addition to two books and numerous articles on early modern England and Ireland, she is the author of a forthcoming book that will explore the political, folkloric, literary, and religious afterlives of Oliver Cromwell in Ireland over three centuries.

Arlene Crampsie is a teaching fellow in the School of Geography at University College Dublin. She is the author of *A Decade of Change: Donegal and Ireland, 1912–23* (2013), and coauthor of 'Environmental History of Ireland, 1550–1730' (*Cambridge History of Ireland, Vol. II, 2018*).

John Cunningham is Lecturer in Early Modern Irish and British History at Queen's University Belfast. His publications include *Conquest and Land in Ireland: the Transplantation to Connacht, 1649–1680* (2011) and the edited collection *Ireland and the World of Early Modern Medicine: Practitioners, Collectors and Contexts* (forthcoming).

Coleman A. Dennehy is research fellow at University College Dublin. Dr. Dennehy has authored and edited a number of publications, including *The Irish Parliament, 1613–89: The Evolution of A Colonial Institution* (2018) and *Law and Revolution in Seventeenth-century Ireland* (2018).

David Edwards is Senior Lecturer in History, University College Cork, and Series Editor of 'Studies in Early Modern Irish History'. A contributor to the *Cambridge History of Ireland*, his most recent book is *The Colonial World of Richard Boyle, 1st Earl of Cork* (2018).

Brendan Kane is Associate Professor of History at the University of Connecticut. Dr. Kane has authored, edited, and coedited numerous publications, including *Elizabeth I and Ireland* (2014). He is currently preparing, with David Edwards, a collection of essays for publication, emerging from the conference 'Tudor Ireland and Renaissance Court Society'.

Francis Ludlow is Assistant Professor of history at Trinity College Dublin. A historical climatologist focusing on the ancient, medieval, and early modern periods, Dr. Ludlow has authored and coauthored a number of publications, including 'Mainstreaming Morality: an Examination of Moral Ecologies as a Form of Resistance' (*Journal for the Study of Religion, Nature and Culture*, 2017) and 'The Past, Present and Future of Irish Environmental History' (*PRIA C*, 2014).

James Lyttleton is the author of numerous publications, including *Jacobean Plantations in Seventeenth-Century Offaly: an Archaeology of a Changing World* (2013), and coeditor of *Plantation Ireland: Settlement and Material Culture, c. 1550-c.1700* (2009).

Willy Maley is Professor of Renaissance Studies at the University of Glasgow. His many publications include *Salvaging Spenser: Colonialism, Culture and Identity* (1997) and *Nation, State and Empire in English Renaissance Literature: Shakespeare to Milton* (2003). He has also coedited a number of collections, including *British Identities and English Renaissance Literature* (2002) and *Celtic Shakespeare: The Bard and the Borderers* (2013).

Valerie McGowan-Doyle is Professor of History at Lorain County Community College and Adjunct Associate Professor of History at Kent State University. She is the author of *The Book of Howth: Elizabethan Conquest and the Old English* (2011) and coeditor of *Elizabeth I and Ireland* (2014). Her current research examines violence against women in early modern Ireland.

Sarah E. McKibben is Associate Professor of Irish Language and Literature, fellow of the Keough-Naughton Institute for Irish Studies and the Nanovic Institute for European Studies, and Concurrent Professor of Gender Studies at the University of Notre Dame. She is the author of *Endangered Masculinities in Irish Poetry, 1540–1780* (2010) as well as a number of essays and is currently preparing a monograph on aspects of the bardic poetic response to political and socioeconomic change, c.1560–1660.

Peter McQuillan is Associate Professor of Irish Language and Literature at the University of Notre Dame. Dr. McQuillan has published widely on Irish language and literature in the medieval and early modern period, including *Native and Natural: Aspects of the Concepts of Right and Freedom in Irish* (2004) and *Modality and Grammar: a History of the Irish Subjunctive* (2002).

Bronagh McShane is a National University of Ireland postdoctoral fellow based at the Moore Institute at NUI, Galway. The author of various articles, including 'Negotiating Religious Change and Conflict: Female Religious Communities in Early Modern Ireland', c. 1530-c.1641 (*British Catholic History*, vol. 33, 2017), she is currently preparing a monograph on the history of early modern Irish nuns.

Jane Ohlmeyer, MRIA, is Erasmus Smith Professor of Modern History at Trinity College, Dublin. Among her numerous publications are *Making Ireland English: the Formation of an Aristocracy in the Seventeenth Century* (2012) and *Cambridge History of Ireland, Vol. II, 1550–1730* (2018), for which she served as editor. Dr. Ohlmeyer is currently preparing an edition of the eighteenth-century text *A shorte view of the state and condicon of the kingdome of Ireland/The History of the Rebellion and Civil Wars in Ireland* by Edward Hyde, earl of Clarendon.

Dr. Micheál Ó Siochrú is Professor of History at Trinity College Dublin. He is the author of numerous books and articles on seventeenth-century Ireland, including *God's Executioner: Oliver Cromwell and the conquest of Ireland* (2009), and was Principal Investigator on the 1641 Depositions and Down Survey of Ireland projects. He is currently preparing a new edition of Oliver Cromwell's letters and papers and is leading the Books of Survey and Distribution project.

Clodagh Tait is Lecturer at Mary Immaculate College in Limerick. She is the author of numerous works, including *Death, Burial and Commemoration in Ireland, 1550–1650* (2002), and coeditor of *Age of Atrocity: violence and political conflict in early modern Ireland* (2007) and *Religion and Politics in Urban Ireland, c. 1500–1750: Essays in Honour of Colm Lennon* (2016).

1 Introduction

The past, present, and future of early modern Ireland

Sarah Covington, Vincent P. Carey, and Valerie McGowan-Doyle

Few historical developments have been as revolutionary as the events which occurred in Ireland over the early modern period. In 1500, the country was a lordship of the English crown, though rule from London was weak, and vast territories outside the Pale were controlled by independent and mighty aristocratic families of Gaelic Irish and Old English stock. By 1700, Ireland was technically a kingdom though also, confusingly, a colony whose conquest had been very much 'consolidated' through wars and dispossession.[1] As for the Gaelic elite, they were well eclipsed from power by 1700, even if their cultural (and with Jacobite poetry, political) world lived on.[2] Catholicism, which was the sole faith in Ireland at the beginning of the sixteenth century, as it was in Europe more generally, continued to be the church of most people in Ireland, though in 1700 it existed under an oppressive regime dominated by the new Anglo-Irish Protestant minority. Ireland's landscape in 1500, meanwhile, was also relatively unknown to the English, at least cartographically; by 1700, the country was the most systematically mapped in Europe, leading to a revolution in property ownership with the small Protestant class owning an enormous majority of the land.[3] In short, anyone who had lived in 1500 and was suddenly propelled forward to 1700 would hardly have recognized the place at all.[4]

Historical and literary scholarship relating to this time has undergone its own transformations as well, particularly in the twentieth century. To generalize (and also bypass some important exceptions, which will be discussed later in this chapter), over sixty years ago it was possible to read a 300-page book on sixteenth-century England that mentioned Ireland in precisely seven pages, with the country indexed under 'rebellion of'.[5] The wars of the mid-seventeenth century, still labeled the 'Civil War', the 'Puritan Revolution', or the 'English Revolution', hardly mentioned related and contributing developments in Ireland. Studies of Ireland were overwhelmingly focused on political and economic history,[6] and with some exceptions, the country's place in the bourgeoning British Empire and larger world was bypassed.[7] It was rare to read of the violence in the period, even if nineteenth-century histories, particularly those of a nationalist orientation, certainly dwelled on it.[8] Women were hardly examined at all, while the social and cultural worlds that animated different groups or men such as Geoffrey Keating tended to be overlooked as well, despite—again—intense interest in the subject during the nineteenth century. Not least, Edmund Spenser was still largely known as the author of the *Faerie Queene*, not as the man who spent significant time in Ireland and whose work was deeply informed by that country.[9]

Our picture of early modern Ireland is entirely different today due in great part to the pioneering efforts of scholars who began to ask new questions of the period in the 1970s. This collection has itself been inspired by the contributions of one of those scholars, Nicholas Canny, for whom three sessions of the Renaissance Society of America (RSA) annual meeting in 2016 were given in honor of his contributions to early modern history. All the panelists at that conference were based in North American universities to underscore our appreciation of how Canny essentially opened up the field for those of us working there. The collection has now moved well beyond those RSA sessions, but its other intent remains the same: to suggest further avenues for research in early modern Ireland and to offer, in the process, new ways of thinking about the approaches and methods of our respective and intermingling disciplines.

To be fair, many scholars before the 1970s offered their own significant contributions to our understanding of the period. But with Canny, Brendan Bradshaw, Ciaran Brady, Colm Lennon, Steven Ellis, and Toby Barnard, followed generationally by Bernadette Cunningham, Mary O'Dowd, Raymond Gillespie, Vincent Carey, and Alan Ford, the field today has now fully arrived and grown. An increasing number of monographs, articles, and collections are published every year on early modern Ireland or (for better and worse) on 'Britain and Ireland'. Volume Two of the recent *Cambridge History of Ireland* is an essential contribution and will be referenced for decades to come.[10] The earlier *New Oxford History of Ireland*, and Volume Three especially, also remains an invaluable reference, along with guides such as *Sources for Modern Irish History 1534–1641*.[11] Digital humanities is flourishing around early modern Ireland, while literary scholarship that focuses on Ireland has especially proliferated in recent years, spurred on in part by the publication of the *Field Day Anthology of Irish Writing* (including Volume Four, on women)[12] and postcolonial studies in the 1990s. The house of Spenser continues to grow (perhaps at the expense of other writers on Ireland), with his Irish dimension deepening our understanding of his work, while new attention paid to Irish-language prose and poetry, exiled continental writings, and material presented on digital humanities platforms—to cite just a few examples—has similarly flourished. Early modern (or rather 'post-medieval') archaeology has also helped us to understand more about plantations, domestic and church structures, artifacts, and other physical survivals, and the clues and conclusions they yield, while material culture has extended more broadly into other disciplines.[13] And historical geography, after the equally seminal efforts of John Andrews and William Smyth, itself represents a cutting edge of scholarship, especially in its focus on cartographers and surveyors such as Richard Bartlett and William Petty.[14]

The chapters in this collection seek on the one hand to build on this existing literature by focusing on new sources, questions, methods, and approaches
that present and future scholars may pursue to possibly field-changing effect.
But pursuing 'new directions' does not simply mean that one presents a fresh
and original topic or source, or applies brilliantly innovative interpretations
to a well-trodden one. It can also involve an overhaul of one's own existing assumptions about what the writing of history, literature, or archaeology
might traditionally mean and the very terms on which we think, in this case,
of Ireland's past. Not least, it calls us to examine our own vested interests
in choosing or framing our subjects and sources the way we do, and the
particular contexts and agendas in which we write. Ireland in the centuries
between 1500 and 1700 may therefore be more known than ever before; yet
it still remains an elusive entity, requiring new tools and methods to widen
its bounds and excavate its other depths. And while no one can truly foresee
what new historical or scholarly turns lie ahead, the interdisciplinary essays
which follow attempt to point the way by asking questions and suggesting
answers. What, for example, are the sources that have yet to be probed, and
how should they be used? In what ways should the disciplines better address
each other? How can political or social history be taken into new territories?
In what ways should Irish-language material be incorporated more deeply
into studies that remain dominated by English-language sources? And what
new theoretical or thematic approaches have not yet been applied to early
modern Ireland or even discovered at all? Not least, how do the questions
we ask ourselves today—or may ask ourselves tomorrow—shape our own
approach to this most turbulent time and place?

Past and current directions

Historians of early modern Ireland hold a particularly poignant relationship
to the period they study, not least because so many sources—with the exception of Irish-language poems and prose works, which are plentiful[15]—are so
scarce or have perished. The most spectacular incident that brought on this
relative dearth was the conflagration of the Public Record Office in 1922,
which was destroyed in the midst of the Civil War, incinerating an incalcu-
lable number of administrative, legislative, ecclesiastical, and court records
relating to Ireland from the thirteenth through nineteenth centuries. For
early modernists especially, it is not too much of an exaggeration to state that
this loss is viewed as comparable to the burning of the Library of Alexandria
or the destruction of the Mayan Codices, even though a project is underway
to digitally reconstruct the archive.[16] Other acts of destruction also occurred,
however, to undermine the source base of pre-1700 records. In 1711, a fire
in the Custom Office reduced privy council books and records from the
surveyor general's office to a charred heap; in 1758, another fire, this time at
Dublin Castle's Birmingham Tower, extinguished central administration records, such as rolls of common pleas and pleas of the crown.[17] Historians have

thus had to rely upon sources such as surviving State Papers, which reflect correspondence between Dublin Castle and the Privy Council in London, resulting in the oft-repeated 'castle-centric' view of Irish history.[18] On the other hand, we know much of early modern Ireland—or rather perceptions of early modern Ireland—because the writing of it extends back to the period itself, in works by Spenser, Edmund Campion, Richard Stanihurst, Mícheál Ó Cléirigh, and Geoffrey Keating.[19]

The eighteenth century also issued its histories or, with the Thomas Carte papers, its repositories. But it was not until the nineteenth century that the period was given renewed attention, spurred on by Catholic emancipation, emergent nationalist and unionist movements, and the tensions around the Land War, which viewed events in early modern Ireland as the source of the current outrageous dispensation.[20] J. P. Prendergast, who changed his positions on such issues as Home Rule later in life, thus offered a (nationalist) study of Ireland in the 1650s that fell on sympathetic ears and, in the words of John Cunningham, made certain that issues such as the 'forced transplantation of peoples west ... now bulked larger in the public consciousness and in histories of mid seventeenth-century Ireland than had previously been the case'.[21] In the wake of the 1922 fire, the works of Prendergast and his contemporaries or near-contemporaries J. A. Froude, Mary Hickson, John Gilbert, P.F. Moran, S.R. Gardiner, and Robert Dunlop—not to mention the local archaeological journals—became especially important as they included in their works material and documents now lost to the flames.[22] On the other hand, while these scholars were careful in their editorial practices, they also intervened in choosing, omitting, or cutting parts of their texts by necessity and sometimes strategy—though what precisely went missing, unfortunately, cannot entirely be discerned, given the loss of those original records.

Richard Bagwell's three-volume *Ireland under the Tudors*, first composed in 1885 and followed by his *Ireland under the Stuarts*, was one of the first systematic histories of the modern period and focused on political, administrative, and military history: unsurprising for a work compiled primarily from the State Papers—though other sources were consulted—and written in an age that privileged the political as the only history which mattered.[23] Bagwell was an acolyte of the great eighteenth-century historian W.E.H. Lecky and contemporary with Lecky's nemesis Froude, and if he lacked the imaginative range and literary style of either, his volumes comprised a valuable narrative survey that embodied the careful textual scholarship of its time.[24] Bagwell's other contemporary, William F.T. Butler—born in Tipperary and described as 'at once dominantly Norman and notably Irish'[25]—found much to dislike in the book, however. Butler's own focus was on the legal and fiscal aspects of land tenure in the late medieval and early modern period, and he found Bagwell's treatment of New English settlements during the Tudor period 'inadequate'. More significantly, Butler, in another work, took the measure of the Gaelic Irish world, thus filling in a subject that had been relatively overlooked in Bagwell.[26]

Despite these fastidious if somewhat parched works, however, it was the nationalist, unionist, or generally sectarian histories that compelled historians in the 1930s to advocate for a new method and approach to Ireland's past. The movement that came to be known as revisionism, which emerged out of Irish scholars' training in London's Institute of Historical Research and found expression in the journal *Irish Historical Studies*, would dominate generations of historians and elicit much controversy, not least in its stated pursuit of what became known as 'value-free' history—a stance which appeared especially egregious to those who believed it minimized or even effaced the very real traumas of Ireland's past.[27] The resurgence of revisionism in a new context—that is, the 1970s and especially the 1980s—provoked yet more controversy. It should be noted that revisionism's founding fathers, Robert Dudley Edwards and Theodore William Moody, never believed that pure objectivity could ever truly be achieved in the consulting of 'neutral' sources. They also divulged, wittingly or not, political biases or convictions of their own. Edwards's *Church and State in Tudor Ireland* (1935) revealed a Catholic and nationalist bias, and Moody's *The Londonderry Plantation, 1609–1641* (1939) reflected what has been called a kind of 'moderate unionism', which would change over the course of the latter's career.[28] Both works, and Edwards' particularly, would continue to be heavily cited by historians such as Steven Ellis, Colm Lennon, Ciaran Brady, and Raymond Gillespie, and they remain significant works today.[29]

Canny has pointed out that an increasing emphasis among revisionists on the history of the nineteenth century, however, led to early modern Ireland being defined in terms of that century's preoccupations, resulting in a kind of 'insularity' with 'primacy ... given to a narrowly defined Irish history that maintained links with an equally narrow version of English history'.[30] It was therefore an enormous step in a different direction when David Beers Quinn, among the first generation of revisionists, transferred his training in Tudor administrative history to the Atlantic world at large, connecting plantations in Ireland, for example, to the larger British imperial global order that was then emerging.[31] Quinn's interest in other disciplines, including anthropology and geography, and perhaps his position on the academic margins (based as he was at the University of Liverpool), gave him a different perspective that allowed him to connect Ireland to the Americas and the North American colonies more specifically. Relatedly, his seminal *The Elizabethans and the Irish* was one of the first to place Elizabeth's relationship with the Irish in overtly colonialist terms, emphasizing the clash of civilizations—English, Old English, and Irish.[32]

Quinn's work was not entirely appreciated in the 1960s, but it would certainly come to influence Canny in its broader comparative approach, and be reinforced by his years as a student under the tutelage of the great Atlanticist Richard Dunn at the University of Pennsylvania. Canny's wide-ranging interests focused, in part, on the expansion of England to Ireland and the Atlantic world, and the ideological, legal, and political mechanisms that propelled and reinforced such an undertaking. But he was equally, and relatedly, interested in intellectual history and ideology, and the particular contexts which determine and are determined by them. His *Elizabethan Conquest of Ireland: A Pattern Established* (1976) used careful archival research to argue for a political, ideological, and legal model for English colonization—one based upon similar enterprises in Europe, even if it radically diverged in the land ruptures that ensued.[33] Canny's *Making Ireland British* was a field-changing study of colonial policy that began with the Munster Plantations of the 1580s and particularly the man—Edmund Spenser—who advocated for them. Ending on the eve of the Cromwellian invasion of 1649, the book connects the processes by which the country was 'made British' during these decades, even as it avoids any kind of teleology in doing so. Canny's contribution in a number of articles on the Old English (mentioned later in this chapter) and Anglo-Irish identity, and Irish-language poetry—as well as his current work on the writing of early modern Ireland—ensures his place as a scholar who set the terms of debate and continues to do so, based on his discovery and insightful readings of the sources.[34]

None of Canny's positions went uncontested, of course, and it was a contemporary of Canny's, Brendan Bradshaw, whose own studies away from Ireland led him also into new directions.[35] Having been trained at the revisionist University College Dublin, Bradshaw proceeded for his graduate work to Cambridge University. His influences, however, were Eóin MacNeill and Edmund Curtis, both of whom preceded the revisionist movement, which Bradshaw famously rejected as being detached and not entirely truthful about the past—and particularly so after the movement enjoyed a resurgence in the wake of the Troubles.[36] Bradshaw was vociferously attacked for this stance and for his related assertion that a 'national consciousness' existed in the sixteenth century and among the Old English community in reaction to the New English settlers, and later in a seventeenth-century Gaelic Irish and Old English 'fusion' (with the latter stance also contested). Aside from these much-debated positions, Bradshaw was not wrong in advocating for alternative ways of presenting the past; for decades, to cite one example, revisionists largely overlooked the contributions of the *Annales* school, also founded in the 1930s. Moreover, Bradshaw's calling attention to the limitations of what had become academic orthodoxy also directly or indirectly led to the challenges of the 'post-revisionists' and the inclusion or rediscovery of subjects such as colonial politics and violence.

Bradshaw was also challenged in an especially acrimonious debate in the 1980s with Steven Ellis,[37] whose own work sought in part to emphasize early modern Ireland 'on its own terms' rather than based on 'modern' assumptions that it was marked by polarized communities and a violence that was exceptional. For Ellis, violence in Ireland was comparable to that experienced in other English borderlands, including Wales, Northern England, or Calais, and while brutality was certainly apparent in Ireland, it reflected an inability to assert crown authority and was largely reflective of an administrative problem.[38] Ellis applied Geoffrey Elton's archival approach as an administrative historian to early modern Ireland, treating the country not as a colony but as a problem of wider royal control for an expanding Tudor state. Criticism of Ellis's borderlands thesis was far-ranging, but his and Christopher Maginn's contributions to understanding Tudor administrative workings in Ireland remain invaluable in their detail and continue to provoke further scholarship around questions of early modern England's relationship to Ireland.

The titanic debates between Canny, Bradshaw, and Ellis, and their separate positions on early modern Ireland, would prove fruitful in inspiring future scholarship, with another powerful response coming from Ciaran Brady, who took issue with (among other things) Bradshaw's stance on the humanist origins of reform policy or the emergence of an incipient nationalism in Ireland, and Canny's on the innovations of Henry Sidney. Similarly contentious was the debate between Brady and Canny over the singular contribution of Spenser's *View of the Present State of Ireland*: a debate which spurred on the enormous growth of interest among literary scholars in Spenser's career in and writings related to Ireland.[39] The question of Irish poetry and its relation to political realities (or not) was also productive, its very ferocity compelling scholars to think through new questions and forcefully argue their own positions in what remains an ongoing yet fertile debate.[40]

Just as representations of Ireland as uncivilized were used to underpin justifications for conquest, so too were representations of the Old English as the cause of failed conquest used to rationalize their displacement at the hands of the increasing numbers of newly arriving administrators, planters, and military personnel in the Tudor period. Old English retention of Catholicism heightened fears of that group's disloyalty, particularly during the Nine Years' War, when Spenser described them as 'much more lawless and licentious than the very wild Irish', following a sixteenth-century trend which attributed the failures and difficulties of completed English conquest to their Gaelicization, or 'degeneration', the term used more frequently to describe their adoption of Gaelic language and customs, their use of Irish wet-nurses, and their marriage to and fosterage with Irish families.[41] As Aidan Clarke wrote in his important 1966 study, by the mid-seventeenth century, the Old English had, as long feared, joined with the Gaelic community in resisting English forces, in the aftermath of suffering significant loss of land and further erosion of their social, economic, and political positions under post-Cromwellian land confiscation and resettlement.[42] (Clarke's other contribution in illuminating the new Protestant community on the eve of the Restoration also ensured his status as canonical.)[43] Understanding the earlier stages of Old English identity formation and displacement in the Tudor period would therefore become important not only in reconstructing their own history but, more crucially, in offering a fundamental plank by which to discern the nature of colonial policy and rhetoric more comprehensively. It was Canny, again, who set the stage for studies of the Old English in this earlier foundational phase of their displacement with his 1974 O'Donnell Lecture at the National University of Ireland, Galway, entitled 'The Formation of the Old English Elite in Ireland'.[44] Ensuing studies focused on individuals and families, beginning with Colm Lennon's 1978 'Richard Stanihurst (1547–1618) and Old English Identity' and being continued by the next generation of historians, notably in Vincent Carey's study of the eleventh Earl of Kildare; David Edwards's study of the Ormond lordship; and Valerie McGowan-Doyle's study of Christopher St. Lawrence, seventh baron of Howth.[45] More recent studies, including those by Ruth Canning and Gerald Power, have returned to broader explorations of the Old English community's experience of and response to Tudor conquest and displacement.[46]

The 1990s also saw important developments crystallize in a 1995 seminar at the Folger Institute in Washington, D.C., under the direction of Hiram Morgan, which brought together established and emerging scholars. Building on the Center for the Study of British Political Thought, this seminar brought Ireland into the forefront of early modern studies and grounded the next wave of approaches to early modern Irish history.[47] Morgan's extensive work on Hugh O'Neill, Earl of Tyrone, and the Nine Years' War also further shifted Ireland into the limelight and away from its place as a 'footnote' in early modern British history to a subject in its own right.[48] His attention to O'Neill's strategy of 'faith and fatherland' signaled the inclusion of yet broader contexts as he compared O'Neill's revolt against English rule to the contemporary Dutch revolt against the Habsburgs.[49] In tandem with studies of O'Neill's subsequent departure from Ireland to the continent, which opened up Ulster to Plantation,[50] attention to continental comparisons and contexts would continue to grow under the guidance of scholars such as Mary Ann Lyons and Thomas O'Connor, mentioned later in the chapter.[51]

While Canny, Brady, and Morgan extended their purview into the seventeenth century, it is also important to note other and earlier innovators, many still active, who added to our understanding of that later time. In 1961, Hugh Kearney transformed the previous benign portrait of Thomas Wentworth, the first Earl of Strafford, and his tenure in 1630s Ireland, arguing instead that the lord deputy often continued previous misconceived policies and contributed much to the disaster to come.[52] Following in the next generation of seventeenth-century historians, Karl Bottigheimer, influenced in part by quantitative history, which enjoyed its heyday in the mid-1970s, applied its methods to seminal books and articles on such subjects as the Cromwellian Adventurers or earlier investors in the conquest of Ireland. While quantitative or data-driven history has allegedly been out of fashion for a while, its methods could well be useful again in approaching such digitally amenable texts as the Down Survey or Books of Survey and Distribution. Meanwhile, Toby Barnard's groundbreaking study of Cromwellian Ireland and its emerging or evolving institutions remains the most important source on the subject, while his explorations of the Anglo-Irish world (and his disruption of traditional periodizations) has also contributed to his impressive scope as a scholar, stretched more recently to include the study of print and material culture.[53]

Another transformation in seventeenth-century scholarship which pushed early modern Ireland beyond its historiographic insularity was the 'archipelagic turn', sometimes known (not unproblematically) as the New British History. In a lecture given in New Zealand, at the farthest reaches of Britain's commonwealth, and (pointedly) delivered a few months after the UK entered the European Economic Committee in 1973, J.G.A. Pocock sought to invest the term 'Britain' with a new kind of political meaning. Specifically, he argued for a 'plural history of a group of cultures situated along an Anglo-Celtic frontier and marked by an increasing English political and cultural domination': an undertaking that would entail, among other things, an exploration of the mutual interactions and interrelations between England and its 'provinces'. Pocock reminded us that such pluralist histories—which could extend oceanically to North America and south to the antipodes— were not new, as he himself was indebted to the Victorian J.R. Seeley. But by recognizing different 'historical consciousnesses' at work in the archipelago, Pocock most forcefully promoted the inherent diversity that could unloosen the kind of monolithic and primarily Anglocentric history that had increasingly become the norm.

It was actually an Irishman, J.C. Beckett, who first coined the term 'wars of the three kingdoms' in reference to the conflicts of the 1640s and early 1650s.[54] But Conrad Russell most famously took up Pocock's call in casting out the 'Civil War' or 'English Revolution' in favor of a larger conflict that acknowledged the intertwined events that occurred in Scotland and Ireland, and became inextricably part of something much more than a civil war.[55] Russell was criticized for providing what John Morrill has called an 'enhanced English history', and indeed, a lingering Anglocentrism has persisted in the years since, particularly in many works of political or cultural history that seek to address a given subject 'in Britain and Ireland'. Even so, the treatment of the three kingdoms—or with Wales, the four nations—has proven extremely fruitful for Ireland, not simply in the discipline of history but in literary studies as well.[56]

The new 'Wars of the Three Kingdoms' assumed an especially dynamic turn with Jane Ohlmeyer, whose earlier scholarship included seminal collections which she supervised, sometimes collaboratively, and which constitute some of the best and most balanced treatments of seventeenth-century military and political history in Ireland, particularly as it pertains to its relations with the archipelago and the continent.[57] Ohlmeyer's personal background is also deeply international, which perhaps influenced her longer and indeed more global perspective when it came to Ireland. In addition to her significant contributions to the study of seventeenth-century political thought in Ireland, or her sweeping study of the Irish peerage, Ohlmeyer's work has emphasized the importance of connections that took place across what she calls the North Channel world, specifically between prominent and titled individuals such as the Marquis of Antrim, who straddled Scotland and Ulster with great facility. Her *Making Ireland English* also convincingly argued that the decline of smaller land proprietors and the rise of a service aristocracy in Ireland fit into larger European trends. Ohlmeyer's current work on the global networks and governmental and colonialist processes that joined early modern Ireland to India promises to open up an entirely new territory as well, as she urges future scholars to 'interrogate eastward enterprises, as well as westward ones, in a more interconnected way'.[58]

The 1980s through the 2000s would thus come to signal the period in which much of this formative scholarship was fully absorbed and sustained, moving into further directions often taken by the original pioneers themselves. But other approaches and methods to writing the past were also assimilated into new monographs, collections, and articles. Social history and anthropologically influenced histories, which had been ascendant since the 1960s and 1970s, found their expression in the work of Raymond Gillespie, who also uncovered new sources or deployed known sources in fresh ways— for example, in his study of popular religion or the social world of print. Clodagh Tait has also contributed to our understanding of such phenomena as martyrdom, the dead, or childbirth, and is one of the few historians, along with Gillespie, to work with (and, in her case, to also be trained in) folklore. The perspective on violence offered by scholars such as Natalie Zemon Davis has also influenced the work of Vincent Carey, who subsequently joined other contributors in the now-classic breakthrough volume edited by David Edwards, Pádraig Lenihan, and Clodagh Tait, entitled *The Age of Atrocity: Violence and Political Conflict in Early Modern Ireland*.[59]

Meanwhile, the related cultural turn of the 1980s and 1990s was also applied to early modern Ireland (often without the accompanying theory, at least when it came to history). Interestingly, many of the best cultural treatments, which brought in the *Annalistes* at last with their exploration of *mentalités*, related to the Gaelic world. These works ranged from Bernadette Cunningham's masterful and now-seminal presentation of (the Old English but Gaelic-sensitive) Geoffrey Keating to Brendan Kane's study of honor, and from Breandán Ó Buachalla's brilliant studies of seventeenth- and eighteenth-century political poetry or literary genres to Marc Caball's work on the early seventeenth-century Gaelic literary and political world. Continuing along this linguistic path, and reflecting the richness of Irish-language material, are Peter McQuillan's studies of the conceptual worlds, primarily of a political nature, contained in words themselves.[60] At the same time, cultural history also inspired scholars to examine questions of representation, which led to a number of interesting studies on the manner in which Ireland was 'read and written'—represented—from English (New and Old) and Irish perspectives.[61] Spenser, of course, was key here. Portrayals of Ireland as uncivilized were inexorably attached to beliefs in the necessity of violence,[62] and in fact, it was literary scholars, including Andrew Hadfield, Clare Carroll, and Patricia Palmer, influenced, in turn, by postcolonial theory, who were among the first to call attention to the rhetorical and actual performance of violence in early modern Ireland after decades of pointed neglect.[63]

Another turn, the so-called religious one that began in the 1990s, might not have been exactly 'new', but it did succeed in pushing religion to the forefront of literary and historical studies after a period in which it was relatively sidelined. Not least, it reframed our understanding of the Reformation or early modern Catholicism.[64] The question of the Reformation's ultimate failure in Ireland, which had first been systematically addressed by Brendan Bradshaw and Canny, was subsequently examined in studies by Karl Bottigheimer, Arthur Murray, and Henry Jeffries.[65] Meanwhile, Toby Barnard, Robert Armstrong and Alan Ford's work on the Church of Ireland, in addition to that of more recent scholars such as Mark Empey, has extended our understanding of the institution and its notable members, including James Ussher and James Ware.[66] Religion during the Cromwellian period was often bypassed (though not by Barnard), but Crawford Gribben has contributed the most extensive study of the many theological (and largely sectarian) debates that raged in those years, while scholars such as Sandra Hynes and Richard Greaves have rejuvenated the study of such groups as the Quakers and other nonconformist dissidents in Ireland.[67] For Catholicism in this period, some of the most important contributions have been offered, in turn, through the many Ireland-related and transnational studies by Tadhg Ó hAannracháin.[68]

Finally, one could speak of another not-altogether-new but still highly reinvigorated turn in the continental one. Of course, this 'turn', like others, simply accords with historical developments of the time, when thousands of merchants, soldiers, religious, and elites maintained contacts with or fled by necessity to Europe. But following the essential work of Louis Cullen,[69] Micheál Mac Craith, Thomas O'Connor, Mary Ann Lyons, and Éamon Ó Ciosáin, and—not least—continental scholars such as Óscar Recio Morales, Igor Pérez Tostado, and Alain Le Noac'h, recent scholarship has displayed a rejuvenated interest in Irish communities in European exile, perhaps influenced by migration, network, diasporic, and transnational studies, not to mention the freer movement of peoples within the borders of the European Union.[70] New sources have been uncovered in continental archives, while the Irish in Europe Project and the special series on the topic published by Four Courts Press allow us greater understanding of Irish communities of priests, scholars, and (to a lesser extent now) soldiers abroad, and the sometimes rivalrous tensions between them. Studies of the Irish in Europe also provide some of the most exciting interdisciplinary approaches in early modern scholarship, focused in great part on Irish-language sources and cultural history. The manner in which Irish and continental cultures informed and transformed each other, particularly through literary genres and across French, Spanish, and Italian regions and cities, is a subject that promises to yield even more benefits in the years to come.[71]

All of these 'turns'—including others, such as the material turn or the older turn to gender—are evident in volume two of the *Cambridge History of Ireland*. A comparison between that volume and the *New Oxford History* might be productive here in tracking the kind of historical and historiographical transformations discussed in this brief and partial survey. The multi-volume *New Oxford History* took many decades to complete, its life span extending from before the Troubles began to the years after they had ended; it was first formulated in the 1960s, with the early modern-related volume three appearing in 1976, and thus bearing the thematic stamp and style of the revisionist generations (including Moody as one of its editors). The *Cambridge History*, on the other hand, was published at a moment in history when a European-Unionized Republic of Ireland located itself firmly in a new, digitized global order (with Northern Ireland tethered, in turn, to the fate of the United Kingdom after Brexit); perhaps as a result, an emphasis in the Cambridge volume is placed on 'global interactions' and 'wider contexts', even if the national or local is recognized as well.[72] In the Oxford volume, politics and the church receive overwhelming coverage, joined by economic and military history, one chapter on the Irish language, and another on coinage. With the revisionist wars having waned, and the 'new history' no longer new, the Cambridge volume, while beginning with political history (thus still privileging it, perhaps), broadens more widely to include cultural history, religion, the Atlantic world, gender, family, material culture, and print and manuscript culture. In other words, the Cambridge volume is of the moment, even as it points ahead to the future. But in the wake of Brexit and with increasing skepticism about the kind of economic, global, political, and technological developments that have dominated the world for the previous twenty years, it can be stated with some certainty that the world will change again and, with it, the questions that scholars apply to the past.

New directions

While the essays in this volume offer new paths of inquiry, other ideas might be acknowledged here. Literary scholars, archaeologists, and historical geographers are well-versed in theory, but historians might use it more extensively than they have in order to bring new interpretations and readings to their sources. The manner in which political or ideological discourse distinct to Ireland is rhetorically shaped and received across a broader public, for example, needs more investigation, with reception theory perhaps serving the latter. Studies of ideological discourse should also address the ways in which that discourse is gendered or uses gendered terms at the level of language (Joan Scott, in other words, might be revisited).[73]

Material culture, as Susan Flavin has pointed out, is also in its 'infancy', at least among historians (though not to archaeologists) of early modern Ireland;[74] yet it would deepen further studies of the subject to incorporate theoretically sophisticated approaches long known by those archaeologists—for example, the works of James Deetz or Tim Ingold, as well as essential contributions by Tadgh O'Keefe, Elizabeth Fitzpatrick, Audrey Horning, and others.[75] Finally, Giorgio Agamben's theoretical ideas about law (including martial law) and violence might be fruitful, while the concept of the 'glocal' or 'glocalization' that emphasizes the local and regional, as well as the universal, could complicate the emphasis placed so often now on a 'globalizing' early modern Ireland.[76] While some may dismiss these approaches as 'trends', an actual reading of the literature behind them could only enrich the questions and perspectives we bring to the sources.

Micheál Ó Siochrú has also pointed out that scholars must move beyond traditional periodizations; for example, many early modern practitioners end their studies at 1660, despite the great continuities that existed up through the end of the century. But why stop at the end of the century? Despite the deep ruptures effected by the Cromwellian, Restoration, and Williamite settlements, continuities also existed across the threshold of 1700, as Ian McBride, Sean Connolly, Toby Barnard, and others have demonstrated. Deana Rankin has also stretched the traditional periodizations by connecting Spenser to Swift.[77] Continuing this trend, a good study could be conducted, for example, that examines the history of 'Present State of Ireland' treatises—of which Spenser and Swift were but two authors—and carries it through the nineteenth century, acknowledging, of course, the different contexts of their production. Or those who work on the *Annals of the Four Masters* might similarly use their expertise to compare the shaping of the text by its nineteenth-century translator, John O'Donovan. In other words, and as Canny and Brady have demonstrated in their own work, early modernists may leap ahead with as much facility as their modernist counterparts who extend themselves backward in time. In this regard, David Armitage's notion of transtemporal history might be especially useful here.[78] Finally, Vincent Morley's *Popular Mind in Eighteenth Century Ireland* offers further alternatives, not simply in its (rightful) advocacy of Irish-language sources but in the way it demonstrates how those sources reveal great swathes of the 'vernacular culture' of the past and its continuities as well. Pre-1700 scholars would be particularly enriched by his iconoclastic approach in reading these sources and in casting off some of the scholarly prejudices that have closed off past approaches—and understandings—of this material.

The essays that follow offer further avenues of research, with established and early-career scholars having been asked to loosely brainstorm their own thoughts on where the field should go. In Chapter 2, Clodagh Tait explores the value of wills as a fertile source for social and cultural history, suggesting methods for finding, utilizing, and applying new frameworks to them. Wills, for example, may account for and illuminate material culture, consumption patterns, and domestic inventories; they also provide a record of economic change and land ownership. In addition to providing insight on early modern networks, Tait also suggests that the flourishing fields of the history of emotions may be applied to these wills, which were 'designed as sites of emotional equilibrium', of acceptance or resignation, even though they also conveyed religiously inflected fear, remorse, terror, love for another, or guilt.[79]

Related to the history of emotions is the pursuit of early modern subjectivity, with Marie-Louise Coolahan, in Chapter 3, investigating life-writings and what they reveal about selfhood and gender across different early modern sources and genres. With some exceptions, including Naomi McAreavey's important work, treatments of subjectivity, Coolahan writes, have yet to fully arrive in sixteenth- and seventeenth-century Irish literary and historical scholarship. But selfhood is an essential topic for historians and literary scholars to consider, not least for its association with modernity. To study such documents as depositions or petitions through its prism may yield great insights about property rights claims, encounters with violence or economic loss, relations between personal experience and the state, experiences of war, or subjective religious experiences.

Wills are one of the sources also utilized by Bronagh McShane in her essay on clerical wives in early modern Ireland (Chapter 4). Though the subject has received extensive attention in England and elsewhere, the study of Church of Ireland wives and widows has been neglected in the story of the Reformation in Ireland.[80] Much of this is due, again, to the thinness of sources, but McShane demonstrates how a new subject of research can be accessed if one mines for alternative and underused (and Irish-language) material. Above all, she demonstrates with her case study that women were not marginal but central to the Reformation in Ireland and elsewhere, and that by studying them, we are given further insight into 'the nature and impact of religious change and reform in early modern Ireland'.

McShane's inclusion of Irish-language sources reminds us of how important it is that scholars engage with that material in order to convey a fuller picture of early modern Ireland. As Brendan Kane reminds us in Chapter 5, however, many continue to resist the need to learn Irish as they either rely upon sometimes-outdated translations or somehow equate Irish with a scholar of England having to learn Latin, despite the fact that Irish continued to be a dominant language of the time. Kane instead argues for the language's vital importance, especially from the thirteenth through seventeenth centuries. Arguing for a 'new linguistic direction', he acknowledges the previous problems of students and scholars being unable to access the educational resources that would allow them to learn Irish; but with the new digital platform of www.léamh.org, Kane presents a 'web-based tutorial and resource that aims to offer guidance for learning the language', with great implications for future scholarship.

In Chapter 6, Sarah McKibben extends Kane's call for scholars to utilize Irish-language sources as she argues for close indexical reading, in this case of bardic poetry. It goes without saying that this literature, especially as it pertains to the social and mental world of the Gaelic Irish, should not be treated superficially, but it certainly has been read in narrowly historicist terms. Bardic poetry might be an undeniably formulaic and 'homogenized' form of literature, and seemingly resistant to close reading, but McKibben offers a method and demonstration of the ways in which such poems can be decoded in their artistic forms and attached more deeply to their cultural and sociopolitical contexts.

Indeed, political understandings in early modern Ireland could carry different meanings across the linguistic divide. In Chapter 7, Peter McQuillan urges scholars to explore more fully the sociocultural and political worlds also embedded in Irish-language sources. If words make up concepts, concepts can also saturate even the most singular word, as McQuillan demonstrates with his analysis of *náision* (or 'nation') and *cine* ('state of being born'), both of which are posited as 'lexical expression[s] of nationhood in seventeenth-century Irish'. Undergirding both is *pobal* (roughly, 'people' or 'race'), another keyword that created the conceptual field around Irish nationhood in writings such as Keating's. McQuillan, in offering a method and a lexical and semantic history, thus demonstrates the powerful ways in which we may understand the complexity of the language and the uses to which it was put in the early modern period.

One of the greatest and more overtly political Irish-language poets of the later period was Aogán Ó Rathaille, who decried what Marc Caball describes as the 'dismal interlopers' of the age. One of those men, Robert Hedges of Munster, is the subject of Caball's essay (Chapter 8), which reflects the new connections being made by scholars between early modern Ireland and India while drawing out broader correlations, in this case between the local and the global, and the families that bridged the two worlds.[81] By presenting the case study of one family, Caball demonstrates how new directions in future research can be forged by taking a 'geographical and cultural perspective [which] illustrates similarities in an early phase of English colonial expansion', one that reflected 'a fascinating process of simultaneous conflict and accommodation'.

The mechanisms of Tudor government have been heavily examined, but David Edwards uncovers new approaches and sources that also promise to transform our understanding of colonial governance. In Chapter 9, Edwards consults the complaints against successive Tudor viceroys and their administrations—a 'type of literature that has not been analysed as much as it should'. As Edwards writes, by placing these complaints front and center in their analyses, scholars may not only move beyond a traditional reliance on viceroys and their viewpoints but be inspired to ask and answer a number of questions that arise from them. Edwards, for instance, identifies the many compelling issues of maladministration that historians may elicit from these sources, including the extent of viceroy financial corruption; the role of self-interest in resisting reform, for example, of the Exchequer; the trampling on Irish-born crown subjects' legal and constitutional rights by viceroys other than the (more well-known) Sussex and Sidney; and, not least, viceroys' provocative diplomatic manipulations against the Irish lords and use of military force that extended into wholesale slaughter.

In Chapter 10, Ruth Canning also looks at neglected sources that complicate our picture of Tudor rule, in her case focusing on those which emerged from the Pale during the Nine Years' War. As Canning writes, petitions, in this case representing the interests of the Old English community, have not been fully exploited by scholars, with records of English administrators generating far more coverage in the State Papers (and in the scholarship). But petitions, she writes, provide 'an alternative and more intimate perspective … by offering insight into how the Palesmen perceived the impact of [the Nine Years' War] on their own community and their relationship with the English crown'.

The history of early modern Ireland's state institutions has also been heavily surveyed, but Coleman Dennehy, in Chapter 11, points out that a traditional emphasis on their political aspects has come at the expense of our fully understanding their no-less-important administrative functions. Dennehy thus offers a fresh blueprint for examining institutional and administrative history during a time of rapid state growth in Ireland, from the Tudor period through the Stuart period. Keeping in mind the relative scarcity of sources (though Dennehy is optimistic about the resurfacing of material), scholars may further scrutinize membership in parliaments, patronage structures, and networks, in order to uncover questions of income, status, and privilege. The impact of parliament and other institutions of state on localities is also important, as is study of the law, and particularly statute law, criminal law, and the courts, especially as they contributed to the colonizing process of early modern Ireland. By further examining the administrative side of institutions, Dennehy writes, we may come to even more insights about the communities and societies they served (and often betrayed).

If the Tudor government has been extensively investigated and debated, the history of medicine, as John Cunningham points out in Chapter 12, has itself been a neglected field in early modern Ireland. The social as opposed to institutional 'top-down' history of medicine, meanwhile, has barely come to early modern Ireland's medical world at all. In his essay, Cunningham asks why this has been the case while offering a wide range of possibilities in topics and methods that future scholars may pursue, including research in medical institutions and personnel; Irish and English medical practices; elite and popular medicine; midwives and healers; and, not least, the many and various sources which offer scholars access to these worlds.

Some medical practices were undoubtedly of a folk nature, and in Chapter 13, Sarah Covington addresses the relative dearth of scholars who explore folkloric material in any depth when it comes to early modern Ireland (Clodagh Tait and Raymond Gillespie being exceptions). The 'folk', she argues, can also extend to any social group, whether families or the bardic class, with its own codes and speech, just as folklore can enter elite texts and return just as easily to popular culture. Early modern scholars must therefore look for the folkloric in both vernacular and 'elite' texts, despite the methodological problems that attend such material. Equally important, she writes, is the necessity for historians and literary scholars to understand the discipline behind folklore—namely, folkloristics and the many critical, theoretical, and methodological traditions and insights it has to offer.

Willy Maley, in Chapter 14, offers another approach to accessing elite and popular culture by tracing the meaning and afterlives of the Irish custom of 'ploughing by the tail'. Much derided by early modern English writers, and outlawed under Wentworth (though not successfully), the practice was transmuted into a resonant cultural image that persisted across the centuries in literature, poetry, and antiquarian and historical writings. Maley incorporates the thriving yet still relatively underused field of animal studies while also displaying the riches that can be found when early modern scholars move across the 1700 divide and enter later centuries.

One of the more exciting interdisciplinary developments in recent years has occurred in the aforementioned field of material culture. James Lyttleton, in Chapter 15, assesses the recent state of historical archaeology in Ireland, particularly after the call to collaboration made by Rolf Loeber. Lyttleton urges scholars, and historians especially, to widen their source field not simply by investigating documentary and cartographic evidence but by incorporating it more closely with material evidence in an approach known as contextual archaeology. Lyttleton also advocates in favor of examining early modern Ireland's archaeological past, not simply in colonial terms (which 'would … deny the complex historical ambiguities of identity formation that were apparent in the country at the time') but in a more European and transatlantic context. Finally, the study of ethnic boundaries also constitutes a rich subject, especially as it is approached 'by building on the respective epistemological strengths of each discipline'.

Another stimulating disciplinary convergence is advocated by Francis Ludlow and Arlene Crampsie (Chapter 16) in their study of the environmental pressures that impacted much of the political, economic, and social turbulences of the sixteenth and seventeenth centuries. Environmental studies and climatic history generally represent two of the most innovative and important developments in early modern studies, and while the *Annalistes* and quantitative historians were forerunners, recent historians have pushed the environment to the forefront, and utilized cutting-edge technology to do so, in their quest to understand how climate affected historical change. After detailing the importance of applying an environmental perspective to early modern Ireland, Ludlow and Crampsie focus on the events around the 1641 uprising, connecting it to extreme weather events and deploying technological, scientific, climatic, and cartographic techniques in order to widen economic and political contexts and outcomes, and forge entirely new understandings around an otherwise heavily researched event.

Finally, Micheál Ó Siochrú and David Brown's essay (Chapter 17) signals another transformative development across scholarship in recent years. If Ireland has sometimes lagged behind other countries in terms of certain scholarly trends, it is at the forefront in the digital humanities (due, not uncoincidentally, to Ireland's technological place in the larger global order). While recognizing other centers and projects in Ireland and elsewhere, Ó Siochrú and Brown describe the efforts, methodologies, and innovations that are required in creating ambitious projects, such as Trinity College Dublin's 1641 Depositions, Down Survey Online, and Books of Survey and Distribution online. While digital projects do not, of course, free scholars from having to dig in the archives, and technology itself is constantly changing, these projects are nevertheless revolutionary in allowing us greater access to a previous black hole of sources, in facilitating our ability to connect data in fascinating ways, and in inspiring us to ask further questions and view the early modern period in an entirely new light.

If early modern Ireland was once the 'laboratory for empire,' it has now become a different kind of laboratory—a locus of innovative research that ranges, sometimes by necessity, across disciplines and, indeed, the world. This volume has been produced at a moment of scholarly verdancy rather than stagnation, with the sixteenth- and seventeenth-century inspiring an unprecedented number of studies, many of which contain or point to further directions that students and scholars may pursue. Of course, one can never wholly predict the directions where the field will go, any more than one can foretell the changing historical contexts or different questions that lie ahead. But by embarking down less-travelled paths or establishing new trails altogether, these essays seek to expand the ground that has been so richly mined by those who came before, and who continue to till it now.

Notes

1 Nicholas Canny, *Making Ireland British, 1580–1650*, rev. edn. (Oxford: Oxford University Press, 2003); Pádraig Lenihan, *Consolidating Conquest: Ireland 1603–1727* (Essex: Pearson, 2008).

2 Breandán Ó Buachalla, *Aisling Ghéar: Na Stíobhartaigh agus an tAos Léinn, 1603–1788* (Dublin: An Clóchomhar, 1996); idem, 'James Our True King: The Ideology of Irish Royalism in the Seventeenth Century', in D. George Boyce et al. (eds.), *Political Thought in Ireland since the Seventeenth Century* (London: Routledge, 1993), esp. pp. 7–8; Mícheál Mac Craith, *Lorg na hIasachta ar na Dánta Grá* (Baile Átha Cliath: An Clóchomhar, 1989); Vincent Morley, *The Popular Mind in Eighteenth-Century Ireland* (Cork: Cork University Press, 2017), esp. pp. 9–10; Éamonn Ó Ciardha, *Ireland and the Jacobite Cause, 1685–1766* (Dublin: Four Courts Press, 2002).

3 For a survey of these transformations, see William Smyth, *Map-making, Landscapes and Memory: A Geography of Colonial and Early Modern Ireland, c.1530–1750* (Cork: Cork University Press, 2007); Brian J. Graham and Lindsay J. Proudfoot, *An Historical Geography of Ireland* (London: Academic Press, 1997), pp. 222–25. For maps of these transformations in the wake of William Petty's Down Survey, see http://downsurvey.tcd.ie/religion.php.

4 For overviews of Ireland in this period, see Jane Ohlmeyer (ed.), *The Cambridge History of Ireland*, vol. II (Cambridge: Cambridge University Press, 2018); see also T.W. Moody, Francis Xavier Martin, and Francis John Byrne (eds.), *A New History of Ireland III 1534–1691*, 3rd ed. (London and Oxford: Oxford University Press, 1976). For longer surveys that reach back into the pre-1700 period, see John Gibney, *A Short History of Ireland 1500–2000* (New Haven: Yale University Press, 2017); Alvin Jackson (ed.), *The Oxford Handbook of Modern Irish History* (Oxford: Oxford University Press, 2014); Thomas Bartlett, *Ireland: A History* (Cambridge: Cambridge University Press, 2010); J.C. Beckett, *The Making of Modern Ireland, 1603–1923* (London:

Faber, 1965); R.F. Foster, *Modern Ireland, 1600–1972* (London: Allen Lane, 1988). For an overview of recent historiography in the later-early modern, see Michelle O'Riordan, 'Ireland 1600–1780: New Approaches', in Katherine O'Donnell et al. (eds.), *Palgrave Advances in Irish History* (New York: Palgrave-Macmillan, 2009), pp. 49–83.

5 Stanley T. Bindoff, *Tudor England* (London: Harmondsworth, 1950); Geoffrey Elton devotes ten pages (out of nearly 500 pages) on Ireland ('Conquest of'). See G.R. Elton, *England Under the Tudors*, 3rd ed. (Abingdon: Routledge, 1991), pp. 384–94. See, however, the relatively more extensive accommodation of Ireland in Susan Brigden, *New Worlds, Lost Worlds: The Rule of the Tudors, 1485–1603* (New York: Penguin, 2000).

6 In economic history especially, the work of Louis Cullen remains extremely important here, even if it tilts toward later centuries. For Cullen, see *The Formation of the Irish Economy* (Cork: Mercier Press, 1979); idem, *An Economic History of Ireland Since 1660* (London: Batford, 1972; 2nd edn, 1988). For more recent work, see also Raymond R. Gillespie, *The Transformation of the Irish Economy, 1550–1700*, 2nd ed. (Dublin: Economic & Social History, 1998); see also Gillespie's overview, 'Economic Life, 1550–1730', in *The Cambridge History of Ireland*, vol. 2, pp. 531–54.

7 But see Nicholas Canny, 'The Origins of Empire: An Introduction', in Nicholas Canny (ed.), *The Oxford History of the British Empire: Volume I: The Origins of Empire: British Overseas Enterprise to the Close of the Seventeenth Century* (Oxford: Oxford University Press, 1998), pp. 1–33.

8 David Edwards, Pádraig Lenihan, and Clodagh Tait (eds.), 'Early Modern Ireland: A History of Violence', in *Age of Atrocity* (Dublin: Four Courts Press, 2010), esp. pp. 14–15.

9 See, however, W.B. Yeats, 'Edmund Spenser' (1902) in *Essays and Introduction* (London: Macmillan, 1961), pp. 356–383; Pauline Henley, *Spenser in Ireland*, (Cork: Cork University Press, 1928).

10 See introduction by Jane Ohlmeyer in *The Cambridge History of Ireland*, vol. II, pp. 1–20.

11 T.W. Moody, F.X. Martin, and F.J. Byrne (eds.), *A New History of Ireland, Volume III: Early Modern Ireland 1534–1691* (Oxford: Oxford University Press, 1976); R.W. Dudley Edwards and Mary O'Dowd (eds.), *Sources for Modern Irish History 1534–1641* (Cambridge: Cambridge University Press, 2003).

12 Angela Bourke (ed.), *The Field Day Anthology of Irish Writing, Vol. IV & V* (Cork: Cork University Press, 2002); see also Margaret Kelleher, 'The Field Day Anthology and Irish Women's Literary Studies', *The Irish Review* 30 (2003), 83–94.

13 For one of the earlier works on the subject, see R.J. Hunter, 'The Bible and the Bawn: An Ulster Planter Inventorised', in Ciaran Brady and Jane Ohlmeyer (eds.), *British Interventions in Early Modern Ireland* (Cambridge: Cambridge University Press, 2005), pp. 116–34; Audrey Horning, Ruairí Ó Baoill, Colm Donnelly, and Paul Logues (eds.), *The Post-Medieval Archaeology of Ireland, 1500–1850* (Dublin: Wordwell, 2001). For more recent treatments, see Tadgh O'Keeffe, *Tristernagh Priory, Co. Westmeath: Colonial Monasticism in Medieval Ireland* (Dublin: Four Courts Press, 2018); Eve Campbell, Elizabeth Fitzpatrick, and Audrey Horning, *Becoming and Belonging in Ireland 1200–1600 AD: Essays on Identity and Cultural Practice* (Cork: Cork University Press, 2018); Audrey Horning, *Ireland in the Virginian Sea: Colonialism in the British Atlantic* (Durham: University of North Carolina Press, 2013); James Lyttleton, *Plantation Ireland: Settlement and Material Culture, c.1550–c.1700* (Dublin: Four Courts, 2009); James Lyttleton, *The Jacobean Plantations in Seventeenth-Century Offaly: An Archaeology of a Changing World* (Dublin: Four Courts Press, 2013). For an outstanding study of Ireland's material

culture from a historian's perspective, see Toby Barnard, *Making the Grand Figure: Lives and Possessions in Ireland, 1641–1770* (London and New Haven: Yale University Press, 2004). See also Susan Flavin's study of 'Domestic Materiality in Ireland, 1550–1730', in *Cambridge History of Ireland*, vol. 2 (Cambridge: Cambridge University Press, 2018), pp. 321–45.

14   William Smyth, *Map-Making*, and J.H. Andrews, *The Queen's Last Mapmaker: A Study of Richard Bartlett* (Dublin: Geography Publications, 2008).

15   Éamonn Ó Ciardha, 'Irish-Language Sources for the History of Early Modern Ireland', in *Oxford Handbook of Modern Irish History* (Oxford: Oxford University Press, 2014), pp. 439–61.

16   Herbert Wood, 'The Public Records of Ireland before and after 1922', *Transactions of the Royal Historical Society*, Fourth Series 13 (1930), 17–49; see also idem, *A Guide to the Records Deposited in the Public Record Office of Ireland* (Dublin: H.M. Stationery Office, 1919); Micheál Ó Siochrú, 'Rebuilding the Past: The Transformation of Early Modern Irish History', *The Seventeenth Century* 33 (2018), 5–9. The Beyond 2022 Project seeks to rebuild and digitize a great part of this archive, however. See https://beyond2022.ie/.

17   Ó Siochrú, 'Rebuilding the Past', 9–18.

18   See Sarah McKibben's essay in this volume for a useful discussion of the sources. Vincent Morley is a pioneer here. See also Morley, *The Popular Mind in Eighteenth-Century Ireland*, especially the introduction; idem, 'Views of the Past in Irish Vernacular Literature, 1650–1850', in Tim Blanning and Hagen Schulze (eds.), '*Unity and Diversity in European Culture c. 1800*' (Oxford: British Academy, 2006), pp. 174–98; idem, 'The Irish Language', in Richard Bourke and Ian McBride (eds.), *The Princeton History of Modern Ireland* (Princeton: Princeton University Press, 2016), pp. 320–42; idem, *Cúrsaí Staire: Aistí ar an Stair, ar Staraithe, agus ar Scríobh na Staire* (Dublin: Coiscéim, 2018). See also the Léamh digital project sponsored by the University of Connecticut, an undertaking to present, translate, and educate in early modern Irish sources: www.léamh.org. The project is described in chapter five of this volume.

19   Nicholas Canny, 'Interpreting the History of Early Modern Ireland: From the Sixteenth Century to the Present', in Ohlmeyer (ed.) *Cambridge History of Ireland*, esp. pp. 638–49.

20   See also Canny, 'Interpreting', p. 652.

21   J.P. Prendergast, *The Cromwellian Settlement of Ireland* (London: Longman, Green, 1865); John Cunningham, *Conquest and Land in Ireland: The Transplantation to Connacht, 1649–1680* (Woodbridge: Boydell and Brewer, 2011), p. 6.

22   Mary Hickson, *Ireland in the Seventeenth Century, or, The Irish Massacres of 1641–2: Their Causes and Results* (London: Longmans, Green, 1884); John Gilbert, *History of the Confederation and War in Ireland, 1641–1649* (Dublin: M.H. Gill, 1882–91); P.F. Moran, *Spicilegium Ossoriense* (Dublin: M.H. Gill, 1878); Robert Dunlop, *Ireland Under the Commonwealth, Being a Collection of Documents Relating to the Government of Ireland from 1651 to 1659*, 2 vols. (Manchester: The University Press, 1913); S.R. Gardiner, 'The Transplantation to Connaught', *English Historical Review* 14 (1899), 700–34; J.A. Froude, *The English in Ireland in the Eighteenth Century*, 3 vols. (New York: Scribner, 1991); W.E.H. Lecky, *A History of Ireland in the Eighteenth Century*, 4 vols. (London: Longmans, Green, 1892/96).

23   See J.G. Simms, 'Early Modern Ireland, 1534–1691', in *A New History of Ireland, 1534–1691*, pp. 634–95; R.W. Dudley Edwards and Mary O'Dowd (eds.), *Sources for Modern Irish History 1534–1641* (Cambridge: Cambridge University Press, 2003), p. 193.

24   For Lecky, see Donal McCartney, *W.E.H. Lecky: Historian and Politician, 1838–1903* (Dublin: Lilliput Press, 1994); for Froude, see Ciaran Brady, *James*

Anthony Froude: An Intellectual Biography of a Victorian Prophet (Oxford: Oxford University Press, 2013).

25 T. Corcoran, 'Dr. William Francis Butler, 1869–1930', *Irish Monthly* 58 (April 1930), 164.

26 William F.T. Butler, *Confiscation in Irish History* (Dublin: The Talbot Press, 1917); and idem, *Gleanings from Irish History* (London: Longmans, 1925).

27 For a general history of revisionism in the 1930s, 1970s, and 1980s, see Ciaran Brady, (ed.), *Interpreting Irish History: The Debate on Historical Revisionism, 1938–1994* (Dublin: Irish Academic Press, 1994); David George Boyce and Alan O'Day (eds.), *The Making of Modern Irish History: Revisionism and the Revisionist Controversy* (London: Routledge, 1996); Evi Gkotzaridis, *Trials of Irish History: Genesis and Evolution of a Reappraisal* (London and New York: Routledge, 2006); Brendan Bradshaw, 'Nationalism and Historical Scholarship in Modern Ireland', *Irish Historical Studies* 26 (1988/89), 329–51. For an early history, see Ciaran Brady, '"Constructive and Instrumental": The Dilemma of Ireland's First "New Historians,"' in Ciaran Brady (ed.), *Interpreting Irish History* (Dublin: Irish Academic Press, 1994), pp. 3–34. See also Roy Foster, 'We Are All Revisionists Now', *The Irish Review* 1 (1986), 1–5.

28 Nicholas Canny, 'Writing Early Modern History: Ireland, Britain, and the Wider World', *The Historical Journal* 46 (2003)', 725; Steven Ellis, 'Historiographical Debate: Representations of the Past in Ireland: Whose Past and Whose Present?' *Irish Historical Studies* 27 (1991), 289–308; Hiram Morgan, 'Writing Up Early Modern Ireland', *Historical Journal* 31 (1988), 701–11; James Murray, 'Historical Revisit: R. Dudley Edwards' Church and State in Tudor Ireland (1935)', *Irish Historical Studies* 30 (1996), 233–41; Aidan Clarke, 'Robert Dudley Edwards (1909–88)', *Irish Historical Studies* 26 (1988), 121–27; T.W. Moody, (ed.) *Irish Historiography, 1936–1970* (Dublin: Irish Committee of Historical Sciences, 1971); J.J. Lee, (ed.), *Irish Historiography, 1970–79* (Cork: Cork University Press, 1981).

29 Others of note in this generation include Patrick Corish and G. A. Hayes-McCoy; J.G. Simms, Kearney and Clarke, who comprised the next cohort.

30 Canny, 'Interpreting', p. 726.

31 Canny would take this up and develop it further, not least by editing *The Oxford History of the British Empire*. See Canny, 'Introduction', in *The Oxford History of the British Empire, Volume I: The Origins of Empire* (Oxford: Oxford University Press, 1988), pp. 1–33.

32 David Beers Quinn, *The Elizabethans and the Irish* (Ithaca: Cornell University Press, 1966). See also Brendan Kane and Valerie McGowan-Doyle (eds.), *Elizabeth I and Ireland* (Cambridge: Cambridge University Press, 2014). For more on Quinn's contributions, see Nicholas Canny and Karen Ordahl Kupperman, 'The Scholarship and Legacy of David Beers Quinn, 1909–2002', *The William and Mary Quarterly* 60 (2003), esp. 849, 851.

33 Vincent Carey, 'The Impact of Nicholas Canny's *The Elizabethan Conquest of Ireland* (1976)', presented at the annual meeting of the Renaissance Society of America, 31 March–2 April, 2016.

34 Among the more notable works, see Nicholas Canny, 'The Ideology of English Colonisation: From Ireland to America', *William and Mary Quarterly* 30 (1973), 575–98; idem, *The Elizabethan Conquest of Ireland: A Pattern Established* (New York: Barnes & Noble, 1976); idem, *Kingdom and Colony: Ireland in the Atlantic World 1560–1800* (Baltimore: Johns Hopkins University Press, 1987); idem, *Making Ireland British, 1580–1650* (Oxford: Oxford University Press, 2001); idem, 'The Formation of the Irish Mind: Religion, Politics and Gaelic Irish Literature, 1580–1750', *Past & Present* 95 (1982), 91–116; idem, 'Edmund Spenser and the Development of an Anglo-Irish Identity', *Yearbook of English Studies* 13 (1983), 1–19.

35 Brendan Bradshaw, *The Dissolution of the Religious Orders in Ireland Under Henry VIII* (Cambridge: Cambridge University Press, 1974); idem, *The Irish Constitutional Revolution of the Sixteenth Century* (Cambridge: Cambridge University Press, 1979).

36 Brendan Bradshaw, 'Interview', in Bradshaw (ed.), *And so Began the Irish Nation: Nationality, Nationalism and National Consciousness in Pre-Modern Ireland* (Farnham and Burlington, VT: Ashgate, 2015), pp. xi–xvii. For Bradshaw's influences, see Mairéad Carew, 'Eoin MacNeill: Revolutionary Cultural Ideologue', *Studies: An Irish Quarterly Review* 105 (2016), 67–75; James Lydon, 'Historical Revisit: Edmund Curtis, A History of Medieval Ireland (1923, 1938)', *Irish Historical Studies* 31 (1999), 535–48. See also a similar position to Bradshaw in Gearóid Ó Tuathaigh, 'State of the Art or Ideological Project?', in Ciaran Brady (ed.), *Interpreting Irish History: The Debate on Historical Revisionism* (Dublin: Irish Academic Press, 1995), 306–26. For other attacks on revisionism, particularly in the wake of the Troubles, see Kevin Whelan, 'The Revisionist Debate in Ireland', *Boundary 2* (2004), 179–205; Willy Maley, 'Nationalism and Revisionism: Ambiviolences and Dissensus', in Scott Brewster and David Alderson (eds.), *Ireland in Proximity: History, Gender, Space* (London: Routledge, 1999), pp. 12–25.

37 Steven Ellis, 'Nationalist Historiography and the English and Gaelic Worlds in the Late Middle Ages', in Ciaran Brady (ed.), *Interpreting Irish History*, pp. 161–80; Brendan Bradshaw, 'Nationalism and Historical Scholarship in Modern Ireland', *Irish Historical Studies* 26 (1988/89), 329–51; Steven Ellis, 'Historiographical Debate – Representations of the Past in Ireland: Whose Past and Whose Present?', *Irish Historical Studies* 27 (1990/91), 280–308; idem, 'More Irish than the Irish Themselves? The "Anglo-Irish" in Tudor Ireland', *History Ireland* 7 (1) (1999), 22–26; Kenneth Nicholls, 'World's Apart?', *History Ireland* 7 (2) (1999), 22–26.

38 For Steven Ellis, see *Ireland in the Age of the Tudors: English Expansion and Gaelic Rule* (London and York: Longman, 1998); idem, *Tudor Frontiers and Noble Power: The Making of the British State* (Oxford: Oxford University Press, 1995); idem, *The Pale and the Far North* (Galway: National University of Ireland, 1988); idem, "Crown, Community, and Government in the English Territories, 1475 to 1575," *History* 71 (1986), 187–204.

39 Ciaran Brady, *The Chief Governors: The Rise and Fall of Reform Government in Tudor Ireland, 1536–1588* (Cambridge: Cambridge University Press, 1994). See also Ciaran Brady, 'Spenser's Irish Crisis: Humanism and Experience in the 1590s', *Past & Present* 111 (1986), 17–49; Nicholas Canny, 'Debate: Spenser's Irish Crisis: Humanism and Experience in the 1590s', *Past & Present* 120 (1988), 201–15. For literary critics and Spenser, see p. 43.

40 T.J. Dunne, 'The Gaelic Response to Conquest and Colonisation: The Evidence of the Poetry', *Studia Hibernica* 20 (1980), 7–30; Nicholas Canny, 'The Formation of the Irish Mind: Religion, Politics and Gaelic Irish literature, 1580–1750', *Past & Present* 95 (1982), 91–116; Michelle O Riordan, *The Gaelic Mind and the Collapse of the Gaelic World* (Cork: Cork University Press, 1990); Breandán Ó Buachalla, 'Na Stíobhartaigh agus an t-aos léinn: Cing Séamas', *Proceedings of the Royal Irish Academy* 83 (1983), sect. C, 81–134; idem, 'Poetry and Politics in Early Modern Ireland', *Eighteenth-Century Ireland* 7 (1992), 149–75; and passim.

41 Andrew Hadfield and Willy Maley (eds.), *Edmund Spenser. A View of the State of Ireland. From the first printed edition* (1633). (Oxford: Oxford University Press, 1997).

42 Aidan Clarke, *The Old English in Ireland, 1625–42* (Ithaca: Cornell University Press, 1966).

43 Ibid.; Aidan Clarke, *Prelude to Restoration in Ireland: The End of the Commonwealth, 1659–1660* (Cambridge: Cambridge University Press, 1999).

44 Published soon thereafter as Aidan Clarke *The Formation of the Old English Elite in Ireland* (Dublin: National University of Ireland, 1975).

45 Colm Lennon, "Richard Stanihurst (1547–1618) and Old English Identity," *Irish Historical Studies* 21 (1978), 121–43; see also Lennon's later book-length study of Stanihurst, *Richard Stanihurst, the Dubliner* (Dublin: Irish Academic Press, 1981). Vincent Carey, *Surviving the Tudors: The 'Wizard' Earl of Kildare and English Rule in Ireland, 1537–1586* (Dublin: Four Courts Press, 2002); Valerie McGowan-Doyle, *The Book of Howth: Elizabethan Conquest and the Old English* (Cork: Cork University Press, 2011); David Edwards, *The Ormond Lordship in County Kilkenny 1515–1642, The Rise and Fall of Butler Feudal Power* (Dublin: Four Courts Press, 2003).

46 Ruth Canning, *The Old English in Early Modern Ireland: The Palesmen and the Nine Years' War, 1594–1603* (Woodbridge: Boydell & Brewer, 2019); Gerald Power, *A European Frontier Elite: The Nobility of the Pale in Tudor Ireland, 1496–1566* (Hannover: Wehrhahn Verlag, 2012); in Kane and McGowan-Doyle (eds.), "Elizabeth I, the Old English, and the Rhetoric of Counsel," *Elizabeth I and Ireland*, 163–83.

47 Hiram Morgan (ed.) *Political Ideology in Ireland, 1541–1641* (Dublin: Four Courts Press, 1999).

48 Hiram Morgan, *Tyrone's Rebellion* (Woodbridge: Boydell Press, 1993); Hiram Morgan (ed.), *The Battle of Kinsale* (Bray: Wordwell Press, 2004).

49 Hiram Morgan, "Hugh O'Neill and the Nine Years War in Tudor Ireland," *The Historical Journal* 36 (1993), 21–37.

50 Éamonn Ó Ciardha and Micheál Ó Siochrú (eds.), *The Plantation of Ulster: Ideology and Practice* (Manchester: Manchester University Press, 2012).

51 Mary Ann Lyons, *Strangers to Citizens: The Irish in Europe, 1600–1800* (Bray: Wordwell Press, 2008); Thomas O'Connor, *The Irish in Europe 1580–1815* (Dublin: Four Courts Press, 2001); Mary Ann Lyons and Thomas O'Connor (eds.), *Irish Communities in Early Modern Europe* (Dublin: Four Courts Press, 2006); *Irish Migrants in Europe after Kinsale, 1602–1820* (Dublin: Four Courts Press, 2003).

52 Hugh F. Kearney, *Strafford in Ireland, 1633–41: A Study in Absolutism*, 2nd ed. (Cambridge: Cambridge University Press, 1989). For Kearney's later reassessment of his important book, see 'Strafford in Ireland 1633–40', *History Today* 39 (1989), 20–25.

53 Toby Barnard, *Cromwellian Ireland: English Government and Reform in Ireland 1649–1660* (Oxford: Clarendon Press, 2000).

54 J.G.A. Pocock, *The Discovery of Islands* (Cambridge: Cambridge University Press, 2005), p. 80.

55 Conrad Russell, *The Fall of the British Monarchies, 1637–1642* (Oxford: Oxford University Press, 1995); see also David Stevenson, 'Cromwell, Scotland, and Ireland', in John Morrill (ed.), *Oliver Cromwell and the English Revolution* (London: Longman, 1990), pp. 149–80.

56 Hugh Kearney, *The British Isles: A History of Four Nations* (Cambridge: Cambridge University Press, 1989); Steven Ellis and Sarah Barber (eds.), *Conquest and Union: Fashioning a British State 1485–1725* (New York and London: Routledge, 1995); Brendan Bradshaw and John Morrill (eds.), *The British Problem, c.1534–1707* (New York: Palgrave Macmillan, 1996); David Scott, *Politics and War in the Three Stuart Kingdoms, 1637–49* (New York: Palgrave Macmillan, 2004).

57 Jane Ohlmeyer (ed.), *Political Thought in Seventeenth-Century Ireland: Kingdom or Colony* (Cambridge: Cambridge University Press, 2000).

58 Jane Ohlmeyer, 'Eastward Enterprises: Colonial Ireland, Colonial India', *Past & Present* 240 (2018), pp. 83–118.

59 Vincent Carey, 'John Derricke's *Image of Ireland*, Sir Henry Sidney, and the massacre at Mullaghmast, 1578', *Irish Historical Studies* 31 (1999), 305–27; David

Edwards, Pádraig Lenihan, and Clodagh Tait (eds.), *The Age of Atrocity: Violence and Political Conflict in Early Modern Ireland* (Dublin: Four Courts, 2007).

60 For works relating to Ireland between 1500 and 1700, see Ó Buachalla, *Aisling Ghéar*; Peter McQuillan, *Native and Natural: Aspects of the Concepts of 'Right' and 'Freedom' in Irish* (Cork: Cork University Press, 2004); Marc Caball, *Poets and Politics: Continuity and Reaction in Irish Poetry, 1558–1625* (Cork: Cork University Press, 1998); Bernadette Cunningham, *The World Of Geoffrey Keating: History, Myth And Religion in Seventeenth Century Ireland* (Dublin: Four Courts Press, 2010); idem, *The Annals of The Four Masters: Irish History, Kingship and Society in the Early Seventeenth Century* (Dublin: Four Courts Press, 2010); Brendan Kane, *The Politics and Culture of Honour in Britain and Ireland, 1541–1641* (Cambridge: Cambridge University Press, 2010); Sarah McKibben, *Endangered Masculinities in Irish Poetry: 1540–1780* (Dublin: University College Dublin Press, 2011).

61 Brendan Bradshaw, Andrew Hadfield, and Willy Maley (eds.), *Representing Ireland: Literature and the Origins of Conflict, 1534–1660* (Cambridge: Cambridge University Press, 1993), pp. 1–23.

62 See essays by Innes, Maley, Arrowsmith et al. in Ashok Bery and Patricia Murray (eds.), *Comparing Postcolonial Literatures: Dislocations* (Basingstoke: St Martin's Press, 2000); Clare Carroll and Patricia King (eds.), *Ireland and Postcolonial Theory* (South Bend: University of Notre Dame Press, 2003).

63 See for example Patricia Coughlin (ed.), *Spenser and Ireland: An Interdisciplinary Perspective* (Cork: Cork University Press, 1990); Clare Carroll, *Circe's Cup: Cultural Transformations in Early Modern Ireland* (Cork: Cork University Press, 2002); Andrew Hadfield, *Edmund Spenser's Irish Experience: Wilde Fruit and Salvage Soyl* (Oxford: Clarendon Press, 1997); Patricia Coughlin, 'The Local Context of Mutabilitie's Plea', *Irish University Review* 26 (1996), 320–41; Thomas Herron. *Spenser's Irish Work: Poetry, Plantation and Colonial Reformation* (Aldershot: Ashgate Publishing Company, 2007).

64 For Ireland and its earlier historiography, see James Murray, Alan Ford, J.I. McGuire, S.J. Connolly, Fergus O'Ferrall, and Kenneth Milne, 'The Church of Ireland: A Critical Bibliography, *Irish Historical Studies* 28 (1993), 345–84. Alan Ford, *The Protestant Reformation in Ireland 1590–1641* (Dublin: Four Courts Press, 1997); James Murray, *Enforcing the English Reformation in Ireland: Clerical Resistance and Political Conflict in the Diocese of Dublin, 1534–1590* (Cambridge: Cambridge University Press, 2011); Henry A. Jeffries, *The Irish Church and the Tudor Reformations* (Dublin: Four Courts Press, 2010); Crawford Gribben, *Enforcing Reformation in Ireland and Scotland, 1550–1700* (London and New York: Routledge, 2016); Tadhg Ó hAnnracháin, *Catholic Reformation in Ireland* (Oxford: Oxford University Press, 2001); Brian MacCuarta, *Catholic Revival in the North of Ireland 1603–41* (Dublin: Four Courts Press, 2007).

65 Nicholas Canny, 'Why the Reformation failed in Ireland: *une question mal posée*', *Journal of Ecclesiastical History* 30 (1979), 423–50; Karl Bottigheimer, 'Why the Reformation Failed in Ireland: *une question bien posée*, *Journal of Ecclesiastical History* 36 (1985), 196–207; Steven Ellis, 'The Irish Reformation Debate in Retrospect', in Mark Empey, Alan Ford, and Miriam Moffitt (eds.), *The Church of Ireland and its Past: History, Interpretation and Identity* (Dublin: Four Courts, 2017), pp. 237–65; and idem, 'Economic Problems of the Church: Why the Reformation Failed in Ireland', *Journal of Ecclesiastical History* 4 (1990), 239–65.

66 See essays in Mark Empey, Alan Ford, and Miriam Moffitt (eds.), *The Church of Ireland and its Past.*

67 Crawford Gribben, *God's Irishmen: Theological Debates in Cromwellian Ireland* (Oxford: Oxford University Press, 2007); Richard L. Greaves, *God's Other Children: Protestant Nonconformists and the Emergence of Denominational Churches in*

Ireland, 1660–1700 (Stanford: Stanford University Press, 1997); Sandra Hynes, 'Dissenters in a Trans-National Context: The Quakers in Ireland 1660–1690', in Claudia Schnurmann (ed.), *Religious Refugees in Europe, Ireland and America from the 6th to the 21st centuries*, Atlantic Cultures Series (Münster: LIT-Verlag, 2007).

68 Tadhg Ó hAnnracháin, *Catholic Reformation in Ireland: The Mission of Rinuccini, 1645–49* (Oxford: Oxford University Press, 2002); Tadhg Ó hAnnracháin and Robert Armstrong (eds.), *Insular Christianity: Alternative Models of the Church in Britain and Ireland c. 1570c. 1700* (Manchester: Manchester University Press, 2013).

69 For Cullen, see L.M. Cullen, 'The Irish Diaspora of the Seventeenth and Eighteenth Centuries', in Nicholas Canny (ed.), *Europeans on the Move: Studies on European Migration, 1500–1800* (Oxford: Oxford University Press, 1994), pp. 113–52; idem, 'Galway Merchants in the Outside World, 1650–1800', in Diarmuid Ó Cearbhaill (ed.), *Galway: Town and Gown, 1484–1984* (Dublin: Gill and Macmillan, 1984), pp. 63–89; idem, 'The Irish Merchant Communities of Bordeux, La Rochelle and Cognac in the Eighteenth Century', in P. Butel and L.M. Cullen (eds.), *Négoce et industrie en France et en Irlande aux xviii et xix siècles* (Paris: National Center for Scientific Research, Bordeaux Regional Publication Center, 1980).

70 See Ellen McWilliams and Tony Murray, 'Irishness and the Culture of the Irish Abroad', *Irish Studies Review* 26 (2018), 1–4; Nicholas Canny (ed.), *Europeans on the Move*. See Canny's excellent overview in Canny, 'Ireland and Continental Europe, c.1600–c.1750', in Alvin Jackson (ed.), *Oxford Handbook of Modern Irish History* (Oxford: Oxford University Press, 2014), pp. 333–53. See also, for example, David Dickson, Jan Parmentier, and Jane Ohlmeyer (eds.), *Irish and Scottish Mercantile Networks in Europe and Overseas in the Seventeenth and Eighteenth Centuries* (Gent: Academia Press, 2007).

71 Among the more recent works, see Thomas O'Connor and Liam Chambers (eds.), *Forming Catholic Communities: Irish, Scots and English College Networks in Europe 1568–1918* (Leiden: Brill, 2018); idem, *Catholic Communities Abroad: Education, Migration and Catholicism in Early Modern Europe* (Manchester: Manchester University Press, 2017); Clare Carroll, *Exiles in a Global City: The Irish and Early Modern Rome, 1609–1783* (Leiden: Brill, 2017); Raymond Gillespie and Ruairí Ó hUiginn (eds.), *Irish Europe, 1600–1650: Writing and Learning* (Dublin: Four Courts, 2013); Thomas O'Connor and Mary Ann Lyons (eds.), *Strangers to Citizens: the Irish in Europe, 1600–1800* (Bray: Wordwell Press, 2008); Brendan Kane, 'Making the Irish European: Gaelic Honor Politics and its Continental Contexts', *Renaissance Quarterly* 61 (2008), 1139–66; J.J. Silke, 'The Irish Abroad', in *New Oxford History of Ireland*, pp. 561–886; Micheál Mac Craith, 'Gaelic Ireland and the Renaissance', in Glanmor Williams and Robert Owen Jones (eds.), *The Celts and the Renaissance; Tradition and Innovation* (Cardiff: University of Wales Press, 1990), pp. 57–89.

72 Jane Ohlmeyer, 'Ireland in the Early Modern World', in Ohlmeyer (ed.) *Cambridge History of Ireland*.

73 Joan Scott, 'Gender: A Useful Category of Historical Analysis', *The American Historical Review* 91 (1986), 1053–75; Joanne Meyerowitz, 'A History of "Gender,"' *The American Historical Review* 113 (2008), 1346–56.

74 The leader in this field is Toby Barnard; see Toby Barnard, *Making the Grand Figure: Lives and Possessions in Ireland, 1641–1770* (London and New Haven: Yale University Press, 2004). See also the very useful reference work of Barnard's, *Guide to the Sources for the History of Material Culture in Ireland, 1500–2000* (Dublin: Four Courts, 2005). For other studies, see Raymond Gillespie, 'The Problems of Plantations: Material Culture and Social Change in Early Modern Ireland', in

James Lyttleton and Colin Rynne (eds.), *Plantation Ireland: Settlement and Material Culture, c.1550–c.1700* (Dublin: Four Courts Press, 2009), pp. 43–60; Susan Flavin, *Consumption and Culture in Sixteenth-Century Ireland: Saffron, Stockings and Silk* (Woodbridge: Boydell & Brewer, 2014); Elizabeth Fitzpatrick and James Kelly (eds.), *Domestic Life in Ireland* (Dublin: Royal Irish Academy, 2011). For an overview, see Susan Flavin, 'Domestic Materiality in Ireland, 1550–1730', *Cambridge History of Ireland*, pp. 321–345.

75 James Deetz, 'Material Culture and Archaeology – What's the Difference?' In Leland Ferguson (ed.), *Historical Archaeology and the Importance of Material Things* (Ottawa: Society for Historical Archaeology, 1977), pp. 9–12; idem, *In Small Things Forgotten: The Archaeology of Early American Life* (New York: Anchor Press, 1977); Henry Glassie, *Material Culture* (Bloomington: Indiana University Press, 1999); Tim Ingold, 'The Temporality of the Landscape', *World Archaeology* 25 (2) (1993), 152–74; Ian Hodder, *Reading the Past: Current Approaches to Interpretation in Archaeology* (Cambridge: Cambridge University Press, 2003). For a literary approach, see Francesco Orlando, *Obsolete Objects in the Literary Imagination* (New Haven: Yale University Press, 2006). For Ireland, see Elizabeth Fitzpatrick, *Royal Inauguration in Gaelic Ireland c.1100–1600: A Cultural Landscape Study* (Woodbridge: Boydell, 2004); and Horning. See also n. 13 above.

76 Giorgio Agamben, *State of Exception* (Chicago: University of Chicago Press, 2003); Victor Roudometof, *Glocalization: A Critical Introduction* (London and New York: Routledge, 2016).

77 Deana Rankin, *Between Spenser and Swift: English Writing in Seventeenth-Century Ireland* (Cambridge: Cambridge University Press, 2005).

78 David Armitage, 'What's the Big Idea? Intellectual History and the Longue Durée', *History of European Ideas* 38 (2012), 493–507.

79 Susan Broomhall, *Early Modern Emotions: An Introduction* (New York and London: Routledge, 2016).

80 See also Mary O'Dowd, *A History of Women in Ireland, 1500–1800* (London and New York: Routledge, 2005); Margaret MacCurtain and Mary O'Dowd (eds.), *Women in Early Modern Ireland* (Edinburgh: Edinburgh University Press, 1991); Marie-Louise Coolahan, *Women, Writing, and Language in Early Modern Ireland* (Oxford: Oxford University Press, 2010).

81 Jane Ohlmeyer, 'Ireland, India and the British Empire', *Studies in People's History* 2 (2) (2015), 169–88.

2 Writing the social and cultural history of Ireland, 1550–1660

Wills as example and inspiration

Clodagh Tait

Despite the fraught political circumstances prevailing when she created her will in January 1650, Honora O'Brien Wingfield, of Smithstown, County Clare, seems to have been sanguine as she anticipated the end to her long life.[1] She designated a grandson, Conor O'Brien of Leamanah, as the heir to Smithstown and her other lands, and set out a series of bequests. Each of her four daughters was remembered with gifts of clothing and jewelry. Seven other grandchildren were mentioned, the girls being given clothing and/ or jewels, and the boys horses, though one granddaughter received a flock of sheep and Honora's 'pacing nag'. While her husband, Richard Wingfield, and eldest son, Edward (both already dead), were probably Protestants, it is clear from her will that Honora was a Catholic. She left bequests to two Catholic priests, two others witnessed her will, and she left her daughter Ellinor 'an amber pair of [rosary] beads'. Honora also owned a fair quantity of other jewelry. There was a big gold ring and three others set with diamond, 'Turkey' (turquoise), and amethyst stones, respectively. She had already given her daughter Mary a quantity of 'jewels'. Among the clothing bequeathed were a black silk gown, a broadcloth gown and cloak, and nine 'gownaghs'. She left livestock to seven women and two men who were probably servants, and she granted Donough O'Hickie a forty-shilling annuity, to 'cherish and maintaine' one of her grandchildren. Any 'cattle, horses, corn and household stuff' not otherwise disposed of were to go to her heir. Honora signed with a mark—she may have been too weak to write or may never have learned. Two of the seven witnesses also used marks.

Though usually relatively short, wills like this one grant us insights into the material, social, political, economic, and religious worlds of sixteenth- and seventeenth-century Irish people. Testators used them to distribute prized possessions and thereby to reward and encourage close friends and family. Bonds of affection are hinted at by the range of Honora's small personal bequests. It was expected that items like rings and clothing would remind the recipient of the donor, thereby continuing bonds beyond death. Honora also bequeathed futures and secured or augmented the status of the recipients. An in-calf cow like those given to her servants, or the flock of sheep given to her granddaughter, provided assets that could help ensure financial well-being, act as collateral for loans, or provide the basis for a dowry. Gifts of clothing appropriate to the recipient's standing were welcome, but even old-fashioned items might be remodeled or sold. Honora's tenure of her lands is interesting too. Though in the medieval period Gaelic women could not inherit land in their own right, Honora's entitlement to the castle and lands at Smithstown survived her marriage and the property was hers to bequeath through the female line.[2] Honora was both a debtor and a creditor: mortgages were owed to and by her, and she owed fifty-six shillings to Slany Ny Loghlen.

Social and cultural history provides us with an opportunity to rummage in the closets, chests, and jewelry coffers of the past in an attempt to recreate the practices, relationships, structures, rituals, and products of everyday experience, its things and spaces, and to consider what these reflect about the inner lives of past populations. This essay offers some thoughts on how the art of rummaging may help further our understanding of how early modern people constructed their place in the world, and negotiated their relationships with others and with the churches and the state. Using wills—especially published versions—as an example, I also hope to suggest some avenues for future research, as well as some ways in which lesser-used sources can be utilized.

The fact remains, however, that historians of early modern Ireland will never be able to reconstruct the experiences and inner lives of their subjects with the same facility and to the same extent as their colleagues working on the same period elsewhere. The possibility of doing so ended with the destruction of most of the contents of the Dublin Public Record Office, including the majority of the wills stored there, as a result of the lamentably ill-considered occupation and siege of the building in 1922 (hard for any historian to think of without wishing they could believe as wholeheartedly as their ancestors did in the vengeful power of the ritual curse). That one event has made it particularly difficult to recover the experiences of women and of the lower sections of society who might, if nowhere else, have been mentioned in such documents as wills, rentals, court proceedings, and parish registers. It has made surviving sources all the more precious and has placed an onus on early modernists to engage robustly with them while accepting that even meticulously researched pieces of work must necessarily remain uncomfortably incomplete. To write early modern Ireland for a wider audience usually necessitates apologetic digressions, reminding the reader of the limits of the possible (written while muttering that ritual curse on the men of 1922): a dilemma for which there is little sympathy within regimes of ranking and rating research and its 'impact'. Historians of Ireland face being told that 'if only you had a few more sources to tie up the loose ends, that article would be fit for *Past and Present*'.[3] They may find themselves contributing to a conference where the person working on a town in Kent has more sources for a similar theme in a similar period than exist for the whole of Ireland.

How then can the writer make peace with—and make the most of—the partial, the half-glimpsed? Several approaches suggest themselves. First, understandings of early modern Ireland can be fed by the insights found in the rich body of scholarship on the cultural and social history of Europe, the Americas, and beyond in the same period. However, comparative history should not be overly imitative and should be attentive to local peculiarities. Second, individual case studies or groups of them can be useful at least in revealing experiences that may have been shared to a greater or lesser degree by contemporaries. Honora O'Brien Wingfield's will may be a rare survivor, and it is problematic to generalize too much from it. But if we shy away from sources that historians elsewhere might find too incomplete or partial, we're left with nothing to say. Third, Irish historians have been somewhat slow to engage with some of the exciting recent developments in historiography, but as this chapter and volume aim to show, histories of the body, space, emotions, and gender (the gendered experience of men as well as women) offer techniques and questions that can be applied fruitfully in an Irish context. Fourth, alternative forms of publication—for example, blogposts, thematic collections of short contributions, shorter book formats, as well as the greater online availability of magazines like *History Ireland* and local history journals—are offering ways to present ideas and episodes not amenable to treatment in the standard article and book word limits to wider audiences.

Many of the sources are gone or mutilated, but others exist. Familiar sources can be approached in new ways. The ongoing excavation of the experiences of those caught up in the 1641 rebellion, recounted in the Trinity College Dublin (TCD) depositions (recently digitized), provides one example of a body of sources whose purpose was ostensibly political and legal, but which can be used to explore the emotional, material, and social worlds of both settlers and natives.[4] There is as much cultural as political history in the State Papers—witness Marie-Louise Coolahan's recent work on women's petitions.[5] Sources for law, land transfers, and administration are full of names, customs, interactions, and anecdotes. Among these I would highlight Irish Fiants and legal records, such as the records of the Court of Castle Chamber and the Court of Chancery (whose potential has been advertised by Jon G. Crawford and Mary O'Dowd, respectively).[6] That material which is available is spread unevenly in geographical and social terms. Old English and New English/British communities have left more extensive bodies of sources that are more suited to the purposes of social and cultural historians. Thus, certain aspects of the experiences of Gaelic populations, especially among the lower sections of society, will inevitably be less recoverable. However, models also exist showing what can be done with Irish-language material and Gaelic material culture—Brendan Kane's comparative work on British and Irish Isles honor cultures, Elizabeth Fitzpatrick's on Gaelic landscapes, and Salvador Ryan's on Catholic faith are all innovative and exciting examples.[7]

Finding and using wills

The indexes to diocesan wills and administration bonds indicate the extent of the material held in the Public Records Office (PRO) before its destruction.[8]

The fragmentary extant corpus takes a variety of forms. Some examples of original wills survive, usually among family papers or in British repositories like the Prerogative Court of Canterbury. Transcripts also exist, the most extensive collection being the Record Commission Deeds and Wills series in the National Archives.[9] We are indebted to the pre-1922 antiquarians who transcribed wills and reproduced them in full or in part in their publications: others linger among their unpublished papers. Abstract collections (e.g., Betham, Crossle, and Thrift) are held in the National Archives of Ireland (NAI). However, these were created for genealogical purposes and thus usually give only sketchy details beyond names, places, and dates.[10] One exception is the Jennings abstracts, mostly dealing with Waterford, which indicate what was bequeathed as well as to whom.[11]

Early modern wills were formulaic, but there was room for elaboration within the formula. Will preambles regularly described the testator's physical and mental state—Donal O'Sullivan More of Dunkieran, County Kerry, was 'at this Instante of perfect witt and memorie' but 'sickely in body' in 1632. Wills tended to be written when the testator was in danger of death. Genet Galwey of Cork was 'of good memorie, in my sicke bed, labouring and drawing towards death naturall'—the notion of dying as a form of labor is interesting here—when she made her short will in June 1582.[12] Warnings by churchmen and lawyers that will-making was too important to be left to the last minute were increasingly heeded. John Blake of Galway was 'ready to goe to sea for the Canarries, and doubting what might happen', when he made a will in 1622. He survived, however, and revoked it in 1636.[13] William Bowen, a soldier from Ballyadams, County Kildare, was in Mayo when he made his will (proved 1594) 'in Respect that I dwell in a dangerous place … employed in her maiesties service amonges Rebels and traytors'.[14]

Most preambles also stated the testators' hopes for their soul and body.[15] While formulaic bequests of the soul 'to God who gave it' or 'Almighty God, my maker and my Redeemer' are common, some took the opportunity for more personal statements. In an impeccably protestant preamble in 1608, Sir Geoffrey Fenton left his soul 'in the hands of my Redeemer Christ Jesus assuring myself that by his death and passion Godes Justice is fully satisfied for my sins and by his resurrection I am fully justified and restored to Godes favor'.[16] By contrast, Donal O'Sullivan More commended his soul 'to the Hollie Trinitie and all the Sc[ain]ts in Heaven'.[17] The testator might then state a preferred burial location. William Nugent of Newhaggard, County Meath, wanted to be buried 'in St Patrick's Church in Tyme [Taghmon] in the Tombe wheren my ancestors for many descents [have] been buried'.[18] In 1652, after the Cromwellian reconquest, Patrick Madan of Waterford merely requested burial 'in Christian grave if possible'.[19]

Wills were usually written in English or Latin (increasingly the former), by a scribe or bystander if the testator was unable to. One rare surviving Irish-language will is that of Edmund Grace of Ballywalter, County Carlow (1606). Grace divided his property into thirds in the traditional manner, leaving a third each to his wife, daughter, and son-in-law, and to activities on behalf of his soul. An attached note recorded that it was proved in June 1609 'being translated by Master Charles Dunn, LL.D'. The translation of other Irish-language wills for administrative purposes may have rendered their original form invisible.[20]

Other aspects of the process of crafting and proving wills (ecclesiastical courts signed off on them once the provisions had been fulfilled) are also largely invisible. However, there are hints to the role of legal professionals and scribes. The transcriber of John Rothe fitzPiers's lengthy will of 1619, G.D. Burtchaell, commented that a lawyer would have been needed to draw it up, and that the finished will itself was probably the work of two or more clerks.[21] Witnesses to wills often included physicians, clergy, and relatives gathered at a deathbed. The Latin will of Sir John MacCoghlan, Chief of Delvin-MacCoghlan, King's County, is prefaced by greetings from the Parish Priest of Fuire, Cormac Dalachan, who wrote it 'having been [therefore] personally appointed'. He noted that it was made 'in the house of Solomon MacEgan, in the town of Cuil', and its witnesses included three who signed in Irish characters.[22] We can thus glimpse something of the circumstances of this will's creation and the deathbed scene, noting again its complex linguistic context.[23]

Much work remains to be done on landed property and succession to it in early modern Ireland, but wills demonstrate some tactics employed to preserve it. The will of Sir Cormac McTeige MacCarthy (1583) began,

> I proteste before God that Johanna Butler is my lawful wedded wife, and that Ellyn Barrett was at the tyme I wed her and before the lawful wife of James fz Morice, and so Cormocke ooge my son is my lawful heire of my body.

He provided for two sons and three daughters. However, the bulk of his possessions—'the whole lordship of Muskry with the towns and hamlets thereof'—he passed to his brother, Kallaghan McTeige, 'for conscience sake'. Richard Caulfield speculated that the testator was conscience-stricken for having 'usurped the chieftainship from his eldest brother … and to have then obtained patents from the Crown granting him the estates according to English law'. More likely he was passing on the lands to his 'tanaiste' by Gaelic custom, and trying to protect his children and wife. To that end he bequeathed them Blarney Castle, appointing three men as chief guards and reserving the 'shott and powder' kept there 'for the warding of that castle to the behoufe of Cormocke ooge'. The will thus illustrates some potential collision points between Gaelic custom and English law as the Elizabethan reconquest gathered pace: Gaelic acceptance of serial marriage; inheritance even by 'illegitimate' offspring versus English privileging of eldest sons born within legally contracted marriage; and Gaelic assigning of lordship to the 'most active and powerful' member of a deceased lord's extended family versus English customs of primogeniture. As Herbert Webb Gillman noted, it also demonstrates how royal policies worked towards 'breaking down the tribal common tenure of the Muskerry lands, and assigning them as private property to the lord of that country'.[24] Willing of property both facilitated and normalized this process.

Other family strategies regarding land transmission are also evident. Until the passing of the Irish Statute of Uses in 1635, wills often reiterated property arrangements (enfeoffment to use) already entered into by landowners in order to ensure descent of landed estates in the male line (entail) and to 'evade the burden of livery and feudal incidents'—customary payments owed by tenants-in-chief to the monarch on inheritance and other alienations (transfers) of lands.[25] Most worrying for Catholic landholders in particular was that under feudal custom, an underage heir became a royal ward during his minority, and the monarch had the right to assign his finances and education to whomever s/he pleased. Wardship was increasingly feared as a tool of Anglicization, with prominent Catholic heirs being assigned protestant guardians.[26] The 1620 will of Sir Christopher Nugent of Moyrath noted that he had 'passed his lands to Edward Dowdale Barnabas Scurlock & [others] for the uses particularly specified in the deed of enfeoffment'. He entailed his estates in the male line, recording the birth order of his five sons and then (in case the descent in these lines failed) expanding the entail to the descendants of his other male relations.[27] The Old English gentry and townsmen were to the fore in utilizing such devices, and O'Dowd has discussed their effects on female inheritance and the disputes arising as a result.[28] In the later seventeenth century, Catholic men continued to stipulate entails in their wills, as William Dobbin of Waterford did in 1663, remaindering his bequests 'to every one of my [five] sons successively one after the other ... and to the heirs male of their bodies lawfully begotten and to be begotten'.[29]

Wills written by women are very scarce. Married women could only make wills with their husbands' consent and thus most female-authored wills are by older widows. Like Honora O'Brien Wingfield, they usually display a good grasp of financial matters. Katherine Butler (1646) noted that her grandchild, Piers Butler of Callan, County Kilkenny, and her son (possibly son-in-law) Theobald, owed her £320 between them for arrears in rents of her jointure lands. As with other female testators, Katherine made small bequests to several relatives.[30] Women are, of course, regularly mentioned in men's wills. Provisions for their wives shed light on economic arrangements for widows (dower and jointure) and their material circumstances.[31] Unmarried daughters might be left contributions towards their dowries: Donal O'Sullivan, 'also O'Sullivan More', of Dunkieran, County Kerry, in 1632 left £300 for the maintenance and 'preferment' of his daughter Syly, £170 for Ellen, and £130 for Mary.[32] Women were also regularly appointed executors of their husbands' and fathers' wills, though usually in conjunction with a male relative, allowing them some agency in protecting their own interests. Very occasionally they appear also as witnesses to wills: for example, Anne Begg witnessed Elizabeth Power of Lismore's will in 1634.[33]

Wills can hint at religious faith and show something of the range of convoluted ways by which Catholics attempted to evade the strictures placed on them. Later medieval wills are filled with provisions for souls, such as bequests to churches, religious orders, and clergy, and charitable donations to the poor and the community that were understood as 'good works' necessary for salvation.[34] In Britain, the Reformation saw such provisions alter rapidly, but it seems to have been fairly easy for Irish Catholics to will money and goods for pious uses up until the 1570s and 1580s. As I have discussed elsewhere, pious bequests became more circumspect thereafter, with Catholics resorting to either charitable works like contributions to almshouses and hospitals, or premortem arrangements that would sidestep scrutiny.[35] To take two examples of many, in 1610, Mary Fitzgerald Nugent, Dowager Baroness of Delvin, left £45 for pious and godly uses 'as she will declare in a letter to her son the Lord of Delvin', while in 1628, Thomas Nugent of Dunferth, County Kildare, left £40 'to be layd outt for the use of my soul according as Thomas Deys will dispose of itt'.[36] In the 1630s, Bishop Andrews of Ferns complained about the collection of 'infinate sumes of monies' by Catholic clerics, including 'legacies given them by the last Will and testament of persons deceased'.[37]

Material culture

Wills say much about things—material culture—allowing us to consider 'the forms, uses and meanings of physical objects in everyday life' and thereby to access aspects of the 'wordless experience' of past populations.[38] Though they provide descriptions rather than the things themselves, and though they privilege things valuable enough to warrant mention, wills crucially provide a sample of the kinds of goods people owned. Furthermore, testators are caught in the act of donation, revealing something of the meaning of certain kinds of items to their owners, ideas about the importance of gift-giving[39] as well as the changing consumption patterns that had put these items into their hands in the first place. Current projects using English wills and probate inventories are revealing a lot about household economies, men's and women's work, eating, drinking, and cooking, and a variety of other topics.[40] There are clear difficulties in using the fragmented body of Irish wills in any similar way. However, Susan Flavin has used a sample of wills and inventories from Cork and elsewhere alongside a variety of other sources to illustrate changing consumption patterns. Other cultural changes—of manners, behavior, and ideas about privacy—can also be observed.[41]

The jewelry and clothing owned by early modern Irish people are known to us mostly from a limited number of portraits, tombs, archaeological fragments, and surviving accounts and inventories. But wills mention quite a lot, helping us to see how wealth and status were displayed as well as indicating the trading connections that brought such objects to Ireland. Like Honora O'Brien Wingfield, Lisagh O'Connor of Leixlip, County Kildare (1626), bequeathed both jewels and clothes to a large number of relatives and friends. He gave a 'Rich Diamond Jewell', a gold chain, and two gold rings to his wife, and his 'amber beades and Crucifix' to his son Carie.[42] Lisagh and Honora's beads indicate the everyday use of religious objects, with Catholics publicly wearing their religious identity.[43] Other testators also mentioned ownership of rosaries, some quite magnificent, such as Richard Walsh of Cork's silver set (1583) 'of nene score graven stones' and 'another pair of beads of christall and silver'.[44] Notably, O'Connor also left valuable bequests to three men, possibly priests, indicated by their designation as 'Mr' and by the items received. One was given a 'wrought golden cup'—presumably either already a chalice, or intended as one—while another, Mr. Peter Geoghegan, was given 'my watch, conditionally that he causeth one hundred masses to be said for my soule' (a very early Irish mention of personal timepieces).[45] Lisagh also left £40 'to be disposed in pious uses'.

Clothing was also important in early modern society.[46] It reflected social identity and social status, no more so than when prestigious roles mandated the wearing of specialized items. Alderman Edward Rothe fitzJohn of Kilkenny (1613 and 1615) expressed his hopes in his sons by leaving the eldest three his violet, scarlet, and black aldermanic gowns, respectively: he clearly hoped that his sons would reach the higher echelons of the new city's corporation.[47] Throughout his life, Richard Boyle assiduously charted additions to his and his wife's costly wardrobes as he rose from obscurity to the earldom of Cork. In his will, he carefully identified recipients for a magnificent succession of outfits that he doubtless expected would assist them, in turn, to present an image appropriate for the standing to which they aspired.[48]

Lisagh O'Connor's wardrobe was less impressive, yet he had thought carefully about its dispersal. He bequeathed a black satin suit, a black cloak lined with velvet, two other lined cloaks, three pairs of silk stockings (red, yellow, and tawny), two Holland shirts, a new broadcloth suit with a cloak and doublet, 'a wrought pair of boothose topps' (decorated tops for stockings, designed to be visible above knee-length boots), a ruff (by then probably somewhat unfashionable), and cuffs (probably lace). O'Connor's background is obscure,[49] but his Anglicized wardrobe was undoubtedly different from the clothing he wore in the Gaelic midlands in his youth. The spread of English fashions is also seen in the 1609 will of the White Knight, Edmund Fitzgibbon. He left his heir 'all me silck English app[ar]ells if he recovers' (if not, his three sons–in–law would get 'an ap[ar]ell le piece').[50] He presumably also had 'Irish apparells' and may have worn different styles under different circumstances. It is tempting to see similar cultural ambidexterity in Honora O'Brien Wingfield's will, which uses both the word 'gown' and its Irish form 'gownagh' (*gúna*) for different pieces of clothing, possibly indicating English- and Irish-style items.[51]

Wills also highlight the agricultural basis of the Irish economy and aspects of economic change. Most of Christopher McCruttyne's limited possessions (Kiltilagh, County Clare, c.1660) were animals. He left his daughter two heifers, six sheep, and six lambs, and, rather charmingly, a large black cow and her calf 'by name duf beg'.[52] Most of the White Knight's very considerable bequests were also in the form of livestock, as befitted an Irish lord of the time. He had 'greate in calfe cowes'; 'yonge cowes'; oxen; great mares; 'horses, mares, caples'; garrens; and 'yonge horses', and employed 'heirds' and other officials to care for and count them. By the time of Lisagh O'Connor's 1626 will, a further distinction had crept in—between newer 'English' breeds and traditional 'Irish' ones. O'Connor bequeathed three English cows with calves, one English bull, and one English heifer.

Some bequests hint at leisure activities. O'Connor owned books, which he left to his son. Others also mention books, but rarely their titles. O'Connor's bequests of a 'stone Crossbow' (a crossbow that fired small bullets, especially for shooting birds) and a 'birding peece' may indicate an interest in hunting. In 1640, Sir Richard Nugent left an annuity of £10 to his falconer, James, and though his son Ignatius was left his lands in Termonbarry, 'the great haukes and eyries of great haukes' were reserved for his grandson and heir. Ignatius was also to pay the heir 200 eels and two salmon yearly. Likewise, in 1602, when Christopher Nugent, Baron of Delvin, bequeathed lands in Roscommon and Sligo, he reserved 'the earie of hawkes that breedethe on the s[ai]d lande' to his son. Hawking was a gentlemanly activity, and hawks were also valuable as gifts to grease the wheels of social and political interactions with other gentlemen. Horses, like hawks, were also regularly exchanged between gentlemen, and they too are frequently referenced in wills.[53]

Few householders gave extensive lists of possessions, but prized objects were often singled out. Silver utensils—especially cups, spoons, and salts—appear frequently, but items did not need to be of high monetary value to be cherished. Susan Flavin has noted that even mundane objects might be 'invested with personal significance beyond their utility'.[54] Thomas Smith of Gillabbey in Cork left his daughter Martha 'a featherbed and bedding, a counterpane made by her deceased mother, and a custing bottle [casting or perfume bottle] which Mr. Dyer gave her'.[55] John MacCoughlan of Delvin MacCoughlan, King's County (1590), gave his son 'the large pan which he lately had of inheritance of his mother'.[56] Christopher Galwey of Cork, in 1582, left his daughter jewels, two crosses, 'and my mother's big coife'.[57] Genet Creaughe left her eldest daughter her best 'roll or breyd' and a broadcloth coat, and her second daughter got another roll and a 'pinke coate with new slyves'. Like the coif, rolls were a form of headwear: lengths of linen were folded and rolled into a cheese shape and worn on top of the head. The women of different Irish towns sported distinctive head coverings, and thus Creaughe's rolls would have represented both sentiment and place.[58]

Some urban wills also mention the more valuable contents of testators' shops and storerooms. Richard Madan of Waterford's will (1602) indicates his stock, including hides, 'aquavita', sweet wine ('bastard' and 'picked bastard'), and Gascony.[59] Nicholas Faggan, a Cork merchant, had eighteen cowhides, thirty-two stones of tallow, one stone of aniseed, sixteen stone of French iron, two bolts of canvas, and a dozen skulls (helmets) among his possessions in 1578.[60] In 1582, Richard Tyrry fitzAdam of Cork was trading in cloth, hides, and haberdashery.[61] In a will made in Bristol in1559, Richard White of Bristol and New Ross bequeathed his daughter Margery his one-third share in *The Julyan* and its appurtenances, and other bequests suggest he traded iron, salt, cloth, and other commodities across the Irish Sea.[62]

As indicated by Madan's stock, wills and their inventories also reveal eating and drinking practices.[63] Nicholas Fagan of Cork's (1578) tablewares included pewter platters, trenchers, and porringers, hinting at the food eaten and how it was served. He had several large and small pans, tablecloths, a brewing pan, an aquavitae pot, and several pewter pots (probably tankards). Items for making and drinking alcohol were regularly mentioned. Several other Cork citizens bequeathed brewing pans, barley, and barley malt.[64] Drinking customs are indicated by specialized drinking vessels. Robert Forstall of Kilferagh, County Kilkenny (1645), owned two silver bowls for beer, one 'cupp of silver' for wine and one 'cupp of silver for Aquavitae'.[65] Robert Blake fitzWalter of Galway (1612) requested that 'one jug of silver for bere and one cup of silver for wine with a brass crock for aqua-vitey be given to every one of my sons'. His daughters' dowries were to be paid in part by his wife, Catherine Darcy, from the 'money of the aqua-vitey that she makes', saved over the previous five years.[66] Drinking and eating were the product of good husbandry and housewifery (note the glimpse in Catherine Darcy Blake's case of women's work and its economic rewards), provided occasions for hospitality that reinforced bonds between those who ate and drank to-gether, and highlighted families' status via the display of craft and vessels. That Roland Savage of Ballygalget, County Antrim, left a brazen pot, silver cups, and 'my harpe' to his third son Patrick may indicate an association in his mind between drinking and music.[67] (Notably, musical instruments are rarely mentioned in wills, though Richard Shee of Kilkenny (1603) had a 'great double pair of virginals' in his 'great chamber'.)[68] Further research on food culture, the production of alcoholic drink, and the contexts (and sound-scape) of its consumption is clearly possible.

Space

Wills and the very few surviving probate and other inventories can be useful in rendering visible the ghosts of domestic and public spaces as they were experienced by early modern inhabitants of Ireland. The inventories of aris-tocratic homes have been used by Jane Fenlon to consider changes to house design and room usage.[69] Wills, meanwhile, can also allow us to peer into the furnishings and layout of some more middling households. Laurence Casse's will (1575), for example, sets out the more noteworthy domestic property of a family from Gowran, County Kilkenny. In addition to a silver salt, a dozen silver spoons, and other pieces of table silver, he had a significant quantity of brass cooking pots and pewter utensils, furniture for a fireplace (andirons, tripods, grate), various beds and bedsteads, sheets, tablecloths, towels, and pillows.[70] He also mentions 'one nut of silver', likely a goblet carved from a coconut with a silver stem.[71] The 1614 will of Walter Wellesley, (feudal) baronet of Norragh, County Kildare, set out half of his livestock and goods to be allocated to his wife, including tables, forms (benches), pewter dishes, two hutches (cupboards), 'my own chest', a 'pot', two featherbeds, sheets, a tablecloth and napkins, a towel, carpet, pillows, candlesticks, two 'kyves' (keeves—vats for brewing or washing), and 'a pann in Irish called lughtery' (*luchtaire* meaning 'to cook').[72]

In 1638, Frances Wadding, a Waterford widow, shared among her sister, three children, and maid 'my father's picture'; a gold cross; a cabinet; various good-quality table linens, including a 'suit of diaper' (heavy linen with a woven pattern); a cupboard cloth; a desk with 'writings and other things in it'; a bed, trunk, chest, and linens; and clothing, including black frieze gowns, smocks, and Holland aprons. Even these limited possessions hint at relatively comfortable material circumstances, as well as her religious faith, possible literacy, and affectionate attachments to objects and people. Her reference to 'what I have at Killagh furniture of chamber there' may indicate that she was allocated houseroom in one or more properties belonging to family members during her widowhood.[73] Detailed terms and conditions were set out by John Rothe fitzPiers in 1619 to facilitate the sharing of his large new Kilkenny house between his widow's and son's families. He described precisely what 'parcel' of the house his wife should inhabit during widowhood, stipulating that she would have the use of one-third of his garden, pigeon-house, furniture, and utensils, and access to the kitchen, gillhouse (for brewing), and well, taking turns with his son's household to use their 'necessarie furniture'. Rothe was very anxious about how his son and wife would get on in their changed living circumstances, expressing his fears of the shame and scandal that could ensue if they clashed.[74] Despite such provisions, disputes over houseroom and other arrangements for elderly and widowed parents regularly ended up before the courts.[75] Thus, wills occasionally reveal not only the layout and furnishings of homes and individual rooms, but the human and power relations expressed in and through them.

The verbal demarcation of plots of land in wills sometimes involved the recitation of both geographical markers and personal memories, allowing us glimpses of 'the material, social, and mental components of space constitution'.[76] Richard Madan of Waterford in 1602 left his son Patrick 'after the decease of his mother my dwelling house with the appurtenances & the garden on the left hand as we go to St Patrick's Gate which I purchased of White of Thomastown'.[77] In these few words, Madan walks us through that city, noticing 'as we go' the property marked out for his son, an act of mental geography in which motion, place, and anecdote intertwine.

Robert Blake fitzWalter of Galway, merchant (1616), recreated snatches of the streetscape of that city as he settled the dispersal of his property in and around it. He left 'my own new dwelling house' to his son Richard; his widow, Catherine, was to live there as long as Richard resided outside the city, but if he chose to relocate, Catherine was to have 'the house wherein we dwelled before'. Blake's second son Peter was left 'my stone house in the Great-Gate street in Galway that I bought of James Roe his son Richard Linch fitzStephen', and Nicholas got 'my stone house near St Nicholas Church in Galway that I bought of my brother [in-law] Nicholas Dorsey [Darcy]'. The properties intended for his three other sons—shops, gardens, and cellars as well as houses—were equally carefully delineated.[78] Nicola Whyte talks about 'the indivisibility of the physical experience of landscape and demarcation of local social and economic relations' in early modern English rural communities.[79] Clearly this member of Galway's elite experienced the spaces and landscape of his city in a similar way. Blake noted his own rise from 'the house wherein we dwelled before' and sought to imprint his ambitions for his descendants on the town through their colonization of its premium buildings, stating, 'I wish to leave a stone house in Galway to every one of my sons'. In Blake's descriptions the spaces of the city are gendered: he earmarked for men buildings that he had acquired from other men. Widows might temporarily control these spaces (in Catherine Darcy Blake's case, only on sufferance), but they ultimately ceded ownership to their husbands' male descendants.[80]

As they set out their burial sites, testators reveal an awareness of both the physical layout of churches and churchyards and their social geography. Burial choices reflected identities in life: family connections, religious faith (for example, through burial near an altar or saint's statue), and social location.[81] Frances Wadding requested a prestigious grave in the chancel of Kilmanagh parish church. Henry fitzJames Walsh (1629) wanted to be buried in his father and grandfather's grave in Christchurch Cathedral, Waterford, 'lying between St Blaise's altar in the north and the pulpit adjoining the body of the said church'—a neat merger of pre- and post-Reformation landmarks.[82] Sir Leonard Blennerhassett of Castlehassett, County Fermanagh, was to be interred 'in my Chappell next unto the wall at the ende of the grave of my [father] Thomas Blennerhassett'.[83] Sir Valentine Blake of Galway (1629) had also created a private chapel, in his case at St. Francis' Abbey in honour of Christ and 'St Mary of Loretto, where I have bene myselfe in person, both there and in Roome'; he asked that masses and prayers be said there regularly 'if it pleaseth God Almightie'. His grandson also requested burial there in 1654.[84] Privatizing parts of sacred buildings, and use of monastic sites in order to avoid surveillance, allowed some Catholics opportunities for freer expression of their faith; both Catholics and Protestants used private chapels to indicate social standing.[85] Glimpsed in the wills, then, but also evident in records of land ownership, parish registers, maps, and archaeological evidence, cultural history's 'spatial turn' holds further potential for enhancing our understandings around experiences of domestic and public space in early modern Ireland.[86]

Networks

As well as mapping some of the things and spaces meaningful to testators, wills above all are charts of meaningful relationships. Wills demonstrate 'who mattered' to early modern individuals, highlighting testators' particularly close relationships among wider groups of relatives and friends. Lisagh O'Connor left bequests to his wife, daughter, two sons, son–in–law, two sisters, four nephews, three cousins, and two brothers (maybe brothers–in–law), various friends, and servants. Patrick Crosby, who transformed himself during the later Elizabethan period from a Gaelic MacCrossan (hereditary bards to the perennially rebellious O'Mores) to an Anglicized government servant and landowner in Kerry, similarly contributed to the dowries of his granddaughter and four nieces, gave £20 to maintain his nephew at the Inns of Court, and provided for his son and daughter and several other kinsmen and women.[87] The testators of early modern Cork mention spouses, siblings, in-laws, and a range of other relatives (including deceased ancestors from whom they had derived lands or with whom they requested burial).

Many male testators acknowledged illegitimate children, and their wills indicate the differential treatment of legitimate and illegitimate half-siblings when it came to inheritance. Piers Gould (1610) left 'my base son Patrick' a frieze jerkin, hose, and forty shillings, and instructed 'my wife to maintain him as long as he shall behave honestly'.[88] Richard Madan of Waterford and Richard Hackett fitz-Thomas of Limerick left small sums to their 'base' daughters.[89] Hackett also left bequests to his foster-father and foster-mother, and wills provide some of the few available glimpses of what seems to have been widespread use of fosterage (possibly involving wet-nursing) by Old English families.[90] The Munster townsmen regularly refer to foster-parents and siblings, indicating that relationships with fosterers were warm and lasting. In 1579, George Galwey fitzEdward of Cork arranged for his foster-brother, Walter Murrough, to live rent-free in 'the house where he now dwells' and left him forty shillings.[91]

Warm sentiments towards servants as key members of the early modern 'family' are also evident. Honora O'Brien Wingfield's will is notable for the long list of servants mentioned. Some testators interceded for valued servants. Sir Geoffrey Fenton left bequests to Jordan Strawbridge, William Osborne, William Woods, and Randall Clayton, and recommended that his wife try to persuade them 'to tarry with her'. Richard Boyle likewise recommended his servants to his heirs, especially noting long-servers like his purse-bearer, William Chettle, to whom he gave £20 per year for life and all of his linens and clothing 'not disposed of' in his will.[92] For Sir Richard Shee of Kilkenny, however, master–servant relationships had soured between 1603, when he left a bequest to his servant Richard Bennet, and the 1608 codicil to his will, when he revoked this legacy as Bennett 'hathe written verie saucie letters … [and] given out maleperte speeches of my wife and of myselfe'.[93]

At a time of significant immigration, wills can reveal something of the social interactions and material circumstances of newcomers to Ireland. Nicholas Pett,

Provost Marshal of Munster, made his will at Carrigaline in 1572. He was un-married and died without family close at hand. His heir was his brother John and 'in his absence here' he made his friend Barnabe Daly an executor, leaving him furniture, a horse, and two pairs of shears. John received Pett's lease of lands in Buttevant, some grand clothing with velvet and gold lace, and a service book. Nicholas had a son, however–perhaps illegitimate–to whom he left a grey horse and £20. Horses and other tokens were left to his two manservants and several acquaintances with Old English names. Those owing him money included Lord Barrymore; James Galwey; Mr. Burgett, Clerk of the Council of Munster; and 'Dick Priest, with one legg', who owed four nobles for a hackney. His property was scattered, indicating something of his travels—items were in Cork, Buttevant, Carrigaline, Dungarvan, Waterford, and Dublin. He gave an apothecary in Bristol two horses. Several women—Daly's wife, several maids, and Adey Wager—received small bequests of livestock and clothing. Pett em-ployed a number of horseboys, one called Meanes (Manus) and a 'little boy galyglas [gallowglass]', to whom he gave money, a rare glimpse of young train-ees in military service. Two other young soldiers were also remembered with items appropriate to their ambitions: his godson John Wager, 'now waiting upon Sir Henry Sydney', and Jasper Wager, 'servant to Sir Warham Sentlegier', were given costly but unostentatious clothing, skulls (helmets), and firearms and other weapons.[94]

Both Pett and Honora O'Brien Wingfield were enmeshed in networks of debt and credit. It was expected that testators would list debts owed and owing so that outstanding monies could be redeemed, and economic misdemeanors would not be charged on their souls. As well as listing his household goods and stock, the inventory of William Verdon (1578) records 'pledges' from nineteen separate debtors of objects against which money or hides were owed. The ob-jects included cups, rings, about eighteen 'crosses', and five 'bedes' (rosaries), varying in value from twenty shillings to seven shillings and six pence. He himself had pledged one silver cup and a silver spoon to others.[95] One of the people who had pawned items to Verdon was David Tyrry fitzEdmund (a sil-ver cross 'for George Skyddy'). Tyrry's own will mentioned further pledges of gold rings 'with' Edmund Gooll, Richard Punch, and Andrew Galwey, while Genet Myaghe had 'the cover of James Roche's [cup]'.[96] The references here to items belonging to third parties being pledged via Tyrry indicate some of the complex ways in which people acquired and circulated money and goods.

Wills sometimes indicate other relationships and networks. George Hart of Templemore, County Donegal (1659), noted the owners of the lands he leased or mortgaged: Lord Chichester, Owen O'Dogherty, Mr. Roper, and the 'Mayrolty of Londonderry'. Business and social networks are also evident in the naming of overseers. These trusted friends and colleagues might be called upon to supervise a will's administration and to intervene in disagreements. Hart made 'Henry and George Cary [his brothers-in-law], Captain Henry Vaughan, Captain Edward Cary, and my loving friend William Warren, Esq., the overseers thereof in whose love and Integritie I have confidence'.[97] Henry

Savage of Ardkeen, County Antrim, in 1655 took an ecumenical approach, appointing 'my singular good friend Lord Viscount Montgomery of Ardes, my wel-beloved friends Lt-Col. Hugh Coghran, Capt W Maxwell, Capt Hugh McGill and Patrick Savage of Ballygalgott' as overseers. Henry Savage was a Catholic but Montgomery and possibly some others were protestant—a surviving account of Savage's death indicates Montgomery approved of his religious moderation.[98]

Emotions

Though wills were designed as sites of emotional equilibrium where the resignation necessary to dying well might be displayed, some struggled to achieve this elevated state. Terror of damnation caused Sir John Fitzgerald of Ballymaloe, County Cork, to reveal in 1640 that he had invented a fee tail 'which was pretended to be done by my grandfather' for the purposes of concealing a large portion of the former church lands of the See of Cloyne (in the family's hands since the 1570s). An inquisition in 1664 heard that Fitzgerald had placed the will in the hands of his heir, and 'as if he had been making his confession to the Priest, he begged pardon of God for concealing his grandfather's will, and detaining his lands from the Church', beating his breast and saying, 'I am damned unless God be merciful for these unjust dealings'.[99]

Fitzgerald's fear, Savage's references to his 'wel-beloved' friends, John Rothe fitzPiers's desire to avert conflict between his wife and son, and Richard Shee's irritation at the actions of Bennett, his former servant, likewise remind us that even these legalistic documents can be places where the emotional lives of past populations can be probed. Emotions are indicated in wills by specific statements of regard, antipathy, or regret, but gestures and silences can also be telling. The "history of emotions" field has grown rapidly in recent years, and promises to assist in explorations of the inner lives of the inhabitants of early modern Ireland. Arguing that in different eras communities may display quite distinct norms around the ways and places in which emotions should be expressed and regulated, historians of emotion also point out that factors such as gender and status can also impact on ideas of 'appropriate' expression of feelings.[100]

As already discussed, items like clothing and especially jewelry were highly valued. A number of testators specifically bequeathed jewels 'that I wear', presumably an indication of their sentimental as much as their material value. Richard Shee of Kilkenny spoke of his 'special love' for one daughter and left her 'the jewel I wear about my neck'.[101] In 1638, Frances Wadding left 'the gold cross that I used wear about my neck' to her daughter.[102] When Richard Boyle, first earl of Cork, wrote his will in 1642, he left his daughter-in-law, Lady Dungarvan, 'my Diamond Ring which my mother at her death gave me, and I have wore it 56 years, praying her to wear it as a happy fortunate and lucky stone during her life and to leave it to her son'. He left £10 each to his daughters and their husbands to buy diamond rings, 'Entreating every and each of them to wear those rings during their lives as a Remembrance of their Deceased and most affectionate Father with God's blessing and my own'. His gift to another daughter-in-law, the recently widowed Lady Kinealmeaky, of silver utensils, including a silver chamber pot, may appear more practical, but the items were likely still of high sentimental value.[103]

Boyle spoke of his grief that the death of his son had divided Lady Kinealmeaky from his family, and others also made outright statements of emotion. Patrick Crosby said of his wife that 'I would ever have her to have favour over and above in respect I have found her faythfull, loving, & dutyfull'.[104] Expressions of affection could be somewhat guarded, however. Edward Wingfield of Powerscourt, (protestant) son of Honora O'Brien Wingfield, left her £5 for a diamond ring in his 1638 will 'as a testimonial of filial duty of affection'. Tellingly, he also left £20 apiece to his 'dear and well beloved friends' Edward Blount and Erasmus Borrowes; £20 to his brother-in-law, Lord Cromwell (Edward's wife was one of Thomas Cromwell's descendants); and a horse to Sir George Wentworth 'as a token of my love and affection'.[105] The differentials in the size of these bequests and the terms used may indicate some degree of estrangement from his (Catholic) mother. Honora's own will likewise signals emotional distance from her Wicklow grandchildren. She does not mention them at all, except to grant the youngest, Cromwell Wingfield, custodianship of her jointure lands at Robertstown, County Limerick, 'until the right heir possesses them'. Physical and political distance, as well as differing religious affiliations, may have been a factor in this seeming estrangement.

Concern for a future from which they would be absent, and fears of rancor between those left behind, also motivated testators. Patriarchs regularly used wills to attempt to control their children's and wives' behavior after their deaths and to head off other difficulties. David Barry of Robertstown in Cork (1627) warned his son to 'well respect, perform and accomplish' the terms of his will. He made his father-in-law, Morris Hurley, 'tutor and warden over my wife and children', and in the case of any variance between them, Hurley and the will's executors were authorized to 'decide and end the same as to their discretion shall be thought meet and convenient'.[106] In 1616, Sir James Hamilton of Bangor, County Down, stipulated that his son's 'breeding and keeping' should be in his wife's hands until he went abroad to school, but if she did not look after his interests or sought to make an 'unfitting' marriage for him, his executors should 'take the child ... and dispose of him for his learning and breeding as they ... shall fynd best'. He specifically forbade—three times—any of his children from marrying the descendants of Sir Hugh Montgomery. He also sought to curb the behavior of his divorced wife Alice Penicook, leaving her £100 'during her life' if she would 'carry herself without troubling of my said wif and son'.[107] William Parsons of Parsonstown, King's County, told his children 'to marry with the consent of their grandmother or any three of my overseers, and not to marry Irish papists', unless they wished to forfeit part of their inheritance.[108] Bequests and requests were sometimes protected by the threat of paternal curses that clearly were understood to be effective even from beyond the grave: Richard

Shee (1603), setting out provisions for the almshouses in Kilkenny that bore his name, warned his son Lucas, with whom he had had previous altercations, 'to avoyde my curse, to look carefullie to my hospitall', and threatened that his heirs would 'answer the same before the tribunall seate of God' if they interfered with his arrangements. Several other Old English patriarchs similarly resorted to threats of rage and vengeance from beyond the grave.[109]

During this 'decade of commemorations', early modernists may lament the irony that the Irish Revolution obliterated the nation's 'dead generations' even as it lauded and co-opted them. The task of dusting off and ordering the remnants is formidable. The surviving wills are a sorry shadow of their former glory. Yet they still allow us to rummage through the earl of Cork's left-behind 'linens' with William Chettle, to stand at the deathbed of Nicholas Pett as his young protégés contemplated their future (perhaps pausing to wonder how Dick Priest had ended up with one leg), and to speculate about what transpired when Lady Kinalmeaky received the news that she had inherited a chamber pot, albeit an exceptionally fancy one. We can be touched by the desire of early modern people to be remembered, by evidence of their remembering their own dead. We can be struck by evidence of family conflict and reconciliation, of loving spouses and parents, and loved and trusted friends. Wills provide glimpses of the layouts of people's houses, the contents of their shops, their drinking habits and leisure activities, their fears, triumphs, and hopes. Robert Blake of Galway gave his nephew Thomas £20 'to begin the world withal'. Honora O'Brien Wingfield saw her rings on other people's fingers; her bequests, big and small, blossoming into other people's futures. Their wills hint at what our surviving sources can reveal if we approach them with caution, respect, and imagination.

Notes

1 John Ainsworth, *The Inchiquin Manuscripts* (Dublin: Irish Manuscripts Commission, 1961), pp. 507–8.
2 Mary O'Dowd, *A History of Women in Ireland, 1500–1800* (Abingdon: Routledge, 2005), p. 81.
3 The 'Beyond 2022' project that aims to reconstruct in virtual form the PRO and some of its contents is to be welcomed (www.beyond2022.ie), but it can never substitute for the vast number of sources that were irretrievably lost.
4 Resource and related bibliographies at www.1641.tcd.ie.
5 Marie-Louise Coolahan, *Women, Writing, and Language in Early Modern Ireland* (Oxford: Oxford University Press, 2010), pp. 180–218.
6 Jon G. Crawford, *A Star Chamber Court in Ireland: The Court of Castle Chamber, 1571–1641* (Dublin: Four Courts, 2005); Mary O'Dowd, 'Women and the Irish Chancery Court in the Late Sixteenth and Early Seventeenth Centuries', *Irish Historical Studies* 31 (1999), 470–87.
7 See Brendan Kane, *The Politics and Culture of Honour in Britain and Ireland, 1541–1641* (Cambridge: Cambridge University Press, 2009); Elizabeth Fitzpatrick, *Royal Inauguration in Gaelic Ireland c1100–1600: A Cultural Landscape Study* (Woodbridge: Boydell and Brewer, 2004); Salvador Ryan, 'The Devotional Landscape of Medieval Irish Cultural Catholicism Inter Hibernicos et Inter Anglicos, c.1200–c.1550',

in Oliver Raffery (ed.), *Irish Catholic Identities* (Manchester: Manchester University Press, 2013), pp. 62–74, and other works by the same authors.

8 These are in the National Archives of Ireland and are available online at www.findmypast.ie. For example, they include the name and address of the testator, year of will, and sometimes a status indicator or occupation. See also John Grenham, *Tracing Your Irish Ancestors* (Dublin: Gill & Macmillan, 2006), pp. 57–71.

9 NAI RC5 and RC10.

10 Also digitized in searchable form at www.findmypast.ie.

11 I am indebted to Julian Walton for copies of many of the Jennings and Wyse abstracts (in Canterbury). His series of contributions to *Decies* (Volumes 16–23) on the Jennings abstracts and other extant Waterford wills is accessible via the Waterford County Council library website, including a very useful introduction on how wills were proved and preserved. The Jennings abstracts, compiled by I.R.B. Jennings, were up until recently in the O'Connell School (Christian Brothers), but the order declined invitations to deposit them in the Waterford County Library and their present location is unknown. They may have been sold. Julian Walton, *pers comm.* There is a copy in the NAI (MS10–41–46). Quotations from them here are from Dr. Walton's transcripts, with pagination he based on the originals. See Julian C. Walton, 'Wills Relating to Waterford II: The Published Abstracts of Ignatius Jennings', *Decies* 17 (1981), 37–52, and subsequent articles in *Decies* 19 and 20 (1982) indexing the unpublished articles.

12 Richard Caulfield, 'Wills and Inventories, Cork, *temp.* Elizabeth. III', *The Gentleman's Magazine* 211 (1861), 257. This series was published across volumes 211 and 212 of the magazine.

13 Martin J. Blake, *Blake Family Records, 1600–1700* (London: Elliot Stock, 1905), pp. 28–30.

14 'The Will of Captain William Bowen of Castlecarra, County Mayo, 1594', *Journal of the Co. Kildare Archaeological Society* 7 (1912/14), 45–46.

15 See Clodagh Tait, *Death, Burial and Commemoration in Ireland, c1550–1650* (Basingstoke: Palgrave Macmillan, 2002), pp. 8–10.

16 Will of Sir Jeffrey Fenton, Dublin, 1608, NAI 999/525(1). Thanks to David Edwards for a transcript of this will.

17 Donal O'Sullivan, 'Ancient History of the Kingdom of Kerry, Chapter II: The O'Sullivans, Culemagort, Cappanacoss, etc.', *Journal of the Cork Historical and Archaeological Society* 4 (1898), 263.

18 Nugent Papers, John Ainsworth and E. Edward MacLysaght, 'Survey of Documents in Private Keeping: Second Series', *Analecta Hibernica* 21 (1958), 139.

19 Patrick Power, 'Old Waterford Wills', *Journal of the Waterford and South-East of Ireland Archaeological Society Journal of the Waterford and South-East of Ireland Archaeological Society* 13 (1910), 27.

20 M.J. McEnery, 'Supplement', *The Catholic Bulletin* 16 (1926), 494–95. See K.W. Nicholls, *The O'Doyne (Ó Duinn) Manuscripts* (Dublin: Irish Manuscripts Commission, 1983). From a Gaelic midlands family, Charles O'Doyne was Master of the Court of Chancery 1602–17 and an official in the prerogative court in Dublin.

21 William Healy, *The History and Antiquities of Kilkenny* (Kilkenny: P.M. Egan, 1893), pp. 381–96.

22 Walter Fitzgerald, 'Notes on Sir John MacCoghlan, Knight, of Cloghan, Chief of Delvin MacCoghlan, Who Died in 1590', *Journal of the Royal Historical and Archaeological Association of Ireland*, 6th ser. 3 (1913), 229–31.

23 On translation see Patricia Palmer, *Language and Conquest in Early Modern Ireland: English Renaissance Literature and Elizabethan Imperial Expansion* (Cambridge: Cambridge University Press, 2001).

24 H. Webb Gillman, 'Sir Cormac McTeige MacCarthy and the Sept Lands of Muskerry, Co. Cork', *Journal of the Cork Historical and Archaeological Society* 1A (1892), 196–98.

25 See http://historyoflaw.co.uk/feudal-incidents/ for a discussion of 'feudal incidents' and their impact.

26 H.F. Kearney, 'The Court of Wards and Liveries in Ireland, 1622–41', *Proceedings of the Royal Irish Academy* 57 (1955), 29–68; Victor Treadwell, 'The Irish Court of Wards Under James I', *HIS* 12 (1960), 1–27; Aidan Clarke, *The Old English in Ireland, 1625–42* (Dublin: Four Courts Press, 2000).

27 Ainsworth and MacLysaght, 'Survey of Documents in Private Keeping: Second Series', 139.

28 O'Dowd, *Women in Ireland*, pp. 80–86.

29 Patrick Power, 'Old Waterford Wills VIII', *Journal of the Waterford & South-East of Ireland Archaeological Society* 11 (1908), 91–98.

30 John Ainsworth, 'Abstracts of 17th Century Irish Wills in the Prerogative Court of Canterbury', *Journal of the Royal Historical and Archaeological Association of Ireland* 78 (1948), 32.

31 O'Dowd, *Women in Ireland*, pp. 98–105.

32 O'Sullivan, 'Ancient History of the Kingdom of Kerry', 263.

33 'Power Papers'; John Ainsworth, 'Survey of Documents in Private Keeping: Third Series', *Analecta Hobernica* 25 (1967), 60. Power was a sister of Richard Boyle, earl of Cork.

34 Mary Ann Lyons, 'Lay Female Piety and Church Patronage in Late-Medieval Ireland', in Brendan Bradshaw and Dáire Keogh (eds.), *Christianity in Ireland: Revisiting the Story* (Dublin: Columba Press, 2002), pp. 57–75; Henry Fitzpatrick Berry (ed.), *Register of Wills and Inventories of the Diocese of Dublin 1457–1483* (Dublin: University Press for the Royal Society of Antiquaries of Ireland, 1898).

35 Clodagh Tait, '"As Legacie Upon my Soule": The Wills of the Irish Catholic Community, c.1550–1660', in Robert Armstrong and Tadhg Ó hAnnracháin (eds.), *Community in Early Modern Ireland* (Dublin: Four Courts, 2006), pp. 179–98.

36 Ainsworth and MacLysaght, 'Survey of Documents in Private Keeping: Second Series', 137, 141, also 144.

37 Philip Herbert Hore, *History of the Town and County of Wexford*, vol. 6 (London: Elliot Stock, 1911), p. 282.

38 Tara Hamling and Catherine Richardson (eds.), *Everyday Objects: Early Modern Material Culture and its Meanings* (Farnham: Ashgate, 2010), p. 10; Karen Harvey (ed.), *History and Material Culture: A Student's Guide to Approaching Alternative Sources* (Abingdon: Routledge, 2009), p. 3. See also Elizabeth Hallam and Jenny Hockey, *Death, Memory and Material Culture* (Oxford: Berg, 2001). On Irish early modern material culture, see especially Susan Flavin, 'Domestic Materiality in Ireland, 1550–1730', in Jane Ohlmeyer (ed.), *The Cambridge History of Ireland, vol. II 1550–1730* (Cambridge: Cambridge University Press, 2018), pp. 231–45; Toby Barnard, *Making the Grand Figure: Lives and Possession in Ireland, 1641–1770* (London and New Haven: Yale University Press, 2004); idem, *A Guide to Sources for the History of Material Culture in Ireland, 1500–2000* (Dublin: Four Courts Press, 2005).

39 Ilana Krausman Ben-Amos, *The Culture of Giving: Informal Support and Gift-Exchange in Early Modern England* (Cambridge: Cambridge University Press, 2008).

40 Sara Pennell, *The Birth of the English Kitchen 1600–1850* (London: Bloomsbury, 2016); Jane Whittle, 'Housewives and Servants in Rural England, 1440–1650: Evidence of Women's Work from Probate Documents', *Transactions of the Royal Historical Society* 15 (2005), 51–74; idem, Enterprising Widows and Active Wives: Women's Unpaid Work in the Household Economy of Early Modern England', *History of the Family* 19 (2014), 283–300; Jane Whittle et al., *Production and Consumption in English Households, 1600–1750* (Abingdon: Routledge, 2004).

41 Susan Flavin, *Consumption and Culture in Sixteenth-Century Ireland: Saffron, Stockings and Silk* (Woodbridge: Boydell and Brewer, 2014); Flavin, 'Domestic Materiality in Ireland'.

42 W. Fitzgerald, 'The Coat-of-Arms of the O'Connors of Offaly, and of Lisagh O'Connor of Leixlip, County Kildare', *Journal of the Kilkenny Archaeological Society* 6 (1909/11), 241–44.

43 Clodagh Tait, 'Irish Images of Jesus, 1550–1650', *Church Monuments* 16 (2001), 44–57.

44 E.E. Waters, 'The Waters Family of Cork', *Journal of the Cork Historical and Archaeological Society* 35 (1930), 40; Caulfield, 'Wills and Inventories VIII', p. 713.

45 Paul Glennie and Nigel Thrift, *Shaping the Day: A History of Timekeeping in England and Wales 1300–1800* (Oxford: Oxford University Press, 2009). Nicholas, Viscount Gormanston, also mentions a watch in his will of 1643. 'Gormanston Papers', Ainsworth, 'Survey of Documents in Private Keeping: Third Series', 481.

46 On clothing, see Mairead Dunlevy, *Dress in Ireland* (Dublin: Collins Press, 2000); Barnard, *Making the Grand Figure*, pp. 251–81; Audrey Horning, 'Clothing and Colonialism: The Dungiven Costume and the Fashioning of Early Modern Identities, *Journal of Social Archaeology* 14 (2014), 296–318; Flavin, *Consumption and Culture*, pp. 70–95; Elizabeth Wincott Heckett, 'Irish Dress and Fashions in the Seventeenth Century', in Crawford Art Gallery, *Portraits and People: Art in Seventeenth-Century Ireland* (Cork: Cork University Press, 2010), pp. 18–21.

47 Caulfield, 'Wills and Inventories V', p. 28–30; George D. Burtchaell, 'The Family of Rothe of Kilkenny', *Journal of the Royal Historical and Archaeological Association of Ireland* 17 (1885/86), 529–33. See Brid McGrath's forthcoming work on the apparel of the members of early modern Irish corporations.

48 On Cork's 'material world', see Jane Fenlon, 'Acquiring Magnificence: Luxury Goods in the Material World of Richard Boyle, First Earl of Cork', in David Edwards and C. Rynne (eds.), *The Colonial World of Richard Boyle, First Earl of Cork* (Dublin: Four Courts Press, 2018), pp. 149–65.

49 He was granted of a pension of 4 shillings per day for life after the Nine Years' War, indicating valued service to the crown. C.W. Russell and J.P Prendergast (eds.), *Calendar of State Papers Ireland [CSPI], 1603–06* (London: Longman, 1880), pp. 254–55; *CSPI 1606–08*, p. 142; *CSPI 1608–10*, p. 168.

50 James Graves and W.M. Hennessey, 'Pedigree of the White Knight', in James Graves (ed.), 'Unpublished Geraldine Documents: The Whyte Knight', *Journal of the Royal Historical and Archaeological Association of Ireland,* 4th ser. 5 (1882), unpaginated appendix.

51 See M. Dunlevy, 'Costume in Co. Clare', www.clarelibrary.ie/eolas/coclare/history/costume.htm, accessed 15 January 2018.

52 Ainsworth, *Inchiquin MSS*, p. 510.

53 Ainsworth and MacLysaght, 'Survey of Documents in Private Keeping: Second Series', 133, 144.

54 Flavin, 'Domestic Materiality', p. 334.

55 Ainsworth, 'Abstracts of 17th Century Irish Wills', p. 29.

56 Fitzgerald, 'Notes on Sir John MacCoghlan', p. 230.

57 Caulfield, 'Wills and Inventories, III', p. 262.

58 Caulfield, 'Wills and Inventories II', p. 34; Flavin, *Consumption and Culture*, pp. 73–77.

59 W. Carrigan, 'Old Waterford Wills XIV', *Journal of the Waterford & South-East of Ireland Archaeological Society* 12 (1909), 169–70.

60 Caulfield, 'Wills and Inventories II', p. 36.

61 Caulfield, 'Wills and Inventories VIII', p. 710.

62 Arthur Sabin (ed.), 'Bristol Wills and Documents', *Bristol and Gloucestershire Archaeological Society* 64 (1943), 125–27. Thanks to David Edwards for a transcript of this will.

63 Rare surviving inventories are scattered, but see especially Jane Fenlon, *Goods and Chattels: A Survey of Early Household Inventories in Ireland* (Dublin: Heritage Council, 2003); Richard Caulfield, 'Appendix A. Inventories of the Goods of

the Citizens of Cork', in Caulfield (ed.), *The Council Book of the Corporation of the City of Cork*. 2 vols. (Guildford: J. Billing and Sons, 1876), pp. 1146–54. On foodways and drinking culture, see Flavin, *Consumption and Culture*, especially chapters 9–11; Flavin, 'Domestic Materiality'; Audrey Horning, '"The Root of All Vice and Bestiality": Exploring the Cultural Role of the Alehouse in the Ulster Plantation', in James Lyttleton and Colin Rynne, *Plantation Ireland: Settlement and Material Culture* (Dublin: Four Courts Press, 2009), pp. 113–31.

64 Caulfield, 'Wills and Inventories II', pp. 35–37; Caulfield, 'Inventories of the Citizens of Cork', 1146–54; Faggan is on 1151.

65 Thomas G. Fewer and Kenneth W. Nicholls, 'The Will of Robert Forstall of Kilferagh, 1645', *Decies* 48 (1993), 14.

66 Blake, *Blake Family Records*, pp. 246, 249.

67 G.F. Savage-Armstrong, *A Genealogical History of the Savage Family in Ulster* (London: Chiswick Press, 1906), p. 280.

68 Power O'Shee Papers, Ainsworth and MacLysaght, 'Survey of Documents in Private Keeping: Second Series', 231.

69 J. Fenlon, 'Moving Towards the Formal House: Room Usage in Early Modern Ireland', *Proceedings of the Royal Irish Academy* 111C (2011), 141–68.

70 Edmund Curtis, *Calendar of the Ormond Deeds*. 6 vols. (Dublin: Irish Manuscripts Commission, 1941), 5, pp. 263–64.

71 Susan Flavin notes the popularity of such coconut cups in late sixteenth-century Cork wills. An English-made Elizabethan coconut flagon survives in Kilkenny. Flavin, *Consumption and Culture*, p. 223; R. Wyse Jackson, 'Old Church Plate of Kilkenny City', *Journal of the Royal Historical and Archaeological Association of Ireland* 81 (1951), 26–28.

72 Walter Lord Fitzgerald, 'Narraghmore and the Barons of Norragh', *Journal of the Kildare Archaeological Society* 7 (1912/14), 259–60.

73 Jennings will abstracts, p. 67.

74 William Healy, *The History and Antiquities of Kilkenny* (Kilkenny: P.M. Egan, 1893), pp. 381–96.

75 O'Dowd, 'Women and the Irish Chancery Court'.

76 Paul Stock, 'Introduction', in Stock (ed.), *The Uses of Space in Early Modern History* (Basingstoke: Palgrave Macmillan, 2015), p. 14.

77 Carrigan, 'Old Waterford Wills XIV', pp. 169–70.

78 Blake, *Blake Family Records*, pp. 247–48.

79 Nicola Whyte, *Inhabiting the Landscape: Place, Custom and Memory, 1500–1800* (Oxford: Oxbow Books, 2009), p. 2.

80 On gender and space, see Amanda Flather, *Gender and Space in Early Modern England* (Woodbridge: Boydell and Brewer, 2006).

81 Tait, *Death, Burial and Commemoration*.

82 Jennings will abstracts, p. 30.

83 RC 5/28, f.11.

84 Blake, *Blake Family Records*, pp. 78, 250–51.

85 Tait, *Death, Burial and Commemoration*, pp. 80–81.

86 See J. Guldi, 'The Spatial Turn in History', http://spatial.scholarslab.org/spatial-turn/the-spatial-turn-in-history/index.html, accessed 1 March 2018.

87 Walter Fitzgerald, 'Notes on the Family of Patrick Crosbie of Maryborough, by Whom the Seven Septs of Leix Were Transplanted to Tarbert in the County Kerry in 1608–9', *Journal of the Royal Historical and Archaeological Association of Ireland*, 6th ser. 13 (1923), 144–45.

88 Caulfield, 'Wills and Inventories', p. 508.

89 Carrigan, 'Old Waterford Wills XIV', 170; Richard Hayes, 'Some Old Limerick Wills', *North Munster Antiquarian Journal* 1 (1936/39), 164.

90 See my forthcoming paper on this topic.

91 Caulfield, 'Wills and Inventories, Cork III', p. 257.
92 Dorothea Townshend, *The Life and Letters of the Great Earl Of Cork* (London: Duckworth, 1904), p. 501.
93 Ainsworth and MacLysaght, 'Survey of Documents in Private Keeping: Second Series', p. 232.
94 Caulfield, 'Wills and Inventories, Cork VI', pp. 165–66.
95 Richard Caulfield, 'Supplement to the Cork Wills', *Gentleman's Magazine* 213 (1862), 299–300.
96 Caulfield, 'Wills and Inventories, Cork VII', p. 444. See also Caulfield, 'Inventories of the Citizens of Cork' for several further examples.
97 Henry Travers Hart, *The Family History of Hart of Donegal* (London: M. Hughes, 1907), pp. 104–5.
98 *Savage Family*, pp. 207–8.
99 'Proceedings', *Journal of the Royal Historical and Archaeological Association of Ireland* 5 (1879/82), pp. 272–73. Keeping the lands and their privileges had been a hard task: Fitzgerald may have perjured himself on occasion—e.g., the Fitzgeralds claimed hereditary succession to the Deanery of Cloyne but in 1628 had to defend this 'right' against the chapter of Cork in Chancery. Mark Empey, 'The Diary of Sir James Ware, 1623–66', *Analecta Hibernica* 45 (2014), 75.
100 On emotions, see Barbara H. Rosenwein, *Generations of Feeling: A History of Emotions, 600–1770* (Cambridge: Cambridge University Press, 2016); Rosenwein, 'Worrying about Emotions in History', *American Historical Review* 107 (2002), 821–45; Susan Broomhall (ed.), *Early Modern Emotions: An Introduction* (Abingdon: Routledge, 2017); Rob Boddice, *The History of Emotions* (Manchester: Manchester University Press, 2018). In an Irish context, see Clodagh Tait, '"Whereat his wife took great greefe and dyed": Dying of Sorrow and Killing in Anger in Seventeenth-Century Ireland', in Phil Withington and Michael Braddick (eds.), *Popular Culture and Political Agency in Early Modern England and Ireland* (Woodbridge: Boydell and Brewer, 2017); idem, 'A print on my body of this day's service: Finding Meaning in Wounding during and after the Nine Years War', in Matthew Woodcock and C. O'Mahony (eds.), *Military Identities in Early Modern Britain and Ireland* (forthcoming, Woodbridge, 2018).
101 Ainsworth and MacLysaght, 'Survey of Documents in Private Keeping: Second Series', p. 232.
102 Jennings will abstracts, p. 67.
103 Townshend, *Life and Letters*, p. 498; Fenlon, 'Acquiring magnificence', pp. 160–61.
104 Fitzgerald, 'Notes on the Family of Patrick Crosbie', p. 145.
105 John Lodge and Mervyn Archdall (eds.), *The Peerage of Ireland* (Dublin: James Moore, 1789), vol. 5, p. 273.
106 Edmond Barry, 'Barrymore', *Journal of the Cork Historical and Archaeological Society* 7 (1901), 79.
107 James Hamilton, 'The Hamilton Manuscripts (continued)', *Ulster Journal of Archaeology* 3 (1855), 242–45; 5 (1857), 28. Information on Hamilton's marriages is very confused. Olive, Lettice, and Margaret Penicook are also mentioned in the will and possibly were his daughters. Hamilton lived a further thirty years and became Viscount Claneboy. See Jane Ohlmeyer, '"Scottish Peers" in Seventeenth-Century Ireland', in David Edwards with Simon Egan (eds.), *The Scots in Early Stuart Ireland* (Manchester: Manchester University Press, 2016), pp. 76–77.
108 Ainsworth, '17th-Century Irish Wills', p. 35.
109 Ainsworth and MacLysaght, 'Survey of Documents in Private Keeping: Second Series', 226–33. See my 'Authority and emotion in seventeenth century Ireland', forthcoming.

3 'I doe add this treatise, as a supplement of mine owne experience'

Subjectivity and life-writing in early modern Ireland

Marie-Louise Coolahan

In the 1620s, the proud Old Englishman John Cusack composed and addressed two legal tracts to King Charles I. These made bold proposals: the first, 'The Kingdomes crye', argued for the arraignment of Sir Edward Coke for high treason; the second, 'Irelands Comfort', sought reformation of the common laws, setting out the distinctions between the Irish and English jurisdictions and the limits of each. Cusack's boldness was avowedly rooted in personal experience. 'Irelands Comfort' opens with a statement of the inherent value of honesty and a declaration of his interest: 'Wherfor Consideringe how my priuat experience of twenty years oppression, on the occasion of my repaire to *your* Maiesties Courts … doth warrant my attempt of bringinge them, & their necessary reformations to light'. Presenting himself as a loyal colonial subject, Cusack cites classical and contemporary authorities, in particular Cicero on the poor execution of natural justice as the cause of rebellion. His own writing is positioned in relation to these precedents: 'Whearevnto I doe add this treatise, as a supplement of mine owne experience, declaring vnto *yor* Maiesty the present imperfect state, & Condition of those Common lawes'. The legal treatise is secondary, derived from bitter experience at the hands of the law: 'ffor the Common lawes of England, & Statuts of Ireland hauinge vniustly denyed me their healps, & a certaine Court, for the recouery of my inheritance'.[1] Cusack had been blocked in his attempts to retrieve legacies from his father and great-uncle, Sir Thomas Cusack, former lord chancellor of Ireland. He had been embroiled for seven years in court (in which he was opposed by Coke, then chief justice of the common pleas) and subsequently imprisoned for twelve years, allegedly a victim of corruption and embezzlement. Cusack's is therefore not a work of autobiography, but it is driven and justified by his own experiences of adversity and sense of injustice. His own life is inextricable from his legal treatise. The narrative frame wears its autobiographical heart on its sleeve, but the manuscript's legal apparatus—not least its structuring around twenty closely argued chapters of precedent and parameter—averts the reader's gaze. Reading Cusack through the prism of autobiography can yield new perspectives on the subjective qualities of writing in this period. This essay draws on recent theories of life-writing and subjectivity in order to illuminate emerging literary-historical scholarship that examines divergent forms of Anglophone autobiographical writing, the articulation of the self, and the gendered subject in early modern Ireland.

The growth in autobiographical studies since the 1980s, combined with the casting of wide nets undertaken for feminist recovery research and the broader expansion of genres attracting literary scholars, has converged to focus attention on the forms of life-writing produced in the early modern period.[2] Philippe Lejeune's classic definition of autobiography as 'a retrospective prose narrative produced by a real person concerning his [sic] own existence, focusing on his individual life, in particular the story of his personality' has become almost ubiquitous, not only for its elegant simplicity in relation to modern autobiography but also as a useful springboard for scholars of earlier periods in which a coherent articulation of the self, and the notion of the retrospective life, are neither agreed nor stable concepts. The publication of Lejeune's essay in 1989 coincided exactly with that of the seminal anthology *Her Own Life*, which located early modern women's voices among such genres as diaries and polemical pamphlets as well as more classically autobiographical works.[3] Researchers of pre-1700 periods were confronted by different realities of textual production and dissemination. Earlier women writers had maneuvered social proscriptions by circulating their writing via manuscript. They had negotiated their way to authorship via the imperatives of their own times, such as religion and contested spiritual identities, and made devotional genres, like meditation and prayer, spiritual accounting and life-writing, more urgent and accessible. If feminist scholars were forced to diversify once they realized where the greatest quantity of writing occurred, this was equally the case for the historian of non-elite culture. Men and women came to writing due to circumstance, and this is starkly evident in the case of Ireland, site of mass and reiterated displacements and warfare. Events drove individuals to formulate a version of themselves for a range of different (often state) audiences.

Feminist recovery research has continued to drive a formative strand of scholarship on autobiography, retaining its focus on the first-person narrative voice but recalibrating it as self-writing, or life-writing, in order to embrace texts that diverge from the linear writing of a life from beginning to end and in hindsight.[4] Shifts in critical thinking about autobiographical writing have expanded the genres under consideration to include letters, petitions, depositions and legal documents, and military memoirs.[5] In tandem with this, early twenty-first-century research has seen an eruption of vibrant scholarship on early modern letter-writing and the materiality of texts. This has consolidated the reframing of autobiographical writing as life-writing, as well as adding further texture and complexity to the range and diversity of texts so considered. Adam Smyth, for example, has considered the ways in which sources such as financial accounts or parish registers contained individuals' experiments with narrating lives.[6] The bulk of this work, however, has focused on life-writing in England and Scotland. Liam Harte's *A History of Irish Autobiography* addresses this critical gap, but mainly in relation to modern

Irish writing. For the early modern period, scholars of women's writing have so far done most to expand understanding of the range of life-writing in early modern Ireland. Julie Eckerle and Naomi McAreavey's essay collection opens up the forms and contexts for women's life-writing in Ireland, supplementing existing studies of letters, petitions, depositions, and conversion narratives.[7]

These developments go hand-in-hand with debates about the nature and emergence of subjectivity across the medieval and early modern periods—debates that have not yet adequately been considered in relation to Ireland. The emergence of the subject, of the self as a conscious agent, was long considered an indelible marker of modernity.[8] Descartes's philosophy of the duality of body and mind, and his now-proverbial *cogito ergo sum* (I think, therefore I am), have been pinpointed as key formulations of a new subjectivity. Jacob Burckhardt's 1958 *The Civilization of the Renaissance in Italy* is the classic study that identified the emergence of individual self-consciousness and self-determination as the defining feature of this period, the break with the past signaled via the concept of 'rebirth'. The question of when a coherent sense of self develops in history is one in which the relevance of periodization is at stake. As David Aers and others have shown, medieval literature and thought were not ignorant of a sense of self.[9] Indeed, the artificiality of the capacious term 'Renaissance' is apparent in its temporal and geographical moving-feast quality, which depends on where and when in Europe, from the fourteenth to seventeenth centuries, we mean.

If we take the longitudinal view, evolution and continuity can be posited rather than the rupture of a clean break. Medieval literary historians such as A.C. Spearing have analyzed the texts of the Middle Ages through the lens of the first-person voice and its performance(s) of self-awareness. Sif Rikhardsdottir has interrogated the interactions between reader and text in producing the effect of emotive interiority. The association of the subject with the emergence of capitalism—so fundamental to the Burckhardtian view—has been dismantled by critics such as Peter Haidu. Meredith Skura has pushed sixteenth-century genre boundaries to argue for interiority in sources that range from court documents to verse, fiction to non-fiction. Barry Windeatt has shown how vibrantly and irrepressibly the first-person voice asserted itself, providing a window into the lives of the commonplace-book compiler, the sermon-diarist, the scholar-annotator, and the theologian whose scriptural commentaries provoke bursts of 'confessional asides'. His argument is that

> modes of auto(bio)graphical activity can be identified as subsumed or implicit, bubbling up across very different medieval genres, which poses the question whether medieval representations of selves in more fragmented forms … may not offer their own compellingly unillusioned readings of how far the self may be represented

This bears extension to the contexts of medieval Irish scribal production,[10] one aspect of their appeal being that such glimpses of subjectivity can illuminate what it felt like to be and to live in these earlier periods.

Interiority has been shown, then, not to be the sole preserve of the modern, or even the early modern. The history of the subject is not linear and progressive; rather, the traces of subjectivity materialize in ways that demand we attend to different modes of expression. Articulations of the self may be found in a range of genres, mediated through generic convention and collaborative processes of writerly production that involved scribes, amanuenses, and authors as agents. Moreover, these traces are themselves subject to the vagaries of historical survival; our gleanings of medieval or early modern subjectivity are fastened to the defining qualities of the texts we have. These debates are coming into focus, in an Irish context, as scholars begin to investigate life-writing in Ireland. Máire Ní Mhaonaigh's study of first-person writing in medieval Ireland emphasizes that the 'individuality which came into view in the eleventh and twelfth centuries ... was above all contextual, the sense of self being defined in relation to an other, as well as communities, and being configured in imitation of earlier models'.[11] This concurs with the more nuanced view of the history of the subject that has emerged in recent years; the qualities of interiority and self-reflection are found in literature from the medieval through to the modern, but this is not to say that the subject is universally constituted.[12]

What can we learn about subjectivity in early modern Ireland from the life-writings it produced? What kinds of subjectivity emerge, and how? The adoption of life-writing as an inclusive category expands the field but embraces the unexamined self as well as reflexive, aware narrators. The insights yielded from the expansion of autobiographical studies alert us to the range of possible sources, but the circumstances of their production may inhibit as well as encourage self-assertion. If adversity and exigency drove many of the non-elite to account for themselves, meaning we have such texts in greater numbers particularly for the seventeenth century, the goal of survival concentrated their accounts and target audiences determined their structure.

Petitions and depositions offer a rich resource of life narratives in early modern Ireland. Compelled to engage with the state bureaucracies of England and Spain, as they sought restoration of property rights, financial compensation, or relief as a result of military and political turmoil, Catholics and protestants turned to the mechanisms of the state in order to make a case grounded in personal experience. Ciaran O'Scea has shown how Irish Gaelic immigrants to the Spanish territories were confronted with 'Europe's most advanced secular state bureaucracy'.[13] Irish immigrants could petition the state for a pension (*entretenimiento*) on the basis of Gaelic nobility and service to the Counter-Reformation cause. Many such petitions survive in the archives, presenting narratives of petitioners' lives framed according to the terms of eligibility. Those submitted by women inevitably relate their menfolks' stories, as the means to establish services rendered. Marina Mahum's 1609 petition, for example, states that 'she is a noblewoman, descended from the house of the O'Briens and that she lost in the service of Your Majesty her husband and two brothers, together with all her estate, in the wars of Ireland'.[14] Exposure to this state bureaucracy entailed a new concern to preserve the documents of one's life; soldiers who sought employment in Spanish forces 'had to produce certificates of payments and time served, along with testimonials of their captain or of other officials'. It also resulted in a new attention to literacy. O'Scea's study of signature ability in La Coruña shows an increase from 55% among first-generation immigrants to 100% in the next generation, 'regardless of gender', observing a 'revolution in Irish women's literacy'.[15] Notwithstanding the thematic parameters dictated by the process itself, these are a rich resource for understanding how individuals represented themselves.

The success of these narratives required conformity to the preordained characteristics of the deserving Irish refugee—a prioritization of collective over individual identity. It is in the specific details, of military service for example, that individuated experience emerges. Where women could avail of a stereotyped gendered subjectivity, founded on female vulnerability and destitution, this served to align the individual with the general. Written in the third-person voice and through the agency of amanuenses, these are life-narratives whose subjectivity is refracted through other agents (yet materializing so compellingly to the modern reader that Micheline Walsh's translations are rendered in the first person).[16] Individual experience is structured according to the formulae set by the state, and calculated to reflect pre-existing perceptions of that community's experience. This balance between community and self is produced by, and at all times attendant upon, function and audience. Petition-letters addressed to the English state were submitted on the basis of individual or group initiative rather than evincing the level of mass organization evident in Spain. However, collective petitions, such as those submitted to Queen Elizabeth by aggrieved Old English nobles or to the Confederate government in Kilkenny by the Poor Clare nuns in Athlone, tended to project corporate identity rather than individual subjectivity.[17] A prolific petitioner such as Eleanor Butler, countess of Desmond, could blur the boundaries of petition and letter to present herself by turns as the distraught wife of a rebellious earl and a loyal subject, as in a 1574 missive to Queen Elizabeth, expressing 'the flame of my tormentid [sic] mynd'. Rather than the synchronic perspective stimulated by the survival of so many petitions to the Spanish state, a petitioner such as Desmond prompts diachronic analysis of change over time, the representation of motive and intention shaped by shifting circumstances as much as petitionary conventions.[18]

The 1641 depositions constitute another rich cache of materials that may be read as life-narratives. A proactive state effort to gather together individual testimonies of suffering resulted from the 1641 to 1642 Catholic rising in order to enable legal prosecutions in the future and inform counter-insurrection efforts in the present. Depositions were made orally and taken down by a commissioner or scribe; the texts consistently, even laboriously, attest to this process via formulae such as 'This deponent sayeth ... and further sayeth that it was a common report'.[19] The self is narrated but according to predetermined parameters and through a distancing filter of narrative voice. They followed a set sequence of questions: the biographical details of name, residence, and occupation were followed by statements of losses incurred and specific information relating to the identities and actions of rebels, robberies and assaults on other victims, details of deaths, and conversions to papistry. The deponent's sparse autobiography formed the point of departure; the formulae of self-identification and economic loss are uniform. But the process elicited 8,000 narratives of widely varying detail, from bare accounts of privation and dispossession to voluble reports of first-hand and third-hand experiences, rumors, and encounters. As with petitions to the Spanish state, bureaucracy shaped form. Their status as legal documents required emendment from the first person of the orally delivered account to the third person of legal documentation. That of Cavan minister Faithfull Teate (father of the puritan poet and grandfather to the royalist laureate Nahum Tate) bears the hallmarks of this transition. First-person pronouns are consistently altered to the third person:

> I *he this deponent* hearing of a rebellion intended by the irish & seeing them begin to arise, put 300 li. sterling in gold & some silver into ~~my~~ *his* pockets, & soe tooke horse, intending with speed both to saue *him* ~~myself~~ from them, & to give notice to the state of their proceedings.[20]

Intentionality is a striking feature, perhaps precisely because of these on-the-spot revisions.

Narrative structure was imposed by the state, but the process actively solicited details of ordeals undergone by traumatized individuals and—given the disparities of length—did not seek to curtail deponents' stories. The deposition of Elizabeth Price is one of the best known for a number of reasons: it is substantial, articulate and moving, covering many of the key events that occurred in Armagh (site of the most egregious violence), including two supernatural apparitions. Price recounted how the land they had bought from Phelim O'Neill was repossessed from herself and her husband; her imprisonment with her five children, their release, and their betrayal; her children's deaths at the massacre of Portadown Bridge; her capture and torture over a period of fifteen months and providential deliverance at the hand of Owen Roe O'Neill (arriving as military commander of the Irish regiment in Spanish Flanders); their witnessing of a vengeful female specter in the Blackwater River; reports of further spectral heads in the river; reports of the mass burning of the congregation inside Blackwater Church; and her further robbery at the hands of the Scottish army. This is harrowing stuff, with many additional details of violence and assault. Emotional affect is held at bay to some degree by the third-person narrative voice; a procedural feature of the deposition-taking process, here it affords the reader distance and filters the distress inherent in the deponent's experiences.

The subjectivity articulated is framed in collective rather than individual terms. In captivity, terror was deliberately inculcated and mutually experienced: 'the deponent and the rest often affrighted with a block and a hatchett: which (to putt them in more feare) was alwaies left with them as the engins of their deaths'. Their encounter with the female apparition—waist-high in the water, with 'skinn as white as snowe', proclaiming revenge—engendered a communal response: 'this deponent and the rest being putt into a strange amazement and fright'. The linking formulae of the 1641 depositions privilege speech over feeling, and it is as witnesses rather than self-conscious subjects that deponents are represented. Price's narrative insists upon the subjectivity of others rather than herself, as, for example, in her account of the prolonged murder of Thomas Mason, who 'being extreamly beaten & wounded', the rebels

> dragged the said Mas{on} into a hole & then and there threw *earth* rub-bish and stone upon him: soe as they *half* buried him: or soe kept him in the earth with that waight vpon him that as the said Masons wiffe tould the deponent, hee cried out & languished about *2 or* three daies in the ground before he died soe as his owne *wiffe* to putt him out of paine & rather then to heare him cry still scraped and pulld the earth & rubbish off his face & tyed her handcarsher over his mowth and ~~soe s to pped there~~ *with* stopped his breath: soe as hee djed.[21]

The extent of suffering and brutality recounted here renders unnecessary—or even unreadable—any more detail. The affective representation of Thomas Mason's suffering is accessed via his wife's account and her anguished experience; we could argue that the story being told is that of wife rather than husband.

Naomi McAreavey has argued for the interpretation of Price's narrative as a manifestation of traumatized subjectivity. 'Reading the depositions as literature of trauma', she suggests, 'allows us to see in the testimonies of the Protestant victims the "truth" of the trauma survivor's experience'. Women's retelling of the stories of other women (as exemplified by Price's reprisal of Mrs. Mason's account) 'reveals the extent to which communicating among friends—both as speakers and listeners—was part of the process by which women came to terms with traumatic experiences'. Moreover, she argues for a gendered subjectivity whereby female deponents related stories of wom-en's dismemberment and murder as a means of articulating their own fears and reconciling themselves to outliving others: the 'dismembered woman thus becomes for the female deponents an emblem of trauma and survival'.[22] McAreavey's approach points to an effective means of teasing out subjec-tivity. The post-Freudian conceptualization of trauma is anachronistic in seventeenth-century terms but insightful for twenty-first-century criticism, opening up new possibilities for our thinking about early modern subjec-tivity. The 1641 depositions are formulaic in terms of structure and phras-ing, but their quantity facilitates analysis of broader patterns, such as those of women's narratives of female dismemberment, and their illumination via modern taxonomies—in this case, of traumatized subjectivity.

However, the extent to which the conventions of a genre shape the subjectivity expressed is most starkly evident in the breach. Two narratives authored and signed by Elizabeth Dowdall survive: her deposition, made in Cork on 3 October 1642, and her 'true note of my several services', endorsed at Kinsale three days later. The differences between the two graphically illustrate the determining role of genre. Dowdall's deposition is typical: narrated in the third person, her economic losses are itemized and tallied. The siege of her home at Kilfinny Castle, Limerick, is described in terms of two offensives and identification of protagonists. Following the commission's terms of reference, she also reported what she heard rebel leaders say and what she knew of forced conversions.[23] On its own terms, this deposition is succinct, to the point, and lacking in emotive detail. It gives no hint of the forceful personality asserted in Dowdall's 'true note'. Written in Dowdall's own hand, this latter account claims military command of defensive forces at Kilfinny. It enumerates four specific services to the cause: three counter-attacks in response to plunder and her final (unsuccessful) defense of the castle—a narrative structure which aligns it with the military memoir, as exemplified by Henry Sidney.[24]

The compelling martial subjectivity that erupts from this account is at odds with the passive inventory of the deposition. Dowdall embodies her forces:

> In the first I was four score strong, obtained at my own cost and charge. I was thirty horse and fifty foot … ready for the field, the wars growing hot … the English coming with an outcry to me that the enemy had taken away their cattle, I sent out twenty horse and thirty foot.[25]

Her first-person narrative abounds in assertiveness, exhibiting a powerfully individual and effective agency that defies stereotypes of female weakness. The contrast, moreover, points to the writing subject's anticipation of, and differentiation between, audiences; the story she tells is designed for different target audiences and changes accordingly. The function of the deposition—to secure future compensation and prosecutions—demanded little by way of self-reflexivity, whereas the autobiographical siege narrative accommodated unapologetic self-representation. Her astute grasp of the specificities of genre and audience in themselves points to a rounded and grounded sense of self. Most importantly, the combination reminds us of the limits of our surviving sources as evidence of early modern subjectivity; Dowdall's 'true note' fills out the picture and cautions us against drawing fixed conclusions from generically circumscribed forms.

Emotion and emotional affect (or the 'passions' in early modern terms) offer another means of apprehending subjectivity. As the history of emotions has burgeoned, its interdisciplinary cast spans across historical periods and has opened up the ways in which experience and interiority are interrogated.[26] The articulation of feeling is hard to find in state-sponsored documents of petition or deposition; indeed, those bureaucracies excise the first-person voice, dampening down any identification with the narrating self. But Clodagh Tait has begun to examine excesses of grief, sorrow, and anger in the depositions.[27] Furthermore, the performance and reportage of emotion were crucial to radical and missionary religion in early modern Ireland. John McCafferty has begun to analyze the activities of Capuchin, Franciscan, and Jesuit missioners in terms of their 'creation of an emotional community' rooted in joy, relief, and compassion, with the aim of establishing a confessional community founded on emotional solidarity. McCafferty points to 'performative crying' as a feature that is 'well attested because of the emphasis the church came to place on inner, personal feeling'.[28]

That emphasis was equally felt in the Protestant churches, which urged members to turn their gaze inward in order to test the quality of their faith and salvation. Admission testimonies were sought of those entering these congregations. In their predetermined formal structures, these were as conventional as a petition or deposition. The 'morphology of conversion' emphasized the steps in a journey from sin and doubt toward assurance, grace, and surrender to God.[29] But these were fundamentally emotional communities, as Rosenwein has shown in relation to the London church whose testimonials were printed as *Spirituall Experiences* in 1653.[30] The safety of the congregational context facilitated an outpouring of emotion and subjective experiences, absorbed by a collective who shared the biographical trajectory of salvation. The congregation led by John Rogers at Christ Church Cathedral in 1650s Dublin drew from Cromwellian soldiers and their families.[31] Rogers published edited versions of his members' conversion narratives on his return to England in 1653, and he did so expressly in order to stimulate evangelization in Ireland.

The individual's subjective experience of awakening is central in these narratives. Raphael Swinfield's story is titled to underscore the point: 'The Testimonial of Raphael Swinfield, or his experience, as was taken out of his own mouth in Dublin'. Similarly, the testimony of Elizabeth Avery is rooted in the authentic self associated with oral delivery: 'out of her own mouth, and declared by her self to the whole Church'. Swinfield related the twists and turns of an inner restlessness that drove him to the Low Countries, England, and New England before returning. Anguished subjectivity, in this context, is crucial to credibility. Hence, Swinfield narrates the to and fro of his spiritual struggle: 'All which things struck me heavily to the heart … And thus I continued till my heart was ready to burst a peeces'. For John Chamberlain, the soldier's life entailed an occupational sense of the sinful, and even suicidal, self:

> being a Souldier, I was thereby brought under many Temptations to sin, especially that vile lust of Drunkennesse, which too much pursued mee, and so strongly, that sometimes I was ready to yeeld, at other times ready to make away my selfe.

Striving for inner epiphany drew the autobiographical gaze inward: John Cooper, having 'longed to enter into this fellowship', presented his account of a dream as evidence of his awakening. Rogers's editorial intervention is clear in this instance, when the narrative voice is switched to the third person following the dream. But the value of these narratives lies in their attestation of individuated first-person experience, requiring that Rogers explicitly assert his fidelity to original utterance.[32]

Conformity of one's emotional journey with elect teleology balances individual subjectivity with the orthodox identity of the group. By and large, the self being expressed by the members of Rogers's Dublin congregation was of a piece with equivalent narratives from the gathered churches in Britain. As with the case of Elizabeth Dowdall, it is in the breach that a more distinctive subjectivity shaped by Irish experience emerges. Frances Curtis told of her experiences during the rising and wars of the 1640s, construing her family's survival of assault and displacement as a sign of election. Major Andrew Manwaring, who 'came into Ireland in the beginning of the Rebellion in the North of Ireland', also integrates these events to his story: 'I passed though great dangers, and many deaths ... for there my Father was killed, my Wife was wounded, and I my selfe with much danger escaped from the bloody Rebels'.[33] However, the paramountcy of the spiritual progress meant that the majority eschewed local description in favor of the more universalizing narrative paradigm.

One of the earliest autobiographies in English, *The Vocacyon of Johan Bale* (1553), uses a different authorizing paradigm to model subjectivity, as well as usefully throwing open questions of 'Irishness'. Bale was a practiced polemicist with impeccably bad timing. Having built an unrivalled reputation as reformer-preacher, not least via his composition and staging of reformist plays modeled on medieval morality drama, he arrived in Ireland in late 1552 as King Edward's new Bishop of Ossory (and was received in Dublin by John Cusack's ancestor, Lord Chancellor Thomas Cusack). Ideological and ecclesiastical confrontation characterized his year in Ireland, which terminated with the accession of the Catholic Queen Mary to the throne, an ambush wherein five of his servants were killed, and flight to the Continent. Bale lays out in detail the parallels between his own life and that of Saint Paul. The saint's life empowers and licenses Bale to assert his own experiences: 'Sanct Paule also reioyced/that God hath so miraculously delyuered him ... Whie shulde I than shrinke or be ashamed to do the lyke/hauinge at Gods hande the lyke miraculouse deliuerance?' The analogies are hammered home to the reader in his account of his flight from Ireland:

> As Paule against his wylle/was put into a shippe ... So was I & my companyon Thomas against our willes taken into a shippe ... As he was for the hope of Israel ledde into captiuite/and at last deliuered/so was I also for the same captiued/and in fine delyuered into Germanie.[34]

Bale's writing is a vehicle for God, his self-abnegation leaving room only for a fallen, stricken subjectivity:

I write not this rude treatise/for that I woulde receyue praise therof/ but that I wolde God to haue all the prayse … ffor I am but a clodde of coruption/felinge in my self as of my self/nothing els but sinne and wickednesse.

In this, he follows the practice of Catholic as well as Protestant life-writing: personal credit is not to be sought; all earthly achievement is divinely ordained. Thus indemnified, Bale's is an unabashed subjectivity—no-holds-barred, furious, righteous, and rambunctious, as in his account of the restoration of Catholicism at Kilkenny:

For they maye now from thens forth / againe deceiue the people as they ded afore tyme / with their Latine momblinges / and make marchaundice of them … They maye make the witlesse sort beleue / that they can make euery daye newe goddes of their lyttle whyte cakes / & that they can fatche their frindes sowles from flaminge purgatory / if nede be with other great miracles els.[35]

The gallop of the narrative is one of events, reportage, and confessional certainty rather than self-doubt or questioning.

The security of his identity rests at least in part on the stability of the paradigms he uses: Pauline deliverance, the binary of religious polemic, received wisdom about the Irish. Sarah Covington has written about the fragility of constructions of subjectivity and its dependence on solid, agreed structures. Comparing the writing of violence in England and Ireland, Covington finds that authors such as Henry Sidney drew upon classical models of military memoir and established assumptions of Irish barbarity. But writers of civil war 'found themselves unable to rely on previous literary frameworks' or established archetypes of the other, circumstances that generated 'a different kind of subjective self' fractured by 'indecision, fear and perplexity'.[36] Bale stands at the opposite end of the spectrum, sure of his rectitude as he regales an international reformed audience with his experiences in and of Ireland. The comparison nudges us toward contemplation of what might be peculiarly Irish about the subjectivities outlined in this essay. Bale's is a case that usefully elucidates the distinction between articulations of the self in early modern Ireland and 'early modern Irish subjectivity'. Bale's persona had been forged long before his appointment in Ireland, immersed in the cut and thrust of reformist politics in England and the Continent. But the subjectivity articulated in his *Vocacyon* is refined and changed by his Irish experiences. Any attempt to capture a singular 'Irish' subjectivity would confound the evidence of an island bursting at the seams with multiple, conflicting, and overlapping identities in a period marked primarily by flux and fluidity. The sheer plurality of identities ushers us instead toward an open-minded probing of different subjectivities, with a view not only to understanding the experience of early modern Ireland but also toward unpicking the imbrications and meanings of those identities. This kind of research must include self-representations that occurred in early modern Ireland as well as those that were produced by early modern Ireland.

The history of the subject in early modern Ireland is necessarily plural. The fact of living in early modern Ireland propelled many toward textual modes of self-representation. The different routes to self-expression and subjectivity outlined here articulate sensibilities that were generated by a specific place at particular moments. Circumstances of extremity and adversity—the threat of displacement or responsibility of conquest, exile, emigration, and flight—produced the individuated subject, and the articulation of that subjectivity is always shaped and delimited by those conditions of production. If literary scholars and historians expand the textual genres they study, that brings into view a broader understanding of the writing of the self, and of the kinds of self we find. But there is a mutual dependency between form and self: subjectivity is shaped by textual genre. The function and audience of the text generate its composition in the first place, but they also mold the self that is projected. Authors such as Dowdall or Bale, who composed in more than one genre, underline this point, as they project different versions of the self tailored to mode of expression and anticipated reader. The very exigency of circumstances forged space for more marginal voices—women's as well as lower-class men's. Female petitioners and deponents were thrust into bureaucracies as wives, widows, daughters, mothers of fully fledged citizens. Associations of female subjectivity with frailty empowered women insofar as they opened up a host of rhetorical possibilities for engendering sympathy. As genres of life-writing, such forms yield patterns and permit the intrusion of individuated details that offer glimpses of early modern subjectivity in Ireland. Moreover, their conformity with genre should point us to analogous practices in other places. The subjectivity expressed in an Independent conversion narrative, for example, bears far greater affinity with that of a member of the gathered churches in England or Scotland than any other confession in contemporary Ireland. The application of methodologies borrowed from other fields, such as trauma literature or the history of emotions, cracks open new approaches to mining and making sense of early modern subjectivities (in Ireland as elsewhere); another fruitful avenue for future research is suggested by the relationship between collective and individual subjectivities.

Notes

1 "The Kingdomes crye', described in 'Irelands Comfort' is not known to survive. Folger Shakespeare Library, Washington, DC, MS G.a.10, fols. 1v-2r, 5r, 6r, respectively.
2 For a recent survey of the field, see Maria Dibattista and Emily O. Whitman (eds.), *The Cambridge Companion to Autobiography* (Cambridge: Cambridge University Press, 2014).
3 Philip Lejeune, 'The Autobiographical Pact', in Paul John Eakin (ed.), *On Autobiography*, trans. Katherine M. Leary (Minneapolis: University of Minnesota

Press, 1989), p. 4; Elspeth Graham, Hilary Hinds, Elaine Hobby, and Helen Wilcox (eds.), *Her Own Life: Autobiographical Writings by Seventeenth-Century Englishwomen* (London: Routledge, 1989).

4   For example, Michelle M. Dowd and Julie A. Eckerle (eds.), *Genre and Women's Life Writing in Early Modern England* (Aldershot: Ashgate, 2007); 'Recent Studies in Early Modern English Life Writing', *English Literary Renaissance* 40 (2010), 132–62; Elspeth Graham, 'Women's Writing and the Self', in Helen Wilcox (ed.), *Women and Literature in Britain, 1500–1700* (Cambridge: Cambridge University Press, 1996), pp. 209–33; David G. Mullan, *Women's Life Writing in Early Modern Scotland: Writing the Evangelical Self, c.1670–c.1730* (Aldershot: Ashgate, 2003).

5   For the military memoir, in particular, see Yuval N. Harari, *Renaissance Military Memoirs: War, History, and Identity, 1450–1600* (Woodbridge: Boydell and Brewer, 2004).

6   Adam Smyth, *Autobiography in Early Modern England* (Cambridge: Cambridge University Press, 2010).

7   Liam Harte (ed.), *A History of Irish Autobiography* (Cambridge: Cambridge University Press, 2018); Julie A. Eckerle and Naomi McAreavey (eds.), *Women's Life Writing and Early Modern Ireland* (Lincoln, NE: University of Nebraska Press, forthcoming); and, *inter alia*, Naomi McAreavey, 'An Epistolary Account of the Irish Rising of 1641 by the Wife of the Mayor of Waterford', *English Literary Renaissance* 42 (2012), 77–109; Vincent Carey, 'What's Love Got to do with it? Gender and Geraldine Power on the Pale Border', in Michael Potterton and Thomas Herron (eds.), *Dublin and the Pale in the Renaissance c.1540–1660* (Dublin: Four Courts, 2011), pp. 93–103; Ruth Connolly, 'A Proselytising Protestant Commonwealth: The Religious and Political Ideals of Katherine Jones, Viscountess Ranelagh', *The Seventeenth Century* 23 (2008), 244–64; Marie-Louise Coolahan, *Women, Writing, and Language in Early Modern Ireland* (Oxford: Oxford University Press, 2010); Felicity Maxwell, 'Calling for Collaboration: Women and Public Service in Dorothy Moore's Transnational Protestant Correspondence', *Literature Compass* 14 (4) (2017), doi:10.1111/lic3.12386.

8   See for example, Michael Mascuch, *Origins of the Individualist Self: Autobiography and Self-Identity in England, 1591–1791* (Cambridge: Polity Press, 1997).

9   Jacob Burckhardt, *The Civilization of the Renaissance in Italy*. 2 vols. (New York: Harper, 1958); David Aers, 'A Whisper in the Ear of Early Modernists; or, Reflections on Literary Critics Writing the "History of the Subject,"' in David Aers (ed.), *Culture and History, 1350–1600: Essays on English Communities, Identities, and Writing* (Detroit: Wayne State University Press, 1992), pp. 177–202.

10 A.C. Spearing, *Textual Subjectivity: The Encoding of Subjectivity on Medieval Narratives and Lyrics* (Oxford: Oxford University Press, 2005); and idem, *Textual Subjectivity and Medieval Autobiographies: The "I" of the Text* (Notre Dame: University of Notre Dame Press, 2012); Sif Rikhardsdottir, 'Medieval Emotionality: The Feeling Subject in Medieval Literature', *Comparative Literature* 69 (2017), 74–90; Peter Haidu, *The Subject Medieval/Modern: Text and Governance in the Middle Ages* (Stanford: Stanford University Press, 2004); Meredith Anne Skura, *Tudor Autobiography: Listening for Inwardness* (Chicago: University of Chicago Press, 2008); Barry Windeatt, 'Medieval Life-Writing: Types, Encomia, Exemplars, Patterns', in Adam Smyth (ed.), *A History of English Autobiography* (Cambridge: Cambridge University Press, 2016), pp. 13–26, at pp. 13–14.

11 Máire Ní Mhaonaigh, 'Writing in Medieval Ireland in the First-Person Voice', in Liam Harte (ed.), *A History of Irish Autobiography*, pp. 23–37, at p. 24.

12 For a philosophical articulation of this view, see Charles Taylor, *Sources of the Self: The Making of the Modern Identity* (Cambridge, MA: Harvard University Press, 1989).

13 Ciaran O'Scea, *Surviving Kinsale: Irish Emigration and Identity Formation in Early Modern Spain, 1601–40* (Manchester: Manchester University Press, 2015), p. 87.

14 Archivo General de Simancas, Spain, Estado, Neg. de España, Legajo 2745, quoted and translated in Coolahan, *Women, Writing, and Language*, p. 131. See also examples printed in Angela Bourke et al. (eds.), *The Field Day Anthology of Irish Writing: Irish Women's Writing and Traditions* (Cork: Cork University Press, 2002), V, pp. 569–70.

15 O'Scea, *Surviving Kinsale*, pp. 90, 89.

16 Micheline Walsh, 'Some Notes towards a History of the Womenfolk of the Wild Geese' and 'Further Notes towards a History of the Womenfolk of the Wild Geese', *The Irish Sword* 5 (1961–1962), 98–106, and 133–45.

17 See Valerie McGowan-Doyle, 'Elizabeth I, the Old English, and the Rhetoric of Counsel', in Brendan Kane and Valerie McGowan-Doyle (eds.), *Elizabeth I and Ireland* (Cambridge: Cambridge University Press, 2014), pp. 163–83; *Calendar of State Papers Ireland, 1633–1647*, p. 662.

18 State Papers [hereafter SP] 63/47/56. For Desmond, see Anne Chambers, *Eleanor, Countess of Desmond, c.1545–1638* (Dublin: Wolfhound Press, 1986) and Coolahan, *Women, Writing, and Language*, pp. 107–16.

19 See Aidan Clarke, 'The 1641 Depositions', in Peter Fox (ed.), *Treasures of the Library: Trinity College Dublin* (Dublin: RIA, 1986), pp. 111–22, and the Irish Manuscript Commission's ongoing print publication of the depositions, edited by Aidan Clarke and Marie-Louise Coolahan, "And this Deponent Further Sayeth": Orality, Print and the 1641 Depositions', in Marc Caball and Andrew Carpenter (eds.), *Oral and Print Cultures in Ireland, 1600–1900* (Dublin: Four Courts, 2010), pp. 69–84; Eamon Darcy, *The Irish Rebellion of 1641 and the Wars of the Three Kingdoms* (London: Royal Historical Society, 2013). For a treatment of women's depositions, see Coolahan, *Women, Writing, and Language*, pp. 141–79.

20 TCD MS fol. 833, fol. 61r; http://1641.tcd.ie/deposition.php?depID=833061r047 (accessed 7 January 2018).

21 TCD MS 836, fols. 102r, 103r, 105r; http://1641.tcd.ie/deposition.php?depID=836101r054 (accessed 6 January 2018).

22 Naomi McAreavey, 'Re(-)Membering Women: Protestant Women's Victim Testimonies During the Irish Rising of 1641', *Journal of the Northern Renaissance* 2 (2010), www.northernrenaissance.org/re-membering-women-protestant-womens-victim-testimonies-during-the-irish-rising-of-1641/ (accessed 11 January 2018).

23 TCD MS 829, fol. 138; http://1641.tcd.ie/deposition.php?depID=829138r082 (accessed 11 January 2018).

24 Ciaran Brady (ed.), *A Viceroy's Vindication?: Sir Henry Sidney's Memoir of Service in Ireland, 1556–78* (Cork: Cork University Press, 2002). For other examples, see David Edwards (ed.), *Campaign Journals of the Elizabethan Irish Wars* (Dublin: Irish Manuscripts Commission, 2014).

25 *Field Day*, V, 22–23; the original holograph manuscript is British Library Sloane MS 1008, fols. 66r–69r.

26 See, for example, the journal *Emotions: History, Culture, Society*, launched by the Society for the History of Emotions in 2017: http://historyofemotions.org.au/society-for-the-history-of-emotions/ (accessed 11 January 2018); Jan Plamper, *The History of Emotions: An Introduction*, trans. Keith Tribe (Oxford: Oxford University Press, 2015).

27 Clodagh Tait, '"Whereat His Wife Tooke Great Greef & Died": Dying of Sorrow and Killing in Anger in Seventeenth-Century Ireland', in Michael J. Braddick and Phil Withington (eds.), *Popular Culture and Political Agency in Early Modern England and Ireland: Essays in Honour of John Walter* (Woodbridge: Boydell, 2017), pp. 267–84.

28 John McCafferty, 'Nosebleeds, Tears and Italianated Hearts: Thinking about the History of Emotions on the Seventeenth-Century Irish Mission', unpublished paper, NUI Galway, October 2017. I am grateful to the author for permission to cite this ongoing work.

29 See Kathleen Lynch, *Protestant Autobiography in the Seventeenth-Century Anglophone World* (Oxford: Oxford University Press, 2012); Tom Webster, 'Writing to Redundancy: Approaches to Spiritual Journals and Early Modern Spirituality', *Historical Journal* 39 (1996), 33–56; Owen Watkins, *The Puritan Conversion Experience* (London: Routledge & Kegan Paul, 1972).

30 Barbara H. Rosenwein, *Generations of Feeling: A History of Emotions, 600–1700* (Cambridge: Cambridge University Press, 2016), pp. 262–74.

31 See Crawford Gribben, *God's Irishmen: Theological Debates in Cromwellian Ireland* (Oxford: Oxford University Press, 2007), pp. 29–53; Coolahan, *Women, Writing, and Language*, pp. 231–37; for the later context, see Richard Greaves, *God's Other Children: Protestant Nonconformists and the Emergence of Denominational Churches in Ireland, 1660–1700* (Stanford: Stanford University Press, 1997).

32 John Rogers, *Ohel, or, Beth-shemesh: A Tabernacle for the Sun, or, Irenicum Evangelicum* (London: R.I. and G. and H. Eversden, 1653), sigs. Fffv, Eee3r, ggg2v–ggg3r, Eee4v, Hhh3r, respectively (the incorrectly paginated numbers are: 402, 397, 8–9, 390, 417).

33 Rogers, *Ohel*, sigs. ggg4r, Fff3v–Fff4r (pp. 11, 2–3).

34 John Bale, *The Vocacyon of Johan Bale* ([Wesel], 1553), sigs. A4r, A5v–6v. For a modern edition, see Peter Happé and John N. King (eds.), *The Vocacyon of Johan Bale* (Binghamton: Medieval & Renaissance Texts & Studies, 1990).

35 Bale, *Vocacyon*, sigs. A7v, D3v.

36 Sarah Covington, 'Realms so Barbarous and Cruell': Writing Violence in Early Modern Ireland and England, *History: The Journal of the Historical Association* 99 (2014), 487–504 (488, 497). See also Brady, *Viceroy's Vindication*, pp. 1–37, countered by Willy Maley in 'Apology for Sidney: Making a Virtue of a Viceroy', *Sidney Journal* 20 (2002), 94–105; Robert Shephard, 'The motives of Sir Henry Sidney's *Memoir* (1583)', *Sidney Journal* 29 (2011), 173–86; Brandie R. Siegfried, 'Rivaling Caesar: The Roman Model in Sir Henry Sidney's *Memoir* (1583)', *Sidney Journal* 29 (2011), 187–208, respectively.

4 Clerical wives in Tudor and early Stuart Ireland

Bronagh McShane

When Leah Mawe, wife of William Bedell (1571–1642), Bishop of Kilmore, passed away on 26 March 1638, Bedell himself preached her funeral sermon in which he eulogized his wife's reputation for piety and virtue. That sermon, according to Gilbert Burnet, Bedell's biographer, was 'such a mixture both of tenderness and moderation [and] touched the whole congregation so much … [that] there were very few dry eyes in the church'.[1] Leah was buried in the churchyard of Kilmore Cathedral where, upon his death in February 1642, according to directions stipulated in his will and in public acknowledgment of the couple's happy union, Bedell was interred next to his 'dear wife Leah'.[2] Twenty years earlier, when George Montgomery, Church of Ireland Bishop of Meath and Clogher, died at Westminster on 15 January 1621, his body was repatriated to Ireland to be interred, in accordance with his will, alongside his first wife, Susan Steynings (d. 1614), in the family vault he had constructed in the parish churchyard of Ardbraccan in County Meath. Complete with effigies of Montgomery, Susan and the couple's daughter Jane, the tomb still stands today.[3] The willingness of Bedell and Montgomery, both senior rank clerics within the Church of Ireland episcopate, to publicly pay tribute to their wives was indicative of the recognition and respect attributed to the role of the clergyman's wife within the Church of Ireland community during the early to mid-Stuart period.

It had not always been so for the wives of clergy in early modern Ireland. Their relatively revered position in the Stuart era contrasted sharply with the uncertainty and ambiguity that had previously shrouded the role and status of women married to clergymen in Tudor Ireland, many of whom, on account of their marriages to members of the reformed clergy, were publicly castigated, ridiculed, and even renounced by their husbands. As Mary Prior has revealed in her study of Tudor bishops' wives in England, because no precedent for the position of clerical wives existed during the early years of the Reformation, their legitimacy remained uncertain as the regime habitually altered its stance on clerical celibacy and the validity of priestly matrimony.[4] Whereas on the Continent the practice of clerical marriage was popularized by leading Protestant reformers—notably Martin Luther, who married Katharina von Bora, a former Cistercian nun—in the Tudor realm, by contrast, the tradition of clerical celibacy continued to be vigorously upheld by the Henrician regime which viewed priestly matrimony with hostility and imposed strict sanctions against it.[5] While the accession of Edward VI in 1547 afforded legal sanction to the institution of sacerdotal marriage, reversion to Catholicism under Queen Mary I rendered it once again obsolete. It was not until the reign of Queen Elizabeth I, when clerical marriage was formally recognized under the Thirty Nine Articles (ratified in 1571), that the wives of clergymen began to enjoy a more stable and recognized position within the Church of England. This was a slow and tentative process, however, and as Helen Parish has shown, attitudes to clerical marriage in England during Elizabeth's reign continued to range from acceptance, uncertainty, and fear to outright opposition.[6]

As in the Church of England, the Church of Ireland during the early years of Tudor reform was at best ambivalent in its attitude to clerical marriage, and was consequently slow to accord clerical wives any official recognition. While the experiences and activities of women married to members of the Church of Ireland clergy during this early reform phase are difficult to reconstruct, owing to their large-scale absence in the historical record, surviving—albeit fragmentary—evidence suggests that desertion, ridicule, and exile character-ized the lives of many clergymen and their wives. For example, Dublin-born Katherine Miagh (d. *c.*1597), wife of George Browne (d. *c.*1556), the first archbishop to be appointed by the Crown in Ireland, was divorced by her husband in 1541.[7] On account of the severe hostility encountered from their Catholic neighbors, in 1553, Dorothy Bale was compelled, together with her husband, John Bale, the Edwardian Bishop of Ossory, to flee Ireland to the relative safety of the exiled Protestant domicile of Wesel in north-west Germany.[8] In Ireland, as in England, it was not until the later Elizabethan and more especially the early Stuart era that the standing of women married to Church of Ireland clerics improved, at least within their own confessional communities: a process that was inextricably linked with the improved insti-tutional position of the Established Church, which became more deeply and strongly rooted in Ireland during that time.[9]

This essay explores the experiences of clerical wives in Tudor and early Stuart Ireland in order to highlight how institutional changes wrought as a result of religious reform, in this case clerical marriage, impacted the lives of women. Indeed, the roles and experiences of the wives and widows of clergymen in early modern Ireland have, to date, received little scholarly at-tention, despite the fact that changes to the institutional and doctrinal status of marriage during this period impacted them profoundly. The historiog-raphy of the Irish Reformation has up to now been largely silent in relation to the experiences of clerical wives, mentioning them only very briefly, if at all.[10] Indeed, the editors of one recent volume on the history of the Church of Ireland clergy lamented the fact that it was not 'possible to include any study of the wives and children of the clergy [within the collection]'.[11] One reason for this neglect is the limited availability of sources. In the case of sources relating to the personnel of the Established Church in Tudor and early Stuart Ireland (which are themselves admittedly scarce), the wives and female relatives of the clergy are often elusive and obscure individuals whose voices and experiences habitually go unrecorded. A case in point is the autobiography of John Bale, Bishop of Ossory—*The Vocacyon of Johan Bale* (1553)—which is notably silent in relation to the experiences of Bale's wife, Dorothy, despite the fact that she accompanied her husband during his year-long sojourn in Ireland.[12]

Notwithstanding their apparent absence within the historical record, this essay will demonstrate how careful mining of a range of underutilized and alternative sources such as funerary monuments and Irish-language poetry,[13] when read with an ear tuned to both women's voices and their silences, can yield significant insights into the experiences of these hitherto overlooked figures. In so doing, it will address a significant lacuna in existing scholarship on early modern Ireland by presenting a case study of how a small but growing number of clerical wives of Gaelic Irish, Old English, and more predominantly New English extraction emerged from a socially stigmatized position during the Tudor era to one of relative visibility and respectability from the early Stuart period onwards. However, as will be discussed, there was also a negative side to this increased visibility and improved status as women married to Church of Ireland clerics, viewed as stalwarts of Protestant evangelization and English conquest in Ireland, were by association regarded as legitimate targets for criticism, derision, and ridicule by members of the lay and religious Catholic community. Furthermore, we will see how the targeting of clerical wives could extend beyond verbal defamation to include physical assault, injury, and abduction, particularly in the context of heightened sectarian tensions. By bringing to light the lives and experiences of these often obscure and elusive figures, this essay thus contributes to a more inclusive and nuanced understanding of the nature and impact of religious change and reform in early modern Ireland. What follows is by no means an exhaustive study but rather sets out new ways to access and interpret this neglected aspect of Irish religious and social history and offers some new directions and approaches for others seeking to reconstruct and evaluate the lives of these shadowy and fleeting figures.

Not surprisingly, the most hostile critics of clerical wives in Tudor and early Stuart Ireland included Catholic clergy and religious, who in their eagerness to uphold the Church's teaching on priestly celibacy and discredit the Protestant institution of clerical marriage, were particularly scathing in their denunciation of women married to clergymen. Those who converted in order to marry were particularly vilified and condemned as apostates who had 'sown heresies and schisms away from the true Catholic faith'.[14] One unique manifestation of the extent of public denunciation experienced by women married to clergymen during the Elizabethan era was a poem composed in Irish by the Gaelic Ulster Franciscan friar Eoghan Ó Dubhthaigh (d. 1590). Ó Dubhthaigh's poem, written around 1578, denounced the wives of three bishops of the Church of Ireland.[15] The clerics in question were William Casey, who served two terms as Church of Ireland Bishop of Limerick (1551–56 and 1571–91); Matthew Sheyne, Bishop of Cork (1572–83); and Meiler Magrath, Archbishop of Cashel (1571–1622). While virtually nothing is known about the wives of Casey[16] and Sheyne, Magrath was married to a Gaelic Irish woman named Anne (or Annie) O'Meara from County Tipperary, and with whom he had five sons and four daughters.[17] Composed just a few years after the marriage of Anne to Magrath (which occurred sometime before 1573), the Ulster friar's scathing satire is directed primarily towards the archbishop and his wife. Indeed, the recurring refrain of the poem is a pun on Meiler's name (in Irish, *Maolmhuire*, 'the devotee of Mary') which Ó Dubhthaigh transliterated into *Mhaol gan Mhuire* or 'Meiler without Mary'.[18] The fact that Magrath was himself formerly a member of the Franciscan order undoubtedly explains why both he and his wife were singled out for especially derisory comment by the Ulster poet who, according to the Catholic historian Philip O'Sullivan Beare (1590–1636), was a personal acquaintance of both Anne and the archbishop.[19]

Entitled 'Léig dod chomhmórtas dúinn ['Cease thine efforts to vie with us'], Ó Dubhthaigh's poem was apparently written in response to a sermon preached by Bishop Sheyne at Cork in October 1578, in which he repudiated the Virgin birth. As Marc Caball has written, the Gaelic friar's poem, which runs to over a hundred quatrains, is significant as one of the earliest extant poems in Irish, manifesting elements of European Counter-Reformation influence.[20] In the context of this essay, the poem is valuable in another way, since it provides a unique insight into the intense criticism leveled upon the personnel of the Established Church and their wives by members of Gaelic Irish society, in this case a Franciscan friar. The poem interweaves a eulogy of the Blessed Virgin Mary with a coarse and caustic attack on the three apostate clerics and their wives. Clerical marriage was derided by Ó Dubhthaigh as 'no aid to piety', while 'cohabitation with a woman' was deemed an 'unbecoming observance for an archbishop'. The clerics were adjudged to be 'blind', 'unclean', and 'befogged churchmen'. Their wives were represented as 'deformed' and 'frantic' women who were the direct antithesis of the 'fair' Blessed Virgin, with their offspring deemed 'illegitimate'. In one revealing insight into the position of clerical wives within the Church of Ireland during the early years of the Elizabethan regime, Ó Dubhthaigh claimed that whereas the Virgin Mary, the 'mother of the High-king', would be afforded a hostile reception at Dublin Castle, receiving 'only a slap on the face', the wives of the episcopate, by contrast, were 'respected there'.[21]

The respect reportedly afforded the women by Dublin Castle authorities contrasted starkly with the damning fate which Ó Dubhthaigh prophesized for them. According to his poetic prediction, on account of their renunciation of Catholicism and their 'unclean' marriages, the women along with their husbands were destined for eternal damnation.[22] Hand in hand with their spouses, Ó Dubhthaigh predicted that the women, in 'piercing flame', would descend into hell, where, confined in 'Lucifer's' 'putrid prison', they would be 'full of hunger, full of thirst … without light, without wine [and] without music'.[23] On account of their blasphemous actions, which in addition to their sacrilegious marriages included iconoclasm and non-observance of Lent, the women together with their husbands would remain 'burning' perpetually in a 'bitter fire'. In another particularly revealing remark, Ó Dubhthaigh claimed that whereas the clerics themselves were 'obsequious' and steeped in 'colossal pretentiousness', their wives had 'ruined the people'.[24]

While it is difficult to assess the reception of Ó Dubhthaigh's poem among contemporary audiences in Elizabethan Ireland, according to Donatus Mooney (1577–1624), historian of the Franciscan order, Ó Dubhthaigh was a 'renowned preacher' whose 'fame extended to the most remote parts of the kingdom'.[25] It therefore seems reasonable to deduce that Anne O'Meara and the two other castigated women heard or were at least aware of the verse. By the early seventeenth century, Ó Dubhthaigh's poetry had certainly circulated beyond Ireland and was known by Irish Catholic scholars on the Continent, among them Luke Wadding (1588–1657), who named the Ulster friar in his 1650 bibliographical list of Franciscan authors.[26] Earlier, in 1621, in his highly polemical *Historiae Catholicae Iberniae compendium*, O'Sullivan Beare made reference to Ó Dubhthaigh's poetry, citing his 'rather incisive poems, written in Irish against Meiler and other heretics'.[27] In his account, O'Sullivan Beare claimed that Anne O'Meara had herself been aware of the poem and that upon hearing it, she was overcome by fear and wept at the prospect of the fate which Ó Dubhthaigh had prophesied for her. When questioned by her husband about why she was upset, Anne allegedly replied that:

> Eugene [Eoghan] who was with me today assured by strong proof and many holy testimonies that I would be condemned to hell if I should die in a state of being your wife, and I am frightened and cannot help crying lest this be true.

Evoking providential rhetoric, O'Sullivan Beare reported that shortly afterwards, Anne, 'consumed with grief', died, whereupon 'the wicked Miler married a second wife' with whom he 'wilfully' lived in sin.[28]

While O'Sullivan Beare's account of Anne O'Meara and her husband's subsequent remarriage must, of course, be treated with caution—he was after all attempting to undermine the Established Church in Ireland and its adherents, whom he castigated as 'heretics'—other sources confirm that Magrath did in fact have a relationship with another woman. According to a papal report written by the Dublin-born Jesuit Christopher Holywood (1559–1626), which is undated but was written sometime between 1605 and 1615, this relationship was conducted while Magrath's wife Anne was still living.[29] The woman involved was therefore castigated by Holywood as a 'concubine'. Furthermore, on account of her illicit relationship with the archbishop, she was reportedly compelled by two Jesuits to endure 'public penance', during which she was 'covered with a white veil' and forced to hold 'a lighted taper' in her hand.[30] The circumstances surrounding the woman's performance of penance are unclear. That she was targeted on account of her relationship with Magrath rather than the archbishop himself suggests that in Ireland, the Catholic Church authorities' punishment of clerical concubinage was biased against women, a trend mirrored elsewhere in post-Tridentine Europe. As Merry Wiesner-Hanks has shown, despite the Catholic Church's best efforts at reform, in Europe, where clerical concubinage continued to be a source of public embarrassment for the Church, women found to be involved in illicit relationships with priests or bishops were forced to endure public humiliation (and sometimes exile), while the clerics themselves were simply fined and/ or at times moved to another parish.[31] The nature of punishments imposed on women who engaged in illicit relationships with clergy (both within the Catholic Church and the Established Church tradition) remains an aspect of Irish Reformation history worthy of further exploration.

Notwithstanding the intense ridicule and derision leveled against clerical wives by Catholic clergy and religious, other indicators suggest that by the early Stuart era, the standing and reputation of clerical wives in Ireland was improving, at least within their own confessional communities. Evidence for this may be gleaned from surviving funerary monuments and epitaphs which, like Irish-language poetry, constitute another fruitful avenue for understanding the experiences and changing status of women married to the personnel of the Established Church in early modern Ireland. The lauded position of 'godly' clerical wives in the early Stuart era, as demonstrated on several funerary monuments, served as an alternative narrative to Catholic representations of them as the antithesis of the Virgin Mary. This was true in the case of Elizabeth Pilsworth, wife of William Pilsworth, a native of London who became vicar of St. David's Church in Naas and was consecrated Bishop of Kildare in September 1604, a position he retained until his death. The couple had four children: three daughters and one son.[32] When Elizabeth died on 31 December 1613 at the age of forty-four, a tomb to her memory was erected in the Church of Dunfert in the barony of Carbury, presumably by her husband who was buried in the same church. Although the tomb is no longer standing, the short inscription (originally in Latin) extolled Elizabeth's laudatory and exemplary attributes and represented her as the epitome of 'ideal' Protestant womanhood. Elizabeth was 'the beloved, chaste and godly wife of Pilsworth' who 'left the world ... seeking a heavenly kingdom'.[33] Emphasis on the chastity of 'godly' wives extended to a cleric's female offspring too, as reflected in the will of Richard Meredith (d. 1597), Church of Ireland Bishop of Leighlin, in which he bequeathed money to his daughters provided that they remained 'chaste' until marriage.[34]

Another example of the respect and status afforded clerical wives was the funerary monument erected to the memory of Jeneta Houston, wife of Archibald Adair (d. 1647), Dean of Raphoe and later Bishop of Waterford and Lismore, who died giving birth to twins, a boy and a girl, in January 1618, at the age of just twenty. Jeneta is represented as a model of exemplary female godliness, a paragon of piety and virtue which her epitaph exhorted others to imitate:

> Her esteemed memory remaining, she outshone others in virtue, far sur-
> passing them in happy piety, in simplicity. Her breeding, voice, soul,
> look, bearing, the other adjuncts of her life as well, sing of a praise not
> likely to pass away.[35]

The epitaphs to the memory of Elizabeth Pilsworth and Jeneta Houston are valuable for what they reveal about the ideals to which clerical wives in early Stuart Ireland were expected to conform. Furthermore, as Clodagh Tait has shown in her pioneering study of burial rituals in early modern Ireland, to contemporaries, these representations on funerary monuments functioned as 'cues' which 'unlocked' a variety of meanings relating to the understanding of the roles held by women in general—and in this case, the wives of clergy-men specifically—in early modern society.[36] More analysis of extant funerary monuments, epitaphs, and sermons—underutilized sources in the study of early modern Irish social and religious history—could yield further valuable insights into the particular ideals to which women in Ireland (including those married to clerics) were expected to conform, and whether those ideals dif-fered between confessions or changed over time.[37] It is important to remem-ber, however, that the women described on monuments and in epitaphs are represented as paragons and exemplars, reflecting the moralizing and didactic nature of funerary architecture. They are concerned with the 'ideal' rather than the actuality, and consequently, they do not give us much sense of the reality of the daily lives of the women in question.

While difficult to reconstruct, it is certain that the daily life of at least some women married to clergymen was far from ideal. In a large majority of cases, the Established Church in Ireland, in the absence of sufficient numbers of native clergy, recruited suitably trained priests and bishops from England, many of whom, upon appointment to benefices within the Irish church, trav-elled to Ireland together with their wives and children. For these women, leaving their family, friends, and familiar surroundings in order to adapt to life in a remote location was a cause of trepidation. Indeed, when London resident Hugh Brady (c.1527–84) was appointed Bishop of Meath in 1563, his first wife (whose identity is unknown but who was a relation of William Cecil) was reportedly apprehensive about relocating to Ireland.[38] On arrival at the episcopal residence in Ardbraccan, County Meath, six kilometers out-side Navan, Brady's wife was undoubtedly shocked to learn that her hus-band, although 'verye poore', was 'charged with a greate house[hold]' that was expected to feed as many as 'any bysshoppe in Englande' but without any 'provysion towarde the same'.[39]

Apprehensions were also expressed by the aforementioned Leah Mawe, the English-born wife of William Bedell, later Bishop of Kilmore. In a letter written to James Ussher (1581–1656), Archbishop of Armagh, in March 1626, Bedell recorded his wife's trepidation about relocating from their comfortable Suffolk abode to Ireland, remarking that Leah

> had rather continue with her friends in her native countrey, than put her self into the hazzard of the seas, and a foreign land, with many casualties in travel, which she perhaps out of fear, apprehends more than there is cause.[40]

Despite her reservations, however, Bedell's wife Leah, 'resolving as she ought to be contented with whatsoever God shall appoint', departed for Ireland in April 1628 in the company of her husband and children.[41] The bishop clearly shared his wife's reservations about the potential risks in travelling; before departing for Dublin, as a precautionary measure, he drew up a will.[42] By July 1628, however, the family was settled in the city where, according to Bedell, they were, 'I thanck God … all well'.[43] After a turbulent tenure as provost of Trinity College William, Leah and their family were once again obliged to move. In 1629, Bedell was appointed bishop of the combined dioceses of Kilmore and Ardagh, and the family settled at the episcopal residence just outside Kilmore, County Cavan. Both Bedell's newly appointed dioceses were in areas that had been recently settled, but as the bishop observed, 'our new plantation is yet raw, the churches ruined' and most of the inhabitants Irish.[44]

In their description of the Kilmore bishop's Irish sojourn, his biographers are largely silent in relation to the experience of Bedell's wife, focusing instead on the bishop's engagement in matters of religious controversy, his attempts to reform the Irish clergy, and his efforts to evangelize among the laity.[45] Although Bedell's proselytizing efforts were largely unsuccessful, he did gain a position of respect among his Irish Catholic parishioners, which, in turn, undoubtedly made life somewhat more tolerable for his wife and children. Indeed, according to Alexander Clogie (1614–98), Bedell's son-in-law and biographer, during Christmas, the Bedell household became a recognized 'place of great hospitality' for 'the poor Irish to feast … both men and women … that scarce had any whole cloathes on their back, or could understand a word of English'.[46] The family's acculturation within the Kilmore community is further highlighted by the fact that Bedell, an avid linguist who promoted evangelization through the medium of Irish, enjoined the couple's children to learn the language as well.[47]

Notwithstanding being surrounded in this remote district by a majority Gaelic Irish and Catholic population, Bedell and his family appear to have been relatively settled in Kilmore, at least until the outbreak of violence in October 1641. The respect afforded the bishop on the occasion of his funeral in early February 1642, during what was a period of extraordinary sectarian tension, is emblematic of the Bedell family being more generally well settled within the predominantly Catholic parish. The rebels, out of respect for the bishop, allowed his family to give him a decent burial, although they prudently avoided use of Protestant rites since, according to Clogie, 'it was not thought advisable to provoke ... [the rebels] so much'.[48] The dutiful reverence afforded Bedell by local Catholic rebels was in stark contrast to the treatment accorded to other deceased members of the Church of Ireland episcopate and their wives during the turbulence of 1641–42, some of whom, in an extreme expression of religious antagonism, were ceremoniously disinterred from their graves. For example, in June 1642, deponent William Vowells reported that the remains of Robert Sibthorpe, Bishop of Kilfenora, and his wife were ceremoniously disinterred from their grave 'in the Chancell of Maynooth' and thrown 'out of the Churchyard (they being buried 3 yeares before)'.[49] Although beyond the scope of this essay, an analysis of the experiences of clerical wives contained in the 1641 depositions represents another fruitful line of scholarly inquiry, one that has, to date, been overlooked in scholarship on women and violence during the 1641 uprising.[50]

Due to her husband's active efforts to engage with the local Irish community, Leah Mawe appears to have lived at relative ease among her Kilmore neighbors. For other women married to members of the Church of Ireland episcopate, acculturation or even coexistence within Irish society was more problematic since, as perceived agents of Protestant evangelization and English conquest in Ireland, they could become targets of physical attacks. Susan Steynings, the wife of George Montgomery, Bishop of Derry, Clogher, and Raphoe from 1605 until his transfer to Meath in 1610, is a case in point. Originally from Somerset in England, Susan moved to Ireland with her husband in October 1606. The couple had one daughter, Jane (d. 1678), who in 1615 married Nicholas St. Lawrence, eleventh Baron Howth, an influential member of the Old English elite.[51] By 1614, Susan and her husband had settled in County Meath, where Montgomery constructed a new episcopal residence at Ardbraccan.[52] By then, however, campaigns of religious coercion, directed by Lord Deputy Arthur Chichester, were aggravating relations between the Catholic community and the personnel of the Established Church and state. During the period of the coercive 'mandate' campaigns initiated by Chichester between 1605–1607 and 1611–15, increasingly harsh measures against religious nonconformity, including punitive fines, arrests, imprisonments, and summary executions, were enforced.[53] These served to accentuate divisions and increase tensions between Catholic communities and members of the Church of Ireland ministry and their families, who, as standard-bearers of the Protestant evangelization mission in Ireland, were often singled out for particularly harsh treatment by disaffected Catholics. Indicative of this hostility, Montgomery reportedly received threats to his life in 1614, prompting his decision to fortify the family residence at Ardbraccan and demonstrating his growing fear for his family's safety.

The bishop's precautionary measures in 1614 were understandable. The Montgomery family residence had previously been targeted by hostile Irish neighbors, as reported in the correspondence of the bishop's wife, Susan. When newly arrived at Derry in October 1606, Susan wrote to her brother-in-law, John Willoughby, reporting that although she and her husband were 'setteled in the Derye, in a verye pretye litell house, built after the Indglesh [English] fashone', their Irish neighbors did 'often troubell our house'.[54] Two years later, in April 1608, following the outbreak of a rebellion in Derry led by Cahir O'Doherty (d. 1608), Lord of Inishowen, the couple's home was once again subjected to attack. During the rebellion, which was driven in large part by Montgomery's policies with regard to land acquisitions in Ulster, the couple's residence was looted and Montgomery's library destroyed.[55] The incident was especially harrowing for Montgomery's wife, however, who was alone at the time of the attack; her husband was in Dublin conducting episcopal duties. Along with Lady Jane Paulet, the wife of the governor of Derry, Sir George Paulet (d. 1608), who was later killed by the rebels, Susan was detained as a hostage and endured almost three months' imprisonment at Burt Castle in County Donegal before being released by her captors.[56]

The deliberate and symbolic attack on the episcopal residence, the destruction of the couple's goods, and the imprisonment of Susan Montgomery in 1608 demonstrate the significant risks confronted by wives of the Church of Ireland episcopate by virtue of their association with public figures who were often ridiculed and vilified within their local communities. Women married to clergymen of lesser ranks could also find themselves victims of violence and hostility. An incident which occurred in the parish of Balrothery, North County Dublin, in November 1607 is a case in point. On 1 June 1608, the Court of Castle Chamber heard the case of Thomas Meredith, an Englishman and minister of Balrothery, against James Barnewall and other defendants accused of orchestrating a riot. Barnewall was a local landowner whose family members were well-known recusants, with several having been educated in the seminaries of Catholic Spain.[57] On Sunday 1 November 1607, Barnewall, along with a group of mourners, prepared to attend the funeral of his mother in the local parish church. According to Meredith's testimony, the service was to be held in an 'idoltarous' fashion which the minister strongly opposed, leading some 200 persons assembled at the church to attack him. Not only was the minister himself targeted; his pregnant wife was also set upon by the mob, who, according to court records, threw the woman to the ground.[58] James Barnewall and others among the rioting party were found guilty. However, in an expression of Catholic solidarity, those involved were evidently unwilling to testify against Barnewall and his counterparts, and the defendants were later dismissed for lack of evidence.[59] Although the outcome of the incident for Minister Meredith's wife is not recorded, the violence that both she and Susan Montgomery experienced during the early Stuart era must be seen in the longer-term context of violence perpetrated against the wives of English officials, and women more generally, in late Elizabethan Ireland.

While the institutional and political impact of the Reformation in Ireland has been the subject of significant scholarly attention, the social implications of that reform remain an under-researched aspect of early modern Irish history. This is especially true in the case of clerical wives whose lives and experiences, owing to their habitual absence from the historical record, are obscure, elusive, and difficult to reconstruct. Nevertheless, as this essay has demonstrated, analysis of a range of underutilized and alternative sources, most notably funerary monuments and Irish-language poetry, can shed light on this hitherto overlooked dimension of Irish Reformation history. While by no means an exhaustive study, this essay has sought to identify new approaches and sources for studying this under-researched topic and to open up new questions for future investigation. As has been highlighted, women married to the personnel of the Established Church in Ireland emerged from an ambiguous, uncertain, and socially stigmatized position during the Tudor era, to one of relative visibility and respectability, at least within their own confessional communities from the early Stuart period onwards. Consequently, by that time, the wives of some of the more senior-ranking clergy were lauded as exemplary 'godly' women and portrayed as paragons of the Protestant evangelization mission in Ireland, as evidenced by the funerary epitaphs dedicated to the memory of Jeneta Houston and Elizabeth Pilsworth. However, although their position and status generally improved during the Stuart era—owing to greater clarity regarding their doctrinal and legislative status—this was a slow and tentative process as clerical wives continued to be regarded as legitimate targets for ridicule and derision, particularly by hostile Catholic commentators who condemned them as apostates. In other more extreme cases, women married to clergymen could sometimes find themselves victims of physical assault. The cases of Susan Montgomery and the wife of Minister Thomas Meredith demonstrate how previously contained antagonisms often found violent expression during periods of heightened tension, and clerical wives, by virtue of their association with the personnel of the Established Church, could become the victims of particularly harsh treatment. Their experiences would serve as salutary precursors to the escalation of violence and hostility experienced by Church of Ireland clerics and their wives, whether those of the episcopate ranks or lower, following the outbreak of sectarian conflict in Ireland in October 1641.

Notes

1 According to Burnet, the sermon was subsequently published under the title 'A good name is better than ointment' but no copies are known to survive: see Gilbert Burnet, *The Life of William Bedell, D.D., Bishop of Kilmore in Ireland* (London: John Southby, 1685), p. 230.

2 E.S. Shuckburgh (ed.), *Two Biographies of William Bedell, Bishop of Kilmore, with a Selection of his Letters and an Unpublished Treatise* (Cambridge: The University Press, 1902), p. 74; Burnet, *The Life of William Bedell*, p. 231.

3 For a discussion of the life and career of George Montgomery, see Henry A. Jefferies, 'George Montgomery, First Protestant Bishop of Derry, Raphoe and Clogher (1605–10)', in Henry A. Jefferies and Ciarán Devlin (eds.), *History of the Diocese of Derry from Earliest Times* (Dublin: Four Courts Press, 2000), pp. 140–66.

4 Mary Prior, 'Reviled and Crucified Marriages: The Position of Tudor Bishops' Wives', in eadem (ed.), *Women in English Society* (London: Routledge, 1985), pp. 118–48.

5 For example, one the main provisions of the Act of Six Articles, ratified by the English parliament in June 1539, was the proscription of clerical marriage. See Susan Wabuda, *Thomas Cranmer* (Abingdon: Routledge, 2017), pp. 142–47.

6 Helen Parish, '"It Was Never Good World Sence Minister Must Have Wyves': Clerical Celibacy, Clerical Marriage, and Anticlericalism in Reformation England', in *Journal of Religious History* 36 (2012), 66. For clerical marriage in early modern England, see also: Eric J. Carlson, 'Clerical Marriage and the English Reformation' in *Journal of British Studies* 31 (1992), 1–31; Jacqueline Eales, 'Female Literacy and Social Identity of the Clergy Family in the Seventeenth Century', *Archaeologia Cantiana* 133 (2013), 67–82; Rachel Basch, 'Reviled to Revered: The Changing Status and Identity of English Bishops' Wives, 1549–1625' (PhD thesis, Royal Holloway, University of London, 2016); Wabuda, *Cranmer*, 143–46.

7 George Browne arrived in Dublin in July 1536 and not long after married a local woman named Katherine Miagh. See James Murray, *Enforcing the English Reformation in Ireland: Clerical Resistance and Political Conflict in the Diocese of Dublin, 1534–1590* (Cambridge: Cambridge University Press, 2009), pp. 141, 154.

8 Bale was appointed Bishop of Ossory in 1552 and travelled to Ireland in the company of his wife in January 1553. The same year he published an account of his Irish sojourn, *The Vocaycon of Johan Bale to the Bishoprick of Ossorie in Irelande.*

9 Alan Ford, *The Protestant Reformation in Ireland, 1590–1641* (Frankfurt: Peter Lang, 1985).

10 One exception is Helen Coburn-Walshe's 1989 article on Hugh Brady, Elizabethan Bishop of Meath, in which she highlights how financial difficulties and public scorn characterized the lives of women married to the Elizabethan episcopate. See Helen Coburn-Walshe 'Enforcing the Elizabethan Settlement: The Vicissitudes of Hugh Brady, Bishop of Meath, 1563–84', *Irish Historical Studies* 26 (1989), 369–70. For a description of women and marriage more generally in early modern Ireland, see Jane Ohlmeyer, *Making Ireland English: The Irish Aristocracy in the Seventeenth Century* (New Haven and London: Yale University Press, 2012), pp. 169–207.

11 Presumably this was due to a lack of available contributors with expertise in this area. See Toby Barnard and W.G. Neely, 'Introduction', in idem (eds.), *The Clergy of the Church of Ireland, 1000–2000: Messengers, Watchmen and Stewards* (Dublin: Four Courts, 2006), p. 4. For an account of women in the Church of Ireland community—both clerical wives and women more generally—during the early modern period, see Bronagh Ann McShane, 'The Roles and Representations of Women in Religious Change and Conflict in Leinster and South-East Munster, *c.*1560–*c.*1641' (PhD Thesis, Maynooth University, 2015), chap. 3.

12 She receives only a passing comment when Bale mentions that he set sail for Ireland with 'my wyfe & one servaunt': *The Vocaycon of Johan Bale*, fol. 17v. See Marie-Louise Coolahan's article in this volume.

13 For a discussion on the ways in which Irish historians have neglected to adequately utilize Irish-language sources, see Nicholas Canny, 'The Formation of the Irish Mind: Religion, Politics and Gaelic Irish Literature 1580–1750', in *Past & Present* 95 (1982), 91–116; and Vincent Morley, *The Popular Mind in Eighteenth-Century Ireland* (Cork: Cork University Press, 2017), pp. 1–14. See Sarah McKibben's article in this volume.

14 'Patent Roll 1 & 2 Mary and Philip, no. 3', in James Morrin (ed.), *Calendar of the Patent and Close Rolls of Ireland, Henry VIII-Elizabeth I* (Dublin: Alex. Thom & Sons, 1861), i, p. 325.

15   The poem is printed in Cuthbert Mhág Craith (ed. and trans.), *Dán na mBráthar Mionúr*. 2 vols (Dublin: Institiúid Árd-Léinn Bhaile Átha Cliath, 1967; 1980), i, pp. 133–38; ii, 60–62. The text and translation of the poem also appear (with minor changes) in Angela Bourke et al. (eds.), *The Field Day Anthology of Irish Writing*. 5 vols (Cork: Cork University Press, 2002), iv, pp. 156–59. I have made use of the *Field Day* edition.

16   For a brief discussion of Casey's wife, see: Henry A. Jefferies, *The Irish Church and the Tudor Reformations* (Dublin: Four Courts Press, 2010), pp. 249–50.

17   For a recent account of the life and career of Miler Magrath, see Patrick J. Ryan, *Archbishop Miler Magrath: The Enigma of Cashel* (Roscrea: Lisheen Publications, 2014).

18   Bourke, *Field Day Anthology*, iv, pp. 157–59.

19   Philip O'Sullivan Beare, *Historiae Catholicae Iberniae Compendium* (Lisbon: excusum a Petro Crasbeeckio, 1621), printed in Matthew Byrne (ed. and trans.), *Ireland Under Elizabeth, Chapters towards a History of Ireland Under the Reign of Elizabeth* (Dublin: Sealy, Bryers and Walker, 1903), chap. 12, pp. 16–17.

20   Marc Caball, *Poets and Politics: Reaction and Continuity in Irish Poetry, 1558–1625* (Cork: Cork University Press, 1998), pp. 77–79, 138.

21   Bourke, *Field Day Anthology*, iv, p. 158.

22   Ibid.

23   Ibid.

24   Ibid., p. 159.

25   Brendan Jennings (ed.), 'Brussels MS. 3947: Donatus Mooneyus, De Provincia Hiberniae S. Francisci', *Analecta Hibernica* 6 (1934), 49–50; translated anonymously in *Franciscan Tertiary* 6 (1984), 196–97. For an account of the Irish Franciscan order, see Edel Bhreathnach, Joseph Mac Mahon, and John McCafferty (eds.), *The Irish Franciscans, 1534–1990* (Dublin: Four Courts Press, 2009); and Benignus Millett, 'The Irish Franciscans and Education in Late Medieval Times and the Early Counter-Reformation, 1230–1630', *Seanchas Ardmhacha: Journal of the Armagh Diocesan Historical Society* 18 (2001), 15–28.

26   Luke Wadding, *Scriptores Ordinis Minorum: quibus accessit syllabus illorum ...* (Rome: Francisci Alberti Tani, 1650), p. 108.

27   O'Sullivan Beare, *Historiae Catholicae*, p. 17. For a discussion of O'Sullivan Beare as an author see Hiram Morgan, 'Making Ireland Spanish: The Political Writings of Philip O'Sullivan Beare', in Jason Harris and Keith Sidwell (eds.), *Making Ireland Roman: Irish Neo-Latin writers and the Republic of Letters* (Cork: Cork University Press, 2009), pp. 86–108.

28   Ibid.

29   Hogan, *Distinguished Irishmen of the Sixteenth Century* (London: Burns and Oates, 1894), pp. 423–28.

30   Hogan, *Distinguished Irishmen*, p. 428.

31   Merry E. Wiesner-Hanks, *Christianity and Sexuality in the Early Modern World: Regulating Desire, Reforming Practice* 2nd edn. (Abingdon: Routledge, 2010), p. 146. For a discussion on clerical concubinage in Ireland during the Henrician era, see Murray, *Enforcing the English Reformation in Ireland*, chap. 4.

32   Their son, Philip Pilsworth (d. 1638), married Amy, daughter of George Fitzgerald of Tecroghan in County Meath. See E. O'Leary, 'John Lye of Clonaugh', *Journal of the County Kildare Archaeological Society* 2 (1896), 134.

33   Walter Fitzgerald, 'Queries', *Journal of the Kildare Archaeological Society* (hereafter *Kildare Arch. Soc. Jn.*) 1 (1893), 342.

34   Richard Meredith was married to Sarah Batho (d. 1650) with whom he had at least three sons and three surviving daughter. Sarah later married Adam Loftus (b. 1568), first Viscount Loftus of Ely. See Helen Coburn Walshe, 'Meredith, Richard (d. 1597)' in *Oxford Dictionary of National Biography* (hereafter ODNB) [doi:10.1093/ref:odnb/18578, accessed 10 Aug. 2017].

35 *Journal of the Association for the Preservation of the Memorials of the Dead* 3 (1895), 419.

36 Clodagh Tait, *Death, Burial and Commemoration in Ireland, 1550–1650* (Basingstoke: Palgrave-Macmillan, 2002), p. 127. On funerary monuments in early Stuart Ireland, see also Rolf Loeber, 'Sculptured Memorials to the Dead in Early Seventeenth Century Ireland: A Survey from "Monumenta Eblanae" and Other Sources', in *Proceedings of the Royal Irish Academy* (hereafter *R.I.A. Proc.*) 81, section c, (1981), 267–93.

37 On funerary monuments in early modern Kilkenny, see Paul Cockerham, "'My Body to be Buried in my Owne Monument': The Social and Religious Context of Co. Kilkenny Funeral Monuments, 1600–1700', in *R.I.A. Proc* 109, section C (2009), 239–365.

38 Coburn-Walshe, 'Enforcing the Elizabethan Settlement', p. 369.

39 'Bishop Hugh Brady to Sir William Cecil, 16 May 1565', in E.P. Shirley (ed.), *Original Letters and Papers in Illustration of the History of the Church in Ireland* (London: F. & J. Rivington, 1851), p. 189.

40 Burnet, *The Life of William Bedell*, pp. 34–35.

41 Bedell and Leah had four children: William (b. 1613), Grace (1614–24), John (b. 1616), and Ambrose (b. 1618). Leah had four children from a former marriage: Nicholas, Leah, Robert, and Edward. See Shuckburgh (ed.), *Two Biographies of William Bedell*, preface, xvi, p. 80.

42 'William Bedell to Ward, 13 May 1628', in Shuckburgh (ed.), *Two Biographies of William Bedell*, p. 293.

43 'William Bedell to Ward, 16 July 1628' in ibid., p. 294.

44 Quoted in Aidan Clarke, 'Bishop William Bedell (1571–1642) and the Irish Reformation', in Ciarán Brady (ed.), *Worsted in the Game: Losers in Irish History* (Dublin: The Lilliput Press Ltd, 1989), p. 66.

45 Knowledge of Bedell's life and career relies on two contemporary biographies: one by his eldest son, also William (b. 1613), and the other by his son-in-law, Alexander Clogie (1614–98). A popular biography written by Bishop Gilbert Burnet (1643–1715) and first published in 1685 was based on the memoirs of Clogie and Bedell's son. See Karl Bottigheimer and Vivienne Larminie, 'Bedell, William (bap. 1572, d. 1642), Church of Ireland bishop of Kilmore', in *ODNB* doi:10.1093/ref:odnb/1924, accessed 27 August 2017.

46 Shuckburgh (ed.), *Two Biographies of William Bedell*, pp. 160–61.

47 'William Bedell to Ward, 24 May 1629', in Shuckburgh (ed.), *Two Biographies of William Bedell*, p. 297. For a discussion of Bedell's career in an Irish context, see Clarke, 'Bishop William Bedell (1571–1642)', 61–70; and John McCafferty, 'Venice in Cavan: The Career of William Bedell, 1572–1642', in Brendan Scott (ed.), *Culture and Society in Early Modern Breifne-Cavan* (Dublin: Four Courts Press, 2009), pp. 173–87.

48 Burnet, *The Life of William Bedell*, p. 218.

49 Deposition of William Vowells, 25 June 1642 (TCD MS 813, fol. 331).

50 On the experiences of clerical wives during the 1641 uprising, see McShane, 'The Roles and Representations of Women', Chap. 4.

51 George E. Cokayne, *Complete Peerage of England, Scotland, Ireland, Great Britain and the United Kingdom*, 8 vols (London: G. Bell & Sons, 1887), vi, p. 608. On the St. Lawrence family in early decades, see Valerie McGowan-Doyle, *The Book of Howth: Elizabethan Conquest and the Old English* (Cork: Cork University Press, 2011).

52 George Hill (ed.), *The Montgomery Manuscripts: 1603–1706* (Belfast: J. Cleeland, 1869), pp. 96–102.

53 For an account of the sporadic spells of state action against religious nonconformity in early Stuart Ireland, see Brian Mac Cuarta, *Catholic Revival in the North of Ireland, 1603–41* (Dublin: Four Courts, 2007).

54 At least nine of Susan's letters survive and are now held in the Somerset Record Office. Three of these letters were printed in the nineteenth century.

Walter C. Trevelyan and Charles E. Trevelyan (eds.), *Trevelyan Papers* (London: Camden Society, 1872), iii, pp. 78–79, 92–94, 99–102. For an extended discussion of her correspondence, see: Marie-Louise Coolahan, 'Ideal Communities and Planter Women's Writing in Seventeenth-Century Ireland', *Parergon* 29 (2012), 69–91.

55   For an account of the 1608 rebellion, see: Henry A. Jefferies, 'Prelude to Plantation: Sir Cahir O'Doherty's Rebellion in 1608', *History Ireland* 17 (2009), 16–19.

56   *Calendar of State Papers Relating to Ireland, 1606–8*, p. 512.

57   By 1608, Patrick Barnwall of Bremore Castle, Balrothery, was a student in Paris, while his brother Robert attended the Irish college at Douai. See 'P. Barnwall to R. Barnwall, 12 Oct. 1608', State Papers 63/225, fol. 222.

58   *Historical Manuscripts Commission: Manuscripts of the Earl of Egmont.* 3 vols. (Dublin, 1920/23) i, pt. 1, 33.

59   Ibid.

5 Making Early Modern Irish studies Irish? Teaching, learning, and researching Early Modern Irish in a digital age[1]

Brendan Kane

In announcing a recent auction for 'the 'oldest-known map of Ireland'', the *Irish Times* described it as being made 'at a time when Ireland was at the edge of the known western world—and travel to this country would have been the 15th-century equivalent of a voyage to the moon'.[2] In this way the article celebrated Ireland's connection to broader European and world history by virtue of its inclusion in a Venetian atlas, and yet simultaneously exoticized it by likening the island to lunar otherness. That tension between seeing Ireland and the Irish as quintessentially European and yet 'owning' and highlighting the designation of European 'other' is a central one in early modern Irish Studies. As the *Times* piece succinctly demonstrates, it is also an element in popular discourse. But while the claim in the article makes good copy, it is inaccurate: connection between Ireland and Britain was strong and operative at the elite and non-elite levels; links with the Continent, while less frequent or sustained, existed in both English and Gaelic parts of the island. Considering the *Times* article in light of this ongoing bifurcated approach to Irish studies, we can, on the one hand, simply conclude 'no harm done', recognizing the obvious hyperbole and not chastising the author or editor for attempting to fool us with false claims. They know better, we know better; the space travel analogy was just for effect. On the other hand, however, I think we can acknowledge that the author does indeed know full well the analogy is inaccurate and respect the needs of journalistic style, while also recognizing that such 'throwaway' lines are symptomatic of the much deeper and complex tension at the heart of Irish studies mentioned earlier—the simultaneous desire to both externally associate and to self-exoticize—and understanding that the inability to effectively balance or erase that tension has hobbled the development of the field.

The study of Early Modern Irish,[3] the dominant language of both quotidian and intellectual life in the period, offers a useful case study in the how that tension between connecting with other national histories while simultaneously identifying as alien affects the production of scholarly knowledge and understanding. The importance of the Irish language is frequently celebrated for its role in the creation of European culture, and the expansion of Christianity and learning more generally. Continental scholars have been as active in charting this narrative as those from Ireland. Where would the study of Old Irish be without the Swiss Rudolf Thurneysen and the German Kuno Meyer? These scholars and others were fascinated by Irish as the language with the oldest, extant vernacular sources in Western Europe. Continuing fascination with the Irish role in European-wide development is revealed in the active media coverage of Trinity College Dublin's recent conference on the medieval manuscript tradition.[4] Modern Irish, too, is an international phenomenon, whether employed in translation at Brussels, exported to North American colleges and universities through initiatives like the Fulbright Foreign Language Teaching Assistant program, or transmitted globally by the 'trad' music industry.

Yet in the space between the heavily studied and celebrated periods of Old Irish and Modern Irish lies the much neglected centuries of Early Modern Irish, home of the (in)famously intricate *dán díreach*, commonly referenced with the broad term of bardic poetry. Old Irish, with its convoluted verb forms and syntactical peculiarities such as the infixed pronoun, is legendary for its difficulty. But one can learn it; there is a dictionary (now online), multiple grammars, and a range of work- and textbooks. Similarly, whatever the claims of Modern Irish as a particularly tricky language to acquire, there is a profusion of materials and courses (face-to-face and online) by which one may gain proficiency. Not so with Irish as it was written *c.* 1200–1650: there exists no dedicated dictionary, no practical grammar, no introductory guide. Bardic poetry, already notorious for its challenging grammar and use of metaphor, is thus rendered all the more otherworldly by virtue of its being largely unreachable to most students, scholars, and interested non-academics. Somehow, a language that was deemed crucial for the development of Western European faith and culture in the Old Irish period is, when we come to the Early Modern, rendered the linguistic equivalent of the sea monsters that populate the edges of period atlases like that on sale at Christies: intriguing to look at and carrying a frisson of danger and mystery, but which can be safely ignored. Come the twentieth century, the Irish language emerges again as a crucial factor in society and politics, and in the current moment it is a driving force of educational innovation and popular culture and art (witness the Gaelscoil phenomenon and TG 4, respectively), and embraced by urban pub culture through the 'Pop-up Gaeltacht' movement. How did we get from, say, the *Lebor Gabála Érenn*, with its celebration *as Gaeilge* of European Irish origins to today's popular press likening a fifteenth-century sail to Ireland to lunar travel? A much needed new direction in early modern Irish studies, then, is normalization of Early Modern Irish and encouragement of deeper engagement with its sources by scholars across disciplines.

In arguing for a linguistic new direction in early modern Irish studies, this essay approaches the paucity of Irish-language research as a pipeline problem. That is to say, the issue is not that scholars are simply choosing to ignore the language; rather it is to claim that given the lack of means to learn Early

Modern Irish we are likely to see even fewer attempts at interdisciplinary engagement with the archive over time. As such, this is a generative problem. What we can know is determined largely by our archive. If we circumscribe that archive to be monolingual, our scholarship will register the effects. From a purely empirical standpoint, the body of data for analysis will be artificially restricted; from a more methodological and interpretive position, it will lack the sorts of conclusions derivable only from thinking multilingually. Consequently, this chapter argues for a new direction that is as much pedagogical/instructional as research focused, which is to say that it is not simply a call to read more Irish, but a call for scholars to take on the challenge of teaching and learning in both of the island's vernaculars and to work in more collaborative modes and with new technologies. Specifically, it focuses on one attempt at linking language acquisition, interdisciplinary collaboration, and digital innovation in the interest of developing new educational and research outcomes: *Léamh.org* (hereafter, Léamh). In doing so, this chapter attempts to argue that a greater engagement with Irish by early modern scholars across fields carries benefits beyond those attainable by simply increasing our database, extensive and promising though those benefits might be. For it is a very curious situation to have an interdisciplinary field of study that largely overlooks the vernacular sources of the society under examination. Increasing the knowledge and thus use of Irish in research and writing, therefore, offers opportunities to intersect with other scholarly, and indeed cultural, conversations related to translation studies and practice, the use of digital humanities in teaching and research, the value of collaborative work in the humanities, and strategies for communicating scholarly knowledge in an age that increasingly is thinking beyond the monograph and journal article when defining acceptable professional 'publication'.[5]

To begin, it should be stressed that this chapter does not claim Irish sources have no presence in the interdisciplinary study of early modern Ireland, but rather that that presence is not commensurate with the richness of the archive. Beyond the significant body of modern scholarship by Irish-language scholars, some of the most influential historical and literary studies of the period draw on Irish sources, as a glance at the work of some of this collection's other contributors reveals. That said, even a fairly cursory look at specialist monographs over the last decade or so reveals very little in the way of serious appeal to Irish sources. Few historical or literary monographs make Irish texts their primary archive. Many dip into printed translations to pluck out illustrative examples, *The Annals of the Four Masters* and Osborn Bergin's modern collection *Irish Bardic Poetry* serving as particularly popular wells from which the non-Irish literate draw. Field surveys operate similarly. There is occasional discussion of Irish sources, and of the culture that produced them, but it is typically marginal to a larger narrative of English imperial expansion and

Irish cultural destruction built out from the State Papers and similar colonial records. Collections of essays tend to offer better integration, as evidenced by the chapters by Marc Caball and Bernadette Cunningham in volume two of the recent *Cambridge History of Ireland* edited by Jane Ohlmeyer.[6] But efforts to weave a multilingual source base into a single-authored, general narrative are rare as a graduate course in bardic poetry.

This understated presence of Irish sources in the scholarship has not gone unnoticed, of course, and there is ongoing debate as to whether or not the language is necessary for studying early modern Ireland. One side of this conversation stresses the facts that Irish was the language of the vast majority of the population, that there is a sizable surviving archive of textual sources, and that there is even a substantial body of relevant secondary literature in Modern Irish.[7] The question typically posed by those favoring this position is whether such a scholarly situation would be acceptable in the study of other societies: for instance, could one be a French historian and not know French, focus on Japan without Japanese, and so on. Occasionally, it is further suggested that historical empathy demands the learning of Irish. Doing so represents not only an intellectual respect for the culture under examination but also an act of solidarity with victims of settler colonialism and cultural imperialism and, thus, an act of resistance.

The counter argument, which is typically expressed casually in conversation or implicitly through practice rather than explicitly articulated in print, is a dual one which also draws historical and transnational analogies. In the first instance, it holds that the vast majority of the material related to early modern Ireland is in English and that, by contrast, extant Irish sources are both few in number and limited in their range and form, and thus only applicable for narrow and specific studies. A second, complementary position contends that the key Irish texts are translated and thus available for use by scholars lacking the skill to read them in the original. Critical examples of such works in modern printed editions with translation include the aforementioned *Annals of the Four Masters* and Bergin's collection, *Irish Bardic Poetry*. When pressed, advocates of this side of the debate also make reference to other cultural settings and languages, but in doing so, the analogy given is not to the study of, say, France without French but rather to the study of England without Latin, the argument being that, like Irish texts, Latin sources are relatively limited in number, useful for narrow and specific areas of study, and given the vastly greater archive of English-language sources, one can enjoy a prolific and ranging career in the field with nary a word of Latin.

There is obvious sense and merit to the position just described, but it is overplayed to the point of rationalization. Taking its various components in order, it is undoubtedly true that there are vastly more surviving English sources than Irish. That is not the same as saying there are no Irish sources, however. Indeed, they are many and varied. There are estimated to be over 2,000 bardic poems in Early Modern Irish, that period of the language's development *c.* 1200–1650.[8] The vast majority of these date from the sixteenth and seventeenth centuries. Beyond the *dán díreach* court poetry of the bards—which is addressed by Sarah McKibben elsewhere in this volume—there is a diversity of other verse genres represented in the corpus, including nature, religious, love, and genealogical and placename poetry. There is similar range and richness in the prose archive: annals, genealogies, histories, religious polemic, medical and scientific tracts, legal texts, satires, origin tales, sagas, diaries, commonplace books, and correspondence. The notion that this corpus of Irish learning is translated in such volume as to obviate the need to learn Irish—the second element of the argument—is wishful thinking. Within the body of printed modern editions, numerous texts remain untranslated, such as the important poetic collections *Leabhar Branach* (poems to the O'Byrnes) and *Leabhar Cloinne Aodha Buidhe* (verse addressing a branch of the O'Neills), and Seathrún Céitinn's long devotional prose tract *Trí Bior-ghaoithe an bháis*.[9] Moreover, a considerable body of material remains in manuscript, untranscribed and thus by definition untranslated.[10]

Similarly, it is wishful thinking to assume that available translations are suitable for the sorts of analytical work scholars today wish to conduct. We may take the example of Eleanor Knott's edition of the corpus of the sixteenth-century poet Tadhg Dall Ó hUiginn.[11] Knott's edition is a landmark piece of scholarship. Produced in the 1920s, it remains of immense value and widely used today. That said, it *is* a product of the 1920s and bears a curious late Victorian literary flare to the English which, as a historical artifact in and of itself, can have a distorting effect as we try to read through it to access the early modern. We should pay proper homage to the pioneering work of scholars like Knott, while simultaneously acknowledging that renderings appropriate to one historical moment may not be so for all.[12] Imagine, for instance, if scholarly access to the *Aeneid* were limited to Victorian translations. Such a situation would never be allowed to stand as acceptable. Nor should it in the case of Early Modern Irish texts. Moreover, if we take seriously the value of interdisciplinarity and collaboration, then we may wish to be cautious in even aspiring to have the full corpus of extant Irish material appear in modern translation. Reliance upon Celticists to provide accurate translation, which can then be added to the source base used by those in other disciplines, is on the one hand a manifestation of professional respect: let the experts do what they do and do not pretend that you can emulate or challenge their findings. Yet, on the other hand, such an approach is problematic for at least two reasons. First, Celticists should not be placed in a 'service' relationship to those working in other areas—that is, asked to translate the texts those without Irish wish to consult. While the following is obvious, it perhaps bears explicit statement: scholars of Irish have their own agendas and interests, and their own publication and professional assessment criteria, which they must follow rather than focusing on producing basic translations for others' projects. Second, while most historians or literary scholars of English texts are unlikely to progress to the level of linguistic and analytical sophistication of their Celticist peers in handling Irish sources, it is conceptually absurd to believe that they could not add to the conversation by virtue of asking new questions, suggesting new renderings, and bringing their own areas of expertise to bear on those sources and their contexts.[13] Indeed, it flies in the face of the current understanding in translation studies, which stresses that there is no such beast as a 'right' translation. Granted, there can be wrong translations, but there is no Platonic perfection of correspondence across languages and glosses.[14] Thus, bearing in mind the editors' charge to be cognizant of the benefits of theory, it is a theoretically impoverished approach to language, especially on the part of humanists, to claim that one must await 'correct' translations produced by others before engaging with Irish texts.

The Irish-as-Latin analogy is particularly problematic, suffering as it does by virtue of category error. As noted earlier, on the face of it, the claim seems sensible: one can indeed research Ireland's historical and literary record with no recourse to Irish, just as one can intimately explore that of England without Latin. However, this is a variety of special pleading based upon removing language from culture. Irish was the insular vernacular, the language of the masses as well as of elite discourse, not an exclusivist *cant* of the intelligentsia. To study the English through Latin is to observe them thinking in the register of international and classical forms and genres. The same applies to the study of Ireland through Latin.[15] By contrast, to study the Irish through Irish—or the English through English, for that matter—is to observe them thinking and communicating in a culturally specific medium. It is true that the form of the language found in written sources was an elite one, not the common spoken idiom, but it was the 'native' language of the vast majority of the population, from *bodach* to *rí*, including numerous bilingual residents who traced their ancestry back to the Anglo-Normans rather than the sons of Míl.[16] To know the vernacular language is a means to know better the people who lived, thought, and experienced the world primarily through the possibilities and constraints offered by that particular grammar. Moreover, for some research areas, Irish texts provide the primary, even only, source. Gaelic élite mentalities, for instance, are accessible through the court poetry but not through anything available in English until well into the seventeenth century, when the imperial language had made serious inroads colonizing indigenous aristocratic culture. English authors, it is true, commented on the great dynasts and their retinues, but those are external, and typically hostile, views. Bardic poetry, by contrast, is indigenous commentary and comes in a variety of (sub)genres, the reading of which offers insight into different modes of thinking, behavior, and values: encomium, genealogy, house poetry, satire, and so on. There exist analogous subgenres of prose which open further the window onto elite culture and mentalities. Much and varied work, then, remains to be done with Irish sources, and much is to be gained. To equate that opportunity with that provided by Latin sources for studying England and the English is to misunderstand fundamentally the place and function of these different languages in context.

All that said, I am sympathetic to this side of the debate and for one reason, already mentioned in this chapter's introduction: learning Early Modern Irish is quite challenging, given the paucity of materials, resources, and opportunities. Frequently, one hears students and colleagues express a desire to learn and research in the language but complain of a lack of opportunities and resources. This is a legitimate complaint. Outside of a very few universities—primarily in Ireland—there are almost no classes to be had.[17] More concerning is the lack of material for self-learners. Again, for Early Modern Irish, there exists no dedicated dictionary, no grammar, and no instructional guide or textbook.[18] Such materials are well developed for Modern Irish, of course, but they are for Old Irish, too. The learner/researcher has access to grammars, guides to the verbal system, multiple textbooks and study guides, and even a long-standing ListServ (Old Irish-L) whereby interested parties can work through a text, ask questions, and the like. But for the period of Irish between Old and Modern, roughly the years 1200–1650, there is nothing the same. In terms of dictionaries, one must triangulate across Patrick Dinneen's *Irish-English Dictionary*, which is more modern in focus; the *Dictionary of the Irish Language*, which is primarily concerned with Old and Middle Irish; and the various glossaries available at the back of such printed editions mentioned earlier (notably, Céitinn's *Trí Baor-Ghaoithe an Bháis*).[19] For grammar assistance, one can consult the brief paradigms and descriptions at the front of those editions, but these are limited both in their depth and breadth of coverage. One must have copies of nearly all the available such primers at hand in order to self-guide through the grammatical and orthographic thicket that is a standard period text.[20] Damian McManus's extraordinary detailing of the Early Modern Irish grammatical system, 'An Nua-Ghaeilge Chlasaiceach', is indispensable but operates more as linguistic description than practical guide.[21] Moreover, its language is technical ... and Irish. Without instructional reference resources for grammar, it is extremely difficult to work through Knott's brilliant short introduction, *An Introduction to Irish Syllabic Poetry of the Period 1200–1600*, let alone tackle a full text encountered in print or manuscript.

The argument over the necessity of Irish for early modern Irish studies, then, is a nonstarter. The situation simply is not analogous to requiring French to study France, for how are we to expect researchers to learn the language under such conditions? Clearly some do, but not many. And doing so is frequently a result of institutional support not available to all, particularly to those studying outside Ireland. The student interested in Early Modern Irish as a research language but studying in the USA, say, or Australia faces significant hurdles in acquiring the language, and it is an unrealistic expectation that either students or established scholars would undertake that journey in any appreciable numbers, whatever the potential benefits to their scholarship. Therefore, for this argument to have any practical bearing on interdisciplinary early modern Irish studies, there needs to be legitimate expectation that people can learn the language. Only then might we reasonably consider avoidance of the language to be a matter of choice. The new direction suggested, therefore, as noted in the introduction, is more than simply advocating for a greater presence of Irish in scholarship, but for increasing our capacity for teaching and learning the language and, in doing so, using that opportunity to think in innovative ways about how we study past societies and how we create and communicate scholarly knowledge more generally.

The construction and ongoing development of the digital humanities collective, Léamh, offers opportunity to reflect upon some of the methodological and theoretical challenges to, and research potentialities of, linking interdisciplinary early modern Irish studies to the Irish archive. It is by no means the only effort at making Irish sources more accessible, and it is certainly not the first. But it is the one that I know best, and, more importantly, it is more a self-consciously instructional tool than a database and, indeed, was conceived so as to work in concert with existing sites such as the pioneering *Bardic Poetry Database* (Trinity College, Dublin/Dublin Institute for Advanced Studies) and the *Corpus of Electronic Texts* (University College Cork).[22] At its most basic, Léamh is a web-based tutorial and resource that aims to offer guidance for learning the language and resources for further study. Its primary audiences include students, nonspecialist scholars, and the general Irish-literate public. In essence, it provides a guide to reading different forms and genres, a practical grammar, and a searchable glossary (see Figure 5.1). All of those features are, unavoidably, expressions of certain pedagogical and epistemological theories and methods determined by its participants, and an attempt is made later to offer some brief explication of choices made by means of briefly addressing those three central features.

Unsurprisingly, some of the most crucial questions facing the site's participants relate to organization and usability.[23] Constructing the glossary page, for instance, seemed on the face of it to be a fairly straightforward matter:

Figure 5.1 Léamh.org landing page.

permissions would need to be secured by the major publishers of Early Modern Irish primary materials—the Dublin Institute for Advanced Studies and the Irish Texts Society—after which glossary entries from individual texts could be entered alphabetically, and thus collated to function as a unified, searchable 'dictionary'. In practice, things were more difficult owing to absence of orthographic and classificatory standards. For instance, what to do with a word that was hyphenated in one glossary but spelled contiguously elsewhere? Make two entries and then hyperlink them internally? List them under one heading and provide some notation signaling that the hyphen was optional? More challenging was the matter of listing verbs. Most editors of printed translations have chosen to list these in first-person singular form: for instance, *cuirim*. However, scholars working on the site believed that listing the third-person singular makes more sense as it is a more regular form: thus, in this instance, *cuiridh*. So, how to adjudicate that disagreement across generations of Irish scholars? Might the site serve as a means to help specialists create modern standards of grammatical explication? In this case, the decision was taken to highlight that scholarly conversation by using *cuiridh* on the 'texts' page (about which more later) and yet retain *cuirim* in the glossary so as to remain faithful to the printed edition being digitized.[24]

The grammar page offers a rather different series of conceptual, pedagogical, and theoretical decisions. As with the glossary, this page is built from a base of collating information found in the (typically) brief grammar descriptions and paradigms found at the beginning of various modern, printed editions of Early Modern Irish texts. Unlike the glossary, however, this page's construction—primarily the labor of Wes Hamrick and Eoin Mac Cárthaigh—required more original constructive work, which necessitated making some crucial choices. An illustrative example involved the very definition of the language the participants wished to make available. 'Early Modern Irish' is not a linguistic designation but rather a chronological one; it denotes a period in the development of the language rather than describing the particular features that mark out that chronological iteration as unique. 'Classical Modern Irish' (CMI) describes linguistic particularity, as set out in the so-called Irish Grammatical Tracts produced in the period and as practiced most notably in *dán díreach* court verse. That said, not all writing in Irish over the period 1200–1650 followed the strictures of CMI I, correspondence offering one noteworthy example.[25] Therefore, how to approach the 'teaching' of grammar for a period that accommodated different linguistics practices in different forms? The decision taken was to structure the grammar on the basis of CMI. Doing so would delineate a recognizable system which, once its basic outlines were grasped, would provide users a sense for both how the language worked in the abstract and how it worked more expansively in practice. To take a concrete example of what this meant, the 'Prepositions' section only lists the nineteen examples described in the period grammatical tracts. It does not, however, list prepositions such as *maille ré* and *dochum/chum/cum*, which were commonly used in practice outside the demands of *dán díreach*: for instance, in prose.[26]

Figure 5.2 Texts/Brian Ó Ruairc landing page.

Perhaps the most complex series of choices arose with the site's 'texts' page (see Figure 5.2), wherein users can access selections of texts, verse, and prose, and of different genres. This is the chief feature of the site, where the instructional work is done, and thus the number of choices in organization and theory are the greatest. They involve matters of translation, instruction/pedagogy, scholarly collaboration, and institutional partnership. Taking these in order, three initial decisions regarding translation were crucial to how the site developed. First, all text selections would be accompanied by translations which would be of the 'literal' variety, cleaving as closely to the language of the original as possible. The thinking behind this decision was, as noted earlier, that there is no 'right' translation and that it was up to users to craft a more 'literary' rendering of their own should they wish. Second, except in one case, only a brief selection of any text would be included on the site, the idea being that learners should become comfortable with one section of text and then use that familiarity to tackle the rest of it on their own.[27] In this way, the site aims to encourage learning rather than simply providing the 'service' of translation. Third, to reinforce that goal, the landing page for texts does not reveal the translation. Rather, a user must decide when to click on that tab, the hope being that they do not do so until they have worked up their own attempt. In this way, the 'Translation' tab serves an 'answer key' function to self-guided instruction.

In terms of instructional theory, the site's participants decided that learners would learn best from other learners. Experts, in their comfort with the language and its forms, may overlook the difficulties that learners encounter: what is a challenge to the nonspecialist may not register as out of the ordinary to the specialist. Thus, it was determined to have people with an intermediate-level facility with the language produce the initial breakdown of the text selections, word-by-word and by semantic unit, and the translation. Their analysis would then be shared with one or two specialists who, in the course of correcting the initial draft, would be able to flag areas wherein their colleagues went astray. That data, then, forms the basis of the 'Detailed Guide' tab, offering assistance on reading the present text, and also the 'General Guide' tab, which is intended to offer broader tips for working with other examples of the same genre and/or form. The overarching goal of this method is that users work closely with a variety of texts, and in doing so, they accumulate a body of experience and skills—that is, a working knowledge— that they can then apply to reading other Early Modern Irish texts, a process assisted by returning to the Léamh site so as to consult the grammar and glossary features.

Crucial to the Léamh experiment, then, is intervention in the growing body of work on collaboration in the humanities and on new directions in scholarly communication.[28] This intervention operates on a number of levels. First, as described earlier, all textual analysis is constructed by teams consisting of 'learners': typically students or scholars in fields other than Irish and 'experts' who uniformly are practicing academics specializing in Irish. To repeat, this decision was primarily one about generating maximum outcomes for learners by virtue of having their 'peers' founder upon, and thus identify, tricky bits and then asking experts to follow up to ensure accuracy and to explain the areas of difficulty. It was also a decision driven by desire to promote connection among scholars, working in different disciplines, but who shared an interest in Early Modern Irish sources and their scholarly uses. Thus, for instance, the initial selection finished—*Brian Ó Ruairc, mo rogha leannán*—was initially translated by the present author (history) and Wes Hamrick (literature) serving in the 'learners' spot, then corrected and augmented by Eoin Mac Cárthaigh (Irish) and Emma Nic Chárthaigh (Irish)—a quartet who may otherwise not have had occasion or reason to work together, but once connected might conceivably do so again in other settings.[29] Second, Léamh is an exercise in institutional collaboration wherein the majority of work is done virtually. Many digital humanities projects are hosted and controlled by one institution. They may have external sponsors, but the work is largely handled in-house, with the credit consequently redounding to the 'home' institution. Léamh, however, was consciously constructed to exist across institutions—many make it happen, all can claim credit as suits their needs. The University of Connecticut acts as data host, and the University of Notre Dame was a crucial early sponsor. Thus, their logos appear in the site's footer. But neither institution 'owns' the project, and indeed it would not exist were it not for the support of those scholars serving on its Advisory Board. More specifically, the text selections and grammar page only exist thanks to permissions granted by partnering institutions and to the efforts of external collaborators. Those scholars are credited for their work, and encouraged to make use of it in ways that fit their or their institution's professional needs.[30] A case in point is the biographical information found on the 'People' page: it is provided by *Ainm.ie*, a joint project of Dublin City University's *Fiontar & Scoil na Gaeilge* and the publisher *Cló Iar-Chonnacht*, both of whom are acknowledged on that page and in the site's running footer. As a general principal, the site promotes active partnership with publishers and other digital projects and makes effort to highlight the work of others. For instance, all of the text selections and the vast majority of the glossary entries, to date, are taken from published volumes, allowed through the generosity and permission of the Irish Texts Society and the Dublin Institute for Advanced Studies. Thus, on the site there is repeated highlighting of the source books, with links directly to the publisher's general webpage and to the book's individual purchase page. Léamh seeks not only to promote further research in Early Modern Irish across disciplines but, in doing so, to help generate further demand for printed editions—a symbiotic relationship its participants believe is healthy for early modern Irish studies, broadly construed.

That is all well and good in theory, but would having more Irish in the scholarly mix make much difference to our understanding of the early modern period? As discussed earlier, one might reasonably grant that at a philosophical level, it is a good thing to have a greater vernacular presence in the scholarship and yet wonder if the payoff for learning would justify the effort. To address that question, it was decided to launch the site by hosting a conference at which a particularly resonant historical event, relevant to those studying across disciplines, could be explored through appeal to Celtic and English sources. The period chosen was 1630–60, the decades of the so-called revolution in Ireland and Britain, over which a tremendous amount of ink has been spilled, and continues to do so, and yet for which there is very little in the way of consideration of Celtic sources—be they Irish, Scottish Gaelic, Welsh, or Cornish—in the interdisciplinary secondary literature. Dubbed 'Re-reading the Revolution: a conference launching Léamh.org', this gathering took the launch of an Irish-language instructional site as opportunity to broaden the scope of inquiry to include the islands' other Celtic vernaculars.[31] Moreover, the instructional approach that informs Léamh's analysis of texts also informed the conference structure. Both Celticists and those working in other disciplines were brought to the table, the idea being that some might know the broader history and historiography but not the vernacular sources, and some might be close to the vernacular sources but less confident about the larger context, and that conversation across areas of expertise would produce unexpected new questions and connections. Keeping with the site's collaborative ethos, the event opened with a crowd-sourcing exercise in translation—dubbed 'One day, one text'—meant to welcome learners and experts alike. The organizers chose a poem to excerpt for the site and invited people to join in a collective translation exercise the day before the conference. In keeping with the broad Celtic approach, the poem chosen, Cathal Mac Muireadhaigh's address to Domhnall Gorm Óg Mac Domhnaill Shléite (c. 1640), *Eireóchthar fós le cloinn gColla*, was one written in Scotland but in the high literary style common across that realm and Ireland.[32] Interested parties were given a quatrain or two to translate in the weeks beforehand, and asked on the day to lead others through their translation and process. The group then worked toward some consensus with an eye to placing the results on the

Léamh site (which will be forthcoming). The conference overall, then, was a practical exercise in the 'new direction' suggested here: introduction to the language for those with interest but limited knowledge or exposure, collaborative generation of new scholarly knowledge, multimodal 'publication' of results, and interdisciplinary network building. A provocative and productive event, 'Re-reading the Revolution' is now planned for further conference settings, with findings to appear both on the Léamh site and in print.

Having just attempted to make a positive case for greater interdisciplinary engagement with Early Modern Irish and its sources, I wish to close by offering a negative argument. That is to say, in addition to asking what we *gain* from promoting the language, what do we *lose* by doing so? I suggest that we stand to lose quite a bit, but that this would amount to addition by subtraction. On a simple reputational point, the field would shed the dubious character of being (perhaps) unique as a nation-focused one that largely shuns vernacular sources. From a disciplinary perspective, the typically firm lines that divide early modern historians, literary scholars, and language specialists would soften considerably, which would likely result in greater collaboration among subfields, participation across specialist conferences, shared supervision of graduate students and the like—precisely the sort of community Léamh and its participants attempt to model and promote. Most importantly, normalization of Early Modern Irish would do much to erase the phenomenon noted at this chapter's beginning, whereby we situate Ireland among the emergent nations of Western Europe while simultaneously perpetuating an ancient trope of its people's otherness, demonstrated by their seemingly unlearnable, alien tongue. In doing so, we at once draw connections to the past, through the birth of the nation narrative, and distance ourselves from it by approaching it almost exclusively through the colonial archive. This is particularly perplexing given that the central problematic in the field, across disciplines, assumes some form of critique of imperialism and celebration of self-determination. Attempting to do so without Irish, however, strikes me less as example of postcolonial critique than of colonial condition: we are hardly going to think ourselves outside of the linguistic, and thus mental/political/social/cultural, matrix constructed by the colonizer by engaging English texts through English. Surely, it represents a limiting way to explore a Gaelic-majority early modern Irish culture and politics, and the range of motivations and mentalities of individuals and groups, and we should not lament its passing.[33]

In a way, then, we might think of the immediate challenge to new directions in early modern Irish studies to be one of methodology rather than theory.[34] The sociologist Theda Skocpol offers a definition particularly useful for the present purpose, stating that methodology 'is understood not as a set of neutral techniques, but as the interrelations of substantive problems, sources of evidence, and larger assumptions about society, history, and the purposes of scholarship'.[35] I think it is safe to say, as just done earlier, that the 'larger assumptions about society, history, and the purposes of scholarship' governing study of the Irish past are concerned, at some basic level, with matters of political self-determination, anti-imperialism and, increasingly in recent decades, social justice. Consequently, the dominant 'substantive problems' focus on how to situate the Irish story in longer, and broader, narratives of imperial expansion and the destruction of indigenous communities and cultures. The industry standard 'sources of evidence' could, however, stand for an upgrade befitting those 'assumptions' and 'problems'. We collectively are in a position to make that happen, to redefine the archive so as to make early modern Irish studies more Irish. To that end, more robust and democratized teaching, learning, and researching in Early Modern Irish qualifies as a new direction for the field, and an imperative one at that. Undoubtedly, doing so comes with significant challenges, both individually and collectively, but, to return to the opening analogy of lunar travel as a benchmark for achievement, we should not allow ourselves to believe them to be of Apollo 11-levels of difficulty. Language acquisition is never easy, but with new technologies, approaches, collaborations, and resources—Léamh being but one of many—engaging with Irish has, arguably, never been easier in the modern age. And, to paraphrase someone who actually *did* journey to the moon, while the learning of Early Modern Irish may be but one small step for a scholar, it is one giant leap for scholarship.

Notes

1 I wish to thank Wes Hamrick for comments on earlier drafts of this chapter.
2 Arminta Wallace, 'Oldest Map of Ireland Puts us on the Edge of the World'. *The Irish Times*, 11 June 2018. www.irishtimes.com/life-and-style/homes-and-property/fine-art-antiques/oldest-map-of-ireland-puts-us-on-the-edge-of-the-world-1.3521408#.Wx4TKy632hQ.facebook. Italics mine.
3 I capitalize 'Early Modern Irish' simply for ease of reading, i.e. to make clear to the reader when I am discussing matters linguistic and when I am using the general historical descriptor 'early modern Irish'.
4 Éanna Ó Caollaí, 'Exhibition Offers Rare Glimpse of Early Medieval Ireland'. *The Irish Times*, 18 May 2018. This story was subsequently picked up, fittingly enough, by *The World News*.
5 I am indebted to Greg Semenza for his generosity in talking through the ideas that became this paragraph and, indeed, the eventual format of this chapter.
6 Marc Caball, 'Language, Print and Literature in Irish, 1550–1630', in Jane Ohlmeyer (ed.), *The Cambridge History of Ireland*, vol. II (Cambridge: Cambridge University Press, 2018), pp. 411–33; Bernadette Cunningham, 'Language, Print and Literature in Irish, 1630–1730', in ibid., pp. 434–57.
7 To take but two now-classic examples, see Breandán Ó Buachalla, *Aisling Ghéar: na Stíobhartaigh agus an t-Aos Léinn 1603–1788* (Baile Átha Cliath: An Clóchomhar, 1996); and Mícheál Mac Craith, *Lorg na hIasachta ar na Dánta Grá* (Baile Átha Cliath: An Clóchomhar, 1989).
8 See Sarah McKibben's succinct discussion of Irish sources and survival rates elsewhere in this volume.

9   Sean Mac Áirt (ed.), *Leabhar Branach: The Book of the O'Byrnes* (Dublin: Dublin Institute for Advanced Studies, 1944); Tadhg Ó Donnchadha (ed.), *Leabhar Cloinne Aodha Buidhe* (Baile Átha Cliath: Coimisiún Lámhscríbhinní na hÉireann, 1931); Osborn Bergin (ed.), *Trí Bior-ghaoithe an Bháis* (Dublin: Dublin Institute for Advanced Studies, 1931; reprint, 1992).

10 See, however, Damian McManus and Eoghan Ó Raghallaigh (eds.), *A Bardic Miscellany* (Dublin: The Department of Irish, Trinity College, Dublin, 2010), which consists of transcriptions of 500 period poems (without translation).

11 Eleanot Knott (ed. and trans.), *The Bardic Poems of Tadhg Dall Ó hUiginn (1550–1591)*, 2 vols. (London: Irish Texts Society, 1922/26).

12 For a recent assessment of Knott's extraordinary achievements and influence, see Pádraigín Riggs (ed.), *Tadhg Dall Ó hUiginn: His Historical and Literary Context* (London: Irish Texts Society, 2010).

13 I say 'most' scholars in other fields as there are obvious exceptions, notably the historians Katherine Simms, Marc Caball, and Mícheál Hoyne.

14 Good starting points for the larger literature include Jeremy Munday, *Introducing Translation Studies*, 4th edn. (New York: Routledge, 2016), and Lawrence Venuti, 'Genealogies of Translation Theory: Jerome', *Boundary 2* (37/3) (2010), 5–28. I wish to thank my colleagues Peter Constantine and Matthew Shelton for these references and guidance on this subject.

15 Although it must be said that the use of Latin in Irish historical scholarship is very limited. As in the case argued here regarding use of Irish sources, it would be of immense benefit to early modern Irish studies if more scholars were trained in Latin and used it in their research. Two prominent examples of new directions opened up through engagement with Latin sources are Jason Harris and Keith Sidwell (eds.) *Making Ireland Roman: Irish Neo-Latin Writers and the Republic of Letters* (Cork: Cork University Press, 2009) and Ian Campbell, *Renaissance Humanism and Ethnicity Before Race: The Irish and the English the Seventeenth Century* (Manchester: Manchester University Press, 2013).

16 On the history of the Irish language generally, see Kim McCone, Damian McManus, Cathal Ó Háinle, Nicholas Williams, and Liam Breatnach (eds.), *Stair na Gaeilge: in Ómós do Pádraig Ó Fiannachta* (Baile Átha Cliath: Roinn na Sean-Ghaeilge, Coláiste Phádraig, 1994); and Aidan Doyle, *A History of the Irish Language: From the Norman Invasion to Independence* (Oxford: Oxford University Press, 2015). On bilingualism see Vincent Carey, 'Neither Good English nor Good Irish: Bilingualism and Identity Formation in Sixteenth-Century Ireland', in Hiram Morgan (ed.) *Political Ideology in Ireland, 1541–1641* (Dublin: Four Courts Press, 1999), pp. 127–57.

17 A crucial opportunity is made available through the Dublin Institute for Advanced Studies' School of Celtic studies 'Summer School' in Irish and Welsh. Attendance at those sessions, however, requires a certain familiarity with the language. One objective of Léamh is to prepare interested parties, internationally, to take advantage of the Summer School and any similar opportunities.

18 Eleanor Knott's short primer on bardic poetry is brilliant and indispensable, but it operates at a very high level and offers no translations, making it most suitable for intermediate and advanced learners. Knott, *An Introduction to Irish Syllabic Poetry of the Period 1200–1600* (Dublin: Dublin Institute for Advanced Studies, 1957).

19 Dinneen's dictionary and the *Dictionary of the Irish Language* are now both available online, at https://celt.ucc.ie//Dinneen1.pdf and www.dil.ie.

20 One could consult the so-called Irish Grammatical Tracts, period guides to what we now refer to as Classical Modern Irish. But these were written for practitioners and are extremely sophisticated texts and thus not suitable as learning tools for the beginner. See Eoin Mac Cárthaigh, *The Art of Bardic Poetry: A New Edition of*

Irish Grammatical Tracts I (Dundalk, Ireland: Dublin Institute for Advanced Studies, 2014).

21 Damian McManus, 'Nua-Ghaeilge Chlasaiceach', in McCone et al. (eds.), *Stair na Gaeilge* (Maigh Nuad: Roinn na Sean-Ghaeilge, Coláiste Phádraig, 1994), pp. 335–445.

22 https://bardic.celt.dias.ie; https://celt.ucc.ie//. These are but two examples. See Sarah McKibben's article in this volume for a more comprehensive overview of the landscape of Irish-focused digital resources.

23 This chapter focuses primarily on the content-side questions of the site's development. The technical and organization requirements are equally varied and fascinating, and offer opportunities for innovative work and experimentation by those in very different areas of expertise. A case in point is the two-toned hover box feature in the texts selections, designed by Andrew Bacon and assisted in conceptualization by Tom Scheinfeldt, the latter of whom directs the technical side of Léamh.

24 Particular credit must be paid to Hilary Bogert-Winkler who tackled with great aplomb and good humor both the pure grunt labor of data entry and the conceptual/ordering questions this paragraph describes.

25 For an example of poetry which lies outside the strict boundaries of CMI and demonstrates aspects of the broader possibilities of EMI, see the close analysis and description of the love poem 'Mór mhilleas an mheanma bhaoth: Dán Grádha 63' (*c.* 1700) by Síle Ní Mhurchú and Mícheál Hoyne: http://léamh.org/texts/dan-gradha-63/.

26 I wish to thank Beatrix Faerber for raising this matter. The site will, in time, include description and discussion of these 'non-classical' prepositions. An interesting exception is in Céitinn's *Trí Baor-Ghaoithe an Bháis*, in which the editor notes the curious exclusion of 'dochum/chum/cum' in spite of the fact that the genre does not require doing so. See Bergin (ed.), *Trí Baor-Ghaoithe an Bháis*, p. xiv.

27 The one exception to this at present is the poem 'Brian Ó Rourke mo rogha leannán', which is only three quatrains long in its entirety.

28 As an exercise in collaborative knowledge production and multimodal dissemination, Léamh has recently teamed with Greenhouse Studios—a Mellon Foundation-funded digital design studio housed at the University of Connecticut—as one of its 'cohort-b' projects: https://greenhousestudios.uconn.edu/projects/leamh/.

29 Further collaboration has indeed occurred. Emma Nic Chárthaigh and Brendan Kane participated in the 'Tudor Ireland and Renaissance Court Society' conference at the Royal Irish Academy (3–4 November 2016), with essays in production; Eoin Mac Cárthaigh, Wes Hamrick, and Kane took part in the 'Re-reading the Revolution' conference held at University of Connecticut (3–5 October 2017).

30 As two cases in point of other greater institutional 'ownership' and direction of the site, Deirdre Nic Chárthaigh of Trinity College, Dublin, has recently joined both the Advisory Board and the content-side 'working group', which handles the day-to-day governance of the site. Dr. Liam Ó hAisibéil of the National University of Ireland, Galway, has worked with an undergraduate class in producing new texts selections for the website.

31 The spur for the conference, in fact, came from Jerry Hunter's 2016 J.V. Kelleher Lecture at the Harvard University, 'The Red Sword, the Sickle and the Author's Revenge: Welsh Literature and Conflict in the Seventeenth Century', which explored Welsh and English commentaries on the wars of the 1640s and their contexts. The essay is now available in Michaela Jacques, Katherine Leach, Joseph Shack, and Joe Wolf (eds.), *Proceedings of the Harvard Celtic Colloquium, 36: 2016* (Cambridge, MA: Harvard University Press, 2018). 'Re-Reading the Revolution', then, was jointly organized by Hunter, Catherine McKenna and the present author—thus keeping with the collaborative ethos of the website being launched.

32 Special thanks to Wilson McLeod for suggesting the poem, supplying the text, and graciously agreeing to oversee the process of publishing the finished product on the website.

33 The translation of Irish texts into English has, of course, had important effect of the development of the modern state and society—for both good and ill. See Maria Tymoczko, 'Translation and Political Engagement', *The Translator* 6 (1) (2000), 23–47. Such translations seemingly have not, however, had the effect over time of increasing the numbers of those learning to read the originals. My thanks to Peter Constantine for this reference.

34 This is not to say that theory is not important or is unnecessary or unwelcome. For sophisticated examples and discussion of the intersection of theory and bardic material, see the contributions of Sarah McKibben and Peter McQuillan in the present volume.

35 Theda Skocpol (ed.), *Vision & Method in Historical Sociology*, 1st edn. (Cambridge: Cambridge University Press, 1984), p. x.

6 Bardic close reading

Sarah E. McKibben

This essay makes a case for close reading of bardic professional praise poetry as an exciting new direction for the study of early modern Ireland in all its artistic, cultural, and sociopolitical complexity.[1] By performing historicized, sociopolitically contextualized, literary close reading of late sixteenth and early seventeenth-century works, we grasp bardic poetry's primary function of praise and counsel, but also gain insight into elite preoccupations and perspectives as well as bardic training, norms, and patronly relations at a time of considerable strain. During our period, the conditions under which poets wrote were rapidly changing, as patrons and patronage became scarcer due to both legislation against the bardic institution and the violently unsettled conditions of the time, with professional poets' increasing precarity and resulting modes of accommodation particularly vivid from the 1560s onward. The intrinsic interest of this material as well as the richer portrait of the society and people it offers suggest that this multifaceted yet underanalyzed literature not only deserves our attention but belongs on the reading list of every scholar and student of early modern Ireland.[2]

To make this case, this essay will give an overview of the poetry and scholarly resources treating it, discuss the poetry's context and function, briefly outline some of the challenges of literary-critical reading as opposed to narrowly historicist, evidentiary use of the material, before closing with a condensed reading of a poem by Domhnall Mac Dáire that illustrates how bardic poems' meanings may ramify under scrutiny, appearing other than superficial reading would have them be. Bardic poems emerge as far more nuanced, witty, engaging, and astute than critics have grasped, thus offering a new set of insights about those who created and consumed them. This underscores the necessity that we sharpen our game to grapple with this subtle and pointed artistic *and* political genre.

Bardic poetry, comprising encomiastic, religious, didactic, genealogical, or historical/narrative verse, was composed by highly trained, hereditary, male literati for around 450 years.[3] Praise poetry, the most extensive extant subgenre, acclaimed and advised elite patrons across Gaelic and gaelicized Ireland and Scotland—or threatened them with satire if they failed to maintain noble norms of comportment.[4] Its primary venue was that of live, public performance: encomiastic verse was declaimed, chanted, or sung at gatherings such as feasts by trained reciters, traditionally accompanied by harps. This means that much bardic poetry was only 'recorded' by its immediate audience, the majority of it dying 'on the lips of the reciter', though the total number of poems composed must have been vast since they marked important occasions for the leaders of the many lordships around the country for centuries.[5] Only select works—particularly works in the most rigorous meters of *dán díreach* ('strict' or 'straight' verse) addressed to great families by master poets—were recorded in a manuscript *duanaire* (pl. *duanairí*) or 'poem-book', chiefly as 'a type of currency and an object of beauty'.[6]

The extant corpus consists of about 2,000 poems, more than half of which date from the early modern period.[7] Bardic poetry provides one of the few substantial sources addressing contemporaneous events from the native Irish point of view. In the absence of the sort of administrative records common elsewhere, we must turn to bardic poetry to learn about native lordships. Given the disparity between the voluminous record-keeping, self-justifications, and jockeying by and under the Tudor-Stuart state and the paucity of recorded material from Irish lordships—not to mention traditions of top-down, statist historiography—counterweights to Anglocentric history have been relatively few. Bardic poetry is not, of course, history or fact. It is aesthetically sophisticated, partisan political work. Nonetheless, it bespeaks the concerns of native lords even as it largely says what they wanted to hear and puts the best gloss on their achievements and aspirations—provided they did not earn warning or critique for straying from noble norms.[8] Standardized poetic language gives few clues as to the date of composition, but because a poem was written to order for a particular patron (or patrons) at or after his inauguration and had to incorporate his name, spouse, and genealogy into the complex meter, the patron and dating (sometimes to the year) are at once ascertainable and hard to counterfeit.[9] Poems have accordingly been mined effectively by historians for evidence of political developments in and between lordships.[10]

Resources for the study of this compelling practice have expanded markedly of late. It is still the case that there are relatively few book-length editions of the complete works of individual bardic poets or collections of poems, though some new studies are forthcoming. Most scholarly publication of bardic poetry occurs in journal articles devoted to single poems, providing manuscript history, historical contextualization, and extensive philological commentary; production of such work has continued steadily. Before the advent of electronic journal access, acquiring these could be laborious. Yet a series of initiatives has transformed the scholarly landscape by making a wealth of catalogued texts, images, and information available in print and online. University College Cork's CELT (Corpus of Electronic Texts) project (celt.ucc.ie), Ireland's longest-running humanities computing project, has published hundreds of texts in a range of fields, languages, and periods, including bardic poetry, online. Katharine Simms's Bardic Poetry Database (bardic.celt.dias.ie), also made available by the School of Celtic Studies, Dublin Institute for Advanced Study, has long offered an essential resource cataloguing the bardic corpus (search page shown in the following) based on her original labor (Figure 6.1).[11]

As can be seen from the search page, the database uses the following fields: the poem's first line (= title), its class or genre, the names and surnames of poet and patron, period (expressed as the beginning, middle, or ending

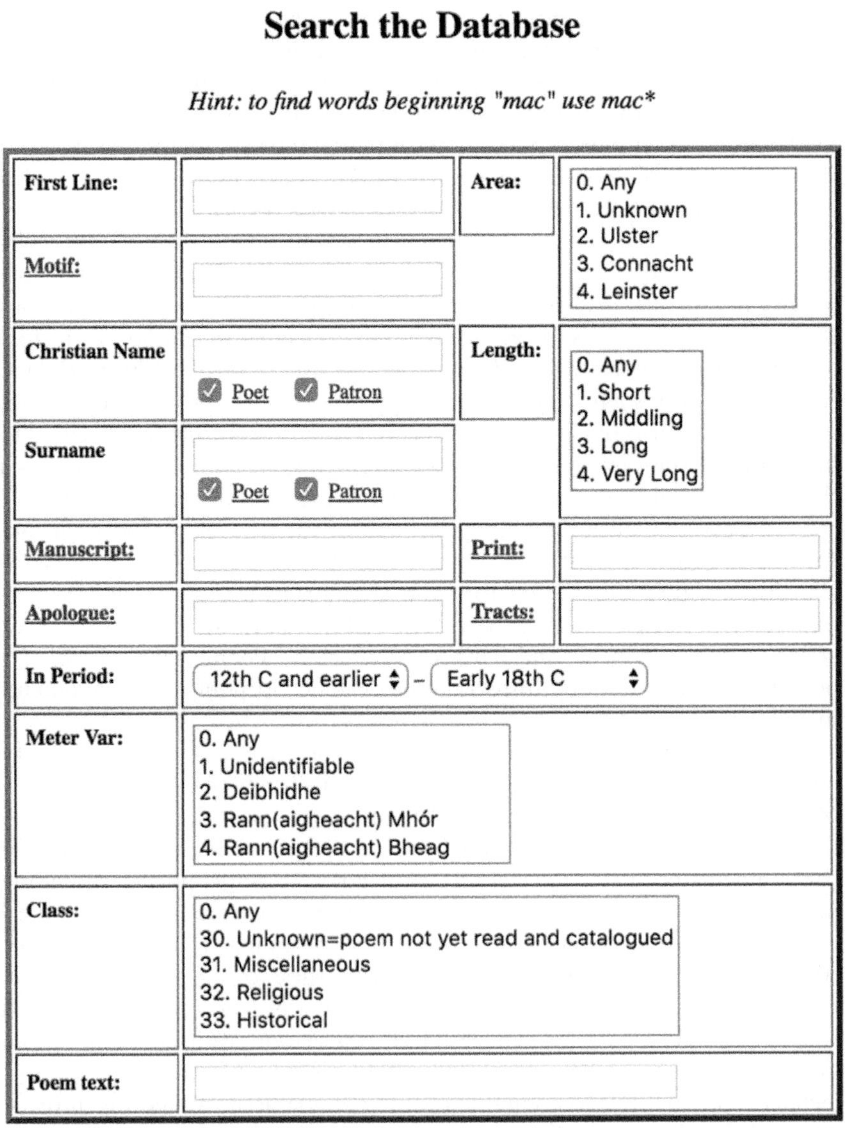

Search the Database

Hint: to find words beginning "mac" use mac*

First Line:		Area:	0. Any
			1. Unknown
			2. Ulster
Motif:			3. Connacht
			4. Leinster
Christian Name		Length:	
	☑ Poet ☑ Patron		0. Any
			1. Short
			2. Middling
Surname			3. Long
	☑ Poet ☑ Patron		4. Very Long
Manuscript:		Print:	
Apologue:		Tracts:	

In Period:	12th C and earlier ↕ – Early 18th C ↕

Meter Var:	0. Any
	1. Unidentifiable
	2. Deibhidhe
	3. Rann(aigheacht) Mhór
	4. Rann(aigheacht) Bheag

Class:	0. Any
	30. Unknown=poem not yet read and catalogued
	31. Miscellaneous
	32. Religious
	33. Historical

Poem text:	

Figure 6.1 Bardic poetry database.

third of the century in which it is believed to have been composed), meter, province/region, length, the five earliest manuscripts in which it is found, print edition (if extant), and an assessment of the degree of certainty of the names and date. In addition, the database lists and classifies up to two of 927 possible apologues the poem might contain, based on Liam P. Ó Caithnia's *Apalóga na bhfilí 1200–1650* (Dublin 1984). Ten fields identify motifs, themes, or rhetorical devices from 985 potential categories. Recently, the database has been updated and expanded by Mícheál Hoyne at the School of Celtic Studies, Dublin Institute of Advanced Studies. Under the direction of Damian McManus, the Department of Irish, Trinity College, Dublin, assembled a full electronic corpus of bardic poetry, generously made available to scholars in a single, 4,700-word, searchable MS Word document. In 2010, McManus and coeditor Eoghan Ó Raghallaigh published a weighty volume of heretofore unpublished poems, *A Bardic Miscellany: Five Hundred Bardic Poems from Manuscripts in Irish and British Libraries*, to prompt the creation of full editions of this rich store.[12] In addition to these enormous contributions, McManus's Bardic Poetry Project at Trinity College Dublin began adding the electronic corpus to the Bardic Database in April 2017, using extant editions or, where poems were unedited, transcripts by Eoghan Ó Raghallaigh, Catherine Saunders, Muiris Ó Raghallaigh, and Eoin Mac Cárthaigh so that the entries for a given poem include the poem's full text, a link to a downloadable PDF, and the source of the edition, just below the database fields. Updates include additional details of new editions, metrical classifications, a note as to whether the poem is cited in metrical tracts, and notice of the existence of further manuscript copies, with plans to append an English translation to each entry as well.

Other key resources include the School of Celtic Studies, Dublin Institute for Advanced Study's Irish Script On Screen / Meamram Páipéar Ríomhaire project (www.isos.dias.ie), founded by Pádraig A. Macháin, which provides high-definition images of Irish manuscripts online, with higher-definition images available to scholars upon registration. The online Dictionary of the Irish Language (dil.ie) is an electronic dictionary of the medieval Irish language based on the Royal Irish Academy's multivolume *Dictionary of the Irish Language*, chiefly based on Old and Middle Irish materials from the period c. 700–c. 1700. In fall 2017, The Royal Irish Academy also launched the Historical Corpus of the Irish Language 1600–1926 (online at http://corpas.ria.ie/), which will be the basis of the Foclóir Stairiúil na Gaeilge / Historical Dictionary of the Irish Language. The digital humanities project MACMORRIS (Modeling Archives and Connections: A Map of Research into Renaissance Ireland in the Sixteenth Century) in development by Patricia Palmer, David Baker, and Willy Maley, promises a deep, comparative investigation into literary production in all languages in sixteenth-century Ireland.[13] A newer resource, founded by Brendan Kane at the University of Connecticut, is the collaborative online site, Léamh: Learn Early Modern Irish (léamh.org), which has begun to offer explicated translations of a wide range of early modern texts and genres, a grammar with basic paradigms and descriptive summaries, and a searchable reference glossary, with plans to offer tutelage in reading manuscripts through a stand-alone guide to paleography in future. Editors involved with the Bardic Poetry Project are also at work on a textbook for third-level students.

Uniquely valuable, bardic poems were 'fashionable portraits in verse'[14] that functioned for generations as 'an expensive prestige purchase' with key sociopolitical functions.[15] Poems produced for patronage enacted a long-standing, largely homosocial exchange understood to be mutually beneficial and essential to the maintenance of the social hierarchy.[16] The professional poet (or *file*, not the lower-ranking *bard* for whom the genre is misleadingly named) proclaimed that, 'in exchange for fleeting wealth' (handsome patronage in tax-free land, livestock, and gear), he offered 'immortal fame (*clú, bladh, ainm, tairm*)', that is, 'the poet's phrases, fashioned and fixed in strict verse and recorded in books which [would] long outlive poet and patron alike'.[17] Within the competitive system of lordly succession, bardic poetry affirmed authority won by force through artistic appeals to supposedly longstanding tradition. Absent primogeniture, recorded contracts, fixed land boundaries or legal title, it was bardic poetry that publicly legitimated a nobleman's lordly authority (or aspirations), affirmed his right to leadership, and confirmed his inherited standing, thus enmeshing him in a web of mutual obligations. (For this reason, the spread of English legal structures spelled the end of the bardic institution as originally constituted, as Marc Caball notes, though poets themselves were also targeted as inciters of rebellion and as dissident cultural critics.[18])

The resulting compositions were highly conventionalized, formal poetry—what an early critic called 'very peculiar and mechanical',[19] and another termed 'a fine, useful, homogenized product'.[20] They employed an artificial literary language, codified in the second half of the twelfth century and based on the language of the time, explicated in minute detail in the bardic grammatical and syntactical tracts probably composed for pedagogical use in the bardic schools run by leading poetic families across Ireland.[21] Classical Modern Irish, as it is known, is at once archaic and rich in permissible dialect and verbal forms, evoking the authority of hoary tradition while facilitating the satisfaction of demanding metrical rules.[22] Prescribed syllabic meters require chiseled quatrains of lines of a fixed syllable count per line (such as seven or eight) with an end-word of a defined syllabic length, ornamented with end-rhyme, internal rhyme, and *aicill* (end-to-internal) rhyme of (only) stressed words, as well as *uaim* (a form of alliteration) between at least one pair of stressed words, among other mandatory features, depending upon the meter.[23] Stanzas function as units of meaning, required to make sense in and of themselves. As a result, whereas 'every quatrain is beautifully wrought and polished ... the connection between them is less strict' than today's readers might expect, the poem evincing 'a certain formlessness', according to Greene, who suggests it may result from its oral composition and the need for memorization.[24] On this question, Gillies remarks that while the poets, 'by taking the rigidly articulated syllabic quatrain as their medium' cut 'themselves off from the whole dimensions of fervour, ecstasy and celebration', they may have sought precisely 'that dampening or braking effect ... to impart solemnity and *gravitas*, or perhaps just to be different'.[25]

Working within strict metrical constraints, poems had to rehearse the noble patron's superiority of body and character, recite his illustrious genealogy, amplify his achievements, affirm his status, legitimate his aims, and capture his circumstances with an elegant conceit accompanied by a well-chosen apologue (or moralizing story) likening the patron to a hero of Irish saga or Classical tradition. Yet the poet had to do all this plausibly and gracefully. Bardic praise was understood to invoke 'poets' truth, *fir filidh*' to legitimate 'the patron's right to rule', avoiding exaggerated 'false praise' bearing 'no relation to the real qualities of the patron', which would both prompt divine retribution and devalue the poet's 'status, and potentially his ability to demand a high price for his endorsement of a magnate's rule'.[26] At the same time, '[p]art of the excellence' of the best such works 'consisted in fulfilling the requirements of the most difficult metres while giving an impression of ease and naturalness', appearing at once utterly traditional and fresh.[27]

While fulfilling their obligations to their patrons, poets also adroitly advocated for themselves. They sought to gain ongoing patronage and protection, defend the bardic institution and patronal structure, and, ideally, win the highest professional poetic rank, that of *ollamh flatha* or chief's poet, the designated poet to a particular lord. This coveted, contractual relationship, often expressed in terms of warmest intimacy and affection, requiring the exchange of ongoing patronage for an annual poem (plus additional works for additional gifts), would last as long as both were amenable, sometimes for the rest of their lives, though poets and patrons did fall out or get supplanted by rivals.[28] A poet's—even a chief's poet's—services were not tendered to one lord exclusively, however; taking advantage of his right of free travel across borders, a poet would compose for others while serving as an ambassador for his lord, when seeking a new patron, or while making regular poetic circuits, though he might append a quatrain dedicated to his main patron to works composed for others.[29] Far from being a supplicant or subordinate, the poet was a high-status professional who offered a mutually beneficial exchange to those he deemed worthy of something precious and unique.[30]

Bardic poetry was thus, for most of its existence, the confident expression of those in power, and was central to that power, the poet 'acting as an instrument of social control and public relations' though 'he reserved the right to bite the hand that fed him'.[31] Consequently, the work was extremely conservative in reiterating and reifying tradition as such through phrasing and imagery intended to please and to affirm. As 'the paid propagandists of the existing order of things', poets were highly attuned to political nuance, avoiding what might give insult, suggest individual or collective dishonor, or even cause awkwardness should they turn to address a patron's rival in a subsequent work.[32] 'Today's enemy might be tomorrow's friend, so that, while there are exceptions, poets praised one man in such generalised terms that they could not thereby incur the disfavour of another'.[33] Unsurprisingly, polished monuments to the political *status quo* deployed a familiar store of concepts, images, and phrases, drawing upon a common store of encomiastic epithets—terming the patron a (heroic) salmon, hawk, or simply branch of his region, or river, or ancestral line, for example.[34] Such epithets were fitted to the metrical demands, 'reflecting the subject's descent, the extent of his power, or some element in his personal or family history'.[35] All subjects are praised, emphatically and repeatedly, for their hospitality and generosity—to encourage more of the same. The male subject of a praise poem is almost unfailingly represented as a paragon of masculine attractiveness, compelling other men's wives to lust or adultery.[36] He exemplifies the noble ideal of manhood in his martial prowess, learning, and judgment:

> The subject is of impeccable ancestry and, unless some measure of re-
> proach is intended, is unfailingly generous. The weather, the harvest, the
> fruits all respond to the justice of his rule. He deserves that his power
> should spread outside his patrimony. His enemies fear him; his courage
> in battle is unparalleled; if he were to get his just deserts he would gain
> possession of Tara and rule all Ireland.
>
> (Carney 1987: 695)

Women are also addressed with high-flown praise of their beauty, elegance, generosity, good humor, mercy, and skill at housekeeping and embroidery.[37] All of this was done at considerable length, thirty quatrains constituting a medium-length poem, a full-blown panegyric extending to seventy or eighty stanzas or more.

If this poetry is so conventional, constrained, and unindividualized—not to mention functional, formulaic, and extraordinarily *long*—why should you—or how can you—subject it to close reading? That is, if the words are in part pre-given, if the poet is so restricted in what he can say and how he can say it, if he does not express powerful, individual emotion, if he (merely) confirms the *status quo* and says what his patron wants to hear, why close read the work? Close reading—most simply defined as a slow exfoliation of individual words, phrases, images, figures of speech, lines, and/or stanzas illustrating interplay of form and meaning—has usually been dedicated to the exposition of distinctively *literary* (and often conveniently compact) texts. That is, close reading has tended to address and celebrate works characterized by individual expression, unique or startling uses of language (often fore-grounding language itself), fictionality, and purely or chiefly aesthetic aims. Hence, in his guide to literary criticism, Jonathan Culler remarks that 'the fact that [a decontextualized] sentence has no obvious practical import is what mainly creates the possibility that it might be literature'.[38] Decontextualized language enables 'readers [to] attend to potential complexities and look for implicit meanings, without assuming, say, that the utterance is telling them to do something'.[39]

But bardic poetry is almost always telling its audience to do something. Its dedication to extraliterary purpose (or, properly, purposes) cannot be evaded, and whatever other desires it might be said to satisfy, that professional purpose defines its generic expression and provides an essential part of its meaning. By the post-Kantian and prototypically Romantic aesthetic measures rehearsed by Culler, including 'the separation from practical contexts of utterance' and 'the fictional relation to the world',[40] bardic poetry is not literature. Indeed, critics have often critiqued bardic poetry for the failure to be sufficiently literary, with 'admiration—for the poets' technical virtuosity' giving way to castigation of 'classical bardic verse variously for being insincere, frigid, artificial, unoriginal, unnecessarily obscure, generally dead, and a massive squandering of talent'.[41]

Yet bardic poetry as highly wrought language that distinguishes itself from other uses, 'language in which the various elements and components of the text are brought into a complex relation'[42] as highly sophisticated rhetorical performance—is indeed literature. And bardic poetry promises to yield satisfying insight when its craft *and* craftiness are analyzed, when we 'look for and exploit relations between form and meaning or theme and grammar and, attempting to understand the contribution each element makes to the effect of the whole, find integration, harmony, tension, or dissonance'.[43] Recall that bardic poetry is hardly alone in being deployed toward extraliterary, functional ends, for early modern Western European literature as a whole overwhelmingly shares this transactional quality and many early modern texts do not or cannot prioritize authorial self-expression.

This returns us to the question of how to close read texts that are functional, conventional, and formulaic, in which numerous images and turns of phrase appear interchangeable (and indeed recur repeatedly both within individual texts and across the corpus), and in which metrical constraints weigh heavily upon the line. Certainly, the critic must attend to the political motives and ends of bardic poetry, which have been historians' primary, and highly illuminating, focus. The close reader will need to learn the vocabulary and nuance of epithets and common turns of phrase to grasp their meaning and implications without misreading them as unique or strange, while remaining alive to the ways that a poet—especially a master-poet—may artfully recast the familiar, such as by elaborating the image or its ornamentation. We may thus grasp the norms of the genre, consider the sociopolitical and cultural contexts with which it is so concerned, discern its constraints and possibilities, preoccupations and characteristics, and find much to interpret in this erudite, complex art. By employing Richard Strier's 'indexical close reading',[44] which connects a richly and variously decoded text to a broadly conceived context, we can rectify the longstanding omission of literary critical treatments of this genre.

The need for this new direction is urgent. Though we depend upon the work of editors, we cannot wait for the completion of full editions of all extant poems—a project that will take many years' painstaking labor—as some Celticists have implied we should, despite others' calls for more attention to bardic texts as literature.[45] Nor can we await scholarly consensus about all the norms, background, and frameworks needed for our work, even concerning such seemingly fundamental questions as, say, the nature of patronage,[46] poetic recitation/performance, or poets' own evaluation of their practice. For the story of early modern Ireland is being rewritten *now*, and these poems and poets need to be part of that complicated, polyvocal, multidimensional tale—not as a fading archaism but as central players. It is not enough for scholars of early modern Ireland to merely gesture at inclusion while remaining monolingual in approach. Even scholars who profess sensitivity to those omitted from official documents, who imagine those missing voices and situate themselves in opposition to dominant narratives, have repeatedly failed to engage with Gaelophone texts or misrepresented key encounters with the 'absent bards' of Patricia Palmer's excoriating 2006 article. Mainstream Anglophone scholars have baldly stated that their definition of Irish discourse does not include Irish-language texts—or have simply proceeded as if their monolingualism needed no explanation at all.[47] It has been too easy for scholars to speak all too sympathetically for the benighted, oppressed Irish without actually attending to their words, as if they did not in fact have voices of their own, and compelling ones at that.

Certainly, turning to bardic poems offers a distinct counter-narrative to Anglophone claims about native Irish society, its poets, and its poetry. In her 2006 critique of the omission of Irish-language texts from discussions of early modern Ireland, Patricia Palmer discusses a poem by Domhnall Mac Dáire Mac Bruaideadha titled *Ní dúal cairde ar creich ngeimhil* ('It is unfitting to postpone a raid for captives').[48] (By convention, titles of bardic poems are italicized, not put in quotation marks, due to their potentially epic length.) Mac Dáire's forty-seven quatrains address Patrick FitzMaurice (aka Pádraigín Mac Muiris) (c. 1550–1600), the eldest son and heir of a lesser Desmond branch, future 17th baron of Kerry and Lixnaw.[49] The poem was probably composed shortly after Mac Muiris's return from the English court after time spent as a child hostage/ward and subsequently as a diplomatic representative for his father, in the middle or late 1560s or so, before the young heir joined the Desmond Rebellion that would radically transform the tranquil landscape of the poem.[50] Mac Dáire begins by seemingly demanding vengeance for an unjust detention through a raid for hostages, initially seeming proof of Edmund Spenser's famous claim that bloodthirsty bardic poets encouraged violence, praised vice only, and spurred unrest and lawlessness (and lacked the 'goodly ornaments of poetry' to boot).[51] Reading on, however, the poem's apparent demand for 'revenge' turns out to be quite the opposite: an elaborate compliment to a generous host, thus illustrating Palmer's point that we must read Irish-language texts rather than finding 'dialogism' within Anglophone texts alone. Evidently, the young heir's hospitality was so enjoyable that the poet and two of his fellows were unable to depart, for which the poet playfully remonstrates with, and thus compliments, him. Not merely 'talking back' to Spenser's caricature, the poem offers a whole picture of otherwise unseen courtly wit and pleasurable patronly exchange, figuring 'worlds that the English text can only caricature but never lead us to'.[52]

Further examination of this exemplary encomium strengthens the case for bardic close reading as a necessary new direction for enriching our understanding of early modern Ireland. Not only is it witty and elegant, bespeaking the artistic sophistication of the genre and its practitioners. The poem is also, as I argue at greater length elsewhere, a compelling enactment and defense of bardic patronage against burgeoning threats, demonstrating the political sophistication of the bardic institution as well. Consider the highly conventionalized, didactic opening that claims it is not 'dúal' ('proper') for there to be 'cairde' ('a delay') in pursuing 'creich ngeimhil' ('a raid for captives'; 1). This line foregrounds the mandatory observance of social norms by dictating correct behavior (seeking vengeance); crafting an aphoristic declarative (ní dúal X = X is not proper) that evokes collective wisdom; and employing a keyword of normativity itself, *dúal* (proper or right, native, hereditary, natural to, meet, fitting), to do so.[53] Thus, the poem begins by confidently rehearsing the sort of prototypical bardic social policing that affirms the *status quo*. Poets, it goes on, have been kept 'i láimh lé leithbliadhain' ('in bondage for half a year'; 6) in violation of norms of bardic autonomy and status, the target has acted 'fada ó riail' ('far from rule', that is, unlawfully; 5), and this outrage causes the poet to speculate what 'geall' ('price, pledge, surety'; 7) would satisfy the need for 'díol' ('payment, recompense or vengeance'; 7). The poet will make a raid for hostages (9–11) 'ar eighre an chláir Chíarroighigh' ('against the heir of the Kerry plain'; 12), and he will make him 'íoc na hainnríaghla' ('pay for his lawbreaking'; 14) in keeping the poets in 'glais' ('fetters'; 15). Following this buildup of seeming outrage and thirst for vengeance, the poet reveals that the patron is in fact the object of precisely the opposite emotions: affection, admiration, and gratitude. The patron has not violated but exceeded norms, so the poet must craft a suitably elaborate poetic recompense. That is the challenging 'revenge' or 'payment' the poet seeks and, in describing, neatly supplies—in the form of the poem itself.

Mac Dáire's praise poem offers additional insights. The poem's sustained conceit bespeaks the self-consciously *captivating* nature of bardic professional poetry: its profound appeal to the patron's status-conscious self-regard, wit, and sociopolitical concerns, as well as its determination to entrap the patron in the reciprocal patronly relationship and in 'immortal' verse.[54] Mac Dáire's poem emphatically affirms that essential noble characteristic of hospitality, thereby confirming the heir's satisfaction of the obligations of his rank, family, and position, and thus his eligibility for leadership. In so doing, Mac Dáire adroitly refigures the presumed difficulty of praising a callow youth as the classic 'challenge' of summoning adequate praise for a superlative subject. By playfully focusing on Mac Muiris's appeal—as superlatively handsome (75), as an 'édáil' or 'prize' desired by all (63), and indeed as a longed-for prisoner throughout—the poet neatly sidesteps the question of the young patron's few or paltry accomplishments. The poet instead makes his praise all desire— troping breathlessly on the urgent hunt for his patronly prey, the impossibility of hiding him from his admirers or finding anywhere he doesn't have parti- sans to rescue him—in a way that is flattering without being inappropriate. At the same time, while the intensity of the pursuit flatters the patron, it also knits him into the intense homosocial bonds that bardic poetry both enacted and reinforced, the poem's thematization of bondage and hunting reminding us of their force.

That said, the play-antagonism is not completely false, for it arguably expresses an underlying tension in the patronly relationship. A poet, de- spite seeking to portray his interests as perfectly aligned with those of his patron, nonetheless may well find himself at odds with him—abandoned or disregarded and in need of the sharper weapons of satire—a potentiality of bardic verse to which Mac Dáire draws repeated attention with refer- ence to sharp blades/spears/arrows/darts of not-weapons-but-verse that supposedly threaten but in fact praise the patron and his family (Stanzas 5, 12, 13, 15), even as he resolves that tension as warm, mutual affection. There is always a danger of satire in bardic poetry, and praise can quickly become satire if the patron does not meet expectations. This reality is sharper given the fact that the poem only works as encomium as long as the patron's generosity is unquestioned—as long as it is unimaginable that the three poets were in fact held against their will by Mac Muiris. If, however, they can be said to have been unwillingly constrained— meagerly wined and dined, unhappily detained, rather than hosted with due lavishness—then the poem's conceit would retroactively sour. The poem of praise would become a sharp complaint. Mac Muiris is thus pre- sented, ever so wittily, with a powerful compliment—and a powerful re- minder of his traditional obligations.

In a final twist, recall that the poet addresses this compliment/reminder to a young patron who had spent years at court as a child hostage un- der the general Tudor policy that sought to Anglicize Irish heirs so they would *not* patronize poets nor go into rebellion—as Mac Muiris nonethe- less later did. The poem acknowledges that time abroad—but does so only in passing, and in so doing neatly binds it to his 'domesticating' praise by making it proof of how valuable Mac Muiris was as a pledge for his kin (st. 19). But the poem supersedes English influence with laudatory excess and a luminous portrait of archaic, noble leisure figured as beyond time and apart from such painful political realities as *actual* violence and raiding. All this is capped off with a vision of bucolic pleasure in its closing stanzas. The poet thus proffers an antediluvian fantasy of what Mac Muiris had missed but could be figured as regaining, making the patron's 'captivity' by a much more eager and appreciative Irish literati and nobility into the master conceit of a poem that welcomes him home. In so doing, Mac Dáire demonstrates bardic resilience and creativity in the daring metaphorical embrace and reworking of the very challenges bardic poets faced. In turn, his poem urges us to attend to bardic poets' captivating and defiantly witty acts of recuperation and resistance as we continue to write the story of early modern Ireland.

Notes

1 There has been little of the sort of sustained, line-by-line close reading familiar in criticism of other literatures of the period, though editors often supply acute commentary on the works they present. Pádraig A. Breatnach's scholarship is exceptional in its simultaneous attention to stylistic and historical elements; see Pádraig A. Breatnach, 'The chief's poet', *Proceedings of the Royal Irish Academy* 83 (1983), 37–79; idem, *Téamaí Taighde Nua-Ghaeilge* (Maigh Nuad: An Sagart, 1997); idem, 'The Aesthetics of Irish Bardic Composition: An Analysis of *Fuaras iongnadh, a fhir chumainn* by Fearghal Óg Mac an Bhaird', *Cambrian Medieval Celtic Studies* 42 (2001), 51–72; idem, 'Poetics and the Bardic Imagination', *Celtica* 27 (2013), 95–113; idem, 'An address to Toirdhealbhach an Fhíona Ó Domhnaill: Edition and critical exposition', *Celtica* 28 (2016), 55–88. Breandán Ó Buachalla's literary history was founded on contextualized close analysis of a characteristically bracing and transformative kind. See Breandán. Ó Buachalla, 'Poetry and Politics in Early Modern Ireland', *Eighteenth-Century Ireland* 7 (1992), 149–75; idem, *Aisling Ghéar: Na Stíobhartaigh agus an tAos Léinn, 1603–1788* (Baile Átha Cliath: An Clóchomhar, 1996). Patricia Palmer has consistently included brief yet acute readings of bardic poetry as counter-narrative in her work. See Patricia Palmer, *Language and Conquest in Early Modern Ireland: English Renaissance Literature and Elizabethan Imperial Expansion* (Cambridge: Cambridge University Press, 2001); idem, 'Missing bodies, absent bards: Spenser, Shakespeare and a crisis in criticism', *English Literary Renaissance* 36 (3) (2006), 376–95; idem, '"A headlesse Ladie" and "a horses loade of heads": Writing the beheading,' *Renaissance Quarterly* 60 (1) (2007), 25–57; idem, *The Severed Head and the Grafted Tongue: Translating Violence in Early Modern Ireland* (Cambridge: Cambridge University Press, 2013).

2 Recent criticism focused on particular bardic poems and/or keywords includes Louis de Paor, 'Do chor chúarta ar gcridhe'. Léamh ar dhán le hEochaidh Ó hEoghusa,' in Pádraigín Riggs, Breandán Ó Conchúir, and Seán Ó Coileáin (eds.), *Saoi na hÉigse: Aistí in ómós do Sheán Ó Tuama* (Baile Átha Cliath: An Clóchomhar, 2000), pp. 35–53; Ann Dooley, 'The Poetic Self-Fashioning of Gofraidh Fionn Ó Dálaigh', in Michael Richter and Jean-Michel Picard (eds.), *Ogma. Essays in Celtic Studies in Honour of Próinséas Ní Chatháin* (Dublin: Four Courts Press, 2001), pp. 211–23; Peter McQuillan, *Native and Natural: Aspects of the Concepts of 'Right' and 'Freedom' in Irish* (Cork: Cork University Press–Field Day, 2004); idem, 'A Bardic Critique of Queen and Court: "Ionmholta malairt bhisigh," Eochaidh Ó hEodhasa, 1603', in Brendan Kane and Valerie McGowan-Doyle (eds.), *Elizabeth I and Ireland* (Cambridge: Cambridge University Press, 2014), pp. 60–85; Sarah McKibben, *Endangered Masculinities in Irish Poetry, 1540–1780* (Dublin: University College Dublin Press, 2010); idem, 'Guaranteeing what cannot be guaranteed: Defending and adapting bardic patronage in *Ag so an chomairce, a Chormaic* (c. 1585) by Tadhg Dall Ó hUiginn',

North American Journal of Celtic Studies 2 (1) (2018), 1–36; Ailbhe Ó Corráin, *The Pearl of the Kingdom. A Study of* A fhir léghtha an leabháin bhig *by Giolla Brighde Ó hEódhasa* (Oslo: Institute for Comparative Research in Human Culture/ Novus Press, 2013); idem, *The Light of the Universe: Poems of Friendship and Consolation by Giolla Brighde Ó hEódhasa* (Oslo: Institute for Comparative Research in Human Culture, Novus Press, 2014); idem, *The Dark Cave and the Divine Light: Verses on the human condition by Giolla Brighde Ó hEódhasa* (Oslo: Institute for Comparative Research in Human Culture, Novus Press, 2016). Joep Leerssen offered important insights on bardic poems but insisted that they were intrinsically self-interested and myopic, while Michelle O Riordan has persisted in applying a decontextualized, apolitical framework to her readings. See Joep Th. Leerssen, *Remembrance and Imagination: Patterns in the Historical and Literary Representation of Ireland in the Nineteenth Century* (Cork: Cork University Press, 1996); Michelle O Riordain, *The Gaelic Mind and the Collapse of the Gaelic World* (Cork: Cork University Press, 1990); idem, *Irish Bardic Poetry and Rhetorical Reality* (Cork: Cork University Press, 2007). See historian Marc Caball's decisive intervention, in Marc Caball, *Poets and Politics: Reaction and Continuity in Irish Poetry, 1558–1625* (Cork: Cork University Press–Field Day, 1998). On the *dánta grá*, see Micheál Mac Craith, '*Féach orm, a inghean Eóghain:* Anailís théamúil agus anailís struchtúrtha', *Studia Hibernica* 21 (1981), 75–94; idem, 'Gearóid Iarla agus *Mairg adeir olc ris na mnáibh*', *Maynooth review* 6 (1) (1982), 72–92; idem, 'Ovid, an Macalla agus Cearbhall Ó Dálaigh', *Éigse* 19 (1982), 103–20; idem, 'A bhean lán de stuaim', *Maynooth Review* 6 (2) (1984), 27–51.

3   See David Greene, 'The Professional Poets', in Brian Ó Cuív (ed.), *Seven Centuries of Irish Learning, 1000–1700* (Cork: Mercier, 1961), pp. 38–49; Brian Ó Cuív, *The Linguistic Training of the Mediaeval Irish Poet* (Dublin: Dublin Institute for Advanced Studies, 1973); idem, *The Irish Bardic Duanaire or 'Poem-Book'* (Dublin: Malton, 1973); Katharine Simms, 'Irish Literature: Bardic Poetry', in Joseph R. Strayer (ed.), *Dictionary of the Middle Ages*, vol. 6 (New York: Charles. Scribner, 1985), pp. 534–39; Pádraig Ó Macháin, 'The Early Modern Irish Prosodic Tracts and the Editing of "Bardic Verse,"' in Hildegard L.C. Tristam (ed.), *Metrik und Medienwechsel/Metrics and Media* (Tübingen: Gunter Narr Verlag, 1991), pp. 273–87; Damian McManus, 'The Bardic Poet as Teacher, Student and Critic. A Context for the Grammatical Tracts', in Cathal G. Ó hÁinle and Donald E. Meek (eds.), *Unity in Diversity. Studies in Irish and Scottish Gaelic language, literature and history* (Dublin: School of Irish, Trinity College Dublin, 2004), pp. 97–123; Katharine Simms, *Medieval Gaelic Sources* (Dublin: Four Courts Press, 2009), pp. 57–72; Mícheál Hoyne, 'Bardic Poetry, Irish', in Siân Echard and Robert Rouse (eds.), *The Encyclopedia of Medieval Literature in Britain* (Hoboken, NJ: Wiley-Blackwell, 2017), pp. 1–6. Women were neither trained nor recognized as professional poets, though they were the subjects of praise poetry (as wives of lords, chiefly) and would have been canny consumers of the art; they must have written some poetry influenced by bardic norms beyond the few examples attributed to them that survived in manuscript. Hoyne, pp. 1–2.

4   Satire posed a serious danger to its target in a society which understood honor to reside in one's good name. Often, the mere threat of satire appears to have been enough to enforce norms of patronly generosity (or ensure that contracts were upheld) without the need for the actual insult and consequent final break with the patron that satire entailed.

5   James Carney, 'Society and the Bardic poet', *Studies* 62 (1973), 247–48, 233–50; 236; cf. Simms, 'Irish Literature: Bardic Poetry', p. 535. Carney suggests that the total production would have amounted to one million poems, conservatively calculated, between 400 and 1400—substantially more when we account for a further 250-plus years of bardic activity after 1400. Carney, 'Society and

the Bardic poet', p. 236. Huge numbers of manuscripts were lost or destroyed, particularly in our period; see Donnchadh Ó Corráin, "Cad d'imigh ar lamh-scribhinni na hEireann?', in Ruairí Ó hUiginn (ed.), *Oidhreacht na Lamhscrib-hinni*, Léachtai Cholm Chille 34 (Maynooth: An Sagart 2004) pp. 7–27; and idem, 'What happened Ireland's medieval manuscripts?' *Peritia* 22–23 (2011), 191–223.

6 James Carney, 'Literature in Irish, 1169–1534', in Art Cosgrove (ed.), *A New History of Ireland ii: Medieval Ireland 1169–1534* (Oxford: Clarendon, 1987), pp. 688–707, at 693; see overview in Simms, *Medieval Gaelic Sources*, pp. 61–64, for a noble family, though poetic lineages and bardic schools also kept manuscript books of verse. 'Only in the sixteenth and seventeenth centuries, with the spread of literacy among cultured laymen, did it become customary to collect poems for their individual literary merits rather than their personal associations' such that 'most of the existing corpus of bardic poems is found in paper manuscripts of the early modern period' (Simms, 'Irish Literature: Bardic Poetry', pp. 535–36). On the duanaire, see Ó Cuív, *Irish Bardic Duanaire*.

7 Katharine Simms, *From Kings to Warlords: The Changing Political Structure of Gaelic Ireland in the Later Middle Ages* (Woodbridge: Boydell and Brewer, 1987), p. 4.

8 Simms writes: [Their] real value [for the historian] lies in their insincerity, even their falsity, if one wants to call it that', since their delivery 'in expectation of a substantial reward meant inevitably that the sentiments it contained were either directly requested by the patron, or the poet confidently expected them to be welcome hearing'. Indeed, 'from another point of view' bardic poems 'are far truer than they pretend to be, since they reflect an existing situation, not merely something the poet would have liked to take place'. Katharine Simms, 'Bardic Poetry as a Historical Source', in Tom Dunne (ed.), *The Writer as Witness: Literature as Historical Evidence* (Cork: Cork University Press, 1987), pp. 60, 63.

9 Simms, 'Bardic Poetry as a Historical Source', p. 58; idem, *From Kings to Warlords*, p. 4; idem, *Medieval Gaelic Sources*, p. 61.

10 Example, Simms, 'Bardic Poetry as a Historical Source'; idem, *From Kings to Warlords*; Caball, *Poets and Politics*; and Brendan Kane, *The Politics and Culture of Honour in Britain and Ireland, 1541–1641* (Cambridge: Cambridge University Press, 2010).

11 See discussion in Simms, *Medieval Gaelic Sources*, pp. 65–66. Permission for image granted by Dr. Mícheál Hoyne, the Bardic Poetry Database.

12 Damian McManus and Eoghan Ó Raghallaigh, *A Bardic Miscellany: Five Hundred Bardic Poems from Manuscripts in Irish and British Libraries* (Dublin: The Irish Department, 2010).

13 David Baker, Willy Maley, and Patricia Palmer, 'What Is My Network? Introducing MACMORRIS: Digitising Cultural Activity and Collaborative Networks in Early Modern Ireland,' *Literature Compass* (forthcoming).

14 Eleanor Knott (ed.), *The Bardic Poems of Tadhg Dall Ó Huiginn (1550–1591)*, 2 vols. (London: Irish Texts Society, 1922–26), p. xxxv.

15 Katharine Simms, 'Poems to the Medieval O'Donnell Chiefs and their Historical Context', *North American Journal of Celtic Studies* 1 (1) (May, 2017), 45–60.

16 On gender and bardic poetry, see Chapters 1 and 2 of McKibben, *Endangered Masculinities*; and McKibben, 'Queering early modern Ireland', *Irish University Review* 43 (1) (Special Issue on Queer Theory and Ireland) (2014), 169–83.

17 McManus, 'The Bardic Poet as Teacher', pp. 105–106.

18 Caball, *Poets and Politics*, pp. 94–95. On violence against poets, see Thomas F. O'Rahilly, 'Irish Poets, Historians, and Judges in English Documents, 1538–1615', *Proceedings of the Royal Irish Academy* 36 C (1922), 86–120; Greene,

'The Professional Poets', p. 45; Brian Ó Cuív, 'The Irish Language in the Early Modern Period', in T.W. Moody, F.X. Martin, and F.J. Byrne (eds.), *A New History of Ireland*, vol. 3: *Early Modern Ireland 1534–1691* (Oxford: Clarendon Press, 1976), pp. 509–45, at pp. 520–21; and Ó Corráin, 'What Happened Ireland's Medieval Manuscripts?', pp. 214–15.

19　O'Donovan 1849, p. 412.

20　Carney, 'Literature in Irish, 1169–1534', p. 694.

21　Aspiring bardic poets had to train at bardic schools, run by prominent poetic families, for seven to twelve terms (or winters, about six months of the year) to hope to achieve mastery. Carney, 'Society and the Bardic Poet', p. 238; Patrick Sims-Williams and Erich Poppe, 'Medieval Irish Literary Theory and Criticism', in Alastair Minnis and Ian Johnson (eds.), *Cambridge History of Literary Criticism*, vol. 2 (Cambridge: Cambridge University Press, 2005), p. 297. Eoin Mac Cárthaigh has freshly edited Irish Grammatical Tracts 1, with commentary, indexes, textual apparatus, and notes to enable the reader to decode this challenging text. Eoin Mac Cárthaigh, *The Art of Bardic Poetry: A New Edition of Irish Grammatical Tracts I* (Dundalk: Dundalgan Press for the Dublin Institute for Advanced Studies, 2014).

22　The language of bardic poetry was, 'generally speaking, understood and intended to be understood by its upper-class audience', there being evidence to show that part of the education of a boy of a princely family would consist in a training in the understanding of the type of verse of which in adult life he was to be a constant recipient. Carney, 'Society and the Bardic Poet', p. 237. For exposition of different meters, see Eleanor Knott, *An Introduction to Irish Syllabic Poetry of the Period 1200–1600*, 2nd edn. (Dublin: Dublin Institute for Advanced Studies, 1957); idem, *Irish Classical Poetry* (Dublin: At the Sign of the Three Candles, 1960); and Cait Ní Dhomhnaill, *Duanaireacht: Rialacha Meadarachta Fhilíocht na mBard* (Baile Átha Cliath: Oifig an tSoláthair, 1975).

23　Rhyme in bardic poetry differs from English perfect rhyme in that words whose consonants belong to the same 'family' (that is, sharing features of linguistic production, such as being voiced stops, voiceless continuants) and which have the same vowel quality are said to rhyme; similarly, 'consonant clusters only rhyme when certain phonetic features (voicelessness, continuation, sibilance) are represented in both the clusters in question' (Hoyne, p. 2). For more on rhyme, see Brian Ó Cuív, 'The phonetic basis of classical modern Irish rhyme', *Ériu* 20 (1966), 94–103.

24　Greene, p. 52.

25　William Gillies, 'The Classical Irish Poetic Tradition', in D. Ellis Evans, John G. Griffith, and E.M. Joyce (eds.), *Proceedings of the Seventh International Congress of Celtic Studies* (Oxford: Oxford University Press, 1986), pp. 112–13.

26　Simms, *Medieval Gaelic Sources*, pp. 68–69.

27　Carney, 'Literature in Irish', p. 694.

28　Breatnach, 'The Chief's Poet'; Carney, 'Society and the Bardic Poet'; Simms, *Medieval Gaelic Sources*, p. 69.

29　Carney, 'Society and the Bardic Poet', p. 238; McManus, 'Celebrating the female in classical Irish poetry: The wife', *Ériu* 65 (2015), 143, 147–58.

30　Bardic poets 'saw themselves, and presented themselves to the outside world, as an elite whose compositions were subtle, elevated and different'. Gillies, 'The Classical Irish Poetic Tradition', p. 112.

31　Sims-Williams and Poppe, p. 292. Speaking of an earlier period, Carney asserts that '[i]n early and medieval Ireland poetry or at least verse was woven into the whole fabric of society, and that society could not exist without it, unless by changing its whole character', which did not occur until the 'military defeat and partial plantation in the seventeenth century', when 'Ireland was irrevocably set on a course of Anglicization'. Carney, 'Society and the Bardic Poet', pp. 238–39.

32 Greene, 'The Professional Poets', p. 57.

33 Carney, 'Literature in Irish', p. 695.

34 See the impressively detailed list of metaphorical terms in Eleanor Knott's foundational edition, *The Bardic Poems of Tadhg Dall Ó Huiginn,* pp. lii–lvi.

35 Carney, 'Literature in Irish', p. 694.

36 See Damian McManus, 'Good–looking and irresistible: The hero from early Irish saga to classical poetry', *Ériu* 59 (2009), 57–109.

37 Carney, 'Literature in Irish', p. 695; McManus, 'Celebrating the Female in Classical Irish Poetry', pp. 137–68; McManus, 'Female ancestry and mother's kin in classical Irish Poetry', *Breatnach & Ní Úrdail* (2015), 193–219.

38 Jonathan Culler, *Literary Theory: A Very Short Introduction* (Oxford: Oxford University Press, 1997), p. 23.

39 Ibid., p. 25.

40 Ibid., p. 32.

41 Gillies, 'The Classical Irish Poetic Tradition', p. 108.

42 Culler, p. 29.

43 Ibid., p. 30.

44 Richard Strier, 'How Formalism Became a Dirty Word, And Why We Can't Do Without It', in Mark D. Rasmussen (ed.), *Renaissance Literature and its Formal Engagements* (New York: Palgrave Macmillan, 2002), pp. 207–15.

45 James Carney, *Studies in Irish Literature and History* (Dublin: Dublin Institute for Advanced Studies, 1955), p. 264; Gillies, 'The Classical Irish Poetic Tradition', p. 108; Breatnach, 'The Aesthetics of Irish Bardic Composition', p. 51; Breatnach, 'Poetics and the Bardic imagination', p. 95.

46 Dooley, 'The Poetic Self-Fashioning of Gofraidh Fionn Ó Dálaigh', p. 211.

47 Patricia Palmer, 'Missing Bodies, Absent Bards: Spenser, Shakespeare and a Crisis in Criticism', *English Literary Criticism* 26 (2006), 383; cf. Clare Carroll, *Circe's Cup: Cultural Transformations in Early Modern Writing about Ireland* (South Bend, IN: University of Notre Dame Press-Field Day. Critical Conditions 11, 2001), p. 2.

48 Mac Dáire's poem is one of several texts by or to historical Mac Muiris/FitzMaurices by which Palmer challenges the stereotyped figures of Shakespeare's Macmorris and Spenser's Irish savages. Text and translation from Osborn Bergin, *Irish Bardic Poetry*, ed. by David Greene and Fergus Kelly (Dublin: Dublin Institute for Advanced Studies, 1984), pp. 52–60, 233–37, with subsequent references to line numbers or pages in parentheses.

49 For biographies of Patrick Fitzmaurice, see Terry Clavin, 'Patrick Fitzmaurice', *Dictionary of Irish Biography Online* (2009), accessed at dib.cambridge.org on Monday, 28 November 2016; and Christopher Maginn, 'Fitzmaurice, Patrick, Seventeenth Baron of Kerry and Lixnaw (c. 1551–1600), Landowner and Rebel', *Oxford Dictionary of National Biography* (Oxford: Oxford University Press, 2004); online edn. Jan 2008, accessed at www.oxforddnb.com/view/article/9616, accessed 28 Nov 2016. Note that Maginn's biographical entry differs from Clavin, assuming that Mac Muiris/FitzMaurice was at court continuously from the 1550s to the early 1570s, which seems inconsistent both with his inclusion in a list of noblemen who traveled to court in 1567 (mentioned by Clavin and Ciaran Brady) and with the fact of his socializing with and patronizing poets for months at a time. Ciaran Brady (ed.), *A Viceroy's Vindication? Sir Henry Sidney's Memoir of Service in Ireland, 1556–1578* (Cork: Cork University Press, 2002), pp. 57–58.

50 The poem cannot be attached to a precise date with any certainty, but editor Bergin suggests persuasively that 'even bardic extravagance could hardly have

pictured such a scene of sport and revelry during the devastations of the Desmond wars' (53), nor likely omitted reference to the patron's laudable martial skill if it had been demonstrated; at the same time, the patron needed to have been old enough to praise and to have partaken in manly pastimes, so he was at least in his teens.

51 Quoted from Palmer, 'Missing Bodies, Absent Bards', 380.
52 Ibid., p. 385.
53 On *dúal*, see McQuillan, *Native and Natural*, pp. 100–108.
54 Cf. McManus.

7 'Nation' as *Pobal* in seventeenth-century Irish

Peter McQuillan

In an essay published in 1993 on the ideology of Irish royalism in the seventeenth century, Breandán Ó Buachalla remarked on some innovations in political vocabulary in the Irish language that accompanied the development of this ideology.[1] One word mentioned was the newly minted borrowing *náision*, or 'nation'. Conversely, I myself have discussed the lexicon, syntax, and rhetoric of the concepts of 'right', especially hereditary right, portrayed as indefeasible, inalienable, and therefore 'natural' as they are expressed by long-established words in the language like *dúthchas* ('native land, heritage').[2] This native lexicon becomes central to the concepts of homeland and patriotism in the Irish of the early colonial period, the sixteenth and early seventeenth centuries. It is an area that has all too often been neglected in the study of early modern Ireland: the intersection of history, literature, and language, specifically the semantics and pragmatics of the original language, Irish, in which that literature is written.

I would like to turn here to the concept of 'nation' in Irish in an effort to provide a single example of how precisely such an approach can enrich our understanding of the period. Or rather, should I say return: in a piece published two years ago, I discussed the fact that the aforementioned word *náision* first appears in Irish in Tadhg Ó Cianáin's 1609 account of the earls' journey to Rome.[3] Irish already had the word *cine* (*cineadh*), 'the state of being born; offspring; children; descendants; tribe; race', which was used to translate Latin *gens*, or 'people, and *natio*, 'nation'.[4] Underlying *cine* as 'nation' is the belief in descent from a common ancestor. On the other hand, *náision* is borrowed as part of the collective 'self-fashioning' that the Irish émigrés who accompanied O'Neill and O'Donnell to Europe in 1607 underwent as they experienced the might and munificence of the Spanish 'nation' in Rome in particular, a Catholic nation that they wished to emulate. In contrast to the long-established *cine*, *náision* seems like a *Modewort*, a 'buzzword' which is associated with a specific context, time, and place, with Franciscan-inspired texts in particular.[5]

Taken together, the two words provide lexical expression for particular aspects of the concept of 'nation' in Irish in the early seventeenth century. Seathrún Céitinn (Geoffrey Keating) uses the word *cine* extensively in both his secular and theological writings, but never *náision*. In *Foras Feasa ar Éirinn* (The Foundation of Knowledge about Ireland), his primary concern is to establish the ancient and unbroken sovereign integrity of the kingdom of Ireland (*ríoghacht Éireann*).[6] At the same time, he adjoins his own historic community of the Old English, descendants of the Anglo-Norman conquistadores of the twelfth century, to the Gaelic Irish as legitimate constituents of that kingdom. The medieval Gaelic origin legend, *Lebor Gabála Érenn* (The Book of the Taking of Ireland), recognized five canonical invasions of Ireland, the culmination of which was that of *maic/clanna Mhíle*, 'the sons/children of Míl', the Milesians, or the Gaelic Irish themselves.[7] To these five canonical invaders of prehistoric Ireland, and not just to the Gaels, Céitinn gives the collective appellation *cine Scuit*, 'the people/children of Scythia', because of the accepted belief that their origins all lay in that ancient kingdom.[8] However, the relationship between this nation and the kingdom of Ireland is asymmetrical in two ways. *Cine Scuit* includes the Gaels of Scotland excluded from the kingdom of Ireland; conversely, it excludes the Old English who are territorially part of that kingdom. Onto the ethnic model of nationhood based on common ancestry encapsulated by *cine*, Céitinn grafts a more civic-territorial one: the twelfth-century *gábhaltas Gall* (conquest by the foreigners) is depicted as a 'Christian-like' (*Críostamhail*) one[9]—that is, one that respected the laws, customs, and language of the previous inhabitants while accepting their (voluntary) submission. The longevity and the success of their tenure conferred its own retrospective and providential legitimacy on the descendants of the Anglo-Normans in Ireland.[10]

As I have argued, the idea expressed by *cine Scuit* nonetheless remains highly serviceable to Céitinn in two complementary functions. New English historians had argued that in the pre-Milesian era, Ireland had been part of a British imperium.[11] The first function of *cine Scuit* as the nation immemorial is to project Gaelic political sovereignty of the historical period into a pre-Milesian antiquity. This means that ultimately, the origins of that sovereignty are not merely Gaelic properly speaking but 'Scotic'.[12] It is to this unbroken sovereign integrity of an Irish kingdom that Céitinn then adjoins the claims of his own Old English community.[13] Second, Céitinn ingeniously deploys the story of the *Lia Fáil* (Stone of Destiny) to chart the further evolution of Gaelic sovereignty in the historical period. Having been brought to Ireland in the pre-Milesian era and used subsequently to inaugurate the high kings of Ireland at Tara, the stone was taken to Scotland to inaugurate its first Gaelic king, Fergus mac Eirc, and was then captured and brought to Westminster Abbey by Edward I of England. The important point for Céitinn is the prophecy that accompanies the stone, derived from Boece's History of Scotland (*do réir mar léaghtar ag Hector Boetius i stáir na hAlban*):[14]

do bhí i gcinneadh don chloich seo, cibé háit ina mbeidheadh, gurab duine do **Chineadh Scoit**, eadhon, do *shíol Mhíleadh Easpáine*, do bheidheadh i bhflaitheas na críche sin.

it was in destiny for this stone whatever place it would be in, that it is a man of the **Scotic nation**, *i.e.* of t*he seed of Míleadh of Spain*, that would be in the sovereignty of that country.

For Céitinn, the accession of James Stuart as James I of England, Ireland, and Scotland in 1603 (*an rí Séamus táinig do Chineadh Scoit*, 'King James who came from the Scotic race') fulfils the prophecy.[15] Not only could the Irish accept James as their legitimate sovereign, but the source of that sovereignty was ultimately Gaelic (or 'Scotic').[16] In effect, therefore, Céitinn's formulation of the idea of a Scotic nation subsumes its historical representatives in Ireland, the Gaelic Irish, in a broader and deeper concept.

There is more here. *Cine* is derived from a verb that means, 'is born'. Céitinn invents the term *Cine Scuit* to encompass both the Milesian and pre-Milesian invaders. He justifies it because it is the common understanding of the historians (*céadfaidh choithcheann na seanchadh*) that the descendants of Gaoidheal (eponymous ancestor of the Gaels) are called the Scotic nation because they come from Scythia:[17]

> gurab uime ghairthear **cine Scuit** do *shliocht Gaedhil* tré bheith ar dteacht ón Scitia dhóibh

Cine is a wider designator than other words denotative of descent, such as *maic* 'sons', *clanna* 'children' (both used extensively with *Míle*) or the two words used earlier: *síol* 'seed' and *slíocht* 'offspring'. Its most typical use, in fact, is in the phrase *cine daonna*, 'the human race' (we are all descended from Noah after all), but it can also be used with more obviously 'national' signifiers, as in *cine Shacsan*, 'the people of England', or in *cine Sacsanach*, 'the English people', in a way that the other items listed here cannot. Therefore, *cine* suits Céitinn's purpose of establishing territorial criteria for nationhood along with the ethnic-genealogical one of common ancestry. Aptly enough, the conclusion of *Foras Feasa*, which clinches Céitinn's argument, uses the word *cine* in conjunction with the inclusive self-designation *Éireannach*, 'Irish', a term which now expressly includes both the Gaelic Irish and the Old English (but excludes the Protestant New English), and here he quotes Sir John Davies, who uses the word *nation* in the original English passage:[18]

> is í so teist do-bheir Seon Dauis ... Ní fhuil **cine** fán ngréin lénar ab annsa ceart is cothram breitheamhnais ní is fearr **ionáid Éireannaigh**.

> this is the testimony that John Davis gives ... There is no **Nation or people** under the sunne, that doth love equall and indifferent justice better **than the Irish**

Crucially, then, 'the state of being born' (*cine*) encompasses both birth *in* a common territory as well as birth *from* a common ancestor, a prerequisite of nationhood.[19]

We might posit in this case a complementary relationship between *náision* and *cine* as the lexical expression of nationhood in seventeenth-century Irish. In this essay, I want to argue for a further lexical realization of the concept of nationhood, the noun *pobal* or 'people (in general); tribe, race; large number of persons bound together by a common interest or forming a society'.[20] Nevertheless, such words are necessary rather than sufficient for the understanding of the idea of nation. Conceptual domains can be constructed through a variety of means, such as myth, images, and metaphors. Therefore, we need to study entire discursive contexts rather than simply the lexicon.[21] Owing to the constraints of space, my main focus here will be on the lexical aspect and on one text; however, my chosen text, Céitinn's poem 'Óm sceól ar ardmhagh Fáil', will also give some idea of the ways in which lexicon and imagery can interact to produce a view of nationhood.

The popularity of this poem has been enduring: it survives in about sixty manuscripts. Here is the poem, text, and translation (there are two instances of the word *pobal*, which I highlight in bold):[22]

> Óm sceól ar ardmhagh Fáil ní chodlaim oíche
> is do bhreoidh go bráth mé dála a **pobail** dílis;
> gé rófhada atáid 'na bhfál ré broscar bíobha,
> fá dheóidh gur fhás a lán den chogal tríthi.

> From my news on Fál's high plain, I cannot sleep at night: the state of
> its faithful people has sickened me eternally; although they have been
> too long a fence against an enemy rabble, eventually a load of weeds has
> grown up through them.

> A Fhódla phráis, is náir nach follas díbhse
> gur córa tál ar sháirshliocht mhodhail Mhíle;
> deór níor fágadh i gclár do bhrollaigh mhínghil
> nár dheólsad ál gach cránach coigríche.

> Brazen Fódla, it is a shame for you not to recognize that it is more
> proper to nurture the surpassing civil descendants of Míl; not a drop
> has been left in the expanse of your gentle fair breast that the brood of
> every foreign sow has not sucked.

> Gach treód gan tásc tar sál dá dtogair síneadh
> go hóirlios álainn ársa Chobhthaigh Chaoil chirt,
> is leó gan ghráscar lámh ár ndonna-bhruíne,
> 's gach fód is fearr dár n-áitibh eochar-aoibhne.

> Every herd without repute that chose to cross the sea to the beautiful
> ancient golden fort of the righteous Cobhthach Caol: our splendid
> abodes are theirs without hand-to-hand combat as well as the best lands
> of our fair-bordered places.

Atáid fóirne ag fás san gclársa Logha líofa
dár chóir beith táir gé hard a rolla scaoile;
síol Eóghain tláith 's an Tálfhuil bodhar claoite
's na hóig ón mBántrath scáinte i gcoigcríochaibh.

There are crews growing in this plain of Lugh the agile who should
be base, though their patent rolls (are wielded) on high; the seed of
Eoghan (is) enfeebled, the blood of Tál bothered and beaten, and the
young men of Strabane dispersed overseas.

Na tóisigh tháisc ón Nás gan bhogadh bhrí-nirt
i ngleó gér gháifeach ágh na lonnabhuíne—
fá shróin an stáit ba gnáth a gcogadh i ndíormaibh;
ní dóibh ba nár ach cách gan chomhall dlí ar bith.

The renowned chiefs of Naas without an ounce of strength, though
fearsome the prowess of that warlike band in combat; under the nose of
the state, customary was their warfare in bands; no shame to them that
no law is observed by any one.

Dá mba beódha ardfhlaith Áine is Droma Daoile
's na leóghain láidre ón Máigh do bhronnadh maoine,
dar ndóigh níorbh áit don táinse in oscaill Bhríde
gan gheóin is gártha ós ard dá dtoghaildhíbirt.

If the great sovereign of Áine and Droim Daoile were alive, or the
mighty lions of the Maigue who would bestow riches, this crowd
would have no place in the bend of the river Bride, without shouts and
cries out loud (while) being destroyed and expelled

Muna bhfóiridh Ceard na n-ardreann **pobal** chrích Chuirc
ar fhoirneart námhad ndána n-ullamh ndíoltach,
ní mór nárbh fhearr gan chairde a bhfoscaindíolaim
's a seoladh slán i bhfán tar tonnaibh Chlíodhna.[23]

If the Craftsman of the high stars does not save the people of Corc's
land from the violence of audacious, ready and vindictive enemies, it
would almost be better to collect and winnow them immediately and
send them out sailing safe, straying over the waves of Clíona.

Marc Caball has analyzed the poem in a more general discussion of Céitinn's
contribution to the development of a sense of Irish cultural identity in his poetry. He sees it as embodying the 'binary complementarity' of Ireland and her
people.[24] However, a hostile presence has violated this natural order; in a biblical
parallel it resembles the weeds that grow in a cornfield, choking the wheat as it
ripens. This image occurs in the first stanza and is resumed in the final verse of

the poem. Because both instances of the image are accompanied by use of the word *pobal*, I will defer to a more detailed discussion of these two stanzas after the content and imagery of the remainder of the poem have been considered.

Another vivid image detailing the collapse of the natural order occurs in Stanza Two, where Ireland is personified as a false maternal figure, here a foster-mother, who has betrayed her own children by ignoring them and suckling the brood of foreigners instead.[25] The poet addresses Ireland as Fódla, along with Banbha and Ériu, one of three eponymous goddesses of Ireland who in *Lebor Gabála Érenn* recognize the Milesian conquest of Ireland following their defeat of their own people, the Tuatha Dé Danann. These are the children whom she has now shunned, the 'ethnic' nation, tracing their descent to Míl Easpáinne (Míl of Spain), instigator of the prehistoric Gaelic invasion of Ireland, the final and culminating conquest in the medieval scheme of *Lebor Gabála Érenn*. We may note too how they are characterized in terms of their civility: they are a *sáirshliocht,* 'an excellent progeny', as well as being *modhail* or 'gentle, gracious, modest', in direct contrast to the brutishness and bestiality ascribed to the 'litter of every foreign sow'.

In Stanzas Three and Four, a heroic Gaelic golden age is evoked which stands in stark contrast to the current reality where Ireland has been ceded without a fight to the foreigner. Emblematic of this golden age are the mythical high kings of Ireland, Cobhthach Caol mBreagh and Lugh Lámhfhada, the latter savior of the Túatha Dé Danann against the tyrannical Fomorians at the second battle of Moytura.[26] Ireland is depicted as the abode ('the fort') of these former high kings. In stark contrast, the present-day Gaelic lords are enfeebled. 'Eoghan's seed' are the Eóghanacht, the preeminent Gaelic sept in Munster until the rise of the Dál gCais in the tenth century. Their principal representatives by the early modern period are the McCarthys and O'Sullivans; here, the reference may be generically to the Gaelic nobility of Munster since so many of those claimed Eóghanacht descent. The *Tálfhuil* are the O'Briens, the principal representatives of the Dál gCais. The O'Neills of Tyrone represent the Gaels of Ulster in the guise of 'the youth of Strabane', described as banished to foreign lands, a reference to the departure of the northern earls for Europe in 1607. While all these Gaelic dynasts have been laid low, lowborn foreigners prosper, brandishing their claims, their patent rolls, on high.

This theme of how Ireland's nobility has been undermined and subverted by upstarts and arrivistes, by those who have flouted the law in their own interest, continues in Stanzas Five and Six. As previously, the contrast is between a heroic nobility and a disreputable rabble who have usurped their place; we may note again the animalistic reference to the latter as a 'herd'. There is an important difference here, however: the references are not to the Gaelic Irish but to the Old English and therefore to the members of the poet's own historic community but acculturated to Gaelic Irish customs and mores in the intervening centuries. Specifically, the references are to the Fitzgeralds, earls of Kildare (Stanza Five), and Desmond (Stanza Six). The Kildare reference is interesting also in light of the phrase in Stanza Five, *fá shróin an stáit* (under the nose of the state), given the position of the Fitzgeralds as border lords between the Gaelic midlands and the English Pale, the 'state'.[27]

In the succeeding stanza, the allusions are all to the toponymy and topography of present-day County Limerick, in the poet's day part, or at least recently part, of the earldom of Desmond. Especially worthy of attention here is the reference to *ardfhlaith Áine*, 'the high prince of Áine'. Áine was the tutelary goddess of the Eoghanacht and her mystical seat was Cnoc Áine (The Hill of Áine, now Knockainey, County Limerick). However, when the Normans arrived, they quickly absorbed, and were absorbed into, her traditions: the first earl of Desmond, Maurice, became known as 'the king of Áine', having according to legend mated with the goddess to produce the third earl, Gerald, known in Gaelic tradition as Gearóid Iarla. This in essence is a reenactment of the myth of her original union with Ailill Ólom, ancestor figure of the Eóghanacht.[28] The rapid association of the Anglo-Norman Fitzgeralds with an original Gaelic topography, pantheon, and myth of dynastic origin expresses the degree to which a shared culture had evolved between the two historic ethnic communities in Ireland after the twelfth century. The phrase *ardfhlaith Áine*, containing as it does the venerable Gaelic term for sovereign (*flaith*), gives this cultural rapprochement succinct poetic expression.

It remains now to examine the opening and closing stanzas, the relationship between them, and their possible implications for the poem's message. The image that unifies the two stanzas is derived from Matthew 13: 24–30, the parable of the wheat and the tares, where the Kingdom of Heaven is compared to field in which a man has sown good seed. In the night, his enemy arrives and sows weeds; as the wheat matures, so do they. When the man's servants inquire of him whether the weeds should be ripped out of the ground, he declares no, for fear that the good crop might be destroyed with them. Better to let both mature together until harvest time when the wheat can be winnowed from the chaff and the remnants of the harvest gleaned; thus, it will be with God on Judgment Day. In Ireland post-1610, the metaphor of sowing seed, of planting in the ground, seems especially apposite, given the words of Sir John Davies, attorney-general of Ireland and principal strategist of the Plantation of Ulster:[29]

> the husbandman must first break the land before it be made capable of good seed, and when it is thoroughly broken and manured, if he do not forthwith cast good seed into it, it will grow wild again and bear nothing but weeds. So a barbarous country must first be broken by a war before it will be capable of good government and when it is fully subdued and conquered, if it be not well planted and governed after the conquest it will eftsoons return to the former barbarism.

Both Irish poet and English official speak the same language but from diametrically opposed positions: what, for Céitinn, is the wheat is, for Davies, the weeds; the cockle of Céitinn is the good seed for Davies. In addition,

Céitinn's use of the parable provides a little twist. Because the poet is suggesting that Ireland cannot wait until Judgment Day: if God sees fit not to intervene now, it might be better to try winnowing and gleaning (compounded as *foscaindíolaim* 'fanning' and 'gathering') the good Irish wheat and sending it safely overseas forthwith.

We might summarize the poem's progression and structure. With their shared biblical imagery, the first and final stanzas act as the poem's frame. The intervening stanzas can be read as a compressed *origo gentis*. The eponymous Fódla represents the Tuatha Dé Danann, the Irish pantheon and penultimate prehistoric invaders, who having accepted the Gaelic Irish (*sliocht Mhíle*) as legitimate conquerors, now reject them. Their descendants are now enervated as a result, as are those of their successors as invaders, the Anglo-Normans, now the Old English. As the poem's treatment of these non-Gaelic conquerors indicates, however, their participation in a shared landscape and culture has made them into one people with the Gaelic Irish. Bradshaw's succinct assessment of the historical import of Céitinn's *Foras Feasa* applies also, albeit in a much more elliptical form, to his poem. It is no less than the transformation of a Gaelic ethnic history, based on the myth of common descent, into a truly national one, founded on allegiance on the part of more than one ethnic community to a common territory, its language, laws, customs, and institutions.[30] By the beginning of the seventeenth century, the key national institution for the Irish was the Catholic Church, and Céitinn himself was a Jesuit-trained secular priest. His poem asserts that the Gaelic Irish and Old English have become one *pobal*, and this lexical feature also links the first and final stanzas. It is to an examination of this lexeme and its implications for a sense of nationhood that we now turn.

Old Irish *popul* (later *pobal*) is an early Christian borrowing from the Latin *populus* and has a similar range of meanings. The Royal Irish Academy's *Dictionary of the Irish language* (DIL or eDIL) gives 'a people, nation, tribe, inhabitants of a country (district, town) taken collectively'; 'people (in general), populace, a crowd'. The dictionary provides a further useful definition where the word is used 'of a large number of persons held together by some common interest or forming a society'.[31] The examples in DIL also illustrate an important feature of the use of *pobal* from its earliest attestations, and that is its gravitation toward religious contexts. This impression is confirmed by a quick examination of available printed sources for the period 1600–1650 as presented in *Corpas na Gaeilge*: of some 250 examples of the word (in its radical or nominative form *pobal* only), 231 (93%) are from texts of a devotional or spiritual nature.[32] By far the largest concentration comes from Ó Domhnaill's 1602 translation of the New Testament (110 instances), while Céitinn makes extensive use of the word in his two theological texts: on the Mass (37 instances) and on death (25 instances). Both texts will be referenced and discussed in the next section.

There is one example that gives us an important clue as to the default semantic and pragmatic setting for *pobal* in the late medieval and early modern periods. It is found in the rather unlikely source of the grammatical tracts on noun declension, compiled for the benefit of aspiring professional praise poets (the so-called 'bardic' poets). Buried in the list of nouns that conform to the inflectional patterns of the first declension (where nominative singular ends in a broad consonant; genitive singular in a slender consonant), we find the following:[33]

> pobal (an aifrinn) l. énrádh air acht sin
> (the) people (of the Mass), incorrect to pronounce it any way but that

This initially cryptic formulation is rendered more transparent by an accompanying gloss in one of the manuscripts: *pubal l. ón chéill sin* '(to say) *pubal* is incorrect in that sense'. The point is that there are two separate nouns in Irish, both derived from Latin, but which have become homophonic. *Pubal* (Old Irish *pupall*) is from *pupilio* 'a tent, pavilion'; what the text is saying here is that in correct poetic diction the stressed first vowel of each must be carefully distinguished, 'o' from 'u'. The real point for present purposes, of course, is that the most succinct way for the grammarian to distinguish the two nouns was to identify *pobal* with *an t-aifreann,* 'the Mass'. That way his point becomes clear. The default medieval and early modern setting for *pobal* is 'congregation'.

Raymond Gillespie has discussed the importance of participation in the liturgy of the Mass for engendering a sense of community in early modern Ireland as Catholics disengaged from parish structures during the Reformation period. This participation engendered 'a wider sense of a sacramental community, based on the experience of the miraculous power of the eucharist, which helped define the nature of Catholicism in a rapidly changing world'.[34] In a like vein, Tadhg Ó hAnnracháin and Robert Armstrong speak of the language of community in early modern Ireland, as in Europe, as deriving from 'Christian principles, as exemplified by the principles of sacramental communion'.[35] As they also point out, in the Ireland of the Reformation, these principles created competing 'sacramental' communities.

If the semantics of *pobal* are straightforward, its pragmatics, its communicative force in the real world, are more interesting. Céitinn's two devotional tracts are instructive and complementary in this respect. Two uses of *pobal* in particular stand out as relevant to a reading of our poem. First, *pobal* is the congregation (*pobal an aifrinn* in other words, as we saw earlier), that part of the sacramental community of the Mass distinct from the celebrant (*sagart,* 'priest') as amply exemplified by the following passage from his tract on the Mass on how the liturgy is concluded:[36]

> Is é chialluigheas '*Ite Missa est*', cead do thabhairt don **phobal** filleadh d'á n-árusaibh féin iar n-éisteacht an Aifrinn, dá chur i gcéill nach dligheann an **pobal** an eaglais d'fhágbháil ó'n oifig dhiadha acht d'aonta an tsagairt, agus is síos bhíos aghaidh an tsagairt re rádh na mbriathar sin, do bhrigh gurab ris an **bpobal** bhíos an sagart ag labhairt. Is é chialluigheas '*Benedicamus Domino*' furáileamh an tsagairt ar an **bpobal** uim altughadh re Dia tar éis íodhbarta an Aifrinn.
>
> (Eoch. 104)

What '*Ite Missa est*' means is the granting of permission to the *people* to return home after hearing the Mass, articulating that the *people* are not allowed to leave the church from the divine office except with the priest's agreement. And the priest's face is cast downward while saying those words because it is to the *people* that the priest is speaking. What '*Benedicamus Domino*' means is the priest's injunction to the *people* to thank God after the sacrifice of the Mass.

Second, *pobal* is collocated with a following noun in the genitive or an adjective in the syntax, 'the people of X' or 'the X people'. This particular usage is more pronounced in Céitinn's other great devotional tract on the *ars moriendi*, *Trí Bior-ghaoithe an Bháis* (The Three Shafts of Death). This text is replete with references to the sufferings of the children of Israel in captivity, as God's chosen people. For instance, the following is from a section of the text that compares physical and spiritual death: in this case, the loss of physical sensation in a corpse is likened to the spiritual death of hardening one's heart to the word of God. The reference here is to Pharaoh's refusal of Moses's request that he release the Israelites from their bondage (see Exodus 5):[37]

> Óir tar éis mar do iarr Maoise air sgaoileadh do **phobal** Dé as an daoirse 'na rabhadar aige, agus tar éis na bplágh ndíoghaltach do imir Dia ar an Éigipt tré bhroid Chloinne Israel, is móide (mar ghreannughadh ar Dhia) do thromuigh ar mhoghsaine Chloinne Israel.

> Because after Moses had asked him to release the people of God from the captivity in which he had them, and after the vengeful plagues that God had visited on Egypt because of the oppression of the children of Israel, he actually increased the slavery of the children of Israel in defiance of God.

In this passage, the Israelites are described in two complementary ways: as *Clann Israel* 'Children of Israel', they are descendants of a common ancestor on the one hand,[38] and as *pobal Dé*, 'people of God', they are a people who have a special relationship with God on the other.[39] The phrase *pobal Israel* occurs also, as in the following passage based on Numbers 14, where God punishes the Israelites in the desert for forty years because of their grumbling against Him as they wander in search of the Promised Land:[40]

> mar do cuireadh **Clann** Israel timcheall ar feadh .40. bliadhan ar an bh-fásach ... Dá chor i gcéill go gcaithfeadh **pobal** Israel, i ndíoghail a n-uilc féin, anmhain bliadhain ar an bhfásach i n-aghaidh gach laoi dá raibhe d'fhiachaibh orra bheith ar an bhfásach.

> as the Children of Israel were sent wandering for forty years in the desert ... meaning that the people of Israel, in recompense for their own evil, would have to spend a year in the wilderness for every day that were compelled to be in the desert.

As in many texts of this period, the Israelites serve as a template for the current predicament of the Irish, and Céitinn makes the analogy explicit: both the Israelites/Jewish people (the adjective *Iúdaidheach* is used here) on the one hand, and the Irish on the other are a *pobal*, a people before God who have, however, been poorly treated. We may note the liberal use of *pobal* in the passage expressly comparing the two peoples in their relationship with God:[41]

> Fa-ríor, is eadh shaoilim nach daoire na dochair do imir Dia, beag nach, ar **phobal** Israel, ioná an daordháil fhuilngeas do thoidheacht ar **phobal** imshníomhach Éireann, ionnus go bhféadaid go dlightheach a n-amfhorrán féin d'fhionnachtain, agus a gcomhmbroid do chasaoid ré Dia, amhail do-rinne Dáibhídh Rí anallód, ré mbeith don **phobal** Iúdaidheach fá éagcomhlann ... Féadaidh gach Catoilice Éireannach a rádh mar an gcéadna, tré bheith fá inghreim éagcoimsigh na n-éagcráibhtheach, ag diúltadh d'fháischreideamh fhollásach Cailbhín₇ Lúitéir₇ lochta a leanamhna.

> Alas, I think that the misfortunes that God had visited upon the people of Israel are almost no more severe than the oppressive bondage that he allows to be inflicted on the distressed people of Ireland, so that they can legitimately establish their misfortune and complain of their oppression to God, as King David did long ago, when the Jewish people suffered tyranny ... Every Irish Catholic can say just the same, being under the egregious persecution of the heretics, rejecting the false and fallacious religion of Calvin and Luther and their followers.

Pobal Éireann, 'the people of Ireland', is thus a Catholic people, comprised of every Irish Catholic (*gach Catoilice Éireannach*), not just Gaelic Irish but Old English like Céitinn himself and opposed to the heretics, the adherents of Luther and Calvin.

When discussing Céitinn's poem initially, we considered a passage from Sir John Davies on the necessity of breaking up the soil and planting the good seed in order to make sure that the weeds do not return and the country revert to wildness. Here is a further passage from *A Discovery* where he rather idealistically praises James I for the latter's advocacy of a 'mixed' plantation in Ulster:[42]

> his Majesty did not utterly exclude the Natives out of this plantation, with a purpose to root them out, as the Irish were excluded out of the First English Colonies but made mixt plantation of Brittish [sic] and Irish, that they might grow up together in one Nation: Only, the Irish were transplanted in some places from Woods and Mountains into the Plains and open countries, that being removed (like wild fruit-trees) they might grow the milder, and bear the better and sweeter fruit ... For when this Plantation hath taken root, and been fixt and settled for a few years, with

the favour and blessing of God (for the Son of God himself hath said in the Gospel, *Omnis plantatio, quam non plantavit pater meus, eradicabitur*), it will secure the Peace of Ireland, assure it to the crown forever.

Here, the idea of Céitinn's first stanza is again inverted and subverted: in the view of Davies, if the 'Brittish' and 'Irish' are planted alongside each other and mature together, the former will 'civilize' the latter and make them members of 'the one Nation', that is, *their* nation, that the good soil and the good crop will prevail. The attorney general also knows his Matthew: this passage expressly quotes his Chapter 15, Verse 13—'every plant which my heavenly Father hath not planted, will be rooted up'.[43]

The parable of the wheat and the tares is explained in Matthew 13: 37–42: the sower of the good seed in the field is the Son of God and the good seed represents the good children of Heaven, whereas the tares have seen sown by the Devil and are the evil children. When the corn ripens, it will be reaped by God's angels and stored in His barn, the tares will be winnowed and burned, and the world will be at an end. Caball interprets the last stanza of Céitinn's poem to mean that Ireland's situation is so dire in facing a superior foe that she will be lost without divine intervention, 'that the reversal of Irish fortunes is now beyond human agency'.[44] What Christ's explanation of the parable does not say expressly, but which seems to be its natural conclusion, is that only God may judge between good and evil, and that on doomsday. From the po-et's perspective, the Irish are God's faithful people (*pobal*), his chosen, the *filii regni*, and all they need is to wait to inherit the kingdom of Heaven.

However, as Matthew 13: 38 has it, 'the field *is the world*' (*ager autem est mundum*) and the poet's concerns are urgently of this world. From a theo-logical perspective, this phrase is not entirely unproblematic,[45] but I would suggest here that Céitinn wishes to seize on a more literal, more worldly, interpretation, potentially eschewing eschatology altogether. The Irish can-not afford to wait until Judgment and let the bad seed grow up around them. Unless God helps them *now*, they need to act, to 'winnow and glean' the harvest themselves and send it to safety abroad. Rather than abandoning the possibility of human agency, the final stanza hints at its potentiality.[46] There is ambivalence though ('it would be *almost* better to winnow and glean'), but the possibility receives added cogency from the Davies passage cited imme-diately before: if the wheat and the tares grow full term together, then what from Céitinn's perspective are the 'weeds' just might prevail. That this is no idle fear is corroborated by his Gaelic Irish contemporary and fellow-poet Fear Flatha Ó Gnímh who, in a poem lamenting the egregious transforma-tions effected upon the material and cultural balance of Gaelic Ulster society by plantation, echoes the Old English poet's anxiety. Compare the following with Céitinn's aforementioned second stanza, as once again Ireland loses her maternal instincts with the attendant transformation of Ireland into another England; note that here she is explicitly identified as Ireland's foster-mother (*buime*), unlike Fódla in Céitinn's poem:[47]

Ní aithneann inis Logha
ní dá faithchibh fonnmhara,
cnuic dhlaoiréidhe i ndiaidh a n-air;
biaidh saoirÉire 'na Saxain

The island of Lugh recognizes none of its pleasant fields, lush-covered
hills have been ploughed; *noble Ireland will become England.*

Ní aithneann aicme Ghaoidheal
Banbha, buime a macdhaoineadh
's ní aithneann Éire iad soin;
tiad re chéile as a gcrothaibh.

The family of the Gaels do not recognize Banbha, their own foster-
mother, and Ireland does not recognize them: they have become mutual
strangers.

Furthermore, Ó Gnímh's penultimate stanza is redolent of Céitinn's conclusion: if God will not intervene positively on Ireland's behalf ('this new
England called Ireland'), it may be time for the Irish to quit their native land:

Má thug an deónughadh dhi,
Saxa nua dan hainm Éire,
bheith re a linn-se i láimh bhiodhbhadh,
don innse is cáir ceileabhradh.

If Providence has decreed that she should be in her time in the hands
of enemies, *this new England called Ireland,* it is proper to bid this island
farewell.

Noteworthy too are the highlighted phrases in Ó Gnímh's verses that give
concrete expression to what is subliminal in Céitinn's final poem that Ireland,
in accordance with the vision of Sir John Davies, will become a new England.
    Another text of the period that foregrounds the conjunction of nationhood
and religion is Aodh Mac Aingil's tract on repentance and confession, *Scáthán
Shacramuinte na hAithridhe* (Mirror of the Sacrament of Repentance), published in
Louvain in 1618. In a passage praising the late departed Franciscan Bonaventura
(Giolla Bhríde) Ó hEoghasa, Mac Aingil uses the neologism *náision* alongside
pobal. It is one of the more evocative passages in the entire work, using as it does
the English loanword *perseacuision,* and providing the context and justification for
Ó hEoghasa's considerable endeavor in the field of religious instruction:[48]

As mór do bhí faoi do sgríobhadh do rachadh a leas anma agus a n-onóir
shaoghalta don *náision* dá maireadh, achd, fá-raor, tré fheirg nDé risan
bpobal bpeacach, do goireadh air a n-ám a thoraidh agus a ttosach a

shaothair do chor a ccló agus suil ráinig leis sinni do theagasg a ttean-
guidh ar máthar, iondus go ttiocfadh dhínn ní éigin do rachadh a leas na
n-anmann do sgríobhadh, ó nách léigthear dhúinn tré bhurba an pher-
seacuision foircheadal do dhénamh ó bheól. Nír fhág ina dhiaidh don
náision duine rér éidir an ní do chor roimhe do dhénamh, ór, gé go
bhfuilid mórán daoine foghlamtha ag ár **náision** (glóir do Dhia) ... ní
bfhuil ... duine coimhdheas₇ comhóirdheirc lé Bonauentura a léighionn,
a nGaoidhealg₇ a ccrábhadh.

There was much that he intended writing to benefit the spiritual welfare
and worldly honour of the nation had he lived. However, because of
God's anger towards the sinful people, he was called when productive
and beginning to publish his work and before he could teach us in our
mother tongue, that we might be able to write something of spiritual
benefit, since we are not permitted through the severity of the perse-
cution to deliver oral instruction. He did not leave behind him anyone
of the nation who could do what he had intended because, though our
nation has many learned people (glory to God), there is no one as fitting
and illustrious as Bonaventura in learning, in Irish and in piety ...

As already mentioned, the word *náision* is first used in Irish in Tadhg Ó
Cianáin's travel narrative of 1608–1609; its first occurrence in Mac Aingil's
aforementioned passage rehearses its most salient association in the former
text which shows an almost obsessive concern with honor (*onóir*) as it affects
the emigré Irish community wending its way through Europe. The word
onóir and its various derivatives occurs over eighty times in Ó Cianáin's text
and provides the context for his use of *náision*: the Irish are a nation like every
other Christian nation, comparable to every other nation especially the most
powerful Catholic nation of all, Spain.[49] On the other hand, *pobal* in the
aforementioned passage again indexes the nation in its relationship with God.

Náision is the public 'face' of the nation as a nation among other nations;
while *cine* is primarily the ethnic nation of time immemorial that includes
the Gaelic Scots as well as the pre-Milesian invaders of Ireland, it also, and
crucially, provides the bridge between the ethnic and the territorial in the
development of nationality. *Pobal*, on the other hand, is the nation to which
the political economy of the Old Testament is applied,[50] a sacramental and
providential community of God's predilection. Here, however, it is applied
with a New Testament imagery that is important for its proper explication
in context. This complementarity is supported by syntactic evidence: while
the Irish are *pobal Dé*, they are never *cine Dé* or *náision Dé* or *clanna Dé*; conversely they are never *cine Mhíle* or *pobal Mhíle* but rather *clanna Mhíle*. All
three words form important parts of the lexical conception of nationhood
in seventeenth-century Irish. The specific appeal of *pobal* is that it conveys a
certain intimacy or solidarity that is derived from a specific sense of common
interest or purpose very topical in the Europe of the Reformation.[51]

Notes

1 Breandán Ó Buachalla, 'James Our True King: The Ideology of Irish Royalism in the Seventeenth Century', in David Boyce, Robert Eccleshall, and Vincent Geoghegan (eds.), *Political Thought in Ireland since the Seventeenth Century* (London: Routledge, 1993), pp. 7–35, 14; see also idem, *The Crown of Ireland* (Galway: Arlen House, 2006).

2 Peter McQuillan, *Native and Natural: Aspects of the Concepts of Right and Freedom in Irish* (Cork: Cork University Press, 2004).

3 Paul Walsh, *The Flight of the Earls* (Dublin: M.H. Gill, 1916).

4 eDIL—Electronic Dictionary of the Irish Language, dil.ie/9138, *ciniud*.

5 Peter McQuillan, "'Nation' as word and concept in seventeenth-century Irish', *Eolas: The Journal of the American Society of Irish Medieval Studies* 8 (2015), 71–88; for the background, see, Clare Carroll, *'Turas na nIarladh as Éire*: International travel and national identity', *History Ireland* 15 (2007), 56–61; Brendan Kane, 'A Dynastic Nation? Rethinking National Consciousness in Early Seventeenth-Century Ireland', in David Finnegan, Éamonn Ó Ciardha, and Marie-Claire Peters (eds.), *The Flight of The Earls. Imeacht na nIarlaí* (Derry: Guildhall Press, 2010), pp. 124–31; for the Franciscans, see Mícheál Mac Craith, 'The false and craft bludsukkers, the Observauntes': ' na súmairí beartacha bréagacha: na hObsarvaintigh, ibid., pp. 208–20.

6 For text and translation, see David Comyn and Patrick S. Dinneen (eds.), *The History of Ireland by Geoffrey Keating D.D.*, 3 vols. (London: Irish Texts Society, 1902–8), hereafter *Foras Feasa*. For context, see Breandán Ó Buachalla, 'Annála Ríoghachta Éireann agus Foras Feasa ar Éirinn: an comhthéacs comhaimseartha', *Studia Hibernica* 22–23 (1982–83), 59–105; Brendan Bradshaw 'Geoffrey Keating: Apologist of Irish Ireland', in Brendan Bradshaw, Andrew Hadfield, and Willie Maley (eds.), *Representing Ireland: Literature and the Origins of Conflict 1534–1600* (Cambridge: Cambridge University Press, 1993), pp. 166–90; Bernadette Cunningham, *The World of Geoffrey Keating* (Dublin: Four Courts Press, 2002).

7 For a summary account of these invasions and their relationship to the Gaelic origin legend as a whole, see Myles Dillon, 'Lebor Gabála Érenn', *Journal of the Royal Society of Antiquaries of Ireland* 86 (1956), 62–72; for the text, see ed. R.A. Macalister (ed.), *Lebor Gabála Érenn: The Book of the Taking of Ireland* (Dublin: Irish Texts Society, 1938).

8 *Foras Feasa*, II, 26.

9 By contrast, the New English conquest is a pagan one, *págánta*, see *Foras Feasa*, I, pp. 34–36.

10 *Foras Feasa*, III, pp. 358–69.

11 Bradshaw 'Geoffrey Keating', 171–72; Colin Kidd, *British Identities before Nationalism: Ethnicity and Identity in the Atlantic World 1600–1800* (Cambridge: Cambridge University Press, 1999), p. 170; see also Andrew Hadfield, 'Briton and Scythian: Tudor representations of Irish origins', *Irish Historical Studies* 112 (1993), 390–408, especially at 390 and 399.

12 I adopt here the coinage of text's editors since the terms 'Irish', 'Scottish', and 'Gaelic' are not broad enough.

13 This is a process aptly described by Kidd as 'Catholic ethnogenesis', *British Identities*, p. 151.

14 *Foras Feasa*, I, 206–208; for the 'stone of destiny' in Scotland, see Nick Aitchison, *Scotland's Stone of Destiny: Myth, History and Nationhood* (Stroud, OK: Tempus Publishing Ltd, 2000). The standing stone commonly portrayed as the *Lia Fáil* is certainly not the original flagstone, *lecc* in Tara, upon which kings-to-be stood. The stone would then scream reflecting the land's acceptance of the aspirant king. The stone probably disappeared early in the Christian period; see also Tomás Ó Broin, 'Lia Fáil: Fact and fiction', *Celtica* 2 (1990), 393–401.

15 *Foras Feasa*, I, 208; note the two different translations of *cineadh* on the editor's part, 'nation' and 'race'.

16 See Breandán Ó Buachalla, *Aisling Ghéar. Na Stíobhartaigh agus an tAos Léinn 1603–1788* (Baile Átha Cliath: An Clóchomhar, 1996).

17 *Foras Feasa*, II, p. 26.

18 *Foras Feasa*, III, p. 368; Sir John Davies, *Historical Relations: or A Discovery of the True Causes why Ireland was never entirely subdued* (Dublin: Samuel Dancer, 1664), p. 225. Early English Books Online, accessed 31 October 2017.

19 The centrality of the idea of birth here means that the nation is 'a community of kinship' in Grosby's phrase; see Steven Grosby, *Nationalism. A Very Short Introduction* (Oxford: Oxford University Press, 2005), pp. 7–26.

20 eDIL: dil.ie/34472, *popul.*

21 This discussion has been occurring over the last number of years between practitioners of different types of conceptual history, in particular, the German *Begriffsgeschichte* as opposed to the 'Cambridge School' of Skinner and Pocock. See Melvin Richter, *The History of Political and Social Concepts: A Critical Introduction* (Oxford: Oxford University Press, 1995), for introduction and discussion.

22 The text given here is from Breandán Ó Buachalla, Tomás Ó Concheanainn, and Pádraig de Brún (eds.), *Nua-Dhuanaire Cuid I* (Bhaile Átha Cliath: Institiúid Ard-Léinn, 1975), p. 18; the translation is by Thomas Kinsella from Seán Ó Tuama and Thomas Kinsella (eds.), *An Duanaire 1600–1900: Poems of the Dispossessed* (Bhaile Átha Cliath: Foras na Gaeilge, 2002), pp. 85, 87.

23 The author wishes to thank the School of Celtic Studies of the Dublin Institute for Advanced Studies for permission to use this poem.

24 Marc Caball, 'Patriotism, Culture and Identity: The Poetry of Geoffrey Keating', in Pádraig Ó Riain (ed.), *Geoffrey's Keating's Foras Feasa, ar Éirinn: Reassessments* (Dublin: Irish Texts Society, 2008), pp. 19–38, 27–29.

25 In another of his poems, Céitinn identifies Éire as 'the old foster-mother of the sons of Míl', *seanbhuime mhaicne Mhílidh.* See Brain Ó Cuív, 'Mo thruaighe mar tá Éire', *Éigse. A Journal of Irish Studies* 8 (4) (1957), 302–308, 305. It is significant in medieval Ireland that the intimate term *muime*, later *buime*, compare English *mummy*, has been transferred from the biological to the foster mother, indicating the pervasiveness and importance of the institution of fosterage. See Fergus Kelly, *A Guide to Early Irish Law* (Dublin: Institute for Advanced Studies, 1988), pp. 86–87.

26 Lugh in particular features in seventeenth-century political poetry as a kind of secular Moses, a messianic figure; see, for example, Tomás Ó Rathile, *Measgra Dánta*, vol. 2 (Corcaigh: Cló Ollscoile Chorcaí, 1977), p. 146.

27 This is one of the first uses of the loanword *stát* in reference to the English state in Ireland.

28 Dáithí Ó hÓgáin, *The Lore of Ireland: an Encyclopedia of Myth, Legend and Romance* (Woodbridge, ON: Boydell Press, 2006), pp. 7–8, 202–204.

29 Davies, *A Discovery of the True Causes*, pp. 4–5.

30 Brendan Bradshaw, 'Reading Seathrún Céitinn's *Foras Feasa ar Éirinn*', in Pádraig O Riain (ed.), *Geoffrey's Keating's Foras Feasa ar Éirinn: Reassessments* (Dublin: Irish Texts Society, 1986), pp. 1–18; for a brief discussion of ethnicity and nationality more generally, see Grosby, *Nationalism*, pp. 7–26.

31 eDIL: dil.ie/34472.

32 *Corpas na Gaeilge 1600–1882* (Baile Átha Cliath: Acadamh Ríoga na hÉireann, 2004).

33 Osborn Bergin (ed.), 'Irish Grammatical Tracts', Supplement to *Ériu* 9 (1921/23), 61–124, 7.

34 Raymond Gillespie 'Catholic Religious Cultures in the Diocese of Dublin, 1614–97', in Dáire Keogh and James Kelly (eds.), *History of the Catholic Diocese of Dublin* (Dublin: Four Courts Press, 2000), pp. 127–43, 143.

35 Tadhg Ó hAnnracháin and Robert M. Armstrong, 'Introduction: Making and Remaking Community', in Tadhg Ó hAnnracháin and Robert M. Armstrong (eds.), *Community in Early Modern Ireland* (Dublin: Four Courts Press, 2006), pp. 13–33, 20.

36 Patrick O'Brien (ed.), *Eochair-sciath an Aifrinn: an Explanatory Defence of the Mass* (Dublin, 1898), p. 104.

37 Osborn Bergin (ed.), *Trí Bior-ghaoithe an Bháis. The Three Shafts of Death* (Dublin: Institute for Advanced Studies, 1992) [reprint from 1931], pp. 62, 20.

38 Jacob, whose name was changed to Israel, see Genesis 32: 24–32.

39 See also Bergin, *Trí Bior-ghaoithe*, pp. 243, 22.

40 Ibid. 154, p. 8.

41 Ibid. 192, p. 19.

42 Davies, *A Discovery of the True Causes*, pp. 250–51.

43 Uttered by Jesus in relation to the Pharisees and their hypocrisy.

44 Caball, 'Patriotism, culture and identity', pp. 28–29.

45 For the differing 'universalist' and 'ecclesiological' readings of this and the entire parable, see Robert I. McIver, 'The parable of the wheat and the weeds (Matthew 13: 24–30, 34–40) and the relationship between the kingdom and the church as portrayed in the gospel of Matthew', *Journal of Biblical Literature* 114 (4) (1995), 643–59.

46 The medieval and early modern exegetical history of this parable is rich in attempts to circumvent its apparent eschatological premises, not least on Luther's part, see Ronald H. Bainton, 'The parable of the wheat and the tares as the proof text for religious liberty until the end of the sixteenth century', *Church History* 1 (1932), 67–89.

47 Ó Rathile, *Measgra* II, pp. 145 and 147.

48 Cainneach Ó Maonaigh (ed.), *Scáthán Shacramuinte na hAithridhe* (Dublin: Dublin for Advanced Studies, 1952), pp. 94, 27.

49 McQuillan 'Nation', pp. 76–78, 88.

50 Adrian Hastings, *The Construction of Nationhood. Ethnicity, Religion and Nationality* (Cambridge: Cambridge University Press, 1997), p. 195.

51 There may also be a further aspect to this. There is a strong exegetical tradition, going back to the Church Fathers, of identifying the tares with heretics, rather than with simple moral delinquents, an interpretation which also tended to favor human agency rather than eschatology, that is, believing they should be rooted out *now*. Along these lines, the age of the Reformation also favors identifying the servants in the parable with ecclesiastical ministers, while exempting the secular authority from Christ's injunction. Both Calvin and Luther supported the execution of heretics on these grounds. One argument was that since heretics were easily identifiable, there was little danger of uprooting the good with the bad. See Bainton, 'The parable of the wheat and the tares'.

8 Munster and India

The local and global in early modern Ireland

Marc Caball

While historians have for some time interpreted early modern Ireland within a broader Atlantic context of expansion and settlement, it will be argued here on the basis of a family-based case study that aspects of the quickly evolving society of the southwestern province of Munster are more profitably comprehended within a global template of colonial capitalism.[1] It is proposed accordingly that an expansive geographical and cultural perspective illustrates similarities in an early phase of English colonial expansion which enriches understanding of a fascinating process of simultaneous conflict and accommodation, and which is suggestive of new research directions in the history of early modern Ireland. The value of family history in a global context has been ably demonstrated by Emma Rothschild in her study of the Johnstone brothers and sisters who lived in Scotland and around the world during tumultuous and rapidly changing times in the eighteenth century. In writing the story of a relatively minor family, Rothschild has aimed to enhance knowledge of new ideas and sentiments which were deeply influential in the context of the period and the eighteenth-century Enlightenment. Presenting her work as a form of microhistory, Rothschild argues that it offers 'new ways of connecting the microhistories of individuals and families to the larger scenes of which they were a part'.[2] Not dissimilarly, the fortunes of the Hedges family of Munster were shaped and influenced by the political and social upheavals of late seventeenth- and early eighteenth-century Britain and Ireland. Moreover, participation by members of the family in the colonial commercial ventures of the East India Company complements their experience in Munster. Therefore, consideration of the experience of the brothers Richard and Robert Hedges results in a combination of local and global perspectives, which enables a textured appreciation of early modern English colonialism. If the following account of Richard and Robert Hedges is fundamentally about their single-minded quest for wealth and influence in Ireland and India, reconstruction of their story also highlights new research themes in early modern Irish material, cultural and economic history, and the allied utility of sources as diverse as Gaelic poetry and legal deeds.

Material traces of India were readily discernible in seventeenth-century Munster. For instance, visitors to the elegant residence of the Percival family at Burton in North Cork in the 1670s might encounter a profusion of Indian textiles. Completed in the early 1670s, Burton was innovative in so far as its design diverged from the previously dominant tradition of castle architecture which had privileged defense above comfort and ostentatious luxury. The external symmetry of Burton's design enshrined prosperity, affluence, and security.[3] An inventory of the possessions of Lady Catherine Percival (d.1679) at Burton and at the family's town house in Kinsale compiled on her death is indicative of the extent to which textiles imported from India constituted an integral element in the decoration and furnishings of the contemporary fashionable domestic interior.[4] Although commodities from the Americas and Asia such as sugar, tea, coffee, porcelain, and textiles featured prominently in the consumer revolution of the eighteenth century, European demand for luxury goods from Asia dated as far back as Roman imports of Chinese silks.

The late seventeenth century, however, witnessed a surge in European demand for Asian goods as stable or decreasing prices resulted in a broader market, which encompassed the middling classes. Demand for Indian fabrics in Europe in the early seventeenth century centered largely on table and bed linens, wall hangings, and domestic furnishings. However, from the 1660s onward, the demand for Indian calicoes for clothing expanded dramatically.[5] Lady Percival's collection of fabrics is illustrative of the domestic function of such materials. In her chamber at Burton, it was noted that one small trunk contained five pieces of painted calico, two painted calico window curtains, two square pieces of calico, one piece of Indian silk and one small piece of coarse calico.[6] Calico was a fabric made from cotton which was said to have originated in Calicut in southwestern India. The diversity of use for calico was further evident in the contents of a large trunk in Lady Perceval's chamber. This trunk contained, among other items, a large painted calico quilt, a painted calico carpet, a small painted calico carpet, two calico testers for beds, and one small piece of calico described as belonging to a bed.[7] Moreover, textiles from India in Lady Percival's chamber were not merely confined to two trunks: the room's great closet accommodated calico sheets and two calico window curtains. Lady Percival's bedroom featured, among other furnishings, two Indian flower mats.[8] Given the frequent arrival of East Indiamen at Kinsale over the course of the seventeenth century, it may be assumed that at an elite level that the presence of such Indian fabrics at Burton was far from atypical in Munster.[9]

The Percival inventory records the presence of one item at the family's Kinsale townhouse which is emblematic of this essay's global focus: 'one great map of the world'.[10] It is suggested that a purely provincial, insular, or British Isles historical focus on early modern Munster risks obscuring global influences and interactions. In this respect, the experience of Anglo-Irish brothers Richard and Robert Hedges of County Cork is discussed with a view to illustrating how these dynamic and socially resilient individuals, Richard in Ireland and Robert in India, negotiated formidable social, cultural, and financial challenges in order to establish and secure their material security and affluence. Reconstruction of the experience of the Hedges brothers further validates the merit of comparative study of Ireland and India on the basis that 'they were zones of hybridity for shifting identities'.[11] In a related vein, Jane Ohlmeyer has suggested that Ireland provided a 'colonial prototype for the early colonisation of India' and more particularly that the Irish background of Gerald Aungier, who was governor of Bombay and president of the Surat Council between 1669 and 1677, requires further consideration in terms of the development of the Bombay colony.[12] In this essay, it is demonstrated that the assiduity of the Hedges brothers in the matter of personal enrichment was informed and tempered by similar cultural and social challenges, notwithstanding their disparate geographical locations.

Although the English lineage of the Hedges family is somewhat obscure, it is assumed they first came to Ireland in the early seventeenth century from Stratton in Wiltshire. Robert Hedges (d.1670) of Youghal was the family's progenitor in Ireland. While little is recorded of Robert's life, it is evident that he was considered an individual of substance in Youghal, where he leased one of the town's most substantial residences, Myrtle Grove, in 1661, and where he was entrusted with high-level municipal business in 1666 in his capacity as a member of the town corporation.[13] The outward focus of the inhabitants of Youghal at this point is evident in the 1666 baptism at St. Mary's Collegiate Church of David, of a youth formerly known as 'Lampo … a negro aged 15 years or thereabout borne in Mountserat one of ye Cariby Islands'.[14] The Hedges were formed within a community which was acutely aware of global opportunity and reward.[15] Robert's sons, William and Robert, definitively inaugurated the family's role in colonial capitalism in India and Ireland. William, the eldest son of Robert, embarked on a career centered on international commerce which resulted in his appointment as the Levant Company's treasurer at Constantinople in 1668 and significantly as the East India Company's agent in the Bay of Bengal, where he arrived in 1682.[16] On his return to England, William was knighted by James II and served as a director of the Bank of England between 1694 and 1700. He was also involved in the affairs of the Royal African Company, which traded in slaves and various commodities along the west coast of Africa.[17] At the time of his death in 1701, Sir William owned land in County Cork, which he may have inherited from his father.[18] While the career of William's younger brother, Robert, was decidedly less expansive, his military appointment, possibly at some time in the 1660s, as the governor of the castle in Borris-in-Ossory in Queen's county or modern County Laois prefigured a similar career path on the part of his son Richard.[19] In fact, the apparently diverse pathways taken by Robert in Bengal and Richard in Munster were not entirely dissimilar in that the brothers manifested a high degree of social agility and financial acumen which enabled them to prosper within environments which were not infrequently hostile, alien, and dangerous. Diverse manifestations of cultural and social resilience required on the part of settlers in early modern Ireland require further scholarly consideration in order to enhance understanding of quotidian interactions between native and newcomers *à longue durée*.

Although Richard Hedges was born around 1670, it is not until the first decade of the eighteenth century that archival material enables a reconstruction of aspects of his experience as military governor of Ross Castle in County Kerry and as an astute man of business intent on his own financial and social aggrandizement.[20] Like his father, Richard was educated at Trinity College Dublin, following a period at a school run by a Mr. Stapleton in Queen's county.[21] Hedges served in the Williamite forces and family tradition held that he took part in the Battle of the Boyne in 1690.[22] With a bond of financial security provided apparently by his London cousin William Hedges, Richard secured an appointment around 1704 as the agent in Cork and Kerry of the Hollow Sword Blade Company.[23] This role positioned Hedges strategically and lucratively within a nexus of land acquisition and financial speculation in southwest Munster. Although the Hollow Sword Blade Company was originally founded in 1691 as a joint stock company for the manufacture of hollow-ground rapiers, it was acquired by a group of businessmen in the early years of the eighteenth century with the objective of deploying the Company's corporate function as a bank.[24] In 1703, the Company embarked on the purchase of Irish estates forfeited in the context of the Williamite settlement, including lands in counties Cork and Kerry previously owned by Donogh MacCarthy, earl of Clancarthy. The establishment of the Registry of Deeds at Dublin in 1708 in order to complement penal legislation in respect of the exclusion of Catholics from the market for land means that Hedges's land dealings are considerably better documented for the years immediately following the launch of the new system of transaction registration.[25] Initially leasing land, as he did from the Percival and Orrery estates in North Cork, Hedges quickly leveraged his Hollow Sword Blade appointment to acquire property in his own name. His purchase in 1710 of an estate centered on the town of Macroom in County Cork from a prominent lawyer, Francis Barnard, was his most significant acquisition, as it would form the nucleus of the family patrimony over succeeding generations.[26] These lands, which had been confiscated from the Earl of Clancarthy, had been sold the previous year by the Hollow Sword Blade Company to Francis Woodley of Dublin, and such changes of ownership within a short period are suggestive of insider dealing.[27] No doubt on the basis of his close knowledge of conditions in Kerry resulting from his function as governor of Ross Castle, Hedges also acquired lands in that county.[28] Energetic and tireless in the pursuit of his advancement, Richard Hedges was indifferent to such prevalent social and ethnic tensions which might have limited his capacity for self-aggrandizement.

Hedges's friendship with Mortogh Griffin of Killarney is suggestive of a social versatility which readily transcended boundaries of ethnicity in a mutually beneficial commitment to profit. Griffin, who originated in County Clare, was a socially ambitious Gaelic Irish convert to the established church who enthusiastically availed of opportunities presented by the Williamite settlement to establish and secure his affluence.[29] A binary template of conquest and colonization too readily risks the extrusion from the historical narrative of numerous individuals like Griffin who shaped new circumstances to their advantage. The attainder of the Jacobite Sir Nicholas Browne had inaugurated a period of uncertainty in the fortunes of the Roman Catholic Browne family, which had long dominated the area around Killarney following the grant of the seigniory of Molahiffe to Sir Valentine Browne (d.1589) under the auspices of the plantation of Munster. Crucially, Griffin served as an administrator to Lady Ellen Browne during the difficult time when her husband was exiled in the Low Countries. The confiscated lands were vested in the Chichester House Trustees on the basis of a life interest, as it was allowed that the estate would revert to Nicholas's son Valentine on the occasion of his father's death. The estate was then purchased on a lifetime basis by a controversial English former politician called John Asgill, who had married Nicholas Browne's eldest daughter Jane, a Protestant.[30] Asgill was a hopelessly inept manager, and when Valentine Browne (d.1736), third viscount of Kenmare, succeeded his father in 1720, he inherited an estate heavily encumbered by debt as a result of Asgill's incompetence.[31] The predatory disposition of Hedges and Griffin was evident as early as 1705, when Asgill sold them timber from the Browne estate to the value of £1,500.[32] It is likely also that Griffin benefited from Hedges's appointment as the local agent of the Hollow Sword Blade Company. For instance, in 1709, Griffin purchased a parcel of land in the Kerry barony of Dunkerron from the Company, which had been previously confiscated from the estate of the earl of Clancarthy.[33] In 1710, Griffin formally witnessed a deed of lease and release between Hedges and Daniel Carthy of County Cork.[34] Clearly, both men not infrequently acted in commercial tandem. Unsurprisingly, Griffin was alert to the prospect of ready profit when he garnered a handsome return on former MacCarthy lands in Magunihy barony, which he purchased in 1709 from the Hollow Sword Blade Company, and which he advantageously resold to Sir Mathew Deane of County Cork the following year.[35] Yet notwithstanding Hedges's and Griffin's avidity for profit and wealth, they were not unopposed locally in their attempts to exploit social, legal, and financial flux with a view to enrichment.

In fact, Hedges and Griffin were bitterly and memorably denounced by a brilliantly outspoken local Gaelic poet. In large measure, both men are only remembered today as victims of the searing satire of Aogán Ó Rathaille who portrayed them as noisome ogres. About the same age as Hedges, Ó Rathaille was born around 1670 in the district of Killarney.[36] Formed both culturally and ideologically within the declining milieu of traditional bardic eulogy, Ó Rathaille infused an antique literary idiom with remarkable verve and insight, which reflected and interpreted a turbulent society. While he composed poetry with a communal focus for members of minor west Munster Catholic gentry families with Jacobite inclinations, Ó Rathaille's poems were also sharply political and their perspective was both local and broader. Influenced by the bardic paradigm of patronage, he was especially devoted to two noble families: the eclipsed Gaelic dynasty of MacCarthy and the Anglo-Irish Brownes of Killarney.[37] Given that Hedges and Griffin had benefited materially from the misfortune of Donough MacCarthy (1668–1734), fourth earl of Clancarthy, who would die in exile in Hamburg, it is hardly surprising that they elicited infuriated disdain from Ó Rathaille. In a poem beginning 'Monuarsa an Chárthfhuil tráite tréithlag' ('My woe – the house of Carthy is exhausted and abject'), Ó Rathaille, while initially bemoaning the fate of the MacCarthy family, quickly moves to an extended reflection on what he perceives as the plunder of Gaelic Ireland by the 'English-speaking gang' ('tír do briseadh le foirinn an Bhéarla'). Divested of its natural bounty, lacking in leadership and marked by the suppression of the church, Ireland is now a country under the sway of enemies, mercenaries and criminals ('fá smacht namhad is amhas is meirleach'). Utilizing the venerable trope of the female personification of Ireland, Ó Rathaille presents a startling image of an abandoned and distressed widow whose life blood is lapped up by the dogs of Bristol and whose body is dismembered by English curs. Two individuals in particular are singled out for personalized reference. The occupation of the ancestral lands of MacCarthy by two such dismal interlopers as Hedges and Griffin was a source of particular torment for the poet.[38] The contemporary significance of Ó Rathaille within a Gaelic cultural milieu is reflected in the scribal transmission of his poems during his own lifetime in Dublin, Cork, and Limerick.[39] Accordingly, it seems that his perspective is not just reflective of an outraged local poet but is also suggestive of an embattled elite Gaelic cohort. The delineation of an early modern Gaelic public sphere requires further elucidation on the part of scholars. However, research to date is indicative of a vibrant culture of communication, knowledge dissemination and news informed by diverse strands of orality, script, and print.[40] Although in recent decades, scholars have made significant progress in attempts to refine understanding of an often elusive and enigmatic early modern Gaelic Ireland on the basis of a relatively large extant corpus of contemporary poetry and prose, the work of interpretation and analysis of literary sources, more often than not accessible only in manuscript format, remains a critical research challenge.

Nonetheless, it would be inaccurate to assume that Richard Hedges was simply a boorish arriviste indifferent to patterns of social status and interaction in the largely Gaelic community in which he lived and operated. In a series of letters written to the administration at Dublin Castle in his capacity as governor of the garrison at Ross Castle, Hedges reveals himself to have been an astute observer of developments in the Cork and Kerry borderlands in the early years of the eighteenth century.[41] Moreover, Hedges was highly energetic in his sustained campaign against local bands of marauding outlaws popularly known as Tories tand rapparees. Typically, Hedges was not slow to assume credit for his efforts in this respect when he claimed in a letter to Joshua Dawson at Dublin Castle in 1704 that nobody of his generation had done more than him to destroy these outlaws.[42] Later in October of the same year, he advised Dawson that 'no English gentleman of note' lived in what he termed the 'barbarous country' of southwest Cork, with the exception of a Protestant clergyman based at Macroom, and accordingly, Hedges maintained that the task of eradicating local miscreants would fall to him alone.[43] In another letter to Dawson composed in late October 1704, Hedges controversially argued that Catholics should be armed in such cases where they could be deployed in his campaign against outlaws. By way of intelligence, Hedges reported on the whereabouts of two leading outlaws: the 'old murderer' Dermot Sullivan was in Kerry, while 'Philip Roonan ye other murderer keeps out of ye way in some other country'.[44] Hedges's intimate local knowledge is evidenced again in March 1707 when the threat of invasion prompted him immediately to arrest a Catholic priest and to issue warrants for the arrest of six other clerics.[45] Writing triumphantly to Dawson in July 1707, Hedges boasted that Daniel Sullivan had turned in the notorious outlaw Dermod Falvey, who had been promptly incarcerated in Tralee jail. The previous week, Hedges had sent the brother of the tory Dermod Bane and what he called 'four more notorious harbourers' to the same prison. In fact, such was Hedges's confidence that he told Dawson that he was close to the outright suppression of such brigands. Claiming that the Irish were now divided among themselves, Hedges reported to Dawson that the gentry were aware that he had what he termed 'just intelligence' about their supposed implication in local banditry and as such they were profoundly compromised. In the event that these gentleman should decline to assist Hedges, he was now determined to 'have those rogues suppressed while ye nights are short'.[46] Notwithstanding Hedges's tendency to exaggeration in his communications with Dawson, it is clear that he was remarkably well informed about local personalities and networks of influence.[47] Such a disposition within a region remote from the authority of the Dublin administration is indicative of a highly resourceful and culturally agile individual.[48]

On 6 January 1698, Robert Hedges was instructed by the senior management of the New East India Company to take passage on board the ship *London* under the command of Captain George Matthews, bound in the first instance for the Coromandel Coast in southeastern India. On arrival there, Hedges was to assist with the loading of cargo to the *London*, and on completion of this and other Company business, he was to proceed to his assigned post in the Bay of Bengal.[49] Established by royal charter in 1600, the East India Company was granted a monopoly of England's Asian trade, which, at the beginning of the seventeenth century, centered on spices, pepper, indigo, and silk. By the end of the century, this trade had expanded exponentially to include textiles such as calicoes.[50] In spite of the considerable logistical, strategic, and resource challenges entailed in such long-distance commercial activity, the Company, which had been founded on a joint stock basis for prescribed voyages or periods, and which was made permanent in 1657, had established itself as a key pillar of London's business environment, with East India stocks and bonds an important part of the city's emergent stock market in the 1690s. The grant of a charter to a New East India Company in 1698 resulted in two English companies trading in Asia for some years. However, it was agreed upon to merge both entities in 1702, and a United East India Company was formed in 1709.[51] While historians traditionally interpreted the Company as a global business enterprise, recent research has considered it from social, cultural, political and intellectual perspectives. Philip Stern, for example, has argued that the Company in the late seventeenth and early eighteenth centuries constituted a form of 'early modern body politic'.[52] Stern has also interrogated what he considers an unhelpful historiographical emphasis on distinctions rather than similarities between the British Atlantic and British Asia.[53] For instance, Stern has argued that the island of St. Helena in the South Atlantic, acquired definitively by the Company in the 1670s as a watering station for Eastindiamen, was to become a plantation colony intimately linked to the Company's activities in Asia. In this respect, the Company was attentive to the creation of a sustainable civil society with a distinct sense of moral order on the island. Moreover, Stern suggests that a pivotal element of the Company leaders' strategy at St. Helena and in Asia was the development of a military-fiscal system to provide local revenues to fund its political and martial administration. In effect, national states were not exclusive agents in the creation of early modern empires.[54]

If India was a land of opportunity and sensual exotic promise for early modern Englishmen, it was also a locus of extraordinary danger, and death was always imminent.[55] John Ovington, an English clergyman who was educated at Trinity College, Dublin, published in 1696 an account of his voyage to India and sojourn in Surat in 1689, in which he stressed the perils to the health of Europeans posed by an apparently extreme Indian climate. Ovington claimed that in Bombay, the mortality rate among Europeans was especially high during the months of September and October in the aftermath of the monsoon season, when 'the rains ferment the air, and raise therein such a sultry heat, that scarce any is able to withstand that feverish effect it has upon their spirits'.[56] Those of a more resilient nature in the service of the Company stood to benefit financially as a result of a decision taken in the mid-seventeenth century when it terminated its inter-Asian trade and focused exclusively on trading to and from England. Company employees and other Englishmen in Asia were now permitted to trade between Asian ports, and such private country trade was often very lucrative.[57] With little to offer other than silver from the New World, Europeans encountered a sophisticated and specialized regional economy, and it has been argued that 'the European advance in Asian waters was parasitic on Asian networks and on Asian trade'.[58]

The survival of details of Robert Hedges's personal account for 1708 indicate that he invested relatively large sums of money in private country trade. For instance, he shipped goods to the port city of Mocha in Yemen in the ship *Godolphin*, where, in return, he presumably purchased coffee.[59] In the same year, with the support of the leading merchant financier and founding director of the New East India Company, Sir James Bateman, Hedges successfully petitioned the Company's Court of Managers for a reduction of the 15% surcharge imposed on 'his goods brought home'.[60]

In 1709, Bateman and the London merchant Alderman John Edmonds agreed to provide security for an astonishing £2,000 in respect of Hedges's Company appointment in the Bay of Bengal. In December of the same year, the Company's Court of Directors allowed Hedges to return to India with 'four thousand ounces of silver and in wrought plate for his own use to the value of £100.[61] It seems likely that such were the profits to be made from private trade that Hedges had secured capital from Bateman and Edmonds to invest in his personal Asian business.[62] However, Bateman's assistance was not restricted to financial matters. In 1710, Sir James sought the permission of the Court of Directors to ship two chests of beer and two chests of wine to Hedges in Bengal on the ship *Dartmouth* free of a freight charge.[63] It seems certain that Robert's uncle Sir William (d.1701), on the basis of his own experience of Company business and as a director of the Bank of England, had first arranged for his nephew to pursue a career in India and had later enabled his access to a nexus of wealthy London financiers and merchants. Crucially, Robert had first served in India when his uncle directed Company affairs in Bengal, but Robert had returned to London with him in 1687.[64] In his will, dictated in 1709, prior to his return to the Bay of Bengal, Robert specified several legacies which are reflective of a web of individuals which enabled him to prosper in the service of the Company. He directed that £50 each be given to Sir John Bateman and John Edmonds, while £20 was to be paid to his cousin Susanna Edmonds, who was John's wife and the daughter of his uncle Sir William. It is surely no coincidence that John Edmonds held shares in the Hollow Sword Blade Company.[65] Evidently, family connections were deployed in the advance of Robert's career. Likewise, smaller sums of money were allocated to his late uncle's second wife Lady Hedges of Finchley and their four sons. Moreover, £20 were reserved for his 'honourable father Major Robert Hedges', while the remainder of his estate was to be divided among 'my dear brother Captain Richard Hedges of Macroom in Ireland' as well as between his three sisters and a niece.[66] Robert's will is suggestive of the importance of kinship networks in early modern Ireland and beyond, and the need for further research to reconstruct patterns of patronage, support, and counsel.

It seems that in the years following his departure for the Bay of Bengal in 1698 that Robert Hedges proved himself an adept and trustworthy Company servant. In 1702, he was one of four New Company employees along with four others from the old Company selected for membership of the council to oversee 'the concerns of the United Trade of both companies' in the Bay of Bengal. Moreover, it had been decided to defer the selection of a local company president for that year and instead to rotate the local leadership between both Companies. It was directed that Hedges, among others, would assume this role on such a rotational basis. Moreover, this was a critical period in relations between the Companies, and it was the responsibility of the council to manage tactfully the removal to Calcutta of the old Company's factory at Hooghly.[67] Ominously, in the same communication from the Court of Managers in London, it was noted that they had also written separately to the serving Company president in Bengal, Sir Edward Littleton, requesting that he 'will apply himself to the adjusting of all matters to satisfaction & give all necessary dispatch therein'. Moreover, the Court of Managers was obliged to acknowledge that Littleton was in possession of the Company's treasury. In the event of dispute, the Court of Managers directed that its council members were to divest Sir Edward of its contents. In conclusion, the council members were admonished to employ an equal number of New Company servants to those of the old Company.[68] It seems these misgivings of the Court of Managers in relation to Edward Littleton represented the early stages of a conflict which would result in a highly pejorative attack by Littleton on Robert Hedges on the basis of his Irish background, as will be seen.

Concerns in the Company's London headquarters as to the financial probity of Littleton were rehearsed in a series of increasingly recriminatory missives to Bengal over a period of several years. In 1703, London informed Hedges and his colleagues on the council that information had reached headquarters to the effect the Company had been subject to fraud on the part of an Indian merchant called Muttradas and his associates. While not explicitly linking Littleton to the latter, London requested that discreet pressure be applied to Sir Edward 'to come to a just accommodation of our affaires'. However, if Littleton proved recalcitrant and if evidence of mismanagement on his part was uncovered, London instructed its Bengal council members to seize Company goods in Littleton's possession as well as securing from him sufficient financial compensation for any financial loss through fraud.[69] However, matters were still unresolved in January 1704, when London admonished Hedges and his council colleagues that, although they had returned completed company accounts to London and had investigated suspect contracts, they had failed to hold Littleton to account in regard to his use of Company funds. London now demanded bluntly that Littleton was to be obliged to render satisfaction 'for the real summes he is debtor to us, & particularly for those summes for which he owns himself to be security'.[70] Matters were still unresolved to the satisfaction of the Company, when, in March 1705, it ordered its agent at Banjarmasin on the southern coast of Borneo, Allen Catchpoole, to seize goods from Littleton's private trade on board three ships *en route* from Bengal. However, these instructions were unlikely to have been implemented as Catchpoole was murdered and the Company's warehouses burned during a mutiny by Malay soldiers that very month.[71]

However, satisfactory progress in matter of Sir Edward Littleton remained elusive as late as 1708, when London yet again complained about the failure to secure compensation for the debts incurred through his fraud and mismanagement.[72] The frustration of officials in London was no doubt compounded by geographical distance and the consequently protracted nature of correspondence, with ships leaving London in December and January in order to catch favorable winds, the voyage around the Cape of Good Hope to India taking up to eight months.[73]

The case of Littleton's corporate corruption is especially interesting as a result of an abusive and ethnically charged tirade which Sir Edward directed at Robert Hedges. In a somewhat desperate attempt to discredit him, Littleton drafted an 'account of the debts owed by Robert Hedges book keeper to the East India Company', which he signed and dated 30 January 1706 in Calcutta.[74] Accusing the 'Irish bookeeper' of entering £200 of saltpeter into the account of a certain Gosseram when, according to Littleton, it should have been correctly entered into his account as it was delivered by him or his servants, Littleton demanded that the Company charge Hedges with this 'villanous Irish forgery' and several other supposed misdemeanors which he termed, respectively, 'another impious Irish forgery' and 'another little Irish forgery' undertaken by the 'devising Irish bookeeper'. Furthermore, Littleton accused Hedges of defrauding the account of an Indian merchant named Gollochand, from which Hedges allegedly withdrew money for his own use. In this respect, Littleton announced to his satisfaction that the 'action of the Irish bookeeper in this affair is no other or not at all short as I conceive not only of damnable forgery ye natural sin of Irishmen'; by stealing from his employer, Hedges was guilty of 'notorious hellish Irish forgery'. Sir Edward demanded hysterically that Hedges be charged for his crimes before a magistrate and declared that he would gladly 'enter into a recognisance to her Majesty to appear and give evidence in any court of judicature of her Majesty's wherein the Irishman your bookeeper shall be prosecuted'. Littleton observed that even an Irishman deserved punishment, although 'some thinke such crimes naturall to them'. In conclusion, Sir Edward declared to his satisfaction that the 'action of the Irish bookeeper I took to be no other or lesse then a most damnable mutinous factious perditious and rebellious villany'. For good measure, Littleton then proceeded to list several instances where Hedges had supposedly deceived a number of Indian individuals. In one instance, he refers to Hedges's having twice defrauded individuals at Cossimbazar on the Hooghly River, which, on the second such occasion, was depicted as 'being a second part to the same tune Lillebolero'. Littleton's allusion to an anti-Catholic and anti-Irish ballad, which was particularly popular during Glorious Revolution of 1688, was intentionally calculated to insult Hedges whose family was Williamite in loyalty and possibly falsely to suggest Jacobite sympathies on his part. For good measure, Littleton claimed that as a result of his actions, Hedges was in debt to the Company to the value of approximately £50,000 sterling.[75] While Littleton's anti-Irish prejudice was not surprising, given the development of deeply malignant ethnic stereotypes, especially in the aftermath of the 1641 rebellion, it does seem unusual that a Protestant of very recent English provenance should be so vilified given the inherently anti-Catholic timbre of an emergent British identity.[76] However, it has been argued that English dread of the Irish was replaced by contempt from the 1680s and 1690s onwards and that, at this stage, English views of

Ireland were 'settling into a more-or-less permanent sneer'.[77] It is possible that such sentiment in this particular context was peculiar to the intemperate personality of Littleton, or it may also reflect a prevailing degree of prejudice against ambitious Irishmen in the Company's service.[78] Ironically, Richard Hedges, who prided himself on being an English gentleman in the wastelands of Gaelic Munster, would surely have recoiled in horror and in disbelief in the face of such colonialist invective turned against the colonizer.

Notwithstanding Sir Edward Littleton's malevolent accusations against him, Robert Hedges prospered in the service of the East India Company. During a period of leave back in London in 1709, Hedges petitioned the Court of Directors to be appointed 'second in Councill in the Bay and to be next in succession to that Presidency'. Following a ballot among the Court of Directors, Hedges was selected to be second-in-command at the Bay of Bengal, with a salary of £40 per annum.[79] Clearly, in favor with the Court of Directors, Hedges was granted permission in December 1709 to transport to India 'two hundred ounces of silver more than the four thousand ounces granted the last Court'.[80] Shortly afterwards, the Court of Directors directed that Hedges be allowed to return to Bengal with two Indian servants who were then on their way over from Ireland, although it was stipulated that Hedges was to pay their passage to India.[81] In due course, Hedges succeeded to the Bengal Presidency and presided over the Company's operations at Fort William in Calcutta.[82] However, Hedges wrote to the Court of Directors on 24 November 1716, seeking permission to travel home due to an illness which had afflicted him over the previous year. While permission to return was granted, the Court of Directors expressed the wish that he might stay longer in Bengal if his health had improved—such was the directors' satisfaction with his 'good management'.[83] Poignantly, Hedges never managed to make it home as he died in Bengal in 1717.[84] Ever reliable, Sir James Bateman undertook his last obligation to Hedges as his executor and accordingly wound up his affairs with a Company distinctly unsentimental when it came to matters of finance.[85] Appropriately for a conventionally pious Protestant, the sole material vestige of Hedges in India today is a reference to his death on 28 December 1717 in an inscription on a monument to former presidents and governors of Fort William in the interior of the late eighteenth-century Anglican St. John's Church in Calcutta.[86]

In Munster, the redoubtable Richard Hedges continued to prosper. No doubt with the assistance of his brother Robert, he pursued an occasional commercial sideline in the sale of Asian textiles and Chinese tea, and this trade was possibly also facilitated by the establishment of East India Company agencies in Cork in 1706 and at Kinsale in 1708.[87] Already by 1702, Company vessels were using Cork as a base from which to ship Irish provisions to India.[88] In 1714, the Court of Directors authorized a payment of approximately £5 to Richard Hedges following a sale of goods sold through private trade, including presumably Robert's merchandise, at the Company's candle or auction.[89] Richard remained active in the land market, selling lands in Kerry and Cork in 1725.[90] Retiring to the appropriately named Snugborough

at Kilcrea in County Cork, Richard Hedges was engaged in property transactions as late as 1736.[91] Predeceased by his wife Frances who died in 1729,
Hedges appears to have passed away as late as 1748.[92]

Yet it would be inaccurate to depict Hedges as a speculator wholly animated by considerations of profit. David Dickson has suggested that Hedges
attempted to develop Macroom as a center of Protestant settlement.[93] On
acquisition of the estate centered on Macroom in 1710, Hedges certainly
inherited a number of English tenants in the town itself, such as George
Lombard, who presided over a small shop, as did Dominick Harding and
George Walters. It was noted that the town's mass house had been demolished
and a Protestant clergyman Richard Browne was listed as a tenant of several
local properties. However, the number of tenants in the town bearing surnames of Gaelic and Old English Munster provenance is perhaps even more
striking.[94] In effect, Hedges inhabited an Irish world where a Gaelic cultural
idiom predominated. Emblematically, it was recorded in 1723 that Timothy
Sullivan served as agent and servant to Hedges.[95] It is likely that Richard
spoke Irish with some degree of competence if only to conduct his business
effectively in an Irish-speaking milieu. Although separated by immense distance and apparent cultural divergence, the worlds of Richard and Robert
Hedges were in some fundamental respects similar. In their commitment to
colonial capitalism, the brothers operated within alien and often dangerous
environments where they effectively served as agents of an intruded foreign
authority within their respective locales. The East India Company decided in
1709 to fund the costs of its employees seeking to learn Indian languages in
order to enable its servants to 'find out the true value of the goods and prevent
the merchants imposing upon you'.[96] The colonial capitalism exemplified
by Richard and Robert Hedges was unconcerned with issues of cultural or
linguistic difference given its overriding focus on the generation of profit.
While such indifference to cultural diversity and integrity seems inconsistent
with a contemporary globalizing dynamic, it is useful for historians of early
modern Ireland to consider that local and global threads of the historical record, when considered in tandem, complement and enhance understanding
of an often elusive but always complex past. If the depredations wrought
by colonial capitalism have been rightly recognized, it is important also to
acknowledge an unparalleled and transformative enrichment of creative experience and knowledge consequent on early modern global encounters.[97]

Notes

1 Jane Ohlmeyer, 'Seventeenth-century Ireland and the New British and Atlantic
   histories', *American Historical Review*, 104 (1999), 446–62; Nicholas Canny, 'Writing Early Modern History: Ireland, Britain, and the Wider World', *The Historical
   Journal* 46 (2003), 723–47; Audrey Horning, *Ireland in the Virginian Sea: Colonialism in the British Atlantic* (Chapel Hill: University of North Carolina Press, 2013).
2 Emma Rothschild, *The Inner Life of Empires: An Eighteenth-Century History* (Princeton, NJ: Princeton University Press, 2011), pp. 2, 7. See also Tonio Andrade,

'A Chinese Farmer, Two African Boys, and a Warlord: Towards A Global Micro-history', *Journal of World History* 21 (2010), 573–91.

3 Rolf Loeber, 'Irish Country Houses and Castles of the Late Caroline Period', *Quarterly Bulletin of the Irish Georgian Society* 16 (1973), 1–70; Rolf Loeber, *A Biographical Dictionary of Architects in Ireland 1600–1720* (London: John Murray Publishers, 1981), pp. 66–67.

4 For examples of Indian textiles generally in seventeenth-century Ireland, see Jane Fenlon, *Goods & Chattels: A Survey of Early Household Inventories in Ireland* (Dublin: Stationery Office, 2003), pp. 113, 115, 117, 119.

5 John E. Wills, 'European Consumption and Asian Production in the Seventeenth and Eighteenth Centuries', in John Brewer and Roy Porter (eds.), *Consumption and the World of Goods* (London and New York: Routledge, 1993), pp. 133–47, 136; P.J. Marshall, 'The English in Asia to 1700', in Nicholas Canny and Alaine Low (eds.), *The Origins of Empire: British Overseas Enterprise to the Close of the Seventeenth Century* (Oxford: Oxford University Press, 1998), pp. 264–85, 275.

6 BL Add. MS 46942, fol.167r.

7 BL Add. MS 46942, fol.167r.

8 BL Add. MS 46942, fol.168v.

9 See, for instance, the Eastindiaman berthed at Kinsale, August 1673, where it moored alongside a fleet of ships bound for Barbados: BL IOR/E/3/34. All dates cited from contemporary manuscript sources are given in their original Old Style format. For the arrival at Kinsale of three Eastindiamen in June 1688, see Edward MacLysaght (ed.), *Calendar of the Orrery Papers* (Dublin: Irish Manuscripts Commission, 1941), pp. 358–59.

10 BL Add. MS 46942, fol.170v.

11 C.A. Bayly, 'Ireland, India and the Empire: 1780–1914', *Transactions of the Royal Historical Society* 10 (2000), 377–97, 378.

12 Jane Ohlmeyer, 'Ireland, India and the British empire', *Studies in People's History* 2 (2015), 169–88, 172. I am grateful to Professor Ohlmeyer for discussing with me her work on colonial enterprises in Ireland and India in the seventeenth century and for providing me with a copy of her article on Gerald Aungier, which is forthcoming in *Past and Present*.

13 Richard Caulfield (ed.), *The Council Book of the Corporation of Youghal* (Guildford, Surrey: J. Billing & Sons, 1878), pp. 314–15, 331; David Kelly and Tadhg O'Keeffe, *Youghal: Irish Historic Towns Atlas No.27* (Dublin: Royal Irish Academy, 2015), p. 27.

14 'The old registry book Youghal from 1665 to 1720', Representative Church Body Library, Dublin, P608/1/1. For adult baptism of Africans, see Miranda Kaufmann, *Black Tudors: The Untold Story* (London: Oneworld, 2017), pp. 159–63.

15 For Irish settlement on Montserrat, see, for instance, Natalie A. Zacek, *Settler Society in the English Leeward Islands, 1670–1776* (Cambridge: Cambridge University Press, 2010).

16 BL IOR/H/803, 349–50.

17 Gary S. De Krey, 'Sir William Hedges (1632–1701)' in H.C.G. Matthew and Brian Harrison (eds.), *Oxford Dictionary of National Biography*, 60 vols. (Oxford: Oxford University Press, 2004), vol. 26, pp. 226–28; William A. Pettigrew, *Freedom's Debt: The Royal African Company and the Politics of the African Slave Trade, 1672–1752* (Chapel Hill: University of North Carolina Press, 2013), p. 76; Jon Wilson, *India Conquered: Britain's Raj and the Chaos of Empire* (London and New York: Simon and Schuster, 2016), pp. 37–43.

18 TNA, prob 11/461/266. Sir William's Cork holdings were located at Clonpriest near Youghal where his father was buried and at Coolclough in the barony of Duhallow.

19 An approximate date for Robert Hedges's military service at Borris-in-Ossory is based on the record of his wife Dorothea's burial at nearby Aghaboe churchyard in 1675. See William Carrigan, *The History and Antiquities of the Diocese of Ossory*, 4 vols. (Dublin: Sealy, Bryers & Walker, 1905), vol. 2, pp. 46, 129; *Journal of the Association for the Preservation of the Memorials of the Dead, Ireland*, 3 (1906), 599–600.

20 In 1710, it was recorded in a legal deed that Richard Hedges and his wife Frances were then aged approximately forty years, and their son Robert was aged around fourteen years. Dublin, Registry of Deeds, henceforth, RD Memorial, 8/35/1705.

21 G.D. Burtchaell and T.U. Sadleir (eds.), *Alumni Dublinenses* (Dublin: A. Thom, 1935), p. 386. Prior to attending TCD, Robert Hedges matriculated at Magdalen Hall, Oxford, in 1651. Joseph Foster (ed.), *Alumni Oxonienses: The Members of the University of Oxford, 1500–1714*. 4 vols. (Oxford and London: Parker & Co., 1891/92), vol. 2, p. 688.

22 Bodleian MS, Top. Ireland. C. 2, p. 21.

23 *An estimate of the value of the present stock of the Governor and Company for Making Hollow Sword-Blades in England* (London, 1705); Edward MacLysaght (ed.), 'Herbert papers', *Analecta Hibernica* 15 (1944), 95–107, 95; Bodleian MS Top. Ireland. C. 2, p. 29; RD, memorial 16/487/7908.

24 Stuart Bell, "A masterpiece of knavery'? The activities of the Sword Blade Company in London's early financial markets', *Business History* 54 (4) (2012), 623–38; Patrick Walsh, *The South Sea Bubble and Ireland: Money, Banking and Investment, 1690–1721* (Woodbridge: Boydell and Brewer, 2014), pp. 29–31.

25 Peter Roebuck, 'The Irish Registry of Deeds: A Comparative Study', *Irish Historical Studies* 18 (1972), 61–73.

26 RD Memorial, 8/35/1705.

27 RD Memorial, 3/167/799.

28 RD Memorial, 44/212/28586.

29 Griffin, in a 1709 land transaction entailing the sale to him by the Hollow Sword Blade Company of lands in the Kerry barony of Magunihy, was careful to have it recorded that he was 'of the Protestant religion'. RD Memorial, 5/211/1581.

30 Edward MacLysaght (ed.), *The Kenmare Manuscripts* (Dublin: Irish Manuscripts Commission, 1942), p. x.

31 MacLysaght, *Kenmare manuscripts*, p. x.

32 MacLysaght, *Kenmare manuscripts*, p. 476.

33 RD Memorial, 5/207/1573.

34 RD Memorial, 6/134/1582.

35 RD Memorial, 5/211/1581; RD Memorial, 6/134/1582).

36 Breandán Ó Buachalla (ed.), *Aogán Ó Rathaille* (Dublin: Field Day, 2007), pp. 1–8.

37 Breandán Ó Buachalla, 'Ó Rathaille, na Cárthaigh agus na Brúnaigh', *Studia Hibernica* 31 (2000/2001), 119–38; Marc Caball, 'Local and Global: A Perspective from Early Eighteenth-Century Munster', *Proceedings of the Harvard Celtic Colloquium* 34 (2014), 35–51.

38 Ó Buachalla, *Aogán Ó Rathaille*, Poem, no. 4, 13–15, 13, lines 16, 20. For a translation to English of this poem, see Patrick S. Dinneen and Tadhg O'Donoghue (eds.), *Dánta Aodhagáin Uí Rathaille* (London: Irish Texts Society, 1911), no. ii, pp. 6–11.

39 Breandán Ó Buachalla, *Dánta Aodhagáin Uí Rathaille: Reassessments* (London: Irish Texts Society, 2004), p. 21.

40 Marc Caball, 'Culture, Politics and Identity in Sixteenth-Century Ireland: The Testimony of Tadhg Dall Ó hUiginn (c.1550–1591)' in Pádraigín Riggs (ed.),

Tadhg Dall Ó hUiginn: His Historical and Literary Context (London: Irish Texts Society, 2010), pp. 1–21; Wes Hamrick, 'The Public Sphere and Eighteenth-Century Ireland', *New Hibernia Review* 18 (2014), 87–100.

41 On Pratt's 1708 map of Ireland, it was noted that two foot companies were based at Ross Castle which made it the largest garrison in county Kerry, BL K Top 50/18 Press 14 A Ireland.

42 Bodleian MS, Top. Ireland. C. 2, 25.

43 Bodleian MS, Top. Ireland. C. 2, 29.

44 Bodleian MS, Top. Ireland. C.2, 29–30.

45 Bodleian MS, Top. Ireland. C.2, 31.

46 Bodleian MS, Top. Ireland. C.2, 33–34.

47 Hedges appears to have continued as governor of Ross Castle down to around 1715. MacLysaght, 'Herbert papers', 97.

48 Marc Caball, *Kerry, 1600–1730: The Emergence of a British Atlantic County* (Dublin: Four Courts Press, 2017), p. 51.

49 BL IOR/E/3/94, 34v.

50 K.N. Chaudhuri, *The Trading World of Asia and the English East India Company* (Cambridge: Cambridge University Press, 1978), pp. 41–56.

51 Marshall, 'The English in Asia to 1700', p. 283.

52 Philip J. Stern, 'History and Historiography of the English East India Company: Past, Present, and Future!' *History Compass* 7 (2009), 1146–80, 1151.

53 Philip J. Stern, 'British Asia and British Atlantic: Comparisons and Connections', *William and Mary Quarterly* 63 (2006), 693–712.

54 Philip J. Stern, 'Politics and Ideology in the Early East India Company-State: The Case of St Helena, 1673–1709', *The Journal of Imperial and Commonwealth History* 35 (2007), 1–23. See also Philip J. Stern, *The Company-state: Corporate Sovereignty and the Early Modern Foundations of the British Empire in India* (Oxford and New York: Oxford University Press, 2011).

55 P.J. Marshall, 'Taming the Exotic: The British and India in the Seventeenth and Eighteenth Centuries', in G.S. Rousseau and Roy Porter (eds.), *Exoticism in the Enlightenment* (Manchester: Manchester University Press, 1990), pp. 46–65.

56 John Ovington, *A voyage to Surat, in the year, 1689* (London, 1696), p. 139.

57 Marshall, 'The English in Asia to 1700', p. 280.

58 Sunil S. Amrith, *Crossing the Bay of Bengal: The Furies of Nature and the Fortunes of Migrants* (Cambridge, MA: Harvard University Press, 2013), p. 61.

59 BL IOR/L/AG/1/1/12, General Ledger B: June 1705-April 1709, fol.229.

60 BL IOR/B/49, 243–44, 274, 347, 445–46. Hedges seems to have maintained a base in London, where, in 1702, he entered into an agreement for seven years in respect of the upkeep of two houses owned by Nicholas Trott in New Street in Bishopsgate: BL IOR/L/L/2/720.

61 BL IOR/B/49, 842.

62 In respect of the importance of private trade, see Emily Erikson, *Between Monopoly and Free Trade: The English East India Company, 1600–1757* (Princeton, NJ: Princeton University Press, 2014), pp. 56–65.

63 BL IOR/E/1/2, 242r.

64 R. Barlow and Henry Yule (eds.), *The Diary of Sir William Hedges, Esq.* 3 vols. (London: Hakluyt Society, 1887–89), vol. 2, pp. cxcvii–cxcix.

65 *A list of the names of the members of the corporation for making Hollow Sword-Blades in England* (London, 1705).

66 TNA, prob 11/565/341.

67 BL IOR/E/3/94, 229v.

68 BL IOR/E/3/94, 230r.

69 BL IOR/E/3/94, 239v.

70 BL IOR/E/3/94, 246v.

71 Stern, *Company-state*, 181.

72 BL IOR/E/3/94, 269v–270r.

73 Miles Ogborn, *Global Lives: Britain and the World 1550–1800* (Cambridge: Cambridge University Press, 2008), p. 84.

74 BL Add. MS 69287.

75 BL Add. MS 69287.

76 Linda Colley, 'Britishness and otherness: an argument', *Journal of British Studies* 3 (1992), 309–29, 316–17.

77 David Hayton, 'From barbarian to burlesque: English images of the Irish c.1660–1750', *Irish Economic and Social History* 15 (1988), 5–31, at 15.

78 For the growing number of Irish personnel in Company service during the eighteenth century, see Barry Crosbie, *Irish Imperial Networks: Migration, Social Communication and Exchange in Nineteenth-Century India* (Cambridge: Cambridge University Press, 2012), pp. 31–42.

79 BL IOR/E/3/96, 337r; IOR/B/49, 813, 821.

80 BL IOR/B/49, 853.

81 BL IOR/B/49, 897.

82 BL IOR/B/53, 122; IOR/B/54, 9.

83 BL IOR/B/54, 541.

84 'Bengal Burials H 1713–1871: IOR indexes Z/N 47, 1717', available in the Asian & African Studies Reading Room, British Library.

85 BL IOR/B/55, 112; IOR/B/57, 33.

86 For example, Hedges donated 500 rupees towards the construction of an English church at Bombay. Richard Cobbe, *Bombay Church: Or, A True Account of the Building and Finishing the English church at Bombay in the East Indies* (London, 1766), p. 68.

87 Bodleian MS, Top. Ireland. C.2, 31, 35–36; James H. Thomas, 'East India Company agency work in the British Isles, 1700–1800', in H.V. Bowen, Margarette Lincoln and Nigel Rigby (eds.), *The Worlds of the East India Company* (Woodbridge: Boydell and Brewer), 2002, pp. 33–47, 33.

88 Crosbie, *Irish Imperial Networks*, p. 43.

89 BL IOR/B/53, 33.

90 RD Memorial, 44/212/28586, RD Memorial, 50/211/32666.

91 RD Memorial, 60/188/40460; RD Memorial, 83/225/58534.

92 Representative Church Body Library, 'Macroom Registers', P137/28/1, 65, 86. However, the 'Richard Hedges Esq' buried at Macroom on 24 May 1748 may have been Richard Hedges's grandson of the same name, who was aged about eleven years in 1731. RD Memorial, 69/4/46888.

93 David Dickson, *Old World Colony: Cork and South Munster 1630–1830* (Cork: Cork University Press, 2005), p. 63.

94 RD Memorial, 8/35/1705.

95 RD Memorial, 42/10/25445.

96 BL IOR/E/3/96, 342r.

97 Miles Ogborn, *Indian Ink: Script and Print in the Making of the English East India Company* (Chicago, IL: University of Chicago Press, 2007); Anna Winterbottom, *Hybrid Knowledge in the Early East India Company* (Basingstoke: Palgrave Macmillan, 2016), pp. 1–25; Shashi Tharoor, *Inglorious Empire: What the British Did to India* (London: Hurst, 2016), pp. 1–16.

9 Questioning the viceroys

Toward a new model of English government in Tudor Ireland, 1536–1594[1]

David Edwards

In February 1574, Elizabeth I addressed a short letter to the viceroy of her kingdom of Ireland, Sir William Fitzwilliam, and to several of the principal administrative officers serving under him in Dublin Castle. Like many of her missives about Ireland, it concerned finance. Tersely, she demanded the immediate reform of the Irish Court of Exchequer to bring its procedures into line with those prevailing in England.[2] Lest Fitzwilliam or his administrators wonder how this might be achieved, she had another document attached, drafted by the lord treasurer of England, William Cecil, Lord Burghley: 'Orders, rules and ordinances for … our Receipts and Revenues of Ireland'. This item was thirty-seven pages long. It listed, under fifty-eight separate headings, the many and various procedures that henceforth should govern the assessment and collection of Irish crown income. Leaving little to chance, it described the specialized functions of every revenue official, from the chief baron of the exchequer to the minor tellers, and—especially important—it also outlined the various means of enforcement available to exchequer and other financial officers in the event of non-payment by the queen's Irish subjects.[3]

Yet it was Elizabeth's short letter that packed the real punch. Her royal highness was irritated, and with good reason. The orders that she had Burghley write up were not new. They had first been delivered to Dublin in the reign of her late father, Henry VIII, probably—she does not give a date—after 1536.[4] Since then they had been virtually ignored by a succession of viceroys and chief governors, 'negligently kept'. But further negligence would not be tolerated. Reform of the exchequer in Dublin must be completed by the following Michaelmas. Viceroy Fitzwilliam had less than seven months to effectuate her orders. Fitzwilliam responded in an interesting way. He did nothing. We know this because twelve years later, in 1586, a letter was addressed to his successor, Sir John Perrot. Written by Burghley, it reiterated, wearily, the queen's previous demand for an overhaul of the Dublin exchequer administration. Attached to the letter was another long list of rules and orders, identical in almost every way to those of 1574.[5]

Regrettably, Burghley does not explain why the new rules had been ignored since February 1574, either by Fitzwilliam, who had vacated the viceroyalty in September 1575, or by any of its more recent incumbents.[6] Nor can an explanation for such neglect be found among any of the other documents that follow in the surviving Irish exchequer records, among which Burghley's 1586 letter and list of orders were later enrolled. All that can be ascertained is that Viceroy Perrot—unlike Fitzwilliam et al.—did not ignore the queen's wishes. The belated shake-up of exchequer administrative practice commenced soon after.[7]

Which is to say, in 1586, Perrot began to implement an important set of royal orders approximately *fifty years* after they had first been issued. Ever since the political earthquake of the Henrician schism and its impact on the government of England and Wales, the exchequer in Ireland had drifted along without serious reform: five decades during which eighteen Englishmen had preceded Perrot in the position of viceroy or acting governor, each solemnly swearing to follow royal orders to the letter, each agreeing to bear full responsibility for the oversight of crown finances, but each in his turn apparently paying no heed whatsoever to royal orders for financial administrative reorganization (Table 9.1).

This scenario becomes more perplexing when the viceroys' backgrounds are considered. With the exception of the churchmen Hugh Curwin and Adam Loftus, those who preceded Perrot over the previous five decades had been socially and politically prominent in England, well known at the

Table 9.1 English viceroys and acting governors of Ireland, 1536–94

Leonard Grey, Viscount Grane	LD	1536–40
Sir William Brereton	LJ	1540
Sir Anthony St. Leger	LD	1540–43, 1544–46, 1547–48, 1550–51, 1553–56
Sir William Brabazon	LJ	1543–44, 1546, 1550
Sir Edward Bellingham	LD	1548–49
Sir Francis Bryan	LJ	1549–50
Sir James Croft	LD	1551–52
Thomas Radcliffe, third earl of Sussex	LL	1556–65
Archbishop Hugh Curwin (with Sidney)	LJ	1557–58
Sir Nicholas Arnold	LJ	1564–66
Sir Henry Sidney	LJ, LD	1557–58, 1558, 1558–59, 1565–67, 1568–71, 1575–78
Sir William Fitzwilliam	LJ, LD	1560, 1561, 1561–62, 1567–68, 1571–75, 1588–94
Sir Robert Weston (with Fitzwilliam)	LJ	1567–68
Sir William Drury	LJ	1578–79
Sir William Pelham	LJ	1579–80
Arthur Grey, fourteenth Baron de Wilton	LD	1580–82
Archbishop Adam Loftus	LJ	1582–84
Sir Henry Wallop	LJ	1582–84
Sir John Perrot	LD	1584–88

Abbreviations: LL, Lord Lieutenant; LD, Lord Deputy; LJ, Lord Justice.

Source: Steven Ellis, *Ireland in the Age of the Tudors: 1447–1603: English Expansion and the End of Gaelic Rule* (London: Routledge, 1998), pp. 368–69.

Tudor court before being asked to serve across the Irish Sea. During the reign of Henry VIII, Sir Francis Bryan had been a royal favorite. Sir Anthony St. Leger too had been one of King Henry's 'boon companions' and long before his posting to Ireland had been a familiar figure at Whitehall and Westminster. Even Sir William Brabazon, the lowest born of the Henrician Irish governors, had spent more than ten years in or near the royal court as a trusted agent of Thomas Cromwell, before setting foot in Dublin.[8] Of the later viceroys, their ties to the monarchy were likewise strong, even intimate. The Edwardian viceroy Sir James Croft had grown up in the royal service, his father a councilor to Mary Tudor when she was Princess of Wales; the Elizabethan viceroy Sir Henry Sidney had been a childhood companion of Edward VI; and his successor, Sir William Fitzwilliam, had been one of the gentlemen of King Edward's privy chamber. One must also not to forget the titled peers who served as viceroys: Lord Leonard Grey, Viscount Grane in the 1530s, and Thomas Radcliffe, third earl of Sussex in the 1550s and 1560s, who had enjoyed positions at the heart of the court virtually by birthright as members of the senior English aristocracy. Though Arthur Grey, fourteenth baron of Wilton, was not nearly as highly placed at court, he was well known to the leaders of Elizabeth's government; besides, during the 1530s and 1540s, his father had been one of the crown's chief military commanders overseas.[9]

As a group, the English viceroys and acting governors of Tudor Ireland were no strangers to the monarchy's need for financial efficiency. All had been raised in a Renaissance culture that revered state service. As young men, whether serving in local government as crown commissioners or in the armed forces in France or Scotland, they had been made familiar with the crown's endless scrutiny of monies paid and received. And of course, as the seminal work of Ciaran Brady has shown, before taking up their appointments to the Irish viceroyalty, they had accepted personal responsibility for the management of royal treasure and had undertaken to pursue the Anglicization of Irish government and society through an evolving series of carefully costed programs of political and military action. Indeed, from Queen Elizabeth's reign onward, they had even been required to present calculated financial projections for their periods of office *before* being appointed, the better to ensure their awareness of proper budgetary discipline and fiscal management.[10]

However, despite many fine studies of Tudor rule in Ireland, few have evinced any awareness that, once in Ireland, all eighteen of Perrot's predecessors, as viceroys or acting governors, shut their eyes to key orders designed to ensure better financial administration. Though Sussex had secured the viceroyalty by exposing the corrupt dealings of his predecessor, and had even for a time toyed with financial reform, he soon lost what little interest he had in the subject. Similarly, his successor Sidney had loudly promised to prioritize better financial management, only to let it slide, upon moving into the viceregal apartments at Dublin Castle.[11] Considering the soaring cost of governing Ireland during these years, with huge subventions out of England needed to keep the civil and military administration going,[12] the viceroys' disregard of exchequer reform in Dublin seems all the more strange. The crown desperately needed to tighten its financial administration. The viceroys' negligence struck at the very heart of the crown's authority. If the king or queen could not even be sure that they would reform the Dublin exchequer, as (repeatedly) instructed, what prospect were the reforms to the wider system of government? Here, surely, is an important topic for investigation, something with implications not only for improving knowledge of how the Tudors' chief representatives in Ireland behaved in office, but also for glimpsing the real nature of the system of government they oversaw.[13]

Yet this is only to scratch the surface. By the time Sir John Perrot received Burghley's letter and orders, the supervision of revenue collection was just one of several core areas of Irish government where viceregal rule was reckoned to have fallen far short of royal expectations. With mounting urgency, each Tudor monarch from Henry VIII to Elizabeth I had received complaints from their subjects and servants in Ireland, alleging major misconduct in office by successive viceroys. Some of this literature of criticism and complaint is quite well known. Numerous histories of the period allude to the detailed charges of misgovernment and oppression laid against Viscount Leonard Grey by his enemies in Dublin in 1540, which contributed to Grey's execution in London the following year.[14] Less dramatically, it is recognized too that the final sacking of Sir Henry Sidney in 1578 was largely the consequence of the torrent of complaints of unfair taxation, corruption, and military excess brought to Queen Elizabeth's attention by the lords and gentry of the Pale and their influential sponsors at her court.[15]

To date, only a few examples of this type of literature have been subjected to careful examination—an extraordinary shortcoming in what is otherwise one of the better developed areas of the historiography.[16] Much remains to be done if the rancor and controversy that surrounded the growth of viceregal government is to be fully appreciated. Complaints and allegations of misgovernment were more widespread than has been realized. In fact, each of the principal viceroys who served in Ireland between the Reformation Parliament of 1536 and the outbreak of Tyrone's rebellion in 1594 often had to face very detailed charges—Viscount Grey, as aforesaid, in 1540; St. Leger in 1547 and again in 1555–56;[17] Croft in 1553;[18] Sussex in 1557–58, 1560, and 1562–64;[19] Sidney in 1570–71 and 1577–78;[20] Arthur, Lord Grey in 1581–82;[21] Perrot in 1585–86 and 1591–92;[22] and Fitzwilliam in 1590 and 1592–94.[23] The contents of these charges were as concerning as they were numerous. A general abuse of power that encompassed tyranny, corruption, and slaughter: the complaints pointed accusingly at all of these and more, and left an abiding impression that the monarchy was not just poorly served but dishonored by the viceroys' wayward behavior. There were even hints of treason.

A fruitful approach to charting the political and administrative history of Tudor rule in Ireland might be to utilize the main complaints against successive viceregal administrations as a readily available component for an interpretative framework. If attempted, it is likely that prevailing views about the day-to-day conduct of Tudor Irish government would require significant modification. Certainly, it is difficult to square the notion of the viceroys and acting governors as essentially 'conservative constitutionalists' who favored 'reform, persuasion and the minimum of coercion'[24] with the sort of allegations that they and their administrations oftentimes faced.

In positioning the complaints nearer the heart of the story, it will be necessary to consider some very serious issues that hitherto have barely featured in scholarly discussions of viceregal government in Ireland—discussions which have sometimes tended to rely unduly on the viceroys' viewpoints, as contained in their official reports and memorials of service, sources designed to enhance the viceroys' image and which barely acknowledged the existence of criticism.[25] Expanding upon the question of financial maladministration with which we began, is it possible that the viceroys were actually complicit in defrauding the crown of revenue, and if so, how much might they have pilfered? It is generally accepted that two of the viceroys, St. Leger and Fitzwilliam, were on the take, but just how corrupt were they, and what of the other viceroys and governors? Was viceregal self-interest—not a lack of interest—the main reason why the exchequer was left unreformed for fifty years after 1536? Turning to wider political matters and the question of tyranny, to what extent were the viceroys and acting governors responsible for suppressing the legal and constitutional rights of Irish-born crown subjects? Sussex and Sidney both faced allegations that they had trampled on subjects' rights. What about the others? Then there is the matter of the viceroys' heavy reliance on force and intimidation, something which, again, was frequently denounced. How often did they turn the army on the ordinary population? When and where did they do so? Going further, is it true that several viceroys and acting governors deliberately drove certain Irish lords into rebellion, by breaking treaties or other agreements previously made with the crown? What effect might this have had on diplomacy between the crown and native rulers? Several Irish rebel leaders insisted that they had taken up arms because they mistrusted the viceroys and their agents, and reckoned that the governors' promises were merely lies to entrap them and their retainers, to lure them to their deaths.[26] Most disturbingly of all, in the course of the military campaigns they commanded, how frequently did the viceroys authorize episodes of deliberate mass killing and starvation of unarmed civilians, acts that would now be termed genocidal? On this last point, some of the complaints and denunciations directed against them insisted that they were too tolerant of indiscriminate killing—charges that are especially notable because they were written by both English and Irish observers, by crown servitors as well as native spokesmen.[27]

The lack of attention paid to the complaints is all the more curious because it is usually acknowledged that some viceroys paid a heavy price for provoking so much anger. Besides the execution of Viscount Grey, Sir John Perrot was attainted and died in the Tower of London, St. Leger was financially ruined, and the reputations of Sidney, Pelham, Arthur, Lord Grey, and

Fitzwilliam never recovered from the malodor clinging to them after their final dismissal from Dublin Castle.

Individual punishment, though, was only part of the story, a quick and easy solution for the monarchy at Whitehall; in the longer term, it was merely a bandage on a festering sore. The constant stream of complaints and allegations tended to touch repeatedly on the same themes; collectively, they strongly implied that the viceroyalty itself had become one of the chief causes of unrest in Ireland. Historians need to make more of this, to build on Brady's perceptive comment that in the growing machinations against Sidney in 1576–78, proposals were advanced by Lord Chancellor Gerrard to rein in the viceroyalty but were subsequently abandoned.[28] More recent research suggests that the appointment of Perrot in December 1583 may have marked the moment when the Elizabethan monarchy came closest to redesigning the viceroyalty.[29] Following the animated intervention of Sir James Croft, himself a former viceroy but, since 1570, a very senior figure at Elizabeth's court, the queen had been persuaded that since her accession to the throne in 1558, *all* of her viceroys and acting governors had served her badly. Echoing some of the most strident critics of viceregal rule, Croft stated that the viceroys had offered no redress whatsoever to the queen's Irish subjects, nor had they given any support to the institutions of law and order, preferring instead the army and brute force, 'whereby by sundry impositions the country groweth poorer and poorer … and the prince's charges spent to the destruction of the best subjects'.[30] Croft was especially alarmed by the growing indiscipline of the army, which preyed on the people, the soldiers 'extending cruelty upon both sexes and upon all ages'. Rather than make Ireland more like England, he claimed the viceroys, by indulging the soldiers, had rendered the country a living hell. Unless it was entirely overhauled, the viceroyalty would remain dangerously unfit for purpose. It made further Irish rebellion inevitable.[31]

Undoubtedly, Croft embellished his case, but that is not the point. His words hit their target. In 1583–84, Elizabeth I was convinced to take the viceroyalty in hand and authorized a series of significant changes to the government of Ireland that bore the imprint of Croft's influence (and, apparently, that of other figures also).[32] Her intervention served to weaken the new governor, Perrot, who was driven to distraction by what he considered unwarranted royal meddling in his conduct of office. Perrot's subsequent political difficulties, which continue to generate intense debate among historians,[33] may perhaps be best explained by the upheaval and ambiguity that flowed from the new direction required by the queen. How was a viceroy to proceed if he could no longer simply dominate the government? What would be the role of the Irish Council, or of more senior government officers such as the lord chancellor, the vice-treasurer, or the marshal of the army? Where might native-born crown officers and loyalist lords fit in, and how much influence would they be allowed? And if Irish elements were to be better accommodated—something Croft insisted upon—how would this affect the growing power of the 'New English' officers who had been serving under the viceroys in ever growing numbers? To an extent, Elizabeth's choice of Fitzwilliam to replace Perrot in 1588 seemed to calm such uncertainties, but Fitzwilliam's own fate, disgraced in 1594, suggests that complaints of mis-government continued to have an impact on the viceroyalty. They merit a prominent place in analysis of the period.

Not that the critics or opponents of the viceroys should alone determine the investigative approach to the problems presented by viceregal rule; that would be misguided. An ideal counterweight to the complaints is readily to hand in the various sets of royal instructions that are extant in the state papers and other associated collections of Tudor government and official records. On their formal appointment to office by the crown, each of the viceroys and acting governors received instructions from the monarch and the Privy Council in London, outlining how they would be expected to proceed upon their arrival in Dublin, and what policies they would be required to prior-itize. In the event of their respective administrations lasting long enough, or if they were confronted with growing native rebellion or the threat of foreign invasion, they often received additional sets of instructions tailored to the changing circumstances. The assertion that these documents contained only 'the vaguest and most general kind' of royal injunction is difficult to accept.[34] The instructions could be very detailed indeed, covering everything from the prosecution of war, and all that that entailed, to the appointment of a mi-nor crown officer in an outlying district. Some royal instructions were very long, encompassing twenty or thirty pages, others fairly short, covering just a sheet or two. Whatever their size, they represent a key source for the ac-curate measurement of viceregal performance. They set out clearly what was expected, and indicate the underlying factors by which a viceroy's reputation could be either burnished or stained. They also provide the best means by which to adjudicate many of the complaints and criticisms that later surfaced against the viceroys. All told (and like the complaints), the royal instructions are much too important to remain neglected any longer.[35]

The instructions merit study for other reasons besides. For more than a generation, historians have been debating the extent to which Tudor rule in Ireland was organized around the political and cultural 'reform' of the coun-try, or its military conquest. While a consensus seems finally to be emerging that they were twin strands of the same overall objective—the subjugation and Anglicization of Ireland and its population[36]—an element of confusion still lingers around a much-supposed decline of reform policy in the latter part of Elizabeth's reign. In particular, the perception continues that sometime between the outbreak of the Desmond Rebellion in 1579 and the Spanish Armada setting sail in 1588, the monarchy and its viceroys abandoned efforts to reduce the Irish to obedience through legal and institutional changes.[37] The viceregal instructions show they did no such thing. Future studies of 're-form' policy in Ireland should pay close attention to the instructions' contents. The crown's desire for new or improved law courts, more officers, and better administrative practices remained in effect under Fitzwilliam (1588–94)—not that he paid much notice—and carried on even in the early stages of the Nine Years' War under his replacement Sir William Russell (1594–97). Moreover, surviving sets of viceregal instructions for the years after 1603 strongly suggest that much of what is deemed early Stuart administrative policy was in many respects a continuation of Tudor 'reform' initiatives.[38]

Peeking out from the pages of all the various sets of instructions is one of the most important questions of all—the extent to which policy was shaped by the monarch and Privy Council in London; by the viceroy and Irish Council in Dublin; or by others, chiefly courtiers and writers, who sought to influence the course of developments in the country through palace-based lobbying and the distribution of specially written advisory texts known as treatises. Although it has been plausibly asserted that the viceroys enjoyed an important role in the construction of some of the very policies that featured in their royal instructions,[39] the extent to which this actually applied has gone mostly untested. Given that several viceroys (Croft, Sussex, Sidney, Perrot, Russell) are known to have penned treatises, it should be a relatively simple task to compare what they wrote with the royal instructions they subsequently received. Did they get the go-ahead to pursue all or most of the policies that they are known to have favored, or did they have to settle for something else? And if it is the latter, might frustration over the terms of their appointment have distorted their experience of office from the very start, and account for any later inclination they may have shown toward insubordination?

Intriguingly, the viceroys' readiness to disregard royal instructions seems to have grown over time. Perhaps it is just a reflection of more ample documentation or (no less likely) simple ignorance on my part, but while exploring the parameters of this essay, I was unable to find clear evidence of Henry VIII's orders being defied by any of his viceroys after 1536, whereas in the reigns of his daughters Mary I and Elizabeth I, several viceroys seem to have committed acts of conscious and calculated disobedience. The most celebrated example of this is the dramatic case of the earl of Essex, who, in 1599, created dozens of English knights in Ireland contrary to Elizabeth's 'pleasure', parleyed with the rebel Tyrone instead of fighting him, and then suddenly vacated his post to return to England, actions which culminated in his official disgrace and his subsequent rebellion, trial, and execution.[40] But the pattern for viceregal willfulness had been established years earlier, in less sensational but equally significant breaches. Take the earl of Sussex's introduction of the new preemptive form of martial law in 1556: the prelude to a major escalation in crown-sponsored violence throughout the country, in which peace-abiding subjects could be summarily killed, the same as rebels in arms, on mere suspicion of disaffection. This initially proceeded, despite Queen Mary's explicit orders to confine martial law to use against rebels only.[41] Then there was Sir William Fitzwilliam's decision to imprison the earl of Desmond in Dublin in 1573, on the earl's return to Ireland after a six-year absence: although Queen Elizabeth had written to Fitzwilliam requiring him to assist in Desmond's restoration to authority in his southern territories, Sir William had preferred to detain the earl in Dublin in order to allow Sir John Perrot, then lord president of Munster, to continue uninterrupted the erosion of Desmond's power-base.[42] Fitzwilliam's disregard of the queen's orders placed an enormous strain on Desmond's loyalty, drawing the earl into an increasingly anxious standoff in Munster in 1574.[43] A final example of viceregal disobedience concerns Perrot himself. As noted earlier, he was greatly frustrated by the queen's (and Sir James Croft's) interference in his government. To assert his authority over the Catholic Irish and, he hoped, secure the backing of Elizabeth's Privy Council for his resolute assertion of Protestant power, a few months into his viceroyalty, he ignored the queen's requirements to tread lightly in religious matters and instead proceeded to impose strong measures against those he called 'Romish thrash' in the country.[44] His action further convinced Elizabeth that he needed to be put on a leash. In the meantime, his clampdown on Catholicism angered the loyalist elements of the general population just as war was beginning with Catholic Spain and Portugal.[45] In the wrong hands, the viceroyalty could be a volatile instrument.

It is widely acknowledged that what made the Irish viceroyalty such a remarkable institution of the Tudor state was the extraordinary range of powers enjoyed by its occupants. While these powers had been trimmed in the 1490s to prevent the then-viceroy, an Irish magnate with a Yorkist past, providing support for the Tudors' enemies,[46] Henry VIII's decision a generation later to raise Ireland to the status of sister kingdom of England (1541) necessarily augmented the authority of subsequent incumbents of the post.[47] Thereafter, the viceroys and acting governors became *de facto* heads of a new Renaissance kingdom in which an English central government in Dublin looked to encompass the entire geographical area of Ireland, and not just 'the four obedient shires' of the late medieval English Pale, or the 'Second Pale' in the mid-south and southeast.[48] Accordingly, although the viceroys never recovered the authority to summon an Irish parliament (resumed into the crown's hands by Poynings' Law of 1494), they were entitled to exercise a suite of rights and powers which, in England, were customarily confined to the person of the monarch. They could make war and peace, proclaim rebels, issue pardons, and approve treaties, all in their own name. No less important, they could embody the majesty of royal government by overseeing the institutions of law and order. They could grant offices in central and local government and, increasingly important as the sixteenth century advanced, they could oversee the crown estate and issue leases of land and property.[49] Capping it all, they commanded a sizeable permanent army, something which meant they were often able to wage war in the country whenever they chose.[50]

There was an important common denominator to these various powers—the royal prerogative, that accumulation of discretionary rights and privileges recognized by contemporaries as the exclusive preserve of the monarchy.[51] By exercising its prerogative, the monarchy asserted its age-old flexibility to set aside law and custom in the interests of *raison d'état* and general contingency. But whereas in Tudor England the use of royal prerogative in practical terms was increasingly held in check by the tendency of the monarchy to govern through the consent of its most important subjects assembled in parliament,[52] in Tudor Ireland its use by the viceroys seems markedly less inhibited. For one thing, parliaments were much less frequent and lasted less time in Ireland; for another, for much of the later sixteenth century, the Tudor 'kingdom' of Ireland was an aspirational dominion only, and required special, and often severe, measures to make it a reality. And, of course, Ireland was more prone to emergencies (invasion scares and rebellions), and so necessitated more frequent recourse to viceregal action that was discretionary, swift, and fearsome.[53] It would be a useful exercise to chart the overlap between the many recorded emergencies and the viceregal use of prerogative power, if only to establish the very frequency of its use, and thereby demonstrate one of the chief ways in which the kingdom of Ireland diverged from England as a state delineated by emergency powers. Very often, viceregal rule was prerogative rule.

This is why martial law looms so large in the political and military history of Tudor Ireland. An application of the prerogative, it enabled successive viceroys to extend the power of the crown by emergency police measures, placing large areas of the country under threat of summary punishment and the hangman's rope. Because after 1556 it was often deployed preemptively, it meant that native territories previously beyond crown control could receive special treatment, and local inhabitants could be killed without trial, via incursions that were presented as security operations but were more like undeclared wars. Moreover, because martial law was self-financing, entitling its enforcers to a generous share of the plunder of its victims, crown officers clamored for the right to use it, thus further ensuring its spread.[54]

One of the most pressing questions about the Tudor viceroys is how they may have availed of martial law commissions to create a second or shadow army in Ireland, one that was separate from the official army paid for by the crown and recorded in the vice-treasurer's accounts (the army 'on the establishment') but which was able to support itself through plunder and coercion. Almost every major viceroy after 1556 had to settle for an establishment army that was smaller than he would have liked in order to comply with the monarch's insistence on cutting costs. Was the recruitment potential of martial law the main reason they acquiesced in a smaller official force, as it enabled them to maintain higher military levels yet keep the extra soldiers off the books? If this was the case, it has important implications for a whole range of issues concerning later Tudor rule in Ireland, from the actual level of military force deployed in the country—a topic that is the subject of growing debate[55]—to the relationship between crown military and policing activity and an evolving subculture of servitor entrepreneurialism. How many 'little wars' were instigated to gain plunder for the officers and soldiers involved? And, overseeing it all, how did the viceroys benefit from the growing violence? Were they content to enjoy the role of patrons of the army and the wider military and policing interest, or did they anticipate material benefits as well?

None of this is to contend that the Tudor viceroys abandoned the extension of English common law or the pursuit of English-style legal and institutional reforms. It is to suggest, though, that the English kingdom they helped create was less and less a replica of England, and more a disturbing variant that was increasingly characterized by repression and violence. Unlike in England, where the Tudors extended the use of martial law but employed it very carefully, through formal legal procedures in response to very particular circumstances,[56] in Ireland the viceroys used martial law constantly and in all manner of situations; indeed, by the 1570s, there were well over 200 commissions in operation around the country, mostly simultaneously, with the then-viceroys Fitzwilliam and Sidney issuing new ones every two or three weeks.[57] In marked contrast, the courts of common law enjoyed no such surge in their use. Although the network of county court sittings was on several occasions extended, its progress was slow, uneven, and intermittent.[58] Future research needs to follow the viceroys' movements to determine the extent to which their 'progresses' and expeditions helped boost local participation in the court system. Drawing chiefly from the self-promotional journals and memoirs of Viceroy Sidney, it is commonly assumed that most viceroys routinely convened court sittings wherever they went. Is this true of all viceregal journeys, or only of some? How long did the viceroys and acting governors spend presiding over court sessions, and what sorts of cases did they hear? Is it possible to determine how many occasions they helped establish new courts in areas previously beyond the common law system? Were their journeys mainly military undertakings or juridical ones?

One way to answer such questions would be study the viceroys' prerogative power to grant pardons. There is much work to be done on this topic. Fifteen years ago, Krista Kesselring published an important study of the function of royal pardons in the government of Tudor England. Her work shows that the provision of clemency through the royal prerogative helped successive monarchs to build political consensus and isolate its opponents during periods of tension and flux, while simultaneously using the sale of general or special-purpose pardons to generate substantial and much-needed additional crown revenues.[59] As yet no Irish historian has responded to Kesselring's study, to examine how pardons may have been used by the viceroys to cultivate acceptance for Tudor rule in Ireland.[60] There is ample evidence in the government papers to show the extent to which pardoning was a major feature of viceregal rule. Although a key source—the records of the assizes—was lost in the 1922 disaster at the Dublin Public Record Office, the surviving (and published) records of government Fiants constitute a store of very detailed information about all types of pardon used in Ireland, especially the general pardon.[61] A rough estimate made in preparation for this paper indicates that during the forty-six years between the arrival of Sir Edward Bellingham in 1548 and the final disgrace and replacement of Sir William Fitzwilliam in 1594, general pardons were granted to approximately 38,000 people in the country (Table 9.2).[62] Initially, as might be

Table 9.2 Approximate numbers pardoned by viceroys in Ireland, 1548–94

Sir Edward Bellingham	May 1548 – Dec. 1549	1,300
Sir Anthony St. Leger	Sept. 1550 – May 1551	370
Sir James Croft	May 1551 – Dec. 1552	1,100
Sir Anthony St. Leger	Nov. 1553 – May 1556	100
Thomas, Earl of Sussex	May 1556 – May 1564	800
Sir Henry Sidney	Jan. 1566 – Apr. 1571	3,900
Sir William Fitzwilliam	Jan. 1572 – Sept. 1575	4,100
Sir Henry Sidney	Sept. 1575 – Sept. 1578	3,500
Sir William Drury	Sept. 1578 – Oct. 1579	360
Sir William Pelham	Oct. 1579 – Sept. 1580	60
Arthur, Lord Grey	Sept. 1580 – Aug. 1582	3,200
Adam Loftus and Sir Henry Wallop	Aug. 1582 – June 1584	2,130
Sir John Perrot	June 1584 – June 1588	9,700
Sir William Fitzwilliam	June 1588 – Aug. 1594	7,200

Source: K.W. Nicholls, ed., *The Irish Fiants of the Tudor Sovereigns: During the Reigns of Henry VIII, Edward VI, Philip & Mary, and Elizabeth I.* 4 vols. (Dublin: Éamonn de Búrca for Edmund Burke, 1994), passim. Table created by author.

expected, the great majority of these pardons were given to subjects who lived in or around the borders of the Dublin Pale or the Second Pale in the southeast. Later, however, it is clear that the availability of viceregal pardons had reached almost every part of the country. By the early 1590s, Fitzwilliam was not only issuing pardons to the inhabitants of all four provinces, but the numbers he pardoned in Munster, Connacht, and even Ulster were surpassing the numbers he pardoned in Leinster.[63] As a measure of Tudor government power, the viceregal pardons had achieved a countrywide impact. It would be a very useful exercise to chart this development, viceroy by viceroy and territory by territory, representing as it does the other side of the Tudor conquest storyline.

The significance of the pardons may be further underlined—and what they reveal of the nature of government expansion greatly sharpened—when they are placed alongside the viceroys' military record. As every student knows, the Tudor viceroys served as commanders-in-chief of the royal forces in numerous campaigns, large and small. Less familiar, however, is the fact that viceregal expeditions were administrative as well as military undertakings, literally government on horseback or by campsite. Even as they labored to track down elusive enemy forces far from the safety of Dublin, the viceroys were expected to continue to conduct all manner of routine official business, from signing orders and decrees to hearing and settling petitions from around the country.[64] Significantly, while campaigning, they also held court sessions and, through their prerogative, took submissions. Reading between the lines, it seems likely that—the Sussex viceroyalty aside—the rapid growth of pardon-granting that is recorded after 1548 was not merely coincidental with the commencement of more frequent military expeditions but was a direct consequence of it.[65] The spread of English legal jurisdiction through viceregal pardons was an outcome of the spread of English force through viceregal soldiering. The 'reform' of Ireland was military-led. It needs to be designated as such.

A final point about the pardons: they were probably a major source of viceregal income, much greater than has been realized. Recalling the persistent disregard for financial administrative reform after 1536, discussed at the beginning of this chapter, it is noteworthy that before that date, successive viceroys had to negotiate with Henry VIII over the scale of their remunerative rights in Ireland. Unwilling to give them a free hand, one of the sources of royal revenue that the king had insisted on controlling was the fines due for pardons, which were to be collected by the officers of the Dublin exchequer and shared out 50:50 between the viceroy and him.[66] This arrangement—if it was ever adhered to—seems to have lapsed after King Henry's death. According to the surviving vice-treasurer accounts, by the reign of Elizabeth I, fines for pardons featured only very rarely in the records of revenue that were officially declared, despite the fact that, as already noted, tens of thousands of pardons were granted by the queen's viceroys and governors. Indeed, it seems that apart from a flurry of fine-gathering in 1571–72, almost no income was declared from pardons before 1588, by which time the long-delayed 'Orders, rules and ordinances for … our Receipts and Revenues of Ireland' were at last being put into effect.[67] Is it possible that, in the interim, the viceroys pocketed nearly all the fines? If they did, it goes to show that service in Ireland had its compensations. It suggests too that viceregal griping about poverty and lack of reward, often repeated by historians, should be treated with skepticism. Having charge of the government of Ireland was an opportunity to become a major political figure in the Tudor composite state, to wield regal powers, and to reap the benefits.

Bearing in mind the oft-held view that the Tudor period constituted an Age of Viceroys in Ireland, much remains to be discovered about how the viceroys actually governed the country. This essay has striven to highlight just some of the gaps in the current state of knowledge. There has not been room to discuss other key aspects of viceregal government such as soldiering and military command,[68] the advancement of religious reform,[69] or the extension of 'soft' state power through the patronage of writing, printing, art, building, and pageantry.[70] All of these, clearly, are topics deserving detailed discussion in their own right. However, as they have all in recent years begun to attract serious attention, it seemed preferable to bypass them here the better to concentrate on elements of the viceroys' story that help expose a rather different model of Tudor Irish government than has been visible hitherto.

The exercise of royal prerogative should receive a more central place in future studies. It is possible that the extent to which the monarchy indulged but then sought to restrain the viceroys over their prerogative powers lies at the heart of the rise and fall of 'programmatic government', that key development in the crown's management of Irish affairs first discovered by Professor Brady that has framed discussion of the viceroyalty for the past thirty years. It may also transpire that the crown's various efforts at oversight from Whitehall will reveal how far it was prepared to permit divergence from English norms in the viceregal conduct of government in Dublin. 'Making Ireland English' may have been the constant refrain of Tudor policy makers, but it allowed for many different interpretations. The viceroys themselves, on assuming office, often followed very different paths, something that was seized on by their critics as further proof of their unfitness to rule, with policy allegedly 'left to every Deputy's Discretion', 'varying every one of them according to fancy and imagination'.[71]

Yet for all their differences of approach, it must be remembered that they served in Ireland in the place of the monarch, *vice roy*. Whether they were styled Lord Lieutenant or Lord Deputy—even Lord Justice—should not obscure this fact. Representing the monarch placed them far above everyone else. If they behaved as though they were above the law, this was because, in practical terms, mostly they were. Only the sovereign, in England, could directly discipline them or intervene in their affairs; the letters they received from the London Privy Council were essentially advisory, with such orders as were contained in them presented either as a summary of the sovereign's wishes, or as having the sovereign's blessing and approval. Regality bound the viceroys together. Indeed, it defined them, wrapping them in the purple cloak of majesty as they went about their everyday tasks, issuing summonses on behalf of the Crown, signing decrees, hearing supplicants, commanding armies. But it did something else too. It gave them a common purpose—to uphold the kingdom that Henry VIII had first announced into life in 1541, to make it a reality. Here, perhaps, is the stuff for a new narrative history of Tudor Ireland—another story of subjugation, admittedly, yet one that can be told in a rather different way than before. It was in the methods that the viceroys and acting governors deployed that the kingdom took shape, methods that often arose from their prerogative power, but which were prone to heavy abuse, and served to antagonize and alienate the crown's Irish subjects as well as overcome them.

Notes

1   An early version of this paper was delivered at the Society for Court Studies conference, London, June 2015.

2   Elizabeth I to Fitzwilliam et al., 12 Feb. 1574, TENA, SP 63/44/41, hereafter SP 63.

3   Orders, etc., n.d., Feb. 1574, ibid., SP 63/44/41(i).

4   King Henry began making changes to the administration of the Irish revenues in that year: D.B. Quinn, 'Guide to English Financial Records for Irish History, 1461–1558', *Analecta Hibernica* 10 (1941), 3. For the organization of the exchequer before that date, see Steven Ellis, *Reform and Revival: English Government in Ireland, 1470–1534* (London: Royal Historical Society, 1986), Chap. 3.

5   The document survives as a nineteenth-century copy, the original having been lost when the Dublin Public Records Office (PRO) was blown up in 1922. Fortunately, it had previously been discovered in a search of the Exchequer Memoranda Rolls by the Victorian Keeper of the Irish Public Records, Samuel Ferguson, who copied it verbatim and filed it away among his private research

papers, National Archives of Ireland (NAI), Ferguson MSS, vii: Memoranda Rolls, Eliz. I, fol. 9r–56v).

6 Elizabeth was especially piqued that a renewed effort at exchequer reform under Lord Justice Drury in 1579 had had no effect: Queen's orders, 28 Feb. 1586, BL Add. MS 37,536, fol. 6r–10v.

7 Some very limited changes had been attempted before: Steven Ellis, *Ireland in the Age of the Tudors, 1447–1603: English Expansion and the End of Gaelic Rule* (London: Routledge, 1998), pp. 179–86.

8 New details of Brabazon's early years are unearthed in Michael Everett, *The Rise of Thomas Cromwell: Power and Politics in the Reign of Henry VIII* (New Haven: Yale University Press, 2015), pp. 77–78, 83, 179–81.

9 For their careers and court status before reaching Dublin, see their respective entries in the *Oxford Dictionary of National Biography*, 60 vols. (Oxford: Oxford University Press, 2004), http://oxforddnb.com.

10 Ciaran Brady, 'Court, Castle and Country: The Framework of Government in Tudor Ireland', in Ciaran Brady and Raymond Gillespie (eds.), *Natives and New-comers: The Making of Irish Colonial Society, 1534–1641* (Dublin: Irish Academic Press, 1986), pp. 45–46.

11 Ciaran Brady, *The Chief Governors: The Rise and Fall of Reform Government in Tudor Ireland, 1536–1588* (Cambridge: Cambridge University Press, 1994), pp. 86, 119.

12 Anthony Sheehan, 'Irish Revenues and English Subventions, 1559–1622,' *Proceedings of the Royal Irish Academy* 90C (1990), 35–65.

13 Hiram Morgan, '"Never any realm worse governed": Queen Elizabeth and Ireland', *Transactions of the Royal Historical Society*, 6th series 14 (2004), 295–308, provides a more wide-ranging interpretation of government shortcomings.

14 Articles against Grey, 1540, *State Papers, Henry VIII*, 11 vols. London, (1830–52), iii, pp. 248–63.

15 David Edwards (ed.), 'A Viceroy's Condemnation: Matters of Inquiry into the Sidney Administration, 1578,' *Analecta Hibernica* 42 (2011), 1–24.

16 For a recent discussion of some of the extant articles of complaint and other related material, see David Heffernan, 'Tudor Reform Treatises and Government Policy in Sixteenth-Century Ireland', PhD thesis, 2 vols., University College Cork, 2012, i, pp. 125–35.

17 Christopher Maginn (ed.), 'A Window on Mid-Tudor Ireland: The Matters against Lord Deputy St Leger, 1547–48', *Historical Research* 78 (2005), 465–82; Brendan Bradshaw (ed.), 'A Treatise for the Reformation of Ireland, 1554–55', *Irish Jurist* 16 (1981), 299–315.

18 Articles concerning the state and affairs of Ireland, n.d., c.1552–53, printed in David Heffernan (ed.), *Reform Treatises on Tudor Ireland, 1537–1599* (Dublin: Irish Manuscripts Commission 2016), no. 3, hereafter, IMC.

19 Primate Dowdall to Archbishop Heath, 1557, TENA, SP 62/1/61, hereafter, SP 62; articles submitted by Primate Dowdall, 1558, SP 62/2/44; Desmond to Mary I, 1558, SP 62/2/11; Jon G. Crawford, *Anglicising the Government of Ireland: The Irish Privy Council and the Expansion of Tudor Rule, 1556–1578* (Dublin: Irish Academic Press,1993), pp. 432–40; Plunket, Cheevers et al. to Elizabeth I, and to Dudley, both 27 May 1562, SP 63/6/12–13; anonymous book of charges addressed to Eliz. I, June 1562, SP 63/6/37.

20 Brady, *The Chief Governors*, pp. 135–36; Edwards (ed.), 'A Viceroy's Condemnation', passim.

21 Ciaran Brady, 'Arthur Grey de Wilton', in A.C. Hamilton (ed.), *The Spenser Encyclopedia* (Toronto, ON: Toronto University Press, 1990), pp. 341–42. See also White to Burghley, 23 Dec. 1581, SP 63/87/55; Note of the disposition of traitors' lands, Nov. 1581, SP 63/86/80(i); Wallop's letter deciphered, 1 Aug. 1582, SP 63/94/85.

22 Roger Turvey, *The Treason and Trial of Sir John Perrot* (Cardiff: University of Wales Press, 2005), pp. 20–21, 24, 123, 135–40.

23 Robert Legge's memoranda, 1590, SP 63/152/2; Legge's 'long book' of accusations, 1593, SP 63/169/3; Thomas Lovell's Beginning and continuance of the rebels of Ireland, n.d., 1592, and Legge's remembrances for the queen, 1594, both in Heffernan, ed., *Reform Treatises*, nos. 58 and 61; Thomas Lee's information against Fitzwilliam's government, 1594, BL, Harley MS 35, fol., 258–65, available at www.ucc.ie/celt/published/E590001-002/index.html.

24 Brady, *The Chief Governors*, p. xii.

25 David Edwards, 'Fashioning Service in a Renaissance State: The Official Journals of the Elizabethan Viceroys in Ireland', in Brendan Dooley (ed.), *Renaissance Now* (Berlin: Peter Lang AG, 2013), pp. 139–63; Willy Maley, '"The Name of the Country I have Forgotten": Remembering and Dismembering in Sir Henry Sidney's Irish *Memoir* (1583)', in Thomas Herron and Michael Potterton (eds.), *Ireland in the Renaissance, c.1540–1660* (Dublin: Four Courts Press, 2007), pp. 52–73; Robert Shepherd, 'The Motives of Sir Henry Sidney's *Memoir* (1583)', in *Sidney Journal* 29, special issue, *Sir Henry Sidney in Ireland and Wales*, eds. Thomas Herron and Willy Maley (2011), 174–86.

26 *Cal. Carew MS., 1515–74*, no. 248; Rory O'More's demands, n.d., autumn, 1577, HMC, *De L'Isle & Dudley MSS*, ii, pp. 70–71; Desmond to Pelham, 31 Oct. 1579, *Cal. Carew MSS, 1575–88*, no. 144; Tyrone's book, 23 Dec. 1597, Bodleian, Laud Misc. 612, fol. 55–59; Hiram Morgan (ed.), 'The 1597 ceasefire documents', *Dúiche Neill: Journal of the O'Neill Country Historical Society* 11 (1997), 19–33.

27 The question of genocide is addressed in Ben Kiernan, *Blood and Soil: A World History of Genocide and Extermination from Sparta to Darfur* (New Haven: Yale University Press, 2007), Chap. 5; David Edwards, 'Tudor Ireland: Anglicization, Mass Killing and Security', in Cathie Carmichael and Richard Maguire (eds.), *The Routledge History of Genocide* (London: Routledge, 2015), Chap. 3.

28 Brady, *The Chief Governors*, pp. 159, 163–66.

29 David Edwards, 'Counselling *in extremis*: Sir James Croft's "Discourse" of 1583 and Elizabethan Irish policy', in David Edwards and Brendan Kane (eds.), *Tudor Ireland and Renaissance Court Societies* (volume in preparation).

30 Croft's discourse, 9 Dec. 1583, Northamptonshire CRO, Fitzwilliam MSS, Irish Papers/67, p. 3.

31 Ibid., p. 6.

32 Such as Robert Dillon and Nicholas White: Heffernan (ed.), *Reform Treatises*, nos. 35–36.

33 Hiram Morgan, 'The Fall of Sir John Perrot', in John Guy (ed.), *The Reign of Elizabeth I: Court and Culture in the Last Decade* (Cambridge: Cambridge University Press, 1995), pp. 109–25; Brady, *The Chief Governors*, pp. 291–300; Turvey, *The Treason*, Chap. 2.

34 Brady, 'Court, Castle and Country', p. 41.

35 The following list of royal instructions is far from comprehensive. It is offered here as a rough guide, to get things started: instructions to Grey and Brereton, 1 April 1540, *State Papers, Henry VIII*, iii, pp. 194–95; to St. Leger in Aug. and Dec. 1540, ibid., iii, pp. 227–30, and *Cal. Carew MSS, i*, no.152; to Bellingham, 6 Jan. 1549, SP 61/2/3, hereafter SP 61, summarized in *Cal. SP, Ire., 1547–1553*, ed. Colm Lennon (Dublin: IMC, 2015), no. 180; to St. Leger in 1550, John Payne Collier (ed.), *The Egerton Papers* (London: Camden Society, 1860), pp. 13–23, and *Cal. Carew MSS, i*, no. 193; to Croft, who received several sets of instructions, SP 61/3/14, ibid., SP 61/3/23, 32, 48, 70, 73–75, and ibid., SP 61/4/48, 51; to Sussex 1556–62, *Cal. Carew MSS, i*, nos. 206, 214, 218, 220, 223–25, 230, 235; to Sidney 1566–70, Tomás Ó Laidhin (ed.), *Sidney State Papers, 1565–70*

(Dublin: IMC, 1962), pp. 16–20, 47–52, 61–77, 90–93, and 124–33; to Weston and Fitzwilliam in Dec. 1567, Bodleian, Carte MS 58, fol. 62, and in Feb. 1568, Ó Laidhin (ed.), *Sidney State Papers*, pp. 84–88; to Fitzwilliam's as viceroy in 1574, *Cal. Carew MSS*, i, nos. 311, 318; to him in his second viceroyalty, in Oct. 1591, Northamptonshire CRO, MS F(M)C 92; to Perrot in Dec. 1583, SP 63/106/37, which, though incomplete, is dated. The full and final (but undated) text is in BL Cotton MS Titus F V, ff 108r–112r. The May 1594 instructions to Russell are in Lambeth Palace Library, MS 632, fol., 112–21, unsatisfactorily summarized in *Cal. Carew MSS*, iii, no. 138.

36 An early synthesis of the trend is provided in Sean J. Connolly, *Contested Island: Ireland, 1460–1630* (Oxford: Oxford University Press, 2007), Chaps. 3–5. See also John P. Montaño, *The Roots of English Colonialism in Ireland* (Cambridge: Cambridge University Press, 2011); and David Heffernan, *Debating Tudor Policy in Sixteenth-Century Ireland: 'Reform' Treatises and Political Discourse* (Manchester: Manchester University Press, 2018, in press).

37 The most recent iteration of this view is Ciaran Brady, 'Coming into the Weigh House: Elizabeth I and the Government of Ireland', in Brendan Kane and Valerie McGowan-Doyle (eds.), *Elizabeth I and Ireland* (Cambridge: Cambridge University Press, 2014), pp. 119–20.

38 For the viceroys of Early Stuart Ireland, several sets of royal instructions c.1609–32 are gathered together in Sheffield City Library, MS WWM, Str. P 1.

39 Brady, 'Court, Castle and Country', p. 41; idem, *The Chief Governors*, p. x.

40 For Essex's knighthoods, see Paul E. J. Hammer, '"Base rogues" and "gentlemen of quality": The Earl of Essex's Irish Knights and Royal Displeasure in 1599', in Kane and McGowan-Doyle (eds.), *Elizabeth I*, pp. 184–208.

41 David Edwards, 'Beyond Reform: Martial Law and the Tudor Reconquest of Ireland', *History Ireland* 5 (1997), 18.

42 Anthony McCormack, *The Earldom of Desmond, 1463–1583: The Decline and Crisis of a Feudal Lordship* (Dublin: Four Courts Press, 2005), pp. 126–32.

43 David Edwards, 'Geraldine Endgame: Reassessing the Origins of the Desmond Rebellion, 1573–9', in Peter Crooks and Seán Duffy (eds.), *The Geraldines and Medieval Ireland* (Dublin: Four Courts Press, 2016), pp. 341–51.

44 Charles McNeill (ed.), 'The Perrot Papers', *Analecta Hibernica* 12 (1943), 11–12, 24, 28, 30–2.

45 It was, of course, partly from concern over the Spanish and Portuguese threat that he adopted this approach: William Palmer, *The Problem of Ireland in Tudor Foreign Policy* (Woodbridge, ON: Boydell, 1994), pp. 116–19; see also Victor Treadwell, 'Sir John Perrot and the Irish parliament of 1585–6', Proceedings of the *Royal Irish Academy* 85C (1985), 259–308.

46 Ellis, *Ireland in the Age of the Tudors*, pp. 162–63.

47 Brendan Bradshaw, *The Irish Constitutional Revolution of the Sixteenth Century* (Cambridge: Cambridge University Press, 1979), remains the main statement of the importance of the 1541 Act, but see also Connolly, *Contested Island*, pp. 111–14.

48 D.B. Quinn and K.W. Nicholls, 'Ireland in 1534', in T.W. Moody, F.X. Martin, and F.J. Byrne (eds.), *A New History of Ireland, iii: Early Modern Ireland, 1534–1691* (Oxford: Oxford University Press, 1976), pp. 1–11, 23–25; the emergence of a Second Pale was first suggested in C.A. Empey, 'The Butler Lordship', *Journal of the Butler Society* 1 (1970–71), 174–87.

49 Brady, 'Court, Castle and Country', p. 41; Ellis, *Reform and Revival*, pp. 13–15.

50 Steven G. Ellis, 'The Tudors and the Origins of the Modern Irish States: A Standing Army', in Thomas Bartlett and Keith Jeffery (eds.), *A Military History of Ireland* (Cambridge: Cambridge University Press, 1996), pp. 116–35; David Edwards,

'The Escalation of Violence in Sixteenth-Century Ireland', in David Edwards, Pádraig Lenihan and Clodagh Tait (eds.), *Age of Atrocity: Violence and Political Conflict in Early Modern Ireland* (Dublin: Four Courts Press, 2007), pp. 64–66.

51   G.R. Elton, *The Tudor Constitution: Documents and Commentary*, 2nd ed. (Cambridge: Cambridge University Press, 1982), pp. 17–20.

52   Penry Williams, *The Tudor Regime* (Oxford: Oxford University Press, 1979), pp. 395–96, 399–405; David Loades, *Tudor Government* (Oxford: Oxford University Press, 1997), pp. 18–19.

53   For an alternative view, see Brady, 'Coming into the weigh house', pp. 118–19. While Brady is correct that invaders from continental Europe only materialized in 1579–80 and 1601–2, I cannot agree that the threat posed to English rule in Ireland by the papacy, Spain, Portugal, France, and Scotland 'amounted to little'. The Scots especially should not be overlooked. The perennial military migration of thousands of galloglasses and redshanks out of the Highlands and Western Isles was perceived by English observers at the time as an ongoing invasive threat to English sovereignty in Ireland; indeed, deliberation of crown policy toward Ulster and north Connacht was largely informed by the desire to stamp it out. Regarding the threat from the Continent, it is important to be mindful of those invasion forces assembled in European ports that were fated not to reach Irish shores. In 1578, several thousand European troops were seemingly destined for Ireland until the king of Portugal had them redirected to his crusade in Morocco, where they were all killed. Similarly, the Spanish Armada had an Irish contingent that was seemingly intent on attacking the Munster Plantation, Niall Fallon, *The Armada in Ireland*, London: Wesleyan, 1978), pp. 221–22. Nor should the *fear* of invasion be overlooked – for instance, the constant rumors of French plans that marked the mid-Tudor years were not without foundation, as careful research has shown, Mary Ann Lyons, *Franco-Irish Relations, 1500–1610* (London: Royal Historical Society, 2003), Chaps. 4–5.

54   Edwards, 'Beyond Reform', pp. 16–21.

55   Besides my own scribblings, see Nicholas Canny, *Making Ireland British, 1580–1650* (Oxford: Oxford University Press, 2001), pp. 49–55, 75–103; Ciaran Brady, 'The Captains' Games: Army and Society in Elizabethan Ireland', in *A Military History*, pp. 136–59; Vincent P. Carey, 'The End of the Gaelic Political Order: The O'More Lordship of Laois', in Pádraig Lane and William Nolan (eds.), *Laois: History and Society* (Dublin: Geography Publications, 1999), pp. 213–56; idem., 'John Derricke's *Image of Ireland*, Sir Henry Sidney, and the massacre of Mullaghmast', *Irish Historical Studies* 31 (1999), 305–27; Montaño, *The Roots of English Colonialism*, Chap. 7; Rory Rapple, *Martial Power and Elizabethan Political Culture: Military Men in England and Ireland, 1558–1594* (Cambridge: Cambridge University Press, 2009), Chap. 5–6.

56   John M. Collins, *Martial Law and English Laws, c.1500–c.1700* (Cambridge: Cambridge University Press, 2016), Chap. 1–2.

57   David Edwards, 'Ideology and Experience: Spenser's *View* and Martial Law in Ireland', in Hiram Morgan (ed.), *Political Ideology in Ireland, 1541–1641* (Dublin: Four Courts Press, 1999), pp. 130–34.

58   The vicissitudes of the sixteenth-century assize circuit also needs detailed study. For a useful starting point, see Crawford, *Anglicizing the Government*, pp. 214–15; see also the explanatory text accompanying Plate 1, 'Counties in Ireland', in his *A Star Chamber Court in Ireland: The Court of Castle Chamber* (Dublin: Four Courts Press, 2005).

59   K.J. Kesselring, *Mercy and Authority in the Tudor State* (Cambridge: Cambridge University Press, 2003).

60   Ellis, *Reform and Revival*, pp. 17, 21, 30–31 provides valuable insights for the pre-1536 period.

61 *Irish Fiants of the Tudor Sovereigns*, 4 vols. (Dublin: de Burca, 1994).

62 I must thank my former student Jack Flynn for helping with the counting; any inaccuracy is my responsibility alone.

63 Between January 1590 and December 1593, Fitzwilliam issued pardons to more than 7,000 people, of which just 500 or thereabouts were inhabitants of Leinster, *Irish Fiants*, iii, Eliz. I, pp. 94–227.

64 David Edwards (ed.), *Campaign Journals of the Elizabethan Irish Wars* (Dublin: Irish Manuscripts Commission, 2014), x–xi.

65 For the growth of campaigning after 1548, see Edwards, 'The escalation', pp. 63–66.

66 Ellis, *Reform and Revival*, pp. 30–31.

67 Sheehan, 'Irish Revenues', pp. 52–59.

68 Edwards, ed., *Campaign Journals*; James O'Neill, *The Nine Years War, 1593–1603: O'Neill, Mountjoy and the Military Revolution* (Dublin: Four Courts Press, 2017); Vincent Carey, '"What Pen Can Paint or Tears Atone?' Mountjoy's Scorched Earth Campaign', in Hiram Morgan (ed.), *The Battle of Kinsale* (Bray: Wordwell, 2004), pp. 205–16; Wayne E. Lee, 'Keeping the Irish down and the Spanish Out: English Strategies of Submission in Ireland, 1594–1603', in Murray Williamson and Peter Mansoor (eds.), *Hybrid Warfare: Fighting Complex Opponents from Ancient Times to the Present* (Cambridge: Cambridge University Press, 2012), pp. 45–71.

69 Ciaran Brady and James Murray, 'Sir Henry Sidney and the Reformation in Ireland', in Elizabethanne Boran and Crawford Gribben (eds.), *Enforcing Reformation in Ireland and Scotland, 1550–1700* (Aldershot: Routledge, 2006), pp. 14–39; Mark A Hutchinson, 'An Irish Perspective on Elizabeth's Religion: Reformation Thought and Henry Sidney's Irish Deputyship, c.1560–1580', in Kane and McGowan-Doyle (eds.), *Elizabeth I*, pp. 142–62.

70 Valerie McGowan-Doyle, 'Fall of Princes: Lydgate, Sir Henry Sidney, and Tudor Conquest in the *Book of Howth*', in Herron and Potterton (eds.), *Ireland in the Renaissance*, pp. 74–87; idem., 'Representations of Sir Henry Sidney: Authority and the Rhetoric of Virtue', in *Sidney Journal* 29, special issue, *Sir Henry Sidney in Ireland and Wales*, eds. Thomas Herron and Willy Maley, 2011, 27–43; Maryclaire Moroney, '"The Sweetness of Due Subjection": Derricke's Image of Irelande (1581) and the Sidneys', and Stuart Kinsella, 'Colonial Commemoration in Tudor Ireland: The Case of Sir Henry Sidney', both in ibid., pp. 105–45 and 147–71; John Bradley, 'Sir Henry Sidney's Bridge at Athlone, 1566–67', in Herron and Potterton, (eds.), Ireland, pp. 173–94; Christopher Burlinson and Andrew Zurcher, '"Secretary to the Lord Grey Lord Deputy here': Edmund Spenser's Irish Papers', *The Library*, 7th series, 6, (2005), 30–69; Edwards, 'Fashioning service', pp. 156–78.

71 Croft's discourse, 9 Dec. 1583, Northamptonshire CRO, Fitzwilliam MSS, Irish Papers/67, p. 2.

10 '[T]hey ... doo nowe resort to the fountaine heade'[1]

The Palesmen's petitions during the Nine Years' War, 1594–1603

Ruth A. Canning

The rapidly declining prosperity of the Pale's urban and rural communities during Ireland's Nine Years' War (1594–1603) provoked great bitterness toward the crown's Irish administration, manifesting itself in a flurry of complaints which increased in both frequency and urgency as the war dragged on. In fact, by the war's closing years, efforts were made to restrain Irish suitors from coming into England, partially because their services were needed in Ireland, but largely because the queen and Privy Council were overwhelmed by the number of Irish suitors coming to court to plead their cases.[2] But the queen's loyal Irish lieges were frustrated. Repeated efforts to obtain recognition, redress, and reward had been made throughout the 1590s, and by 1600, the overburdened Palesmen were determined to dispatch a formal embassy to the English Court. Though they had hoped to send three men from every Pale shire to impress upon the queen the magnitude of their situation, the Palesmen could ill afford such an impressive commission at this time, and so they sent the three most qualified. In June 1600, a delegation led by Nicholas St. Lawrence, the Baron of Howth, Sir Patrick Barnewall, and a Mr. Rocheford traveled to the English Court to represent a petition containing the grievances of Ireland's loyalist Old English community.[3] Like many petitions before it, this 1600 supplication focused on three interrelated wartime problems: first, the endless and unfair demands placed upon the Palesmen's resources and bodies to support the crown's war machine; second, the corruptions of 'bad gouernors' and the abusive behavior of soldiers who had been appointed to defend them; and third, the infinite accusations of backwardness and disloyalty leveled at them by those corrupt officers. While all three issues greatly troubled the Palesmen, according to at least one Pale lord, it was the third 'which toucheth them neerer at the hart, then the losse of theire goodes, the ruyne of theire houses, and spoile of theire lands occasioned thereby'.[4]

The 1600 Pale embassy and the petition they presented highlight the importance of petitioning for the Old English community of Ireland. There are many examples of personal and corporate petitions to be found amongst the Irish State Papers, but the significance of these documents as sources which specifically represent the views of the Old English community has not been adequately explored. Records written by English administrators are far more numerous, and while they detail specific events, comment on individuals, and discuss government policy, they are typically the views of outsiders who could not possibly understand the innermost workings and concerns of Ireland's native populations: the Gaelic Irish and Old English. Unfortunately, the views of Gaelic Irish individuals and groups are poorly represented in the State Papers, but there are a substantial number of personal and corporate petitions submitted by Old English individuals, towns, and the wider Pale community. These, along with the personal letters which often accompanied petitions or were directed to patrons at court, reveal social, political, economic, cultural, and religious concerns specific to the supplicants and their community which cannot be gleaned in such intimate detail from the correspondence of New English crown officials. This is especially true during the Nine Years' War, when the crown administration's continual military and supply demands, along with the extortions of soldiers and the depredations of rebels, placed enormous strain on the loyal Pale community. The letters and reports of crown administrators certainly shed light on the sufferings and consequences of war within the Pale, but they also tend to be highly critical of Old English allegiances and behavior and are clouded by a general dislike and distrust of all things Irish. Consequently, when the hardships of war were acknowledged, they were often accompanied by comments on the unreliability and shortcomings of the Palesmen's loyalties and services. The petitions and treatises composed by Old English supplicants, however, offer an alternative and more intimate perspective on this war by offering insight into how the Palesmen perceived the impact of this conflict on their own community and their relationship with the English crown. The fact that the burdens of war feature so prominently in every single letter and petition submitted by Palesmen during this interval indicates the centrality of this conflict to their daily lives and its consequences for their relationship with the state. But what is particularly noteworthy about these petitions and complaints is that in seeking recognition for their services and justice for their suffering, they also served as stubborn declarations of loyalty. Their sufferings were many, and this chapter will focus on the three main grievances raised in the 1600 petition, all of which appear in other personal and communal supplications during this period.

It is impossible to address every grievance in a study of this length because, as a 1597 petition from the inhabitants of Kildare declared, the 'manifould other abuses & innovacions [are] not conteynable in any forme of peticion'.[5] Thus, this chapter will outline the material burdens of war and the manner in which the crown's loyal Irish subjects were exploited. It will then discuss how, in airing their grievances on these issues, the Palesmen used petitions to assert their unfaltering loyalty to the crown. In doing so, it will also explore how the Palesmen deployed these complaints to affirm their rights as subjects and exert influence on the administrative process. Indeed, as one Palesman so aptly explained in 1577, 'to complain was the very gate of obedience through which they must enter with humble petition'.[6]

Before proceeding, it is necessary to establish the purpose of petitions. As explained by David Zaret, the petition was 'a traditional instrument of communication' which had 'medieval origins and traditions that upheld norms of secrecy and privilege in political communication'.[7] They could serve multiple purposes, and their contents, requests, and grievances depended on the supplicant and the time in which they were composed. The petitions themselves addressed matters that were beyond common law procedures and ones which required some permission, grant, or intervention by the monarch. Individual petitions usually contained requests for office, soldiers, lands, salaries, military or financial succor, licenses, trading privileges, or more general forms of favor. Corporate and community petitions frequently sought the granting of civic rights, privileges, immunities, building licenses, exemptions from the impositions of central authority, funding for hospitals, educational and religious initiatives, or other special grants which might benefit the well-being of the community. Petitions could also contain details of personal or local grievances, which often included criticisms of the central authority and the monarch's representatives. This was especially true during periods of economic or physical dislocation when petitions tended to focus on issues of ill treatment by government or military personnel, inequitable taxation, moneys owed, uncompensated services, and blatant discrimination. In Ireland, petitions may have been presented to a monarch's viceroy, but because they often contained complaints about the social and political situation in Ireland, they were usually directed to the monarch and his or her chief councilors. In fact, the Palesmen had a long tradition of petitioning the crown, and this had proven in the past to be a rather successful method of lobbying for reward and registering opposition to governors. Thus, petitions were political communications between subjects and monarchs (or their representatives), and they can be viewed as an early form of popular politics. Studied in this manner, petitions can reveal much about the attitudes and experiences of supplicants as well as the nature of crown–community relations.

Historians have addressed the drain on England's manpower and resources during the Nine Years' War, and much has been said about the miserable condition of English soldiers operating in Ireland during this period.[8] Yet the same expenditure of Ireland's population and resources, along with the impressive efforts of the queen's loyal Irish subjects in sustaining the crown's military machine, has not received the same attention. The reality was that the Nine Years' War initiated an unprecedented drain on the Pale's human, agricultural, and financial resources. The Palesmen provided the crown with active military service; lent huge sums of money; provided laborers, materials, and victuals; and billeted crown soldiers in their own homes. To these voluntary and mandatory contributions must be added the depredations of rebels and the illegal and extortionate appropriations of soldiers and military personnel. Not only were Palesmen killed in combat, but they died of famine and disease, their lands were spoiled, their goods stolen, and money borrowed never repaid. Unfortunately, it is impossible to compile a comprehensive assessment of the actual physical and economic impact of war on the Pale. Preserved in the Irish State Papers are scores of warrants directed to the mayors, sheriffs, and gentlemen of Pale towns and counties, some of which itemize the number of soldiers, cows, sheep, hens, pigs, horses, and laborers to be levied within Pale shires. There are also numerous reports specifying to what extent certain warrants were answered, but these almost always allege that government requirements were unsatisfactorily met by Irish subjects.[9] These complaints cannot be verified because they rarely accounted for what was in fact delivered, and, according to the sheriffs of Pale shires, government-appointed receivers often refused to issue bills of receipt for the supplies delivered.[10] In most instances, warrants and recorded deliveries do not correspond, and there is no telling how many warrants, auditor reports, and complaints have not survived or were never recorded.[11] Notwithstanding these documentary deficiencies, however, existing State Paper evidence indicates that the Palesmen's contribution to the war effort, whether voluntary, mandatory, or illegally seized, far exceeded what could be reasonably expected from a community laboring under the physical and economic hardships of war. In fact, even the English chronicler, Sir James Perrott, wrote in hindsight that educated approximations of the charges imposed upon the Palesmen would greatly underestimate the actual burden they bore because '[t]he poore English pale did beare many secret and heauie burdens aboue the charges imposed by publicke authoritie'.[12] Although petitions cannot fill the statistical void, they can offer the personal observations and sentiments of those who bore these burdens along with some of the 'secret and heauie burdens' which escaped comment— intentionally or otherwise—in the official record.

Probably the greatest and most persistent problem facing the Palesmen during the Nine Years' War was feeding and provisioning the crown's ever-growing army. Shortages and delays in English shipments of food and treasure meant that the crown's Irish administration was unable to meet the increasing needs of the army without the help of Ireland's loyal inhabitants, the vast majority of whom were resident within the Pale.[13] Like in England, supplies were levied through a series of warrants which, initially, were executed in accordance with the Palesmen's annual service and taxation obligations. As the war unfolded and the army's needs continued to escalate, government levies quickly surpassed the Palesmen's regular obligations with the result that the Dublin administration and its agents were driven to circulate supplementary warrants—some legal, some not.[14] Most of the evidence for these extralegal charges comes from the petitions submitted by Palesmen, and, over the course of the war, their supplications increasingly complained that huge amounts of money, food, supplies, and housing had been unfairly impressed upon them, and even forcibly seized, by the very soldiers and military officers appointed for their defense.[15]

The greatest culprits of abuse were those soldiers who were billeted amongst the local population. In theory, billeting served a dual purpose. Rebel raids on the Pale threatened lives by the sword and starvation through the destruction of crops and property. In addition to being the sustenance of its permanent residents, the Pale's agricultural output was the chief food supply of the English army, and it therefore had to be protected. Rather conveniently, in return for a protective barrier of billeted soldiers, the inhabitants were required to satisfy their daily needs, thereby relieving the crown of that responsibility.[16] But in practice, this was not the symbiotic relationship envisioned by administrators, and the system was regularly abused by disgruntled soldiers and frustrated officials who felt their needs were not being satisfied by either their employer or their hosts.[17] Although soldiers and officers were supposed to pay their hosts for all goods consumed, they rarely received their dietary allowances and, even if they had, as the war progressed and prices inflated, these sums were not sufficient to meet their daily needs. The soldier's diet had been established at six pence per day, but as early as 1596, the Palesmen were given to complain that the common soldier consumed more than six pence for a single meal, officers consumed up to three shillings a meal,[18] and one officer's diet allegedly cost eighteen shillings six pence a day.[19] Forces stationed in nearby garrisons took advantage of the inhabitants in a similar manner. In order to support the warders, weekly levies of beef, mutton, and grain, along with horses and men to deliver them, had been imposed upon the Palesmen. Little regard was had for whether the country could actually afford to surrender these provisions and, if the inhabitants failed to deliver the demanded supplies, 'the soildiors straight runneth into the contry'.[20] According to petitioners, deficits in supplies were merely a pretext for overrunning the country because even when they had fully complied with government orders, the soldiers still 'vex[ed] and opresse[d] thenhabytaunts ... moste extreamelie, consumyng wastfullie and needles[sly] suche provision as the people do make for the relief of them selves and their famylies'.[21]

The Palesmen bore a higher proportion of these supply and accommodation costs than other regions because crown soldiers were disproportionately concentrated within the Pale. This was largely due to their recent arrival at the Dublin port, calls to muster, and times of cessation. For instance, during the war's frequent cessations, it was common for 2,000 or 3,000 soldiers to be drawn into the Pale, during which time it fell to the inhabitants to feed and house them.[22] Army discipline was generally appalling and, even after being reassigned to other regions, the soldiers were in the habit of leaving 'a path of destruction in their wake'.[23] Although traveling forces were expected to cover a minimum of ten miles each day, horse companies were known to travel less than four, repeatedly deviating from their course in search of habitations to loot, while foot companies journeyed a maximum of three, often detouring 'thirty myles aboute'.[24] And the queen's soldiers were not the only problem. By mid-1599, the crown's military presence stood at 19,000 men, and one can well imagine the devastation wrought by these extra bodies in a region suffering from considerable political and economic instability. This figure, however, only accounts for enlisted men[25]; it does not include the army's sizable entourage of soldiers' attendants, wives, and mistresses.[26] Army regulations permitted six women to follow each company; each horseman was entitled to one horseboy; and foot soldiers were restricted to one boy for every two men.[27] Yet the Palesmen commonly complained that every horseman maintained 'dobble horses, some officers treble, each of them one boy … some two', and a few employed as many as three.[28] Foot companies were little better, 'eache soildior with his boy at leaste, and for a greate parte with their woman, and many horses aswell of their owne, as of the contrie violentlie taken'.[29] Although official decrees stipulated that these noncombatants 'shalbe no waie chargeable to the Countrie',[30] these people, like the soldiers they followed, took their maintenance and more from the inhabitants.[31]

Whether they were billeted, garrisoned, or just passing through, the Palesmen's complaints remained the same: soldiers and officers demanded and illegally seized food, drink, lodging, money, and goods, declaring that 'their drom and collors [were] a sufficiant[t] warrant'.[32] Worse still, one 1598 group complaint asserted that if the soldiers were

> not satisfied with meate and money according their outradgious demaundes, then doe they beate their poore hostes … ransackinge their howses, taking away chattell and goodes of all sortes, not leaving soe muche as … the garments to their backes, or clothes on their beddes.[33]

The petitioners further alleged that if any person dared resist or lodged a formal complaint, then the soldiers 'not onelie excersies all the crueltie they can against them, but … procure other companies to set a fresh vpon the poore Inhabytaunts and spoyle them in farre worse sorte … in nature of a Revendge'.[34] Unsurprisingly, the Palesmen were distraught that they were being 'assaulted and as Rigouroslie vsed as if they were disobedient, and disloyall Subiects'.[35] This was hardly the way to win the hearts and minds of the people of Ireland and, as Lord Gormanston so succinctly noted in 1596, 'I pray your L. remember wee are Christians, and therfore good L. vse vs as xpians [Christians]'.[36]

The oppressions of soldiers and the supply demands of the administration were only some of the burdens endured by the Palesmen during the Nine Years' War. To these must be added the destruction of property and goods during rebel raids, several years of unseasonable weather, and the depletion of men and equipment for sowing and harvesting crops as a result of enlistment or conscription by crown forces. All of these issues contributed to a dangerous decline in agricultural productivity. The war also precipitated a serious debt crisis for which the Palesmen bore more than their fair share. Over the course of the war, huge sums of money were borrowed and never repaid, prices soared, currency was debased, and international trade nearly halted. Merchants and corporations advanced loans and supplies on unfulfilled promises of repayment with the result that the debts owed to Palesmen increased rapidly. For instance, in August 1598, the administration owed the merchants and corporation of Dublin £8,000;[37] by December 1600, that debt had risen to nearly £62,000.[38] Naturally, the Palesmen desired satisfaction of these debts, but remuneration required persistent solicitation by patrons and representatives at home and at the English court.[39] This could be prohibitively expensive for most would-be supplicants; in fact, the Pale delegation of 1600 was reduced from three representatives from each shire to three representatives in total for this very reason.[40] Moreover, those who did journey to Court met with varying success; Dublin Alderman Nicholas Weston managed to obtain several bills for repayment, but Patrick Typper, who had long battled for the welfare of the inhabitants of County Kildare, was confined to prison for a period.[41] The cost of petitioning the crown and the possibility of falling out of favor served as a deterrent for some, yet much to the annoyance of the queen and Privy Council, Irish suitors and country agents continued to flock to the English Court, seeking redress and restitution.[42]

But for all the bitterness and frustration embedded in the Palesmen's petitions, they cleverly harnessed the bearing of all these hardships and injustices as proof of their crown allegiance. To emphasize this, they deliberately noted that

> although the alurements of this vnhappie tyme did offer provocacions to carry vnstaied myndes astray, yet we [are] as vnremoveable from our loyalties, doe remayne stedfast and constant, contynuallie accepting, and making choise, of all callamities, misseries, and mischiefes what soever, rather then to be disloyall.[43]

Prominent in every petition was a statement of loyalty and a reference to ancestral traditions of obedience and service. The sacrifices of past generations were also frequently noted; for instance, one 1598 group petition recounted the lives lost serving against numerous crown enemies in recent decades:

> by the deathes of sondry gentlemen of the englishe Race of the Pale that have spent their bloode and lost their lives in these late tumoltes in resisting the Rebells and enemyes, by that also that moste of the Notablest Rebells that have borne Armes here against your Maiesty since the begynynge of your Highenes Raigne, have ben slayne and overthrowen by your subiects of this contry byrth, as the Earle of Desmonde, James fitz Morrishe, Callough O Connor, Rory oge, and divers others.[44]

Both personal and corporate petitions consistently glorified wartime sacrifices like these, and they drew on their suffering as testament to their unwavering dedication to crown interests.[45] For instance, the Baron of Dunsany lamented the death of his brother, who died 'of a former hurt receaued in her Maiesites seruice, with Eight more of his name and kynred slaine, besyde Thirtie of his followers and servants, havinge all his landes & his kynsmens vpon that border vtterlie spoiled'.[46] Dunsany was, nonetheless, insistent that:

Yf ... pouertie, whose propertie is to dryve men hedlonge to mischieves, which ... a desperate mynde is always reddye to entertayne and wherewith the most soled [solid] mynde is often moved, yet [I] did never yield thereby to be a iott removed from that loyaltie that my sincere duttie, the honour of my stock and deere vertue hath tyed me vnto.[47]

Like Dunsany, many other Pale petitioners announced that no amount of anguish endured for the advancement of the crown could remove them from their natural affection for their English monarch.

Having made their allegiances clear through detailed accounts of sacrifices and services, which could even include the number of rebel heads delivered,[48] the Palesmen expressed optimism that '(... your Maiesty will conceave) what faithfull and harty affection we carrie towardes your Maiesty vpon whose gracious care and regarde of vs our whole hope do altogether depend'.[49] That hope was that they would be granted some sort of relief or reward. The petitions themselves, being the Palesmen's favored course for redress, provide valuable insight into the sociopolitical workings of the Old English Pale community. Rather remarkably, the State Papers contain no formal description of any major clash between civilians and military personnel within the Pale during these war years.[50] Instead, it seems the Palesmen's preferred mode of protest was to exercise their constitutional rights by submitting petitions directly to the queen and Privy Council in which they detailed their grievances and expressed their hopes of arbitration and remedy. The very fact that the Palesmen continued to solicit the crown for the easing of their suffering indicates that they regarded themselves as crown subjects and that, as subjects, it was their inalienable right to expect those complaints to be heard and answered by their monarch.[51] This sentiment was clearly expressed in the 1600 group petition: 'We humblie expect from your [Royal Majesty] that comfforte and redresse in these our calamities, which our Loyalties at all tymes and readines to extend our vttermost endevoures to the Advancement of your highnes service ... doth deserve'.[52] That the Palesmen regarded the queen as a protector concerned for their welfare is also clear by the fact that they laid the blame for their unaddressed condition on Irish administrators, not the queen, and expressed hope that those officials would be held accountable. In fact, many petitions were presented under the assumption that Elizabeth did not fully comprehend just how distressed her Irish subjects were because her delegates in Ireland had either neglected to inform her or had purposely tried to deceive her. To make their petitions more effective, supplicants were careful to note that the abuses and corruptions of officials in Ireland obstructed the queen's service as much as their own well-being, '[s]oe as her Maiestis bounty (if yt might be) is dishonored & dispised, the souldier beggered and defrauded, thinhabytants of the country robbed spoyled and abused, and all this wrought thorough the auarietie and abuse of the same'.[53] In order to help the queen preserve her subjects and her service from these corruptions, the Palesmen felt it was their duty, as subjects, to inform her of the many abuses committed in her name, 'the vyolacion wherof must be most offencyve vnto her highnes'.[54] Thus, their persistent lists of grievances were not the tiresome whingings of ungrateful subordinates, but the true reports of devoted crown servants.

The Palesmen were not entirely naïve, and their petitions did give the queen cause for concern. As early as 1596, she reprimanded her Irish council for its weak efforts in addressing and reforming government and soldier misconducts because this neglect provided 'so lytle shewe to the People of any purpose to right them, as ether they must needes thincke our hart allyenated from doeing them Iustice, or you our Governor ill chosen that haue not better dealt in it'.[55] Yet the chief officers in the queen's Irish administration almost always offered her the same explanation. They routinely dismissed the Palesmen's complaints, insisting that the petitioners were grossly exaggerating soldier misconduct and their own sufferings. According to these officials, the real problem was the Palesmen's backward and changeable dispositions.[56] Prominent among this type of official was Lord Deputy Burgh who ridiculed the Palesmen's complaints:

> Place Garisons emongst them, they cry owt of oppression. If the enimie runne them, they wishe a company, wher 50 ensignes cannot impeach the passadge of everie Bogg & Woodde, which geves safetie to a fewe lewde persons to steale vppon pertycular mens goods; Pursue the Rebbells, one or other releives them; seeke to defend soome, other drawe draughts vppon them, so as being false among themselves, & wauering in everie condicion, none can tell howe to proceede to theyre contentment.[57]

Several years later, Lord Deputy Mountjoy likewise dismissed the Palesmen's protests because:

> Clamorous they are above all nations in the world, and that for little or no cause, whereof I have had many trials in my journeys, when, the army marching through the country, the people have run out of the villages with open mouth, crying out that they were utterly spoiled and nothing left them, when upon examination I have found that they had nothing taken from them, but, for fear of that which might happen, they complained of that which never happened ... But the manner of this country is to cry out in general that they are spoiled, and not to lay down in particular by whom, whereby envy is raised against the Government, and no course can be taken for redress.[58]

But Burgh and Mountjoy were not entirely correct about the impossibility of redress because the Palesmen often offered their own suggestions to this end. And this, like the act of complaining to their monarch, was considered both a right and a duty of subjects. Mindful that remuneration was rarely forthcoming, some Pale petitions proposed alternative solutions which might see them partially appeased. For example, in June 1597, the corporation of Dublin petitioned the queen 'to grant vnto them and their Successors their humble requestes conteyned in the annexed articles'.[59] Discounting substantial outstanding loans and independently supplied materials advanced by members of the Corporation,[60] the citizens of Dublin city claimed the government owed them £890 for billeting soldiers and a further £3,000 for their assistance 'maintaining armed companies in the field'.[61] But this was only a fraction of their financial woes because the damages caused by the recent gunpowder explosion amounted to an estimated £14,076 sterling.[62] Also contributing to their difficulties were constant calls for military service, which far exceeded their forty-day annual service obligation, and the need to provide watchmen and guards to be on duty round the clock.[63] The inhabitants and civic corporation were overextended, and so they sought some solution which might help offset all these charges. Instead of demanding direct satisfaction from the crown, the annexed articles included the confirmation of certain judicial and commercial privileges; exemptions from English customs duties; and the restoration of fee farms, which had since fallen into abeyance or the hands of peculating government officials.[64] The supplicants were conscious that financial restitution would not be forthcoming from England at this time; however, the suggestion that their debts could be satisfied within Ireland might persuade the queen to grant them some relief. Equally important, though, was that having endured all these hardships, such a grant would serve as a token of acknowledgment for all their sacrifices, 'for their better encouragement & inhablinge to contynue their accustomed forwardnes in the furtherance of her Maiesties seruice wherein they wilbe readie to bestowe their accustomed lyves lands and goodes if occasion be offered'.[65] It is unclear if or to what extent these specific requests were granted.

A significant feature of the Dublin Corporation's petition is that the supplicants were offering their own proposals for easing the ills of Elizabeth's Irish subjects. This was important to the Palesmen because, as Valerie McGowan-Doyle has demonstrated, 'oppositional appeals to Elizabeth' can be considered 'a function of lost counsel'.[66] Over the course of the sixteenth century, the Old English had lost considerable influence over the direction of government policy as they found themselves being gradually displaced from positions of authority by English Protestant newcomers. Yet, as subjects, they believed they still had certain responsibilities to assist their monarch and her government, and that included offering advice based on their local expertise and special experience. Petitioners frequently reminded the queen and Council that generations of Irish residence had endowed them with certain abilities and knowledge which would greatly benefit crown service, if only those in power would listen. For instance, when seeking military office, the Baron of Dunsany noted that his experience of Irish warfare, linguistic knowledge, and near relations with rebels were all valuable assets for the service.[67] Similarly, the Pale embassy of 1600 drew on how the Palesmen's expertise, along with their vested interest in Irish affairs, made them the best placed to offer guidance. As their petition asserted,

> it is impossible, that any should so well right the Causes of the Poore, as those that are best acquainted with their condition, the nature of theire griefes, and causes of their complaints, or that any should so much tender their good & Estate of any Kingdome, as he, whom nature doth oblige thereto, having no other place of refuge, & retruit.[68]

Unfortunately, during the Nine Years' War, very few of the Palesmen's petitions achieved their desired result. The administration's efforts to curb army abuses remained weak throughout the war, financial compensation was uncommon, recognition for services was infrequent, promises of reward were rarely fulfilled, and local advice was seldom heeded. Nevertheless, for Old English Palesmen, petitioning remained an important avenue of communication with their monarch, and it was symbolic of their status as subjects of the English crown. Although most wartime petitions were complaints against the administration, army, and the exploitation of loyal subjects, they also provide evidence of how the Palesmen experienced the war and how they understood their relationship with the English crown. By the very act of complaining, the Palesmen were exercising their rights as crown subjects to provide both information and counsel to their prince.[69] In doing so, petitions were important expressions of allegiance through peaceful constitutional protest. Instead of taking up arms against the many injustices they described, they sought the protection and assistance of their queen. These were the symbols of their loyalty.

Notes

1 Dunsany to R. Cecil, 15 June 1600, State Papers (hereafter SP) 63/207(3)/108.
2 For example, Certain instructions conceived, June 1600, SP 63/207(3)/139. Also see, G. Carew to Privy Council, Dec. 16 1600, SP 63/207(6)/75; Fenton to R. Cecil, 25 May 1601, SP 63/208(2)/93; Mountjoy to R. Cecil, 10 Aug. 1602, SP 63/212/8.
3 Dunsany to R. Cecil, 15 June 1600, SP 63/207(3)/108; N. St. Lawrence, Baron of Howth, to R. Cecil, 14 Sept. 1600, SP 63/207(5)/23. In an excellent study on the Old English and rhetoric of counsel, Valerie McGowan-Doyle addressed the significance of this 1600 embassy and petition, highlighting how the Palesmen attempted to use this opportunity to elevate one or more of their own to positions of authority whereby they might help direct crown policy in Ireland. See Valerie McGowan-Doyle, 'Elizabeth I, the Old English, and the rhetoric of counsel', in Brendan Kane and Valerie McGowan-Doyle (eds.), *Elizabeth I and Ireland* (Cambridge: Cambridge University Press, 2014), pp. 163–83.
4 Dunsany to R. Cecil, 15 June 1600, SP 63/207(3)/108.
5 Petition of the inhabitants of Co. Kildare, 24 July 1597, SP 63/200/53; Charges and impositions on inhabitants of Co. Kildare, 24 July 1597, SP 63/200/53(I); Sir Patrick Barnewall to R. Cecil, 10 Aug. 1600, SP 63/207(4)/62. For a more comprehensive assessment of the Palesmen's other wartime grievances, such as military and religious, see R. A. Canning, *The Old English in Early Modern Ireland: The Palesmen and the Nine Years' War, 1594–1603* (Woodbridge, Suffolk: Boydell, forthcoming).

6 Cited in McGowan-Doyle, 'Elizabeth I, the Old English, and the rhetoric of counsel', p. 177.

7 D. Zaret, 'Petitions and the "invention" of public opinion in the English Revolution', *American Journal of Sociology* 101 (6) (1996), 1497.

8 J. McGurk, *The Elizabethan Conquest of Ireland: The 1590s Crisis* (Manchester: Manchester University Press, 1997); Cyril Falls, *Elizabeth's Irish Wars* (London: Constable, 1996), Chap. 3, see Vincent P. Carey, 'As Life to go to the gallows as to the Irish wars: Human rights and the abuse of the Elizabethan soldier in Ireland', *History, The Journal of the Historical Association* 99 (2014), 468–86.

9 G. Harvey to Russell in Russell's Journal, 10 Oct. 1595, Carew MS. 612, 270; H. Brouncker to Cecil, 22 Jan. 1598, SP 63/202(1)/29; Heads of things, 27 Oct. 1600, SP 63/207(5)/116.

10 See the certificates submitted by the sheriffs of Dublin, Meath, and Westmeath: Russell's Journal, Carew MS. 612, No. 270. See also, Answers to complaints, Dec. 1600, SP 63/207(6)/123; Privy Council to Mountjoy, 20 Feb., BL Add. MS. 4757, Milles Collection, III, fol. 27r–27v.

11 For example, Fenton to Burghley, 14 Aug. 1595, SP 63/182/35.

12 Collections made by Sir James Perrott, BL Add. MS. 4819, fol. 75v. See also, Fenton to Burghley, Aug. 14, SP 63/182/35.

13 For a more detailed study of the physical and material burdens of this war, see Canning, *The Old English in Early Modern Ireland*, Chaps. Four and Five.

14 This was the case in July 1596 when Norreys and Fenton urged the Lord Deputy and Council to issue writs to Meath and Westmeath to deliver 300 beeves for garrisoned forces in Connacht. Norreys and Fenton to Lord Deputy and Council, 3 July 1596, SP 63/191/15(v).

15 For example, for one particularly detailed episode which led to complaint, see petitions about Sir John Norreys's forces by the inhabitants of County Meath. Petition of the inhabitants of Co. Meath, 1597, SP 63/201/146; Note of the abuses committed by certain soldiers of the Lord General's troop in the county of Meath, 22 May 1596, SP 63/189/46(x).

16 For instance, in early 1595, the Earl of Ormond had reportedly established several crown garrisons, at Ballinacor, Castlekevin, Ballimore, and Talbotstown, totaling 500 soldiers, 'of which 300 were at the contrey chardge, and the other 200 at hir maiesties allowance for their vitling onely, withowt further pay, and yet wee hope to haue them wholly borne of the Contrey by some courss of contrybucion withowt anie chardg to hir maiestie or at least verie little.' Russell and Council to Privy Council, 26 Feb. 1595, SP 63/178/54.

17 Ciaran Brady, *The Chief Governors: The Rise and Fall of Reform Government in Tudor Ireland, 1536–1588* (Cambridge: Cambridge University Press, 1994), pp. 209–44; Nicholas P. Canny, *Making Ireland British, 1580–1650* (Oxford: Oxford University Press, 2001), pp. 66–67.

18 Petition of the County of Kildare, 8 May 1596, Lansdowne MSS. 81 fol. 181.

19 Note of the abuses, 22 May 1596, SP 63/189/46(x).

20 The greevances of the Englishe Pale [hereafter Greevances], 1598, SP 63/202(4)/60.

21 Ibid.

22 Ibid., and also, 'A discourse to show "that planting of colonies, and that to be begun only by the Dutch, will give best entrance to the reformation of Ulster,"' 1598, SP 63/202(4)/75.

23 The humble requests of the Captains of Ireland, 18 May 1598, SP 63/202(2)/38; Copie of a warrant for executing a soldier by marshall Lawe, Carew MS. 612, No. 270. Canny, *Making Ireland British*, p. 67. For the treatment of the English soldiers, see Carey, 'As lief to go to the gallows as to the Irish wars'.

24 Greevances. See also, Petition of the inhabitants of Co. Kildare, 24 July, 1597, SP 63/200/53, hereafter, Petition of the inhabitants of Co. Kildare.

25 J.S. Nolan, 'The Militarization of the Elizabethan State', *The Journal of Military History* 58 (1994), 391–420, esp. 418.

26 Brady, *The Chief Governors*, p. 221. See also Ciaran Brady, 'Conservative Subversives: The Community of the Pale and the Dublin Administration, 1556–86', in Patrick J. Corish (ed.), *Radicals, Rebels and Establishments* (Belfast: Appletree Press, 1985), p. 18; Canny, *Making Ireland British*, pp. 68–69.

27 Orders to be observed, 18 Apr. 1596, SP 63/189/46(ix). McGurk, *The Elizabethan Conquest of Ireland*, p. 199; Falls, *Elizabeth's Irish Wars*, p. 37.

28 Greevances; note of the abuses.

29 Greevances.

30 Orders to be observed.

31 For example, the inhabitants of Kildare complained that each woman demanded 4d. or 6d. and each boy consumed 3d. per meal. Petition of the County of Kildare. It should be noted that the rates given by the Kildare petitioners were significantly lower than those listed by the inhabitants of Meath. See note of the abuses.

32 Greevances.

33 Ibid. See also, N. St. Lawrence, Baron of Howth, to R. Cecil, 14 Sept. 1600, SP 63/207(5)/23.

34 SP 63/202(4)/60 1598; 'Greevances'.

35 Ibid., A declaracion of the presente state of the Englishe Pale, June 1597, Carew MS. 632, 271. See also, T. Lee, 'The Discovery and Recovery of Ireland with the Author's Apology, c. 1599–1600', BL Add. MS. 33743, ed., J. McGurk (CELT, 2009), fol. 71–72.

36 Memorial, 7 Dec. 1596, SP 63/196/13(i).

37 Irish Council to Privy Council, 2 Aug. 1598, SP 63/202(3)/1.

38 Reckoning of moneys borrowed from City of Dublin, Dec 1600, SP 63/207(6)/114.

39 Stephen Barron, acting on behalf of the citizens of Dublin City, submitted multiple suits to the state for compensation in 1594. Suits presented by S. Barran, Feb.–Mar. 1594, SP 63/173/49; 58; 58(I); 59; 71; Countess of Ormond to Cecil, 8 May, SP 63/207(3)/24.

40 Dunsany to R. Cecil, 15 June 1600, SP 63/207(3)/108.

41 Loftus and Irish Council to Privy Council, 20 July 1597, SP 63/200/40; Privy Council Meeting, 17 Aug. 1597, SP 2/22/217; BL Lansdowne MSS. 81, fol. 181; 8 May 1596, Petition of the County of Kildare; HMC Salisbury MSS. 8, pp. 420–21. See also Ruth Canning, 'Profits and patriotism: Nicholas Weston, Old English merchants, and Ireland's Nine Years' War, 1594–1603', *Irish Economic and Social History*, 43 (2016), 1–28.

42 ULC MS. Kk. I. 15, fol. 207–209; Cecil to Lord Deputy Russell, 10 July 1596, Carew MS. 612, 270. Irish Council to Privy Council, 2 Aug. 1598, SP 63/202(3)/1.

43 Greevances.

44 Ibid.

45 For example, Dunsany to Burghley, Feb. 1595, SP 63/178/65; Humble suit of the Baron of Dunsany, 1597, SP 63/201/144.

46 Humble suit of the Baron of Dunsany.

47 Baron of Dunsany to Burghley, Feb. 1595, SP 63/178/65.

48 Services done by Delvin from 1596 to Feb. 1, 1600, 1600, SP 63/207/88(i).

49 Greevances.

50 The most detailed incident of local aggression toward the establishment occurred in Limerick in 1600; no similar incidents were recorded within the Pale. See Articles against the town of Limerick, 3 Mar. 1600, SP 63/207(2)/7.

51 This was a continuation of methods used before the war. According to Ciaran Brady, the Old English 'showed both in word and deed a clear awareness of their status as loyal subjects of the crown who were possessed of the right to seek redress for their grievances in the conventional manner long before the painful issue of their recusancy was forced upon them. Politically, at least, they were countrymen before they were Catholic.' Brady, *The Chief Governors*, pp. 212–13.

52 Petition of noblemen and gentlemen of the English Pale to the Queen, 13 June 1600, SP 63/207(4)/5(i).

53 Petition of the inhabitants of Co. Kildare; Charges and impositions on inhabitants of Co. Kildare, 24 July 1597, SP 63/200/53(i); Barnewall to R. Cecil, 10 Aug. 1600, SP 63/207(4)/62.

54 Petition of the inhabitants of Co. Kildare.

55 Queen Elizabeth to Lord Deputy and Council, 25 May 1596, SP 63/189/43.

56 'Observations' endorsed by R. Cecil, 1598, SP 63/202(4)/81.

57 Burgh to Loftus and Irish Council, 26 Sept. 1597, SP 63/201/25(i).

58 CSPI, 1600, p. 508.

59 Petition of mayor and citizens of Dublin, June 1597, SP 63/199/127.

60 One of many examples is Dublin Alderman James Bellew who was owed '660 and odd poundes' for supplying 'dyvers of hir Maiesties Army with apparrell and other necessaries'. Loftus to R. Cecil, 7 April, SP 63/198/78.

61 HMC Salisbury MSS. 14, p. 35; Petition of Mayor and Citizens of Dublin to Burghley, June 1597, SP 63/199/127. See also Mayor and Sheriffs of Dublin to Burghley, 6 May 1597, SP 63/199/11; Mayor and Sheriffs of Dublin to R. Cecil, 6 May 1597, SP 63/199/12.

62 In addition to extensive damages done to the physical geography of the city, the explosion killed 126 people, 76 of whom were confirmed citizens of the Dublin Corporation.

63 For instance, between January and September 1595, the Dublin administration called upon the Palesmen for at least four separate risings, the first of which the city of Dublin supplied 100 men 'Armed, paied and vitled at their owne chardges for 2 monthes to aunswere this prosequcion'. Irish Council to Privy Council, 23 Jan. 1595, SP 63/178/14; Canning, *The Old English in Early Modern Ireland*, Chap. 4; HMC Salisbury MSS. 14, p. 35; Petition of Mayor and Citizens of Dublin to Burghley, June 1597, SP 63/199/127. Colm Lennon, 'The great explosion in Dublin, 1597', *Dublin Historical Record*, 42, 1988, esp., 14–15.

64 Petition of mayor and citizens of Dublin to Burghley, June 1597, SP 63/199/127; HMC Salisbury MSS 15, p. 95.

65 Petition of mayor and citizens of Dublin.

66 McGowan-Doyle, 'Elizabeth I, the Old English, and the Rhetoric of Counsel', p. 177.

67 Lye to R. Cecil, 5 Dec. 1600, SP 63/207(6)/59.

68 Petition of the inhabitants of the Pale.

69 Baron of Howth to Cecil 14 Sept., SP 63/207(5)/23. McGowan-Doyle, 'Elizabeth I, the Old English, and the Rhetoric of Counsel', pp. 177–78.

11 Institutional history and the early modern Irish state

Coleman A. Dennehy[1]

Typically, the study of courts, parliament, and local, shrieval, provincial, and national administrations has been used to provide material for traditional history—that is, the history of great men, wars and territorial disputes, and religious, constitutional, and political contests. Irish history has generally followed many of the main trends within historiography to be found outside of Ireland (usually from Britain), except perhaps with the exception of the lurch to Marxist or strong leftist history in the second half of the twentieth century.[2] In Ireland, such orthodox history, as in most countries, has been undertaken in order to produce a broad national history—the story of Ireland and how it got to where it was when such histories were written.[3] This inevitably has led historians toward understanding the relationship between native and newcomer; England and Ireland; Catholic and Protestant; or, in short, conflict and resolution.

While the general history of politics, governance, and the state has been relatively well-attended by historians writing political history in the past, and this trend is likely to continue, there still is need for an improvement of knowledge as to how institutions worked and how they developed over time, either in the shadow of change inspired by crisis or by ongoing evolutionary adaption. There have certainly been some enthusiastic institutional historians, yet there is still space for historians looking not just at how these organs of state functioned—a valuable exercise in itself—but how various societies in the kingdom viewed and interacted with them.[4] The tendency of historians in the past and sometimes in the present to study just the political nature of such institutions has meant, to a degree, that we have spent less time on how these institutions worked and developed outside of times when political moments of high drama demand attention. This chapter will take the opportunity to consider the understanding of how the state and all of its institutions functioned over a long time frame and how they may have affected the societies in which they worked. It will also suggest areas where attention might be focused and how trends in institutional history might be fruitful in attempts to understand the past.

We know that as time progressed, the state expanded, not just in the geographical sense but also administratively. Raymond Gillespie points out that in the thirty years on either side of the turn of the seventeenth century, chancery adjudications increased in excess of threefold; we also know that assize justice was extended over the island, and parliament expanded exponentially in terms of both representation and jurisdiction.[5] By the early 1600s, the army had garrisons all over the island for the first time, sheriffs were active in their newly established counties, and taxation was regularly contributed from all corners of the kingdom.[6] Whilst the island of Ireland remained the same size, the kingdom grew considerably from its origins in the early 1540s, both in terms of territorial reach and also its growing influence over the population. It was therefore almost inevitable that the state and its constituent parts would play a substantial role in the Anglicization of the parts of Ireland which had remained outside the orbit of Dublin Castle before this point, and that institutions would be adapted to meet this change in the process.

While we have two postgraduate theses that are biographical dictionaries for the lower house of parliament of 1613–15 and 1640–41, we are still somewhat in the dark as to membership for early modern parliament more generally.[7] Precise membership lists exist for almost all the Stuart parliaments, usually in their journals, the exception being the attendance at the House of Lords in the Jacobean and Jacobite parliaments, and some records for the membership in the Tudor parliaments.[8] Such a study covering at least the parliaments of 1634–35, 1661–66, and 1689 is viable, along with constituency studies. The lords must also be included in such studies—Johnston-Liik's six-volume study of eighteenth-century parliamentary membership did not include the lords at all, though there has been some exploration of their involvement in recent years.[9] Parliamentary-like assemblies, such as the early Restoration convention and the confederate assembly, may be best approached in such a fashion, and indeed have already been conducted in the case of the former.[10]

Connected to such studies, of course, should be networks and connections, which would generally inform historians' understanding of political, familial, and regional links in early modern Ireland generally. Some of these will become obvious with studies of memberships alone, but they can be better informed if they are combined with a closer examination, for example, of activity on committees and of the distribution of voting proxies in the upper house.[11] In the same fashion, it is important to ask ourselves who is driving parliamentary politics at this stage. On the one hand, there is a century-old school of thought that the Commons had taken the initiative in seventeenth-century English politics, yet more recently, the peers are viewed as having far more influence than previously acknowledged.[12] How Ireland compares with this outlook needs more examination. In a similar fashion, a study akin to Michael Graves's work on management of government patronage, of both houses of parliament, will in all likelihood produce informative results relating both to parliamentary politics and governmental organization, and to tactics generally.[13] Just how much can this institution be regarded as 'the king's parliament' and to what extent would the business of parliament represent one which is primarily working toward royal governments' wants and needs—or might it be more the planter's parliament? Many of these questions have been answered in studies of particular parliaments or issues, but a longer study may bear a different fruit.

A case can be made as well for studies of how parliaments (and indeed any other institutions of the state) impact on their locations. It is worthy of note that after parliament had been somewhat restricted to assemble in either Dublin or Drogheda, there was an 'inability of [the latter city] to bear the train of a parliament' in Sir John Perrot's parliament (1585–86).[14] This is a reminder of the necessity of having an urban environment that could manage to host such a gathering, especially one that was to grow considerably in the seventeenth century. We might remind ourselves that Ballydoyle had been chosen as a location in 1371 by William of Windsor, partially because it was so miserable, in the hopes that the (not so) great council would vote the necessary funds in a more speedy fashion.[15] As to how this has been done effectively elsewhere, we might consult the work of Henry Cohn on the German imperial diet.[16] It is without a doubt that parliament did impact the urban space where it gathered in a variety of ways, even though not all members of both houses attended every day that parliament sat, just as there were certain days when a considerable majority of them did gather, such as the opening of sessions or the giving of the royal assent. While some members of parliament (MPs) were undoubtedly of modest means, for other peers of substantial income and status, medieval retinues of retainers were replaced by substantial families and a bevy of assistants and servants. Investigations into this sudden growth of population in Dublin in the sixteenth and particularly the seventeenth centuries would surely yield interesting insights into the effect that such an influx had on accommodation and the price of food. While we have always understood that there is a strong connection between the assembling of parliament and the necessity of finance for war, the war of the 1640s in Ireland impacted on parliament more than most others.[17] Parliament had been sitting in Dublin Castle, which was not only an administrative center and home to the lord lieutenant, but also a garrison and fortress. While most of the wars of the sixteenth century did not, for the most part, come close to Dublin, parliament in the 1640s sat in an environment where considerable military engagements took place just a few miles away. The influence of the Jacobite/Williamite war and the general security situation also had an impact on the 1689 parliament that is worthy of further investigation.

Somewhat related to the impact of parliament on the local economy and environment of the city is the issue of parliamentary privilege. Though recent studies on early modern privilege in England have centered around an MP's right not to be arrested during parliament time, there is room for a more thorough study of privilege in parliament across several centuries.[18] Privilege covered many issues in parliament such as the right to free speech and collective rights of the lower house to select its own speaker, but also the right not to be pursued in any legal action during parliament time, and to extend that protection to servants, later stipulated to only manual servants. The fact that this restriction needed to be reiterated regularly and that legislation was submitted before parliament for suspending privilege surely means that there was friction between the states, the members of both houses, and the citizens of Dublin and the rest of the kingdom.[19] By the early eighteenth century, the earl of Roscommon had no less than eighty-five unqualified individuals under his protection.[20] Having such a number of protected people, who could refuse to pay bills and honor debts and not be proceeded against in the courts, impacted on the local economy and could be an interesting window on public perceptions of parliament outside of the normal contest between native and newcomer. In August 1642, one man was prosecuted by the Commons for asking publicly, 'would this parliament never be at an end?', reflecting the general public's exasperation with parliamentary privilege, and the nuisance and burden it became on the city.[21]

While a more thorough study of privilege of this manner would be beneficial, so too would a larger study, where possible, about how a representative body such as parliament actually impacted upon the lives of the communities of the kingdom. Obviously, in political and confessional terms, the ability of parliament to be truly representative becomes less convincing after the total exclusion of Catholic members from 1692 onward, as it had been for the Gaelic community (which it had never sought to represent) before surrender and regrant in the 1540s. Some parliamentary boroughs and the county franchises were established and kept intentionally small with a view to exclusion and control as in many of James I's creations, but others, such as those medieval urban centers on the south Wexford coast, tended to wither away more naturally, frequently due to the kind of environmental change discussed elsewhere in this volume by Francis Ludlow and Arlene Crampsie.[22]

But parliament and particularly its work can be viewed through a broader definition of 'representation' than many of us might adhere to above. Studies concerning the reach and impact of parliament, whether through its representation or its law-creating functions, would give us a different view of its role and its effect on the Irish society and economy. For example, although the 1613–15 parliament is clearly important in terms of the breakdown of the relationship between the Old English political community and the king and his government, we might do well to ask if it made any significant change in the kingdom. This parliament passed just ten acts, and some of these were largely symbolic or of little practical effect.[23] The following parliament, however, passed a total of seventy-two acts, many of which may well have made significant changes in Ireland. It can always be difficult to ascertain the manner in which legislation may be effective even today, but a thorough study of such legislation (public versus private and governmental versus commonweal) would at least give an indication as to the extent that parliament and new laws impacted people, in agricultural practices, economic changes, taxation, or bridge- or road-building. In the same fashion, we might acknowledge the multiplicity of ways in which an MP might want to influence his constituents. For example, a Protestant MP who might rail against Jesuits would surely not want to see his Catholic tenants in economic difficulty, as it would clearly affect his own prosperity. Ethnic or sectarian divide is evident at times, but there are also alternative groupings and concerns in parliament based around regional or economic interdependencies.[24]

We might also consider just how those represented saw the gathering. The comments in 1642, quoted earlier, represent exasperation at the length of parliament and the impact of the parliamentary privilege of members, but there are hints that the importance or indeed interest in parliament by the general population could well be overrated. Restoration Ennis, it would appear, elected one of its MPs on the basis that he would promise to serve without expense to the town.[25] The borough of Knocktopher in Kilkenny held the election for the Jacobite parliament some two weeks after its commencement.[26] While there may have been issues surrounding the reconstitution of the borough membership, it would suggest that sending representatives to parliament may not have been as high a priority as it might otherwise have been. Such a disconnect between the people and their MPs, where it did exist, was surely exaggerated by the nature of government place-men representing towns that they may have had no vested interest in, and possibly had never visited, despite legislation insisting that they had to be resident. For example, Athenry was a strange location for Hooker's election, considering the influence of Clanricarde and the east Galway legal community in representing the town at other parliaments, and may have reflected an attempt by Sidney to pack the parliament.[27]

Moving on from representation, we may arrive at towns in Ireland. As has been commented upon, there has been a strange neglect generally in urban history in Ireland up until recently.[28] Urban history and particularly borough governance and organization can, even with minimal amounts of contemporary source material, allow for a much stronger understanding of town governance, economy, local politics, and governmental policies than previously known. As the Historic Towns Atlas project and McGrath (among others) have recently shown, for example, there are vast swathes of urban history to be mined in the early modern period.[29] This can extend from population estimates and local taxation to borough governance, composition of urban elites, internal and external urban economies, and trade organization and government. Political concerns and developments were frequently addressed in town politics, and they became especially relevant in the seventeenth century. Because of the historiographical slant toward the rural land settlement, a study of the shifting ground of urban composition and interference by Cromwellian and Restoration central government is sorely needed.[30] It is also viable, as we have a relatively wide range of archival material relating to urban records.[31] In the same fashion, further examination of the role of the sheriff and also provincial governors, and their administrative and financial responsibilities, will produce a knowledge of the offices and their work that we do not, as of yet, have.

While the colonial project sought to create a Little England to the west, imposing English manners, customs, religious beliefs, and civilization,

English law was an essential part of this, and frequently a vehicle for the other processes of adaption and consolidation. However, at the same time, it was abundantly clear that Ireland and the subjects in the kingdom, be they Protestant or Catholic, could not be allowed to have exactly the same laws as in the imperial mother country for fear that Ireland might become a kingdom equal to England under a common monarch. This is why the section of Poynings' Law that extended all pre-1495 English public legislation to Ireland would not be repeated again, even though it would have made the process of extending English legislation to Ireland quite simple. For example, had the king's Irish subjects enjoyed the benefit of the English statute of limitations (1623), the pressures felt by Catholic landowners in the 1630s would have been obviated, and the subsequent history of their involvement in the rebellion might have been considerably different.[32]

A study that ascertains exactly what the statute law in Ireland was would allow us to understand the process of colonization and governmental policy over a longer period. For example, the English parliament in the reign of James I produced in excess of 300 acts as opposed to Ireland's mere eleven acts in the same reign. Leaving the less (but not ir-)relevant private acts aside, it is clear that there must be a considerable divergence in statute law in Ireland by the end of the period. In a similar manner, the divergence in the application of and political interference with law in Ireland is worthy of further study. The English attorney general noted in 1578 about the relation of the treasonous activity of Richard Sassanach Burke, second earl of Clanricarde, whether if proceedings might be brought, 'half the evidence would have served against any subject of England'.[33] We might normally assume, considering the reputation of English administrators and soldiers in later Elizabethan Ireland, that the law would have been enforced more rigorously if anything, but on this occasion it was not, despite having the apparent support of the English legal establishment. Of course, this is not an isolated example. Governors of Ireland frequently complained that they were hamstrung by restrictions in applying certain laws placed upon them either by authorities in London or by practical concerns, such as lack of sufficient personnel to ensure enforcement. The most obvious example of this is the almost consistent failure by the state to ensure that the anti-recusancy laws were enforced from the Elizabethan period until well into the eighteenth century.[34]

Ireland, in generally replicating the English model of law and general legal culture, is perhaps a little surprising in that the law reports that one might expect to find in Ireland are quite sparse.[35] Well known are the reports of Sir John Davies, which are a most valuable source, being quite informative, but are nevertheless laudatory of his own abilities and achievements in Ireland. There is certainly 'a certain propagandistic element in tone and style', doubtless used to curry favor and position back in England.[36] After this point, we wait until Michaelmas 1716 for the next reports, which emerge from the court of exchequer for the years 1716–34.[37] This means, in effect, that we are bereft of anything resembling law reporting for the vast majority of activity in the king's courts in the Tudor and Stuart periods.

Obviously this can make judicial oversight, administration, and creation of law a difficult subject for study, but it does not make all aspects of the law impossible, and indeed there has been some excellent work on law in early modern Ireland in recent years.[38] But what can replace these missing sources, the equivalents of which are so plentiful in other jurisdictions?[39] Outside of some remains of the early modern court of chancery in Ireland (more than some realize), which have luckily survived the Public Record Office fire of 1922, there is really very little left of the original source material for the central common law and equity courts.[40] From what little material there is, historians have extrapolated much about lawyers, their clients, and the nature of the disputes.[41] Recent extensive research by this author in the Parliamentary Archives at the Palace of Westminster, for example, makes it clear that there is a lot of material relevant to Ireland, and the printed cases of the early eighteenth century will frequently look back to the origins of disputes in the seventeenth century.

The other three central courts of the kingdom are much less accessible, and their operation and influence tend to be restricted to whatever we might pick up from casual comments and informal reports of its work from a variety of sources. Even the trial details in King's Bench of a celebrity case, such as that against John Atherton, the Bishop of Waterford—the 1640 politically motivated trial and execution of a bishop for sodomy—are largely unknown to us still, certainly when compared with a similar case in England a few years earlier.[42] In all likelihood, considering the training of Irish lawyers and judges taking place at least partially in London along with the general Anglicization of government and state in early modern Ireland, it probably resembled the English model in large part. However, there is always a danger in making such an assumption and sometimes Irish administrative norms can be quite different from England's. For example, the prevalence of the Irish system to appoint lord chancellors who were bishops (Loftus of Dublin, Jones of Dublin, Boyle of Armagh, to name but a few) or other unsuitably qualified men (such as Fitton) as lord chancellor in the early modern period, long after appointments in England of common lawyers became standard, may well have produced a variant form of a particular Irish equity.

The study of the criminal law should not be of interest just to legal historians, where it has in the past been written off as being of little interest and limited development ('The miserable history of crime in England can be shortly told. Nothing worth-while was created'); it also carries interest to historians of society, gender, and the urban and rural localities.[43] There have been some studies for the early modern period, but the area seems to be somewhat underdeveloped, certainly compared with its English equivalent.[44] Assize records and quarter sessions records are not available to the historian of Irish criminal justice in the manner in which they were for J.S. Cockburn and other historians of the English equivalent.[45] There is, to the best of my knowledge, just one substantial collection of assize records (Tipperary) for the later seventeenth-century, some scraps of quarter sessions (Longford and Kilkenny), jury lists for mid-Ulster, and what presumably are the last active vestiges of court leets in rural Dublin. These will never be satisfactory, but they can provide for a decent, if limited, study. The records for Tipperary, containing in excess of 1,600 hearings on everything up to and including murder, include grand jury lists, indictment details, pleadings, and punishments.[46] These may give a skewed impression and may not necessarily be representative of Irish criminal justice generally in the period, but they are still worthy of more thorough examination than they have gotten to date. Surprisingly little use has been made, for example, of Bolton's guide for justices of the peace.[47]

Punishment, being a distinctly public process and one that the common people were encouraged to observe and enjoy, is naturally more plentiful in source material. While it has been observed that we are devoid of any detail of Bishop Atherton's trial, we do have considerable detail as to the manner of his dispatch, as we do for Bishop O'Devany, the 1663 Dublin plotters, and many others. There is, naturally, less material for the execution and punishment of the unexceptional convicts. The punishments available and sometimes handed down by the various courts were quite varied, from imprisonment in the newly created houses of correction to the hanging, drawing, and quartering of men convicted of murder (a harsher punishment than in England).[48] Yet for the sources we have, it would appear that juries are, as in England, most reluctant to render a guilty verdict when the punishment is death, even in the ethnically and confessionally divided Ireland of the early modern period. All of this would suggest that a substantial study of crime and punishment in Ireland is feasible and worthy.

Although the central government has generally been well represented in the history of early modern Ireland, there is still some room for further investigation. Several of the politicians left substantial archives, the duke of Ormond's Carte Collection at the Bodleian, Oxford, being the most impressive. The State Papers at Kew represent the state archive, and a series of papers are gathered specifically around Irish issues.[49] Due to the prohibitive nature of the cost of State Papers online, only a select few universities across Ireland and Britain can afford to subscribe either partially or fully. Thus, without the funds or time to spend long periods in London, many researchers depend upon the calendars, which are of course useful, but do not fully represent the wealth and detail of the Irish material there.

As has been mentioned elsewhere in this volume, petitions represent an insightful window into the public's interaction with government, whether those are by an individual, a regional group of subjects, or a corporate body.[50] Of particular prominence in the State Papers is the English secretary of state for the southern department, who generally controlled communications between Ireland and the king and his government in Whitehall. In particular, the nature of appointments can be insightful when studying networks and connections, as well as more generally considering statecraft, corruption, and governance within Ireland in the period.[51] The appointments to the various offices relating to customs, and how much the second earl of Cork received for them in the early Restoration period, make for fascinating reading.[52] In particular, the growth of taxation and state formation is worthy of further examination in Ireland, extending the work of the later Stuart period back into Tudor Ireland.[53]

The investigation of both the civil and military lists might be a good place to address the issue of prosopography. Gerald Aylmer describes this process as 'the historical technique of collective biography, seeking to collect, verify, and present a minimum amount of information about the lives and careers of a relatively large number of people', and then suggests that it has 'now been long established both in history and in applied social studies'.[54] The value of such studies rests in the fact that while the nature of appointments and networks associated with them are not always obvious to the historians of a specific appointment, a systematic examination of large numbers of appointments will allow us to garner a strong semblance of exactly what was and what was not essential or desirable criteria in the appointment of state servants. The technique also allows us to observe the trajectory of a career. Obviously the technique can be used for any groups of people, and has been to great effect.[55] So too, we have had some excellent works in Irish history that have worked toward the biographical and veered into the prosopographical—the earlier work of Brid McGrath and that of F.E. Ball being two fine examples at either end of the twentieth century.[56] The critical aspect of the work is the cross-examination of the various strands or important criteria in the many careers under examination. Indeed, although it has not had much impact in Ireland, there is also a case for applying social network theory to the actors in early modern Irish politics and administration.[57]

Biographical lists, something quite different from mature prosopography, have come in for substantial criticism in the past. George Sayles, a champion of the history of medieval government in Ireland, described the approach as comprising the 'sparse and uninformative details of the obscure lives of obscure men [that] are laboriously collected because they made a fitful appearance'.[58] Geoffrey Elton, also a constitutional historian of government, and parliament in particular, criticized Sir Lewis Namier's obsession with the persons of individuals—his belief that the history of parliament equals the history of individual members of the commons'.[59] The critical issue here is that the biographical details must be considered part of a whole membership of a given profession or group with a view to ascertaining commonalities, and it tends to be best done within a more comprehensive study of the institution also. Biographical lists alone can remain as those described by Elton and Sayles.

Although it would be a substantial project, or, in all likelihood, several projects, a long history of office holders in Ireland would be most useful. The raw materials in terms of lists are largely available in collections such as Lascalles' *Liber munerum publicorum Hiberniæ* and Hughes' *Patentee Officers in*

Ireland.[60] Obviously the more important offices, such as that of lord lieutenant, have gotten more substantial amounts of attention, but there are still many officers of state, both great and minor, in whom we are less well-versed.[61] While we have articles and books on individual office holders, prosopographical studies of the men (it was very rare that women were invited to partake in government) who undertook this work of government are less prevalent, but such an approach will surely garner at least some illumination as to office holders and the nature of their appointments.

While considering the usefulness of the prosopography of each office holder, we might also consider the necessity of a long history of each office, defining the role that each office holder was expected to execute, and the same for certain crucial roles within the English system such as secretary of state for the south. For example, we might consider Sir Anthony Hart's study of the Serjeants-at-Law, an office of substantial prestige and initially great importance, but of dwindling influence compared with the growing responsibility of the attorney general or the solicitor general.[62] Hart's work traces the history of the office from its medieval origins up to the dissolution of the office with the establishment of the Irish Free State. A number of chapters chart the development of the office, the nature of appointments and responsibilities, the growth of the office into a second and then third serjeant in the seventeenth century, and the political involvements that the earlier serjeants naturally were involved in. Following this, there are succession lists from Roger Owen in 1261 to Alexander Sullivan (the 'last serjeant') in 1919.[63] Biographical notes then follow this list on each serjeant, and finally indications as to the fees, earnings, privileges, and perquisites related to the post, in as much as they are possible to figure.[64]

A similar approach might be taken toward all the major and many of the minor officers of the state—executive, judicial, administrative, military, and financial—although obviously the roles were not as keenly distinct in the sixteenth or seventeenth centuries. A history of the sheriff, the secretary of state, the chief remembrancer of the exchequer or the Ulster king of arms would all be well worth the time and effort with a view to understanding the nature of the role and interconnected manner in which many of these officers must have worked. The nature of the appointment to office, the cost of the sinecure, the responsibilities that the holder should execute, and the benefits that accrued from such offices are not always readily available to students and researchers and would be of undoubted benefit. A small handbook with even a modest description of the role would be worthwhile for those historians who do not work in legal or constitutional history, but who regularly find mention of such offices in their sources for the history of religion, society, or ideas. An alternative way to consider the same problem might be to take Aylmer's approach and write a history of the civil service generally over a shorter period of time.[65] While it may not provide the same insight that a longer history of each office can, it would allow for a closer examination of how the civil service worked in a more integrated fashion.

In suggesting possible gaps in the established bibliography of the institutional history of Ireland more generally, it might be suggested that as a community of historians so aware of the nature of the Irish constitution and its impact on the development of the kingdom in the early modern period, we are still devoid of a constitutional history textbook for the early modern period. This may seem a little strange as Irish history has such a fine tradition of constitutional studies both in the early modern period[66] and also in other eras.[67] This all is the stranger, considering the strong intellectual connections between the Irish academy and Oxford and Cambridge, where undergraduate courses on constitutional history were standard, making use of equivalent textbooks by Kenyon and Elton.[68] In truth, such a textbook may not produce anything that is not already known to most historians in the area, but it would be of great use in promoting constitutional history more generally.

While we are all too aware of the limitations of source material in Ireland and the fact that institutional and constitutional history is far from a 'new' topic, it is patently clear that there is still much work to do and new avenues and opportunities to consider when we look at courts, parliament, government, and all other state institutions. These new (or perhaps new to Irish history) approaches to old institutions will add to our understanding as to how institutions functioned and also how they interacted with the people on the island.

Perhaps we should not be too cynical as to the possibility of discovering or rediscovering material that was not previously known to us—always keeping in mind that what may be unknown to historians may well be known to librarians and archivists. Material will inevitably surface or resurface in Ireland and abroad, as has been the case with the court martial records from the 1650s at Marsh's Library, or indeed the useful transcription and publication of the Cromwellian high court of justice in recent years.[69] In all likelihood, such material, such as King's Bench records, may not be fully discovered if at all; but it is not outside the possibilities that some significant material will become available. The Irish Research Council-funded project entitled *Beyond 2022*, based at Trinity College, Dublin, and with cooperation from many archives abroad, clearly has the strong likelihood of coughing up material once thought lost or forgotten.

The benefits of such new discoveries or even just a greater exploitation of those available to us already are twofold. As mentioned earlier, a greater understanding of administrative systems and institutions in early modern Ireland is, in itself, a thoroughly worthwhile endeavor. There are also secondary benefits that may well outweigh the primary ones, since institutional histories always inform the societies, communities, and economies that these institutions sought to regulate, judge, control, and serve.

Notes

1   While preparing this chapter, the author was an Irish Research Council Marie Skłodowska-Curie Elevate Fellow, based in Das Institut für Rechts- und Verfassungsgeschichte, at the Faculty of Law, University of Vienna. The author would like to acknowledge this support.

2 Brian Manning, a student of Christopher Hill, was relatively rare in being quite left-wing in his approach to history, but wrote mostly on English history and rarely on Irish. Ivan Roots, 'Obituary: Professor Brian Manning: Marxist Historian of the English Civil Wars and Student of Christopher Hill', *The Independent*, 11 May 2004. One of the more fascinating forays into this wilderness-like genre in Irish history is surely E.F. Telegina, 'Osno vopolozhniki Marksizma ob Angliiskoi kolonialoi politike v Irlandii v Period Restauratsii (1660–1688)', in E.V. Kuznetsov (ed.), *Problemy razlozheniia feodalizma i genezisa kapitalisma v Anglii* (Gorkii: Gorkovskogo Universiteta, 1980), pp. 3–16, [Written in Cyrillic script, it translates roughly as: 'The Founders of Marxism on English Colonial Policy in Ireland during the Restoration Period', in *Studies in the Disintegration of Feudalism and the Origins of Capitalism in England*].

3 For example, we might consider Richard Bagwell, *Ireland under the Stuarts and during the Interregnum* (3 vols., London: Longmans, Green, 1909–16); W.E.H. Lecky, *A History of Ireland in the Eighteenth Century*, 4 vols. (London: Longmans, Green, 1872–96); J.P. Prendergast, *Ireland from the Restoration to the Revolution, 1660–1690* (London: Longmans, Green, 1887). Regardless of their whig, unionist, or nationalist outlook, their books are laid out in a similar fashion and cover political history.

4 For example, see the classic S.G. Ellis, *Reform and Revival: English Government in Ireland, 1470–1534* (London: Royal Historical Society, 1986).

5 Raymond Gillespie, *Seventeenth-century Ireland: Making Ireland Modern* (Dublin: Gill, 2006), pp. 34–35.

6 Anthony Sheehan, 'Irish Revenues and English Subventions, 1559–1622', *Proceedings of the Royal Irish Academy* 90C (1990), 35–65; Victor Treadwell, 'The Establishment of the Farm of the Irish Customs, 1603–16', *English Historical Review* 93 (1978), 580–602.

7 Brid McGrath, 'A Bibliographical Dictionary of the Membership of the Irish House of Commons, 1640–41'. PhD thesis, Trinity College, Dublin, 1997; idem, 'The Membership of the Irish House of Commons, 1613–15', M.Litt. thesis, Trinity College, Dublin, 1985.

8 *Tracts relating to Ireland printed for the Irish Archaeological Society* (Dublin: Irish Archaeological Society, 1843), vol. 2, pp. 134–42. British Library, MS Add. 4814, ff. 56–57; British Library, MS Cotton Titus B.XIII, ff. 388–89.

9 Coleman A. Dennehy, 'Privilege, Organization, and Aristocratic Identity in the Seventeenth-Century Irish House of Lords', in Francesco Soddu and Annamari Nieddu (eds.), *Assemblee rappresentative, autonomie territoriali, culture politiche* (Sassari: Editrice Democratica Sarda, 2011); E.M. Johnston-Liik, *History of the Irish Parliament, 1692–1800* (Belfast: Ulster Historical Foundation, 2002), vol. 1, p. 7; Jane H. Ohlmeyer, *Making Ireland English: The Irish Aristocracy in the Seventeenth Century* (New Haven, CT: Yale University Press, 2012), chaps. 8 and 12.

10 Aidan Clarke, *Prelude to Restoration in Ireland: The End of the Commonwealth, 1659–1660* (Cambridge: Cambridge University Press, 1999), c. 6; Micheál Ó Siochrú, *Confederate Ireland, 1642–1649* (Dublin: Four Courts Press, 1999), pp. 251–68.

11 Chris Kyle and Jason Peacey, *Parliament at Work: Parliamentary Committees, Political Power, and Public Access in Early Modern England* (Woodbridge: Boydell and Brewer, 2002). See also the various publications (with quality varying over the decades) of the history of Parliament Trust.

12 John Adamson, *The Noble Revolt: The Overthrow of Charles I* (London: Weidenfeld, 2007); G.R. Elton, *The Parliament of England, 1559–1581* (Cambridge: Cambridge University Press, 1986), pp. 350–55; Wallace Notestein, *The Winning of the Initiative by the House of Commons* (London: The British Academy, 1924); Ohlmeyer, *Making Ireland English*.

13 M.A.R. Graves, 'The Management of the Elizabethan House of Commons: The Council's "men-of-business"', *Parliamentary History* 2 (1983), 8–21.

14 C.L. Falkiner, 'The Parliament of Ireland under the Tudor Sovereigns', *Proceedings of the Royal Irish Academy* 25 (1905), p. 514; Victor Treadwell, 'Sir John Perrot and the Irish parliament of 1585–86', *Proceedings of the Royal Irish Academy* 85 (1985), 259–308.

15 H.G. Richardson and G.O. Sayles, *The Irish Parliament in the Middle Ages* (Philadelphia: University of Pennsylvania Press, 1952), p. 190. James Lydon, 'William of Windsor and the Irish parliament', *English Historical Review* 80 (1965), 258. By the Tudor period, an archaism existed of disputed function (particular where tax and cess was concerned) and membership, but in the 1370s, it was an assembly with parliamentary powers and responsibilities to vote taxation and represent grievances, but with a representation of the local region of concern and without the normal forty-day notice to convene.

16 Henry Cohn, 'Representing Political Space at a Political Site: The Imperial Diets of the Sixteenth Century' in Beat Kümin (ed.), *Political Space in Pre-Industrial Europe* (Abingdon: Routledge, 2009).

17 Coleman A. Dennehy, 'Parliament in Ireland, 1641–48', in Patrick Little and P. Little (eds.), *Ireland in Crisis: War, Politics, and Religion, 1641–1651* (Manchester: Manchester University Press, forthcoming).

18 Paul M. Hunneyball, 'The Development of Parliamentary Privilege, 1604–29', in Chris Kyle (ed.), *Managing Tudor and Stuart Parliaments: Essays in Memory of Michael Graves* (Oxford: Oxford University Press, 2015); K.A.T. Stapylton, 'The Parliamentary Privilege of Freedom from Arrest, 1603–29', PhD thesis, University of London, 2016.

19 *Commons' Journals, Ireland,* 7, 11 July 1666.

20 F.G. James, *Lords of the Ascendancy: The Irish House of Lords and its Members, 1660–1800* (Dublin: Blackrock, 1995), p. 85.

21 *Commons' Journals, Ireland,* 9 August 1642.

22 Coleman A. Dennehy, 'Representation in Later Medieval and Early Modern Ireland', in Mario Damen, Jelle Haemers, and Alastair J. Mann (eds.), *Political Representation: Communities, Ideas and Institutions in Europe, c. 1200–c. 1650* (Leiden: Brill, 2018).

23 The more symbolic (and of less absolute legal necessity) might be the act recognizing James I's right to the crown, while of greater import was the act for a subsidy. 11, 12, & 13 Jas I, c. I, X [Ire.].

24 See Coleman A. Dennehy, 'Representation in later medieval and early modern Ireland'.

25 *Commons' Journals, Ireland,* 9 April 1666.

26 National Archives of Ireland, MS M239.

27 James Hardiman, *Tracts relating to Ireland* (Dublin: Irish Archaeological Society, 1843), vol. 2, app. 2. *Holinshed's Chronicles of England, Scotland and Ireland,* 6 vols. (London: J. Johnson, 1807), vol. 6, p. 344; Victor Treadwell, 'The Irish parliament of 1569–71', *Proceedings of the Royal Irish Academy* 65 (1966/67), 64, n. 55; 67, n. 64.

28 Micheál Ó Siochrú, 'Civil autonomy and military power in Ireland', *Journal of Early Modern History* 15 (2011), 32–33, n. 1.

29 Brid McGrath, 'A Fragment of the Minute Book of the Corporation of New Ross, 1635', *Journal of the Royal Society of Antiquaries of Ireland* 144–45 (2014–15), 100–112; idem, 'Managing the Windsor of Ireland: The composition of Galway's town council, 1603–1653', *Journal of Galway Archaeological and Historical Society* 70 (2018, forthcoming); 'Archbishop John Bramhall and Church lands in Athboy, 1641–1663', *Ríocht na Midhe* 28 (2017), 91–113; Colm Lennon, *The Lords of Dublin in the Age of the Reformation* (Dublin: Irish Academic Press, 1989).

30 John Cunningham, *Conquest and Land in Ireland: The Transplantation to Connacht, 1649–1680* (Woodbridge: Boydell and Brewer, 2011).

31 Some records remain for Belfast, Coleraine, Youghal, Dublin, Cork, Clonmel, New Ross, Athboy, Knocktopher, Belturbet, Waterford, and Irishtown in Kilkenny.

32 21 Jas 1, c 16 [Eng.]. William Ballantine, *A Treatise on the Statute of Limitations (21 Jac. I. c. 16.)* (New York: C. Wiley, 1812).

33 State Papers 63/63/42.

34 Elizabethanne Boran and Crawford Gribben, *Enforcing Reformation in Ireland and Scotland, 1550–1700* (Aldershot: Ashgate, 2006); Brendan Bradshaw, 'Sword, Word, and Strategy in the Reformation in Ireland', *Historical Journal* 21 (1978), 475–502.

35 L.W. Abbott, *Law Reporting in England, 1485–1585* (New York: Humanities Press, 1973). John Baker, *An Introduction to English Legal History* (London: Butterworths, 1990, 3rd edn.), pp. 204–14.

36 Hans S. Pawlisch, *Sir John Davies and the Conquest of Ireland: A Study in Legal Imperialism* (Cambridge: Cambridge University Press, 1985), p. 34; John Davies, *Le primer report des cases in les courts del roy* (Dublin: Iohn Franckton, 1615); *A report of cases and matters in law resolved and abridged in the king's courts in Ireland* (Dublin, 1762).

37 Andrew Lyall (ed.), *Irish Exchequer Reports: Reports of Cases in the Courts of Exchequer and Chancery in Ireland* 125 (London: Selden Society, 2008).

38 Jon G. Crawford, *A Star Chamber Court in Ireland: The Court of Castle Chamber, 1571–1641* (Dublin: Four Courts Press, 2005).

39 W.N. Osborough, 'In search of Irish legal history: a map for explorers', *Long Room* 35 (1990), 28–38.

40 Jane H. Ohlmeyer, 'Records of the Irish Court of Chancery: A Preliminary Report for 1627–1634', in D.S. Greer and N.M. Dawson (eds.), *Mysteries and Solutions in Irish Legal History* (Dublin: Four Courts Press, 2001), app. 1. Ken Nicholls has produced a most useful, but unpublished, calendar of Chancery-related material at the National Archives of Ireland.

41 Hazel Maynard, 'The Irish Legal Profession and the Catholic Revival', in J. Kelly, J. McCafferty, and C.I. McGrath (eds.), *People, Politics and Power: Essays on Irish History 1660–1850 in Honour of James I. McGuire* (Dublin: University College Dublin Press, 2009); Mary O'Dowd, 'Women and the Irish Chancery Court in the Late Sixteenth and Early Seventeenth Centuries', *Irish Historical Studies* 31 (1999), 470–87.

42 Cynthia Herrup, *A House in Gross Disorder: Sex, Law, and the 2nd Earl of Castlehaven* (Oxford: Oxford University Press, 2001); Peter Marshall, *Mother Leakey and the Bishop: A Ghost Story* (Oxford: Oxford University Press, 2008).

43 S.F.C. Milsom, *Historical Foundation of the Common Law* (2nd edn, London: Butterworth-Heinemann, 1981), p. 403. While his assessment on the development of criminal law, and the law of the criminal trial, evidence, and counsel, stands reasonably true until well into the eighteenth century, for the most part, there has been much work in England on the nature of society, gender, policing, and crime by J.S. Cockburn, Malcolm Gaskill, J.M. Beattie, and Karen Jones.

44 Raymond Gillespie, 'Women and Crime in Seventeenth-Century Ireland', in Margaret MacCurtain and Mary O'Dowd (eds.), *Women in Early Modern Ireland* (Edinburgh: Edinburgh University Press, 1991), 43–52.

45 J.S. Cockburn, *A History of English Assizes, 1558–1714* (Cambridge: Cambridge University Press, 1972).

46 National Library of Ireland, MSS 4908–9.

47 Richard Bolton, *A Justice of the Peace for Ireland* (Dublin, 1638).

48 10 Henry VII, c. XXI [Ire.].

49 National Archives, Kew, SP 60–63.

50 Brian Weiser, *Charles II and the Politics of Access* (Woodbridge: Boydell and Brewer, 2003).

51 It is worthy of note that Laetitia Chichester, wife of the lord deputy Sir Arthur, and the rest of 'the femall sex bares too great a swaye in altering his mynd' when it came to appointments and the disposal of patronage. *The Trevelyan Papers*, ed. W.C. Trevelyan and C.E. Trevelyan (London: Camden Society, 1872), pt. 3, p. 131.

52 'Diaries of the second earl of Cork, first earl of Burlington', Chatsworth House Archives, Lismore MS Misc Box 1, vol. 1, Dec. 1660, n.p.

53 Michael Braddick, *State Formation in Early Modern England, c.1550–1700* (Cambridge: Cambridge University Press, 2000); Aaron Graham and Patrick Walsh (eds.), *The British Fiscal-Military States, 1660–c.1783* (Abingdon: Routledge, 2016); Neil Johnston, 'State Formation in Seventeenth-Century Ireland: The Restoration Financial Settlement, 1660–62', *Parliaments, Estates and Representation* 36 (2016), 115–36.

54 G.E. Aylmer, *The Crown's Servants: Government and Civil Service under Charles II, 1660–1685* (Oxford: Oxford University Press, 2002), p. 242.

55 For some thoughts on the issue, see Lawrence Stone, 'Prosopography', *Daedalus* 100 (1971), 46–79. See also the work of the Prosopograhy Project at the Modern History Research Unit at Oxford.

56 Brid McGrath, 'A Bibliographical Dictionary of the Membership of the Irish House of Commons, 1640–1', PhD thesis, Trinity College, Dublin (1997); 'The Membership of the Irish House of Commons, 1613–5', M.Litt. thesis, Trinity College, Dublin (1985); F.E. Ball, *The Judges in Ireland, 1221–1921*. 2 vols. (Dublin: Round Hall, 1993). One might also include, C.A. Dennehy 'Speakers in the seventeenth-century Irish parliament', in Paul Seaward, *Speakers and the Speakership: Presiding Officers and the Management of Business from the Middle Ages to the 21st Century* (Oxford, 2010).

57 Charles Wethrell, 'Historical social network analysis', *International Review of Social History* 43 (1998), 125–44.

58 G.O. Sayles, *The King's Parliament of England* (New York: Norton, 1975), p. 18.

59 G.R. Elton, *Political History: Principles and Practices* (New York: Basic Books, 1970), p. 35.

60 Rowley Lascalles, *Liber munerum publicorum Hiberniae, ab an. 1152 usque ad 1827: or, the establishments of Ireland, from the nineteenth of King Stephen to the seventh of George IV., during a period of six hundred and seventy-five years* (London, 1824–30); J.L.J. Huges, *Patentee Officers in Ireland, 1173–1826: Including High Sheriffs, 1661–1684 and 1761–1816* (Dublin: Irish Manuscripts Commission, 1960); T.W. Moody, F.X. Martin, F.J. Byrne, *A New History of Ireland, Vol. 9: Maps, Genealogies, Lists: A Companion to Irish History, Part II* (Oxford: Oxford University Press, 1989), pp. 469–537.

61 For example, see Ciaran Brady, *The Chief Governors: The Rise and Fall of Reform Government in Tudor Ireland 1536–1588* (Cambridge: Cambridge University Press, 1994); Peter Gray and Olwen Purdue (eds.), *The Irish Lord Lieutenancy, c. 1541–1922* (Dublin: University College Dublin Press, 2012).

62 A.R. Hart, *A History of the King's Serjeants at Law in Ireland: Honour rather than Advantage?* (Dublin: Four Courts Press, 2000).

63 Ibid., pp. 143–58.

64 Ibid., pp. 161–84, 185–94.

65 G.E. Aylmer, *The Crown's Servants*; *The King's Servants: The Civil Service of Charles I, 1625–1642* (New York: Columbia University Press, 1961); idem, *The State's Servants: The Civil Service of the English Republic, 1649–1660* (London: Routledge and Kegan Paul, 1973).

66 For just a few examples amongst many, see Brendan Bradshaw, *The Irish Constitutional Revolution of the Sixteenth Century* (Cambridge: Cambridge University Press, 1979); Aidan Clarke, *The Old English in Ireland, 1625–42* (2nd edn, Dublin: Four Courts, 2000); Steven G. Ellis, *Reform and Revival: English Government in Ireland, 1470–1534* (London: Royal Historical Society, 1986).

67 For example, see Donal Coffey, *Constitutionalism in Ireland 1932–1938: National, Commonwealth, and International Perspectives* (New York: Palgrave Macmillan 2018); idem, *Drafting the Irish Constitution, 1935–1937: Transnational Influences in Inter-war Europe* (New York: Palgrave Macmillan, 2018); H.G. Richardson and G.O. Sayles, *The Administration of Ireland, 1172–1377* (Dublin: Irish Manuscripts Commission, 1963); idem, *The Irish Parliament in the Middle Ages* (Philadelphia: University of Pennsylvania Press, 1952); A.J. Ward, *The Irish Constitutional Tradition: Responsible Government and Modern Ireland, 1782–1992* (Washington, DC: Catholic University of America Press, 1994).

68 G.R. Elton, *The Tudor Constitution: Documents and Commentary* (Cambridge: Cambridge University Press, 1960); J.P. Kenyon, *The Stuart Constitution: Documents and Commentary* (Cambridge: Cambridge University Press, 1986); E. Neville Williams, *The Eighteenth-Century Constitution, 1688–1815: Documents and Commentary* (Cambridge: Cambridge University Press, 1960).

69 Heather Maclean, Ian Gentles, and Micheál Ó Siochrú (eds.), 'Minutes of courts martial held in Dublin, 1651–53 [with index]', *Archivium Hibernicum* 64 (2011), 56–164; Jennifer Wells (ed.), 'Proceedings at the High Court of Justice at Dublin and Cork, 1652–1654 [Part 1, with index]', *Archivium Hibernicum* 66 (2013), 63–260; 'Proceedings at the high court of justice at Dublin and Cork, 1652–1654 [Part 1, with index], *Archivium Hibernicum* 67 (2014), 76–274.

12 The history of medicine in early modern Ireland

Some research problems and opportunities

John Cunningham

The early modern volume of the nine-part *New History of Ireland*, published in 1976, stands as an important historiographical landmark. Yet its 633 pages contained just four paragraphs relating to the history of medicine: two each in its chapters on the Irish language and Irish literature in Latin, respectively.[1] The comparable volume of the four-part *Cambridge History of Ireland*, published in 2018, provides a welcome up-to-date synopsis of the period 1550–1730, one that in many ways reflects the fruits of scholarly endeavor since the 1970s. In the latter publication, new areas of focus include environmental history, material culture, and art history. But there is still no chapter on the history of medicine. In fact, the subject receives even less attention than it did in 1976.[2] In what follows, I will first try to account for this situation by sketching an outline of the relevant historiographical context. I will then signpost some of the 'new directions' that might be pursued as part of a worthwhile effort to promote research into the history of medicine in early modern Ireland. The chapter is largely informed by my own work on, and interest in, medical practitioners.[3] Yet because of the breadth and complexity of the history of medicine, there is little sense in proposing anything like a prescriptive agenda for future activity. The more sensible approach is to encourage continued collective effort by a range of scholars. Ideally, this will entail research across a wide variety of relevant topics, in a manner that pays due cognizance to historiographical developments in the history of medicine more generally.

Historiography

The past twenty years have witnessed a notable intensification of research activity on the history of medicine in Ireland. This has been partly due to institutional developments, especially the establishment in 2006 of the Centre for the History of Medicine in Ireland at University College Dublin and Ulster University. A significant multiauthored essay collection from 1999, edited by Greta Jones and Elizabeth Malcolm, also provided impetus.[4] In their introduction to *Medicine, Disease and the State in Ireland, 1650–1940*, Jones and Malcolm surveyed Irish medical historiography and highlighted some of the perceived shortcomings of earlier publications. They portrayed work on Ireland as largely out of step with scholarship on other countries. In particular, the 'social history of medicine' that had transformed the field in England and elsewhere had made little impact.[5] The history of medicine in Ireland instead continued to be dominated by a 'traditional' focus on topics such as institutions, the lives and achievements of prominent doctors, and the role of the state. With their collection of essays, Jones and Malcolm sought to launch the project of bringing research on Ireland up to date.[6] The ways in which that project has been successful was usefully captured in a 'discursive essay' published by Catherine Cox in 2013. Cox highlighted some of the areas where she and other scholars had made significant inroads, for example in relation to the rise of lunatic asylums in the nineteenth century. At the same time, she noted 'some very basic lacunae in our knowledge', particularly concerning the years before 1800.[7]

The same problem was recognized by James Kelly and Fiona Clark in 2010 in their introduction to another important edited collection. The preponderance of work on the nineteenth and twentieth centuries meant that 'the modern period overwhelms the early modern'.[8] Their remarks prefaced a volume of essays on *Ireland and Medicine in the Seventeenth and Eighteenth Centuries*, which made a significant contribution to our knowledge of a range of subjects. The publication of a number of other articles and essays in recent years has further deepened our understanding of medicine in early modern Ireland. Here, the work of James Kelly has been of particular importance.[9] But a synthetic chapter of the kind that might usefully have found a home in the *Cambridge History of Ireland* remains to be written. Why is this the case?

Kelly and Clark argued that the sheer 'diversity' of the subject meant that a great deal of further research was needed before any new and well-grounded overview could be produced.[10] This remains the case as of this writing. It is clear, moreover, that the challenge posed by this diversity can be best met by collective effort. This is the case for several reasons. First, few, if any, individual scholars can combine the expertise needed to study texts and sources in Irish, Latin, and English on the one hand, with a solid grounding in the history and historiography of medicine on the other. Second, there is a need to create a 'critical mass' of secondary literature.[11] This is essential to underpinning university teaching of the subject and attracting the interest of research students. It is also crucial in securing greater attention for early modern medicine within developing scholarly narratives and analyses of Irish history more broadly. Therefore, the continuation of specialized research, by those best equipped to do it, into sources such as Gaelic medical manuscripts or relevant tracts in Latin ought to be prioritized over any premature effort to produce a neat overarching synthesis.

Recent developments indicate the emergence of the years around 1750 as a key dividing line in the historiography. It has come to mark a division not only between early modern and modern medicine in Ireland, respectively, but also between an earlier period that attracts relatively few researchers and a later one where scholarship is very much thriving. For some evidence of this, we can again look to the contents of an important collection of essays, namely, the *Cambridge Social History of Modern Ireland* published in 2017. The chapters include Catherine Cox's 'Health and Welfare, 1750–2000' as well as a number of other contributions with a similar timeline that are also relevant to the history of medicine broadly defined.[12] Another significant recent essay collection, *Cultures of Care in Irish Medical History*, also takes 1750 as it starting point.[13] Most of the growing number of historical monographs on Irish medicine focus on the nineteenth and twentieth centuries, with coverage pre-1750 a less common occurrence.[14] Given the underdeveloped state of research on the earlier period, the task of providing a longer-term analysis that spans the mid-eighteenth century divide while retaining scholarly coherence is one that appears to present some considerable difficulties.

One context where scholars have successfully integrated at least part of the earlier period is in histories focused around important institutions. The establishment of a fraternity of physicians in Dublin in 1654 and the setting up of the school of medicine at Trinity College Dublin in 1711 stand out as key dates. They serve as the chronological starting points for a number of relevant publications.[15] The fraternity of physicians was the precursor to the Dublin College of Physicians. The latter body received its royal charter in 1667, and it continues to exist today as the Royal College of Physicians of Ireland (RCPI). Its prominent role since the seventeenth century has supplied scholars with a means of imposing some order on at least one extended strand of Irish medical history. For example, the 350th anniversary of the 1667 charter saw the launch of a 'Lives of the Presidents' website; it contains biographical articles on 141 of the men who have headed that institution, 'celebrating their medical careers, accomplishments and widely varied interests'.[16] Amongst other things, this project highlights the potential that exists for further prosopographical research on the history of Irish medicine.

While this top-down 'great men' approach has been out of fashion for some time in the historiography of medicine in other countries, the paucity of research to date on many of the individuals concerned ensures that it still has a useful role to play in the Irish case, especially for the period before 1750. It is also worth highlighting one of the potential advantages that has accrued from what Jones and Malcolm depicted as the persistent use of outdated methodologies by historians of Irish medicine, long after scholars elsewhere had adopted new approaches.[17] Those researchers now training their sights on the history of Irish medicine can use as a stimulus the scholarship generated by long-running international debates around questions of theory and methodology. These debates encompass, for example, the conflicting claims made about the social history of medicine since 1990. The field has been variously described by some scholars as still in its infancy, and by others as having reached maturity; Roger Cooter has, by contrast, pronounced it dead.[18] The debates in question also reflect the impact of cultural history as well as the postmodern challenge, not least in the form of the approaches advocated by Michel Foucault to the issue of mental illness.[19]

Historians of medicine tend toward a greater degree of soul searching than is usually the case in early modern Irish and British historiography. The resulting reflective and critical writings can serve as a very useful map for navigating what is a large, lively, and contested field.[20] Due attention to this map can enable early modern Irish historians to engage more fully with broader debates, something that scholars of the modern period have already succeeded in doing quite well. Just as the personnel, practices, and ideas that shaped Irish medicine in the early modern period cannot be properly understood without reference to international contexts, the resulting historiography ought also to be responsive to the methods pursued and subjects explored by the large global community of medical historians. For example, the emphasis currently placed on carefully contextualized and detailed case studies should be seen as an opportunity by scholars of medicine in early modern Ireland.[21] In some ways, it renders less problematic the many gaps in the available archives. We cannot reasonably aspire to write a history of medicine that is as detailed and broadly focused as what has been achieved for early modern England and some other parts of Europe.[22] At the same time, the pursuit of case studies and what the sources allow offer one way for Irish historians to make a meaningful contribution to ongoing debates, to offer new insights, and to integrate Irish perspectives into a range of comparative analyses and wider frameworks.

Gaelic Ireland and English Ireland

The 2017 celebration of the history of the RCPI's founders and long line of presidents, mentioned earlier, in some ways draws attention to the difficulty that surrounds the task of situating its origins in a meaningful longer-term Irish medical context. After all, the fourteen fellows named in the 1667 charter were mostly English-born, and all of them were Protestants.[23] This arrangement partly reflected the political situation in the 1660s, following the Catholic loss of land and power under Cromwell.[24] The picture of Irish medicine suggested by the fourteen names listed in the College's charter is not representative of physicians in Ireland more generally, not to mention the wider medical milieu on the island. The latter included surgeons, apothecaries, midwives, and a host of other practitioners, both male and female, both learned and popular. A focus on the mid-seventeenth century and the origins of the RCPI thus throws up some of the same historiographical problems as the period *circa* 1750. It is possible to work forward in a coherent manner from these points of departure but much more difficult to bridge them. Perhaps the first to attempt to do so was made by Dr. Aquilla Smith. In 1841, he published an article entitled 'Some Account of the Origin and Early History of the College of Physicians in Ireland'.[25] To set the scene for developments post-1654, he had to look beyond Ireland and to the prominence achieved by some Irish doctors as royal physicians in early modern Europe. These included Niall

O'Glacan in Spain, France, and Italy, and Bernard O'Connor in Poland.[26] Although little was known about the practice of medicine in Ireland prior to the mid-seventeenth century, the careers of men such as O'Glacan were 'sufficient to establish the high estimation in which our countrymen were held both in England and on the continent'.[27] Smith was also very much aware of the survival of numerous Gaelic medical manuscripts from earlier periods, but he could do no more than lament the fact that 'no Irish scholar has been hitherto induced' to examine them.[28]

The manuscripts to which Smith referred have received a good amount of attention in recent decades, in the work of Aoibheann Nic Dhonnchadha and others.[29] We now have a reasonably good understanding of their contents, which largely consist of translations into Irish of medical texts widely used elsewhere in Europe. These included the aphorisms of Hippocrates and Bernard of Gordon's *Lilium Medicinae* (1303). Jason Harris has very helpfully situated this manuscript tradition within a broader process of 'vernacularization' across northern Europe in the late medieval period.[30] The identities and locations of the hereditary Gaelic medical families have also been explored in some detail: for example, in the work of Áine Sheehan.[31] Yet the gulf that Aquilla Smith encountered between an obscure Gaelic world on the one hand and Irish medicine after 1654 on the other has yet to be satisfactorily bridged. One aspect that needs to be explored in particular is how medics from Gaelic families adjusted to the new order in Ireland after 1603. Mary Ann Lyons and Jason Harris have identified the 1610s as a crucial decade, with the emergence of figures such as Dermot O'Meara. Harris has pointed to O'Meara as 'one of a new breed of Irish physician', publishing in Latin, boasting an MD from Rheims, and insisting on the superiority of university-educated physicians.[32] The ways in which Gaelic doctors in general were able to negotiate this cultural shift ought to repay further investigation. An extra layer of interest is added by the fact that the character of Gaelic medicine and the competence of its practitioners were issues that became intertwined with the wider English critique of Gaelic culture and society in the early modern period. This aspect was especially pronounced in the works published by the Old English humanist Richard Stanihurst in the 1570s and 1580s, arguing that Gaelic practitioners were trained inadequately and did not have a proper understanding of Latin and learned medicine.[33] Philip O'Sullivan Beare's response to Stanihurst duly included a defense of Gaelic medicine, which the latter was seen to have maligned.[34]

It is well known that O'Sullivan Beare was just one of a large number of Gaelic Irish men who pursued careers on the continent in the seventeenth century, as clergy, soldiers, and doctors.[35] But the number of Gaelic doctors who seem to have prospered at home in Ireland, especially after 1660, is striking. At least five of them, all apparently Catholic, were admitted to the Dublin College of Physicians in the decade after 1667.[36] This belies the impression of that body given by the 1667 charter, with its list of fourteen

Protestant fellows.[37] The election of a cluster of Catholic fellows meant that the composition of the College had quickly evolved to reflect the relatively relaxed confessional environment of the 1660s and early 1670s in Ireland. At the same time, the prominence of Gaelic practitioners was out of step with the wider political environment, where those of Gaelic background generally fared worst in their efforts to recover land under the Restoration settlement.[38]

The notable presence of Gaelic doctors in Restoration Ireland can be at least partly explained by the endurance of patron-physician relationships at the elite level, notwithstanding the collapse of independent Gaelic lordships. This is an aspect that merits further study. An example from 1637 is the appointment of Donell O'Shiell as physician to the earl of Antrim and his heirs, for which service he was to receive an annuity of £20.[39] The O'Shiells were a hereditary medical family, and there appears to have been at least two physicians from that family in Dublin in the 1670s. O'Shiell doctors can also be traced in Galway and Derry in the 1680s.[40] The political connections of Dermot O'Meara and his son Edmund are reasonably well known; the latter physician maintained strong ties to the duke of Ormond and his circle in the Restoration period.[41] Yet other relationships between physicians and their traditional patrons must surely have been disrupted by the widespread upheaval of the seventeenth century. In this context, the rapid growth of Dublin's population after 1660 may have been an important factor in attracting and sustaining Gaelic doctors. One of them, William Hickey, married Elizabeth Jans, the daughter of a Dublin alderman, while their daughter, in turn, married Thomas Connor. Hickey and Connor were two of the medical doctors of Gaelic background active in the College of Physicians in the 1670s.[42]

Another issue worth exploring is the extent to which the transformation of Irish society in the sixteenth and seventeenth centuries helped to make medicine an attractive option for men of Gaelic background who came from outside the circle of hereditary medical families. One of the difficulties here is to establish how wide that circle was in the first place. A figure of around twenty lineages has been generally accepted for some time, but Nollaig Ó Muraíle has recently drawn attention to a number of others mentioned in various sources.[43] Loss of land and power and the resulting difficulty in maintaining social status may have pushed some Gaelic Irishmen in particular toward medicine. One seeming example is Dr. Thady Fitzpatrick, who was elected an honorary fellow of the College of Physicians in 1667 and died in Dublin in 1674.[44] He was the son of Teige Oge Fitzpatrick of Akip in Queen's County, whose estate had been confiscated after 1641. Dr. Fitzpatrick's heraldic funeral entry is considerably more detailed than was the norm for such records, something that perhaps reflects a degree of status anxiety. It is arguably more reminiscent of a genealogy, commencing with his great-grandfather Teige Oge McTeige of Mondrehid and detailing five generations in all.[45] This branch of the Fitzpatrick family seems to have been quite successful in managing the transition from land to medicine; Thady's eldest son Patrick was probably the MD of that name who practiced in Dublin until his death in 1719.[46]

The recovery and study of a much wider cohort of physicians beyond the relatively few whose backgrounds and careers have been to date examined in detail is crucial to deepening our understanding of the medical world of seventeenth-century Ireland. This necessarily encompasses a focus on men of Gaelic, Old English, New English, Scottish, Dutch, and French origins, and ought also to include those who pursued their careers abroad.[47] There are, of course, limits to what the surviving sources can tell us about many individuals' educations and medical practices, their travels and intellectual pursuits, their wider social and professional networks, and their patients. Exploration of these aspects and due attention to social, confessional, and other contexts can, however, help us to develop a much richer picture of this medical environment. The objective is not simply to reinforce or to extend further back in time a linear narrative of progress underpinned by professionalization and Anglicization but instead to more fully recognize and comprehend at least some of the 'diversity' stressed by Kelly and Clark.[48]

Beyond physicians

Although the numbers of university-trained physicians in Ireland undoubtedly increased as the seventeenth-century progressed, they were of course always just a minority among medical practitioners as a whole. The relatively high level of visibility enjoyed by elite physicians in various sources is one of the factors that has ensured their dominant position in Irish medical historiography. This imbalance can be at least partly corrected by focusing more scholarly attention on the urban setting and on the medical trades, namely the barber-surgeons and the apothecaries.[49] The source limitations that exist mean that for the period before 1700, the only urban center where the medical trades can be examined in some detail is Dublin. Some aspects of medical personnel and organization in Cork can be reconstructed from the 1650s onward, but for other towns the available evidence is extremely patchy.[50] For Dublin, the most valuable set of guild records is that of the barber-surgeons, which run from the 1530s until the nineteenth century.[51] Unfortunately, most of the sixteenth-century content relates merely to the payment of fees by guild members, although this does allow their identities and some other details of guild size and organization to be ascertained.[52] Even more unfortunate is the lack of any records for the guild between the late 1580s and 1688. The fate of the relevant manuscripts from this period is unknown; they may perhaps have been lost during the upheaval caused by the Jacobite-Williamite War. This gap in the archive can be partly remedied by using the evidence that exists relating to admissions to freedom in Dublin. The roll of freemen for the period 1600–1700 contains some 11,291 entries, including around 250 barber-surgeons and almost 80 surgeons. The Dublin roll contains the names of freemen and the dates of admission; in some cases, it is the only evidence for an individual barber-surgeon having existed.[53]

Among the medical trades in Dublin, apprenticeship was the most common route to freedom, and the relevant masters can sometimes be identified.[54] In certain instances, it is possible to reconstruct various aspects of an individual's trade and familial networks; these very often overlapped. The barber-surgeon John Morphy, for example, commenced his apprenticeship with William Kelly in 1576 and gained his freedom in due course.[55] He then married Margaret Segerson and took on her nephew, a shoemaker's son, as an apprentice.[56] Morphy became master of the barber-surgeons in 1588 and was eventually elected an alderman in 1596.[57] The careful pulling together of scattered details of individual lives and families in this way can allow us a range of insights into the social and occupational world of the medical trades in early modern Dublin.

Morphy's election as an alderman seems to have been an unusual achievement for a Dublin barber-surgeon. It was more common for apothecaries to play a role in the upper levels of urban government, in Dublin and elsewhere on the island.[58] One example is Mark Quin, who completed his apprenticeship in 1644. His prominence and prosperity were demonstrated by his election as lord mayor of Dublin in 1667 and his sending two sons up to Trinity College Dublin a year later.[59] Although apothecaries were often wealthy and high profile, the task of identifying them is more problematic than for other male practitioners. This is so because apothecaries in Ireland did not belong to stand-alone guilds. Until the late seventeenth century they were everywhere subsumed within larger merchants' guilds. In Dublin from 1687, and in Cork from at least the early 1700s, the apothecaries were joined with the barber-surgeons.[60] But it was not until 1745 that the first guild consisting solely of apothecaries was established in Dublin.[61] The problem for much of the early modern period is the ubiquitous occupational label of 'merchant' in many surviving sources. As a consequence, it is not always possible to identify the apothecary behind this general label. As Mark Quin became free of the merchant's guild in 1644, the freemen's roll records him simply as a 'merchant'.[62] While this tendency to return apothecaries simply as merchants was not always adhered to, the occurrence of just thirty-eight apothecaries in the Dublin freemen's roll between 1576 and 1700 is undoubtedly an underrepresentation of their actual numbers.[63] The use of disparate sources to piece together a more complete picture ought to allow for better understanding of the size and wider significance of this important group of practitioners.

Another of the difficulties in researching early modern Dublin is the fact that an unknown number of practitioners lived and practiced outside of the confined area governed by the corporation. One of the migrants who set up south of the city walls in St. Kevin's Parish was the Dutch apothecary and perfumer Jacob or James Rickman.[64] Some decades later, Rickman's former apprentice Adrian Huyberts recalled that his old master had been 'the ablest apothecary' in 1630s Dublin.[65] An intriguing possible connection to Rickman has recently been unearthed on an archaeological site off Kevin Street. During excavations directed by Alan Hayden, a cesspit was uncovered that contained a large amount of elaborate materials from an apothecary's shop, including a pot inscribed with the date 1639.[66] While the link to Rickman is necessarily speculative on my part, the find itself promises to open up an invaluably fresh perspective on the material culture of medicine in seventeenth-century Dublin. It points to the undoubted potential of archaeology to enrich our historical understanding of early modern Irish medicine.

The problems associated with identifying apothecaries pale into significance when compared to those surrounding any attempt to research female practitioners, among whom midwives were an important cohort. Evidence for ecclesiastical licensing of midwives, a useful source in the English context, is close to nonexistent for Ireland.[67] It is not clear, however, whether this reflects a general lack of such regulation or rather a major deficiency in surviving records. The fellows of the College of Physicians showed scant interest in exercising their right to examine prospective midwives, which means that the relatively detailed archives of that institution also offer little insight.[68] In any case, midwives tended to be excluded from the domain of elite learned medicine, as represented by the College. Further difficulty arises because in some sources where midwives are mentioned, their names are not recorded. The account book of William King, Archbishop of Dublin, supplies a useful example. In August 1718, he paid '2 guineys and a crown' to the unnamed 'Nurs Middwife and Nurs Keepr at Mr Cusacks Childs Christning'.[69] Nonetheless, the papers of elites such as Archbishop King appear to offer one of the better prospects for identifying and locating midwives in early modern Ireland. At the same time, the paucity of the surviving sources suggests that there is little scope for gaining more detailed insights into the practices and lives of midwives, especially prior to 1700.

Beyond Dublin

The exploration of the surviving papers of elite landed families inevitably takes us beyond Dublin. They can also be used to trace some of the connections that existed between the medical world of Dublin and other parts of the island. A prominent example of these connections is Dr. John Madden, thrice president of the RCPI, who owned a substantial estate at Manorwaterhouse in County Fermanagh.[70] Patronage networks could also entail travel far beyond the capital, as in 1667, when the duchess of Ormond prevailed on Edmund Meara to journey to County Longford with Sir George Lane to treat the latter's ailing wife, Dorcas.[71] The transmission of medical knowledge can also be traced in some cases. From County Mayo in 1704, Patrick Fergus wrote to Dublin seeking a copy of 'Sydnams treatis or practice of phisick'.[72] Fergus's letter gives some insight into the workings of a Gaelic medical family that continued to prosper into the eighteenth century.[73] Unfortunately, such clues about medical practice in rural Ireland are all too rare. As might be expected, the 1641 depositions contain mentions of numerous medics from across the island, many of whom are not mentioned in any other sources.[74] These include, for example, Alexander Stewart, a 'Doctor of Phissick' in the Scottish plantation at St. Johnstown in County Longford.[75] But as is well known, the sort of detailed and diverse information found in the depositions is in many ways exceptional.

While the depositions are of use for the 1640s, outside of that decade considerable difficulties attend any effort to identify medical practitioners across large parts of the island. The usefulness of the sources that survive for the various cities and towns varies widely, with Cork and Youghal among the better documented.[76] For rural Ireland, the Tudor Fiants are of use as far as 1603, but subsequent to that date the archival evidence for medics practicing in rural settings is sparse. Our sources are not sufficient to support even an attempt to estimate how many practitioners of various types, regular and irregular, might have lived in various regions of the country in the seventeenth century.[77] It was undoubtedly the case that the maintenance or recovery of health was a basic concern at the level of the early modern household. This must have been the case even more so in areas where recognized medical practitioners were scarce, assuming that they very often were. Surviving recipe books can tell us much about how some elite women sought to preserve the health of their families, and these sources have recently begun to attract more attention.[78]

Evidence for the nature and extent of medical provision available to the majority of the rural population is obviously harder to come by. Healers from rural areas were likely to make a mark in the archive only when they attracted wider attention.[79] One example is an O'Sullivan woman from County Kerry who appeared in Dublin in 1674. She reportedly cured the earl of Carlingford and the Bishop of Meath of the gout, swiftly prompting accusations of witchcraft from some physicians in the city.[80] Such hostile responses to this sort of healing were, of course, common throughout Europe. From County Galway, the Restoration-era story of Morogh O'Lee is well known. He claimed to have picked up his medical knowledge, and an elaborate manuscript, on the mythical Atlantic island of Hy Brasil.[81] Cases such as these inevitably tend toward the exotic.[82] A great deal about the more mundane and the everyday of medical care in the early modern Irish countryside seems destined to remain a mystery.

Revealing works such as that published by Michael Harward in 1673 are all too rare. Harward was an 'ox-leech' from Cheshire, and his book, *The herds-man's mate*, recounts details of his treatment both of animals and humans following his relocation to King's County (County Offaly) in the mid-seventeenth century. In the aftermath of the devastation wrought by the Cromwellian conquest, his ability to treat victims of attacks by rabid wolves and dogs seems to have been especially valuable. Harward boasted of several cases where patients had come to him as a last resort. By combining a course of bloodletting with a medicine comprised of tormentil roots, beer, and several other ingredients, he claimed success where 'physick, Priests charms, and … [being] … cast into the sea' had already failed. He insisted too on the efficacy of a method with ancient origins, whereby the victim was required to eat the cooked liver of the offending animal: 'a present remedy; often proved'.[83] Harward was also an astrologer, an interest widespread among early modern medical practitioners (Girolamo Cardano most famously), and he stressed 'the influence of the malevolent aspects of Stars' in causing disease.[84] The range of approaches mentioned by Harward is a useful reminder of the need to guard against simply privileging ideas and practices that can be read as marking progress or as anticipating modern 'scientific medicine'. Early modern medical culture was permeated by much that may seem strange and irrational today, and these aspects demand careful scholarly attention.[85]

Conclusion

The ground covered in this chapter is necessarily selective; I have sought to draw attention to some questions and suggest areas for further research, and to point toward some of the many sources that might be exploited. The suggested focus on medical practitioners makes sense for several reasons, not least because it builds upon the foundation provided by the existing historiography. Practitioners are of interest in their own right, both individually and collectively, but they can also be utilized as points of entry into a broad range of complex research problems, texts, and debates. They provide a basis too for situating aspects of Irish medicine in broader comparative contexts. While the spotlight here has been on practitioners, this essay is not intended to discourage alternative approaches; the history of medicine is a field diverse enough to accommodate a variety of methodologies and emphases. The main purpose of this essay is simply to encourage greater scholarly interest in its subject, one that is widely recognized as underdeveloped and under-researched. It stakes a claim for the history of medicine as having potential to constitute a significant and intellectually rewarding direction for new research in early modern Irish history.

Notes

1 Brian Ó Cuív, 'The Irish Language in the Early Modern Period' and Benignus Millett, 'Irish Literature in Latin, 1550–1700', in T.W. Moody, F.X. Martin and F.J. Byrne (eds.), *A New History of Ireland: iii, Early Modern Ireland, 1534–1691* (Oxford: Oxford University Press, 1976), pp. 518–20, 565–66.

2 Jane Ohlmeyer (ed.), *The Cambridge History of Ireland: ii, 1550–1730* (Cambridge: Cambridge University Press, 2018).

3 This research was conducted as part of a project at the University of Exeter: 'The Medical World of Early Modern England, Wales and Ireland, c. 1500–1715'. The project was funded by the Wellcome Trust (Grant 097782/Z/11/Z). See practitioners.exeter.ac.uk.

4 Greta Jones and Elizabeth Malcolm (eds.), *Medicine, Disease and the State in Ireland, 1650–1940* (Cork: Cork University Press, 1999).
5 Much important research has appeared, for example, in the journal *Social History of Medicine*, first published in 1988.
6 Greta Jones and Elizabeth Malcolm, 'Introduction: An Anatomy of Irish Medical History', in *Medicine, Disease and the State*, pp. 1–17.
7 Catherine Cox, 'Discursive Essay: A Better Known Territory? Medical History in Ireland', *Proceedings of the Royal Irish Academy* 113C (2013), 341–62.
8 James Kelly and Fiona Clark, 'Introduction', in James Kelly and Fiona Clark (eds.), *Ireland and Medicine in the Seventeenth and Eighteenth Centuries* (Farnham: Ashgate, 2010), p. 3.
9 For example, James Kelly, 'The Emergence of Scientific and Institutional Medical Practice in Ireland, 1650–1800', in Jones and Malcolm (eds.), *Medicine, Disease and the State*, pp. 21–39; James Kelly, 'Health for Sale: Mountebanks, Doctors, Printers and the Supply of Medication in Eighteenth-Century Ireland', *Proceedings of the Royal Irish Academy* 108C (2008), 75–113; Andrew Sneddon, 'Medicine, Belief, Witchcraft and Demonic Possession in Late Seventeenth-Century Ulster', *Medical Humanities* 42 (2016), 81–86; Marian Lyons, 'The Limits of Old English Liberty: The Case of Thomas Arthur, MD (1593–1674) in Dublin and Limerick', in Salvador Ryan and Clodagh Tait (eds.), *Religion and Politics in Urban Ireland, c.1500–c.1750: Essays in Honour of Colm Lennon* (Dublin: Four Courts Press, 2016), pp. 70–88; Pierce Grace, 'Patronage and Health Care in Eighteenth-Century Irish County Infirmaries', *Irish Historical Studies* 41 (2017), 1–21; Danielle Westerhof (ed.), *The Alchemy of Medicine and Print: The Edward Worth Library, Dublin* (Dublin: Four Courts Press, 2010).
10 Kelly and Clark, 'Introduction', p. 4.
11 For some useful insights on such challenges, see Ludmilla Jordanova, 'Has the Social History of Medicine Come of Age?' *Historical Journal* 36 (1993), 437–49.
12 Catherine Cox, 'Health and Welfare, 1750–2000', in Mary Daly and Eugenio Biagini (eds), *Cambridge Social History of Modern Ireland* (Cambridge: Cambridge University Press, 2017), pp. 261–81.
13 Catherine Cox and Maria Luddy (eds), *Cultures of Care in Irish Medical History, 1750–1970* (Basingstoke: Palgrave Macmillan, 2010).
14 One that spans the divide is Laurence Geary, *Medicine and Charity in Ireland, 1718–1851* (Dublin: University College Dublin Press, 2004). Recent monographs on the modern period include Laura Kelly, *Irish Medical Education and Student Culture, c.1850–c.1950* (Liverpool: Liverpool University Press, 2017).
15 John Widdess, *A History of the Royal College of Physicians of Ireland, 1654–1963* (Edinburgh and London: E. & S. Livingstone, 1964); Tony Farmar, *Patients, Potions and Physician: A Social History of Medicine in Ireland, 1654–2004* (Dublin: A. & A. Farmer in Association with the Royal College of Physicians of Ireland, 2004); Thomas Percy Claude Kirkpatrick, *History of the Medical Teaching in Trinity College, and of the School of Physic in Ireland* (Dublin: Hanna and Neale, 1912); Davis Coakley (ed.), *Medicine in Trinity College Dublin: An Illustrated History* (Dublin: Trinity College Dublin, 2014).
16 'Lives of the presidents', www.rcpi.ie/heritage-centre/lives-of-the-presidents/ (accessed 24 Nov. 2017).
17 Jones and Malcolm, 'Introduction', pp. 1–17.
18 Andrew Wear, 'Introduction', in Andrew Wear (ed.), *Medicine in Society: Historical Essays* (Cambridge: Cambridge University Press, 1992), p. 1; Jordanova, 'Has the Social History of Medicine Come of Age?; Roger Cooter, '"Framing" the End of the Social History of Medicine', in Frank Huisman and John Harley Warner (eds), *Locating Medical History: The Stories and Their Meanings* (Baltimore,

MD: Johns Hopkins University Press, 2004), pp. 309–337; Mary Lindemann, *Medicine and Society in Early Modern Europe* (Cambridge: Cambridge University Press, 2010).

19 Charles Rosenberg and Janet Golden (eds.), *Framing Disease: Studies in Cultural History* (New Brunswick, NJ: Rutgers University Press, 1992); On Foucault, see Roger Cooter, 'After Death/After – "life": The Social History of Medicine in Post-Postmodernity', *Social History of Medicine* 20 (2007), 441–64 and Jonathan Toms, 'So What? A Reply to Roger Cooter's "After Death/After-'life': The Social History of Medicine in Post-Postmodernity"', *Social History of Medicine* 22 (2009), 609–15; for a useful recent collection on mental health in modern Ireland, see Pauline Prior (ed.), *Asylums, Mental Health Care and the Irish: 1800–2010* (Dublin: Irish Academic Press, 2017).

20 One useful brief sketch of early modern historiography is Thomas Rütten, 'Early Modern Medicine' in Mark Jackson (ed.), *The Oxford Handbook of the History of Medicine* (Oxford: Oxford University Press, 2011), pp. 60–81.

21 Ibid., p. 71; Cox, 'A Better Known Territory?', p. 361.

22 For an example of some of the detailed sources available for England, see 'The Casebooks Project: A Digital Edition of Simon Forman's & Richard Napier's Medical Records 1596–1634', www.magicandmedicine.hps.cam.ac.uk/ (accessed 24 Nov. 2017); for a German example, see Michael Stolberg, 'A Sixteenth-Century Physician and His Patients: The Practice Journal of Hiob Finzel, 1565–1589', *Social History of Medicine* (advance publication online, 8 Sept. 2017), https://academic.oup.com/shm/advance-article/doi/10.1093/shm/hkx063/4108110 (accessed 24 Nov. 2017); On France, see Laurence Brockliss and Colin Jones, *The Medical World of Early Modern France* (Oxford: Oxford University Press, 2007).

23 Thomas Belcher, *Register of the King's and Queen's College of Physicians in Ireland, with Historical Introduction* (Dublin: Hodges, Smith, and Co., 1866), pp. 105–106.

24 John Cunningham, *Conquest and Land in Ireland: The Transplantation to Connacht, 1649–1680* (Woodbridge: Boydell and Brewer, 2011).

25 Aquilla Smith, 'Some Account of the Origin and Early History of the College of Physicians in Ireland', *Dublin Journal of Medical and Chemical Science* 19 (Mar. 1841), 81–96.

26 O'Glacan was from County Donegal; little is known of his early years. O'Connor was from County Kerry and may have studied at Montpelier, before graduating at Rheims. The *Dictionary of Irish Biography* contains articles on both men.

27 Ibid., pp. 82–83.

28 Ibid., pp. 83–84.

29 Aoibheann Nic Dhonnachadha, 'The "Book of the O'Lees" and Other Medical Manuscripts and Astronomical Tracts', in Bernadette Cunningham and Siobhán Fitzpatrick (eds.), *Treasures of the Royal Irish Academy Library* (Dublin: Royal Irish Academy, 2009), pp. 81–91; Aoibheann Nic Dhonnchadha, 'The Medical School of Aghmacart, Queen's County', *Ossory, Laois and Leinster* 2 (2006), pp. 11–43; Eithne Ní Ghallchobhair (ed.), *Anathomia Gydo* (London: Irish Texts Society, 2014); Liam Ó Murchú (ed.), *Rosa Anglica: Reassessments* (London: Irish Texts Society, 2016).

30 Jason Harris, 'Latin Learning and Irish Physicians, *c*.1350–*c*.1610', in Ó Murchú (ed.), *Rosa Anglica: Reassessments*, p. 19.

31 Áine Sheehan, 'Locating the Medical Families in Elizabethan Ireland', in John Cunningham (ed.), *Early Modern Ireland and the World of Medicine: Practitioners, Collectors and Contexts* (forthcoming).

32 Harris, 'Latin Learning and Irish Physicians', p. 24; Marian Lyons, 'The Role of Graduate Physicians in Professionalising Medical Practice in Ireland, *c*. 1619–54',

in Kelly and Clark (eds.), *Ireland and Medicine*, pp. 17–37; Charlie Dillon, 'Medical Practice and Gaelic Ireland', in ibid., pp. 39–52.

33 Liam Miller and Eileen Power (eds.), *Holinshed's Irish Chronicle* (Dublin: Dolmen Press, 1979), p. 114; Richard Stanihurst, *Great Deeds in Ireland: Richard Stanihurst's De Rebus in Hibernia Gestis*, Hiram Morgan and John Barry (eds.), (Cork: Cork University Press, 2013), pp. 126–31.

34 Thomas J. O'Donnell (ed.), *Selections from the Zoilomastix of Philip O'Sullivan Beare* (Dublin: Irish Manuscripts Commission, 1961), pp. 89–91.

35 See Benjamin Hazard, 'Early Modern Medical Practitioners and Military Hospitals in Flanders and the South-west of Ireland', in Cunningham (ed.), *Early Modern Ireland and the World of Medicine* (forthcoming).

36 Belcher, *Register of the King's and Queen's College of Physicians in Ireland*, p. 106; Certificate of the election of Thady Patrick MD as honorary fellow of the College of Physicians of Dublin, 7 Dec. 1667, Bodleian Library, Oxford, Carte MS 173, fol. 29; Account book beginning 21 Jan. 1672, Royal College of Physicians of Ireland (RCPI), RCPI/3/3/1.

37 It perhaps also lends further weight to the argument against the once fashionable thesis that put 'Puritans' at the forefront of medicine in this period. See Peter Elmer, 'Medicine, Religion and the Puritan Revolution', in Roger French and Andrew Wear (eds.), *The Medical Revolution of the Seventeenth Century* (Cambridge: Cambridge University Press, 1989), pp. 10–45.

38 Cunningham, *Conquest and Land*, pp. 119–49.

39 Grant by Randall, earl of Antrim to Donnell O'Shyell, 20 July, 1637, Public Record Office of Northern Ireland, Earl of Antrim Estate Papers, D2977/5/1/2/2.

40 Bills for medicines from Gerald Colley, apothecary to Gerald Dillon, 1677, National Library of Ireland (NLI), Westport MS 40,895/7(4A); Index of prerogative court grants of administration on estates of intestates, NLI, GO MS 260, p. 19; List of freemen sworn, 18 Nov. 1687, Hardiman Library, Galway, Galway Corporation Books, Liber C, p. 174; Extracts from Tuam grant book, 1696–1715, NLI, GO MS 707; Walter Harris, *The History of the Life and Reign of William-Henry, Prince of Nassau and Orange* (Dublin: Edward Bate, 1749), appendix, xiv. For a detailed insight on one O'Sheill doctor, see the will of Patrick O'Shiell of Brendrum, County Mayo, Doctor of Physick, 31 July 1728, National Archives of Ireland, Will and grant book 1728–1729, pp. 359B–364A.

41 Patrick Logan, 'Dermot and Edmund O'Meara, Father and Son', *Journal of the Irish Medical Association* 43 (1958), 312–17.

42 Will of Thomasine Chamberlaine, alias Crolly, alias Jans, of Dublin, widow, 5 May 1670, NLI, GO MS 529, p. 183; Funeral entry of Mary Hickey, 1665, and William Hickey MD, 1677, NLI, GO MS 225, pp. 128 and 141; Will of William Hickey MD, 1 Sept. 1677, RCPI, TPCK/5/3/1, no. 1, p. 71; Chancery bill of Thomas Connor, Doctor in Physick, and others, Jan. 1685, NAI, RC 6/3, Repertory to chancery decrees, vol. iii, 1685–1732, p. 23; Belcher, *Register of the King's and Queen's College of Physicians in Ireland*, p. 106; Account book, RCPI/3/3/1.

43 Nollaig Ó Muraíle, 'The Hereditary Medical Families of Early Modern Ireland', in Ó Murchú (ed.), *Rosa Anglica: Reassessments*, pp. 85–113.

44 Election of Thady Patrick, MD, 7 Dec. 1667, Bodleian Library, Oxford, Carte MS 173, fo. 29; Funeral entry of Thady Fitzpatrick, doctor of physick, 1674, NLI, GO MS 67, fo. 202r.

45 Funeral entry of Thady Fitzpatrick, Doctor of Physick, 1674, NLI, GO MS 67, fo. 202r.

46 Abstract of the will of Thady Fitzpatrick MD, 1674, NLI, GO MS 225, p. 56; Patrick Fitzpatrick was at Rheims in 1681. I am grateful to Professor Laurence

Brockliss for providing me with a copy of his file on Rheims students, derived from the records of that institution. He returned to Ireland the same year, securing letters of denization on 24 Dec. See NAI, Lodge MSS, MFS 42/8, p. 31; Arthur Vicars, *Index to the Prerogative Wills of Ireland, 1536–1810* (Dublin: Edward Ponsonby, 1897), p. 172.

47 For a study of one Irish doctor abroad, see Liam Chambers, 'Medicine and Miracles in the Late Seventeenth Century: Bernard Connor's *Evangelicum Medici* (1697)', in Kelly and Clark (eds.), *Ireland and Medicine*, pp. 53–72.

48 Kelly and Clark, 'Introduction', p. 3.

49 For a study of the medical guilds in eighteenth-century Dublin, see Susan Mullaney, 'The Evolution of the Medical Professions in Eighteenth-Century Dublin', in Cunningham (ed.), *Early Modern Ireland and the World of Medicine* (forthcoming).

50 Richard Caulfield's transcript of the Cork Court of D'oyer Hundred records, 1656–1730, is especially useful. See Cork City and County Archives (CCCA), U/127.

51 Papers of the Guild of Barber-Surgeons, Trinity College Dublin (TCD), MS 1447.

52 Papers of the Guild of Barber-Surgeons, 1530–1607, TCD, MS 1447/6.

53 The transcript of the Dublin freemen's roll made by Gertrude Thrift has been digitized and is accessible at 'Ancient Freemen of Dublin', http://databases.dublincity.ie/freemen/about.php (accessed 24 Nov. 2017).

54 Ibid.

55 Ibid., where he is listed as 'Johes Morcho'; Memo relating to John Morphie, 10 May 1576, TCD, MS 1447/6, fol. 30v.

56 Note of John Segerson's indenture of apprenticeship to John Morphy, 23 May 1582, TCD, MS 1447/6, fol. 34r; 'Ancient Freemen of Dublin', http://databases.dublincity.ie/freemen/about.php (accessed 24 Nov. 2017); Abstract of the will of John Morphy of Dublin, alderman, 17 Apr. 1603, NLI, GO MS 225, p. 264.

57 List of guild members, 1588, TCD, MS 1447/6, fol. 40v; John Gilbert and Rosa Gilbert (eds.), *Calendar of the Ancient Records of Dublin* (19 Vols, Dublin: Joseph Dollard, 1889–1944), ii, p. 306.

58 Harris, *The History of the Life and Reign of William-Henry*, appendix.

59 'Ancient Freemen of Dublin', http://databases.dublincity.ie/freemen/about.php (accessed 24 Nov. 2017); Gilbert and Gilbert (eds.), *Calendar of Ancient Records of Dublin*, iv, p. 413; George Burtchaell and Thomas Sadleir (eds.), *Alumni Dublinenses* (London: Williams & Norgate, 1924), p. 689.

60 K. Theodore Hoppen, *The Common Scientist in the Seventeenth Century: A Study of the Dublin Philosophical Society, 1683–1708* (London: Routledge & Kegal Paul 1970), p. 18; Transcript of the Cork Court of D'oyer Hundred records, 1656–1730, CCCA, U/127, p. 98A.

61 Mullaney, 'The Evolution of the Medical Professions in Eighteenth-Century Dublin'.

62 'Ancient Freemen of Dublin', http://databases.dublincity.ie/freemen/about.php (accessed 24 Nov. 2017).

63 Ibid.; From 1700 to 1746, just two are recorded.

64 William Arthur Shaw (ed.), *Letters of Denization and Naturalization for England and Ireland, 1603–1700* (London: Lymington, 1911), p. 337; Brian Mac Cuarta, 'A Planter's Funeral, Legacies and Inventory: Sir Matthew De Renzy (1577–1634)', *Journal of the Royal Society of Antiquaries of Ireland*, 127 (1997), 18–33.

65 Adrian Huyberts, *A Cornerstone Laid towards the Building of a New College (That Is To Say, A New Body of Physicians) in London* (London: Printed for the Author, 1675). Huyberts was admitted to freedom in Dublin in 1639.

66 'Apothecary's Shop Found in Dublin Excavation', *Archaeology Ireland* (Summer 2017), https://archaeologyireland.ie/recent-issues/summer-2017/ (accessed 24 Nov. 2017). I am grateful to Alan Hayden for sharing some of his preliminary findings with me.

67 A rare example for Dublin is Susanna Sterling, licensed as a midwife in 1664. *Twenty-Sixth Report of the Deputy Keeper of the Public Records in Ireland* (Dublin: Alexander Thom & Co., 1894), p. 811.

68 Blank form of a license for a midwife, 1697, RCPI/1/1/3, Dun's Book, p. 75; Proceedings of the College of Physicians, 3 Feb. 1697, RCPI, Typescript of college journals, i, p. 67.

69 Payment dated 28 Aug. 1718, Account book of Archbishop William King, TCD, MS 751/3, fo. 79v.

70 John Cunningham, 'John Madden MD, 1649–1703', https://rcpi-live-cdn.s3.am-azonaws.com/wp-content/uploads/2017/09/8-John-Madden.pdf (accessed 25 Nov. 2017).

71 Sir George Lane to Lady Dorcas Lane, Dublin, 25 May 1667, NLI, Lane MS 8643/10.

72 Patrick Fa[rgus?] to Father [Patrick] Duffy, 28 Feb. 1704, NLI, Westport MS 40,904/7(19).

73 Diarmaid Ó Catháin, 'John Fergus MD: Eighteenth-Century Doctor, Book Collector and Irish Scholar', *Journal of the Royal Society of Antiquaries of Ireland* 118 (1988), 139–62.

74 John Cunningham, 'Sickness, Disease and Medical Practitioners in 1640s Ireland', in Cunningham (ed.), *Early Modern Ireland and the World of Medicine* (forthcoming).

75 Deposition of Elizabeth Stewart, 26 Aug. 1642, TCD MS 817, fol. 200r-v.

76 There is not space here to discuss towns in any detail. On Youghal, see Clodagh Tait, 'Causes of Death and Cultures of Care in Co. Cork, 1660–1720: The Evidence of the Youghal Parish Registers', in Cunningham (ed.), *Early Modern Ireland and the World of Medicine* (forthcoming).

77 'Irregular' here refers to practitioners who did not possess a recognized qualification, such as a medical degree or completion of an apprenticeship and membership in a relevant guild.

78 Madeline Shanahan, *Manuscript Recipe Books As Archaeological Objects: Text and Food in the Early Modern World* (Lexington, IL: Lanham, 2014).

79 The best-known healer from seventeenth-century Ireland is probably Valentine Greatrakes, who enjoyed an unusually high-profile career due to the perceived success of his healing methods. See Peter Elmer, *The Miraculous Conformist: Valentine Greatrakes, the Body Politic, and the Politics of Healing in Restoration Britain* (Oxford: Oxford University Press, 2012).

80 Richard Bellings to the duke of Ormond, Dublin, 28 Sept. 1674, Bodleian Library, Oxford, Carte MS 243, fol. 156.

81 Dhonnchadha, 'The "Book of the O'Lee's"', pp. 81–91.

82 On holy wells, miracles, and much more of interest, see Raymond Gillespie, *Devoted People: Belief and Religion in Early Modern Ireland* (Manchester: Manchester University Press, 2007).

83 Michael Harward, *The Herds-Man's Mate, Or, a Guide for Herds-Men Teaching How to Cure All Diseases in Bulls, Oxen, Cows and Calves, Gathered from Sundry Good Authors, and Well Approved by the Authour, in His Thirty Years Practice* (Dublin: Benjamin Tooke,1673), pp. 117–21. Animal medicine in early modern Ireland is another topic that deserves greater attention. For England, see Louise Hill Curth, *The Care of Brute Beasts: A Social and Cultural Study of Veterinary Medicine in Early Modern England* (Leiden: Brill, 2010).

84 Harward, *The Herds-Man's Mate*, p. 6. On astrology see Paola Zambelli, *Astrology and Magic from the Medieval Latin and Islamic World to Renaissance Europe: Theories and Approaches* (Farnham: Ashgate, 2012).

85 Elaine Leong and Alisha Rankin (eds.), *Secrets and Knowledge in Medicine and Science, 1500–1800* (Farnham: Ashgate, 2011); see also Nancy Siraisi, *Medieval and Early Renaissance Medicine: An Introduction* (Chicago: University of Chicago Press, 1990).

13 Dung beetles and the 'Vulgar Traditions'

Applying folkloric sources and methods to early modern Ireland[1]

Sarah Covington

One of the more exciting developments in the study of early modern Ireland over the last twenty years has been a turn toward (or perhaps a return to) interdisciplinarity. History, literature, archaeology, and historical geography have converged to deepen our understanding of the transformative period from 1500 to 1700. Yet for all this, scholars of early modern Ireland, with a couple of notable exceptions, remain hesitant to engage on any deep level with folklore, or the oral and written tales and proverbs, superstitions and riddles, material artifacts and culture which provide clues into an otherwise elusive past.[2] This lacuna is disappointing, given the pioneering studies of Guy Beiner, who not only advocated for the use of folklore in Irish history, but provided a sophisticated methodology for doing so. It is true that early modern scholars might pay heed to the folkloric by quoting from a few quaint and colorful tales, though they do so only in a supplementary way, as illustrative (or as Gramsci once put it, 'picturesque') matter; folklore in general may be thought important for social history or popular culture studies, though it goes ignored with regard to political, literary, or other 'elite' expressions which can very much be informed by popular oral traditions, however indirectly.[3] Meanwhile, the highly sophisticated and theoretically rich field of folkloristics tends to be neglected altogether—sometimes to historians' embarrassment. Peter Burke once famously recalled an episode from an academic conference in the 1970s, in which the great historian Emmanuel Le Roy Ladurie offered what he thought was a new approach to folktales. Unfortunately, Le Roy Ladurie was 'gently', though devastatingly, informed by a Scandinavian scholar in the audience that the 'new approach' was 'effectively a revival of the methods of the Finnish historical-geographical school', which had been in existence for decades.[4]

Scholars, of course, must tread carefully in using folkloric (or vernacular) material,[5] with pre-1700 early modernists facing a greater challenge, given the narrower source base of antiquarian accounts, travel literature, local histories, and popular ballad and folkloric books that capture oral traditions occurring at the time. Applying the word 'folklore' to the period before the late eighteenth century, decades before it was first invented as a term, is also problematic, with more accurate contemporary renderings being 'popular antiquities', 'popular superstitions', or 'popular traditions'.[6] Not least, and as will be seen, the term 'folklore' itself has today become a highly contentious word among folklorists themselves.

Nevertheless, materials that we would today consider of a folkloric as well as mythological nature were recorded well before the term and the field existed. The twelfth-century *Book of Leinster* was one of the earliest to classify mythological and legendary tale types, such as battles, voyages, and cattle-raids, many of which would enter into popular narratives. Ancient or medieval scholars such as Alan Bruford and Dáithí Ó hÓgáin—himself a folklorist—have engaged heavily in folklore, though from a primarily literary perspective.[7] Meanwhile, T.P. Cross's *Motif-Index of Early Irish Literature* remains an invaluable resource and supplement to the Aarne-Thompson motif-index.[8] Popular traditions also indirectly pervade writings important to early modernists, from Geraldus Cambrensis to Richard Stanihurst, Spenser, and James Ware.[9] Geoffrey Keating, from the Gaelic-Irish and Old English perspective, might have loathed folkloric and popular traditions, though they could creep into his texts, however indirectly; nor are they absent from the work of the great antiquarian Charles O'Conor, who continued Keating's mission in the very different context of the late eighteenth century, even though he too, like John Lynch before him, spurned the Cambrensis-inspired 'crude tales' and 'popular amusements for the vulgar' that allegedly defined popular Gaelic culture to the English.[10]

Following the efforts of Beiner, this essay will argue for the recognition of folkloric material in pursuing both elite and popular sources related to early modern Ireland. Even more, it will urge scholars to engage more deeply with the discipline itself. It should be pointed out that folklore—or vernacular culture, or ethnology, however it is known—is not quite synonymous with the study of non-elite 'popular culture', though it is certainly part of it.[11] Unlike popular culture studies, students of folklore set out to understand the function, transmission, or reception of a very particular set of cultural beliefs, narratives, and practices, just as they seek to trace stories, customs, or forms to tale-types, motifs, and deeper narrative genealogies. For historians and literary scholars to therefore understand folklore on its own terms, they must become conversant in the field's debates and know its basic terms and noteworthy practitioners. Without knowledge of the deeper critical discourse that has informed the field of folkloristics, they will remain amateurs no matter how frequently they utilize those sources, and therefore do a disservice not only to that discipline but to their own.[12] While much of the following will be obvious to experts in the discipline, this essay thus seeks to push folklore to the forefront, and suggest future directions for how it can be uniquely applied to a range of subjects and inquiries in Ireland over the course of the early modern period and beyond.

It was Geoffrey Keating—Old English but Irish-speaking and living in Munster—who most notably protested those popular tales, legends, and superstitions that came to be known as 'folklore'.[13] Keating's *Foras Feasa ar Éirinn* offered, at least in part, a response to the *Topographia Hibernica* of Geraldus

Cambrensis, whose sometimes-lurid descriptions of twelfth-century Ireland contained many allusions to tales that could be classified today as folkloric: talking she-wolves, or suicidal mice that plunge into the sea. For Keating, such stories served Cambrensis's essentially denunciatory purposes in portraying Ireland as 'wild and inhospitable', and its people as easily susceptible. As a result of his book's influence, Geraldus's images were appropriated by Spenser, Stanihurst, and others, thus making him, in Keating's words, 'the bull of the herd of those who write the false history of Ireland'.[14] For Keating, if these stories were not invented by Geraldus himself, then they came from the imaginations of 'inferiors and wretched little hags', thus creating an untruthful picture of Ireland. Instead, Keating and his contemporary, Mícheál Ó Clérigh, embarked on a corrective, legitimating history, defined on distinctly Irish, Catholic, and elitist terms.[15] Despite his disdain for the popular, this did not mean, however, that Keating spurned evidence from oral culture himself. It is somewhat ironic that he is credited with inventing the term—*béaloideas*—that came to be so associated with 'folklore', including the modern journal of that name.[16] Keating, however, intended the word to connote oral tradition, by which he meant *seanchas*, or the acceptable historical, genealogical, or legal lore preserved by bardic elites or *fili*.[17] In other words, Keating reminds us that 'not all oral traditions are folk', if one means by 'folk' the 'common' people alone.[18]

Two hundred years later, Keating's stance toward the 'vulgar traditions' would influence the great Irish-language scholar John O'Donovan, who commented frequently and derisively about the popular tales he encountered over the course of his work for the Ordnance Survey. For O'Donovan, the *Annals of the Four Masters*, which he translated and edited, was the dominant authority on Ireland's past, as it contained previous texts such as the eleventh-century *Lebor Gabála Érenn*;[19] against this source base, all else, for O'Donovan, was to be discarded, though he added elsewhere that 'I don't believe in any other authority upon Irish antiquities but Keating and Moses'. Next to this, living oral tradition was nearly worthless, since 'it has only mushroom existence and no foundation in fact or [even] early superstition, serving as it does to illustrate nothing'. Unfortunately, and to his endless frustration, O'Donovan's 'old antagonist', popular oral tradition, continued to confront him at every turn during his perambulations through the country, with him describing it as 'a blundering Booby who has a clouded memory and muddy brains'.[20] In O'Donovan's estimation, the collector Charles Vallancey—today called 'the first practitioner of ethnology in Ireland'—was 'full of error';[21] the great folklorist Thomas Crofton Croker, meanwhile, was dismissed as that 'little fairy elf' who practiced 'fairyology'.[22] For all of O'Donovan's brilliance and mastery of the Irish language and history, one can only speculate as to how much pre-famine folk material was lost by its being deemed not worthy of inclusion in his letters and memoirs.

Traces of O'Donovan's proto-positivist rhetoric echoed into the next century with the movement that became known as revisionism.[23] It too sought to purge Irish history of its 'servitude to myth', including those myths which even O'Donovan and his Ordnance Survey colleague George Petrie, for all their historio-scientific allegiance, upheld. Intersecting with the profession-alization of academic history in the 1930s, and assuming renewed vigor in the 1980s, the movement's founders, T.W. Moody and Robert Dudley Edwards, took their cue and training from the British model of empirical scholarship, and aimed to pursue a more 'scientific' study of history based on archival evi-dence, often emanating from on high and centered upon 'neutral', 'objective' fact.[24] It should be emphasized that revisionism was and remains necessary for correcting the overly nationalist historiography that had prevailed be-fore, and that the practitioners themselves did not seek after pure objectivity per se—they were not as naïve as all that.[25] But does 'facing the facts of the Irish past'—Moody's phrase—always entail the exclusion of sources that are methodologically problematic but no less instructive? Does consulting folkloric sources necessarily return us to the nationalism that revisionists so greatly spurned—particularly given the sheer and often *un*-nationalistic di-versity that is actually contained in that material?[26]

In focusing so intently on Anglophone methods of writing history, re-visionism also ignored major developments emerging elsewhere, primarily in France, where the *Annales* school devoted as much attention to *culture folklorique* as it did to the driest of statistical sources (indeed, it was a folklife-minded historical geographer, E. Estyn Evans, who adopted *annaliste* ap-proaches to Irish culture before any historian of Ireland did). Revisionism's fetish for the printed or written source at the expense of much else also led to egregious errors such as Marianne Elliott's statement that 'the oral history of 1798 was almost nil': a statement rebutted by Richard Hayes as well as Guy Beiner, who uncovered enormous amounts of lore around the events.[27] Distressing historical ruptures in Ireland's past also tended to be overlooked or minimized by revisionists,[28] though more recent studies are now ad-dressing those subjects, due in great part to Vincent Carey, David Edwards, and others.[29] Revisionist debates, however, have now faded[30] as the idea of 'value-free' history, which masks its own ideological impulses, has been questioned and some say overturned. By the same token, some of the more 1990s' era post-structuralist aspects of postcolonialism are also showing their age, even if the continued contentiousness around Ireland and postcoloni-ality keeps the approach alive.[31] While many assume the revisionist/post-revisionist debate is thus on the wane, the attachment to revisionism remains, however, whenever any historian, wittingly or not, relies on predominantly English-language archival, textual, and printed sources to the exclusion of more problematic oral-vernacular material.[32]

Though Douglas Hyde once described folklore as important in its liter-ary rather than 'scientific' dimensions,[33] it is therefore misguided to equate folklore with 'falsity, wrongness, fantasy, distortion and error', not to men-tion 'emotion', as opposed to 'dispassionate' hard fact.[34] For one, there is, of course, a heavily positivist history—even a hyper-positivist history—behind the discipline of folkloristics, which paralleled the professionalization of history as well. Books such as *Folklore as a Historical Science* were published in the beginning of the twentieth century, even if folklorists themselves later dismissed such an approach. Exhaustive categorizations and catalogings were also undertaken and ranged from Stith Thompson's motif index to Seán Ó Súilleabháin and Radar Th. Christiansen's *Types of the Irish Folktale.*[35] Arnold Van Gennep, whose 'rites of passage' idea influenced so many anthropologically-minded historians from the 1970s onward, considered folklore a science that synthesized different elements,[36] while analytical and theoretical interpretive methods continue to deepen and widen the field. While much of the systematic folklore collecting and archiving in 1920s- and 1930s-Ireland coincided with nationalism—Ireland is hardly unique in that[37]—the process was also deeply informed by international and cross-cultural contributions and influences. Séamus Ó Duilearga (James Delargy) studied in Lund and Uppsala after a momentous encounter with the pioneering Swedish practitioner of folklore Max von Sydow, who himself lived for a time in Ireland and contributed deeply to the National Folklore Collection.[38] After Ó Duilearga's retirement, the chair of the National Folklore Collection fell to the late Swedish scholar, Bo Almqvist, who also edited *Béaloideas* and served many years as Professor of Folklore at University College Dublin.

That said, there has long been 'trouble in the house of folklore', with programs and departments being cut, and scholars redefining themselves as ethnologists, ethnographers, cultural anthropologists, or scholars of the verbal arts.[39] The term 'folklore' itself remains unstable, especially when it is treated unquestioningly, or not distinguished from pseudo-folklore, or 'fakelore'.[40] As Dan Ben-Amos has pointed out, the word is deployed archaically by those outside the field to connote a *gesunkenes Kulturgut*—roughly translated as a 'primitive' or peasant communal culture.[41] Folklorists no longer hold this view, nor the 'affable condescension to the common people' implied by it.[42] In addition, 'folklore' is neither static nor self-enclosed, nor are 'the people' a homogenous entity, whether at elite or at lower levels. Terminological muddle and misunderstanding that has gathered around the term has also led some in the field of folkloristics to advocate for a reinvention of the name. Barbara Kirshenblatt-Gimblett once wrote that 'folklore' should be changed 'to enhance our survival' (she preferred 'vernacular culture'),[43] while Regina Bendix advocates 'a Frazerian ritual slaying of the name folklore to make room for the installation of one or more new names'.[44]

It is necessary for those who wish to venture into folklore to be aware of this disciplinary history as well as many of the extremely valuable questions from the field—what is folklore precisely? who are the 'folk'? how do we define or extend the perimeters of each?—that could send history and literature into new directions. But it is equally important that non-folklorists define their terms precisely and not use 'folklore' as self-evident, or simply present folkloric examples without delineating the categories and social contexts to which they belong. Historians, literary scholars, and others may use the word 'folklore' freely, unaware perhaps that it has been defined at various times as a communicative event and analytical construct (Dan Ben Amos), 'human creativity in its own context' (Henry Glassie), 'action' and 'performance' (Richard Bauman), and 'process' (Lauri Honko).[45] According to Alan Dundes, the 'folk' can also be 'any group of people whatsoever who share one common factor ... and some traditions which it calls its own'—even though this might appear incongruous at first, given the associations around the word 'folk'.[46] Folklore has also been perceived as too often privileging the verbal arts, even though it also encompasses folklife (pioneered by Estyn Evans in the North) as well as music, dance, rituals, folk theater, and other activities.[47] Non-folklorists should also be cognizant of narrative conventions, with myth referring to that which is sacred and originary, an epic as a long narrative with cultural heroes, or a legend as a historically based story, albeit with supernatural borrowings. Furthermore, folktales can be complex or simple, *Märchen* (wonder tales) or jokes, a general or personal-experience narrative.[48] These distinctions are important in tending to the conventions that determine a particular tale, and in this sense, historians in particular might revisit Hayden White and Paul Ricoeur to understand how real events of the past are narratively organized into genres, tropes, and interpretative frameworks—not only in folkloric tales but in the act of history writing itself. Indeed, if history encompasses 'both the facts of the matter and the narrative of those facts', both 'what happened' and 'that which is said to have happened', then it is incumbent upon historians especially to acknowledge this difference, paying more attention to the formal conventions not only behind folkloric tales but their own writing of the past.[49]

Despite the aforementioned paucity of pre-1700 sources that focus in any overt way on popular oral traditions, possibilities nevertheless present themselves to early modernists who seek to trace folkloric narratives and forms across discourses. Scholars, however, must confront the problem of mediation, or the invariably shaped transcriptions made by literate and often elite observers who thought to write these traditions down. Folkloric tales were also not simply oral but performative, with speakers constantly shaping material for the audience and occasion, even if that material often contained within itself a core of narrative and formal consistency. To capture these tales in writing or print was to therefore convey them in the narrowest of ways, akin to pinning a butterfly to a mounting board, its once-wild movements now dead or at least frozen.[50] One might further add the linguistic mediation that occurs when tales moved from Irish to English; as Seán Ó Súilleabháin put it, when 'ordinary folktales passed through the language' and 'meshed' into English, they became 'but faint echoes of the former glories of Irish storytelling'.[51] Antiquarians, chapbook authors, or travel writers who directly or indirectly captured these oral tales finally inserted themselves as mediators by way of editorial intervention or omission, in accordance with their own interests and agendas.

The process by which an author worked off these motifs or these narrative forms can itself be a productive approach, however. Scholars, for example, might perform a close reading of primary literary and historical texts themselves—a method advocated elsewhere in this volume by Sarah McKibben—in order to discern the appearance of folkloric tropes (saints' handprints on rocks, wise-talking animals). If the author has invented a tale or, one could say, created fakelore, that itself is valuable too, particularly since those tales have been known to enter into the culture at large and thereby become folklore, just as orality and textuality move back and forth in a fluid zone.[52] In addition to medieval literary scholars who have worked on this approach, a good general model here might be Bakhtin's old study of Rabelais, even if early modern Ireland did not have its equivalent author. By analyzing the rituals, carnival rites, or culture of laughter that appeared in Rabelais, for example, Bakhtin was able to locate a 'folkloristic consciousness' within *Gargantua* and *Pantagruel*: a mediated one, certainly, and distilled in turn from a popular chapbook of the time but no less important in offering clues both to the popular culture and to other dimensions within the text itself.[53] Motifs and topoi from folkloric tradition, checked against other contemporary texts or the Stith-Thompson Motif Index or Aarne-Thompson Classification of Folk-Tales, may similarly be traced against texts by John Derricke, specifically his image of the woodkerne in Rory Óg O'More; Spenser's well-trodden *View of the Present State of Ireland* could also be explored through its vernacular aspects, in addition to the folkloric elements in the pastoral elegy 'Colin Clouts Come Home Again'.[54]

Bardic poets and prose writers loosened their own formulaic rigidity in the seventeenth century, which led to the indirect adaptation of folk or popular elements.[55] Their poems could therefore be analyzed through this prism. Dáibhí Ó Bruadair, who dismissed what he called *sráidéigse*, or street poetry, nevertheless borrowed from popular culture, as did Aogán Ó Rathaille, while earlier historical literature, such as Tadhg Ó Cianáin's *Imeacht na nIarlaí* (The Departure of the Earls) or Lughaidh Ó Cléirigh's life of Red Hugh O'Donnell, entitled 'Beatha Aodha Rua Uí Dhomhnaill', adopt both elite and popular, local and universal motifs such as exile.[56] The seventeenth-century social satire entitled *Páirlement Chloinne Tomáis*, while written from a condemnatory elite perspective, may also reveal aspects of the 'lower' orders. Meanwhile, Guy Beiner has demonstrated that traditions of prophecy circulated as much in folkloric social memory as much as they served, in Breandán Ó Buachalla's words, as 'validatory mechanisms' in *seanchas* accounts.[57]

Possibilities also open if one is to accept Dundes' aforementioned definition of a given 'folk' as encompassing any social group with a common identity and shared traditions, as well as a 'distinctive folk speech and other traditions—the lingo and lore which set [it] apart from others'.[58] Families which preserved their own stories and traditions—for example, of land lost or of exile—perpetuated a kind of insider 'kinship folklore', with narratives preserved in genealogical records, memoirs, and letters. For poets and prose writers, qualities such as honor, as explored by Brendan Kane, may also be considered part of a shared 'folklore' and 'folk speech', providing a distinct 'intergroup essence'. Masculinity, examined by Sarah McKibben, constitutes another approach, especially as it was contained within certain resonant cultural symbols understood by the group.[59] Framed in this way, shared 'linguistic codes' that mark a group's verbal communications across texts and social interactions merit further investigation, especially as those codes and communications migrated over to the continent or endured in different forms across time.

Following the examples of largely post-1700 scholars such as James Donnelly or Niall Ó Ciosáin, more popular customs could also be accessed, however obliquely, through other textual channels.[60] Legal or ecclesiastical records and condemnations, for example, may reveal attitudes about witchcraft, magical potions, or behavior at patron-day festivals (or patterns);[61] unfortunately, earlier quarter sessions, assize, and King's Bench court records up to the mid-eighteenth century are relatively rare, as are many Church of Ireland parish and institutional sources. As Neal Garnham has written, historians of early modern Ireland must therefore rely on 'aggregations of examples drawn from [contemporaries], or [on] the wealth of anecdotal evidence contained in the private papers of prominent individuals'.[62] Pre-1700 travel or antiquarian writings, for example, can offer suggestive material related to popular traditions.[63] The writings of Edmund Campion and Stanihurst misunderstood or manipulated (or invented) traditions, but their own folklore or fakelore influenced English perceptions back home. Campion, for example, noted the 'shamrock' (spelled 'shamrote'), while John Derricke referred to the woodkernes and their 'wild shamrock manners'. Stanihurst, who built on Campion and claimed that his knowledge also came from 'certain gentlemen of our acquaintance', went further in asserting that the people of Ireland ate shamrocks. There also appears to have existed a custom of eating a 'sprig' of shamrock on St. Patrick's Day, perhaps for luck or, as the antiquarian Thomas Dineley would write of 'shamroges' in 1681, 'to cause a sweet breath'.[64] And so the chain of references proceeds forward, as the shamrock becomes for the English at least an indelible instance of what would today be termed popular folklife.

Antiquarianism has been a vibrant field of study for twenty years, with the seventeenth century represented by Bernadette Cunningham's work on Geoffrey Keating, Mark Empey's on James Ware, and Graham Parry's more generally. But the specifically folkloric aspects of these writings could be pursued at more length, just as a good study awaits of the tragic Roderic O'Flaherty or comic Thomas Dineley. Also important is the printer and bookseller John Dunton, whose *Dublin Scuffle* was one of the more idiosyncratic works of the time, along with his often-unreliable yet still useful *Teague Land or a Merry Ramble to the Wild Irish* (1698).[65] Both have received excellent editions undertaken by Andrew Carpenter and Four Courts Press; while readers must remain aware of both books' fictive (and, in *Dublin Scuffle*'s case, plagiarized) elements, not to mention Dunton's 'pompous self-importance',[66] the books nevertheless remain valuable in reflecting the author's travels or 'rambles' through the country—not to mention the interactions with all segments of society and the popular tales that resulted from the encounter.

A related approach in accessing the era's popular and folkloric beliefs and customs is through Marc Bloch's famous regressive method, in which one begins with a later source base and systematically traces the motifs or themes back to the early modern, recognizing in the process that no folktales are ever fully stable.[67] Clodagh Tait (along with Raymond Gillespie the leading historian of social history, and trained in part as a folklorist), as well as Andrew Sneddon, have employed such methods productively, using later antiquarian or other texts to trace back or confirm earlier customs, particularly around the dead, popular religion, or witchcraft.[68] In England, Ronald Hutton also used the evidence of eighteenth- and nineteenth-century folklore collections to forge new conclusions about the Reformation in England, while Andy Wood and Daniel Woolf have utilized later folkloric records in particularly interesting and theoretically rich ways, to analyze popular memory and custom in England.[69]

But the regressive method must be used very carefully; as Peter Burke once put it, one must not '[take] descriptions of relatively recent situations and cheerfully [assume] that they apply equally well to earlier situations'. By working back through the centuries and sources methodically, reconstructing contexts along the way, scholars should utilize the modern material indirectly at best, to interrogate and 'suggest connections' with the earlier material.[70] And the outdated nineteenth-century idea of survivals should be forsaken altogether, especially as it assumes that the earlier material reflects any kind of purer, more 'primitive' originary source of these customs and traditions. Gillespie, for example, maintains his focus on the writings of Barnaby Rich, Edmund Campion, Philip O'Sullivan Beare, and Keating in order to uncover popular folkloric beliefs; antiquarian records are minimized in comparison, though they serve to reinforce the actual existence as well as transmission and reception of those beliefs.[71]

There is an abundance of modern sources which early modernists can nevertheless use as their initial source base in tracing popular traditions backward or forward, as the case may be. In addition to the nineteenth-century folkloric collections by Crofton Croker, William Carleton, Patrick Kennedy, Yeats, Lady Gregory, and Jeremiah Curtin, an even bigger goldmine can be found within the National Folklore Collection, containing one of the world's greatest collections of vernacular recordings and transcriptions.[72] Much (though by no means all) of its material is now available on www. duchas.ie. With stories transcribed or recorded in the 1920s and 1930s, it would be tempting to assume that many of the themes that run through them reflected the interests pervading that period or perhaps the late nineteenth century of the elder storytellers. Yet while this is true, it also takes too restricted a view of folklore and historical memory. Why, for example, do some historical figures—Elizabeth I; Hugh O'Neill; Cromwell, above all—appear in the first place if they did not carry a longer historical resonance? Were they simply and solely picked up from books, only to circulate in the oral culture? If nineteenth- and early twentieth-century land grievances were reflected in many of the National Folklore Collection sources, why were they given an origin story attributable to fairly specific early modern dispossessions? Historical referents, in other words, did not simply emerge *ex nihilo*, but were transmitted across generations, orally and to texts and back again.

One challenge for any historian or literary scholar who works on this material is that the National Folklore Collection comprises raw data, with material that is open-ended, narratively unstable, often opaque, and sometimes jokey, with minimal information on context except for mention of the location (town, county) and date of transcription. What does it mean, for example, that Cromwell appears as a king of Ireland who then lives in exile in England, only to return 'home' and exact his revenge? Or that he is depicted in some tales or mummers plays as harmlessly comical? Interpretative methods borrowed from folkloristics (or literary scholarship) might be helpful here: for example, where non-folklorists might dismiss such tales or avoid unpacking their meanings, folklorists would point out that in the case of the Cromwellian tales, these narratives are standard and common devices in depicting inversions of the hierarchy, and therefore weighted with symbolic and historical meaning.[73] As for the question of their instability—their inventiveness or changeability over time—Brian Earls, Guy Beiner, and even John O'Donovan in a more tolerant mood pointed out that an internal consistency, regularity, and 'a glimmer of truth' undergird the often wild narrative variations in these stories. They may not be factual, but they are truthful in reflecting *mentalités* and social memory, and even then, they are often not too far off the mark in referencing what actually occurred. Scholars may therefore track this inner narrative core while also accounting for the variability and instability inherent to the form.

If Peter Burke implores historians to utilize the regressive method sparingly and indirectly with regard to modern sources, those same sources may also be pushed to the forefront when one examines the subject of memory.[74] There is still much to be explored about the memorializations of figures and events from early modern Ireland, particularly in their folkloric and popular iterations, though one must be careful not to conflate 'memory' with 'historiography', as so many historians do. Pádraig Lenihan has already explored the 'folklorizing' of Aughrim, for example, while Vincent Carey has traced the transmission of a sixteenth-century episode of murder through the centuries up to the National Folklore Collection archives. The late Brian Earls, who specialized in folkloric transmissions, traced references to the 1577 massacre at Mullaghmast across manuscript texts owned by the Rev. James O'Neill, a priest from Maryborough, and the Rev. John Whelan, and finally the late Walter Fitzgerald, who transcribed the more detailed story 'from the lips of an old man'.[75] As for historical figures, Hugh O'Neill turns up as a legend in the National Folklore Collection; Cromwell—'Cromail' in the Irish sources—appears more than any other historical figure except for Daniel O'Connell,[76] and Redmond O'Hanlon lives on throughout the centuries, and in the National Folklore Collection as well.[77] Eoghan Ruadh Ó Néill, the great military leader of the Ulster army in the 1640s, accumulated a number of tales around himself (and he too appears in the National Folklore Collection): a famous one involves his setting a last remaining bullock on fire, which causes a neighboring herd—future provisions for the army—to wander over, lured by the creature's wail. This is not simply a quaint 'story of Ireland', however; rather it is a superimposition of a historical figure—Eoghan—onto an existing epic and historical template, recalling as it does the story of the Daghda getting their cattle from the Fomhóire, or of Hannibal's own cattle trick in his battle against the Romans.[78] The very familiarity of the narrative template—the placement of Eoghan onto existing and familiar stories—thus ensures the story's survival and Eoghan's own memorialization. At the same time, it is crucial that scholars attend to the particular historical contexts in which these legends were transcribed, and the functions they served for those who lived in a later time. To quote Jan Vansina, such figures as Eoghan 'serve the interests of the society' that finds him, in turn, convenient in addressing those interests.[79]

Early modernists might use this later and earlier material to build on the recent surge in animal studies, discussed in this volume by Willy Maley. Many indeed have written on the mythic, legendary, and folkloric meanings in Irish culture of horses (magical and powerful), asses (sacred), or black beetles (the 'worst of all animals'). But some animals were intensely connected to a particular historical moment. One thinks of the folklorically resonant wolf, significantly depleted over the early modern time period.[80] Even the beetle, or 'dung beetle', made a rhetorically sharp appearance in Keating, who drew on its folkloric and naturalistic associations, likening Giraldus, Moryson, Spenser, and others to the insect which 'lifts its head in the summertime, to go about fluttering' not to 'any delicate flower that may be in the field' but to the 'dung of horse or cow,' after which it then 'proceeds to roll itself therein'.[81] The regressive method, in addition to tale type and motif-indexes, may again offer reference points of study in excavating the deeper meanings of these topoi, keeping in mind that particular motifs may constitute just one indivisible element in a given narrative or within an entire episode from a longer tale.[82] Extending the idea further, ecological studies might also be utilized toward folkloristic and historical analysis; Nigel Everett's recent book on the woods of Ireland, not to mention the work of William Smyth, offers excellent treatment of early modern Ireland's timberland catastrophes; much more could be pursued on the subject from a literary and folkloric perspective.[83] And the historical significance of weather, discussed in this volume by Francis Ludlow and Arlene Crampsie, might also be enriched when viewed through a folkloric prism, as the authors occasionally do.

Finally, the methods and interpretive theories specific to the discipline of folkloristics—sparing the psychoanalytical approach, perhaps—would be useful to historians, even if many have been subsequently criticized and even discarded.[84] The Finnish historical-geographical method, previously mentioned with regard to Emmanuel Le Roy Ladurie's embarrassment, seeks to resist ideas of polygenesis by tracking a tale's diffusion across time and space. Similar to the regressive method, this requires the painstaking assemblage and subsequent cataloging of texts in archives, literature, and printed and manuscript collections in order to track the manner in which a tale (or event, or personage) changes—rather than remains stable—over time, while also retaining its essential identity. The idea of the variant is key here; as Richard Dorson once pointed out, earlier folklorists 'employed the nearest text at hand to illustrate their discussion', not realizing that 'every text is a variant captured at some point in time and place, and undergoing change at every point'.[85] Structuralists, on the other hand, elaborated upon the seminal work of Vladimir Propp by focusing on narrative elements, and while the approach is now dated, interest in Propp's morphology and story grammar has revived in recent years, especially as they have been systematized and coded with computer technology, thereby 'computerizing Propp'.[86] The problem with such systematization, however, is that while it may organize great masses of detail, it tends to 'overstress similarities and undervalue differences'.[87]

Finally, functionalists have much to offer as they seek to understand the ways in which the verbal arts dynamically performed in a given society: satires masking hostilities, proverbs carrying judicial functions, mythical narratives validating belief systems, and so forth. A good study awaits, for example, on how popular and elite folktales functioned in the wake of the ruptures of early modern Ireland. The question of land and its confiscation, as mentioned, haunts the National Folklore Collection, especially as dispossessions were attributed to Elizabeth and Cromwell as well as the Williamite settlement. Indeed, land (or rather confiscated property) elicits more attention in the folkloric memory of Cromwell than the massacres at Drogheda and Wexford. The surveying and mapping undertaken by Elizabethans through William Petty have also justifiably merited much attention, due in part to Trinity College Dublin's Down Survey online and contributions from innovative and theoretically sophisticated historical geographers such as Nessa Cronin. In contrast, evidence from oral and folkloric traditions reveals that a kind of oral 'counter-mapping' continued to persist, refusing to recognize the new territorial dispensations or place names.[88] A valuable if challenging study awaits on this subject as well.

None of these folkloric approaches, it should be emphasized, are alien to historians or literary scholars. Students of medieval literary texts have used many of these methods, just as early modernists in general once borrowed heavily from the structuralist-functionalist approach of Clifford Geertz. More recently, Marc Caball has applied Max von Sydow's concept of the ecotype (or oicotype) to the cultural hybridity of Seaán Ó Cearnaigh's protestant Irish primer. Others continue to apply (and in some cases reject) the application of Milman Parry and Albert Lord's oral-formulaic method, particularly when it comes to the ongoing question of orality (as Marie-Louise Coolahan has brilliantly demonstrated with the 1641 depositions).[89] Yet greater attention to these methods, and a sensitivity to the way a narrative is imbued with folkloric elements in a given historical moment, would benefit scholars who wish to take the study of popular and elite culture further, pursuing sources that could also include pre-1700 (and pre-Jacobite) ballads or the depositions and related literature around the events of 1641.[90]

While formidable challenges thus await those scholars who seek to dig more deeply into oral vernacular culture and its many forms, the results could prove transformative in raising new questions and offering fresh approaches to the pre-1700 past and its texts, uncovering topics that have yet to be explored.[91] Approaching oral-based sources through the methods offered by the field of folkloristics does not simply reveal a relatively neglected early modern past but also offers us insight into what tales, festivals, or popular proverbs meant to the culture at large. Folkloristics also reveals the longer histories and narrative gene-alogies behind these Irish and English-language stories, and how they adapted to specific historical contexts while conveying a resonance beyond themselves. None of this means that one must necessarily return to Daniel Corkery's much derided *Hidden Ireland*, which sought to uncover the oppressed Gaelic world of Ireland's eighteenth-century peasantry and its now-reduced poets—even though recent scholars such as Vincent Morley have made a convincing case for the worthy aspects of that writer's emphasis on the Irish language, the 'popular mind', and 'an fear ar an gcnoc'.[92] But in moving beyond the strictly empirical approaches that have constricted much of early modern Irish history, one may address the historical silences that haunt a past which is still presented primarily through administrative records and State Papers, texts, and maps. The previously maligned and historiographically dismissed field of folklore—and knowledge of its attendant discipline—may in this way illuminate early modern Ireland's netherworld, and elucidate great parts of its known world as well.[93]

Notes

1 I wish to thank Jane Kelton for her conversations with me on folkloristics and for her comments on this essay. I also wish to thank Clodagh Tait for helping me to see the value of folklore and early modern Ireland, and for her sharing Cromwell references with me. In addition, I am grateful to Vincent Carey and especially Críostóir Mac Cárthaigh of the National Folklore Collection for his invaluable help in the NFC archive and through the years.

2 Guy Beiner, *Remembering the Year of the French: Irish Folk History and Social Memory* (Madison: University of Wisconsin Press, 2007).

3 For a more nuanced understanding of Gramsci and folklore, see Stephen Olbrys Gencarella, 'Gramsci, Good Sense, and Critical Folklore Studies', *Journal of Folklore Research* 47 (2010), 221–52; for Gramsci and folklore in general see Diarmuid Ó Giolláin, *Locating Irish Folklore' Tradition, Modernity, Identity* (Cork: Cork University Press, 2000), pp. 153–59.

4 To be fair, Ladurie was very much interested in and utilized folklore, including Occitan folklore. See Emmanuel Le Roy Ladurie. *L'argent, l'amour, et la mort en pays d'oc; Précédé du roman de l'abbé Fabre, Jean-l'ont-pris (1756)* (Paris: Éditions du Seuil, 1980). For historians on folklore, see Peter Burke, 'History and Folklore: A Historiographical Survey', *Folklore* 115 (2004), 137; William G. Pooley, 'Native to the Past: History, Anthropology and Folklore in *Past and Present*', *Past and*

Present 239 (2015), 13. See also Caoimhín Ó Danachair, 'Oral Tradition and the Printed Word', *Irish University Review* 9 (1979), 31–41.

5 Kevin Danaher, *A Bibliography of Irish Ethnology and Folk Tradition* (Dublin: Mercier, 1978); Ruth Finnegan, *Oral Traditions and the Verbal Arts: A Guide to Research Practices* (London and New York: Routledge, 2003).

6 Ó Giolláin, *Locating Irish Folklore*, p. 32. See also Henry Glassie, 'Folklore and History', *Minnesota History* 50 (1987), 188–92; 'Folklore and History', in Hilda Ellis Davidson (ed.), *Patterns of Folklore* (Ipswich: D.S. Brewer, 1960), pp. 1–20.

7 See among other works, Dáithí Ó hÓgáin, *Fionn mac Cumhaill: Images of the Gaelic Hero* (Dublin: Gill and MacMillan, 1988); idem, 'Fionn féin: pearsa agus ideal', in Pádraig Ó Fiannachta (ed.), *An fhiannaíocht, Léachtaí Cholm Cille* 25 (Maynooth: An Sagart, 1995), pp. 144–64; idem, *The Hero in Irish Folk History* (Dublin: Gill & Macmillan 1985); idem, Migratory Legends in Medieval Irish Literature', *Béaloideas* 60–61 (1992–1993), 57–74.

8 Alan Bruford, *Gaelic Folktales and Medieval Romances* (Dublin: Folklore Society of Ireland, 1969); T.P. Cross, *Motif-Index of Early Irish Literature* (Bloomington: Indiana University Press, 1952); see also Dorothy Ann Bray, *A List of Motifs in the Lives of the Early Irish Saints* (Helsinki: Academia Scientiarum Fennica, 1992); Dáithí Ó hÓgáin, *The Lore of Ireland: An Encyclopaedia of Myth, Legend and Romance* (Woodbridge: Boydell Press, 2006).

9 For seventeenth-century antiquarians in Ireland, see Graham Parry, *The Trophies of Time: English Antiquarians of the Seventeenth Century* (Oxford: Oxford University Press, 1995); for Ware, see Mark Empey, 'Value-free' History? The Scholarly Network of Sir James Ware', *History Ireland* 20 (2012), 20–23; idem, '"A real credit to Ireland, and to Dublin": The Scholarly Achievements of Sir James Ware', in Kathleen Miller and Crawford Gribben (eds.), *Dublin: Renaissance City of Literature* (Oxford: Oxford University Press, 2017). See also Richard Dorson, *The British Folklorists* (London: Routledge and Kegan Paul, 1968), p. 23.

10 Charles O'Conor, 'Observations on the Heathen State and Ancient Topography of Ireland', in Charles Vallencey (ed.), *Collectanea de Rebus Hibernicis*, vols. 3, 12 ([1783] Dublin: R. Marchbank, 1786), pp. 653–54. For O'Conor generally, see Luke Gibbons and Kieran Denis O'Conor (eds.), *Charles O'Conor of Ballinagare, 1710–91: Life and Works* (Dublin: Four Courts, 2015). For John Lynch, see *Cambrensis Everus: The History of Ancient Ireland Vindicated ...* vols. 2. (Dublin: Printed for the Celtic Society, 1848–1852).

11 Peter Burke, *Popular Culture in Early Modern Europe*, 3rd edn. (New York: Routledge, 2016); R.W. Scribner, 'Is a History of Popular Culture Popular?' in Lyndal Roper (ed.), *Religion and Culture in Germany (1400–1800)* (Leiden: Brill, 2001), p. 40; Robert Muchembled, *Popular Culture and Elite Culture in France, 1400–1750*, trans. Lydia Cochrane (Baton Rouge: Louisiana State University Press, 1985). For more recent treatments, see Andrew Hadfield and Matthew Dimmock (eds.), *The Ashgate Research Companion to Popular Culture in Early Modern England* (New York and London: Routledge, 2016); and idem, *Literature and Popular Culture in Early Modern England* (Burlington, VT: Ashgate, 2009). For Ireland (and with a focus on later centuries), see Niall Ó Ciosáin, *Print and Popular Culture in Ireland, 1750–1850* (Basingstoke: Macmillan, 1997); J.S. Donnelly, *Irish Popular Culture 1650–1850* (Dublin: Irish Academic Press, 1998); Michael Willem De Nie and Sean Farrell (eds.), *Power and Popular Culture in Modern Ireland* (Dublin: Irish Academic Press, 2010).

12 Examples of journals in folkloristics, many of which are open access, include *Cultural Analysis* (Berkeley); *Folklore* (Taylor & Francis), *Journal of Folklore Research* (Indiana University); *Journal of Ethnology and Folkloristics* (De Gruyter), *Journal of American Folklore* (American Folklore Society), and *Material Culture Review* (Cape Breton University). In Ireland, see *Béaloideas* (An Cumann Le Béaloideas

Éireann/Folklore of Ireland Society). Many of the local journals as well as *Éire-Ireland* also publish folkloric articles.

13 Breandán Ó Buachalla, 'James Our True King: The Ideology of Irish Royalism in the Seventeenth Century', in D. George Boyce et al. (eds.), *Political Thought in Ireland since the Seventeenth Century* (Abingdon: Routledge, 1993), pp. 17–18.

14 See also Bernadette Cunningham, 'Seventeenth-Century Interpretations of the Past: The Case of Geoffrey Keating', *Irish Historical Studies* 25 (1986), esp. 122–23; Bernadette Cunningham, *The World of Geoffrey Keating: History, Myth and Religion in Seventeenth-Century Ireland* (Dublin: Four Courts, 2000).

15 Brendan Bradshaw, 'Geoffrey Keating: Apologist of Irish Ireland', in Brendan Bradshaw, Andrew Hadfield, and Willy Maley (eds.), *Representing Ireland: Literature and the Origins of Conflict, 1534–1660* (Cambridge: Cambridge University Press, 1993), p. 167; see also Brendan Kane, 'Domesticating the Counter-Reformation: Bridging the Bardic and Catholic Traditions in Geoffrey Keating's "The Three Shafts of Death"', *Sixteenth Century Journal* 40 (2009), 1029–44; Pádraig Ó Riain (ed.), *Geoffrey Keating's Foras Feasa ar Éirinn: Reassessments* (London: Irish Texts Society, 2008).

16 Dáithí Ó hÓgáin, '"Béaloideas": Notes on the History of a Word', *Béaloideas* 70 (2002), 83–98.

17 Cunningham, *World of Geoffrey Keating*, pp. 22, 60. See also for example Francis John Byrne, 'Senchas: The Nature of Gaelic Historical Tradition', in J. G. Barry (ed.), *Historical Studies 9* (Belfast: Blackstaff Press, 1974), pp. 137–59; Edel Bhreathnach, 'The *Seanchas*: Tradition in Late Medieval Ireland', in Edel Bhreathnach and Bernadette Cunningham (eds.), *Writing Irish History: The Four Masters and their World* (Dublin: Wordwell, 2007), pp. 19–23.

18 Cristina Bacchilega, 'Folklore and Literature', in Regina F. Bendix and Galit Hasan-Rokem (eds.), *A Companion to Folklore* (Oxford: Wiley-Blackwell, 2012), p. 450; Cunningham, *World of Geoffrey Keating*, p. 116; Ó Giolláin, pp. 46–48; D.R. Woolf, 'The "Common Voice": History, Folklore and Oral Tradition in Early Modern England', *Past & Present* 120 (1988), esp. 39–40.

19 For the *Annals of the Four Masters*, see Bernadette Cunningham, *The Annals of the Four Masters: Irish History, Kingship and Society in the Early Seventeenth Century* (Dublin: Four Courts, 2010); Ó Buachalla, pp. 20–22. See also John O'Donovan, *Annals of the Kingdom of Ireland by the Four Masters* (Dublin: Hodges and Smith, 1833).

20 Michael Herrity (ed.), *Ordnance Survey Letters Donegal* (Dublin: Four Masters Press, 2000), pp. 75, 74, 48; Graham Mawhinney (ed.), *John O'Donovan's Letters from County Londonderry (1834)*, (Draperstown: Ballinascreen Historical Society, 1992), p. 55; Michael O'Flannagan (ed.), *Letters Containing Information Relative to the Antiquities of the Counties of Ireland: Westmeath* (Bray: Typescript, National Library of Ireland, 1926), p. 58; 'blundering booby' quoted from Stiofán O Cadhla, *Civilizing Ireland: Ordnance Survey 1824–1842: Ethnography, Cartography, Translation* (Dublin: Irish Academic Press, 2007), p. 148.

21 Caoimhín Ó Danachair, 'The Progress of Irish Ethnology 1783–1982', *Ulster Folklife* 29 (1983), p. 4.

22 Gillian Doherty, *The Ordnance Survey: History, Culture and Memory* (Dublin: Four Courts Press, 2006).

23 See Evi Gkotzaridis, *Trials of Irish History: Genesis and Evolution of a Reappraisal 1938–2000* (Abingdon: Routledge, 2006).

24 G.R. Elton, *The Practice of History*, 2nd ed. (Oxford: Blackwell, 2002), p. 109.

25 David George Boyce and Alan O'Day (eds.), *The Making of Modern Irish History: Revisionism and the Revisionist Controversy* (London: Routledge, 1996); Brendan Bradshaw, 'Nationalism and Historical Scholarship in Modern Ireland', *Irish Historical Studies* 26 (1988–89), 329–51.

26 See new readings of nationalism(s) in Thomas E. Hachey and Lawrence J. McCaffrey (eds.), *Perspectives On Irish Nationalism* (Lexington: University Press of Kentucky, 2015).

27 Beiner, p. 9.

28 See Mary Daly, 'Revisionism and Irish History: The Great Famine', in David George Boyce and Alan O'Day (eds.), *The Making of Modern Irish History: Revisionism and the Revisionist Controversy* (London and Routledge, 1996), p. 86.

29 David Edwards, Pádraig Lenihan, and Clodagh Tait (eds.), *Age of Atrocity: Violence and Political Conflict in Early Modern Ireland* (Dublin: Four Courts, 2007); see also Rory Rapple, 'Writing about Violence in the Tudor Kingdoms', *Historical Journal* 54 (2011), 829–54.

30 Ciaran Brady, 'Constructive and Instrumental: The Dilemma of Ireland's First "New Historians,"' in Ciaran Brady (ed.), *Interpreting Irish History: The Debate on Historical Revisionism 1938–1994* (Dublin: Irish Academic Press, 1994), p. 413; R. D. Edwards, 'An Agenda for Irish History, 1978–2018', in *Interpreting Irish History*, p. 56; Guy Beiner and Joep Leersen, 'Why Irish History Starved: A Virtual History', *Field Day Review* 3 (2007), 67–81; Roy Foster, 'We Are All Revisionists Now', *Irish Review* 1 (1986), 1–5; Kevin Whelan, 'The Revisionist Debate in Ireland', *Boundary* 2 (2004), 179–205.

31 For postcolonial theory and Ireland, see Eoin Flannery, 'Irish Cultural Studies and Postcolonial Theory', *Postcolonial Text* 3 (2007), 1–9; Joe Cleary, 'Misplaced Ideas? Colonialism, Location and Dislocation in Irish Studies', in Clare Carroll and Patricia King (eds.), *Ireland and Postcolonial Theory* (Cork: Cork University Press, 2003), pp. 16–45.

32 Aiden Clarke once wondered whether revisionists 'were not too literal and mechanistic in their exposition of the creed, too intolerant of the undocumented statement, too unappreciative of the contribution that the historian himself can make to the understanding of the past'. See Aidan Clarke, 'Robert Dudley Edwards (1909–1989)', *Irish Historical Studies* 26 (102) (1988), 126–27.

33 Douglas Hyde, *Beside the Fire* (London: D. Nutt, 1890), p. x.

34 See Daly, p. 86.

35 Antti Aarne and Stith Thompson, *The Types of the Folktale: A Classification and Bibliography* (Helsinki: Suomalainen Tiedeakatemia, 1964); David S. Azzolina, *Tale Type and Motif Indexes: An Annotated Bibliography* (New York: Garland Publishing, 1987); Hans-Jörg Uther, *The Types of International Folktales: A Classification and Bibliography* (Helsinki: Finnish Academy of Science and Letters, 2011); Diarmiud Ó Giolláin, 'Archives and Artefacts: Collecting, Collections and Ethnography in an Irish Comparative European Context', in Séamas Ó Síocháin, Pauline Garvey, and Adam Drazin (eds.), *Exhibit Ireland: Ethnographic Collections in Irish Museums* (Dublin: Wordwell, 2012), esp. pp. 94–96.

36 H.A. Sen, 'Arnold van Gennep: Structuralist and Apologist for the Study of Folklore in France', *Folklore* 85 (4) (1974), pp. 229–43.

37 See Ó Giolláin, *Locating Irish Folklore*, pp. 71–93; idem, 'An Béaloideas agus An Stát', *Béaloideas* 57 (1989), 151–63. For nationalism and folklore generally, see Timothy Baycroft and David M. Hopkin (eds.), *Folklore and Nationalism in Europe during the Long Nineteenth Century* (Leiden: Brill, 2012); Benedict Anderson, *Imagined Communities: Reflections on the Origin and Spread of Nationalism*, rev. edn. (London: Verso, 2006), p. 77.

38 Nils-Arvid Bringéus, *Carl Wilhelm von Sydow: A Swedish Pioneer in Folklore*. Trans. John Irons (Helsinki: Academia Scientiarum Fennica/Suomalainen Tiedeakatemia, 2009); Bo Almqvist, 'C.W. von Sydow agus Éire: Scoláire Sualannach agus an Léann Ceilteach', *Béaloideas* 70 (2002), 3–49.

39 For the state of folkloristics, see Alan Dundes's acerbic remarks in 'Folkloristics in the Twenty-First Century', *Journal of American Folklore* 118 (2005), 385–408; see

also Elliott Oring, 'On the Future of American Folklore Studies: A Response', *Western Folklore* 50 (1991), 75–81; Gregory Hanson, 'The End of Folklore and the Task of Thinking', *Folklore Forum* 28 (1997), 99–101. For the terminology, see Dan Ben-Amos, 'The Name is the Thing', *Journal of American Folklore* 111 (1998), 257–80; Regina Bendix, 'Of Names, Professional Identities, and Disciplinary Futures', *Journal of American Folklore* 111 (1998), 235–46; Barbara Kirshenblatt-Gimblett, 'Di Folkloristik: A Good Yiddish Word', *Journal of American Folklore* 98 (1985), 245–54; Gottfried Korff, 'Change of Name as a Change of Paradigm: The Renaming of Folklore Studies Departments at German Universities as an Attempt at 'Denationalization', *Europaea* 2 (1996), 9–32. See also 'Is Folklore a Discipline?' in Richard Dorson (ed.), *Folklore and Fakelore: Essays toward a Discipline of Folk Studies* (Cambridge, MA: Harvard University Press, 1976), pp. 101–24. For the verbal arts, see William Bascom, 'Folklore, Verbal Art and Culture', *Journal of American Folklore* 86 (1973), 374–81.

40 See also Dundes, 'Folkloristics', p. 393.

41 James R. Dow, 'Hans Naumann's *gesunkenes Kulturgut* and primitive *Gemeinschaftskultur*', *Journal of Folklore Research* 51 (2014), 49–100.

42 A. Robinson Wright, *English Folklore* (New York: Robert M. McBride, 1931), p. 31.

43 I wish to thank Jane Kelton for our many conversations here.

44 Elliott Oring, 'Anti Anti-"folklore,"' *The Journal of American Folklore* 111 (1998), 328–38.

45 Lauri Honko, 'The Folklore Process', in Pekka Hakamies and Anneli Honko (eds.), *Theoretical Milestones: Selected Writings of Lauri Honko* (Helsinki: Academia Scientiarum, 2013), pp. 39–53. For an explication of how this process played out in Ireland, see Gearóid Ó Crualaoich, 'Folkloristic-Ethnological Studies in Ireland', in Diarmuid Ó Giolláin (ed.), *Irish Ethnologies* (South Bend: University of Notre Dame Press, 2017), pp. 75–89.

46 Alan Dundes, *Interpreting Folklore* (Bloomington: Indiana University Press, 1980), pp. 6–7.

47 See E. Estyn Evans, *The Personality of Ireland: Habitat, Heritage and History* (Cambridge: Cambridge University Press, 1973); E. Estyn Evans, 'The Cultural Geographer and Folklife Research', in Richard M. Dorson, (ed.), *Folklore and Folklife: An Introduction* (Chicago, IL: University of Chicago Press, 1982), pp. 517–32; Ray Cashman, 'E. Estyn Evans and His Lasting Importance to the Study of Folklore', *Folklore Forum* 27 (1) (1996), 3–19.

48 See William Bascom, 'The Forms of Folklore: Prose Narratives', *Journal of American Folklore* 78 (1965), 3–20.

49 Michel-Rolph Trouillot, *Silencing the Past: Power and the Production of History* (Boston, MA: Beacon Press, 1995), p. 2; Hayden White, *Metahistory: The Historical Imagination in Nineteenth-Century Europe* (Baltimore and London: Johns Hopkins University Press, 1973); Paul Ricoeur, *Time and Narrative*, vols. 1 (Chicago: University of Chicago Press, 1984); Wulf Kansteiner, 'Hayden White's Critique of the Writing of History', *History and Theory* 32 (1993), 273–95; Angelos Mouzakitis, 'From Narrative to Action: Paul Ricoeur's Reflections on History', *Rethinking History* 19 (2015), 393–408.

50 Henry Glassie, *Irish Folktales*, (New York: Pantheon Books, 1985), p. 11.

51 Seán Ó Súilleabháin, *Storytelling in Irish Tradition* (Cork: Cork University Press, 1973), p. 12.

52 For the transmission of medieval Irish romances into folklore, see, for example, Bruford. See also Richard M. Dorson, 'Fakelore', *Zeitschrift fur Volkskunde* 69 (1969), 56–64; for a critique, see Alan Dundes, 'Nationalistic Inferiority Complexes and the Fabrication of Fakelore: A Reconsideration of Ossian, the Kinder- und Hausmärchen, the Kalevala, and Paul Bunyan', *Journal of Folklore Research* 22 (1985), 5–18.

53 Mikhail Bakhtin, *Rabelais and His World* (Bloomington: Indiana University Press, 1984), esp. pp. 98, 391, 424, 434.

54 See also Andrew Hadfield's brief mention of the folkloric in Spenser's 'Colin Clouts Come Home Againe', in Andrew Hadfield, *Edmund Spenser: A Life* (Oxford: Oxford University Press, 2012), p. 223.

55 Bruce A. Rosenberg, 'Reconstructed Folktales As Literary Sources', in Jerome McGann (ed.), *Historical Studies and Literary Criticism* (Madison, WI: University of Wisconsin Press, 1986), pp. 76–89; Bruce A. Rosenberg, *Folklore and Literature: Rival Siblings* (Knoxville, TN: University of Tennessee Press, 1991).

56 Joep Leersen, *Mere Irish and Fíor-Ghael* (Cork: Cork University Press, 1996), pp. 202–203, 246.

57 Beiner, pp. 106–109 ff; Ó Buachalla, pp. 18, 26.

58 Alan Dundes, *Interpeting Folklore* (Bloomington: Indiana University Press, 1980), p. 7; see also Simon J. Bronner (ed.), *Meaning of Folklore: The Analytical Essays of Alan Dundes* (Logan: Utah State University Press, 2007).

59 Brendan Kane, *The Politics and Culture of Honour in Britain and Ireland, 1541–1641* (Cambridge: Cambridge University Press, 2010); Sarah McKibben, *Endangered Masculinities in Irish Poetry: 1540–1780* (Dublin: University College Dublin Press, 2011). See also Jan Brunvand, *The Study of American Folklore* (New York: W.W. Norton, 1968), pp. 21–22; Richard Bauman, 'Differential Identity and the Social Base of Folklore', *Journal of American Folklore* 84 (1971), 32, 41. See also Stanley Brandes, *Metaphors of Masculinity: Sex and Status in Andalusian Folklore* (Philadelphia: University of Pennsylvania Press, 1980).

60 See the important essays in James S. Donnelly, Jr., and Kerby A. Miller (eds.), *Irish Popular Culture, 1650–1850,* (Dublin: Irish Academic Press, 1998).

61 See Natalie Zemon Davis, *Fiction in the Archives: Pardon Tales and Their Tellers in Sixteenth-Century France* (Stanford: Stanford University Press, 1987); Carlo Ginzburg, *The Cheese and the Worms: The Cosmos of a Sixteenth-Century Miller* (Baltimore: Johns Hopkins University Press, 1992).

62 Neil Garnham, 'How Violent Was Eighteenth-Century Ireland?' *Irish Historical Studies* 30 (1997), 378.

63 C.J. Woods, *Travellers' Accounts as Source-Materials for Irish Historians.* Maynooth Research Guides for Irish Local History (Dublin: Four Courts, 2009).

64 Edmund Campion, *A Historie of Ireland Written in the Year 1871* (Dublin: Hibernia Press, 1809), p. 25; Richard Stanihurst, 'A Treatise Containing a Plain and Perfect Description of Ireland', in Raphael Holinshed (ed.), *The Chronicles of England, Scotland and Ireland and Ireland*, vol. vi (London: J. Johnson, 1807), p. 67; John Derricke, *The Image of Ireland: With a Discovery of Woodkarne*, F. J. Sypher (ed.) (Delmar, NY: Scholars' Facsimiles and Reprints, 1998), p. 8; J.P. Prendergast (ed.), 'Extracts from the Journal of Thomas Dineley, Esquire, Giving Some Account of His Visit to Ireland in the Reign of Charles II', *The Journal of the Kilkenny and South-East of Ireland Archaeological Society* 1 (1856), 183. See also James Britten, 'The Shamrock', *The Month* 137 (1921), 193–205; idem, 'Vindication of the Shamrock Legend', *The Month* 137 (1921), 541; Nathaniel Colgan, 'The Shamrock in Literature', *The Journal of the Royal Society of Antiquaries of Ireland* 6 (5th ser.) (1896), 217.

65 See the relatively recent edition of and excellent introduction in John Dunton, *Teague Land or A Merry Ramble to the Wild Irish (1698)*, Andrew Carpenter (ed.) (Dublin: Four Courts, 2003). See also Ríonach uí Ógáin, 'John Dunton and Irish Folklore: A Brief Note', in idem, pp. 21–26.

66 Brean Hammond, *Professional Imaginative Writing in England* (Oxford: Clarendon Press, 1997), p. 159; Andrew Carpenter, 'Introduction', in John Dunton (ed.), *The Dublin Scuffle* (Dublin: Four Courts, 2000), p. xxiv.

67 For an older critique of Thompson, see Christine Goldberg, 'The Construction of Folktales', *Journal of Folklore Research* 23 (1986), 163–64.

68 Raymond Gillespie, *Devoted People: Belief and Religion in Early Modern Ireland* (Manchester: Manchester University Press, 1997); Andrew Sneddon, *Witchcraft and Magic in Ireland* (Basingstoke: Palgrave Macmillan, 2015); Clodagh Tait, *Death, Burial and Commemoration in Ireland, 1550–1650* (Basingstoke: Palgrave-Macmillan, 2002), p. 75, pp. 110–11.

69 Ronald Hutton, 'The English Reformation and the Evidence of Folklore' *Past and Present* 148 (1995), 89–116; D.R. Woolf, 'The "Common Voice": History, Folklore and Oral Tradition in Early Modern England', *Past and Present* 120 (1988), 26–52; William Pooley, 'Native to the Past: History, Anthropology, and Folklore in Past and Present', *Past and Present* 239 (2015), 1–15. See also Andy Wood, 'Five Swans over Littleport: Fenland Folklore and Popular Memory, c. 1810–1978', in John Arnold, Matthew Hilton, and Jan Ruger (eds.), *History After Hobsbawm: Writing the Past for the Twenty-First Century* (Oxford: Oxford University Press, 2017), pp. 225–41; see also Andy Wood, *The Memory of the People: Custom and Popular Senses of the Past in Early Modern England* (Cambridge: Cambridge University Press, 2013).

70 Peter Burke, *Popular Culture in Early Modern Europe* (New York: Harper & Row, 1978), pp. 83–84.

71 Raymond Gillespie, 'Popular and Unpopular Religion: A View from Early Modern Ireland', in Donnelly and Miller, pp. 30–49.

72 Micheál Briody, *The Irish Folklore Commission, 1935–1970: History, Ideology, Methodology* (Helsinki: Finnish Literature Society, 2007).

73 See Barbara Babcock, *The Reversible World: Symbolic Inversion in Art and Society* (Ithaca, NY: Cornell University Press, 1978). I wish to thank Jane Kelton for this reference.

74 In examining the memory or afterlives of such figures or events, it is important, however, that scholars keep in mind the problematic term 'collective memory', with its implication of homogeneity and timelessness. Beiner uses 'social memory' and emphasizes the importance of keeping in mind forgetting (or social forgetting). See Beiner, Chap. 16.

75 Brian Earls, 'Voices of the Dispossessed', *Dublin Review of Books* (www.drb.ie/ essays/voices-of-the-dispossessed).

76 For Cromwell in the folklore, see Alan Smith, 'The Image of Cromwell in Folklore and Tradition', *Folklore* 79 (1968), 17–39.

77 For more on the legend in folklore, see Heda Jason, 'Concerning the "Historical" and the "Local" Legends and their Relatives', in Américo Paredes and Richard Bauman (eds.), *Toward New Perspectives in Folklore* (Austin: University of Texas Press, 1975), pp. 134–44; for historical legends, see H. R. Ellis Davidson, 'Folklore and History', *Folklore* 85 (1974), 73–92. For O'Hanlon, see Ray Cashman, 'The Heroic Outlaw in Irish Folklore and Popular Literature', *Folklore* 111/2 (2000), 191–215.

78 Dáithí Ó hÓgáin, *The Lore of Ireland: An Encyclopedia of Myth, Legend and Romance* (Woodbridge: Woodbridge the Boydell Press, 2006), pp. 399–400.

79 Jan Vansina, *Oral Tradition: A Study in Historical Methodology* (Chicago: Aldine, 1965).

80 Ellen Powell Thompson, 'Folk-lore from Ireland I', *Journal of American Folklore* 6 (1893), 264–65.

81 See Geoffrey Keating, *Foras feasa ar Éirinn: The History of Ireland*, ed. David Comyn and P.S. Dinneen, 4 vols. (London: ITS, 1902–14), pp. 3–5. I am grateful to Peter McQuillan's comments on the dung beetle and Keating at the symposium

entitled 'Re-Viewing Edmund Spenser's *A View of the Present State of Ireland*', Case Western Reserve University, May 15–16, 2018.

82 Goldberg, p. 167.

83 Nigel Everett, *The Woods of Ireland: A History, 700–1800* (Dublin: Four Courts, 2014); William J. Smyth, *Map-Making, Landscapes and Memory: A Geography of Colonial and Early Modern Ireland c. 1530–1750* (South Bend, IN: University of Notre Dame Press, 2006).

84 For a good general overview, describing as well the problems in each approach, see Robert A. Georges and Michael Owen Jones, *Folkloristics: An Introduction* (Bloomington: Indiana University Press, 1995).

85 Richard Dorson, *Folklore and Folklife* (Chicago, IL: University of Chicago Press, 1972), p. 11.

86 Gregory Hanson, 'Computerizing Propp's Morphology: A Forward-Thinking Retrospect on Structuralism', *New Directions in Folklore* 13 (2015), 3–43; see also David K. Elson, 'Modeling Narrative Discourse'. M.A. Thesis. Columbia University, https://academiccommons.columbia.edu/catalog/ac:146913. For a brief mention of Propp, see also Roy Foster, *The Irish Story: Telling Tales and Making It Up in Ireland* (Oxford: Oxford University Press, 2002), pp. 5–7.

87 Goldberg, p. 165.

88 See Nancy Lee Peluso, 'Whose Woods Are These? Counter-Mapping Forest Territories in Kalimantan, Indonesia', *Antipode* 27 (1995), 383–406. See also Gerry Smyth, *Space and the Irish Cultural Imagination* (Basingstoke: Palgrave MacMillan, 2001), esp. chapter 2. Placenames are also a vibrant field of study. See Catherine Nash, 'Irish Placenames: Post-Colonial Locations, *Transactions of the Institute of British Geographers* 24 (1999), 457–80.

89 Marie-Louise Coolahan, '"And This Deponent Further Sayeth": Orality, Print and the 1641 Depositions', in Marc Caball and Andrew Carpenter (eds.), *Oral and Print Cultures in Ireland, 1600–1900* (Dublin: Four Courts Press, 2010), pp. 69–84. For Milman Parry, see Milman Parry, 'Studies in the Epic Technique of Oral Verse-Making. I: Homer and Homeric Style', *Harvard Studies in Classical Philology* 41 (1930), 73–143; idem, 'Studies in the Epic Technique of Oral Verse-Making. II: The Homeric Language as the Language of an Oral Poetry', *Harvard Studies in Classical Philology* 43 (1932), 1–50. For Albert Lord, see Albert B. Lord, *The Singer of Tales* (Cambridge, MA: Harvard University Press, 1960).

90 Julie Henigan, *Literacy and Orality in Eighteenth-Century Irish Song* (New York: Routledge, 2012); for an excellent incorporation of Jacobite ballads, see Éamonn Ó Ciardha, *Ireland and the Jacobite Cause, 1685–1766: A Fatal Attachment* (Dublin: Four Courts, 2004).

91 Anne O'Connor, *The Blessed and the Damned: Sinful Women and Unbaptised Children in Irish Folklore* (New York: Peter Lang. 2005).

92 Vincent Morley, *The Popular Mind in Eighteenth-Century Ireland* (Cork: Cork University Press, 2017), pp. 1–8. See also Patrick Walsh, 'Daniel Corkery's *The Hidden Ireland* and Revisionism', *New Hibernia Review* 5 (2) (2001), 27–44.

93 Michel-Rolph Trouillot, *Silencing the Past: Power and the Production of History* (Boston, MA: Beacon Press, 1995); Raphael Samuel, *Theatres of Memory: Past and Present in Contemporary Culture* (London: Verso, 2012), p. 6.

14 'Barbarisme and obdurate wilfulnesse'

Agricultural materialism, animal welfare, and Irish studies[1]

Willy Maley

Opening the field

In dialogue with Joep Leerssen, Guy Beiner claimed that *The New History of Ireland* marginalized antiquarian and folklorist studies.[2] Beiner was building on previous comments about the 'professionalization of Irish history' being 'grounded in the debunking of popular "mythology"', with the effect that a crucial dimension, oral tradition, was downplayed or dismissed.[3] Scholars also ignore or underplay evidence relating to practices and pastimes, deeming it amateurish, nationalistic, or subjective.[4] In what follows, I take one agricultural custom in Ireland—'ploughing by the tail'—and survey responses by anthropologists, antiquarians, archaeologists, ethnologists, geographers, historians, and creative writers. Uncovering fault lines in early modern Irish history, extending forward through the centuries, and working at the intersection of different fields of study, I focus on how critics—polemicists, historians of the seventeenth-century, experts in Animal Studies, scholars of husbandry—responded to a farming method condemned by colonists, but understandable in the context of contemporary animal welfare, animal warfare, and agricultural history in Ireland. In tracing this practice—background, prohibition, afterlife—I harness multiple cross-disciplinary responses, including what I call 'agricultural materialism', pushing beyond colonial ideology toward an understanding of environmental factors in the broadest sense. In this particular case I aim to show that an Irish agricultural practice condemned as barbaric had its roots not only in a resourceful response to a culture of conflict and economic hardship, nor merely in an act of resistance to colonial power, but in a workable and workaday solution to the challenges of rough terrain and farm animals limited in the weight they could bear.

Cultural materialism has two strands, one from American anthropologist Marvin Harris—who coined the term—and the other from Welsh Marxist Raymond Williams. Both drew on historical materialism, developed by Engels out of Marx's materialist conception of history. For Harris, 'cultural materialism ... directs attention to the interaction between behaviour and environment as mediated by the human organism and its cultural apparatus'.[5] Crucially, this approach 'opposes numerous strategies that set forth from words, ideas, high moral values, and aesthetic and religious beliefs to understand the everyday events of ordinary human life' by, among other things, looking at 'ecological variables'.[6] For Williams, it is 'a theory of the specificities of material cultural and literary production within historical materialism'.[7] Famously, for Marx and Engels, humans 'distinguish themselves from animals as soon as they begin to *produce* their means of subsistence'.[8] Agricultural materialism foregrounds the part played by animals in social transformation, interrogates the problematic separation of humans into productive and unproductive categories within colonial discourse, and charts the representation of farming practices across periods and borders.

I first used the term 'agricultural materialism' to refer to material aspects of 'planting' in reviewing a book on Edmund Spenser's pastoralism.[9] My purpose here is to challenge colonial moralizing by homing in on criticism cognizant of the material culture of farming practices and the relevant environmental factors facing early modern natives (and settlers). In doing so, I offer here a brief, preliminary and impressionistic survey that present and future scholars may pursue and apply to other colonialist and cultural images, in this case utilizing but also extending the field of Animal Studies, which thrives in early modern scholarship though not yet fully in Ireland, and which has not always been alert to the hypocrisy of humanitarian claims in a colonial context. Part of a larger project, this essay will chart the practice's progress beyond legal and historical debate, tracking its literary impact through early modern playwrights, Romantic novelists, and contemporary poets.

The path to prohibition

In 1634, Thomas Wentworth, lord deputy of Ireland, 'gave Order unto his Majesty's learned Counsel ... for restraining the barbarous Custom[] of Plowing by the Tail'—reference to a practice in which a short plow was attached to the horse's tail.[10] Wentworth's act is considered the earliest animal welfare legislation in the English-speaking world, and Piers Beirne has plotted its impact in immense detail.[11] William Brereton's 1635 visit to Dublin Castle suggests that Wentworth's own concern for horses was thoroughgoing, with the Lord Deputy having 'erected a gallant stately stable as any I have seen in the King's dominions; it is a double stable, there being a strong wall in the middle, to either side, whereof stand the horses' heads'.[12] The context is complex, however. The legislative background suggests this was more about colonial exploitation than humane practice.[13] For example, we can trace Wentworth's legislation from a 1606 Act of Council,[14] with William Pinkerton, in an essay in the *Ulster Journal of Archaeology*, reminding us that Wentworth's act began as Jacobean policy. Even so, James I alluded in 1620 to ploughing by the tail as a 'barbarous custome commonly used in the Northerne parts'.[15]

Earlier English writers had also denounced the practice. Barnaby Rich listed 'loathsome observations ... used by the Irish ... but especially in the ploughing of their land … every horse by his owne taile'.[16] According to Fynes Moryson, the Irish 'draw carts and like things … by a withe to the tails of their horses, and to the rumps when the tails be pulled off, which had been forbidden by laws, yet could never be altered'.[17] The practice also generated outrage, since shorn of its local meaning and function, the practice could be held up as proof of the barbarity typical of a backward society. Settlers were required instead to plough in the English manner using a harness.[18] Even so, Pilib Ó Mórdha notes that Hugh O'Reilly, granted land in Cavan, continued the practice and violated the conditions of the Articles of Plantation, having 'made no estates but from year to year, and all his tenants do plough by the tail'.[19] As a result, financial gain and cultural improvement could often go hand in hand, as outlawing ploughing by the tail also generated income through fines.

This injunction, as we shall see, did not take into account the lighter breed of Irish horses. Whereas in England heavier horses bred for warfare had found their way into farming, in Ireland smaller steeds were common. John Langdon suggested England's 'selective breeding programmes to produce large horses for warfare … perhaps … rubbed off onto agricultural horses'.[20] According to Edward Wentworth, 'types suitable as chargers, chariot animals, and bearers of armor were identified long before those desirable for saddle transportation, cartage, plow, and racing were set apart'.[21] Thomas Blundeville, on the other hand, admired the Irish horses' slightness, which also held different implications for ploughing: 'The Iryshe Hobby is a pretye fyne horse', he wrote.[22] Robert Payne also observed that 'Their chiefe horsses are of as great price as in England, but carthorsses mares, and little hackneyes are of very small price'.[23] Gervase Markham, on the other hand, censured Ireland's loose horse husbandry: 'That your Mares which you preserue for your studd should runne wilde and vntamed, as I haue seene them doe in … *Ireland* … I vtterly dislike … such wildnesse indangers them as oft as they are driuen … from ground to ground'.[24]

Native protests that the practice was commensurate with the quality of Irish soil fell on deaf ears. The 1613 commission of inquiry into the state of Ireland declared: 'Although divers of the natives pretend a necessity to continue the said manner of ploughing, as more fit for stony and mountainous ground, yet we are of opinion it is not fit to be continued'.[25] William Lithgow's 1619 sojourn decried as perverse 'Ploughes drawne by Horse-tayles, wanting harnesse', and 'onely fastned with straw, or wooden Ropes to their bare Rumps, marching all side for side, three or foure in a ranke, and as many men hanging by the ends of that untoward Labour'. It was 'as bad a husbandry … as ever I found among the wildest Savages alive', especially since 'the *Irish* have thousands of both Kingdomes daily labouring beside them, yet … will not learne to use harnesse, as they doe in *England*, so obstinate and perverse they are in their Barbarous consuetude'. Despite these injunctions, couched in a familiar colonialist metaphor, and while 'punishment and penalties were inflicted', most husbandmen, again, were 'content to pay twenty shillings a yeare, before they will change their custome'.[26] Opposition to Wentworth's act was also swift.[27] Its repeal appeared as item four among 'Additional Propositions' by Confederate Catholics in 1644, and as item nineteen of thirty articles of peace drawn up by Ormond in 1646.[28]

In the most quoted passage of *Observations upon the articles of peace made with the Irish Rebels* (1649), John Milton responded to the legislation which sought to repeal Wentworth's act against ploughing by the tail, characterizing this custom as 'more ridiculous then dangerous'. For Milton, the practice proved the Irish were

> averse from all Civility and amendment ... who rejecting the ingenuity of all other Nations to improve and waxe more civill by a civilizing Conquest, though all these many yeares better shown and taught, [preferred] their own absurd and savage Customes before the most convincing evidence of reason and demonstration: a testimony of their true Barbarisme and obdurate wilfulnesse to be expected no lesse in other matters of greatest moment.[29]

Most Milton scholars, confronted with this passage, only scratch the surface. Merritt Hughes is an exception. For Hughes, Wentworth's act reflected English self-interest: 'the famous Twenty-second Article ... [asserted] Parliament's authority over popular mores and economics at points where English civilizing pretensions in Ireland had long been sorely challenged'.[30] 'Thomas Corns argues that Milton deftly plays upon what he assumes to be his readers' sense of national superiority' by asserting that 'Such a practice, besides being cruel (not a point Milton makes), could be perceived as evidence of primitivism' since 'who but a savage couldn't manufacture a functional collar, especially after he'd seen one being used? And proof, too, of idiocy: who but a fool would ruin a good horse by mistreating it in this way?'[31] Corns blithely endorses the view of the practice as barbaric, unnecessary, and harmful to horses. Joad Raymond, on the other hand, seeks to rationalize Milton's statement when he argues that 'Milton professed shock not only at the savagery of a culture that ... attached a plough to a horse's tail, but at the stupidity of a people that continued to do so even after having had demonstrated to them the principle of the neck collar'. For Raymond, however, 'Though this passage has been read as a literal expression of Milton's personal hatred of the Irish and a call for their extirpation, Milton was objecting instead to the repeal of Caroline, not republican policy, and the only one of its kind in the Articles ... wrested from Charles's representative in return for military support'. Indeed, 'Despite the name-calling, Milton remained relatively unexercised on the Irish, as if their shortcomings could be left unsaid'.[32]

Except that they were not left 'unsaid'. Milton's anti-Irish sentiments go back to 1641, when he railed against 'these murdrous Irish the enemies of God and mankind, a cursed off-spring'.[33] Piers Beirne's groundbreaking essay tamely accepts Raymond's claim that '[t]hat Milton would not have supported Cromwell's slaughter of the Irish' either.[34] But in fact, Milton once cried out for 'Justice to avenge the dead' and exaggerated the 1641 victims beyond any contemporary, accusing the Irish of shedding 'the bloud of more then 200000 ... Subjects'.[35] This related to ploughing-by-the-tail, according to Karen Edwards, who writes of Milton's attack on Article 22 that 'the vehemence with which [he] ... condemns the practice suggests ... he regards it as another Irish "crime"'.[36]

Other seventeenth-century writers also protested the custom. Richard Bolton included the practice under 'abuses and enormities tending to ... prejudice of the Common-wealth'.[37] Thomas Waring considered the natives 'meerly a kind of *Reptilia*, things creeping on their bellies, and feeding on the dust of the earth'. Waring's comment on Article 22—'O ridiculous indulgence and servill compliances'—confirms his dehumanizing rhetoric.[38] Meanwhile, the practice continued. In a convoluted passage in his *Essay upon the advancement of trade in Ireland* (1673), William Temple—son of Sir John, author of *The Irish Rebellion* (1646), the theory to which Drogheda was the practice—demonstrated how proscription of this practice could turn a handsome profit for the crown as 'Statutes against that barbarous custom of Plowing by the tayl, ought to be renewed', and 'a Tax might be laid upon every Horse of draught throughout the Kingdom, which ... would encrease the Kings Revenue by one of the easiest ways that is any where in use'.[39]

David Norbrook, observing that English republicans such as Milton 'tended to find in Ireland the epitome of everything that was backward', cites an earlier letter from Sir Cheney Culpeper to Samuel Hartlib on 17 February 1646, which states that 'I see in the generalitie of mens dispositions ... an analogicall Irishe humor which nothing but an acte of [parliament] can break from drawinge by the horses tayle'. The practice thus becomes a metaphor for stubbornness or 'obdurate wilfulnesse'.[40] But the Hartlib Circle's angle on husbandry is more complex. 'A Large letter concerning the Defects and Remedies of English Husbandry' prefixed to *Samuel Hartlib his legacie* (1651), sometimes attributed to Robert Child, pleads for a new invention to '*facilitate* the going of the *Plough* and lighten our ordinary *Carriages*'.[41] The author laments the variety of methods used for ploughing in 'every *Countrey*, yea almost every *County*', in the absence of any standardized technique:

> Some with wheels, others without; some turning the *Rest* (as they call it) as in *Kent*, *Picardy* and *Normandy*), others not; some having *Coulters* of one fashion, others of another; others as the *Dutch*, having an Iron wheele or circle for that purpose; some having their *sheares* broad at point; some not; some being round, as in *Kent*, others flat; some tying their horses by the taile, as in *Ireland*.[42]

Here, the sense of what is progressive is unclear, and the note of condemnation directed specifically at Ireland is absent. But characteristic of the Hartlib Circle is the strenuous pursuit of standardization and the frustration with national and regional differences.

Tailgate

Later antiquarians picked up on the custom and varied their denunciations and descriptions. These writers were visitors and scholars rather than settlers and investors, which afforded a degree of detachment. English antiquarian Thomas Dineley is a case in point. Better known for his reflections on Wales, Dineley's 1680 tour of Ireland remarks of the barony of Burren, County Clare:

> Here Horses 4 abrest draw the Plough by the Tayles, which was the custome all over Ireland, untill a Statute forbad it. Yett they are tollerated this custome here because they cannot mannage their land otherwise, their Plough Geers, tackle, and traces being [...] of Gadds or withs of twiggs twisted, which here would break to pieces by the Plough Share so often jubbing against the Rock, which, the Geers being fastened by wattles or wispes the horses being sensible stop untill the Plowman lifts it over.[43]

Dineley's eye for detail and eagerness to interpret rather than condemn goes against the grain of earlier commentators. Indeed, the nineteenth-century note on this passage by Robert O'Brien concludes:

> It is curious that ... in the treaty of March 25, 1646, between the Supreme Council of the Confederates and Lord Ormond, it was provided that ... prohibiting ploughing by the horses' tails ... should be repealed, proving what a hold these customs had taken, when such great issues were at stake at that moment.[44]

The great issues at stake included ploughing by the tail, a key locus of cultural and economic contestation, since that particular practice was bound up with land use and land ownership at the heart of the Anglo-Irish conflict in the period. As Toby Barnard has remarked: 'Since by the end of the seventeenth century what was at stake for the Catholic Irish ... was whether they were to own lands at all, the niceties about how they should be laid out and cultivated looked crassly inappropriate. The English might garden while the Irish starved'.[45]

Horses had long been a vital resource whose value went beyond husbandry, and in Ireland they assumed a special symbolism. According to Maria Pramaggiore, 'The horse ... served as a metaphor for validating and renegotiating Irish identities from the middle ages ... to late twentieth-century popular culture'.[46] Ulf Dantanus insists on the particularity of equine Ireland and its impact on literature.[47] Seizure of horses for military purposes was also common. Gavin Robinson's study of the part played by horses in the conflicts of the mid-seventeenth century makes this point clear: 'As the wars continued, horses were increasingly taken from anyone who had them'.[48]

Long after large-scale seizure of horses in England had ceased, the practice persisted in Ireland, with the Lord Lieutenant in 1715 ordering justices of the peace 'to seize and take all serviceable horses, geldings and mares ... found in the possession of any papist'.[49]

Historians in general often fail to provide context for Irish customs, accepting at face value the claims of colonial commentators. In *The Siege of Derry*, for example, Patrick Macrory writes:

> arable farming [...] was carried on by methods which seemed primitive by English standards. There were no enclosed fields and the Irish, to the horrified indignation of the English, 'ploughed by the tail'.[50]

Here there is no recognition of the fact that Irish land is being confiscated on the pretext of agricultural improvement while the natives are being forced onto stony ground and hunted down in a manner that made mobile and fluid farming methods essential. The 'horrified indignation' invoked by Macrory seldom extended to the harrowing treatment of humans.

Restoration horseplay

Inevitably, creative writers found in the practice of ploughing by the tail a rich metaphorical resource. J.O. Bartley's celebrated study of dramatic depictions of Celtic figures, however, asserts that 'the Irish practice of attaching the plough to the horse's tail ... is not mentioned in drama before *Love and a Bottle*'.[51] Bartley's allusion is to an exchange in George Farquhar's Restoration comedy between Pamphlet the bookseller and Lyric the poet:

> Faith, I have often wonder'd how your Muse cou'd take such flights, yoak'd to such a Cartload as she is.
> Oh, they are like the Irish Horses, they draw best by the Tail.[52]

Bartley refers in the same passage to John Michelborne's play about the Siege of Derry, *Ireland Preserved*, where Irish colonel Sir Neil defiantly declares:

> Your English customs shall no more prevail,
> And Gads instead of Ropes do never fail,
> Our horses shall again plow by the tail.[53]

Horses appeared onstage, as themselves and as metaphors.[54] Horse racing was, like theater, also associated with nefarious activities, and periodically outlawed,[55] even though Cromwell's own ban on horse racing in Ireland was disregarded.[56] Unsurprisingly, an Irish dramatist penned 'the first racing play on record'. While providing entertainment for Wentworth at the St. Werburgh Street Theatre in Dublin in the late 1630s, James Shirley published his 1632 London horse racing comedy, *Hide Parke*, featuring a race between English and Irish footmen.[57] In *A strange horse-race* (1613), Thomas Dekker offers an aside on the Irish reputation for being fleet-footed: 'I thinke the wilde Irish are best at it in these latter times'.[58] According to Kevin De Ornellas, 'Tropings of the horse in early modern culture ... nearly always engage with human society'. But never mind 'horse-based metaphors' and 'equine allusions', which deserve much more extensive study—what about actual horses?[59]

Animal historians

One could begin with what animal historians make of ploughing by the tail. For many, links between empire and animal welfare are bound up with competing colonial discourses of cruelty and concern. As Kathryn Shevelow remarks in *For the Love of Animals*, 'Protestant landowners despised their tenant farmers as savages – or as animals'. Linda Kalof, on the other hand, sees the 1635 act as part of 'the new sentimentality toward animals'.[60] Other experts in the field discern expropriation and dehumanization of native communities based on human warfare rather than animal welfare.[61] Colonialism and religion also combined to produce a discourse specific to planter communities. As Robert Watson observes, 'the legal history of animal protection suggests a strong Protestant tendency'. Robert Boyle, for example, 'performed animal dissection from the late 1640s when he was barely twenty years old', yet 'gratuitous suffering of animals was, in Boyle's understanding, a blasphemy'.[62]

For Keith Thomas, 'The same element of self-interest runs through all the legislation against animal cruelty ... And it underlay attempts in the same period to prohibit the Irish practice of yoking horses to the plough by their tails'. Thomas also puts English concern in context: 'England was proverbially a hell for horses and ... many were literally ridden to death'.[63] Clearly, England was not a nation of animal lovers either. According to Piers Beirne, Wentworth's act itself 'had little or nothing to do with its self-stated intent to protect horses from cruelty and was, instead, much more connected with the dominance of English nationalism and culture and the pursuit of private profit'.[64] Beirne thus reminds us that 'the object of anti-cruelty legislation is not always the welfare of animals', and suggests Wentworth's act 'was one small weapon among many forcefully used by the English to impose their cultural norms (on animal husbandry, on the ideal war horse, on efficient horse furniture and so on) and their search for economic profit, extirpating the backward customs of the barbaric Irish'.[65] 'Against old-fashioned teleological and Whiggish accounts of the history of anti-cruelty legislation', Beirne sees 'an urgent need ... for new ... postcolonial histories of anti-cruelty legislation from the late eighteenth century to the present'.[66] In an Irish context—a colonial context—it is therefore vital to view attitudes to animals alongside attitudes to natives since not only can concern for livestock sit comfortably with cruelty to human communities, but often customs condemned by colonists are decontextualized in order to be characterized as barbaric.

Romantic Ireland

Ploughing by the tail also surfaced in Irish fiction. In Lady Morgan's *The O'Briens and the O'Flahertys* (1827), Trinity College Dublin student Murrogh O'Brien receives a breathless letter from aunts Mable and Monica, 'The Miss Mac Taffes', who 'spelled as they spoke', urging him to come home and decrying 'them mushrooms and Williamites', who declare that 'it's a barbarous custom, ploughing, harrowing, and drawing horses, garans, and colts by the tail, after th' ould Connaught fashion … whereby … the breed of horses is impoverished in the county, and such like talk; as if none ever ploughed, till the new undertakers of Moycullen came among us'.[67] According to Helen O'Connell, Morgan also 'associates "the barbarous custom" … with backward agriculture and the consequent development of "impoverished" breeds of Irish horses', but the novel's treatment of the practice is more subtle because it ties the attack on Irish customs to plantation and expropriation, and the wording of Wentworth's act is invoked for the purposes of mockery.[68] Likewise, in Maria Edgeworth's novel *Ormond* (1833), Sir Ulick O'Shane commends his cousin Cornelius on 'the economy of your ploughing tackle' before adding, 'Tis a pity you don't continue the old Irish style of ploughing by the tail', to which 'Corny' replies, 'That is against humanity to brute *bastes*, which, without any sickening palaver of sentiment, I practise. Also, it's against an act of parliament … which, the way you parliament gentlemen draw them up, is not always particularly intelligible to plain common sense'.[69] Here, animal welfare is detached from 'any sickening palaver of sentiment' and from legislation worded to confound.

Enlightenment and after

Eighteenth- and nineteenth-century perspectives accompanied developments in antiquarianism, husbandry, and travel writing, but these developments were not necessarily advances, for while some scholars and visitors adopted a neutral tone, others simply regurgitated the colonial prejudice. In *A Tour of Ireland* (1780), agricultural reformer Arthur Young foregrounded the practice as a perennial feature of the Irish landscape:

> Here let it be remarked, that *they very commonly plough and harrow with their horses* DRAWING BY THE TAIL: it is done every season. Nothing can put them beside this, and they insist that, take a horse tired in traces, and put him to work by the tail, he will draw better: quite fresh again. Indignant reader! this is no jest of mine, but cruel, stubborn, barbarous truth. It is so all over Cavan.[70]

Young's terms—'cruel, stubborn, barbarous'—exemplify the high-handed moral attitude to the ploughing by the tail. This went hand in hand with an approach more neutral in tone that stressed the antiquity of the practice. In *The Antiquities of Ireland* (1804) Edward Ledwich observes:

> Our manner of plowing Cambrensis does not describe; it certainly was by the tail, and is as yet practised in remote parts .... Probably the custom was introduced by the Picts, for it prevails in the Northern parts of Scotland.[71]

This not only reflects the urge at the time to search for origins, but also the recognition of common geological terrain in the north of Ireland and Scotland.

But the charge of barbarism persisted. Looking back on Wentworth's 1635 Act, Thomas Dunham Whitaker offers a footnote: 'the whole enumeration proves that the common people must have been cruel, mischievous, and filthy in the highest degree'.[72] Thomas Wood calls it a law 'enacted ... for the civilization of the Irish ... such as would be naturally expected for the improvement of any barbarous country'.[73] John Barrow's travelogue of 1836 declares that 'travelling in Ireland has no doubt wonderfully improved of late years' as he expressed relief that the 'horrid practice of ploughing by the tail' has passed into history. Reviewing Barrow's book, Tim Bobbin mocks this passage: 'We certainly should feel much obliged to our author for thus making known our improvements in travelling, as well as our advancement in civilization'.[74] Rather than concurring with Barrow that progress has been achieved, this sarcastic comment by Bobbin takes aim at the patronizing tone of a man whose *Dictionary of National Biography* entry describes him as '[a]n ardent imperialist'.

John Stuart Mill's 1838 critique of Jeremy Bentham invoked the act as emblematic of piecemeal reform in legal history. While this, of course, reflects a very nineteenth-century historical and legal context, at the same time that it continues the rhetoric of John Davies (law as civilizing), the trope served Mill's present-day purposes and drew on a geological metaphor—'irregularity of strata'—relevant to the agricultural practice invoked:

> In the English law ... the adaptations of barbarous laws to the growth of civilised society were made chiefly by stealth .... The result of this mode of improving social institutions was ... the laws were improved with much the same effect as if, in the improvement of agriculture ... the primeval practice of ploughing by the horse's tail gave way to the innovation of harness, the tail, for form's sake, had still remained attached to the plough.[75]

Piers Beirne cites an earlier instance of Mill's use of the practice in a speech at the London Debating Society. There, Mill declares: 'The Irish, who had always been in the habit of tying the plough to the horse's tail, regarded the very idea of employing harness with horror'.[76]

Caesar Otway, on the other hand, spoke archly of 'the custom of making horses draw by the tail, which certainly is not only ancient but economical, for it saves all manner of tackle, except the hair of the animal'.[77] The implication here is that poverty underpins the practice, reflecting a kind of utilitarianism, but this remark refuses to engage with the colonial context of insecure land tenure, the light breed of horses, or the obdurate nature of the soil. The practice had a prehistory that also engaged agriculturally-minded writers. John Langdon mentions 'A possible example of a horse ploughing by the tail in prehistoric Sweden (i.e., from a rock carving)'.[78] James Allen Ransome himself declared that 'our Saxon forefathers were wont to fasten their horses to the plough by the tail; a barbarous custom ... formerly practised in Ireland to such an extent that the legislature in 1634 found it necessary to interfere'.[79] Picking up on Ransome, Sarah Tomlinson rehearses primitive ploughing methods in other countries, claiming the English method owes its civility to the Romans, whose taxes spurred economic improvement, providing a great advertisement for colonialism.[80]

George Nicholls, in *A History of the Irish Poor Law* (1856), offers a nuanced reading of the legislation. His position as commissioner influences his words, which serve the purpose of providing a brief contextual grounding for the practice in which objective analysis or the laying out of possible reasons supplants moralizing, ridicule, and abuse:

> These Acts certainly indicate ... rude and barbarous practices in some parts of Ireland – so rude ... one finds some difficulty in giving credence to them; ... but how far this backwardness was owing to 'a natural lazie disposition' in the Irish tenantry, or whether it was the 'better to enable them to be flitting from their lands to deceive their landlords of their rents' ... or occasioned by the oppressive conduct of the landlords ... is impossible to say ... Most likely all these causes were in operation.[81]

John O'Donovan, on the other hand, is one commentator who 'finds some difficulty in giving credence' to the custom:

> What 'ploughing by the tail' actually means, none of our writers have as yet cleared up.... I hold it impossible that they could drag the plough through the land, if yoked to their tails only ... but the subject has not received that degree of historic and scientific investigation which it deserves.[82]

O'Donovan set great store by the 'historic and scientific' and their application to Ireland's customs and past. Here, rather than investigate the grounds of the practice, O'Donovan invokes scientific proof as a challenge to its very existence.

Antiquarian notes and queries

O'Donovan's skepticism was shared. A one-line query in the *Ulster Journal of Archaeology* in 1855—'Is it the fact that at one period the Ulster Irish, in ploughing, fastened the plough to the horse's tail?'[83]—elicited a flurry of responses, including this enlightening answer:

> There is no doubt that this was at one time actually a common practice in Ireland; but ploughing, in those days, was a very different thing from what it is now. The old plough was a slightly made wooden implement, with a stone plough-share, and only calculated to scratch the surface of the ground.[84]

This last remark reflects emerging archaeological knowledge. The *Ulster Journal of Archaeology*, founded in 1853, was at the leading edge, with excavation reports and a materially evidenced approach to antiquarianism. Even so, another respondent observed:

> In 1642, Sir George Hamilton, ancestor to the Marquis of Abercorn, had a grant for life of all the penalties accruing to the Crown under this act. Did the Merry Monarch intend this as a joke? or is it possible that the penalties under the act in question could have been of any considerable value?[85]

We know such fines were fruitful.[86] But the incredulity here feels forced, and fits with efforts to ridicule rather than look for reasons. A later respondent, 'Cuthbert Bede' (pseudonym of English novelist Edward Bradley), takes a more historicist approach, suggesting that horsehair extensions were crucial to the practice:

> Harrowing, if not ploughing, by the horse's tail was practised at a more recent date than 1649, both in Ireland and in the Scottish Highlands. This, at any rate, is the testimony of Capt. Burt in 1754, and since then of the author of *Paddiana*, and also of Lord George Hill, in his *Facts from Gweedore*. The horse's tail would seem to have been tied to the harrow without the further aid of harness or ropes; and when the tail had become too much docked for the work, it was artificially lengthened by twisted sticks.[87]

Here one sees the coming together of strands of agricultural, antiquarian, and historicist approaches, but the tendency to hark back to unexamined colonial condemnation proved hard to shake off. Other commentators cited the relevant article of peace from 1649, which 'drew forth from Milton a severe remark', referencing the poet's observation, or noted the practice's persistence in mid-nineteenth-century Cavan.[88] J.R. Haig offered a comparative perspective:

> In Caithness and Sutherland ... they always ploughed by attaching the plough, a wooden one-stilted thing, to the horse's tail. Ropes were made of twisted rushes which, though they did not last long, were cheap.[89]

This adds economy and improvisation to geology and breed of horse as a way of rationalizing the practice.

Later critics picked up on Dineley's identification of stony soil as key to the practice, sometimes entwined with an acknowledgment that straitened circumstances played a part too. Michael Duignan, in his study of 'Irish Agriculture in Early Historic Times', links the Irish breed of light horses to the practice of harrowing without harness in a way that suggests that ploughing in the English manner would have been the crueler custom:

> the Irish horse of the period was a very light animal indeed, no bigger than a pony of the Connemara or Antrim type ... horses could not profitably be harnessed to a plough prior to the adoption of the stiff horse-collar which rests on the shoulders. [...] The older type of collar ... was of soft leather and worn in such a way that it pressed on the trachean artery and hindered the horse's breathing.... Incidentally we may have here the ultimate explanation of the alleged Irish custom of ploughing by the horse's tail.[90]

Here we are back here with Blundeville, Payne, and Markham and the recognition of the lightness of Irish horses. Writing in 1955, Bernard O'Daly commented:

> The practice was defended by its advocates on the ground that, to avoid hurting themselves, the horses stopped instantly whenever the soc of the plough struck against anything solid. [...] In Ulster, at least, the people generally were too poor to buy either ploughs or harness, and took the view that ploughing was bad for the soil.[91]

Other observers, noting the custom's persistence in Ulster, neglected to dig deeper. Harold Masterson remarked: 'The English attempted to abolish this practice by imposing fines, but in Fermanagh it took them a century and a half to do so completely'.[92] Taking a cross-section, what we find in critical responses to ploughing by the tail is 'irregularity of strata'. Some seek to understand through scholarly excavation; others accept the 1635 act as fair and final judgment. While it would be tempting to see the persistence of ploughing by the tail as a form of obstinate cultural resistance or native stubbornness, the arguments of agriculturalists assure us that the practice had its advantages, suited as it was to the nature of the soil and the breed of horse.

From antiquarianism to ethnology

Within ethnology, ploughing by the tail has a vexed history.[93] Citing a 1943 essay in *The Irish Book Lover* by J.J. McAuliffe, E. Estyn Evans bemoaned Irish defensiveness:

> A striking example of Irish sensitivity and ingenuity is the denial, against all the evidence, that the practice ever existed ... that the English invented this Irish vice and that the sole purpose of the laws passed against

it since the seventeenth century was to prove that it must have existed. In fact the custom was not so barbarous as might be thought.[94]

Evans seeks to replace denial, which he sees as bound up with nationalist narratives, with understanding. His point is that English representations of the practice as barbarous have prompted some Irish commentators to refute its existence, which paradoxically places them on the same side as those who condemn the practice as beyond the pale. Evans's own strategy is to understand more and condemn less.

Revisiting the topic in a subsequent defense of the continuing relevance of 'human geography, ethnology, and social anthropology' to Irish history, Evans neither flinched from exacting scrutiny nor accepted the colonial context as the whole story: 'It is fatally easy to blame the poverty of folk artifacts on landlordism, and to scorn them instead of describing them'. Interestingly, using the ploughing-tail as part of a revisionist debate shows the flexibility of the trope toward different polemical purposes. Evans' revisionist agenda entails a corrective approach to Irish nationalist historiography: 'Some patriotic Irish writers have denied that it was ever practised, just as they have hotly denied the well-known marital infidelities of some of their political heroes'.

These patriotic writers, Evans wryly notes, not only deny the practice but maintain that 'the English also invented the Gaelic term for it'. Evans insists that 'it is also clear from the early literature that horses were occasionally used in pre-Norman Ireland, and if the implements they pulled were light the tail would have been the most efficient and even perhaps the most humane form of traction'. Such a practice was 'simple and capable of only scratching the surface'. Evans argues that 'while poverty provides the easiest explanation, there were probably practical advantages and possibly – in the beginning – ritual reasons for a practice that should be regarded as a cultural phenomenon rather than as a mark of disgrace, something to be forgotten or even denied'. He concludes, 'So late as 1938, in Donegal, I spoke to a man who told me that the tail was secured by a difficult knot which in his youth only a few men knew'.

In a note tucked away at the back of his essay, Evans adds something germane to this whole debate:

> One explanation … is that in glacial soils where the plough might strike a hidden boulder, the tail-tied horse would immediately stop if this happened, whereas plough, horse and ploughman might suffer harm if the horse had no such immediate warning. Cultural as well as political opposition to the English planters may be seen in the complaints of their Irish tenants in the early seventeenth century that they did not like their animals 'loaded by English horse-collars.[95]

Again, here is the claim that the aversion to English horse collars was based on the light breed of Irish horses, unsuitable to heavy harnesses.

Social anthropologist May McCann, reviewing *Folk and Farm*, in which Evans' essay appeared, commented: 'The example of ploughing by the tail must be viewed in the light of the wider problem of the slow acceptance of ... folk life studies in Ireland by scholars and others whose attitudes ... led people to prefer to believe that the Irish did not employ this technique of ploughing because it seemed degrading and a slight on the Irish nation'.[96] Likewise, anthropologist Eugenia Shanklin, reflecting on Evans's intervention, remarks, 'This kind of reasoning is the quintessence of Irish thinking about tradition'.[97]

Locking horns with Nicholas Canny's landmark essay 'Migration and Opportunity', Raymond Gillespie also questioned 'the criteria used to measure comparative development': 'Ploughing by the tail ... was taken up by settlers in Ulster, not because they did not know any better, as Canny implies, but rather because it was a technique well suited to stony Ulster soil'.[98] The very ground itself is obdurate (*Oxford* English Dictionary: 'hardened'). Surveying Irish agricultural history, Cormac Ó Gráda was also bemused by Gillespie's rejection of 'the implicit claim that the immigrants had nothing to learn from native techniques, [with Gillespie] drawing attention to how Ulster planters copied the native method of ploughing by the tail'.[99] Ó Gráda's exclamation is disingenuous insofar as he has seen how Gillespie situates the practice but chooses merely to sensationalize it himself.

But Gillespie furnishes the relevant context, bound up with the environmental conditions—the soil—of Ireland. That factor, the environment, is also linked to the type of land that natives were compelled to farm and within a context of conflict. As Clodagh Tait recently remarked, 'decisions about the alteration of farming methods and the adoption of new crops such as potatoes were made by cottiers partly in response to troubled times'.[100] The relationship between political conflict and fluid farming practices was known in the seventeenth century. Gervase Markham recognized that special methods of tillage and storage were 'much in vse in Ireland and other Countries where warre rageth'.[101]

Brian Smith, in *The Horse in Ireland* (1991), also supports Gillespie's view: 'There were substantial reasons for ploughing ... in what was called by English writers "the Irish manner," since much of the country where the practice occurred was hilly and the ground stony'.[102] The earth's obduracy is countered by expert husbandry, and this aspect of ingenuity is captured beautifully in a poem by Michael Longley:

> Whoever plucks wool in thrifty skeins from his sheep [...]
> Is likely to do without a halter and reins
> And plough by the tail, if the hairs are strong enough
> And he has learned to tie the complicated knot.[103]

Paul Muldoon's poetic response, 'Hinge', presents Longley and himself as bards versed in local lore, 'never losing sight of what was meant/ by "ploughing by the tail", or the workings of some far-flung farm-implement'.[104]

Tailpiece

When William Hamilton Drummond, Larne-born Unitarian Minister and Honorary Member of the Belfast Natural History Society published *The Rights of Animals* (1838),[105] he chose an epigraph from *Paradise Lost*:

> Is not the earth
> With various living creatures, and the air
> Replenished, and all these at thy command
> To come and play before thee? Know'st thou not
> Their language and their ways? They also know
> And reason not contemptibly; with these
> Find pastime and bear rule; thy realm is large.
>
> *Paradise Lost*, viii. 369–75

The enslavement of animals for 'pastime and … rule' is in this way bound up with the enslavement of people. From Milton to Muldoon, ploughing by the tail is a practice that the topsoil of traditional scholarship serves to conceal. Horses remain crucial to Irish history.[106]

Notes

1 Work for this article was undertaken during a research fellowship from the Leverhulme Trust for which I am most grateful. I am also grateful to Thomas Herron and Colin Lahive for the opportunity to air these ideas in a plenary paper for 'Reading Ireland, 1500–1700: An Interdisciplinary Conference', Marsh's Library, Dublin, 31 May 2018.
2 Guy Beiner and Joep Leerssen, 'Why Irish History Starved? A Virtual Historiography', *Field Day Review* 3 (2007), 70–75.
3 Guy Beiner, 'Recycling the Dustbin of Irish History: The Radical Challenge of "folk memory,"' *History Ireland* 14 (1) (2006), 42–47. See also the essay in this volume by Sarah Covington.
4 The 2018 *Cambridge History of Ireland*, Volume 2, does include some folkloric material in Clodagh Tait's essay. See Clodagh Tait, 'Society, 1550–1700', in Jane Ohlmeyer (ed.), *The Cambridge History of Ireland. Vol. 2, 1550–1730* (Cambridge: Cambridge University Press, 2018).
5 Marvin Harris, *The Rise of Anthropological Theory: A History of Theories of Culture* (New York: Thomas Y. Crowell, 1968; updated edition, Walnut Creek, CA: Altamira Press, 2001), p. 659.
6 Marvin Harris, *Cultural Materialism: The Struggle for a Science of Culture* (New York: Random House, 1979; updated edition, Walnut Creek, CA: Altamira Press, 2001), pp. viii; xv.
7 Raymond Williams, *Marxism and Literature* (Oxford: Oxford University Press, 1977), p. 5.
8 Karl Marx and Frederick Engels, *The German Ideology*, ed. C.J. Arthur (London: Lawrence and Wishart, 1970), p. 42; emphasis in original.
9 Willy Maley, review of Richard Chamberlain, *Radical Spenser: Pastoral, Politics and the New Aestheticism* (Edinburgh: Edinburgh University Press, 2005), in *English Studies* 88 (6) (2007), 728.

10 William Knowler, ed., *The Earl of Strafforde's Letters and Dispatches: With an Essay towards His Life by Sir George Radcliffe*, vols. 2 (London: William Bowyer, 1739), vol. 1, p. 291.

11 Piers Beirne, 'Against Cruelty? Understanding the Act against Plowing by the Tayle (Ireland, 1635)', in *Confronting Animal Abuse: Law, Criminology, and Human-Animal Relationships* (Lanham, MD and Plymouth: Rowman & Littlefield Publishers, 2009), pp. 21–67.

12 R.J. Kelly, 'Dublin in 1635', *The Irish Monthly* 45 (1917), 301.

13 Pinkerton, pp. 212–13.

14 Evelyn Philip Shirley, Robert O'Brien, and James Graves, 'Extracts from the Journal of Thomas Dineley, Esquire, Giving Some Account of His Visit to Ireland in the Reign of Charles II (Continued)', *The Journal of the Kilkenny and South-East of Ireland Archaeological Society* 6 (1) (1867), 191–2, n. 24.

15 William Pinkerton, 'Ploughing by the Horse's Tail', *Ulster Journal of Archaeology* 1st series 6 (1858), 212–13. Pinkerton suggested the light plough fitted the task of gently turning the soil: 'As late as the beginning of the present century, the people of Cork believed that much or deep ploughing *weakened* the land; and even then they still carried out their old practice of sowing barley, oats, and wheat "under the plough", (as they termed it), that was, scattering the seed on the untilled ground prior to ploughing'. Idem, 220, emphasis in original. Pinkerton is the sole source mentioned by the most recent editors of Milton's *Observations*. N.H. Keeble and Nicholas McDowell (eds.), *Complete Works of John Milton Vol. VI: Vernacular Regicide and Republican Writings* (Oxford: Oxford University Press, Oxford, 2013), p. 212.

16 Barnaby Rich, *A New Description of Ireland* (London: William Jaggard, 1610), p. 26.

17 Cited in C. Litton Falkiner (ed.), *Illustrations of Irish History and Topography, Mainly of The Seventeenth Century* (London: Longmans, Green, & Co., 1904), p. 263.

18 Beirne, 'Against Cruelty?' p. 58, n. 32.

19 Pilib Ó Mórdha, 'The Mac Mahons of Monaghan (1603–1640)', *Clogher Record* 2 (1) (1957), p. 163.

20 John Langdon, *Horses, Oxen and Technological Innovation: The Use of Draught Animals in English Farming from 1066 to 1500* (Cambridge: Cambridge University Press, 1986), p. 19.

21 Edward N. Wentworth, 'A Livestock Specialist Looks at Agricultural History', *Agricultural History* 25 (2) (1951), 52.

22 Thomas Blundeville, *The fower chiefyst offices belongyng to horsemanshippe* (London: William Seres, 1566), Di^v–Dii^r.

23 Robert Payne, *A Briefe Description of Ireland* (London: Thomas Dawson, 1589), p. 10.

24 Gervase Markham, *Cauelarice, or The English Horseman* (London: Edward Allde and W. Jaggard, 1607), p. 30.

25 Shirley, O'Brien and Graves, pp. 191–2, n. 24.

26 William Lithgow, *The Totall Discourse, of the Rare Adventures, and Painefull Peregrinations* (London: John Okes, 1640), p. 436.

27 W.N. Osborough, 'The Irish Custom of Tracts', *Irish Jurist* 32 (1997), 453.

28 *The Propositions of the Roman Catholicks of Ireland* (Waterford: Thomas Bourke, 1644); George Digby, Earl of Bristol, *Two Remarkable Letters Concerning the Kings Correspondence with the Irish Rebels* (London: Francis Neile, 1645), p. 10 [mispaginated as 8]); James Butler, Marquess of Ormond, *The Last Articles of Peace Made, Concluded, Accorded, and Agreed Upon the 30 Day of July, 1646* (London: Edward Husband, 1646), p. 15.

29 John Milton, *Articles of Peace Made and Concluded with the Irish Rebels … Upon All Which Are Added Observations* (London: Matthew Simmons, 1649), p. 47.

30 Merritt Y. Hughes, 'The Historical Setting of Milton's *Observations on the Articles of Peace*', *Proceedings of the Modern Language Association* 64 (5) (1949), 1051–52, n. 6.

31 Thomas N. Corns, 'Milton's *Observations Upon the Articles of Peace*: Ireland Under English Eyes', in David Loewenstein and James Grantham Turner (eds.), *Politics, Poetics, and Hermeneutics in Milton's Prose* (Cambridge: Cambridge University Press, 1990), pp. 125–26.

32 Joad Raymond, 'Complications of Interest: Milton, Scotland, Ireland, and National Identity in 1649', *Review of English Studies* 55 (220) (2004), 319–20.

33 John Milton, *The Reason of Church-Government Urg'd against Prelaty* (London: John Rothwell, 1641), p. 31.

34 Beirne, 'Against Cruelty?' p. 66, n. 127.

35 Milton, *Articles of Peace Made and Concluded*, p. 49.

36 Karen Edwards, 'Horse', in 'Milton's Reformed Animals: An Early Modern Bestiary H-K', *Milton Quarterly* 41 (2) (2007), 79–129, at 108.

37 Richard Bolton, *A Justice of Peace for Ireland* (Dublin: Society of Stationers, 1638), p. 21.

38 Thomas Waring, *A Brief Narration of the Plotting, Beginning & Carrying On of That Execrable Rebellion and Butcherie in Ireland* (London: Bernard Alsop and Thomas Dunster, 1650), pp. 41–42, 60.

39 William Temple, *An Essay Upon the Advancement of Trade in Ireland* [Dublin?: s.n., 1673?], pp. 18–19.

40 David Norbrook, *Writing and the English Republic: Poetry, Rhetoric, and Politics, 1627–1660* (Cambridge: Cambridge University Press, 1998), p. 246.

41 Samuel Hartlib, *Samuel Hartlib His Legacie* (London: Henry Hills, 1651), p. 5.

42 Ibid., pp. 4–5. In 1652, Peter Heylyn, discussing Samogitia (now part of Lithuania), spoke of 'An humour like that of the present *Irish* in ploughing with their *Horses tayles* … So pertinacious for the most part are ignorant and superstitious people in standing to their antient customes, though absurd and hurtfull'. Peter Heylyn, *Cosmographie in Four Books* (London: Henry Seile, 1652), p. 169.

43 Shirley, O'Brien and Graves, pp. 191–92.

44 Ibid., pp. 191–92, n. 24.

45 T.C. Barnard, 'Gardening, Diet and "Improvement" in Later Seventeenth-Century Ireland', *The Journal of Garden History* 101 (1990), 71.

46 Maria Pramaggiore, 'The Celtic Tiger's Equine Imaginary', in Kathryn Kirkpatrick and Borbála Faragó (eds.), *Animals in Irish Literature and Culture* (Basingstoke: Palgrave Macmillan, 2015), p. 214.

47 Ulf Dantanus, 'Equus and Eloquence: The Irish Horse as Transcendent Symbol', in Alison O'Malley-Younger and John Strachan (eds.), *Ireland at War and Peace* (Newcastle upon Tyne: Cambridge Scholars Publishing, 2011), p. 168.

48 Gavin Robinson, *Horses, People and Parliament in the English Civil War: Extracting Resources and Constructing Allegiance* (Farnham: Ashgate Publishing Limited, 2012), p. 117.

49 Dantanus, 'Equus and Eloquence', p. 172.

50 Patrick Macrory, *The Siege of Derry* (Oxford: Oxford University Press, 1989), p. 49.

51 J.O. Bartley, *Teague, Shenkin, and Sawney: Being An Historical Study of the Earliest Irish, Welsh and Scottish Characters in English Plays* (Cork: Cork University Press, 1954), pp. 120–21.

52 George Farquhar, *Love and a Bottle* (London: Richard Standfast … and Francis Coggen, 1699), p. 32.

53 John Michelborne, *Ireland Preserved; Or, the Siege of London-Derry* (Belfast: James Magee, 1759), p. 10.

54 W.J. Lawrence, 'Horses upon the Elizabethan Stage', *Times Literary Supplement* (5 June 1919), 312.

55 Oliver Cromwell, *A Proclamation Prohibiting Horse-Races* (London: Henry Hills and John Field, 1655).
56 Patrick Little, 'Uncovering a Protectoral Stud: Horses and Horse-Breeding at the Court of Oliver Cromwell, 1653–8', *Historical Research* 82 (2009), 255.
57 James Shirley, *Hide Parke a Comedie* (London: Thomas Cotes, for Andrew Crooke, and William Cooke, 1637), p. E4^v; Kevin De Ornellas, 'Laying the World on Your Mare: The Corrupt Horse Race in Shirley's *Hide Parke*', in *The Horse in Early Modern English Culture: Bridled, Curbed, and Tamed* (Madison, NJ, Teaneck: Fairleigh Dickinson University Press, 2014), pp. 95–124.
58 Thomas Dekker, *A Strange Horse-Race* (London: Nicholas Okes, 1613), p. B3^r.
59 de Ornellas, p. 117.
60 Kathryn Shevelow, *For the Love of Animals: The Rise of the Animal Protection Movement* (New York: Henry Holt, 2003), p. 187; Linda Kalof, *Looking at Animals in Human History* (London: Reaktion Books, 2007), p. 125.
61 Jennifer Maher, Harriet Pierpoint, and Piers Beirne (eds.), *The Palgrave International Handbook of Animal Abuse Studies* (London: Palgrave Macmillan, 2017), p. 2.
62 Robert N. Watson, 'Protestant Animals: Puritan Sects and English Animal-Protection Sentiment, 1550–1650', *ELH* 81 (4) (2014), 1115; Malcolm R. Oster, '"The beame of divinity": Animal Suffering in the Early Thought of Robert Boyle', *British Journal for the History of Science* 22 (2) (1989), 151–72.
63 Keith Thomas, *Man and the Natural World: Changing Attitudes in England 1500–1800* (London: Allen Lane, 1983; rept. Penguin, 1984), pp. 189, 100.
64 Piers Beirne, *Hogarth's Art of Animal Cruelty: Satire, Suffering and Pictorial Propaganda* (Houndmills, Basingstoke: Palgrave Macmillan, 2015), p. 8, n. 2.
65 Piers Beirne, *Murdering Animals: Writings on Theriocide, Homicide and Nonspeciesist Criminology* (Houndmills, Basingstoke: Palgrave Macmillan, 2018), p. 26.
66 Ibid., p. 27.
67 Lady Morgan (Sydney Owenson), *The O'Briens and the O'Flaherty's; A National Tale*, vols. 4 (London: Henry Colburn, 1827), pp. 31–32.
68 Helen O'Connell, 'Animal Welfare in Post-Union Ireland', *New Hibernia Review* 19 (1) (2015), 38.
69 Maria Edgeworth, *Ormond*, in *Tales and Novels*, vols. 18 (London: Baldwin and Cradock, 1833), p. 66.
70 Arthur Young, *A Tour in Ireland*, vols. 2 (Dublin: James Williams, 1780), I, 292; emphasis in original.
71 Edward Ledwich, *The Antiquities of Ireland*, 2nd ed. (Dublin: John Jones, 1804), p. 373.
72 Thomas Dunham Whitaker, *The Life and Original Correspondence of Sir George Radcliffe, the Friend of the Earl of Strafford* (London: John Nichols and Son, 1810), pp. 270–71.
73 Thomas Wood, 'Fable and Fact in the Early Annals of Ireland, and on the Best Mode of Ascertaining What Degree of Credit These Ancient Documents Are Justly Entitled to', *The Transactions of the Royal Irish Academy* 13 (1818), 76–77, 77, n. 197.
74 John Barrow, *A Tour Round Ireland, Through the Sea-coast Counties in the Autumn of 1835* (London: John Murray, 1836), pp. 197–98; Tim Bobbin, 'A Tour Round Ireland', *The Dublin Penny Journal* 4 (203) (May 21, 1836), 369–76, 374.
75 John Stuart Mill, *An Estimate of Bentham's Philosophy* (London: C. Reynell, 1838), pp. 28–29.
76 Beirne, 'Against Cruelty?' p. 67, n. 133; John Stuart Mill, 'A Hitherto Unprinted Speech on the Influence of Lawyers (1825)', *Economica* 13 (1925), 3.
77 Caesar Otway, *Sketches in Erris and Tyrawly* (Dublin: William Curry, Jr. and Company, 1841, p. 369.

78 Langdon, *Horses, Oxen and Technological* Innovation, p. 19, n. 47.

79 James Allen Ransome, *The Implements of Agriculture* (London: J. Ridgway, 1843), pp. 10–11.

80 Sarah Tomlinson, *Sketches of Rural Affairs* (London: Society for Promoting Christian Knowledge, 1848), pp. 10–11.

81 George Nicholls, *A History of the Irish Poor Law* (London: John Murray, 1856), pp. 32–34.

82 John O'Donovan, 'Additional Notes on Bawns', *Ulster Journal of Archaeology*, 1st ser., 6 (1858), 135.

83 'Senex', 'Antiquarian Notes and Queries', *Ulster Journal of Archaeology*, 1st ser., 3 (1855), 254.

84 'Ollamh Fodhla', 'Horses Ploughing by the Tail', *Ulster Journal of Archaeology*, 1st ser., 4 (1856), 275.

85 E. H. D. D., 'Ploughing by the Horse's Tail', *Notes and Queries*, ser. 2, 7, 169 (1859), 257.

86 'In 1612, the Lord Deputy ordered the penalty to be levied in all Ulster, which, amounting to £870, was employed for public uses. The profits under the grant to Sir William Uvedale within Ulster has produced £800, though they were informed the charge on the people was more'. Shirley, O'Brien and Graves, 191–92, n. 24.

87 Cuthbert Bede, 'Ploughing by the Horse's Tail', *Notes and Queries*, 5th ser., 10, 260 (1878), 503.

88 Abhba, 'Ploughing by the Horse's Tail', *Notes and Queries* 5th ser., 10, 254 (1878), 366; E. C. G., 'Ploughing (or rather harrowing) by the Horse's Tail', *Notes and Queries*, 5th ser., 12, 290 (1879), 57; 'Sussexiensis', 'Ploughing by the Horse's Yail', *Notes and Queries* 5th ser., 11, 265 (1879), 77.

89 J.R. Haig, 'Ploughing by the Horse's Tail', *Notes and Queries* 5th ser., 12 (1879), 35–36.

90 Michael Duignan, 'Irish Agriculture in Early Historic Times'. *The Journal of the Royal Society of Antiquaries of Ireland* 14 (3) (1944), 138–39.

91 Bernard O'Daly, 'Material for a History of the Parish of Kilskeery', *Clogher Record* 1 (3) (1955), 93.

92 Harold T. Masterson, 'Land Use Patterns and Farming Practice in County Fermanagh 1609–1845', *Clogher Record* 7 (1) (1969), 63, n. 21.

93 E.E. Evans, 'Some Problems of Irish Ethnology: The Example of Ploughing by the Tail', in Caoimhín Ó Danachair (ed.), *Folk & Farm: Essays in Honour of A. T. Lucas* (Dublin: Royal Society of Antiquaries of Ireland, 1976), p. 34.

94 E. Estyn Evans, *The Personality of Ireland: Habitat, Heritage and History* (Cambridge: Cambridge University Press, 1973), p. 107, n. 22; J.J. McAuliffe, 'Ploughing by the Horses' Tails', *The Irish Book Lover* 29 (1943), 1–11.

95 Evans, 1976, p. 30, 31, 33, pp. 34–37; 39, n.27.

96 May McCann, Review of *Folk and Farm: Royal Society of Antiquaries of Ireland, 1976, Fortnight* 134 (1976), 9.

97 Eugenia Shanklin, *Donegal's Changing Traditions: An Ethnographic Study* (London: Routledge, 2016; first published Gordon and Branch, 1985), p. 30.

98 Raymond Gillespie, 'Migration and Opportunity: A Comment', *Irish Economic and Social History* 13 (1) (1986), 93; Nicholas Canny, 'Migration and Opportunity: Britain, Ireland and the New World', *Irish Economic and Social History* 12 (1985), 7–32.

99 Cormac Ó Gráda, 'Irish Agricultural History: Recent Research', *The Agricultural History Review* 38 (2) (1990), 165.

100 Clodagh Tait, 'Society', p. 285.

101 Gervase Markham, *Markhams Farwell to Husbandry* (London: Roger Jackson, 1620), p. 108.

102 Brian Smith, *The Horse in Ireland* (Dublin: Wolfhound Press, 1991), pp. 185–86.
103 Michael Longley, 'Ploughing by the Tail', *The Echo Gate: Poems, 1975–79* (London: Secker and Warburg, 1979), p. 25.
104 Paul Muldoon, 'Hinge: for Michael Longley', *The Honest Ulsterman* 110 (2001), 12.
105 William Hamilton Drummond, *The Rights of Animals: And Man's Obligation to Treat Them with Humanity* (London: John Mardon, 1838).
106 Colin A. Lewis and Mary E. McCarthy, 'The Horse Breeding Industry in Ireland', *Irish Geography* 10 (1) (1977), 72–89.

15 Archaeologies of early modern Ireland—crossing the disciplinary divide

James Lyttleton

Historical archaeology, or post-medieval archaeology as it is more commonly known in Ireland, has emerged as a vibrant subdiscipline in the last couple of decades. Aspects of early modern society and settlement are now taught in undergraduate courses and researched by graduates in all of Ireland's archaeology departments. The establishment of the Irish PostMedieval Archaeology Group in 1999, drawing membership from the academic, state, and commercial sectors as well as from the general public, has continued to promote the growth of this vibrant subdiscipline. Archaeological research, with its emphasis on material remains, including buildings and their surroundings, can offer provocative and insightful views on the physical environment of that time. Indeed, twenty years ago, Rolf Loeber, a leading figure in the study of early modern settlement in Ireland, called for a multidisciplinary approach, a view very much informed by his own work on the compilation of documentary sources for sixteenth- and seventeenth-century settlements.[1]

The study of society in early modern Ireland offers significant potential for collaborative work between archaeologists and historians. With such work it is possible to draw on the different fields of enquiry—documentary sources, paintings, architecture (both formal and vernacular), landscapes (for example, pleasure gardens and field enclosure), artifacts, cartographic sources, and excavated remains—to build up a more holistic appraisal of this past society. A good example of this collaborative effort was a conference jointly hosted by the Ireland Post-Medieval Archaeology Group (IPMAG) and the Group for the Study of Irish Historical Settlement (GSIHS) in 2006. The papers of this conference, presented by historians, geographers, archaeologists, and one literary scholar, were subsequently published in an edited volume by Colin Rynne and this author in 2009, entitled *Plantation Ireland: Settlement and Material Culture, c.1550–c.1700*. Without a doubt, collaborative strengths can be used to fill in the gaps in our knowledge, providing comprehensive and varied insights into one of the most contested eras of Irish history. This article will discuss the challenges faced in using documentary sources, followed by the issues encountered in the archaeological evidence. The relationship between archaeology and history will be discussed with a view toward developing a dynamic that draws on the best each discipline has to offer. This is followed by an elaboration of what is meant by an archaeo-logical study of the early modern era, and what such studies have to offer academia, and indeed the wider public. A couple of interdisciplinary case studies are highlighted, namely Andrew Hadfield's work on Edmund Spenser and Raymond Gillespie's work on material consumption and culture in early modern Roscrea in County Tipperary. Further collaborative approaches are put forward, based on either a regional or a thematic perspective, such as colonialism, ethnicity, religion, modernity, or the opening of the English Atlantic world.

Challenges in using documentary sources

Historical scholarship, by its nature, focuses on the study of the written word. Compared to earlier periods, research on sixteenth- and seventeenth-century Ireland is able to draw upon a greater variety of documentary sources, whether in the guise of State Papers, municipal records, estates papers, and personal correspondence. While early modern documents are more extensive and bet-ter preserved than earlier sources, they can still be fragmentary in survival, hindering a more comprehensive appraisal of society and culture at the time. In a study of the Jacobean plantations in County Offaly that utilized various documentary and cartographic sources, it was found that the Civil Survey (1654) for the county was long missing and that some baronial and parish maps from the Down Survey (1657) could no longer be found, illustrating the prob-lem of partial survival.[2] Indeed, most of the documentary sources of the period take the form of grants, deeds, and leases, which typically detail the various townlands held by individuals, without any further elaboration except maybe for a breakdown of acreage into profitable and unprofitable land. Such records have much to say on changing patterns of landownership, but provide little insight on, for example, the process of enclosing the Irish landscape.

The alleged impartiality of written sources is also an issue. Such writings, whether in the form of government legislation, correspondence between officials, household inventories, estate rentals, indentures or private corre-spondence between individuals, originated from literate sources that were overwhelmingly representative of the wealthy landholding classes. These documents were designed to serve the economic and administrative inter-ests of the social and political elites, and, obviously, were never compiled with the intention of answering questions posed by academic scholarship. People in the lower social classes were certainly underrepresented in these documents and consequently have much less visibility in academic discourse. This is not surprising, given that in 1500, 90% of the male population and 99% of the female population in neighboring Britain were unable to read or write and this had changed little by the late seventeenth century—in 1680, 70% of males and 90% of females were still illiterate.[3] Literacy was clearly a socially restricted practice that was largely confined to the elites. A complete reliance on documentary sources can create a top-heavy bias in the study of early modern society in Ireland, which ignores the greater proportion of the population, reducing people to passive participation on a stage where political, economic, and social forces held perpetual sway over them. Archaeology, with its emphasis on material culture, the built environment, and historic landscapes, can help to address this bias in early modern studies by providing case studies, examples of which are cited in the following.

Another feature of historical (and admittedly archaeological) writing is its essentialism, which regards the cultural identity of the population as neatly divided between the Gaelic Irish, the Anglo-Irish (or the Old English), and the New English. Documentary sources such as the State Papers compiled in Dublin Castle, or private correspondence between prospective planters, tend to reinforce a view that the population of sixteenth- and seventeenth-century Ireland was divided into three different (at times antagonistic) populations. Modern academic studies can absorb these essentialist ethnic constructs, which have influenced approaches and debates on the period. It has been suggested that there is far greater value in an alternative model in which divisions of class and social order mattered much more than perceived divisions between native and colonizer.[4] Archaeology, with its emphasis on artifacts, buildings, and landscapes, can provide new insights on social organization and cultural identity free from an over-reliance on arbitrary ethnic assignations.

Challenges on the archaeological front

Without a doubt, there has been a tendency in archaeological research to focus on the most visible monuments, which are overwhelmingly of elite status. Nevertheless, approaches which seek to explore settlement and material culture associated with the lower social orders are compromised by poor levels of archaeological (and indeed historical) visibility. This is symptomatic of an environment which has militated against the survival of low-status early modern buildings, presumably due to the comparatively flimsy nature of domestic buildings in the period. Whether in Munster, the midlands, or in Ulster, the earliest architectural survivals of lower-status dwellings tend to be the households of well-to-do farmers, established more often than not during the latter half of the seventeenth century; the farmstead at Berwick Hall in County Down (built *c*.1682–85) comes to mind, though a number of less-preserved examples can be found elsewhere across the Irish countryside.[5] Therefore, as in historical sources, there is a clear bias in survival and preservation toward sites associated with the literate elite, with ordinary farmers, laborers, and artisans largely invisible.

Fortunately, there have been notable exceptions to this; for example, in 2001, the remains of five domestic houses dating to the seventeenth century were excavated at Rough Point in Killybegs Harbour, County Donegal, in advance of harbor improvements. These houses, built of stone, were dated on the basis of pottery imported from England and the European continent, and may have been related to the initial phase of the plantation of the area by incoming settlers.[6] Elsewhere in Ulster, the extensive remains of a village lie in the shadow of Dunluce Castle, the chief household of the earls of Antrim during the first half of the seventeenth century. The footprint of the settlement remains largely intact due to the fact that no ploughing had taken place in recent years, and that estate agents through the eighteenth and nineteenth centuries had been instructed to protect the field and prevent the removal of any building stone. The layout of the village was assessed through the use of topographical surveys, utilizing both GPS and airborne high-resolution LiDAR. Extensive areas of the village were also subject to geophysical prospection, including resistivity and ground-penetrating radar. Aerial photography complemented the aforementioned data sets. This work was followed by excavation in selected areas to gauge the broader development of the site.[7] Consequently, an exceptionally well-preserved plantation period village was uncovered, with the remains of stone-built and timber-framed houses flanking the sides of cobbled streets. Particular buildings were examined including a merchant's home and a blacksmithy, the focus of the village being a cobbled market place of triangular plan known as a diamond. While the fieldwork by the archaeologists has been completed, the material, spatial, and temporal information available for such settlements can complement further work by historians who are working on aspects of colonialism, class relations, and economics in seventeenth-century Ulster.

The relationship between archaeology and history

Traditionally, archaeology has been perceived as complementing the documentary sources, with the suggestion (implicit or otherwise) that archaeology is 'an expensive way of telling us what we know already'.[8] Indeed, archaeology was also described as the handmaiden of history with archaeological interpretations supported on a historical epistemological framework—in effect the archaeologists supplying the relics to illustrate historians' texts and to add flavor to historical narratives constructed on documentary evidence.[9] However, archaeological discourse, based on its own epistemological structures and data, does possess an inherent value. It can utilize contemporary writings and cartographic sources as just one aspect of the evidence available, depending on its relevance to the archaeological analysis.[10]

The more traditional approach has been to treat the written and material sources as separate categories of data, which can be consulted in parallel—in effect, using one as an empirical control for the veracity of the other. Archaeology was used to add texture to terse references in documents, while history was used to fill in the gaps in the archaeological record.[11] However, a more contextual approach would be to include the idea that people and communities constructed themselves through engagement with both texts and materials, transcending the disciplinary boundaries between history and archaeology.[12] Human relations directly impact upon the environment, both natural and built, as people use space and form as an active agent to create and reproduce social relations. Material and documentary remains such as a collection of artifacts, the ruins of a manor house, or a household inventory are not some passive reflection or residue of a more substantial past. Instead, the creation of material and textual forms such as these allowed for the communication and expression of meaning and behavioral norms. Accepting Pierre Bourdieu's notion of habitus, cultural norms tend to be installed and reproduced through the use of materials and daily practice, with such modes of behavior being construed by contemporaries as common sense. Material culture and textual forms can allow for the creation of a context for discourse, defining the social and cultural mores in a given place and time.[13] Like other forms of human creativity, documents were also active in the production, negotiation, and transformation of social relations: for example, the early maps created of Ulster in the run-up to plantation contributed to the creation and reproduction of technologies of domination.[14] Other textual sources also provided opportunities for modes of resistance, such as Geoffrey Keating's *Foras Feasa ar Éirinn*, otherwise known as the Compendium of Wisdom of Ireland. This was a national history probably completed by 1634, and which provided a sense of what it meant to be Irish and Catholic at the time.[15] It has been suggested that local traditions and knowledge were sidelined by such national histories—that tales of local monuments, landscapes, and people fell in the face of written accounts of occurrences of national significance.[16]

A detailed examination of the material remains within a perspective that sees them as something more than reflecting identity or adaptive responses has been called 'contextual archaeology'. Contextual archaeology demands a close and detailed engagement with all the data available, including written sources. Archaeologists must recognize that people in the historical past constructed their identities not only from the objects that they created and used, but through texts as well—written words were not some neutral form of recording. Even illiterate populations were deeply entangled within social relations and structures underpinned by writing; one only has to think of the numerous tenants who farmed on Sir Richard Boyle's extensive estate in Munster, paying rents to his agents and middlemen across the province— payments which were dutifully recorded in rent rolls held by Boyle himself.[17]

Archaeologies of the early modern era

Tadhg O'Keeffe, in a recent review of the archaeological excavations of seventeenth-, eighteenth-, and nineteenth-century sites carried out over the course of motorway construction in Ireland during the last twenty years, observed that what has been revealed has not forced a radical rethinking of how the Irish rural settlement and the landscape evolved in recent centuries. Post-medieval archaeology, in effect, has not been fully established in the archaeological imagination in Ireland to challenge the grand narrative inherited from historians, albeit with one exception, in the realm of plantation studies.[18] Post-medieval archaeology, he argues, is still largely a subdiscipline that is focused on the collection, description, and identification of data, and on the site-specific description of the same, though again, there are notable exceptions—Charles Orser's *A Historical Archaeology of the Modern World* (1996) embraces an explanation of the modern world through the prisms of modernity, colonialism, and capitalism.[19] Most archaeologists would support the principle that archaeological studies, once confined to prehistory alone, now include the historical era, including the sixteenth and seventeenth centuries, and even more recent times, as it is materiality, not temporality, that defines the boundaries of archaeological practice.[20]

O'Keeffe also makes an interesting observation that unlike medieval historians, all of whom would at least acknowledge the contribution that archaeology makes, modern historians, starting with the plantations (especially of the post-Restoration era), express far more rarely any appreciation of the archaeological research into that era.[21] In an Irish context, there are notable exceptions such as Clodagh Tait and Raymond Gillespie, who have delved into material aspects of devotion and commemoration in the period.[22] It is important to point out though that this lack of appreciation can work both ways—it has been observed that because of the anthropological training of American archaeologists, they may not be as familiar with historians' work as they should be. Ivor Noël Hume, one of the leading pioneers of Historical Archaeology in the 1960s, was never in doubt about the close relationship between history and archaeology, but as someone whose career started in English archaeology and who did not come from an anthropological background, he did not represent the mainstream of American thought at the time.[23] Another prominent figure in the development of historical archaeology was James Deetz, who did encourage his students to read historical scholarly work and indeed study documentary sources. This challenge was taken up by his early students such as Mary Beaudry and Marley Brown III, who did pioneering work on probate inventories from an anthropological and archaeological perspective.[24]

A number of works published by American archaeologists have been highlighted as marking a high point in the joining of archaeological and historical research, including Anne Yentsch's *A Chesapeake Family and their Slaves* (1994) and Kathleen Deagan's *Puerto Real: The Archaeology of a 16th-Century Spanish Town in Hispaniola* (1995).[25] Calls for a multidisciplinary approach to the study of post-medieval societies have been long aired. Matthew Johnson called for changes in the way post-medieval archaeology was practiced and written about. He suggested four steps: first, that our writing of the past must be at a human scale of time and space—that too many archaeological depictions of the landscape have almost nothing to with how it was experienced; second, that the views of the economy and the environment in the past should be respected, which meant a move beyond formalist economic models in the interpretation of archaeological data; third, that archaeologists should think more imaginatively about the nature of archaeological materials, including a consideration of the material conditions in which texts were produced; and fourth, that scholars should take up Michel Foucault's metaphor of archaeology, which means excavating below the surface of documented history.[26] Johnson noted that recent historical work exhibited the same interpretative tensions between generations of scholars as in archaeology, and that there was a need to build alliances within interdisciplinary work in social and cultural history. Such research would place an emphasis on the subjective nature of everyday living, and on the importance of material things, giving post-medieval archaeology the potential to be central to a critical interdisciplinary enquiry into the Renaissance and early modern periods.[27] Audrey Horning's article on archaeology and contemporary identity in Northern Ireland has been put forward as an example of how an archaeologist can produce reflections which are far more radically revisionist and critically reflexive than most of the reflections published by historians. Her observations point the way forward for how archaeology might challenge commonly held notions of colonialism and postcolonialism, and in the process increase public knowledge and discourse on early modern Irish history, as well as on the political and social values of heritage.[28]

However, there can be negative comment on such cross-disciplinary approaches, a good example of which was criticism of Audrey Horning's book on English colonialism in the North Atlantic. It was argued that Horning's view of non-hostile collaboration between native and newcomer was over-emphasized and overlooked the contentious and at times hostile nature of the relationship between the two groups in Ulster.[29] In another instance, a literary scholar wondered whether the archaeological excavation of Edmund Spenser's castle in Kilcolman, County Cork, was really going to reveal more of Spenser as a poet and writer.[30] However, in counterpoint to these critiques, the most recent biographer of Spenser, Andrew Hadfield, has made significant use of the information retrieved from the excavation of Spenser's Irish castle.[31] The point here to be made is that archaeology's contribution to early modern studies was not always readily appreciated by specialists in early modern studies. This is reflective of the traditional boundaries between the disciplines, which has discouraged scholars from engaging with research from outside their field of studies. Collaborative projects involving historians and archaeologists drawing upon the epistemological strengths of their respective disciplines offer a way forward.

Interdisciplinary case studies

Excavation is the quintessential method attributed to archaeology, since it is the method most exclusive to the discipline. And while it is a method of data retrieval, the interpretation of the results allows unique insights into material and cultural environments that would not necessarily be readily apparent from documentary sources. The difference between prehistoric and historic archaeologists is that in the case of the former, they have uncontested control of the interpretation and therefore ownership of the narrative, whereas with the latter, the narrative is constructed by others, namely the historians, though this needs to be considered. O'Keeffe believes that archaeologists need their own 'bespoke frame of interpretation' which recognizes that human societies are constituted materially and spatially, and hence the archaeological enquiry must highlight the patterns of material and spatial formations. As part of that paradigm, the written record obviously cannot be ignored but it needs to be recognized as an artifact in its own right, one in which people recorded and communicated ideas through the process of writing and printing.[32] O'Keeffe cites John Moreland, who asserts that 'a rapprochement between the disciplines can be achieved only if we begin to think of texts and objects as having had efficacy in the past rather than just as evidence about it'.[33]

As mentioned, Andrew Hadfield in his biography of Edmund Spenser includes a chapter on the poet's Irish castle and 3,000 acre estate—Kilcolman in north County Cork—which was granted as one of the seigneuries that made up the Munster Plantation. This scheme had been established following the Desmond Rebellion and the confiscation of the escheated lands of the earl of Desmond. Hadfield draws on archaeological, historical, geographical, and literary evidence to paint a picture of what everyday life would have been like on the Spenser estate. When he was formally granted Kilcolman on 26 October 1590, Spenser's choice of name for his new lands—'Hap Hazard'—reflected the complicated and uncertain route by which he had acquired it.[34] Hadfield as a literary scholar draws on quotes from Spenser's works which illustrate the poet / planter's knowledge of the local geography, and to a lesser degree the Irish language. Such knowledge would have been necessary for anyone who owned an estate, even if the running of it was delegated to a local middleman, as was the case on this property. Evidence from Klingelhofer's excavation and geophysical work at Kilcolman Castle is drawn upon to reimagine what Spenser's residence originally looked like—the fair house built by him (as described in a 1622 government survey) beside the later medieval tower house, and the sort of furnishings that would have existed in the household. Faunal evidence (animal and bird bone) is used to provide insights into the diet at the time and the agricultural economy on the estate (in which sheep rearing appears to have been important). Historical evidence and the knowledge of the local topography, including the locations of various castles and churches, are used to tease out the local familial connections that Spenser and his offspring would have developed over time. This drawing together of various strands of evidence from different disciplinary interests produces a richer, more thorough account which gets closer to creating what life would have been like for the subject at hand. The chapter sets the stage for a discussion on the sort of library Spenser would have kept in Kilcolman Castle, plying his art as a poet and writer.[35]

Insights into the material and cultural world of the Munster Plantation can be gained by emphasizing the Irish content of Spenser's poetry, and indeed the Irish context in which it was written. In the words of Thomas Herron, a literary scholar, 'Spenser's poetry has much to offer the archaeologist and archaeology the Spensarian'.[36] Spenser set out his ideas on colonizing Ireland in the dialogue *A View of the Present State of Ireland* (written *c.*1596, though published much later in 1633) and in verse, most notably in his romance epic *The Faerie Queene* and shorter poems, such as his wedding poem 'Epithalamion'.[37]

Faunal evidence, including high-quality wheat, recovered from archaeological excavation at Kilcolman, suggests that Spenser's 'idealization of the arduous georgic way of life and tillage husbandry was not therefore sheer fantasy but had roots in actual practice in Munster.'[38] The postulated garden within the bawn in the shadow of the tower house at Kilcolman can be paralleled with the ideologically fraught functions of Spenser's famous Garden of Adonis in Book III of *The Faerie Queene*. The Garden has a colonial, plantation resonance in that Spenser fantasizes a civic, fruitful garden that is beneficial to wider society—an idea that is likely to have been cultivated within the protected surrounds of Kilcolman Castle.[39]

Raymond Gillespie, writing on material culture and social change in early modern Ireland, has observed how the various plantation schemes have not proved equal to the expectation that they brought about social, economic, and political changes. Such transformations like commercialization or architectural change were not driven solely by formal plantation schemes, although they may well have been linked with such developments.[40] Similar changes took place in areas that had not been planted; archaeological investigations at Roscrea Castle, for example, indicate that in the two centuries after 1500, much of the castle and town were transformed—the castle had seen refurbishment, aligning its appearance more with fashionable Jacobean manor houses seen elsewhere in Ireland, while pottery, glassware, and tobacco pipes became more commonly used, imported from various areas of England and further afield, representing an ever greater diversity of materials available in the local market. The appearance of more material goods in Roscrea from the early seventeenth-century onward suggests that a shift had taken place in the production, distribution, and consumption of goods, and like architectural change, this may have reflected a fundamental social and economic shift, with Roscrea entering a much wider world than before.[41] Plantation had a limited role in bringing about such changes, due to the lack of enthusiasm for its social reform agenda among the undertakers who were charged with implementing those plans. Most of the social reshaping instead was brought about by the market and the goods that were exchanged in it as new values came to be attached to persons and items.[42] The plantation-driven models fail to allow for agency among the natives and newcomers, and underestimate the capacity of social and economic change to spread in ways other than in centrally planned schemes.[43]

Further collaborative approaches

The archaeological examination of material culture can be complemented by documentary sources and published scholarly work on political, social, religious, economic, and architectural developments where relevant. Such a multidisciplinary approach has allowed the archaeology of early modern Ireland to be placed against the background of a Europe that was experiencing transformation on many fronts. In recent years, there has been a greater appreciation of the changes taking place in the material culture of the period, and an appraisal of it is fundamental to our understanding of how society developed in early modern Ireland.

One concern that is shared by both archaeologists and historians is colonialism—how useful is such a concept in elucidating the nature of social relations in early modern Ireland? The dominant effect of analyzing archaeology in purely colonial terms would be to deny the complex historical ambiguities of identity formation that were apparent in the country at the time. A more useful approach could be to situate sixteenth- and seventeenth-century Ireland in a European context. While the Gaelic lordships of early modern Ireland witnessed the appropriation and colonization of their territories by English and Scottish settlers, such events were not unexceptional in a European context as other peripheral regions, such as Brittany and Catalonia, were also assimilated by more powerful neighbors in the process of building modern nation-states.[44] On the other hand, aspects of Ireland's experiences were not shared by other Western European countries; instead, like many native societies in the New World, Ireland saw its language, legal systems, territorial organization, settlement patterns, social structures, and artistic expression either replaced or radically reconfigured by an English-speaking state and culture.[45]

Much of the published literature on material culture and settlement has only gauged impressionistic trends, with little opportunity to take into account regional differences. In recent years, the publications of Colin Breen's *The Gaelic Lordship of the O'Sullivan Beare* (2005) and *The Jacobean Plantations in Seventeenth-Century Offaly* (2013) by this author have looked at specific regions, encompassing all aspects of local society, and how the activities of the different groups, whether native or newcomer, contributed to the development of the built environment and the surrounding landscape.[46] Such studies, on a regional level, while answering questions, invariably raise more.

Further studies, based on either a regional or thematic approach, should be welcomed. A collaborative project was jointly hosted by the Departments of History and Archaeology in University College Cork, which focused upon the colonial landscape of Sir Richard Boyle, first earl of Cork. Utilizing documentary sources and fieldwork, new insights have been gained into aspects of life on Boyle's extensive estates, including architecture, landscape, economy, political networks, and transatlantic connections, providing much important contextual information at a local and regional level.[47] This is particularly important given the emphasis in academic writing on the 'high' politics of the period which can ignore the material environment of these elite individuals and their families, whose names abound in the same literature.

Another area of concern which archaeologists and historians share is how notions of ethnicity developed and evolved over the course of the sixteenth and seventeenth centuries. Economic realities meant that mutual interdependence between the different ethnic groups was a necessity. Most British landowners were dependent on native tenants to varying degrees, while native landowners recognized the need to import skilled English tenants if their estates were to survive in the new economic dispensation, in effect abandoning their traditional titles, tributes, and exactions to become English-style landlords. This meant that there were regular face-to-face meetings between the settlers and natives across most of the country. Such encounters allowed for cultural identities to be subsumed into a process of appropriation, subversion, and transformation, resulting in hybridization between the different ethnic groupings. Emblematic of this hybridization is the Jacobean manor house traditionally associated by architectural historians with the waves of British settlers that arrived in Ireland following the demise of the Gaelic lordships. Yet some of the finest examples of plantation-era architecture are to be found at the seats of prominent native families. Two such examples can be found in County Offaly: Kilcolgan More was described in 1650 as a 'faire house belonging to Terence Coghlan', and Ballymooney Castle was constructed *c*.1622 by Donell O'Carroll.[48] These were fine buildings, the sort of residences expected of individuals who were well versed in the virtues of gentility and polite living. Through the architecture, we can see that material culture was in a continual process of reproduction and transformation in changing social and historical contexts. This is at variance with the essentialist perspective that places an emphasis on the one-to-one correlation between material culture and ethnicity. Consideration of both documentary and archaeological sources illustrates that ethnic boundaries were not rigidly enforced as people at the time had the propensity to adopt language, social etiquette, and material culture from beyond. Such boundaries could be porous, with the importance of ethnic identity varying significantly in different social contexts and between individuals.[49]

Collaborative studies can also focus upon issues of religious beliefs and practices in early modern Ireland. Church buildings and commemorative monuments provide visual testimony of people's earnest aspirations and religious beliefs. While the political, social, and economic instabilities of the period conspired against the patronage and maintenance of church building, the indifference of lay impropriators who held much of the church lands and revenues was also a decisive factor. Indeed, the contribution of the latter to the pace of church reform and the fate of individual church buildings at parish level has not been fully appreciated. Archaeological studies of particular planter families or individuals such as the Parsons of Birr in County Offaly or Sir Richard Boyle in Counties Waterford and Cork reveal evidence for investment and continued maintenance of church buildings as part of a strategy to promote their standing in local communities, as well as to enable the development of villages and towns on their estates.[50]

Despite prohibitions of the public display of Catholic worship, however, churches could be reedified by native landed families at times when Protestant hegemony was being openly challenged, as in the 1640s, with the outbreak of widespread rebellion, and in the 1680s, under the reign of the Catholic monarch James II. In the instance of the ancient monastic site of Clonmacnoise in County Offaly, the restoration of certain church buildings for the celebration of Catholic liturgy, namely, Clonmacnoise Cathedral, Temple

Ciarán, and Temple Dowling, suggests that there was a conscious revival of past cultural accomplishments. Just as the native elite was well versed in old literary and oral traditions, such interest in the past may have also extended to ancient church buildings.[51] While formal Catholic worship took place within churches, serving the spiritual needs of local communities, there was still a strong tradition of holy places in popular Catholic devotion. These places were associated with saints' legends in which the actions of a particular saint had sanctified a location—holy wells, sacred trees, and rocks; such locations became in turn the object of pilgrimages and specific devotions. By their nature, however, it is difficult to quantify by morphological or documentary analysis alone the use of such sites in the early modern period, but the challenge has been taken up by historians.[52]

Another area of cross-disciplinary interest is the impact of modernity on early modern Ireland. The sixteenth and seventeenth centuries witnessed an emerging modernity in which Gaelic Irish lordship, embedded in land, tradition, and past custom, was transformed by an emerging and expanding state. Government officials in Dublin and London were keen to regularize the status of the native lords according to the norms of civil living, common law, and the market economy. Such an agenda was to be supported by the introduction of English forms of tenure, estate organization, settlement, and education. With the rights and liberties of lordships being strongly encroached upon, there was a need for the Gaelic landed elites to redefine and present themselves as landlords in the English tradition. As mentioned earlier, such concerns persuaded native families like the O'Carrolls and the MacCoghlans to erect fortified manor houses, the very epitome of the English country estate and a precursor to the Big House of the eighteenth and nineteenth centuries. The conversion of communal open-field systems into individually worked enclosed fields was symptomatic of a more capitalist-orientated economy. The foundations for the modern estate system had thus been laid, and this agricultural revolution was to shape the reforming agenda in Ireland.[53] Studies on the evolution of estates, from both an archaeological and historical perspective, can yield invaluable insights into how the Irish landscape was affected by the political, social, and economic changes of the early modern era.

It is not coincidental that this process was taking place in the context of an embryonic capitalist economy that was developing on both sides of the North Atlantic. Spanning this ocean, very different peoples were linked through cultural encounters, exchange and trade, political alliances, enslavement in some areas, incursions upon their territories, and the unintentional spread of disease. As a result, an Atlantic world was created, a geographical entity varied and complicated in its nature. The establishment of the plantations in Ireland was largely contemporary with the first colonial endeavors in North America, with many of the same aspirations and prejudices being brought to bear in both environments. Taking this more global (and multidisciplinary) approach is Audrey Horning's transatlantic comparative study *Ireland in the Virginian Sea: colonialism in the British Atlantic* (2013) which has examined the experience of

British colonialism in the Ulster Plantation and the Jamestown colony in Virginia, challenging the notion that Ireland merely served as a stepping stone or laboratory for a more ambitious expansion into North America.[54]

Another transatlantic project is a comparative study of the colonial activities of Sir George Calvert, first Lord Baltimore in Ireland and North America during the 1620s and early 1630s. At the time, he contemporaneously managed his various estates in England, Ireland, and Newfoundland, which included the construction of manor houses in Kiplin Hall in North Yorkshire; Clohamon, County Wexford in Ireland; and Ferryland on the Avalon Peninsula in Newfoundland. Differences in the form and layout of these buildings reflect the challenges and opportunities posed in developing settlements in the various regions, and offer insights into the commonalities and divergences experienced in the English colonization of the Atlantic world in the early seventeenth century.[55]

While archaeologists typically examine local and regional settings, given the nature of the archaeological record, a wider view provided by other disciplines such as the history of the influences, social processes, and connections operating upon the local populations can be informative. Consequently, the concept of an Atlantic world can play an important role in the study of sixteenth- and seventeenth-century English colonization and Gaelic Irish responses to it, as well as other cultural processes that were transforming early modern European society, such as capitalism and religious schism.

Conclusion

Work on the various themes enunciated earlier can and should be carried out on a cross-disciplinary basis, building on the respective epistemological strengths of each discipline. The early modern world was a complex one in which various political, social, economic, and cultural ideas and trends intermeshed with each other, profoundly influencing the lives of the various peoples who lived in it. Bearing in mind this complexity, it is surely appropriate that the epistemological strengths of different scholarly disciplines, and not just archaeology and history, should be brought to bear on developing more nuanced and reflexive understandings of how society evolved. This is a challenge to all scholars who seek to understand Ireland's place in the early modern world.

Notes

1   Rolf Loeber, *The Geography and Practice of English Colonisation in Ireland from 1534 to 1609* (Athlone: Group for the Study of Irish Historic Settlement, 1991).
2   James Lyttleton, *The Jacobean Plantations in Seventeenth-Century Offaly: An Archaeology of a Changing World* (Dublin: Four Courts Press, 2013), p. 7.
3   Nigel Wheale, *Writing and Society, Literacy, Print and Politics in Britain 1590–1660* (London and New York: Routledge, 1999).
4   Tadhg O'Keeffe, 'Irish "Post-medieval" Archaeology: Time to Lose Our Innocence?', in Audrey Horning and Marilyn Palmer (eds.), *Crossing Paths or Sharing*

Tracks: Future Directions in the Archaeological Study of Post-1550 Britain and Ireland (Woodbridge, Suffolk: Boydell, 2009), pp. 65–80 at p. 72.

5 Lyttleton, *Jacobean Plantations in Offaly*, p. 200, Figure 7.29.

6 Frank Coyne and Tracy Collins, *Excavation of a Post-medieval Settlement at Rough Point, Killybegs, County Donegal, Aegis Archaeology Reports 2* (Limerick: Aegis Archaeology Limited, 2004).

7 Colin Breen, *Dunluce Castle: Archaeology and History* (Dublin: Four Courts Press, 2012), p. 134.

8 Anders Andrén, *Between Artifacts and Texts: Historical Archaeology in Global Perspective* (New York: Springer, 1998), p. 3.

9 John Moreland, *Archaeology and Text. Duckworth Debates in Archaeology* (London: Bloomsbury, 2001), p. 10; ibid., 'Archaeology and Texts: Subservience or Enlightenment', *Annual Review of Anthropology* 35 (2006), 135–51 at 136.

10 David Austin, 'The "Proper Study" of Medieval Archaeology' in David Austin and Leslie Alcock (eds.), *From the Baltic to the Black Sea: Studies in Medieval Archaeology* (London: Unwin Hyman, 1990), pp. 9–42 at pp. 13–14, 18.

11 Moreland, 'Archaeology and Texts', pp. 137–38.

12 Ibid., p. 142.

13 Lyttleton, *Jacobean Plantations in Offaly*, p. 259.

14 Annaleigh Margery, 'Representing Plantation Landscapes: the Mapping of Ulster, *c.*1560–1640' in James Lyttleton and Colin Rynne (eds.), *Plantation Ireland, Settlement and Material Culture, c.1550–c.1700* (Dublin: Four Courts Press, 2009), pp. 140–64.

15 Bernadette Cunningham, *The World of Geoffrey Keating: History, Myth and Religion in Seventeenth-century Ireland* (Dublin: Four Courts Press, 2004).

16 Moreland, *Archaeology and Text*, pp. 72–73.

17 Ibid., pp. 82–84.

18 Tadhg O'Keeffe, 'Routes Across the Familiar Past: Reflections on NRA-funded Excavations and the Challenge Facing the "Post-medieval" Archaeology of Rural Ireland' in Michael Stanley, Rónán Swan, and Aidan O'Sullivan (eds.), *Stories of Ireland's Past, Knowledge Gained from NRA Roads Archaeology, TII Heritage 5* (Dublin: Transport Infrastructure Ireland, 2017), pp. 153–64 at p. 154.

19 O'Keeffe, 'Routes Across the Familiar Past', p. 158.

20 Ibid., p. 161.

21 Ibid., p. 161.

22 Clodagh Tait, 'Manipulations of Death, Burial and Commemoration in the Career of Richard Boyle, First Earl of Cork (1566–1643)', *Proceedings of the Royal Irish Academy* 101C (2001), 107–34; Raymond Gillespie, 'Irish Funeral Monuments and Social Change, 1500–1700: Perceptions of Death' in Raymond Gillespie and B.P. Kennedy (eds.), *Ireland, Art into History* (Dublin, 1994), pp. 155–68.

23 Paul Courtney, '"Different Strokes for Different Folks": The Transatlantic Development of Historical and Post Medieval Archaeology', in Geoff Egan and R.L. Michael (eds.), *Old and New Worlds, Historical / Post Medieval Archaeology Papers from the Societies' Joint Conferences at Williamsburg and London 1997 to Mark Thirty Years of Work and Achievement* (Oxford: Oxbow Books, 1999), pp. 1–9 at p. 4.

24 Courtney, 'Different Strokes for Different Folks', p. 4.

25 Ibid., p. 4.

26 Matthew Johnson, 'The New Postmedieval Archaeology', in Egan and Michael (eds.), *Old and New Worlds, Historical / Post Medieval Archaeology Papers from the Societies' Joint Conferences at Williamsburg and London 1997*, pp. 17–22 at pp. 18–19.

27 Johnson, 'The New Postmedieval Archaeology', pp. 19–20.

28 O'Keeffe, 'Irish "Post-medieval" Archaeology', pp. 66–67, citing Audrey Horning, 'Archaeology, Conflict, and Contemporary Identity in the North of Ireland:

Implications for Theory and Practice in Irish Historical Archaeology', *Archaeological Dialogues* 13 (2006), 18–99.

29 Nicholas Canny, 'Reconciled to Colonialism?: Ireland in the Virginian Sea', *Irish Times*, 24 May 2014. Review of Audrey Horning, *Ireland in the Virginian Sea, Colonialism in the British Atlantic World* (Chapel Hill: University of North Carolina Press, 2013).

30 Willy Maley, *Salvaging Spenser: Colonialism, Culture and Identity* (Basingstoke: Palgrave Macmillan, 1997).

31 Andrew Hadfield, *Edmund Spenser: A Life* (Oxford: Oxford University Press, 2012).

32 O'Keeffe, 'Routes Across the Familiar Past', p. 164.

33 Ibid., citing Moreland, 'Archaeology and Texts', p. 135.

34 Hadfield, *Edmund Spenser: A Life*, p. 205.

35 Ibid., pp. 197–230.

36 Thomas Herron, 'Irish Archaeology and the Poetry of Edmund Spenser: Content and Context', in James Lyttleton and Colin Rynne (eds.), *Plantation Ireland: Settlement and Material Culture, c.1550 – c.1700* (Dublin: Four Courts Press, 2009), pp. 229–47.

37 Ibid., p. 229.

38 Ibid., p. 244.

39 Ibid., pp 245–46.

40 Raymond Gillespie, 'The Problems of Plantations: Material Culture and Social Change in Early Modern Ireland', in Lyttleton and Rynne (eds.), *Plantation Ireland*, pp. 43–60 at p. 49.

41 Ibid., pp. 52–54.

42 Ibid., p. 57.

43 Ibid., p. 60.

44 Liam Kennedy, *Colonialism, Religion and Nationalism in Ireland* (Belfast: Institute of Irish Studies, 1996), p. 175.

45 William J. Smyth, *Map-making, Landscapes and Memory: A Geography of Colonial and Early Modern Ireland, c.1530–1750* (Cork: Cork University Press, 2006), p. 16.

46 Colin Breen, *The Gaelic Lordship of the O'Sullivan Beare* (Dublin: Four Courts Press, 2005); James Lyttleton, *Jacobean Plantations in Offaly* (Dublin: Four Courts Press, 2013).

47 David Edwards and Colin Rynne (eds.), *The Colonial World of Richard Boyle, First Earl of Cork* (Dublin: Four Courts Press, 2018).

48 Caimin O'Brien and P. David Sweetman, *Archaeological Inventory of County Offaly* (Dublin: Stationery Office, 1997), pp. 157, 159–60.

49 Siân Jones, *The Archaeology of Ethnicity: Constructing Identities in the Past and Present* (London: Routledge, 1997), p. 69.

50 Lyttleton, *Jacobean Plantations in Offaly*, pp. 222–25; James Lyttleton, '"A godly resolucon to rebuild": Richard Boyle's Patronage of Elite Architecture', in Edwards and Rynne (eds.), *The Colonial World of Richard Boyle*, pp. 121–48.

51 Ibid., pp 233–44.

52 Micheal P. Carroll, *Irish Pilgrimage, Holy Wells and Popular Catholic Devotion* (Baltimore, MD: Johns Hopkins University Press, 1999); David Fleming, 'The "Mass Rock" in Eighteenth-century Ireland: The Symbolic and Historical Past', in James Lyttleton and Matthew Stout (eds.), *Church and Settlement in Medieval and Early Modern Ireland*, forthcoming.

53 Smyth, *Map-making, Landscapes and Memory*, p. 96.

54 Horning, *Ireland in the Virginian Sea*.

55 James Lyttleton, 'The Manor Houses of the 1st Lord Baltimore in an English Atlantic world', *Post-Medieval Archaeology* 51 (2017), 43–61.

16 Climate, debt, and conflict: environmental history as a new direction in understanding early modern Ireland

Francis Ludlow and Arlene Crampsie[1]

Introduction

The early modern period is recognized as one of the most tumultuous in Ireland's political, socioeconomic, and cultural history, resulting in transformations to power structures, land ownership, economic activity, settlement patterns, and demographic and sociocultural profiles—all of which took place alongside the accelerating incorporation of the island into globalized flows of goods, ideas, and people. This same period is also acknowledged as experiencing the coldest sustained period of the broader Little Ice Age (c.1350–1850), with prolonged changes in background average temperature and precipitation accompanied by an increased frequency and severity of extreme and potentially global weather events.[2] These natural and human-driven upheavals combined to transform the Irish physical landscape beyond recognition between 1550 and 1730. Despite an awareness of the broader significance of these political, economic, social, and cultural alterations, interest in this aspect of early modern Ireland has been largely confined to historical geographers, social and economic historians, and, more recently, environmental historians. Yet even a cursory examination of the political history of this period makes clear that extreme weather events and environmental destruction from decades of warfare formed a significant context for and backdrop to contemporary commentators' experiences of the continually evolving political landscape. To uncritically consign such accounts to the realm of irrelevant hyperbole is to severely underestimate the dependence, even in peacetime, of a predominantly agricultural society on favorable environmental conditions. In a period marked by unrest, uncertainty, and upheaval, environmental deteriorations and uncertainty added exponentially to the already substantial challenges faced by natives and newcomers alike.

Studies from many regions have shown suggestive links between violence, conflict, climatic changes, and extreme weather; studies of the modern era have also identified associations.[3] The mechanisms underlying these associations are contested, however, and considerably more complex than allowed for by some studies, often with an absence of input from the humanities and social sciences.[4] A need therefore exists for nuanced historical analyses that assess the role of environmental pressures in the inception, severity, spatio-temporal evolution, and outcomes of conflict, alongside political, socioeconomic, and wider cultural factors. In this chapter, we utilize a case study approach to both develop our recent work outlining the wealth of human accounts and natural proxy sources available to reconstruct the period's environmental history, and to highlight the array of advantages inherent in an approach integrating environmental history with social, economic, and political history.[5] In doing so, this chapter illuminates a range of potential new directions for the wider historiography of the period as well as for environmental historians and those working in cognate disciplines. In particular, we illustrate the means by which abrupt climatic changes, extreme weather, and other hazards can act as 'revelatory crises' that expose hidden or latent cultural, economic, and political fault lines and tensions, and test the extent to which extreme weather events may be identified and characterized as a force in catalyzing or hastening societal change in early modern Ireland.[6]

Environmental history of Ireland, 1550–1730

Despite significant contributions from historical geographers, historical cartographers, and social and economic historians to the historiography of Ireland's early modern period,[7] the environmental and climatic transformations of the period are still treated as largely tangential to, or the product of, the traumatic political upheavals of the period. But divesting the landscape and environment of agency in this respect ignores their potential to act as more than a canvas on which historical events unfold. In this section we provide a brief overview of current understandings regarding the environmental history of early modern Ireland, situating our recent work chronicling climatic variability and extreme weather events in the context of more well-known landscape transformations, and identifying a number of key periods when significant environmental deterioration coincided with or closely preceded severe political turmoil. Placing Ireland's political history in conversation with its environmental history also forces us to situate Ireland in its wider European and global context, highlighting the increasingly interlinked nature of environment, politics, economy, and society, particularly across Europe in this period.

In elevating Henry VIII of England and his successors from lords to kings of Ireland, the Kingship Act of 1541 marked the onset of a renewed campaign by the English monarchy to gain full control of the island of Ireland. The attendant policy of 'surrender and regrant', followed by the dispossession of the Irish landholder and the plantation of loyal new English settlers, initiated a sustained period of warfare, rebellion, and unrest that resulted initially in stark landscape degradation occurring against the backdrop of extreme weather events. Knowledge of the timing and extent of these extremes has been revolutionized in recent years as techniques utilizing a combination of primary source materials and natural archives—including physical (e.g., ice core) and biological (e.g., tree-ring and pollen) proxies—have allowed for paleoclimatic reconstructions at fine temporal and spatial scales.[8] These have produced new understandings of the extent and severity of weather extremes globally in this period as well as their spatial variations and likely origins in volcanic activity, solar variability, and other mechanisms.[9]

As Geoffrey Parker illustrates, impacts from extreme weather, in particular droughts, flooding, and sustained cold spells, were felt not just across Europe in the seventeenth century but as far afield as China, Japan, India, Africa, and North America,[10] all of which had devastating effects on harvests, markets, and economic activity at a time when political turmoil and warfare were rife across Europe. It would appear that the people who lived through these events were more appreciative of the widespread nature of the climatic turmoil they were experiencing and its influence on society than many modern historians. Writing from Oxford in 1638, Robert Burton commented on regular reports of

> War, plagues, fires, inundations, thefts, murders, massacres, meteors, comets, spectrums, prodigies, apparitions; of towns taken, cities besieged in France, Germany, Turkey, Persia, Poland, etc; daily musters and preparations, and such like, which these tempestuous times afford; battles fought, so many men slain, monomachies, shipwrecks and sea-fights, peace, leagues, stratagems, and fresh alarms.[11]

Similarly, in 1653, historian Jean-Nicolas de Parival described how multiple natural disasters appeared to be occurring simultaneously: 'The elements, servants of an irate God, combine to snuff out the rest of humankind: mountains spew out fire, the earth shakes, plague contaminates the air', and 'the continuous rain causes rivers to flood'.[12] Tempting though it is to suggest a directly causal relationship between environmental disruption and political turmoil in the century, it is important that environmental historians do not indulge in 'neo-environmental determinism' in approaching the period.[13] Extreme weather events in one location were not necessarily negative for an entire country or even continent, and in an increasingly interlinked world, a harvest crisis in one territory might provide trade and other economic opportunities in another, while disproportionately impacting different classes and societal groups dependent on a range of other factors. One key role of the environmental historian is therefore to provide a holistic context for political narratives, incorporating the challenges and possibilities that individuals and societies faced as a result of environmental upheavals into the wider historiography, and when asserting that environmental change may have had an influence, to tease out the evidence of its extent.

In the context of Ireland's early modern period, this first requires an understanding of the timing and extent of extreme weather, and a sense of the practical societal implications of an age often cited as experiencing the coldest sustained period of the Little Ice Age. These can begin to be understood when the variable temperature and precipitation rates over time and

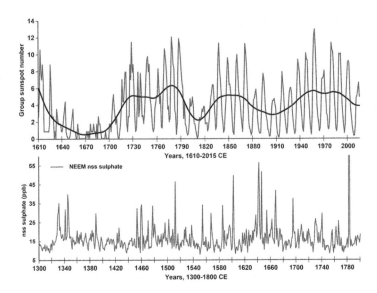

Figure 16.1 Solar and volcanic forcing. The *top panel* shows solar forcing as reflected
in annual counts of the group sunspot number beginning with telescopic
observations from 1610, revealing the ~11-year sunspot cycle (light
grey line). The dark gray line depicts the longer-term trend, using an
8.3-point spline smoothing.[14] The *bottom panel* shows annual (non-sea-
salt, nss) sulfate values from the North Greenland Eemian Ice Drilling
(NEEM) ice core, Greenland, covering 1300–1800. The large sulfate
values for the Laki (Iceland) fissure eruption (starting 1783) are trun-
cated for clarity, with its sulfate deposition exaggerated by the volcano's
proximity to Greenland.[15] Figure redrawn after Ludlow and Crampsie.[16]

space are examined alongside the 'forcing factors' most likely to cause these
variations—the level of solar energy reaching the Earth and the frequency
and magnitude of explosive volcanism.[17] The energy that drives the Earth's
climate system is provided by the Sun and is often measured as 'total solar
irradiance' (TSI), the levels of which vary, or cycle, continually on a range
of time-scales with a complex and contested influence on climate. Perhaps
most famous is the ~11-year sunspot cycle. When sunspots are at their most
numerous, solar irradiance peaks. Although the small scale of irradiance
change associated with this cycle is generally held to have a small direct
impact on climate, the existence of 'grand solar minima', when the 11-year
cycle weakens for extended periods, may induce more pronounced impacts,
including an increased probability of cold winters in Europe and the northeast Atlantic.[18] The 'Maunder Minimum',[19] a grand minimum that occurred
during the early modern period, is traditionally cited as spanning c.1645 to
c.1715, but with a decline in TSI output arguably setting in from c.1625 (as
per Figure 16.1). The Maunder Minimum is one of only twenty-seven grand
minima to have occurred in the past 11,000 years and was closely preceded

by the even deeper Spörer Minimum from c.1450 to c.1550, suggesting that the late medieval and early modern periods were subject to notable volatility from solar forcing.

Compounding this is the fact that the period from 1550 to 1730 is also distinguished for its high frequency and magnitude of explosive volcanic eruptions, with sulfate concentrations in polar ice sheets indicating the occurrence of twenty-four major eruptions, in comparison to the fourteen often smaller eruptions in the preceding 181 years (Figure 16.1).[20] These eruptions are perhaps the most important of many potential contributors to the climatic changes of the period, driving in particular the occurrence of severely cold summers. This is accomplished primarily through the explosive release of large volumes of sulfur dioxide gas into the high atmosphere, where it oxidizes to form sulfate aerosol particles that efficiently reflect solar radiation back to space and thereby cool the Earth's surface,[21] with the impact on summer temperatures (and often late spring and early autumn) lasting for several years post-eruption.[22] These eruptions are likely to have been responsible for some of the coldest summers of the period, with their influence identifiable in most decades and notably in relation to the two largest eruptions occurring in 1600 and 1640. Volcanic impacts on winter climate are less straightforward and less often discussed, but could still be of critical importance to early modern Irish agriculture. It is possible that tropical eruptions may in fact induce a winter season warming for some regions of Europe, but in Ireland both tropical and high-latitude eruptions have been shown to induce cold winters historically.[23] The many tropical and high-latitude Northern Hemispheric explosive eruptions identifiable in polar ice-cores between 1550 and 1730 would, in sum, have resulted in multiple years of substantially below average temperatures, even without the onset of notably declining solar irradiance.

Although important, the knowledge that reduced levels of total solar irradiance and explosive volcanic eruptions occurred on a scale likely to promote sustained cooler periods in Europe throughout the early modern period does not by itself provide the fine-grained evidence that allows for temporally and spatially specific understandings of the climatic conditions experienced in Ireland. For this we must turn to 'high resolution' natural archives such as annual tree-ring growth records. A recent landmark tree-ring-based reconstruction of summer air temperatures tailored for the European region, including Ireland,[24] reveals a relentless downward trajectory in summer temperatures from the mid-1560s that reached a nadir in the late 1590s and early 1600s. Although a rapid partial recovery occurred in the 1610s, persistently below average temperatures continued until the 1720s. Specific summers are of note within this broader period, the most severely cold being in 1601, while in chronological order the ten coldest took place in 1587, 1596, 1601, 1606, 1608, 1633, 1641, 1663, 1675, and 1695 (Figure 16.2).[25] Of these, at least four can be readily associated with major volcanic eruptions, occurring in 1586, 1601, 1641, and 1695 (Figure 16.1). Examining the ring widths of precipitation-sensitive Irish oaks has also recently allowed a landmark reconstruction of spring-summer soil moisture availability for the entirety of the Common Era for Ireland.[26] This reconstruction reveals the sixteenth and early seventeenth centuries to be of sustained, if variable, above average wetness (or more formally, of increased soil moisture availability), with values peaking in the 1580s and 1590s before subsiding toward the 1630s. They also indicate a period of significant below average soil-moisture availability in the early 1650s and in the 1680s, followed by a return to wetter conditions by the early 1700s (Figure 16.2). The availability of oak tree-ring data across Europe also allows the examination of the spatial extent of periods of anomalous drought or

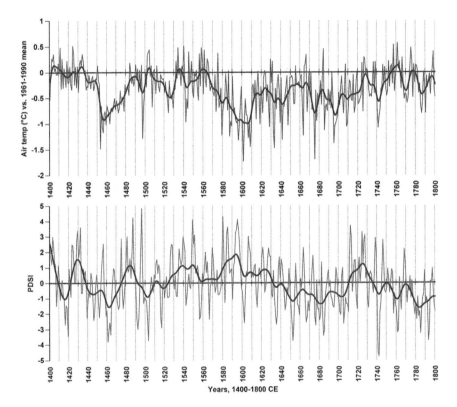

Figure 16.2 *Top panel*: European summer air temperature reconstruction, in which the annual values represent departures from the 1961–1990 mean (in °C), for the years 1400–1800.[27] On the vertical axis, positive values indicate increasing temperatures, and negative values the opposite. The thin line shows the resolution at an annual resolution, with longer-term trends shown in the thick line (using a 7-point spline smoothing). *Bottom panel*: Palmer Drought Severity Index (PDSI) reflecting spring-summer soil moisture, based upon Irish oak tree-ring growth-width measurements, 1400–1800.[28] Positive values on the vertical axis represent increasing soil moisture, and negative values the opposite (in standardized scPDSI units). The thin line shows the annual PDSI values, with longer-term trends represented by the thick line (using an 8-point spline smoothing).

wetness, as per Figure 16.3. This shows the severe and persistent drought conditions that prevailed across northwestern and northern Europe in the early 1650s, coinciding with wet weather in southern and southeastern Europe, a pattern that often repeats and reverses depending upon the region experiencing drought.

Combining such evidence from natural archives with evidence of weather extremes preserved within the rich array of documentary sources surviving

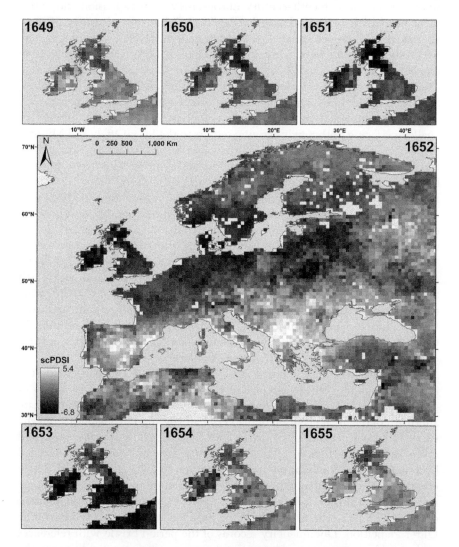

Figure 16.3 Palmer Drought Severity Index (PDSI) reflecting spring-summer soil moisture,[29] based upon European oak tree-ring growth-width measurements for the years between 1649 and 1655, with notable drought conditions prevailing from 1650 to 1654. Here, darker equates to drier conditions, and lighter equates to wetter.

from the early modern period, it is evident that many of the first-person testimonies of extreme weather are more than narrative embellishments; they are windows into a tremendously unsettled climatic era. Sustained engagement with the environmental details preserved within these sources can further aid our understanding of these extreme events by introducing evidence of locally and temporally specific variations in their duration, geographical extent, and societal impact. Extreme weather would have exacerbated the challenges of sixteenth- and seventeenth-century European overseas expansion and settlement plans both in Ireland and the Americas,[30] but they also may offer an alternative and little-considered interpretation of the motives encouraging settlers to uproot to 'terra incognita'.[31] In the Irish context, these unpredictable climatic variations occurred as a backdrop to dramatic societal and landscape changes as the native population was dispossessed and displaced by English, Scots, and Welsh settlers in formal and informal state plantation schemes.

Variable climatic conditions likely complicated the already significant challenges facing both newly arriving settlers to the Leix-Offaly and Munster plantations of the later sixteenth century, and natives forced to seek alternative living spaces in marginal, bog, and upland regions. The native population's reluctance to forsake traditional pastoral agricultural practices and the newcomers' struggles to introduce 'civilized' crop production methods may well have been influenced by these unfavorable weather conditions, undoubtedly contributing to the multiple grain shortages and harvest-related crises of the first half of the seventeenth century, namely in 1600–1603, 1607–1608, 1621–1624, 1627–1629, 1630–1633, 1639–1641.[32] Yet agricultural difficulties cannot solely be blamed on weather, given the proliferation of scorched-earth tactics by both the Gaelic Irish and English armies as they traversed the country. While a focus on cattle likely insulated (to a degree) Gaelic Ireland from harvest failures arising from cold and damp Irish summers and autumns, in Gaelic territories, where cattle were often reliant on winter pastures in place of fodder, severe winters could bring particularly heavy losses.[33]

As we have written elsewhere, the Nine Years' War and particularly the events surrounding the Battle of Kinsale occurred against the backdrop of severe weather.[34] The critical winter of 1601/1602 occurred in the immediate aftermath of the great eruption of the Peruvian volcano Huaynaputina in February 1600, with eruptions recurring into March.[35] This event is considered one of the largest eruptions of the last thousand years and was closely preceded by a smaller though substantial tropical eruption in 1595 (Figure 16.1). These eruptions can be credited with a sizeable contribution to the coldest sustained run of years in this period, from c.1595 to c.1610, and spanning the duration of the Nine Years' War, the Flight of the Earls, and the commencement of the Ulster Plantation. Documentary records of the period bristle with references to the problems encountered by armies due to excessive wet conditions in the late 1500s, with the *Annals of the Four Masters* highlighting an engagement between O'Donnell and crown forces near Carbury, County Sligo, in 1597, when 'there fell a shower of rain in such torrents that the forces on either side could not use or wield their arms, so drenched with wet were their powder-pouches and the apparatus of their fine guns'.[36] Similar accounts have survived not only in the documentary record but also in folklore, of the earlier-than-usual winter of 1601, the severe cold, and the pressure it placed on the armies on all sides prior to, during, and immediately after the Battle of Kinsale. An account from the National Folklore Collection details how Hugh O'Neill's crossing of Logbreach Bog was interrupted 'because he could not cross the bogs with his heavy artillery. The bogs were too soft. That night it froze very heavily and early next morning Hugh crossed the frozen bogs safely and proceeded to Kinsale'.[37] This notably poor weather, in tandem with ongoing multiyear conflict and environmental degradation, diminished the Irish environment's capacity to provision armies and the general population. As Colm Lennon notes, 'closely allied to intemperate weather as a harbinger of death … was disease', with visitations of plague in 1597 and 1602–1604.[38]

The period immediately after the Nine Years' War witnessed a gradual improvement in temperatures, precipitation, and a brief respite from major volcanic activity, leading to a gap in harvest crises between 1608 and 1621. This period witnessed the Anglicization of the Irish landscape through the rejuvenation of the Munster plantation and the initiation of the Ulster plantation and, in the 1610s and 1620s, a series of smaller plantations in Wexford and across the Midlands.[39] Urban centers were created, land reclamation began in earnest, new agricultural techniques were trialed, industry was established, the population grew rapidly, and the Irish economy was modernized with a consequent increase in imports and exports that enmeshed Ireland in deepening trade networks across the Irish Sea to Europe and the Americas.[40] The 1620s, however, witnessed a return to more unsettled climatic conditions, the effects of which are evidenced by the reemergence of poor harvests in the absence of any widespread military campaigns. The additional stresses that this placed on a settler society still in its infancy and surrounded by a discontented native population likely contributed to the undercurrent of unrest, characterized by David Edwards as a 'near-constant spark and crackle of localized rebellion',[41] which spiraled into large-scale open rebellion in October 1641. As weather conditions deteriorated with the deepening of the Maunder Minimum and the impact of further volcanic eruptions in 1637 and 1640, it is unsurprising that the 1641 Depositions abound with references to the severe weather and the attendant loss of life as a result of exposure to harsh winter conditions.

The extreme weather that characterized the start and end of the 1640s and the early 1650s was not unique to Ireland, with unsettled climatic and political conditions at play almost globally.[42] Thus, the Eleven Years' War in Ireland, with its consequent massive depopulation,[43] driven by wartime atrocities, famine, exposure, disease, and out-migration of settlers returning to Britain, occurred largely coterminously with the English Civil War and toward the end of the Thirty Years' War in Europe. The extreme cold of the early 1640s was superseded by severe drought conditions across Northern Europe from 1649 to 1654, exacerbating the plight of a population suffering the twin onslaughts of plague—which reached Galway from Spain in 1649 and lasted in some regions until as late as 1653—and the Cromwellian conquest.[44] It seems likely that a lack of clean drinking water accelerated the success of Cromwellian siege tactics in this period, acting as an additional stressor to an already overburdened population.

While the environmental destruction of a sustained period of warfare and poor weather conditions made a return to normality at the immediate conclusion of the war unlikely, the ensuing significant land transfers, dispossession, displacement, and forced transplantation of the Gaelic Irish and Old English population made it an impossibility.[45] The Ireland that emerged in the aftermath of the Eleven Years' War had been firmly removed from the Catholic Irish. New and returning settler populations were rebuilt from the foundations established pre-1641 and, in the context of generally improving weather conditions, continued to expand Ireland's produce and export rates. Neither a brief but significant return to unsettled weather in the late 1670s and early 1680s, with a precipitous decline in both temperatures and precipitation, nor the Williamite Wars of 1689 to 1691, generated the same level of societal stress as earlier periods. A return thereafter to relatively more stable political and environmental conditions ensured that by 1730, the face of the Irish landscape was transformed. The ruined villages and nucleated settlements of Catholic Ireland stood juxtaposed against new urban centers, while the rural landscape was largely deforested, both to remove the hiding places of the Gaelic Irish and profit from British market demands. Meanwhile, drainage works had been enacted, improving bogs and marshlands, as fields were enclosed and agriculture practices were altered and became increasingly and regionally specialized. The unfortified nature of the big houses and demesnes of the Protestant Ascendancy spoke to the stability and security of the new landowners and wider society.[46]

Climate, debt, and the 1641 rising/rebellion[47]

In providing a general environmental history of the early modern period, the preceding section highlights a number of key periods where the coincidence of environmental upheaval and political unrest suggest the need for further research. In this section we take a case study approach to the 1641 Rebellion that explores its climatic context, spatializes this examination, and integrates evidence of socioeconomic context to interrogate what we have identified as a possible period in which extremes of weather may have acted as revelatory crises. The influence of weather on violence and conflict is, however, always mediated by the interplay of underlying cultural, social, and political contexts that differ, depending upon the manner of weather and violence or conflict under consideration. Climatic conditions may thus trigger or worsen some kinds of violence and conflict, including more spontaneous or diffuse internal unrest and civil revolt by promoting contestation over increasingly scarce resources.[48] This may be particularly so in contexts that have reduced social resilience to extreme weather as when given political, religious, or ethnic groups are marginalized and more limited in their ability to mitigate the impacts of extreme weather and adapt to longer-term changes in climate (e.g., by switching to alternative income and food sources).[49] Other regions and eras furnish evidence that extreme weather repeatedly acted to suppress certain forms of conflict, such as organized inter-state warfare that necessitated large armies and could be sustained only by access to considerable natural resources.[50]

As noted earlier, accounts contained in the 1641 Depositions abound with testimony concerning the harsh climatic circumstances prevailing during the rebellion in the 1641–42 winter season. Many deponents, often widows from Ulster and Leinster, attested to 'cold snowy weather' and 'the extremity of the winter', exacerbating the consequences of rebel practices that included the destruction of Protestant homes, stripping the inhabitants naked, and forcing them to flee.[51] Thus, Katherin Cooke of Armagh recalled

> such frost [and] snow that the deponents children and divers other children … present at that battle would[,] where they saw the warm blood of any fall on the ground[,] [tread] therein with their bare feet to keep them from freezing and starving such was the extremity of the weather.[52]

Inhabitants forced to traverse the country in frost and snow, naked, homeless, and in search of shelter resulted in predictably harrowing outcomes. As another deponent recalled:

> Whereupon the deponent and his wife and 5 small children going away were stripped of all their clothes … one poor daughter of his seeing him … grieve for their general miseries in way of comforting said she was not cold nor would cry although presently after … she died by that cold and want: and the first night this deponent and his wife creeping for shelter into a poor crate were glad to lie upon their children to keep in them heat and save them alive.[53]

As noted, ice core data reveal a substantial eruption in Greenland in 1637, with the source volcano most probably located in the mid- to high-latitudes of the Northern Hemisphere. The cold summer of 1639, seen in Figure 16.4, may have partly resulted from this event, contributing to documented agricultural difficulties from 1639 to 1641, with an additional contribution by the much greater eruption that deposited high volumes of sulfate in Greenland between 1641 and 1642 (Figure 16.4).[54] The source volcano is considered to have been located in the tropics because notable sulfate was also deposited in Antarctica.[55] One candidate is Parker Volcano, Mindanao island, in the Philippines, which erupted violently between December 1640 and January 1641, reaching Volcanic Explosivity Index (VEI) Point 5 ('Paroxysmic'). Hokkaido-Komagatake in Japan is a further potential contributor, erupting from July to October 1640, and similarly reaching VEI Point 5.[56]

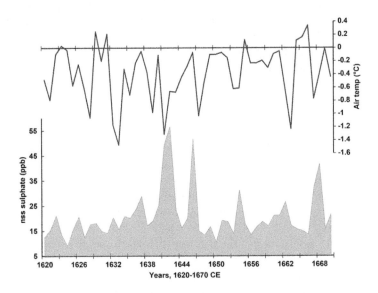

Figure 16.4 Close-up of the climatic context of the 1641 Rebellion. The *top panel* shows reconstructed European summer temperatures for 1620 to 1670 relative to the 1960 to 1990 mean (PAGES 2k Consortium data). The *bottom panel* shows Greenland non-sea-salt sulfate levels from the NEEM ice-core in solid shading. Deposition from volcanic eruptions is identifiable as large spikes above the background average depositional levels.

The declining solar activity of the Maunder sunspot minimum (Figure 16.1) potentially amplified the temperature impact of these eruptions in 1641, which the PAGES 2k temperature reconstruction reveals as having the second coldest European summer in the fifty-year period (plotted in Figure 16.4). The broader geographical impacts of the eruption(s) at this time can be identified in high-altitude Bristlecone pine trees from western North America, where unusually narrow growth registers for 1641,[57] indicating a severely cold growing season there. A tree-ring-density summer temperature reconstruction for the wider Northern Hemisphere also places 1641 as the third coldest summer since the start of this record in 1400, with only 1601 and the 1816 European 'year without a summer' that followed the 1815 eruption of Tambora in Indonesia (VEI Point 7, 'Super-Colossal') ranking colder.[58]

Documentary sources that furnish quantitative economic data (e.g., wages, grain prices, yields) are invaluable in assessing the impacts of extreme weather on society. Early modern Ireland often lacks such data, which economic historians in England and elsewhere have profitably exploited, but a provisional list of years experiencing harvest-related difficulties can, however, be compiled from various sources for Ireland up to the end of the seventeenth century,[59] before price series start to become available.[60] Our provisional list of years is 1496–1497, 1499–1500, 1502, 1505, 1538–1539, 1541, 1545, 1552,

1557, 1561, 1574, 1585–1587, 1600–1603, 1607–1608, 1621–1624, 1627–1629, 1630–1633, 1639–1641, 1652, 1672–1673, 1687–1689, and 1698. While likely incomplete and requiring further research to evidence a distinction between the severity and geography of each respective episode, this listing is sufficient to allow a preliminary investigation of the potential association between extreme weather and societal stress of this form in early modern Ireland. To do this, years of experiencing harvest-related difficulties are set statistically against years of notable heat and cold identifiable from Figure 16.2, in an approach known as a superposed epoch analysis (hereafter SEA) that provides a robust means of examining the frequency and timing of correspondences between sets of events (Figure 16.5).[61]

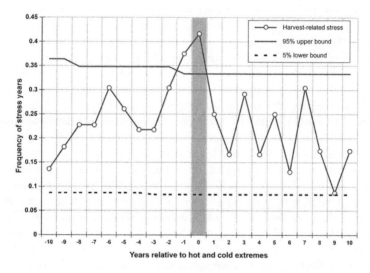

Figure 16.5 Superposed epoch analysis, showing the average frequency of years (dotted line), with known or inferred harvest-related difficulties (forty-four years in total) composited relative to years (31 in total) that fall at least 1.5 standard deviations above (i.e., hot) and below (i.e., cold) the reconstructed mean spring-summer air temperatures from 1496 to 1700 in the PAGES 2k data (Figure 16.2). These averages are shown for each of the ten years preceding the occurrence of extreme weather (points −10 to −1 on the horizontal axis), the average during the years of extreme weather (point 0), and each of the ten years following (points 1–10). Frequencies on the vertical axis can be read as percentages: for example, the frequency for superposed year 0 (i.e., point 0 on the horizontal axis, representing the years in which extreme weather actually occurred) is 0.417, meaning that 41.7% of these years also experienced harvest-related difficulties. The value for superposed year +1, that is, the first year following the occurrence of the extreme weather is 0.25, that is, 25% of these years also experienced harvest-related difficulties.[62] Statistical significance is estimated using Monte Carlo randomization, wherein any frequency values observed below or above the solid or dashed lines are estimated to have less than a 5% probability of having occurred purely by chance.[63]

This analysis reveals that approximately 42% of years with notably hot or cold summers experienced harvest-related difficulties, greater than in any years closely preceding or following and sufficiently high as to have just a 1.4% chance ($p = 0.014$) of occurring randomly. Also notable is the high frequency of years that apparently experienced harvest-related difficulties in the first year *before* the occurrence of extreme weather, nominally suggesting that effect precedes cause. This is, however, a well-known potential artifact of SEA that can arise for multiple reasons, often relating to the character of data available for analysis. In this case, the approach employed to identify years of extreme summer weather is a likely contributor, with deteriorating weather severe enough to impact harvest, having already begun in some instances in the preceding year.[64] Overall, these results indicate a long-term role, at least between 1496 and 1700, for extreme weather in episodes of societal stress related to harvest difficulties. This includes the decades immediately preceding the 1641 Rebellion, during which multiple extreme cold summers occurred (Figures 16.2 and 16.4), further suggesting a longer-term contributory role for weather extremes in the tensions and stresses building toward the Rebellion.

One of the few quantitative sources of economic data for seventeenth-century Ireland are the statute staple books, edited by Jane Ohlmeyer and Éamonn Ó Ciardha, with data extracted into a relational database covering the years 1597 to 1687.[65] The statute staple comprises a register of recognizances of debts made to secure loans under the authority of various staple towns, the most active, after Dublin, being Cork.[66] Loans were sought by multiple sectors of society from a range of wealthy creditors,[67] often but not solely landed gentry who lent for many reasons, including 'as a means of increasing their landed bases'[68] when debtors defaulted upon their loans and thus forfeited their title to lands they had used as security. Variations in the number of transactions recorded in the staple are certainly of complex origin, partly reflecting record completeness and consistency.[69] Ohlmeyer has, however, identified socioeconomic stressors, including harvest crises, as driving several prominent increases in transactions, 'as people, deprived of their landed revenues, turned to the staple for credit'.[70] One such harvest crisis associated with a peak in transaction numbers is that of 1639–1641, clearly visible even despite the loss of the Dublin staple volumes covering 1638 to 1660.

Figure 16.6 shows the number of transactions registered in the extant statute staple books up to 1645, in which one of the most prominent features is an upward 'step change' in yearly transactions from the 1620s, broadly sustained to the date of the 1641 Rebellion. Assuming this is not solely a product of change in the character of recording, it suggests either investment and economic expansion or a mounting need to compensate for losses induced by weather, conflict, and other misfortunes, though these are not necessarily mutually exclusive. With a return in the 1620s to more unsettled weather and harvest difficulties after the comparative stability of the 1610s (Figure 16.2), it is particularly notable that the percentage of transactions known to have been referred to the chancery court or sheriff grows strikingly from the 1620s, plausibly reflecting an increase

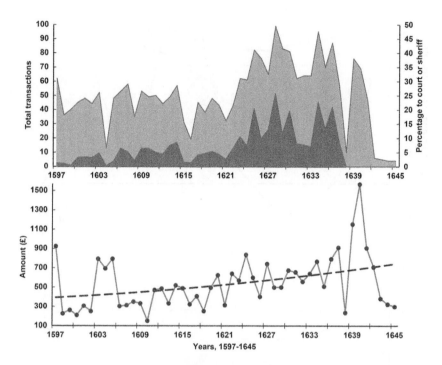

Figure 16.6 *Top panel:* Total transactions recorded in the staple books (light shading), and the percentage recorded as referred to court (primarily the
Chancery court) or sheriff (darker shading). Note that the Dublin staple
volumes are missing for the years 1638–1660, which impacts the number
of transactions known through time, and also the recording of the fate
of loans regarding their referral to court or sheriff. *Bottom panel:* Annual
average (mean) amount (£) of transactions recorded on the Irish statute
staple books (solid dotted line) and trend line (a second-order polyno-
mial, dashed line).

in loan repayment difficulties. Average transaction amounts also show an ongoing increase through the early decades of the seventeenth century, accelerating
from the early 1630s before collapsing in the 1640s, attributed by Ohlmeyer to
the disruption arising from the Eleven Years' War from 1641 onward.[71] While
other contributory factors, such as the rate of inflation, require consideration,
this longer-term increase may at least partly reflect a mounting indebtedness in
the lead-up to the 1641 Rebellion, not only for the settler populations establishing and expanding their livelihood, but perhaps especially for the Gaelic Irish
and Old English facing ongoing economic and political marginalization, compounding the stresses prevailing in these pivotal years and increasing societal
vulnerability to extreme weather and other shocks.

Comparing reconstructed temperatures against the evidence of the staple
volumes (Figure 16.7) reveals a tendency for transaction numbers to spike

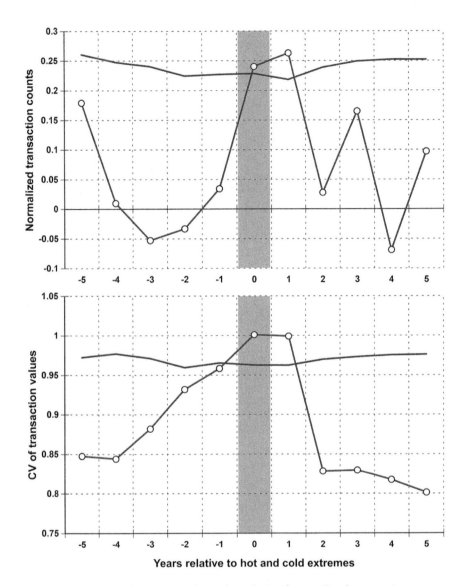

Figure 16.7 Top panel: Superposed epoch analysis of normalized transaction counts (dotted line) relative to twenty-one years falling at least 1.5 standard deviations above and below the long-term reconstructed mean summer temperatures, 1597–1687. *Bottom panel:* Variation in the mean size of loans (measured by the coefficient of variation, CV) relative to all extreme years falling at least 1.25 standard deviations above and below the mean reconstructed temperatures for the same period. Statistical significance in both panels is tested via Monte Carlo randomizations with 10,000 iterations. The solid (un-dotted) line represents the 95% upper bound of the distribution generated by these randomizations.[72]

significantly during and immediately following years of extreme heat and cold. With the likelihood of these spikes' having occurred purely by chance being just 4.4% ($p = 0.044$) and 2.9% ($p = 0.029$), respectively, the tree-ring-based data thus provides independent corroboration of the usage of the staples during times of stress. Although not sufficiently large to be statistically significant, a tendency toward lower mean transaction values also occurs in extreme years. Examining the variation in transaction sizes relative to the dates of extreme summers reveals a notable increase in the range of values during these years and in the first years following, sufficiently large to have a respective probability of just 1.8% ($p = 0.018$) and 1.6% ($p = 0.016$) of occurring purely by chance. Considered in sum, these results suggest that extreme summers could provoke increased borrowing of a notably greater range, including smaller loans, perhaps indicating a greater likelihood of borrowing for subsistence rather than investment. As people from all classes could avail of the staple, from farmers to members of the peerage, further examination of the occupations of creditors listed in the staple books will likely prove revealing of the class (and religious) dimensions of borrowing during and following years of climatic stress.

The application of Geographical Information System (GIS) methodologies to the staple data, a source that is as revealing of variability through space as through time, is recommended by Ohlmeyer and Ó Ciardha and allows for an examination of regional variations across Ireland.[73] Figure 16.8 thus offers an initial spatial visualization of staple data for the years 1597 to 1641. Mapping the total number and values of transactions per county in this period reveals the highest level of interaction with the staple in Dublin and Meath, with lower but still comparatively high values in Louth, Westmeath, and Kildare reflecting the traditional core area of English colonial influence, and greater economic activity reflecting Dublin's merchants and traders, with their national and international trade links. Proximity to the ports of Cork and Limerick may contribute to the slightly elevated values in these counties, but the biasing influence of Dublin and Cork as the two most active Irish staple towns should be borne in mind. Accounting for this, mapping mean transaction values provides a contrast, with some of the lowest values observed for the core region of Meath, Kildare, and Westmeath. Taken together with the variability around each mean, mapped using the coefficient of variation, this might be interpreted as a region with a sustained engagement in the market economy and frequent use of staples among debtors of more diverse occupation, taking on average smaller loans, but with a reasonably high degree of variability relative to this mean. By contrast, some of the largest mean values are found concentrated in parts of Ulster and a contiguous region further south, comprising Offaly, Laois, and Kilkenny, mapping almost directly onto the leading locations of the outbreak of the 1641 Rebellion.[74] While much caution and further research are required before making categorical links between these two facts, this spatialization implies mounting indebtedness

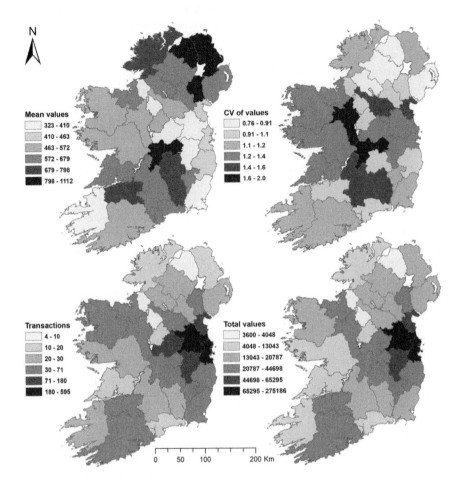

Figure 16.8 Map bottom left: The number of statute staples transactions per county, where identifiable, according to the address of the debtor, for all years 1597 to 1641, inclusive. *Map bottom right:* The total value of bonds in £ sterling for all transactions for these years. *Map top left:* The average (mean) value of bonds in £ sterling. *Map top right:* The variation of bond values around the mean, as measured by the CV. Gradation into intervals in all maps is accomplished using the Jenks Natural Breaks methodology as implemented in ArcMap.[75]

(potentially across a wide class spectrum) in these areas, suggesting a diverse demographic under stress before the outbreak of rebellion.

The application of similar GIS methodologies to the 1641 Depositions, facilitated by their recent digitization (1641.tcd.ie), enables an interrogation of the spatial patterns of weather conditions reportedly experienced during the Rebellion, potentially providing a unique insight for climate historians into the Irish early modern climatic response to the major explosive eruptions detailed earlier, and reflecting regions in which vulnerability to extreme weather may have been particularly marked. If, as we have argued, extreme weather should be considered part of the suite of triggers for the Rebellion itself, then potential variability in the severity of the cold conditions across Ireland can perhaps also be expected to have played a role in the geographical patterning of violence.[76]

The value of the depositions in this matter can be illustrated by mapping a selection of weather referenced therein, as per Figure 16.9, including references to 'snow' and 'weather' (when described as severe explicitly or by implication).[78] The map of weather is underlain by shading that depicts the variation in depositions gathered, itself partly reflecting the methodology employed by the various commissioners in charge and the geography of New English settlement. Because of the large variation in the number of depositions (and examinations, recognizances, and other relevant documents) available per county, weather references are mapped as percentages, rather than absolute numbers, to avoid the biasing 'population effect' of counties with large numbers of depositions. Our mapping reveals the wide spatial extent of references to snowfall and severe weather, which can be seen to represent a small but persistent substratum of content in the Depositions. The greater percentage concentration of references in the north, midlands, and east of Ireland makes considerable climatological sense, with the influence of the

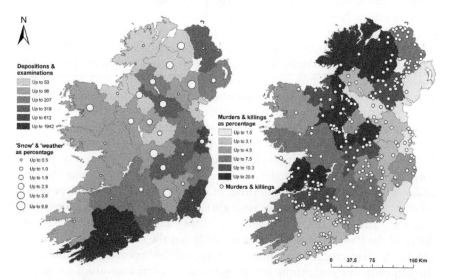

Figure 16.9 *Map left:* Total depositions, examinations, recognizances, etc., per county (gray shading), as listed on 1641.tcd.ie (accessed 10/10/15). The percentage of these referencing 'snow' and severe 'weather' is shown in graduated dots. *Map right:* Murders and killings reported in the depositions, as mapped by William J. Smyth are shown as white dots,[77] and expressed as a percentage of the total depositions per county (gray shading). Gradation into intervals in both maps is accomplished using the Jenks Natural Breaks methodology as implemented in ArcMap.

Atlantic in western and southern coastal counties known to frequently moderate the severity of cold spells here;[79] however, all this is also reflective of the geography of the Rebellion itself. It is little surprise that extreme weather was in the forefront of the minds of people removed from their homes, stripped naked, and forced to travel to seek shelter.

To explore the role of weather, we draw upon William J. Smyth's mapping of murders and killings from the depositions (Figure 16.9), comprising one of the most numerous categories of reported violence.[80] As with references to weather, we map murders and killings as percentages of control for the effect of variations in the total number of depositions per county. While some 'mismatches' are apparent between the percentages of weather and murders and killings per county,[81] a suggestive visual association exists overall—for example, in Offaly, Armagh, and particularly Derry, where reports of both are numerous.[82] A more systematic comparison between extreme weather and murders and killings is shown in Figure 16.10. This scatterplot reveals a general positive correlation, with counties exhibiting higher percentages of murders and killings tending to exhibit a higher percentage of references to severe weather, as evidenced by the upward-sloping trend line. This is a tendency rather than an absolute. As noted from the visual inspection of Figure 16.9, certain counties are outliers from this general pattern, showing only a modest increase in the percentage of reported violence and killing for a relatively large percentage increase in references to severe weather. Nonetheless, a strongly positive overall correlation ($r = 0.596$) can be observed, with only a 0.3% ($p = 0.003$) chance of having occurred randomly.[83] An association between scarcity-induced resource competition and violence is well attested in Irish history,[84] and this result suggests that geographically variable susceptibility of Catholic populations to extreme weather may have partly driven the violence seen during the Rebellion, with years of mounting tensions and grievances making settler populations the natural targets for much of the violence. These results should not be interpreted to suggest that extreme weather acted as the only driver of geographical variations in violence.[85] Indeed the correlation analysis clearly signals this. With a maximum possible correlation coefficient of 1.0, the observed value of 0.596 implies that there are additional influences on the patterning of violence reported in the depositions, whether acting independently or synergistically with weather conditions.

If the variable geographical severity of weather conditions may have influenced the levels of violence, this is clearly not the end of the story, and we can further interrogate the spatial patterns of the reporting of violence in the Depositions by returning to the spatialized information from the staples. Taking the mean value of transactions per county between 1597 and 1641, and correlating these with the percentage of murders and killing per county return a value of $r = 0.409$, a moderate positive correlation with only a 2.0% ($p = 0.02$) probability of having occurred purely by chance. Average transaction values must be interpreted cautiously as a metric of indebtedness and stress. An unknown number of loans may have been repaid without undue difficulty and, dependent upon the purpose of the loan, might have been

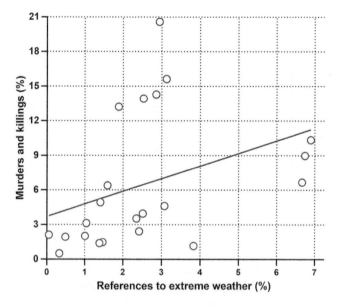

Figure 16.10 Scatterplot of references to 'snow' and extreme 'weather' per county
(horizontal axis) versus the frequency of murders and killings reported
in the depositions (quantified by William J. Smyth[86]) on the vertical
axis.[87] Both are expressed as a percentage of total depositions and examinations per county. Each dot represents a county, while the straight
line represents a linear trend line indicating a positive correlation between frequency of references to extreme weather and the reported
number of murders and killings.

invested successfully to improve returns on land or mercantile activity. It is
known, however, that loans were lent to debtors under stress, including loans
taken to repay previous loans or for potentially frivolous expenditures.[88] The
evidence of Figure 16.7 also suggests that loans may have been necessitated
by the impacts of extreme weather, which, with an interest rate of 10%, may
have initiated some debtors into spiraling indebtedness, eventual insolvency,
and the prospective loss of properties and lands. This doubtless promoted tensions that would play into the scale and geographical foci of violence in 1641.
The staple books themselves identify many Catholic gentry in danger of for-
feiting their properties, with a growing number of loans referred by creditors to the Chancery Court or sheriff (Figure 16.6) in the years before the
Rebellion, including by Protestant settlers and gentry attempting to increase
their landholdings in Ireland.[89] It hence seems credible to consider mean
transaction values registered on the staple in the run up to the 1641 Rebellion
to be a reflection (albeit imperfect) of indebtedness and societal stress. Indeed,
a growing realization of the apparent permanence of land confiscations, social dislocation, loss of local hegemony, and displacement, combined with

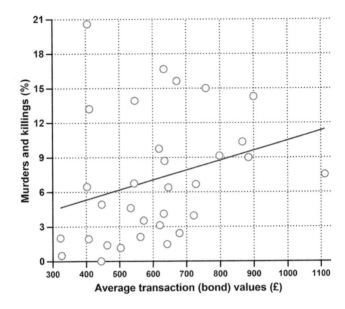

Figure 16.11 Scatterplot of average (mean) transaction values per county for the period 1598 to 1641 (horizontal axis) versus the frequency of murders
and killings reported in the depositions (as quantified by William J.
Smyth[90]) expressed as a percentage of the total depositions and examinations per county (vertical axis). Each dot represents a county, while
the line represents a linear trend line showing a positive correlation
between average transaction values and the percentage of reported murders and killings.

the growing burden of increasingly poor weather conditions and a return to
harvest crises and increasing indebtedness, makes it unsurprising that sim-
mering political unrest became manifest in October 1641. That concerns over
personal indebtedness formed one chief concern for the rebels is evident in
accounts from the depositions, outlining how some actively sought out their
bonds to destroy them (Figure 16.11).[91]

Conclusion

Irish climate between 1550 and 1730 experienced some of the most profound changes, often toward colder and less stable conditions, of the second
millennium; but it also exhibited a recovery from the deepest trough of the
Little Ice Age in the early decades of the eighteenth century, coinciding with
a period of economic growth, the growing fortunes of the Ascendancy, and
the remaking of the Irish landscape. Caution must be exercised to avoid en-
vironmentally deterministic interpretations, but situating the political upheavals of the late sixteenth and early seventeenth centuries in an appropriate

environmental context offers an opportunity to better understand the challenges and opportunities faced by the new settlers and the dispossessed Irish. In this chapter we have provided an overview of social-environmental relations in early modern Ireland, noting questions and concerns that will benefit from further research, and offering a detailed illustration of the potential of a mixed methods approach through its ability to unlock spatiotemporally specific detail about the role of climate and extreme weather as a political and socioeconomic stressor. In this regard, we offer further suggestions for new directions in the study of environmental history in early modern Ireland.

Natural archives such as tree-rings, from which temperature and precipitation reconstructions can be developed, clearly provide valuable and relevant datasets for historians of this period. Taking advantage of the long temporal span provided by these reconstructions may allow the identification of periods and regions in which extremes of a given severity are and are not followed by the same degree of societal stress,[92] implying varying levels of resilience and offering new questions for historians to pursue in understanding what may be previously unrecognized patterns. Extremes of wet, dry, hot, cold, or windy weather, occurring in different seasons, with different durations and severities, with variable levels of societal preparedness (such as grain storage from preceding years) and fragility (not least indebtedness)—all can interact to influence societal responses to extreme weather, and must be the subjects of interrogation by environmental historians using as diverse an array of written and natural archives as possible. New palaeoclimatic reconstructions continue to emerge with increasing relevance for Ireland, as exemplified by the development of Scottish pine tree-ring chronologies that may hold more climatically relevant information for Ireland than trees growing more distantly in Scandinavia or the Alps and which have formed the mainstay of European tree-ring-based temperature reconstructions to date.[93]

The superposed epoch analysis illustrated here is just one statistical tool that can be adapted for use by historians and offers great potential for the identification and examination of interactions between extreme weather and society as reflected in a vast range of variables. Taking the Irish staple data, both lending and borrowing behaviors can be examined for responses to extreme weather. Further nuance can be gained by examining this behavior according to class (listed occupation), gender, and, where identifiable, the religion of debtors and creditors, as well as loan sizes and their referral to the Court of Chancery or sheriff. Such analyses will provide considerable insight into the differing vulnerabilities of these groups to extreme weather and, by potential extension, other socioeconomic shocks. Extremes of weather can also be examined according to type, severity, and frequency in order to examine, for example, whether multiple closely spaced versus singular ('out of the blue') extremes triggered more or less of a societal response. Examining the evolution of responses and vulnerabilities throughout the period of coverage provided by the staple, including before and after 1641 and the Eleven Years' War, can improve our understanding of how changing historical and socioeconomic contexts may mediate the impact of extreme weather over a longer time span and with class, gender, and geographically specific outcomes. Such work can deliver on the analytical promise that extreme weather events hold as 'revelatory crises' that expose latent tensions and otherwise hidden fault lines to the scrutiny of scholars.[94]

Building on the foundations laid by historical geographers such as William J. Smyth, GIS-based mapmaking and methods of spatial analysis have been put to increasingly effective use by scholars of early modern Ireland, as evidenced by the Down Survey Project,[95] Jane Ohlmeyer's maps of seventeenth-century landholding,[96] and others.[97] The growth in digitized primary sources greatly increases the possible integration of early modern documentary sources with natural archives and their combined representation and interrogation in GIS. With the staples alone, the potential exists to parse out regional variations in loan activity in the aftermath of extreme weather while continuing to account for class, gender, and religion. Within GIS, such patterns can be cross-referenced against other spatial information, such as soil quality, elevation, aspect, drainage, and infrastructure to identify other potentially meaningful patterns of resilience, vulnerability, and response. Such spatializing can also crucially allow for an understanding of both the isolation and interconnectedness of people and places in early modern Ireland, providing further nuanced understandings of the impacts of political and environmental upheavals on the physical and human landscapes of Ireland.

Perhaps most importantly, any attempt to understand the societal impacts of extreme weather in this period is immediately suggestive of the need to situate Ireland's weather (and political and socioeconomic history) in a wider continental and global context, highlighting an array of factors that speak to the interconnectedness of early modern Ireland to the outside world. This is an area rich in possibilities for further research since detailed comparative studies are, as yet, limited. The seventeenth century is an intriguing period internationally, but the increasing incorporation of Ireland into European and global trade networks in this period raises a range of questions about how this altered or exacerbated the impact of environmental stressors within Ireland. Indeed, there is scope to expand this to an examination of the different regional interactions within Europe. How, for example, did the severe northern European drought of the early 1650s (Figure 16.3) influence trade and prices across an increasingly interconnected Europe when at the same time southern Europe experienced above average rainfall?

While these are only a selection of potential avenues for future environmental histories of early modern Ireland, they are indicative of the increasing richness of both methodologies and sources relevant to the period, despite an overall lack of engagement by Irish historians with these topics. We hope that this chapter will motivate others to begin to address these myriad possibilities so that the rich documentary and natural archives for the period can be utilized to their full potential.

Notes

1 We thank the editors for their input and great patience during the production of this chapter. We also thank Jane Ohlmeyer for her support and input into the interpretation of the 1641 Depositions and Statute Staple data, as well as access to unpublished work. In addition, we are grateful to Raymond Gillespie for guidance on harvest crisis dates in the later seventeenth century; Brianán Nolan for her assistance in proofing and referencing and for the extraction of data from the 1641 Depositions; Al Matthews for his assistance with the superposed epoch analyses and the manipulation of the statute staples database; Patrick Hayes for discussion of early modern Irish primary sources, and Bruce Campbell for discussion of pan-European climatic patterns in the oak tree-ring record. Francis Ludlow further acknowledges the support of colleagues at the Trinity Centre for Environmental Humanities (tcd.ie/tceh) and the Volcanic Impacts on Climate and Society (VICS) Working Group of PAGES (Past Global Changes). This paper is a contribution to the 'Historical Dynamics of Violence, Conflict and Extreme Weather in Medieval Ireland' (CLIMCONFLICT) project, which has received funding from the European Union's Horizon 2020 research and innovation program under the Marie Skłodowska-Curie grant agreement No 709185.
2 For a review of the spatial extent of Little Ice Age conditions, see John A. Matthews and Keith R. Briffa, 'The 'Little Ice Age': Re-Evaluation of An Evolving Concept', *Geografiska Annaler* 87 (2005), 17–36. For a skeptical view concerning the global coherence and definition of the 'Little Ice Age', see Astrid E. J. Ogilvie, 'Historical Climatology, Climatic Change, and Implications for Climate Science in the 21st Century', *Climatic Change* 100 (2010), 33–47.
3 See, e.g., Zhibin Zhang et al., 'Periodic Climate Cooling Enhanced Natural Disasters and Wars in China during AD 10–1900', *Proceedings of the Royal Society* 277 (2010), 3745–53; David D. Zhang et al., 'The Causality Analysis of Climate Change and Large-Scale Human Crisis', *Proceedings of the National Academy of Sciences* 108 (42) (2011), 17296–301; R.S.J. Tol and S. Wagner, 'Climate Change and Violent Conflict in Europe over the Last Millennium', *Climatic Change* 99 (2011), 65–79.
4 See, e.g., the critical commentary by Ka-wai Fan, 'Climatic Change and Dynastic Cycles: A Review Essay', *Climatic Change* 101 (2010), 565–73. For more general comment, see Francis Ludlow and Charles Travis, 'STEAM Approaches to Climate Change, Extreme Weather and Social-Political conflict', in Armida de la Garza and Charles Travis (eds.), *STEAM: Transdisciplinary Approaches to Science, Arts, Humanities & Technology Studies* (Heidelberg: Springer, 2018).
5 For detailed discussion of human accounts and natural proxy sources that allow environmental reconstructions of the early modern period, see Francis Ludlow and Arlene Crampsie, 'Environmental History of Ireland, 1550–1730', in Jane Ohlmeyer (ed.), *The Cambridge History of Ireland, Vol II, 1550–1730* (Cambridge: Cambridge University Press, 2018), pp. 608–37.
6 Jacqueline S. Solway, 'Drought As a Revelatory Crisis: An Exploration of Shifting Entitlements and Hierarchies in the Kalahari, Botswana', *Development and Change* 25 (1994), 471–95.
7 Of particular note is the seminal work by William J. Smyth, *Map-Making, Landscapes and Memory: A Geography of Colonial and Early Modern Ireland c.1530–1750* (Cork: Cork University Press, 2006); a selection (not exhaustive) of other important contributions include Raymond Gillespie, 'Meal and Money: The Harvest Crisis of 1621–4 and the Irish Economy', in E. Margaret Crawford (ed.), *Famine: The Irish Experience, 900–1900: Subsistence Crises and Famines in Ireland* (Edinburgh: J. Donald, 1989), pp. 75–95; John H. Andrews, 'Colonial Cartography in a European Setting: The Case of Tudor Ireland', in David Woodward (ed.), *History of Cartography, Vol.*

3: *Cartography in the European Renaissance* (Chicago, IL: Chicago University Press, 2007), pp. 1670–83; Annaleigh Margey, 'Representing Plantation Landscapes: The Mapping of Ulster, c1560–1640', in James Lyttleton and Colin Rynne (eds.), *Plantation Ireland: Settlement and Material Culture, c.1550–1700* (Dublin: Four Courts Press, 2009), pp. 140–64; Raymond Gillespie, 'Economic Life, 1550–1730', in Jane Ohlmeyer (ed.), *The Cambridge History of Ireland,* pp. 531–54; William Nolan, *Fassadinin: Land, Settlement and Society in Southeast Ireland c.1600–1850* (Dublin: Geography Publications, 1979), as well as the path-breaking multivolume *County History and Society* series of which William Nolan is Series Editor (geographypublications.com). Further relevant work is cited in Juliana Adelman and Francis Ludlow, 'The Past, Present and Future of Environmental History in Ireland', *Proceedings of the Royal Irish Academy* 114C (2014), 359–91.

8 For a review of palaeoclimatic reconstructions and methods, see Raymond S. Bradley, *Paleoclimatology: Reconstructing Climates of the Quaternary* (3rd edn), (Amsterdam: Elsevier, 2015).

9 Recent works examine these environmental-political linkages in a wider context, e.g., Sam White, *The Climate of Rebellion in the Early Modern Ottoman Empire* (Cambridge: Cambridge University Press, 2011); Sam White, *A Cold Welcome: The Little Ice Age and Europe's Encounter with North America* (Cambridge, MA: Harvard University Press, 2017); and Geoffrey Parker, *Global Crisis: War, Climate Change and Catastrophe in the Seventeenth Century* (New Haven, CT and London: Yale University Press, 2013).

10 Parker, *Global Crisis,* p. xxii.

11 Robert Burton, *The Anatomy of Melancholy* (1638), cited in Parker, *Global Crisis,* p. xxi. We have modernized the spellings here and throughout.

12 Jean-Nicolas de Parival, *Abrégé, Au lecteur* (1653) cited in Parker, *Global Crisis,* p. xxii.

13 Gabriel Judkins, Marissa Smith, and Eric Keys, 'Determinism within Human-Environment Research and the Rediscovery of Environmental Causation', *The Geographical Journal* 174 (2008), 17–29.

14 Group sunspot number (v2.0, 1st July 2015) from SILSO, the Sunspot Index and Long- term Solar Observations World Data Centre, Royal Observatory of Belgium, Brussels, sidc.be/s ilso (accessed 13 July 2015). See Frédéric Clette et al., 'Revisiting the Sunspot Number. A 400-Year Perspective on the Solar Cycle', *Space Science Reviews* 186 (2014), 35–103.

15 Michael Sigl et al., 'Timing and Climate Forcing'.

16 Ludlow and Crampsie, 'Environmental History of Ireland, 1550–1730'. Figures 16.2 and 16.4 are also redrawn.

17 An account of the mechanisms underlying these factors is provided in Ludlow and Crampsie, 'Environmental History of Ireland, 1550–1730', pp. 617–27.

18 This partly operates by increasing the number of large-scale anticyclonic pressure systems with cold northerly or northeasterly winds over the northeast Atlantic and northwest Europe, with clearer skies also allowing greater loss of heat to space. Michael Lockwood et al., 'Are Cold Winters in Europe Associated with Low Solar Activity?' *Environmental Research Letters* 5 (2010), 024001; Michael Lockwood et al., 'The Solar Influence on the Probability of Relatively Cold UK Winters in the Future', *Environmental Research Letters* 6 (2011), 034004.

19 This takes its name from astronomer Edward Walter Maunder (1851–1928), who noted the reduction of visible sunspots at this time. Annie Russell Maunder (1868–1947), Walter's wife, also contributed, but has not been widely acknowledged.

20 Excluding Southern Hemisphere mid- to high-latitude eruptions.

21 For general mechanisms, see Alan Robock, 'Volcanic Eruptions and Climate', *Reviews of Geophysics* 38 (2000), 191–219, and Jihong Cole-Dai, 'Volcanoes and Climate', *WIREs: Climate Change* 1 (2010), 824–39.

22 Stephen D. Galvin, Kieran R. Hickey, and Aaron P. Potito, 'Identifying Volcanic Signals in Irish Temperature Observations since AD 1800', *Irish Geography* 44 (2012), 97–110.

23 Francis Ludlow et al., 'Medieval Irish Chronicles Reveal Persistent Volcanic Forcing of Severe Winter Cold Events, 431–1649 CE', *Environmental Research Letters* 8 (2013), 024035. It is possible that winter warming following tropical eruptions may be confined to the first post-eruption winter season, thereafter reverting to a net cooling impact in subsequent winters. See Brian Zambri and Alan Robock, 'Winter Warming and Summer Monsoon Reduction after Volcanic Eruptions in Coupled Model Intercomparison Project 5 (CMIP5) Simulations', *Geophysical Research Letters* 43 (2016), 10,920–28.

24 PAGES 2k Consortium, 'Continental-Scale Temperature Variability during the Past Two Millennia', *Nature Geoscience* 6 (2013), 339–46.

25 In order of severity, these are 1601, 1675, 1633, 1608, 1695, 1596, 1641, 1606, 1587, and 1663.

26 More specifically, this is a reconstruction of the self-calibrating PDSI (scPDSI), and has been extended by to Europe, North Africa, and the Middle East by Edward R. Cook et al., 'Old World Megadroughts and Pluvials during the Common Era', *Science Advances* 1 (10) (2015), e1500561. We thank E.R. Cook for supplying data for Ireland.

27 PAGES 2k Consortium, 'Continental-Scale Temperature Variability during the Past Two Millennia', *Nature Geoscience* 6 (2013), 339–46.

28 Cook et al., 'Old World Megadroughts and Pluvials during the Common Era'.

29 Ibid.

30 White, *A Cold Welcome*.

31 Dean Guntner White, 'The Tudor Plantations in Ireland before 1571', unpublished PhD thesis, Trinity College Dublin (1968), pp. 245–48, cited in Margey, 'Plantations, 1550–1641' 555–83, at 562.

32 Jane Ohlmeyer, 'The Statute Staple in Early Modern Ireland', *History Ireland* 6 (4) (1998), 36–40; see also Gillespie, 'Meal and Money', 75–95.

33 This is made repeatedly clear in the Irish Annals. For example, in 1502 (the date of a likely high-latitude explosive eruption), a 'Very great inclemency [of weather occurred] … so that it killed very much of the cattle of Ireland and hindered the husbandry of the land …' See William M. Hennessy and Bartholomew MacCarthy (eds.), *Annala Uladh: Annals of Ulster Otherwise Annala Senait, Annals of Senat: A Chronicle of Irish Affairs from A.D. 431 to A.D. 1540* (Dublin: Printed for H. M. Stationery Office by A. Thom, 1887–1901), vol. 3, p. 461. This does not imply that grain was unimportant, and 'Grain certainly played a significant part in the expanding Irish trade in the early seventeenth century, perhaps up to 10 per cent by value by the 1620s'. Gillespie, 'Meal and Money', 75–95, at 75.

34 Ludlow and Crampsie, 'Environmental History of Ireland, 1550–1730'.

35 Jean Claude Thouret, 'Reconstruction of the AD 1600 Huaynaputina Eruption Based on the Correlation of Geologic Evidence with Early Spanish Chronicles', *Journal of Volcanology and Geothermal Research* 115 (2002), 529–70.

36 John O'Donovan (ed.), *Annala Rioghachta Eireann*, vol. 5 (Dublin: AMS Press, 1966), pp. 2033–35.

37 National Folklore Collection, The Schools' Collection, Volume 0537, Page 004, available at www.duchas.ie/en/cbes/4922143/4856167/5015381 (accessed 08 June 2018). Although this account is slightly misdated to 1599, it illustrates both the strength of local memory around the Battle of Kinsale and the significance of

the weather extremes in the period. It suggests the merit of a greater consideration of folklore in studies of this period. See Sarah Covington's essay in this volume.

38 Colm Lennon, *Sixteenth-Century Ireland: The Incomplete Conquest* (Dublin: Gill and Macmillan, 1994), p. 8.

39 Margey, 'Plantations, 1550–1641', 578.

40 Gillespie, 'Economic Life, 1550–1730', pp. 531–54.

41 David Edwards, 'Out of the Blue? Provincial Unrest in Ireland Before 1641', in Micheál Ó Siochrú and Jane Ohlmeyer (eds.), *Ireland, 1641: Contexts and Reactions* (Manchester: Manchester University Press, 2013), pp. 95–114.

42 Parker, *Global Crisis*.

43 Smyth estimates that the island's population had fallen from a high of between 1.8 and 2.1 million by 1641 to just 1.3 million by 1653, a decrease of almost 25%. Smyth, *Map-Making, Landscapes and Memory*, pp. 160–61. William Petty accredited the population decrease to 'the sword, plague, famine and hardship', as cited in Sean O'Callaghan, *To Hell or Barbados: The Ethnic Cleansing of Ireland* (Dingle: Brandon, 2000), p. 52.

44 Smyth, *Map-Making, Landscapes and Memory*, p. 158.

45 Ibid., pp. 178–88 suggests that the planned transplantation of the native population was significantly more extensive than that actually achieved.

46 Adelman and Ludlow, 'The Past, Present and Future of Environmental History in Ireland'.

47 Smyth, *Map-Making Landscapes and Memory*, p. 105, cautions of the need to qualify the title of this event, viewed generally by the Irish as an uprising and by the British as rebellion. For brevity, hereafter, we will simply use the title 1641 Rebellion.

48 Ludlow and Travis, 'STEAM Approaches to Climate Change'.

49 The integrity and representativeness of government, provision of fair property rights, and equitable access to natural resources and markets are also important contextual factors, historically, in societal sensitivity to extreme weather, and consequently, the efficacy with which weather-induced stresses such as food scarcity might trigger violence and conflict.

50 This has been long suggested, e.g., Frank E. Huggett, *The Land Question and European Society* (London: Thames and Hudson, 1975), p. 58.

51 For the first quotation, see Ms 836, f. 89r, and the second, see MS 831, f. 77v. All are available at 1641.tcd.ie. We thank Jane Ohlmeyer for supplying these citations.

52 Spelling has been modernized. MS 836, f. 92v.

53 Spelling has been modernized. Deposition of Thomas Richardson, Down, MS 837, f. 013r.

54 Michael Sigl et al., 'Timing and Climate Forcing of Volcanic Eruptions during the Past 2,500 Years', *Nature* 523 (2015), 543–49.

55 Low-latitude tropical eruptions are capable of injecting sulfate into the stratosphere of both hemispheres, whereas sulfate from eruptions in higher latitudes of either hemisphere will generally be confined to that hemisphere. Whether a sulfate signal is detected simultaneously in polar ice-core records from both hemispheres, or only in one hemisphere, thus provides a strong indication of the hemispheric location of the eruption. See Michael Sigl et al., 'Timing and Climate Forcing'.

56 See the Global Volcanism Program entry for Parker at www.volcano.si.edu/volcano.cfm?vn=271011 and for www.Hokkaido-Komagatake at volcano.si.edu/volcano.cfm?vn=285020. Both eruptions may have contributed to the elevated sulfate in Greenland, and indeed further contributions are possible, such as from the 1641 Kelud eruption in Indonesia, reaching point 4, 'Cataclysmic', on the VEI (www.volcano.si.edu/volcano.cfm?vn=263280). Entries were accessed 02 May 2016.

57 Matthew W. Salzer and Malcolm K. Hughes, 'Bristlecone Pine Tree Rings and Volcanic Eruptions over the Last 5000 Years', *Quaternary Research* 67 (2007), 57–68. Frost-damaged rings are also identified for 1640. In presumably forming during the spring-summer growing season and hence before the December 1640 Mt. Parker eruption, it further highlights the cold experienced in general at this time, and the need for further research into its origins.

58 Keith R. Briffa et al., 'Influence of Volcanic Eruptions on Northern Hemisphere Summer Temperature over the Past 600 Years', *Nature* 393 (1998), 450–55. See also www.volcano.si.edu/volcano.cfm?vn=264040 (accessed 02 May 2016).

59 Ohlmeyer, 'The Statute Staple', and Gillespie, 'Meal and Money', offer a list of harvest crises for the latter half of the sixteenth and first half of the seventeenth centuries. Ohlmeyer cites 1600–1602, while Gillespie cites 1601–1603. We rationalize this difference by taking 1600–1603 as our date. To achieve greater statistical power, we extend our record of harvest-related difficulties back to 1496 on the basis of testimony from the Irish Annals (see Francis Ludlow, 'The Utility of the Irish Annals as a Source for the Reconstruction of Climate', unpublished PhD thesis, University of Dublin (2010)), and forward to the end of the seventeenth century using references compiled by William Wilde, *Census of Ireland 1851*, vol. 1, Part 5 (Dublin: Thom, 1851).

60 See the appended price tables in Liam Kennedy and Martin W. Dowling, 'Prices and Wages in Ireland, 1700–1850', *Irish Economic and Social History* 24 (1997), 62–104. See also dunaire.ie, 'A Treasury of Digital Data for Irish Economic History' (accessed 09 June 2018).

61 The general approach was outlined by C. Chree, 'Some Phenomena of Sunspots and of Terrestrial Magnetism at Kew Observatory', *Philosophical Transactions of the Royal Society of London* 212A (1913), 75–116. It was elaborated upon by J. Stanford Willie, 'Measuring the Association of a Time Series and a Point Process', *Journal of Applied Probability* 19 (3) (1982), 597–608; and Michael H. Prager and John Hoenig, 'Superposed Epoch Analysis: A Randomization Test of Environmental Effects on Recruitment with Application to Chub Mackerel', *Transactions of the American Fisheries Society* 118 (1980), 608–18. It was more recently popularized by J. Brad Adams, Michael E. Mann, and Caspar M. Ammann, 'Proxy Evidence for an El Niño-Like Response to Volcanic Forcing', *Nature* 426 (2003), 274–78, and has been adapted to the use of climatic and societal information derived from documentary sources, e.g., see Zhihong Zhuo, Chaochao Gao, and Yuqing Pan, 'Proxy Evidence for China's Monsoon Precipitation Response to Volcanic Aerosols over the Past Seven Centuries', *Journal of Geophysical Research: Atmospheres* 119 (11) (2014), 6638–52; and Joseph Manning et al. 'Volcanic Suppression of Nile Summer Flooding Triggers Revolt and Constrains Interstate Conflict in Ancient Egypt', *Nature Communications* 8 (2017), Article 900.

62 This is because the time series of harvest-related difficulties is in binary (0, 1) format: a year either experienced harvest-related difficulties or it did not. The maximum theoretical value that can be obtained for any given superposed year (-10 to $+10$) is thus 1.0, in which case 100% of these years would have experienced harvest-related difficulties. Note that the results of the SEA presented in Figure 5 cannot be read as percentages in this way, because the relevant time-series data are not binary.

63 The solid and dashed lines represent the 5th and 95th percentile boundaries in a distribution of values that is generated by making 10,000 randomized sets of forty-four years (i.e., the same number as identified as experiencing harvest-related difficulties) and counting the number of correspondences at each superposed year (-10 to -1, 0, and 1 to 10) relative to the dates of the thirty-one years experiencing temperature extremes in the 1496–1700 period. Any value observed in

reality that crosses these boundaries thus occurred in less than 5% of the 10,000 sets of randomizations.

64 We identify extreme years using a static threshold in which any year falling at least 1.5 standard deviations distant from the long-term average reconstructed temperature is used in the analysis. This is an expedient means of identifying anomalous years. However, while variations in weather year by year are always partly stochastic, they may also be cyclical, and years selected for inclusion may thus have been directly preceded by years that were also potentially severe enough to impact harvests, but which do not strictly meet our static threshold. This will tend to register in our analysis as an elevation in harvest-related difficulties in superposed year -1. Future work can employ multiple or adaptive thresholds to gain insight into the level of severity of weather at which harvest difficulties begin to register in the documentary sources of the period. Other potential contributions to this issue include the possibility of small dating uncertainties in our list of harvest crises, an issue also meriting further study.

65 Jane Ohlmeyer and Éamonn Ó Ciardha (eds.), *The Irish Statute Staple Books, 1596–1687* (Dublin: Dublin Corporation, 1998). And for a concise introduction, see Ohlmeyer, 'The Statute Staple'.

66 For terminology relating to the staple, see Ohlmeyer and Ó Ciardha, *The Irish Statute Staple Books*, pp. xvii–xviii. See also these authors, p. 4, for the relative activity of the Irish staple towns.

67 The staple books do not record the loan values themselves, but rather the value of the bond securing the loan, customarily double the loan value. See Ohlmeyer and Ó Ciardha, *The Irish Statute Staple Books*. This allows us to infer loan values with reasonable confidence, but we report the bond values as standard in this chapter.

68 Ohlmeyer, 'The Statute Staple', p. 38.

69 Particularly notable in this respect are the absence of Dublin volumes between 1638 and 1660. The number of towns that functioned as designated staple towns also increased through time, although Dublin remains dominant, with creditors traveling widely to use the Dublin staple even if a different staple town was closer. Ohlmeyer and Ó Ciardha, *The Irish Statute Staple Books*.

70 Ohlmeyer, 'The Statute Staple', p. 37.

71 Ibid.

72 For the top panel of Figure 16.7, each yearly count of transactions in the extant staple volumes has been normalized relative to itself and the preceding nine years. The units on the vertical axis thus represent z-scores. Rather than using raw counts of transaction numbers as shown in Figure 16.6, this normalization is undertaken to prevent bias in the superposed epoch analysis by allowing comparability in the transaction count response to extreme weather throughout the 1597–1687 period. Large step-changes in the time series of raw transaction counts, as well as other influences on the counts from the growing numbers of staple towns through time, will otherwise render incomparable a response to extreme weather at the start of the period to the middle or end. For the bottom panel, the coefficient of variation (the standard deviation divided by the mean value of transactions for each year) is used as a measure of variability because the standard deviation itself scales alongside each year's mean value, hence again biasing a comparison of responses to extremes at different points between 1597 and 1687. For both panels, the years 1642–1652 (inclusive) are excluded from this analysis in having artificially low transaction counts relating to the missing Dublin volumes between 1638 and 1660 and the impact of the Eleven Years' War. The lower bound (5th percentile) significance line is not shown in these figures because no value was sufficiently low as to approach this boundary.

73 Ohlmeyer and Ó Ciardha, *The Irish Statute Staple Books*, p. 12.
74 While it might be argued that this is an artifact of indebtedness simply as a result of plantation, the lack of similarly high values in Munster suggests an alternative hypothesis is more appropriate.
75 Described neatly by David W. Franzen, 'Jenks Natural Breaks is a Procedure That Groups Data into Classes That are Relatively Separate of the Other Classes, Relying on the Natural Grouping of the Data Instead of a More Subjective Division'. See David W. Franzen, 'Nitrogen Management in Sugar Beet Using Remote Sensing and GIS', in Francis J. Pierce and David Clay (eds.), *GIS Applications in Agriculture* (London: CRC Press, 2007), pp. 35–47, at p. 39.
76 Even widespread episodes of severe cold, as in December of 2000, exhibited spatial variability, with southern and western coastal regions experiencing less marked cold, for example. See Edward Graham, 'The Emerald Isle Turns White: Snow and Very Low Temperatures over Ireland during Christmas 2000', *Weather* 59 (2004), 15–19.
77 William J. Smyth, 'Towards a Cultural Geography of the 1641 Rising/Rebellion', in Micheál Ó Siochrú and Jane Ohlmeyer (eds.), *Ireland 1641: Contexts and Reactions* (Manchester: Manchester University Press, 2013), pp. 71–94.
78 References are identified using the free text search function at 1641.tcd.ie. This approach should ideally be complemented by a full reading of the texts, essential for a fuller understanding of the context (historical, geographical, textual) in which weather conditions were reported.
79 John Sweeney, 'Ireland', in Julian Mayes and Dennis Wheeler (eds.), *Regional Climates of the British Isles* (London and New York: Routledge, 1997), pp. 254–75.
80 Smyth's mapping appears broadly consistent with the mapping of murders for (primarily) Ulster by the Down Survey Project. See www.downsurvey.tcd. ie/1641-depositions.php (accessed 11 June 2018).
81 See, e.g., Cavan, where there are low reports of killings but relatively numerous reports of severe weather, and Donegal, where reports of weather are fewer, but one-fifth of all depositions relate to murders and killings.
82 Also notable is an apparent association between counties with lower numbers of overall depositions and higher levels of reported murder and violence, e.g., Donegal, Derry, Tyrone, Leitrim, and Westmeath, suggesting that in counties with lower rates of deponents only the most severe violence was reported.
83 We use Spearman's Rank Correlation coefficient because it is robust to datasets with outliers. The merits of different forms of correlation analysis (including the advantages of Spearman's Rank Correlation when the assumptions [e.g., in the normality of residuals] of the popular Pearson's correlation are not met) is introduced by Danny McCarroll, *Simple Statistical Tests for Geography* (London: CRC Press, 2017).
84 See, e.g., the following account from the *Annals of Connacht* for 1465 CE, which describes 'Exceeding great frost and snow and stormy weather this year, so that no herb grew in the ground and no leaf budded on a tree until the feast of St. Brendan [May 16], but a man, if he were the stronger, would forcibly carry away the food from the priest in church'. Further examples are provided by Donnchadh Ó Corráin, 'Aspects of Society, c.800', in Dáibhí Ó Cróinín (ed.), *A New History of Ireland*, vol. 1 (Oxford: Oxford University Press, 2005), pp. 549–608. See also Ludlow and Travis, 'STEAM Approaches to Climate Change'.
85 As well as assessing other potential explanatory variables, future research must examine factors that might bias (either upward or downward) the results of a correlation analysis between weather and violence. Such biases may arise from factors internal to the documents and the processes of their creation, not least the changing scope of the investigations, the potential influence of the various commissioners, the differing lengths of time between events and the actual depositions being recorded, and even the length (i.e., word count) of each deposition

itself. Even with a percentage approach, the length of the deposition may still, for example, bias a correlation analysis given that a longer deposition will have more space to reference both weather and violence than shorter submissions. If identified, such potential biases can, however, be statistically controlled.

86 Smyth, 'Towards a Cultural Geography'.

87 A subset of counties reporting no references to weather is excluded from this analysis to prevent bias.

88 'Dermot MacCarthy, an esquire from North Cork appears to have sunk into debt thanks to his determination to remodel his mansion house at Kanturk'. See Ohlmeyer and Ó Ciardha, *The Irish Statute Staple Books*, p. 23.

89 See the case of Sir Philip Percival's pursuit of an Irish debtor's castle and lands, ibid. p. 30, and also pp. 10–11.

90 Smyth, 'Towards a Cultural Geography'.

91 We thank Jane Ohlmeyer for this information. See also Nicholas Canny, *Making Ireland British, 1580–1650* (Oxford: Oxford University Press, 2001), p. 476; Nicholas Canny, 'What Really Happened in Ireland in 1641?' in Jane H. Ohlmeyer (ed.), *Ireland from Independence to Occupation, 1641–1660* (Cambridge: Cambridge University Press, 1995), pp. 24–42, at p. 32.

92 The same result presented in Figure 16.5 suggests that ~58% of extreme years did not experience harvest-related difficulties. Even assuming, reasonably, that not all such years are known, this result suggests that early modern Irish society was, to a considerable degree, robust to shocks from extreme weather.

93 Britain and Ireland have quite a few long tree-ring chronologies that are principally temperature-sensitive, with the exception of Scottish pine, which is now finding increased usage in palaeoclimatic reconstruction, e.g., Miloš Rydval et al., 'Reconstructing 800 Years of Summer Temperatures in Scotland from Tree Rings', *Climate Dynamics* 49 (2017), 2951–74.

94 Solway, 'Drought as a Revelatory Crisis'.

95 See www.downsurvey.tcd.ie

96 Jane Ohlmeyer, *Making Ireland English: The Irish Aristocracy in the Seventeenth Century* (New Haven, CT: Yale University Press, 2012).

97 See, e.g., Charles Travis, *Abstract Machine: Humanities GIS* (Redlands, CA: ESRI Press, 2015); Ian N. Gregory et al., *Troubled Geographies: A Spatial History of Religion and Society in Ireland* (Bloomington: Indiana University Press, 2013).

17 Mapping the past

Geographical information systems and the exploitation of linked historical data

Micheál Ó Siochrú and David Brown

In the last twenty years, a series of high-profile projects in the Digital Humanities have revolutionized the research and teaching environments of British and Irish history. The accessibility of material electronically enables students wherever they are situated to conduct much of their archival research online, without having to leave the comfort of their office. Early English Books Online, State Papers Online, and British History Online, among others, provide easy access (with an institutional subscription) to an enormous body of primary source material, albeit as stand-alone resources. The majority of these digital archives, however, are essentially image repositories, with limited functionality beyond a basic word search and image enhancement.[1] Moreover, there is no means of comparing or integrating data outside of these research silos. The latest challenge, therefore, for those working in the field of Digital Humanities is to move beyond these early prototypes and develop something more sophisticated, with a greater potential for tackling complex research questions. A high degree of interoperability is absolutely crucial, linking data across a number of different archives and datasets. In particular, projects comprising visual material and tabular data require a highly structured methodological approach to enable their effective use as a research tool.

The creation of structured data is a necessary first step. Structured data is a standardized format for providing information about objects that allows a database search to find common attributes across platforms. This means that if a person or place occurs in the database of more than one project, it should be possible for the search tool to find both instances, establishing a link between them and enabling a more complex query to be made using the information associated with both entries. Linking data in this manner from the outset, however, depends on a deep level of cooperation between scholars and institutions. At Trinity College Dublin (TCD), research teams have taken a lead in developing integrated resources for early modern Irish history, using a succession of datasets from ongoing projects that, although not originally designed to be linked, are sufficiently similar in structure to enable this process to take place. This chapter will explore a variety of methodological approaches required to exploit linked data through a case-study of projects relating to the

Cromwellian land settlement of Ireland, one of the largest transfers of land anywhere in Western Europe during the early modern period.

Historians of early modern Ireland constantly bemoan the enormous gap in surviving primary sources compared to the abundance of material available to their counterparts in Britain or elsewhere in Europe. An explosion and subsequent fire in the Public Records Office in Dublin at the outset of the Irish Civil War in June 1922 destroyed almost 700 years of historical records. The Irish past literally went up in smoke, and for weeks afterward, fragments of medieval and early modern manuscripts littered the streets of the city.[2] The seventeenth century suffered particularly badly, with the loss of much of the material relating to the Cromwellian conquest and subsequent land settlement. Fortunately, archivists and historians such as J.T. Gilbert, J.P. Prendergast, and Robert Dunlop had already transcribed and, in many cases, published some of this documentation, but a significant amount could not be retrieved.[3]

This loss, perhaps, explains why the mid-seventeenth century remained relatively neglected by academics, despite its obvious political, military, social, and cultural significance. From the 1990s, however, a new generation of scholars began to revisit this controversial period, producing a number of important monographs but also seeking out any surviving original material or nineteenth-century transcriptions.[4] This activity generated new projects in Digital Humanities, starting in 2007 with the digitization and transcription of thousands of witness statements, known as the 1641 Depositions, taken by the colonial authorities from Protestant refugees fleeing their homes following the outbreak of a rebellion in Ulster.[5] This chapter, however, focuses on a source central to the Cromwellian land settlement of the mid-1650s: namely, the Down Survey of Ireland, which, like the 1641 Depositions, has begun to open up exciting new avenues for research as well as demonstrating how future schemes in Digital Humanities can be developed to sophisticated new levels.[6]

Launched in 2013, the Down Survey of Ireland Project (http://downsurvey. tcd.ie) rendered over 1,300 manuscript survey maps into digital form and integrated them with data on 50,000 landholdings and 8,000 individual landowners, mined from the contemporaneous Books of Survey and Distribution by means of a bespoke Geographic Information System (GIS) and relational database.[7] In addition to novel data management techniques adapted for dealing with seventeenth-century material, considerable effort was devoted to the website's design to accommodate a range of users from professional academics to the general public who might not be familiar with premodern material. The website also incorporates a number of normalization techniques to render the manuscript sources into a machine-readable format, which enables material to be properly identified, quantified, and mapped to a modern GIS. This approach also opens up the possibility of interacting with any historical text structured around place names, employing spatial analysis tools on a variety of sources, spanning a wide chronological and thematic range. The Down Survey website already integrates data from additional tabular sources, providing a detailed schema and roadmap for future exploitation of digitized historical material. The ongoing nature of the project will transform the current repository of images and data into an active online research platform, exploiting recent technological advances to enable the user to begin asking the types of questions that hitherto would have been impossible to address, let alone answer. The specific methodologies outlined here have a broad application relevant to any historical period, with the potential to produce equally exciting and transformative results.

The Down Survey is crucial for an understanding of Irish history, as control and ownership of the land helped define the nature of the English conquest of Ireland in the early modern period.[8] A series of plantations from the mid-sixteenth century, in the Midlands, Munster, and Ulster, resulted in the displacement of the native Catholic population by a new Protestant settler class, with varying degrees of success. By 1640, despite decades of widespread dispossession and systematic ethnic and religious discrimination in all areas of life, the majority of the land still remained in the hands of the Catholic Irish. A revolt in October 1641 by the Ulster Irish, marked in the initial stages at least by extreme violence on all sides, triggered a war that lasted for over twelve years.[9] The outbreak in the summer of 1642 of civil war in England between king and parliament prevented military resources from reaching Ireland, forcing the colonial government in Dublin to adopt a largely defensive strategy for the next seven years. No side could win an absolute victory, but the execution of King Charles in January 1649 enabled the English parliament to focus exclusively on the reconquest of Ireland. In March, Oliver Cromwell agreed to lead an invasion on behalf of the new Commonwealth regime, to crush all royalist opposition and avenge the alleged massacres of Protestant settlers in 1641–42. Over the next four years, his army engaged in a series of bloody sieges and battles, as well as targeting Catholic Irish civilians in an effort to demoralize enemy forces and deny them local support. By 1653, the English had emerged victorious but at a high price, with the population decimated and the economic infrastructure of the country destroyed.[10]

Ireland, in the alleged words of Cromwell, was now 'as a clean paper' upon which a new society could be constructed, a process underpinned by a series of legislative measures.[11] At the beginning of the conflict in March 1642, the English parliament had passed the Adventurers Act, which sought to raise money for a military campaign in Ireland, to be repaid with land forfeited by the defeated Catholic rebels.[12] Despite the distraction of the civil war in England throughout the 1640s, the conquest of Ireland remained a political, military, and economic necessity, particularly with the 'Adventurers'—mainly London merchants, who parliament promised to pay off the arrears of tens of thousands of English soldiers with Irish land. In August 1652, as the conflict in Ireland drew to a conclusion, the Act of Settlement specified who exactly would forfeit land, including those who had supported the rebellion in any way.[13] Technically, almost the entire male Catholic population could have been encompassed within the terms of the act, but it soon became clear that landowners constituted the primary target. In July

1653, the Commonwealth regime issued an order for the transplantation of all Catholic landowners westward across the Shannon to Connacht, which was considered to be the poorest of the four Irish provinces. Two months later, in September 1653, the Act of Satisfaction began the process of distributing forfeited lands among the Adventurers and disbanded soldiers.[14]

The Acts of Settlement and Satisfaction may well have provided the immediate legal framework for the Cromwellian land settlement, but such an extensive redistribution urgently required a major survey of the forfeited estates. This began in 1653 with the Gross Survey, which (as the name implies) provided a rough estimate of the extent of the confiscated lands, with some mapped areas, followed by the entirely textual Civil Survey (1654–56).[15] The Civil Survey, ordered by the civil authorities in Dublin, sought to assess the precise value of those lands assigned to satisfy the claims of soldiers and Adventurers. Overseen by the Surveyor-General Benjamin Worsley, this survey consisted of a collation of landowner records for both forfeited and unforfeited land at townland level, with the value of each townland determined as it stood at the outbreak of the Ulster Rebellion in October 1641.[16] The Civil Survey did not involve the making of maps but instead provided a detailed boundary description for each barony and parish, alongside the name of the owners prior to the rebellion.[17]

Worsley's work, based mainly on the records of the original owners, attracted significant criticism because of purported inaccuracies. In response, the government appointed William Petty, former Physician-General of the English army in Ireland and a man with no practical surveying experience whatsoever, to conduct a new, more extensive evaluation. The Down Survey (1656–59), so called because a chain was laid down and a scale made, was a mapped survey. Using the Civil Survey as a guide, teams of soldier-surveyors sent out under Petty's direction measured every townland to be forfeited, organized by parish. The results were truly revolutionary, with nothing as systematic or on such a large scale appearing anywhere else in the world.[18] The cadastral maps, at barony and parish level, were also rich in topographical detail, showing among other things rivers, woodlands, roads, castles, churches, houses, and military fortifications. The survey was restricted to forfeited land in Ulster, Leinster, and most of Munster, relying on Thomas Wentworth's 1636 survey (better known as the Strafford Survey) for coverage of Connacht and parts of Munster. The surveyors did not measure Protestant-held lands, so as John Andrews shrewdly notes, the Down Survey was essentially a survey of Catholic Ireland, not of the entire island.[19] More limiting, perhaps, is what the surveyors omitted from the maps. The sole purpose of the survey was to measure areas that were converted to a monetary value and used to settle debts. Woodlands and fisheries could be licensed separately to raise badly needed funds, and those buildings depicted on the maps are there primarily as landmarks. The surveyors did not show Irish habitations, as the intention at the time was to clear the land of that population. The maps do not, therefore, present the landscape as the surveyors found it, but are representative of Cromwell's 'blank canvas' more than anything else (Figure 17.1).

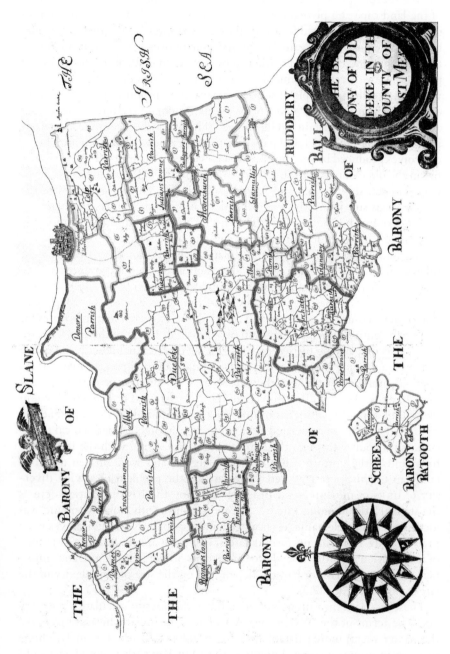

Figure 17.1 Barony of Duleek, County Meath. The image is reproduced courtesy of the Library of Trinity College, Dublin.[20]

Despite these limitations, the Down Survey was one of the most ambitious and technically accomplished mapping projects of the early modern period, and the source can reveal new directions in understanding the transformation of the landscape at a pivotal time in Ireland's history. A major component of the TCD project involved locating all extant maps relating to this survey and bringing them together again for the first time in over 300 years. It was a tantalizing prospect, enabling a marker to be laid down that Irish historians were perhaps not as bereft of primary sources as they claimed. Dogged detective work, an excellent example of source retrieval in unpromising circumstances, enabled the project team to identify surviving copies scattered throughout archives in Ireland, Britain, and Europe.[21] The original set comprised approximately 250 barony and 1,400 parish maps, with at least three contemporaneous copies produced before the end of the seventeenth century (Figure 17.1). A fire in the old records office in Dublin in 1711 partially destroyed the Surveyor General's set, the original and largest collection.[22] Three partial sets of the barony maps survive in the Bibliothèque Nationale de France, the National Archives of Ireland, and the British Library.[23] Not surprisingly, the stunningly impressive cartographic material remains the most recognizable part of the Down Survey, but the beauty of these maps as objects should not obscure their role in facilitating the large-scale redistribution of Catholic-owned land to English soldiers, investors, and other claimants (Figure 17.2).

The result of all the project team's effort can be viewed on the 'Maps' section of the website. As new material is added, it is expected that surrogates for almost the entire Down Survey will be recovered. Many of the parishes also have an accompanying terrier, providing a detailed textual description of the territory, alongside the names of the landowners of each parcel of land and a reference number that allows the parcel to be located on the corresponding map. In effect, William Petty invented the Geographical Information System in 1656 by providing a means of linking a geographical area to a potentially unlimited amount of associated attributes. Petty adopted a hierarchical structure, from county through the barony and parish levels, with the individual townland at the bottom. Enrolments of large estates were broken down to conform to this hierarchy. Petty also tackled the problem of a wide diversity of units of measurement, insisting on using the Irish plantation acre as the standard throughout. Finally, and most significantly, each townland was identified by a single name, even when a number of possible alternatives were in use locally. From his uniform datasets, Petty was able to link a broad range of information recorded elsewhere to his maps, using a simple reference number unique to a parish or barony, depending on the size or complexity of the larger parcel (Figure 17.3).

These standard measurements aided the authorities to calculate a property tax. The terms of the Adventurers Act of 1642 included a measure to make the arrangements more palatable to a skeptical King Charles I: namely, a huge increase in crown income, known as the Quit Rent, that would accrue to him. To collect these rents, Charles II established the Quit Rent Office in

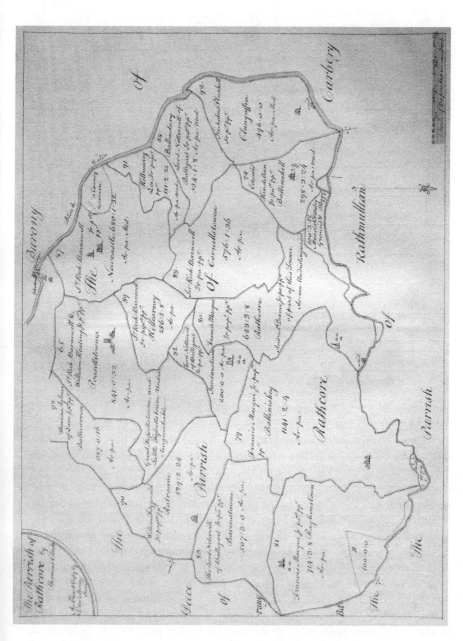

Figure 17.2 The Parish of Rathcore, Barony of Moyfenrath, County Meath. The image is reproduced courtesy of the National Library of Ireland.[24]

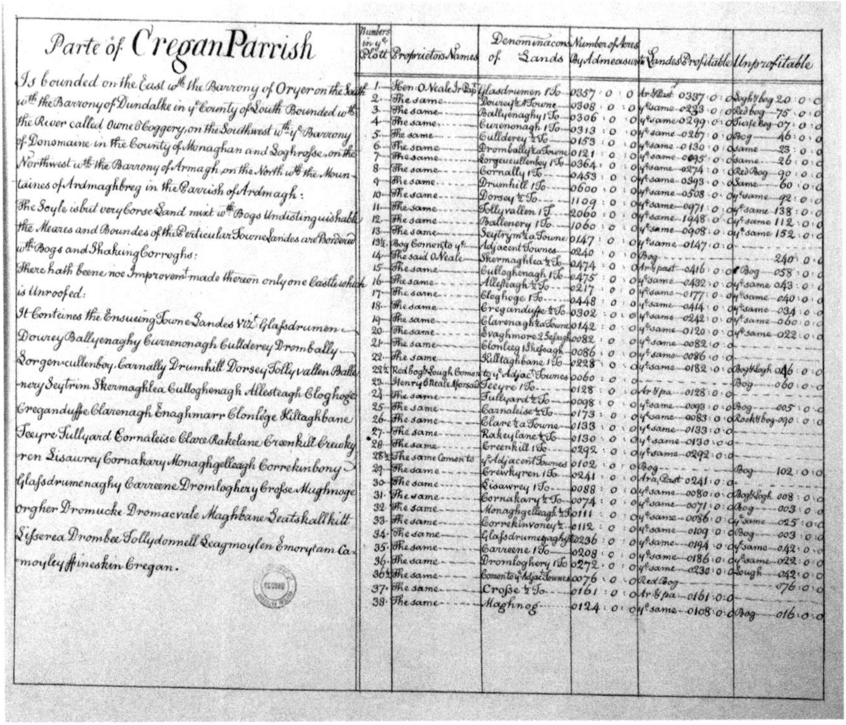

Figure 17.3 Terrier for Parish Map of Cregan, the Barony of Fews, County Armagh.[25]
The image is reproduced courtesy of the Public Record Office of
Northern Ireland.

Dublin shortly after his restoration in 1660. It is to this office that we owe
the survival of so much of the Cromwellian land surveys. In the late 1660s,
the office commissioned an abstract of all of the material that recorded the
landowners in 1641, together with a list of the corresponding owners at the
date of compilation. The resultant data make up the Books of Survey and
Distribution.[26] Fortunately for future generations of researchers, the compil-
ers also included Petty's reference number for each townland depicted on the
Down Survey parish maps and terriers, providing a means by which the two
sources could be linked. The Books of Survey and Distribution remained as
working documents for decades afterward, and major changes in the pattern
of landholding continued to be recorded in the manuscript volumes. The
position of Catholic landowners, for example, deteriorated further following
the Williamite confiscations of 1691–1703.[27] Land owned by the deposed
monarch, James VII and II, and his supporters was sold by public auction, and
by the end of this process, Catholic landownership had shrunk to less than
15% of the total.[28] This newly forfeited land had to be mapped and measured
using techniques very similar to those employed by Petty, with changes in
ownership carefully recorded in the Books of Survey and Distribution.[29] The

books, therefore, chart the rise of the Protestant Ascendancy, which by the early eighteenth century had consolidated its control of every aspect of Irish political, legal, and socioeconomic life (Figure 17.4).[30]

In addition to the Books of Survey and Distribution, the Quit Rent Office also became the custodian of a set of tracings of all of the surviving Down Survey parish maps, created for the Griffiths' Boundary Survey of 1824 to confirm the location of townland boundaries. The Ordnance Survey office subsequently used this material in the 1830s to create its first edition of six-inch to one-mile maps.[32] The Ordnance Survey had the authority to survey townland boundaries, but not to create new townlands or delete existing ones, thus ensuring strong continuity between the work of Petty's surveyors and their nineteenth-century counterparts.[33] The following year, these became Statute Boundaries, meaning that they could only be altered through legislation, preserving most of Petty's delineations of townlands up to the present day, although many of the place names changed over time. The stability of these boundaries provides a useful source of long range data, statistically independent of shifts in population, language, and governance.[34] This data, therefore, will facilitate the study of continuities in Irish history, breaking through the rigid periodization that has characterized much of the historical research to date. As soon as the Ordnance Survey completed its project, the Quit Rent Office reclaimed the map tracings, together with a set of Ordnance Survey sheets marked with the Down Survey boundaries. This entire collection, together

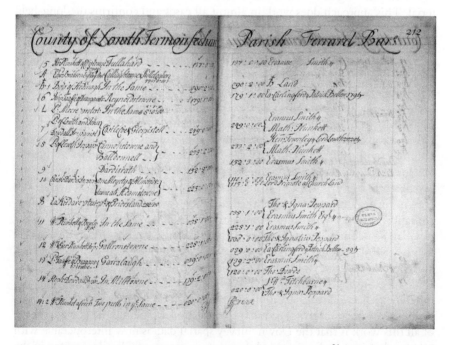

Figure 17.4 Books of Survey and Distribution, County Louth.[31] Reproduced with permission from the Irish Manuscripts Commission.

with the historical archive of the Ordnance Survey of Ireland for the Republic of Ireland, now resides in the National Archives of Ireland in Dublin. The Ordnance Survey archive covering Northern Ireland, however, is housed in the Public Record Office of Northern Ireland in Belfast.

Unlike the maps, the Quit Rent Office set of the Books of Survey and Distribution, covering the entire country, now resides in a single location in the National Archives of Ireland. The manuscript is in good condition and written in a clear hand and follows a consistent layout, reducing the need for an interpretative analysis prior to converting the text into a database format. Nonetheless, despite recent advances in Handwritten Text Recognition (HTR) technology, the first phase of the Down Survey project involved creating a modern, machine-readable dataset from this historical material through the time-consuming process of manual transcription, with some important additions.[35] Crucially, the seventeenth-century townland names are matched to their modern equivalents using spatial coordinates and areas provided by the Ordnance Surveys of Ireland and Northern Ireland, amalgamated for the first time. This process, however, proved to be both challenging and controversial, generating an enormous volume of correspondence following the launch of the website.[36] Despite relying heavily on the Down Survey maps, the Ordinance Survey material clearly demonstrates the technical limitations of the former in terms of delineating boundaries. The two do not overlay directly onto one another, and a considerable amount of interpretation is required to match them together, utilizing both visual (maps) and textual (townland name-books) material. This approach does work in almost all cases and confirms the long-held belief regarding the accuracy of the survey undertaken by Petty, whose surveyors used relatively primitive tools and labored in very difficult circumstances.

All the variant spellings of place names and personal names within the Books of Survey and Distribution have also been normalized into a modern form to render it 'machine readable'. Petty's surveyors interpreted names phonetically, as their work pre-dated the publication of gazetteers, and led to a wide variance in spelling, even within a single source document. As the Books of Survey and Distribution comprise the work of many surveyors, tidying up all the variations required significant manual effort. The resulting database provides an identifier for each townland with its modern spelling, which is then linked to the seventeenth-century name. The area in hectares is also recorded, alongside the Down Survey's measurement of that same area, with the names and religious affiliation of the owner in 1641 and from 1670. A further table includes the townland's geometry expressed in Latlong coordinates for display in Google maps.[37] Most national mapping agencies use proprietary coordinate systems. The Ordnance Survey of Ireland conforms to the Irish National Grid, but the Ordnance Survey of Northern Ireland conforms to the UK grid. Both use different projections to the Latlong system common to most web-based applications, which meant that a geometric translation was required. The advantage of all this work is that the Down Survey spatial data is now interoperable with other web-based applications and the existing corpus of GIS silos created in the past around their respective national grids.

The GIS section of the website links the normalized data from the Books of Survey and Distribution with Ordnance Survey spatial data, with the familiar Google maps interface as the default. The user may also switch to Google's satellite view, a useful feature to ascertain the type of terrain for a particular parcel of land, which might not be obvious from looking at the Down Survey map. This section also provides the facility to view the original Down Survey maps in the context of this modern representation. The project team departed from an emerging trend to use proprietary software such as ARC/GIS as a platform and opted to develop the system from scratch using the open source tools provided by Google. This was mainly driven by a desire to ensure free public access with open source topographic and satellite imagery on an interface that Google provides with an unlimited dissemination license. An added advantage is that the Google platform quickly became dominant in the marketplace, meaning that most users have found it a familiar environment that they do not need to learn in order to access the Down Survey's GIS data. The GIS allows the user to search for landowners throughout the seventeenth century. When zoomed out, a simple label represents each townland, but as the user zooms in, this transforms into a polygon, marking the exact boundary of each townland, accurate to less than five meters in real space (Figure 17.5).

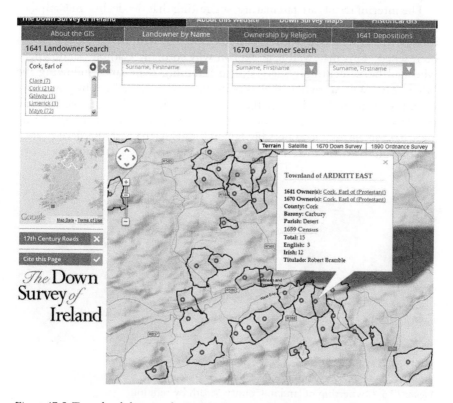

Figure 17.5 Townland data on the Down Survey website.

The GIS thus reveals not only the location but also the precise shape of every landholding in Ireland in the seventeenth century. A panel for every townland displays more information from the database. For the first time, therefore, it is possible to see the full extent of estates for thousands of landowners, something that would have been impossible a few years ago. This will enable scholars to track over time the continual process of land redistribution throughout the early modern period and to assess the wealth of individual families on a case-by-case basis. The potential for new and exciting research avenues is limitless.

In addition to this dynamic data, the project team also prepared static maps showing the shift in landownership by religion that occurred during the Wars of the Three Kingdoms (1637–53). This demonstrates in a dramatically visual manner the collapse in Catholic landownership at a previously unimaginable level of detail. According to the existing historiography, the Protestants emerged as the clear victors from the upheavals of the mid-seventeenth century, with Catholics left in possession of a mere one-fifth of the land total, a huge reduction from the 60% they owned prior to the 1641 rebellion.[38] By reuniting the tabular and cartographic evidence for the first time in 300 years, the Down Survey project is in the process of reexamining these figures (Figure 17.6).

The interim results are fascinating, suggesting that the decline in Catholic-ownership prior to 1641 was in fact far greater than hitherto understood, although further research is still required before any definitive conclusions can be reached. This may well help explain why so many Catholic landowners, who had been seemingly successful in retaining their lands following the Nine Years' War, were nonetheless prepared to risk everything by going into open revolt in 1641. Whatever the outcome of these deliberations, the land transfers of the 1650s still represent the single largest shift in land ownership anywhere in Europe (and possibly beyond) during the early modern period, and proved to be Cromwell's lasting legacy in Ireland.

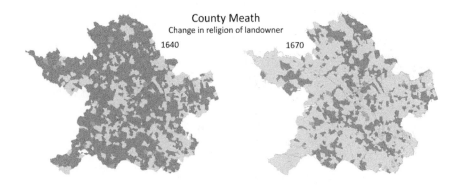

Figure 17.6 Ownership of land in County Meath by religion.

This historical humanities resource has generated an unprecedented level of public interest and engagement, with over 100,000 people spending a meaningful length of time on the site weeks after it went live. Intensive media attention accompanied the launch, and Fintan O'Toole, a leading social commentator and literary editor of *The Irish Times*, neatly encapsulated the intent of the initial version of the site:

> This is a new kind of knowledge. It is not a product but a process. It consists not of conclusions but of an open-ended invitation to explore. And it does not separate the idea of research from the idea of communication. Every aspect of the project is about research and about the making public of the documents, tools and methods through which this research can be done.[39]

With this endorsement, and a feature on the national evening news, the Down Survey became one of the first early modern Irish research projects to move from scholarly circles into the public consciousness. All that was required was to make it accessible. By 2018, over 400,000 people across the globe had accessed the site, and this sustained position in the public eye since 2013 has been its most significant achievement. Nearly all local history groups in Ireland link to it, and at least 100 people with an interest in Irish history from all over the world are logged onto the site every day. The site has provoked thousands of written comments, good and bad, provided material for use in schools throughout the country, and attracted significant heritage tourism as well.

Key to the project's success is the empowerment of the user to conduct personalized research, not only for historians but for historical geographers, economists, literary scholars, and others. The Down Survey site is not simply a data silo, a repository of interesting material, but rather serves as the foundation stone of a far more ambitious endeavor to create a dynamic research platform connected to a range of other early modern data sources. As discussed earlier, the process of matching early modern townlands to a modern equivalent enables linkage to any resource using Ordnance Survey placenames, including all manner of census, economic, and land-use data. Two further early modern sources that rely heavily on townland names have already been linked to the site on a trial basis in order to test out the methodology. Despite its name, the 1659 'Census' in fact relates to a poll tax, with 'English' and 'Irish' tenants enumerated by individual townland. It covers twenty-seven of the thirty-two Irish counties, although the quantity and quality of the data varies widely throughout.[40] Comparison of the census data with land-ownership information in the Books of Survey and Distribution reveals the limitations of the former, which, with very few exceptions, is restricted to the populations of forfeited townlands, the same as those enumerated in the Down Survey. Consequently, the population data for almost half the country, mainly on un-forfeited Protestant-owned estates, is not recorded. Nonetheless, the comparative approach has already revealed new patterns of distribution, potentially transforming our understanding of population trends in early modern Ireland.

The 1641 Depositions collection is the second early modern source linked to the Down Survey project data. Images of the original documents with an accompanying transcription are available online at http://1641.tcd.ie, while the Irish Manuscripts Commission has produced an ongoing print edition in twelve volumes.[41] The depositions are witness testimonies by Protestants from all social backgrounds, concerning their experiences of the 1641 Irish rebellion. They document the loss of goods, military activity, and the alleged crimes committed by the Irish insurgents, including assault, stripping, imprisonment, and murder. This body of material is unparalleled anywhere in early modern Europe, and provides a unique source of information for the causes and events surrounding the 1641 rebellion and for the social, economic, cultural, religious, and political history of seventeenth-century Ireland, England, and Scotland.[42] Merging information abstracted from the 1641 Depositions with the Down Survey data has also divulged surprising new results. The project geo-referenced any mention of a murder in the Ulster volumes of the 1641 Depositions and presented the results using the same clustering approach developed for the display of landholdings (Figure 17.7).

1641 Depositions

Figure 17.7 Reported murders in Ulster with an overlay of seventeenth-century roads.

Another layer depicting the approximate location of seventeenth-century roads, derived from Petty's published atlas, *Hibernia Delineatio*, graphically illustrates how many of the recorded murders followed along the major transportation routes, a fact not recorded in the witness statements. The addition of further layers of data, therefore, from complementary sources provides exciting possibilities for new interpretations.

While the potential is clear, a wide divergence currently exists between the pace of change in the technology sector and the adoption of these technologies by historians, partly because of the costs involved. The Down Survey project was fortunate to run concurrently with a European Seventh-Framework Programme (FP7)-funded project called 'CULTURA' (CULTivating Understanding and Research through Adaptivity), also based at TCD and involving many of the same people.[43] CULTURA aimed to move beyond a simple imaging and delivery model, developing natural language processing tools in partnership with IBM to enable early modern printed texts to be searched by machine without the need for manual normalization of the variant spellings. The project also created an adaptive, personalized interface that anticipates the needs of a range of users, as well as a social network analysis framework to explore the different layers of relationships of named individuals within the source material. A crucial element of CULTURA's success was its interdisciplinary nature, involving colleagues from History and Computer Science. The Down Survey project adopted a similar interdisciplinary model, with Google's mapping division and a Dublin-based web design company, *Language*, acting as the industry partners. As a result, historians engaged from the outset with the latest relevant advances in technology, exploring with computer scientists how they might be adapted to work on early modern sources.[44]

Ongoing development work will enable users not only to access data but to conduct their own research online. For example, there are approximately 50,000 townlands and 10,000 names of Catholic and Protestant landowners from 1641 to 1703 recorded in the Books of Survey and Distribution. The first version of the website integrated early modern and modern spatial data through the normalization of townland names. The new phase of the project assigns a unique identifier to each landowner as a first step toward linking them to a range of other historical sources where they are referenced. For this to happen, however, it has been necessary to manually tabulate the corpus of printed sources available for Cromwellian Ireland. This process now enables researchers to address a far more complex range of historical queries. The first implementation of this data source also automatically generated indexes for an edited transcription of the Books of Survey and Distribution for the Irish Manuscripts Commission.[45] As a productivity tool, automatic indexing of such a large project has obvious benefits, and this technology can be applied to any future published work involving significant amounts of tabular data.

Moreover, as search technology moves away from simple keyword searches toward the ability to parse questions and return phrases as answers, the potential for searching for relationships between individuals, actions, and concepts becomes ever more real.[46] The sheer number of potential attributes to be found within phrases, however, introduces an urgent need to impose some order by means of classification. This can be achieved by generating a grammar comprising a lead-word, such as a single landowner, with hyponyms in a concept hierarchy that enable the user, through a search engine, to interpret the text. The challenge for historians is to ensure that the results are accurate and relevant, smoothing large-scale data into more manageable parcels. Thousands of townlands, for example, can be grouped into one county and the aggregated data presented as a single entity. Similarly, landowners can be grouped together, and their behavior can be examined at a local, regional, or national level. Accounts of military engagements or economic activities can also be included to test for commonalities. The discipline of Digital Humanities, therefore, is moving beyond a straightforward digital version of historical sources toward the integration of this material with useful technology. The most powerful software tools available to industry for many years include statistical, design, and presentation applications, all of which are now ready to be applied to the humanities. Perhaps, therefore, it is time to change the perception of Digital Humanities from an expensive dissemination tool to something which not only enables research but also reduces its costs.

Despite all the exciting developments outlined earlier, historians must not expect technology to fully automate research methodology, providing all the answers at the push of a button. Accessibility is unquestionably important, but before scholars and others can properly exploit any newly available historical source, it needs to be made machine-readable. Optical Character Recognition (OCR) can assist with printed material, but even here, manual normalization is still required for any premodern texts, to deal with the problem of variant spellings. Moreover, non-published manuscripts must first be manually transcribed. This is an extremely costly and time-consuming process, as is the restructuring of tabular data, and may well explain why many projects in Digital Humanities appear to aspire to little beyond digital imaging. This material can indeed be accessed on a computer, but it is then read in exactly the same way as any printed or manuscript source. Once newly searchable digital content has been created, however, technology can start to significantly alter the research environment. The key here is to adopt a fully multidisciplinary approach. An application of HTR technology enables keyword spotting over large quantities of images, eliminating the need to transcribe the text before searching it for useful information.[47] Amalgamating several engineering and humanities disciplines has the potential for further transformative results.

The launch of the Down Survey of Ireland project in 2013 proved to be a landmark in Historical GIS, bringing together a large archive of manuscript maps, formerly thought lost, and integrating it with a complementary textual source, namely the Books of Survey and Distribution. This, however, was only the beginning, and the second phase is far more ambitious, providing links to other contemporaneous sources of information, including text from existing published works and data from largely forgotten digital projects. Recent advances in search technology and database query will not only transform our understanding of a particularly controversial and pivotal period in the Irish past but enable us to ask a series of new and challenging research questions.

While the potential for early modern Irish history is obvious, the projects outlined earlier will also inform the methodological approach to linked data across the discipline of history more generally. Those involved in similar projects worldwide, or hoping to develop a similar project, need to engage more effectively with one another to share insights, approaches, and experiences as well as crucial data standards. There is nothing proprietorial about the TCD projects, all of which are open access, making use of widely available technologies. Major challenges do remain, particularly in the areas of cost and the long-term preservation of digitized material, which will require resources beyond the capacity of any single institution. Cooperation and collaboration are key to the success of all future projects, not only within history but also with colleagues in computer science, historical geography, and a host of other disciplines, as well as institutionally across the third-level sector, working closely with industry. Recent experience, however, suggests that we can expect to see exciting new developments over the coming years in these rapidly expanding and constantly evolving fields of study.

Notes

1 Most Digitial Humanites sites fall into this category. There is, of course, considerable further work performed on a project-by-project basis on each DH dataset, as every project has a set of research questions to answer. For overviews, see, for example, Laura Estill, Diane K. Jakacki, and Michael Ullyot (eds.), *Early Modern Studies after the Digital Turn* (Temple, AZ: Arizona Center for Medieval and Renaissance Studies, 2016); Christian Rollinger, Marten During, Martin Stark, and Robert Gramsch (eds.), 'Editor's Introduction', *Journal of Historical Network Research* 1 (2017), 1–7; Alexander von Lunen and Charles Travis (eds.), *History and GIS: Epistemologies, Considerations and Reflections* (Dordrecht: Springer, 2013).

2 As part of the decade of commemorations in Ireland (1912–22), Trinity College Dublin's 'Beyond 2022: Ireland's National Memory' project, in partnership with the National Archives of Ireland, is attempting to catalog the extent of the loss while at the same time bringing together all the material that has survived in a virtual archive. See https://histories-humanities.tcd.ie/research/Beyond-2022/. An associated project, 'Commonwealth Records 1651–9', funded by faculty benefactions within TCD, is concentrating on rebuilding the records of the 1650s.

3 Robert Dunlop (ed.), *Ireland under the Commonwealth*, 2 vols. (Manchester: Manchester University Press, 1913); J.T. Gilbert (ed.), *A Contemporary History of Affairs in Ireland from 1641 to 1652*, 3 vols. (Dublin: Irish Archaeological and Celtic Society, 1879–80); J.T. Gilbert (ed.), *History of the Irish Confederation and the War in Ireland*, 7 vols. (Dublin: M.H. Gill & Son, 1882–91); J.P. Prendergast, *The Cromwellian Settlement of Ireland* (London: P.M. Haverty, 1865).

4 See for example, Robert Armstrong, *Protestant War: The British of Ireland and the Wars of the Three Kingdoms* (Manchester: Manchester University Press, 2005); Pádraig Lenihan, *Confederate Catholics at War, 1641–49* (Cork: Cork University Press, 2001); Micheál Ó Siochrú, *Confederate Ireland, 1642–1649: A Constitutional and Political Analysis*, 2nd edn. (Dublin: Four Courts Press, 2008); Jane Ohlmeyer,

Civil War and Restoration in the Three Stuart Kingdoms: The Career of Randal Mac-Donnell, Marquis of Antrim (Cambridge: Cambridge University Press, 1993).

5   This project may be found online at http://1641.tcd.ie.

6   This TCD-based project was informed by the Historical GIS Research Framework, established in the UK, led by Ian Gregory, and supported with a small but vibrant emerging literature. Running concurrently, and of great help to the Down Survey project in terms of data and methodologies, were the Landed Estates Database project at NUI Galway, the Northern Ireland Placenames Project, and the Irish Placenames Project. See www.landedestates.ie; www.placenamesni.org; www.logainm.ie.

7   The Irish Manuscripts Commission published the Books of Survey and Distribution for Counties Mayo, Galway, Roscommon, and Clare over fifty years ago, but progress proved painfully slow. See Robert C. Simington (ed.), *Books of Survey and Distribution: Being Abstracts of Various Surveys and Instruments of Title, 1636–1703*, vols. 1–4 (Dublin: Stationery Office, 1949–67).

8   See John H. Andrews, *Plantation Acres: An Historical Study of the Irish Land Surveyor and his Maps* (Belfast: Ulster Historical Foundation, 1985); Toby Barnard, *Cromwellian Ireland: English Government and Reform in Ireland 1649–1660* (Oxford: Oxford University Press, 2000); Karl S. Bottigheimer, *English Money and Irish Land* (Oxford: Oxford University Press, 1971); John Cunningham, *Conquest and Land in Ireland: The Transplantation to Connaught, 1649–1680* (Woodbridge: Boydell and Brewer, 2011); Pádraig Lenihan, *Consolidating Conquest, Ireland 1603–1727* (London: Pearson Longman, 2007); Michael MacCarthy-Morrogh, *The Munster Plantation: English Migration to Southern Ireland, 1583–1641* (Oxford: Oxford University Press, 1986); and Jane Ohlmeyer, *Making Ireland English: the Irish Aristocracy in the Seventeenth Century* (London and New Haven, CT: Yale University Press, 2012) for various perspectives on the Cromwellian conquest and subsequent land settlement.

9   For an account of the early stages of the revolt and the establishment of the Catholic confederate association in 1642, see Ó Siochrú, *Confederate Ireland, 1642–1649*, pp. 27–54.

10 There are a number of accounts of the Cromwellian conquest, including James Scott Wheeler, *Cromwell in Ireland* (Dublin: Gill & Macmillan, 1999), and Micheál Ó Siochrú, *God's Executioner: Oliver Cromwell and the Conquest of Ireland* (London: Faber, 2009).

11 Cromwell's alleged words appear in Edmund Ludlow, *Memoirs of Edmund Ludlow Esq.*, vols. 2 (Vivay, 1698), vol. 1, p. 319.

12 'An Act for the speedy and effectual reducing of the Rebells in his Majesties Kingdome of Ireland to theire due obedience to his Majestie & the Crowne of England' in *Statutes of the Realm: Volume 5: 1628–80* (London: Great Britain Record Commission, 1819), pp. 168–72.

13 *An Act for the Setling of Ireland Thursday 12, August, 1652* (London, 1652).

14 *An Act for the Speedy and Effectual Satisfaction of the Adventurers for Lands in Ireland: and of the Arrears Due to the Soldiery There, and of Other Publique Debts; and for the Encouragement of Protestants to Plant and Inhabit Ireland* (London, 1653). The numbers of people who actually moved to Connacht is unclear. For the most recent study of the transplantation see Cunningham, *Conquest and Land in Ireland*.

15 The Gross Survey map of Crumlin parish, County Dublin, is in the Library of Trinity College Dublin, TCD MS 7394; the Survey of Mullingar may be found in David Brown and Micheál Ó Siochrú, 'The Cromwellian Urban Surveys', *Archivium Hibernicum* 69 (2016), 37–150.

16 A townland was the smallest administrative division of land, probably based on an earlier native Irish system of landholding. See J.H Andrews, *Shapes of Ireland: Maps and Their Makers, 1564–1839* (Dublin: Geography Publications, 1997), pp. 18–20.

17 The Irish Manuscripts Commission published the surviving material from the Civil Survey. See *The Civil Survey*, 10 vols. (Dublin: Irish Manuscripts Commission, 1931–61).

18 For Petty as a representative of the New Science, see Ted McCormick, *William Petty and the Ambitions of Political Arithmetic* (Oxford: Oxford University Press, 2009) and Nessa Cronin, 'Writing the 'New Geography': Cartographic Discourse and Colonial Governmentality in William Petty's Political Anatomy of Ireland (1672)', *Historical Geography* 42 (2014), 58–71.

19 Andrews, *Shapes of Ireland*, p. 147. The most complete published account of the various surveys is still to be found in W. H. Hardinge, 'On Manuscript Mapped and Other Townland Surveys in Ireland of a Public Character, Embracing the Gross, Civil and Down Surveys, from 1640 to 1688', *Transactions of the Royal Irish Academy* 24 (1873), 3–118.

20 See http://downsurvey.tcd.ie.

21 The Down Survey project team is extremely grateful to all those archivists who assisted with this search and who subsequently provided images for the website. The project simply would not have been possible without their generous cooperation.

22 Bibliothèque Nationale de France Ms Anglais 1,2; Claude de l'Isle, *Cabinet des manuscripts de la Bibliotheque Imperiale* (Paris: Léopold Victor Delisle, 1868), p. 333; PROI 2B-33-25; PROI v20-57; PROI 2A-12-51; BL Harley Ms 4784, ff 7-8; BL Add. Mss 41550–41557.

23 PROI 2B-33-25; PROI v20-57; PROI 2A-12-51; BL Harley Ms 4784, ff 7-8; BL Add. Mss 41550–41557.

24 Ibid.

25 Ibid.

26 National Archives of Ireland (NAI) QRO 1/1/3 vols. 1–20.

27 For further reading on this topic see J. G. Simms, *The Williamite Confiscation in Ireland, 1690–1703* (London: Faber & Faber, 1956).

28 J.G. Simms, 'Land Owned by Catholics in Ireland in 1688', *Irish Historical Studies* 7 (1951), 180–90.

29 The original maps of the Williamite land forfeitures, the Trustees Survey (so called as the land was vested in trustees prior to sale), no longer survive. The Quit Rent Office, however, also made tracings of these maps. Some copies survive in the British Library, Add. Mss 13,956, 14,405 and 41,159. For a copy of the printed abstract of Trustee's sales, see the National Archives of Ireland, M 2578.

30 The best account of these developments from 1660 is still David Dickson, *New Foundations: Ireland 1660–1800*, 2nd edn. (Dublin: Irish Academic Press, 2000).

31 The image is from the National Archives of Ireland, QRO/1/1/3/17/p. 453, Books of Survey and Distribution, vol. 17, Meath & Louth.

32 See J.H. Andrews, *A Paper Landscape: The Ordnance Survey in Nineteenth-Century Ireland*, 2nd edn. (Dublin: Four Courts Press, 2006).

33 For a discussion of these links see Andrews, *Shapes of Ireland*, passim.

34 Gojko Barjamovic, Thomas Chaney, Kerem A. Coşar, and Ali Hortaçsu, 'Trade, Merchants, and the Lost Cities of the Bronze Age', Working Paper No. 23992 (Cambridge, MA: National Bureau of Economic Research, 2017).

35 Research into HTR is prioritized by the European Commission's H2020 research fund, offering the revolutionary prospect of turning handwritten documents into machine readable, and therefore searchable text. It requires a very different methodological approach to widely used Optical Character Recognition (OCR) tools, interpreting bitmaps of stored character sets. HTR uses artificial intelligence to 'learn' handwriting styles and quirks, such as abbreviations, from large samples of matched text and images and applies these patterns, using probabilities and other techniques, to additional images. See https://read.transkribus.eu/.

36   The matching of historical townlands with their modern equivalent generated the vast bulk of correspondence. In a handful of instances, errors were identified, but most people simply misunderstood the sources, believing that the project team rather than Petty were responsible for the historical information.

37   Latlong is the global coordinate system used in software based on the Global Positioning System, developed by the US military in the 1970s. Now open source, it is the coordinate system of choice for most location-based services, including Google maps and mobile phone apps. Its advantages, in addition to its ubiquity, are that it is independent of the proliferation of national coordinate systems used by each mapping agency, and that it is free.

38   These figures are based primarily on the pioneering work of Simms. See 'The Restoration, 1660–85', in T.W. Moody, F.X. Martin, and F.J. Byrne (eds.), *New History of Ireland: Vol. III: Early Modern Ireland 1534–1691* (Oxford: Oxford University Press, 2009), p. 428.

39   *The Irish Times*, 11 May 2013.

40   For a published version of the census, see Séamus Pender (ed.), *A Census of Ireland Circa 1659* (Dublin: Irish Manuscripts Commission, 2002). No data survives for Galway, Mayo, Cavan, Tyrone and Wicklow, as well as significant parts of Cork and Meath.

41   For the originals, see Trinity College Dublin, MSS 809–841. The depositions for all of the Ulster counties and Louth have been published by the Irish Manuscripts Commission. See Aidan Clarke et al. (eds.), *1641 Depositions*, vols. 1–3 (Dublin: Irish Manuscripts Commission, 2014).

42   There is a growing scholarship on 1641, but for recent edited collections on the subject, see Eamon Darcy, Annaleigh Margey, and Elaine Murphy (eds.), *The 1641 Depositions and the Irish Rebellion* (London: Pickering and Chatto, 2012) and Micheál Ó Siochrú and Jane Ohlmeyer (eds.), *Ireland 1641: Contexts and Reactions* (Manchester: Manchester University Press, 2013).

43   See www.cultura-strep.eu/. Huygens Institute for the History of the Netherlands, www.huygens.knaw.nl, produces a broad range of research platforms for early modern research. University College London's Centre for Digital Humanities, with the Transcribe Bentham project, www.ucl.ac.uk/transcribe-bentham, is developing highly innovative tools aimed at crowd-sourcing and textual analysis. Stanford University has made available innovative tools for spatial network analysis, http://hdlab.stanford.edu/palladio/, while The Folger Library has undertaken a major literary analysis project www.folger.edu/folger-digital-texts, using its unique collection of Shakespeare editions. What all of these projects have in common is a willingness to cross the boundaries between the academic communities and the wider public.

44   These insights cannot be overstated. In 2012, at the outset of the project, Google predicted the ubiquitous use of maps on smartphones. The website was subsequently developed with a view to ensuring that it would work on what were then quite new devices.

45   It is interesting to note that despite all this new technology, historians are still keen for project outputs to appear in traditional print format.

46   For current research on this topic, see Sunita Sarawagi et al., 'Discovering Structure in the Universe of Attribute Names', *Proceedings of the 25th International World Wide Web Conference* (Bombay, 2016), http://static.googleusercontent.com/media/research.google.com/en//pubs/archive/45245.pdf.

47   www.citlab.uni-rostock.de/en/, the Computational Intelligence laboratory at the University of Rostock.

Afterword

'Revising anew' early modern Irish history[1]

Jane Ohlmeyer

At a speech in April 2018 to mark the launch of *The Cambridge History of Ireland*, President Michael D. Higgins spoke passionately about the importance of knowing the past. 'A knowledge and understanding of history', he observed, 'is intrinsic to our shared citizenship. To be without such knowledge is to be permanently burdened with a lack of perspective, empathy and wisdom'. He continued that 'to be without historical training, the careful and necessary capability to filter and critically interpret a variety of sources, is to leave citizens desperately ill-equipped to confront a world in which information is increasingly disseminated without historical perspective or even regard for the truth.'[2] In short, history matters now more than ever.[3]

Early Modern Ireland: New Sources, Methods, and Perspectives and *The Cambridge History of Ireland* are being published at a particularly sensitive moment.[4] They are appearing on the eve of Brexit and in the midst of Ireland's Decade of Centenaries (2012–22).[5] After the great dignity that marked the centenary commemoration of the outbreak of World War I (1914) and the Easter Rising (1916), Brexit now provides the backdrop to some particularly contested anniversaries: the twentieth anniversary of the Good Friday Agreement (1998), the fiftieth anniversary of the outbreak of the Troubles (1969), the 100th anniversary of the political partition of the island (1920), and the outbreak of civil war (1922).

Brexit itself illustrates how the 'Irish Question' never dies; it just gets reformulated. Of course, the historic and human links between Ireland and England date back to the early Middle Ages. Ireland, though an integral part first of the English and later British Empire, was also England's first overseas colony. From the mid-sixteenth century, approximately 350,000 people—from England, Scotland, and Wales—migrated to Ireland. By the early eighteenth century, society in Ireland was ethnically diverse, with nearly one-third of the population of immigrant stock. People from Ireland have also been settling the world for centuries, particularly from the early modern period onward. The 2011 UK Census shows that 395,000 people living in Great Britain were born in the Republic of Ireland and that roughly six million people living there had an Irish-born grandparent. In the United States, nearly 250,000 residents as of 2015 were born in Ireland, while thirty-six million Americans claim Irish ancestry. After 2008, and for the first time, a majority of Irish emigrants, mostly of a younger demographic, chose to settle not in Britain or the United States but in Australia, New Zealand, Canada, and European Union countries as well as the Middle East and Asia.[6]

In keeping with this pattern of intertwined historic and contemporary destinies, a significant number of scholars of early modern Ireland are now internationally based. It will, as a consequence, come as little surprise that the academic community around the world would prefer Brexit not to happen. We are, as a recent survey published by the Royal Irish Academy highlights, deeply apprehensive about the impact it might have on education, research, and the ongoing Peace Process.[7] At the same time, the welcome injection of funding for doctoral and postdoctoral research into all aspects of history has had a positive impact on the extraordinary growth of high-quality history publications.[8] Tom Bartlett has estimated that today approximately 3,000 books and articles relating to Irish history are published annually, whereas in the 1970s, this figure stood at around 500. 'As a result', Bartlett suggests, 'we are seriously in danger of not being able to see the wood for the trees'.[9]

Up until the 1930s, Irish history writing was vigorously partisan, biased, and used to win an argument or prove a case. For example, the Norman invasion was either a 'good thing' or 'bad thing'; the same held true for the plantations of the early modern period. There was little interest in engaging in a careful evaluation of evidence or in searching for appropriate sources. As a result, nuance, complexity, and measured judgments were rigorously avoided. Today, this approach characterizes history writing in some countries where the state strives to use the past to construct a narrative that justifies its politics in the present. Thankfully, this is no longer the case in Ireland. There is no longer a consensus view of Irish history; indeed, there are sometimes conflicting interpretations of the same event and heated debates, which, in turn, generate further scholarship.

Despite these diverse approaches, there are at least five broad themes that concern students of early modern Ireland, and will affect future scholarship as well. These relate to evidence, method, interdisciplinarity, technology, and wider contexts. Let us take a closer look at each.

First, researchers of the period are acutely aware of the limitations of the evidence and the dangers of over-relying on the English-language archives of the state. History is all too often written by the winners. To invoke the Nigerian writer Chinua Achebe, 'Until lions produce their own historian, the story of the hunt will glorify only the hunter'. Every effort has been made to interrogate all available evidence in whatever language it exists and in every form that it survives—written, visual, material, physical, and oral. The hope is that current and future work will provoke debate, discussion, and further research as new archival riches become available. This applies as much to original research on familiar topics—like the nature and operation of government or the institutions of state—as to imaginative use of well-known sources, like petitions or testamentary records, that have been previously disregarded.[10] In this volume, Canning's chapter on individual, collective, civic, and corporate petitions during the Nine Years' War of the 1590s invites comparable evaluation of the body of petitions submitted to the king, parliament, the confederates, and Ormond in the immediate aftermath of the 1641 Rebellion and throughout the civil wars of the 1640s.[11] Testamentary records, as Tait's analysis highlights, affords the scholar an opportunity to 'rummage in the closets, chests, and jewelry coffers of the past to recreate the practices, relationships, structures, rituals and products of everyday experience' of early modern men and women. McShane, meanwhile, demonstrates how a variety of sources, including material objects such as monuments and Irish-language sources, may allow us to access the overlooked lives of early modern clerical wives in Ireland.

As some contributors to this volume remind us, rather than lamenting what was lost in 1922, we need to focus on what has survived, including transcriptions often dating from the nineteenth century.[12] This is the goal of an ambitious project, 'Beyond 2022', which has the potential to offer a virtual reconstruction of the destroyed Treasury in the Public Record Office of Ireland (PROI) and the collections it housed.[13] The quantum of financing required to realize the full opportunity afforded by 'Beyond 2020' is way beyond the budget of the Irish Research Council, which has funded the pilot, and requires significant investment on the part of the Irish, and possibly British, government. As we approach the 100th anniversary of the destruction of the PROI, it is hard to imagine a more fitting cultural intervention.

The second theme relates to method. Current scholars, for example, have responded to wider historiographical debates and adapted methodologies developed by the historians of countries where the archival landscape is richer, and applied them to Ireland, often with great effect. The chapter by Cunningham on the history of medicine and Tait's analysis of emotion serve as fine examples of this. In a similar vein, Covington's fascinating account of folkloric sources and methods draws inspiration from the pioneering research by scholars working on the post-1700 period, while Willy Maley's essay incorporates folklore, literature, history, and the burgeoning field of animal studies to track one colonialist motif across time. Coolahan analyzes the 1641 Depositions through the lens of life narratives and draws attention to pioneering work by Naomi McAreavey who has used trauma theory to interrogate these women's narratives as 'literature of trauma'. Reading the depositions as literature of trauma allows us to see in the testimonies of the Protestant victims the 'truth' of the trauma survivor's experience, which must be differentiated from the objective 'facts' of the rising.[14]

Approaches pioneered by literary scholars have greatly influenced my current work and especially the edition of 'A short view of the state and condition of the kingdom of Ireland from the yeare 1640 to this tyme' by Edward

Hyde, earl of Clarendon, that I am editing for Oxford University Press. Scholars of seventeenth-century Ireland generally recognize Clarendon's importance as a royalist historian and that of his magnum opus, *The History of the Rebellion and Civil Wars in England*. Only rarely do they even acknowledge 'A short view', which takes the form of a chronological narrative of Irish affairs between 1640 and 1652. At one level this should not surprise since 'A short view' was far from being a comprehensive history of these years, and coverage of events was patchy and at times muddled. Instead, it is a work about honor and reputation, and stands as the first substantial defense of James Butler's (the duke of Ormond's) conduct as lord lieutenant.[15] The purpose of 'A short view' was to reclaim the memory of the war, to vindicate Charles I of any wrongdoing in his associations with the Irish, and to portray Ormond as a man of honor and a loyal servant to the Stuarts.[16] As such, it needs to be reevaluated in the context of wider discussions of honor and reputation, and of history and memory, especially during the 1650s and 1660s but also at the height of the Popish Plot and Exclusion Crisis during the 1670s and early 1680s. Interestingly, 'A short view' had a long shelf life. Written in the 1650s, it became a 'best seller', circulating widely (but anonymously) in manuscript.[17] It was printed under the title *History of the rebellion and civil wars in Ireland* in multiple editions in the eighteenth and nineteenth centuries, often at moments of political crisis when issues of loyalty and reputation were being debated and challenged.[18] 'A short view' clearly influenced other 'histories' written during the later decades of the seventeenth century both by Protestants, like Edmund Borlase and John Nalson, and Catholics, especially Richard Bellings, where authors sought to justify actions and decisions taken during the civil war years. A few annotated copies survive, which provide insights into how contemporaries read and responded to 'A short view'. Significantly, these included an (incomplete) copy annotated by Arthur Annesley, earl of Anglesey, who was Ormond's nemesis during the late 1670s and early 1680s.[19]

The third theme is interdisciplinarity. Over the course of the last few decades, cross-pollination has taken place between, on the one hand, history and, on the other, disciplines such as archaeology, folklore, geography, literature, gender studies, and computer and natural science. In this volume, Lyttleton articulates the importance of archaeology to our understanding of material culture, landscapes, and the physical world and illustrates how it frames historical narratives.[20] Perspectives afforded by literary studies also feature in this volume. The chapters by Coolahan, Kane, McKibben, and McQuillan highlight how the close reading of a text provides insights into identity, mind-sets, behaviors, motivation, and emotion.[21] In her chapter on bardic poetry, McKibben outlines the richness of Irish-language resources and the research opportunities that these afford in providing 'a distinct counter-narrative to Anglophone claims about native Irish society, its poets and poetry'. Kane does likewise and reminds us of the importance of also engaging with sources in Irish to understand the past more completely.

Crampsie and Ludlow have used the 1641 Depositions, along with scientific data on tree-ring-based precipitation and volcanic activity, to better understand the environmental history of early modern Ireland and the role that extreme weather played in major historical events like the Nine Years' War and the 1641 Rebellion.[22] In their contribution to this volume, they have also interrogated the Irish statute staple, records of credit and debt from the 1590s until the 1680s, to establish the intimate relationship between extreme weather, violence, and indebtedness.[23]

Of course, achieving meaningful conversations across disciplines is not easy, and flagged across many of these chapters are concrete suggestions of how to build trust, reciprocity, and collaborations across and between disciplines. This is especially true for technology, our fourth theme. Thanks to technology, many archives are now more accessible than ever before. Scholars enjoy unprecedented access to commercial, digital collections of state papers, correspondence, newspapers, and pamphlets (especially Early English Books Online);[24] to more niche but open access corpuses, like the CELT project (Corpus of Electronic Text),[25] the Bardic Poetry Project,[26] the 1641 Depositions,[27] and the Down Survey (which reconstitutes Sir William Petty's remarkable maps);[28] and to 'big data', like the records of the statute staple and the Books of Survey and Distribution, which are the equivalent of the Doomsday books in recording Irish landholding in 1641 and after 1670.[29] Access to these archives is, however, just the beginning and it is critical to heed Canny's health warning in the foreword to this volume: that 'an increasing number of scholars [not] consider the creation of data sets and on-line compilations to be ends in themselves [but] rather … resources … to address research questions'. Undoubtedly, as the chapter by Brown and Ó Siochrú highlights, innovative use of technology and the development of user-friendly tools that allow us to interrogate these resources mean that we can ask questions of sources that were previously unimaginable.[30] For example, the development of powerful platforms like Léamh.org, which is a web-based resource for learning early modern Irish, facilitates the interrogation of Irish-language sources in CELT and in the Bardic Poetry database.[31]

However, 'digital humanities' projects also pose challenges. Take, for example, my own research on widows and the 1641 Depositions which illustrates both the value of these resources and the complexities inherent in using them. The online publication of the 1641 Depositions provides unprecedented access to the archive, while the development of a suite of tools, especially under the auspices of CULTRA (CULTivating Understanding and Research through Adaptivity), facilitated their interrogation and visualization.[32] Particularly valuable was the development of a set of algorithms that allowed for the 'normalization' of seventeenth-century English. This meant that a simple search for 'widow' returned all of the variant spellings: widowe, widdow, widdowe, wydow, wyddow, wyddowe, wydowe, widows, widdows, widdowes, wido, widoe, widos, widdos, widdoe, widdos, and widdoes.

So, how many widows actually deposed? An occupation search for 'widow' at 1641.tcd.ie (the 'original' 1641 website that is most commonly used) returned 497 widows, 386 of whom deposed (the other 111 were depositions where a widow featured but was not the actual deponent). A CULTURA search for 'widow' across the normalized text yielded thirty-five additional women, making 421 in all. However, a close reading of the 1641 Depositions quickly revealed that a search for 'widow' (and its variants) had failed to return all of the widows who deposed. Why? In the seventeenth century, people used a variety of related words to describe a widow. These included 'relict' and 'late wife', along with 'late the wife' and 'formerly wife'.[33] A widow might also be identified in relation to her 'late husband', 'former husband', 'husband deceased', or as 'formerly married'. Finally, we need to ask: when is a widow not a widow? The answer is when she remarries. So, a close reading of the depositions yielded an additional ninety-one widows, making a grand total of 512 or nearly 20% more than a basic search revealed. This is a sober reminder of the fundamental importance of context and of reading, rather than doing word searches or mining, the 1641 Depositions.

The 1641 Depositions Project, CULTURA, and the related CIRCE project (Collaborative Linguistic Research and Learning Environment) also point to the dangers of creating digital silos.[34] CULTURA, CIRCE, and the Down Survey have all built on the original 1641 project, but there is no interoperability between them, and the long-term future of each is uncertain. Thus, issues of interoperability, sustainability, and long-term preservation of digital resources continue to bedevil, which make it important, as Brown and Ó Siochrú urge, to create structured data in a standard format. In some instances, it is already too late. For example, the records of the statute staple, published during the first wave of 'historical computing' in the late 1990s as a CD-ROM using an Access database, are now effectively redundant in their digital, but not printed, format. So it is critical that we 'future proof' these digital resources and the tools developed, often at considerable expense, used to interrogate them and to invest in infrastructure that supports best practice and long-term preservation.[35] In addition, the digital age poses challenges around the shape and form of future libraries, and archives and how electronic resources might be sustained and conserved. We know that volumes like these or paper records will be around in 100 years, but what of tweets, blogs, websites, and emails?

The fifth theme is that every effort is made to situate Ireland in wider contexts, while never losing sight of the local. The openness of Ireland to outside influences, and its capacity to influence the world beyond its shores, are recurring features in much scholarship today, including studies by those based in universities on the continent. From the late fifteenth century, Irish people engaged in global expansionism. William Eris (or Ayres) from Galway sailed with Christopher Columbus on his historic voyage of 1492 to the Americas; others from Galway voyaged with Ferdinand Magellan on his circumnavigation of the globe (1519–1522). By the turn of the seventeenth century,

Irish migrants, merchants, missionaries, and mercenaries were to be found in Britain and continental Europe as well as in the French Caribbean, the Portuguese and later Dutch Amazon, Spanish Mexico, and English settlements in North America and India. Without wishing to become embroiled in debates around 'glocal' or 'glocalization', approaches which emphasize the local and regional as well as the universal, these global interactions undoubtedly transformed commerce and facilitated the rise of cosmopolitanism and of cultural and intellectual exchange. Caball's account in this volume of Richard and Robert Hedges, brothers who spent their lives in Ireland and India, respectively, illustrates this.[36]

In my own research on early modern Ireland and India, I reexamine the biography of Gerald Aungier, governor of Bombay and president of Surat (1669–1677), through the lens of early modern Ireland.[37] Given Aungier's importance as the 'founding father' of Bombay, his career is reasonably well documented. Yet few scholars acknowledge the fact that he was born in Dublin during the later 1630s, of Protestant planter stock (the grandson of the Archbishop of Dublin and of a legal imperialist); none have assessed how this might have shaped the formation of the Bombay colony. Equally to historians of Ireland, Aungier remains an obscure figure, the younger son of a younger son, whose life was overshadowed by his elder brother, Francis, earl of Longford, the leading property developer in Restoration Dublin. I am interested in exploring how Ireland, England's oldest overseas colony, might have influenced the development of Bombay and how a Protestant from Ireland contributed to the formation of empire in Asia, in a period long before the Irish were associated with imperialism in India. I also argue that in a number of key areas, Ireland served as a 'laboratory for empire' for seventeenth-century Bombay, much as it did for India in the nineteenth century.[38] By focusing on processes and practices of government, especially legal and landed ones and others relating to Anglicization, it is possible to distinguish what characterized the implementation of English imperial authority in both Ireland and Bombay.

I would also like to invite scholars to interrogate eastward enterprises, as well as westward ones, in a more interconnected way. To date, the emphasis has been on situating Irish colonial experiences in the context of the English Atlantic world, and here, the scholarship of Canny and D. B. Quinn has been pioneering. This is understandable given the scale of migration to the Caribbean and American colonies, the importance of commercial links especially to the West Indies, and the extent to which Ireland influenced the plantations of English North America. Closely linked to this is the intimate interplay between commerce and colonization and the importance of challenging, much as Philip Stern has done, the traditional distinctions between the commercial and imperial eras in British India, as well as distinct notions of a colonial Atlantic world and a 'trading world' of Asia.[39] What becomes immediately apparent in any wider study of the Atlantic colonies, Ireland, and Bombay is the extent to which colonization and commerce went hand in hand.

Let me conclude by returning to President Higgins, who closed his remarks by inviting 'young historians … to revise anew these volumes. That, I believe, will be the measure of our success in the coming years'.[40] This collection of essays represents another important step in 'revising anew' the early modern period more generally. It will serve as a springboard for further research and reflection.

Notes

1 Jane Ohlmeyer (ed.), *The Cambridge History of Ireland, Volume II: 1550–1730* (Cambridge: Cambridge University Press, 2018). For the series, see Thomas Bartlett (gen. ed.), *The Cambridge History of Ireland*. 4 vols. (Cambridge: Cambridge University Press, 2018). This article draws on Jane Ohlmeyer's contribution to www. irishtimes.com/culture/books/bolder-and-wiser-our-new-and-improved-history-of-ireland-1.3479285, accessed 10 June 2018.
2 www.president.ie/en/media-library/speeches/speech-at-the-launch-of-the-cambridge-history-of-ireland, accessed 10 June 2018.
3 The speech circulated widely on social media and fed into an opinion pieces by Sir David Cannadine (see Note 4) and Diarmuid Ferriter in the *Irish Times* (www. irishtimes.com/opinion/higgins-is-right-that-history-should-be-compulsory-for-junior-cert-1.3484386, accessed 10 June 2018).
4 www.theguardian.com/uk-news/2018/may/11/john-major-customs-union-brexit-hard-border-northern-ireland, accessed 10 June 2018. Also see Sir David Cannadine in the *Evening Standard* (www.standard.co.uk/comment/comment/today-s-lesson-for-politicians-is-to-learn-from-history-a3854621.html, accessed 10 June 2018).
5 www.decadeofcentenaries.com, accessed 10 June 2018.
6 Department of Foreign Affairs and Trade (Ireland), 'Irish Emigration Patterns and Citizens Abroad', www.dfa.ie/media/dfa/alldfawebsitemedia/newspress/publications/ministersbrief-june2017/1--Global-Irish-in-Numbers.pdf; Office for National Statistics (UK), '2011 Census: Key Statistics and Quick Statistics for Local Authorities in the United Kingdom': www.ons.gov.uk/people-populationandcommunity/populationandmigration/populationestimates/bulletins/keystatisticsandquickstatisticsforlocalauthoritiesintheunitedkingdom/2013-10-11#ethnicity-and-country-of-birth.
7 www.ria.ie/sites/default/files/ria_brexit_taskforce_survey_results_report_final. pdf, accessed 10 June 2018.
8 The research funding landscape was transformed by the establishment in 2000 of the Irish Research Council for the Humanities and Social Sciences (it became the Irish Research Council in 2012).
9 Tom Bartlett's contribution to www.irishtimes.com/culture/books/bolder-and-wiser-our-new-and-improved-history-of-ireland-1.3479285, accessed 10 June 2018.
10 See the chapters in this volume by Edwards, Dennehy, Canning, McShane, and Tait.
11 See, for example, Charles Edwards Gifford, 'Calendar of Petitions to Ormonde in 1649 and 1650', *Irish Genealogist* 6 (4) (1983), 423–44; 6 (5) (1984), 577–600; 6 (6) (1985), 724–47 and Oxford, Bodleian Library, Carte MSS 155–57.
12 Micheál Ó Siochrú, 'Rebuilding the Past: The transformation of early modern Irish history', *The Seventeenth Century* (2018), doi:10.1080/02681 17X.2018.1445552, accessed 18 June 2018.
13 https://beyond2022.ie, accessed 10 June 2018.

14 Also see Marie Louise Coolahan, *Women, Writing, and Language in Early Modern Ireland* (Oxford: Oxford University Press, 2010), p. 142. Naomi McAreavey, 'Re(-) Membering women: Protestant women's victim testimonies during the Irish Rising of 1641', *Journal of the Northern Renaissance* 2 (2010). www.northernrenaissance.org/re-membering-women-protestant-womens-victim-testimonies-during-the-irish-rising-of-1641/, accessed 15 June 2018. Also see the chapters by Diane Hall and Sarah Covington in Fionnuala Dillane, Naomi McAreavey and Emilie Pine (eds.), *The Body in Pain in Irish Literature and Culture* (New York and London: Palgrave Macmillan, 2016).

15 Jane Ohlmeyer and Steven Zwicker, 'Patronage and Restoration politics: John Dryden and the House of Ormond' in *Historical Journal* 49 (2006), 677–706 and M. Perceval-Maxwell, 'Sir Robert Southwell and the Duke of Ormond's Reflections on the 1640s', in Micheál Ó Siochrú (ed.), *Kingdoms in Crisis: Ireland in the 1640s* (Dublin: Four Courts Press, 2001), pp. 229–47.

16 Mark R. F. Williams, *The King's Irishmen. The Irish in the Exiled Court of Charles II 1649–1660* (Woodbridge, Suffolk: Boydell & Brewer, 2014), pp. 251–52.

17 In addition to Clarendon's autograph text, there are five partial and eighteen complete copies. There are also between two and five 'untraced' copies, making a total of between twenty-five and twenty-eight copies (in folio and quarto). Only twenty-four of these are listed in the online 'Catalogue of English Literary Manuscripts, 1450–1700' (CELM).

18 Willis Addison Belford, 'A Survey of the Writings of Edward Hyde, Earl of Clarendon' (University of Denver, PhD thesis 1972), pp. 388–89. It was 1719–20 before 'A short view' appeared in print for the first time. Despite being repeatedly reprinted in the eighteenth and nineteenth centuries, Macray did not include it in his 1888 edition.

19 Cambridge University Library, Ms Add 4348.

20 Many of the contributors to Volume 1 of *The Cambridge History* do likewise.

21 See the chapters in this volume by Coolahan, Kane, McKibben and McQuillan.

22 See their chapter in *The Cambridge History of Ireland, Volume II*.

23 Jane Ohlmeyer and Éamonn Ó Ciardha, (eds.), *The Irish Statute Staple Books, 1596–1687* (Dublin: Four Courts Press, 1998).

24 https://eebo.chadwyck.com/home, accessed 18 June 2018.

25 https://celt.ucc.ie//, accessed on 15 June 2018.

26 https://bardic.celt.dias.ie, accessed 15 June 2018.

27 http://1641.tcd.ie, accessed 15 June 2018.

28 http://downsurvey.tcd.ie/down-survey-maps.php, accessed 15 June 2018.

29 Ohlmeyer and Ó Ciardha, (eds.), *The Irish Statute Staple Books*.

30 See the chapter in this volume by Brown and Ó Siochrú.

31 See the chapter in this volume by Kane.

32 www.cultura-strep.eu, accessed 15 June 2018.

33 There are nine variant spellings of the word 'wife' (wiffe, wyfe, wyffe, wyve, wifes, wive, wiffes, wyfes).

34 http://1641dep.abdn.ac.uk, accessed 16 June 2018.

35 It also makes EU-funded initiatives like Digital Research Infrastructure for the Arts and Humanities (DARIAH) so important, in addition to nationally funded ones like the Digital Repository of Ireland (DRI), www.dariah.eu and http://dri.ie, accessed 18 June 2018.

36 See the chapter in this volume by Caball.

37 Jane Ohlmeyer, 'Eastward enterprises: Colonial Ireland, colonial India', *Past & Present* 240 (2018), 83–118.

38 Scott B. Cook, *Imperial Affinities: Nineteenth-Century Analogies and Exchanges between India and Ireland* (New Delhi: Sage Publications, 1993); Christopher A.

Bayly, 'Ireland, India and the Empire: 1780–1914', *Transactions of the Royal Historical Society*, vii series, 10 (2000), 377–97 and Jane Ohlmeyer, 'Ireland, India and the British Empire', *Studies in People's History*, ii (2015), 169–88.

39 Philip J. Stern, *The Company-State. Corporate Sovereignty and the Early Modern Foundations of the British Empire in India* (Oxford: Oxford University Press, 2011) and *ibid.*, 'British Asia and British Atlantic: Comparisons and connections', *The William and Mary Quarterly* 63 (2006), 693–712.

40 www.president.ie/en/media-library/speeches/speech-at-the-launch-of-the-cambridge-history-of-ireland, accessed 10 June 2018.

Index